HISTORICAL RECORD

OF

THE SEVENTH

OR

ROYAL REGIMENT OF FUSILIERS

COMPILED AT THE REQUEST AND WITH THE ASSISTANCE OF THE

OFFICERS OF THE REGIMENT

BY

W. WHEATER

PRINTED FOR PRIVATE CIRCULATION

LEEDS:

1875.

PREFACE.

THE Record of the Royal Regiment of Fusiliers contained in the following pages may not be without some errors of omission as regards facts in the history of the Regiment. Every effort, however, has been made to obtain all the available authentic evidence, every official document that was accessible having been consulted. In the later period of the history, which has been written in a much more detailed manner, the narrative has been revised, and the facts authenticated by officers who were then serving, as well as by those who are now serving, in the Regiment; and the compiler can state with confidence that it is the most complete and reliable record of the services of this distinguished Regiment that has yet been published.

HISTORICAL RECORD

OF THE

ROYAL REGIMENT OF FUSILIERS.

THE Royal Regiment of Fusiliers, the Seventh Regiment of the British Line, was formed by King James II., on the augmentation of the army in consequence of the rebellion of the Duke of Monmouth, in the summer of 1685. At the period of its formation the regiment was singular both in its duties and armament. It was raised as an Ordnance Regiment, its peculiar duties being the protection of the guns of the Royal Artillery, then often worked by privates of Infantry Regiments, and without sufficient defensive means to repel a hand-to-hand attack. In its armament it was also to be superior to the ordinary Infantry Regiments of the period.* At that period Line Regiments were composed of three different kinds of soldiers: Musketeers, armed with muskets and swords; pikemen, armed with a long pike and a sword; and grenadiers, armed with hand grenades, muskets and bayonets, swords, and small hatchets. As will be seen from the different arms of the men, a regiment thus composed was weak for offensive and defensive purposes, as only one-half of it could act on any given emergency; and it was to remedy this weakness, as far as possible, that another species of arm was introduced, and another order of soldier created.

<small>Establishment of the Regiment.</small>

The Fusiliers, all armed with a superior kind of musket, called a Fusil, were the new troops, and, as the regiment was the first of its kind in the English service, the King publicly patronised it by entitling it the "Royal Fusiliers."

<small>The Armament of the Fusiliers.</small>

---

* We give the following curious remarks from the *Gentleman's Dictionary*—"The first design of the Fusiliers was to guard the Artillery, for which end the regiment of English Fusiliers was first raised. To supply the want of pikes, and to secure themselves against horse, the Fusiliers used to carry turnpikes along with them, which in a camp were placed along the front of a battalion, and on a march were carried by the soldiers, each carrying one of the short pikes and two by turns the spar through which they were thrust, so that they were quickly put together."

The regiment had not the proportion of colours usually given to other regiments, viz., one to each company, and on that account it had no need for an ensign in its commissioned ranks. But as its duties were considered of a superior kind to those of the ordinary Infantry Regiments, and as the responsibility of its subaltern officers was great, each company obtained two subalterns, who were both styled lieutenants, and placed on the same rate of pay, the junior being called the second lieutenant, and the senior the first lieutenant. These terms were used in their commissions for several years, but were afterwards discontinued, the distinction between first and second lieutenant being abandoned.

<small>Both Subalterns to be Lieutenants</small>

The regiment was to consist of thirteen companies, twelve of fusiliers, and one of miners; each battalion company being composed of three officers, three sergeants, three corporals, two drummers, and 100 private soldiers. George, Lord Dartmouth, then Master-General of the Ordnance, was appointed colonel, by the following commission:—

<small>Strength of the Regiment.</small>

> "JAMES R.—To our right trusty and well-beloved counsellor, George Lord Dartmouth, Major-General of our Ordnance, greeting. We, reposing especial trust and confidence in your loyalty, courage, and good conduct, do by these presents constitute and appoint you to be Colonel of our Royal Regiment of Fusiliers, raised and to be raised for our service, and likewise to be Captain of a Company in the said Regiment. You are, therefore, to take the said Regiment as Colonel, and the said Company as Captain into your care and charge, and duly to exercise as well the officers and the soldiers in arms, and to use your best endeavours to keep them in good order and discipline. And we hereby command them to obey you as their Colonel and Captain respectively, and you to observe and follow such orders and directions from time to time as you shall receive from us, or any of your superior officers, according to the rules and discipline of war in pursuance of the trust we hereby repose in you.
>
> "Given at our Court at Whitehall, the 11th day of June, 1685.
> "By His Majesty's Command,
>
> "SUNDERLAND."

The field officers of the regiment, with their subalterns and the captain of the miners, were appointed on the same day, and two days later Thomas Whalley, the senior of the newly-appointed captains, received his commission. The first two companies were old independent companies, which had long garrisoned the Tower of London; the other ten companies were to be raised in London, by the several captains appointed to them. The company of miners appears to have been first raised, not as a company of the Royal Fusiliers, but for the "service of our ordnance," and at the outset was certainly different both in its status and organisation from the battalion companies of the regiment.

Warrant for raising the Company of Miners:—

"JAMES R.—These are to authorise you to raise forty volunteers to be employed as miners for the service of our Ordnance, under your command; and, as you raise the said Volunteers, you are to quarter them within our Tower of London, where they are to do such duty as you shall direct.
"15th June, 1685.
"By His Majesty's Command,
"W. BLATHWAYTE.
"To our trusty and well-beloved Cousin, George, Lord Dartmouth."

Within a week, however, the organisation of the regiment was fully completed, and the somewhat independent career of the company of miners brought to a close by its incorporation with the Royal Fusiliers. The following is the warrant for raising the colonel's company:— *The Regiment finally organised.*

"JAMES R.—To our trusty and well-beloved counsellor, George Lord Dartmouth, Colonel of our Royal Regiment of Fusiliers, and Captain of a Company in the said Regiment.
"These are to authorise you, by beat of drum or otherwise, to raise volunteers to serve for soldiers in your own company in our Royal Regiment of Fusiliers, which we have appointed to be raised, and whereof you are colonel; which company is to consist of 100 private soldiers, three sergeants, three corporals, and two drummers. And as the said soldiers shall be respectively raised in the said company, they are to be produced to muster, to the intent that they may be received into our pay and entertainment; and when that number shall be fully or nearly completed, they are to march to the general rendezvous of their regiment, where they are also to be mustered. And you are to appoint such person or persons as you shall think fit to receive arms for the said soldiers, and halberts for the said sergeants, out of the stores of our ordnance. And we do hereby require all magistrates, justices of the peace, constables, and others, our officers whom it may concern, at all places where you shall raise, march, or rendezvous our said company, to be assisting therein as there shall be occasion.
"Given at our Court at Whitehall, the 20th day of June, 1685.
"By His Majesty's Command,
"WILLIAM BLATHWAYTE."

A week later came the order to arm the regiment:—

"Our will and pleasure is that out of the stores which are, or shall be, in the office of our Ordnance you cause to be delivered to the several Captains of our Royal Regiment of Fusiliers under your command, or such person or persons as shall be appointed to receive the same, 100 fusees, musket bore, 100 cartridge boxes, with bayonet, belt, and apron; 100 swords, 3 partisans, 3 halberts, and 2 drums for each company.
"27th June, 1685.
"By His Majesty's Order,
"SUNDERLAND.
"To our trusty and well-beloved Cousin, George, Lord Dartmouth."

The lieutenant-colonel of the regiment was Thomas Talmash, a young soldier who had gained a knowledge of war in the rude Tangier fights, as well as on the plains of Flanders; who had commanded a company of the Coldstreams, and thence passed to the lieutenant-colonelcy of an Infantry Regiment, disbanded at *The Company Officers appointed.*

the peace of Nimeguen; he subsequently became a celebrated general and the colonel of the Coldstream Guards. The major was Robert St. Clair,* who commanded one of the independent companies.

The following is a list of officers appointed to raise the several companies of the regiment, compiled from the Commission Books at the War Office, and placed in order according to the dates of the captains' commissions; we may state that, at this period, the appointment of subalterns was to a specified company, their transfer to another company could only be effected by a new commission:—

CAPTAINS.			1st. LIEUTENANTS.			2nd LIEUTENANTS.		
Col. Lord Dartmouth,	11th June, 1685					—— Seymour,	11th June, 1685	
Lt.-Col. Thomas Talmash,	,,	,,	Frederick Mole,	11th June, 1685		Thos. Orby,	,,	,,
Major Robert St. Clair,	,,	,,	Theophilus Garlick,	,,	,,	Francis Devenish,	,,	,,
Capt. James Adams,	,,	,,						
Thomas Soper,			Edward Vincent,	14th,	,,	Henry Fleetwood,	12th	,,
Martin Beckman,			John Pitt,	,,	,,	David Williams,	14th	,,
Thomas Whalley,	13th	,,				Michael Chivers,	13th	,,
Charles Fitzwilliam,	15th	,,	Thomas Hart,	15th,	,,			
Richard Fowler,	16th	,,				John Shales,	16th	,,
John Boys,	19th	,,	John Salter,	18th,	,,	Daniel Sutton,	18th	,,
William Freeman,	19th	,,	Robert Dancy,	19th,	,,	Richard Betesworth,	19th	,,
John Pennington,	21st	,,				John Livesay,	20th	,,
Henry Vaughan,	21st	,,	Rupert Kempthorne,	17th ·	,,	William Frowde,	21st	,,
Adjt. Christr. Worthevale,	11th	,,	Surgeon, Andrew Heriot,	11th	,,	Chaplain, Knightley Chetewood, June 11th		,,

On the 23rd August Adjutant Worthevale was promoted to First Lieutenant in Captain Whalley's Company, and was succeeded in the Adjutancy by John Shackleton, whose commission is dated the same day.

<small>The Uniform of the Regiment.</small> The uniform was scarlet coats, lined with yellow, grey breeches and grey stockings, yellow cloth caps ornamented with military devices, similar to those afterwards adopted for Grenadiers. The regiment was speedily raised, and on the 4th July the several companies were directed to proceed to the Tower of London to perform the duties of that fortress.

<small>Three Companies sent to Sheerness</small> On the 3rd September three companies of the regiment were sent *via* Dartford and Rochester to Sheerness, "to do duty there as the governor shall direct."

* It will be observed that only one major was appointed to the regiment, the duties of the present "senior" major being at that time discharged by the lieutenant-colonel, while the colonel was really a combatant officer, and in actual command of his regiment.

"WINDSOR, 7th Sept., 1685.

"SIR,—The King having ordered three companies of the Royal Regiment of Fusiliers to remain in garrison at Sheerness, instead of the three companies that were usually lodged there, and the quarters being too strait, unless some of the officers be lodged in the navy dock, His Majesty thinks fit that you signify his pleasure to the officers of the dock that they afford quarters to such of the officers of those companies as need them. Being all I have in command, I remain, &c.,

"To Mr. Pepys."   "WILLIAM BLATHWAYTE.

These companies remained there only until October, when being relieved by a detachment of the Queen Dowager's Regiment, they returned to the Tower, where the whole regiment spent the winter. Before the close of the year the establishment was reduced to eleven companies of fusiliers, with the same complement of officers and non-commissioned officers, but only fifty private soldiers; and one company of miners with two officers, one sergeant, two corporals, one drummer, and forty privates. *Reduction of the Establishment.*

1686.

The spring of this year was spent by the regiment in the Tower. On the 25th May the company of miners, with a detachment of fusiliers, was ordered to convey the tents and other necessaries to Hounslow Heath, and to mark out the camp that the King proposed to establish there. Evil times were then falling upon the country; the King's rule was creating great dissatisfaction and fear, and among the first to express discontent was the Lieutenant-Colonel of the Fusiliers, Talmash, who, on the 1st May, resigned his commission and left the country. On the same day Captain William Freeman also left the regiment; Major St. Clair was promoted to the Lieutenant-Colonelcy, and Captain Soper to the Majority. On the 13th June, Lord Dartmouth was ordered to send such other detachments of the Fusiliers with convoys to Hounslow Heath as were necessary. One of these detachments was an escort to 30 guns, which on the 19th proceeded from the Tower to the camp. The weather was then very unfavourable; a succession of storms and rain, succeeded by excessive heat, so reduced the health of the camp that a great many men were sick, and not a few died. But still James persisted in seizing every opportunity of making strong military demonstrations to overawe the people. Before proceeding to Hounslow the Fusiliers had been reviewed by the King in Hyde Park on the 16th March, when 6000 troops were present; but this exhibition had failed of its object. The camp, therefore, was to shew the people the still greater strength, readiness, and devotion of the army. *Camp at Hounslow Heath.*

Description of Camp Life.

At first it was regarded with awe; but this feeling soon died away. Macaulay says: "The Londoners saw this great force assembled in their neighbourhood with a terror which familiarity soon diminished. A visit to Hounslow Heath became their favourite amusement on holidays. The camp presented the appearance of a vast fair. Mingled with the musketeers and dragoons, a multitude of fine gentlemen and ladies from Soho Square, sharpers and painted women from Whitefriars, invalids in sedans, monks in hoods and gowns, lacqueys in rich liveries, pedlars, orange girls, mischievous apprentices, and gaping clowns, were constantly passing and repassing through the long lanes of tents. From some pavilions were heard the noises of drunken revelry, from others the curses of gamblers. In truth, the place was merely a gay suburb of the capital. The King, as was amply proved two years later, had greatly miscalculated. He had forgotten that vicinity operates in more ways than one. He had hoped that his army would overawe London; but the result of his policy was that the feeling and opinions of the Londoners took complete possession of his army."* The regiment did not, however, remain long in this strange training ground, where it had 590 men present and doing duty. The Royal Fusiliers left the camp on the

Return to the Tower.

evening of Monday the 9th August, and entered the Tower next morning, where they were stationed for the winter. In "A List of King James's Army at Hounslow Heath, 30th June, 1686, with the names of the General Officers, Field Officers, Colour of their Clothes and Number of Men," the regiment is thus noticed:—

Colonel Lord Dartmouth	Red lined with yellow	12 Companies.
Lieutenant-Colonel St. Clair	Grey breeches and stockings	50 Officers.
Major Soper		600 Men.

* Macaulay's History of England. We have a description of the camp, which shows the position of the Royal Fusiliers: "The horse, foot, and dragoons are encamped in a straight line; the intervals between the foot are seventy paces; the intervals between each regiment of horse about fifty paces, and the intervals between the horse on the left and the dragoons (because of the ground) is near half a mile. The lieutenants' and ensigns' tents are in the rear of the respective companies in a direct line, seventeen paces from the soldiers' huts or tents; the captains' tents twelve paces behind the lieutenants'; the colonels' tents behind the captains, ten paces; the lieutenant-colonel on the right of the colonel, and the major on the left in a direct line. The brigadier-generals have their tents twenty paces behind the colonels. The King's tent and chapel is in the rear of the left of the horse on the left, and the general officers' tents behind the King's. The Fusiliers are encamped in the rear of the line, a good distance behind the interval between the Earl of Craven's regiment and the Scots Guards; and in several places about the horse carriages. The guns are planted about one hundred paces before the line, before the interval between the Scots Guards and Prince George's regiment, guarded by a party of Fusiliers; each gun having two gunners and a matross to attend to it. The suttling booths are about two hundred paces in rear of the line."

1687.

While the regiment was lying in the Tower, the establishment was again increased in accordance with the following warrant issued to the Paymaster General:— {Establishment increased.}

"JAMES R.—Whereas we have thought fit to add one Company more to Our Royal Regiment of Fusiliers, and to apply the pay of one of the non-regimented companies mentioned in our establishment to the entertainment of the said company of Fusiliers, with the addition of one shilling per diem to the youngest lieutenant, and one shilling and sixpence for the pay of one sergeant, and one shilling for one drummer more. Our will and pleasure is that you include the pay of the said company, and additional allowances, within the certificates or debentures you shall from time to time make out for the pay of Our said Royal Regiment of Fusiliers, to commence from the 1st January last; and for so doing this shall be your sufficient warrant.

"Given at our Court at Whitehall, this 12th day of March, 1686-7, in the third year of our reign."

Captain Cheek was appointed to the command of this company; on the 9th June he was succeeded by Captain St. Ange.

At the end of April the regiment marched from the Tower to Blackheath to guard the mortars and stores sent there for the purpose of making experiments before His Majesty. The proceedings, which curiously illustrate the history of artillery, are thus quaintly reported by Lutterell: "The 29th, was tried an experiment on Blackheath of bombs with two mines; mortars of 300 weight, one with 9 cylinders, to shoot as many bullets; as also a sort of fiery hott bullett, to burn ships." At the expiration of the service the men were each paid 6d. per day in addition to their pay, and the regiment returned to the Tower. {Artillery experiments at Blackheath.}

The summer saw the Fusiliers again in camp at Hounslow, and the camp again in the condition described by Macaulay. Evelyn, in his diary, under date 6th June, says, "the camp was again pitched at Hounslow, the commanders profusely vying in the expense and magnificence of tents." The regiment did not, however, assemble there with the infantry regiments, for it was not until the 15th of June when it left the Tower, on which day it escorted the train of artillery, "with ammunition and other provisions for the camp," through the city of London. On the 19th August, a grand military spectacle "was performed at the camp, the taking of Buda, to the satisfaction of the spectators." During this month the Fusiliers left the camp, and returned to the Tower, and to quarters in the neighbourhood of that fortress. {In Camp at Hounslow Heath.}

That the whole of the regiment cannot have resided in the Tower, but was scattered over the neighbouring taverns as was the case with the other regiments garrisoning London, is clear from the following order:—

<small>General Order regulating the Pay of the Regiment.</small>

General Order.

"Whitehall, Nov. 27th, 1687.

"JAMES R.—For the better preventing all complaints that may be made touching any debts that shall be hereafter contracted by private soldiers of Foot within Our pay and entertainment, we have thought fit hereby to declare Our Royal pleasure to all persons whom it may concern within our garrisons or elsewhere, that no private soldier of any regiment or company of foot be trusted on any account whatsoever in these quarters; and to the end every private soldier may be enabled duly and constantly to discharge his quarters, and pay for what shall be necessary for him, we do hereby further direct and require every respective captain or officer in chief with any company of foot to pay and satisfy unto each private soldier under their command three shillings per week, at two equal payments to be made at the beginning and middle of each week, as *subsistence money*, without any deduction whatsoever; and that they do likewise account every two months with each soldier for sixpence *per week* more, allowed by us for the providing such necessaries for each soldier to which the off-reckonings to be employed by the Colonel of each respective regiment for the clothing and poundage, and satisfying all other remaining expenses, for which a due account is likewise to be made unto each soldier at the time of every clothing. It being nevertheless Our pleasure that the officers of Our Regiments of Foot Guards do pay by advance four shillings per week; and the officers of Our Royal Regiment of Fusiliers three shillings and sixpence per week, allowed by Us to each private soldier in the respective regiments for their subsistence; and do also account with the soldiers under their command for the remainder of their pay as above mentioned. And We do hereby strictly charge and command all governors, lieutenant-governors, and commanders-in-chief of Our garrisons, or of any regiment or company of foot in Our Service to take especial care that these Our Orders be duly observed and put in execution.

"Given at our Court at Whitehall, the 27th day of November, 1687, in the third year of Our reign.

"By His Majesty's Command,

"W. BLATHWAYTE."

<small>Description of the Arms of the Fusiliers and Miners.</small>

The armament of the regiment was this year thus settled:—

"Musquetiers of all other regiments of foot (excepting our Regiment of Fuziliers, the Granadiers, and the Company of Miners) to have matchlock and Snaphance musquetts; the barrells whereof to be 3 foot 6 inches long, good swords, and bandiliers.

"Our Royal Regiment of Fuziliers to have Snaphance musquetts strapt, with bright barrells of 3 foot 8 inches long, with good swords, cartouch boxes, and bionetts.

"The Companies of Miners to have long carabines, strapt; the barrells to be 3 foot 2 inches in length; cartouch boxes, bionetts, and extraordinary hammer hatchets."

During this year the regiment was in a greatly troubled state. Some of the old officers were so dissatisfied with the King's measures that they threw up their commissions. Among these was Sir John Morgan, who, on leaving the regiment, gave his allegiance to the Whig party. His career during the

Revolution we have not traced, but, it being accomplished, he came into favour. On the 28th May, 1689, he was made governor of Chester, which appointment he held till his death in 1693.

Capt. St. Ange, the junior captain, was a Frenchman, a Roman Catholic, and, no doubt, one of Louis's emissaries. His appointment, and indeed the very enrolment of the company, was a part of the fatal effort James made to place the military power of the country in the hands of the members of his church; and, as a menace to their religious liberty, was one of the strongest causes of discord betwixt him, his army, and people. Its effect both on the regiment and the nation was soon realised.

The first official list of officers of the Royal Fusiliers that we have been able to obtain is from the Harl. MS., 4847: it refers to this year:—

CAPTAINS.	1st LIEUTENANTS.	2nd LIEUTENANTS.
Geo. Lord Dartmouth, Col.	Sir Francis Windebank.	Thomas Orby.
Robert St. Clair, Lieut.-Col.	Frederick Mole.	Fras. Devenish.
Thomas Soper, Major.	Edwd. Vincent.	Henry Fleetwood.
Thomas Whalley.	Christ. Worthevale.	Michael Chivers.
Sir Martin Beckman.	Theoph. Garlick.	David Williams.
Richard Fowler.	Wm. Richardson.	John Shales.
John Boys.	John Salter.	Daniel Sutton.
John Pennington.	Anthony Brown.	John Livesay.
Henry Vaughan.	Rupert Kempthorne.	Wm. Frowde.
Edmund Wilson.	Thomas Hart.	Patrick Seaton.
Will. Seymour.	Robert Dancy.	Richd. Betesworth.
Thos. Haggerston.	Edwd. Haggerston.	Robt. Lowick.
Anthony St. Ange.	Benj. Blewer.	Thos. Richardson.
James Adams (Miners).	John Pitt.	

Chaplain: Knightley Chetwood.   Adjt.: John Shackleton.
Chirugeon: Andrew Herriott.   Qr.-Mas.: Christopher Simpson.

On the 20th December Thomas Phillips was appointed Captain of the Company of Miners *vice* James Adams, who is believed to have been promoted. He did not long retain the command, but, as "Engineer" Phillips, was known in William's Wars.

The careers of others of the above can be traced out of the regiment, and through the stormy period so rapidly approaching. Robert Lowick was the Major Lowick who was executed for high treason in 1696, as one of the plotters of the assassination of King William, after having fought under James in Ireland. His comrades, the Haggerstons, will soon come before us as Jacobites, who had to be removed from the regiment, and who, like him, then took up arms in the service of James.

1688.

Discontent in the Regiment.
Though the occupation of the Fusiliers during the tranquil portion of the reign of King James was a monotonous repetition of the camp at Hounslow in summer, and quarters in the Tower in winter, the inner life of the regiment was not without excitement. The men, all Englishmen, though soldiers, had not surrendered all ideas of their civil rights. Amongst them there was the same disgust at the behaviour of the King that was manifested in civil life. The King had raised them mainly to support his authority; but a curious incident in their career, shows how little they, as well as the rest of the army, were disposed to do so at the expense of the national liberties. When, at the time of the trial of the Seven Bishops in June, the Fusiliers were guarding the prisoners in the Tower, they openly avowed their sympathy for the persecuted dignitaries. Burnet tells us that the king's order for the imprisonment of the prelates, "set the whole city in the highest fermentation that was ever known in memory of man. The bishops were sent by water to the Tower: and all along, as they passed, the banks of the river were full of people, who kneeled down and asked their blessing, and with loud shouts expressed their good wishes for them, and their concern in their preservation. The soldiers and other officers in the Tower did the same. A universal consternation appeared in all people's looks. But the king was not moved with all this." While the bishops remained under their guard in the Tower, the Fusiliers repeatedly insisted on drinking their health. "When Sir Edward Hales, the Constable of the Tower, heard of these proceedings, he sent orders to the Captain of the Guard to check them; but the answer given was, that they were doing it at that very instant, and would drink that health, and no other, while the bishops were there. The bishops were brought before the judges in the King's Bench on the 29th June, and were acquitted to the great joy of the whole country. On the same day, detachments of several Irish regiments, under Sir Charles Carney, were sent to the Tower to relieve the Fusiliers, who were sent to the camp then just formed on Hounslow Heath.*

*See Burnet's *History of his Own Times*, and Gen. Hamilton's *History of the Grenadier Guards*. Vol. I, p. 295.

[1688—London.] *Record of the Royal Regiment of Fusiliers.* 11

On the 10th August, the Fusiliers returned to the Tower; but though the regiment, notwithstanding the recent émeute, was more loyal to the king than most of the regiments in the service, and, as a mark of its loyalty, its Lieut.-Colonel, St. Clair, was in July made governor of Tilbury Fort, it still contained a large proportion of malcontents. On the 1st September, when collision between the King and the nation became inevitable, a general augmentation of the army took place; ten men were added to each company of the Fusiliers. The regiment then consisted of twelve companies of fusiliers, one of grenadiers, and one of miners. At this time it appears to have been entirely quartered in the tower, the officers being lodged in the house of Owen Wynn, Esq., Warden of the Mint, with whom an agreement was entered into for the hire of his house for £40 per annum, for their use while quartered there. *Augmentation of the Regiment.*

These preparations hurried on the crisis they were intended to avert. The temper of the people could no longer be doubted. At the end of September Lord Dartmouth was ordered to send a lieutenant, with forty fusiliers and a proportion of non-commissioned officers, on board the fleet, to serve as marines against the anticipated invasion of the Dutch. Lieutenant Livesay was sent in command. In November the King and nation were at open hostility. William, Prince of Orange, had been invited to assist the people, and he had accepted the invitation. The fleet was then commanded by the Colonel of the Fusiliers, Admiral Lord Dartmouth, a man whose loyalty to the King was not doubted; but the Rear-Admiral, Sir John Berry, many of the captains, and most of the seamen were favourable to the people. Lieutenant Livesay was also found to be disloyal; he was sent up to London in custody, on suspicion of going over to the Dutch.* In the meantime the invaders had sailed from Holland, and accomplished their landing in England. *A Detachment sent to serve as Marines.* *Lieutenant Livesay Arrested for Disloyalty.*

The regiment was still in the Tower waiting to be called into action to resist the invaders, when, on the 5th November, the very day that William's ships were debarking the first troops in the harbour of Torbay, an order whose meaning is now lost in mystery was issued to the regiment; the Adjutant, Mr. *Secret Service to be performed.*

---

*He is believed to have regained his commission under William, and to have become a Major-General; if so, he served in Marlborough's campaigns, and died at his seat in Bedfordshire on the 23rd Feb., 1718. Of this there can be but little doubt.

Shackleton, was ordered "to be supplied with a pair of pistols and a dark lantern, to be returned at the end of the service." Three days later the regiment seemed on the point of leaving its quarters. On the 8th, the Justices of Essex were ordered to press four teams of able horses and wagons, as may be intimated to them by the Lieutenant-Colonel or Major of the Royal Fusiliers, for carrying the baggage and ammunition of the regiment, then ordered to march from the Tower with the Royal train of Artillery. But the regiment did not move; its presence in London growing not less pressing, its services not less mysterious. On the 10th, when London was in revolt, and James's authority crumbling to pieces, eighteen pairs of pistols were served out to the sergeants of the regiment—for a purpose that we cannot announce.

The story of the downfall of a worthless King, when he was deserted by his people, need not be told here, for the Royal Fusiliers performed but a small part in the events of the change. They remained in the Tower, with little change to themselves, until the 11th December, when James dropped down the river from Somerset House in the first stage of his flight, and the lords spiritual and temporal met at the Guildhall, and having declared for the Prince of Orange, sent down "to the Tower to demand the keyes thereof, which were sent to their lordships, and they appointed the Lord Lucas governour thereof." Their first action was "to secure the peace in London and Westminster, by disarming papists and secureing all Romish priests." This involved the immediate dismissal from the regiment of Captain Haggerston, Lieutenant Haggerston, one sergeant, and some privates, known Roman Catholics. The Haggerstons were the sons of Sir Thomas Haggerston, an active agent of King James, whom that monarch had appointed governor of Berwick. Captain Haggerston, who commanded the grenadiers of the regiment, afterwards lost his life in Ireland, fighting under the banner of his King. His brother took holy orders in the Roman Catholic Church.

Roman Catholic Officers Dismissed.

With the delivery of the keys of the Tower to the Privy Council, the regiment seems to have left the fortress, but only for a very short time. After James had fled to France, and the reins of Government had fallen into William's hands, the regiment remained only for a short time in London. It was then under the command of Major Soper, a most determined adherent of King James, who, on the 13th December, was ordered by the Privy Council to march his regiment into the Tower and adjacent hamlets, but this order was soon revoked, and the regiment sent to Barnet, the metropolis being emptied of English troops to make room for the Dutch. Captain St. Ange, a Frenchman and a Roman Catholic, was seized at Court and sent prisoner to Newgate. The regiment did not stay long at Barnet. On the 29th December, the thirteen companies were ordered to leave that town, seven of them being sent to Norwich, and six, under the command of Captain Pennington, to Yarmouth. *The Fusiliers sent to Barnet. thence to Norwich and Yarmouth.*

During this eventful year several changes had taken place in the regiment. Without knowing the exact fate of their predecessors we find that on the 3rd October, W. Forbes was appointed Lieutenant in Major Soper's Company, Henry Fleetwood became 1st Lieutenant of Lord Dartmouth's Company, James Lucas, Lieutenant of Captain John Pennington's Company, Charles Hacon of Captain Fowler's Company, and John Shackleton, the Adjutant of Captain Haggerston's Company. The officers in whose places they were appointed were Sir Francis Windebank, John Livesay, John Shales, and Robert Lowick. Sir Francis we know was in trouble some years later for his Jacobite principles; Livesay appears to have lost his commission for the reason which caused his arrest as already stated; of Shales we know nothing further than that he was of a Jacobite family; and Lowick's fate has already been given. Of Forbes and Hacon, nothing certainly can be said; but it is more than probable they were Roman Catholics, and owed their commissions solely to their creed. Lucas became a Captain in the regiment. *Promotion and appointment of Officers.*

From the period of the Revolution, the Royal Fusiliers ceased to be considered exclusively an Ordnance Regiment, and took their turn of duty with the regular regiments of the line. Their arms and organisation were not, however, changed; they still continued to be without pikemen, and every man remained armed with a fusil. About this time, also, the company of Miners passed from the command of Captain Phillips into that of Captain Pitts, whose Lieutenant was also named Pitts, and appears to have been his son; it proceeded to Flanders and served to the end of the war. *The Regiment ceases to be exclusively an Ordnance Regiment.*

In November, the establishment and cost of the regiment were as follow:—

Royal Regiment of Fusiliers, consisting of 11 Companies of 50 men, and one of 40 miners; in all 590, besides officers.

FIELD AND STAFF OFFICERS.	PER DIEM. £ s. d.	PER ANNUM. £ s. d.
Colonel, as Colonel	0 12 0	219 0 0
Lieutenant-Colonel, as Lieutenant-Col.	0 7 0	127 15 0
Major, as Major	0 5 0	91 5 0
Chirugeon, 4s.; and 1 mate, 2s. 6d.	0 6 6	118 12 6
Adjutant	0 4 0	73 0 0
Chaplain	0 6 8	121 13 4
Quarter-Master and Marshal	0 4 0	73 0 0
Gunsmith, 4s.; his servant, 1s.	0 5 0	91 5 0
	£2 10 2	£915 10 10
(One Company)		
Captain	0 8 0	146 0 0
Two Lieutenants at 4s. each	0 8 0	146 0 0
Three Sergeants at 1s. 6d. each	0 4 6	82 2 6
Three Corporals at 1s. each	0 3 0	54 15 0
Two Drummers at 1s. each	0 2 0	36 10 0
Fifty Soldiers at 8d. each	1 13 4	608 6 8
	£2 18 10	£1073 14 2
The pay of Ten Companies more at the rates and numbers above expressed	29 8 4	£10737 1 8
(One Company of Miners belonging to this Regiment.)		
Captain	0 5 0	91 5 0
Lieutenant	0 4 0	73 0 0
One Sergeant	0 2 6	45 12 6
Two Corporals at 2s. each	0 4 0	73 0 0
One Drummer	0 1 0	18 5 0
Forty Miners at 1s. 6d. each	3 0 0	1095 0 0
Total for this Regiment	£38 13 10	£14122 9 2

1689.

In February the companies at Yarmouth took part in the proclamation of the accession of King William III. and Queen Mary to the throne. On the 1st March the companies at Yarmouth, as well as those at Norwich, were ordered to march to Mendlesham, Debenham, Framlingham, Saxmundham, and Wickham,

Change of Quarter.

and to these stations the Royal Fusiliers proceeded. At this period the effects of the political changes were still operating; discipline had not entirely resumed its sway over the individual preferences of the soldiery; the regiment, like several other regiments in the Service, was in a disaffected state, and losing many men by desertion. Finding this disaffection to be, in some cases, deeply rooted, William resolved to send the disaffected corps over to Holland, and to replace Ordered to Holland. them with Dutch troops, which, as uninfluenced by factious differences, he intended to keep about him in England until tranquillity should be restored, and the stability of his throne ensured. The Royal Fusiliers and the Royal Scots were two of the regiments ordered to embark. Harwich was the port selected for embarkation, and there they were marched. The insubordination of the Royal Scots at Ipswich, on the receipt of this order, is an event well known in the history of the British army, but it is not so well known that they had, as sympathisers, many men from the Royal Fusiliers, some of whom openly joined the Scots in their revolt, while the remainder seemed ready to imitate their example. The greater part of the regiment was however embarked; Captain John Pennington being left at home to secure the deserters, who were to be taken to Harwich.

The Royal Fusiliers joined the Dutch Army at Tongres, and served the campaign under Prince Waldeck. No general action took place; but in a succession of combats the advantage was on the side of the Confederates. Of these combats the most important was that which occurred at Walcourt. On the 25th August, a picket of the 16th Regiment, under Colonel Hodges, was attacked in Combat of Walcourt. the village of Forgé, near Walcourt. Hodges, a stout Tangier veteran, accepted battle, and made so fierce a fight that the two armies became engaged. The details of the affair are not given with sufficient clearness for us to ascertain the exact services of the Royal Fusiliers; but the result was that the French were beaten with considerable loss. The English troops, and especially their commander, the Earl of Marlborough, gained great praise. "The testimony which Waldeck, in his despatch, bore to the gallant conduct of the islanders was read with delight by their countrymen. The fight, indeed, was no more than a skirmish: but it was a sharp and bloody skirmish. There had within living memory been no equally serious encounter between the English and French; and our ancestors were naturally elated by finding that many years of inaction and vassalage did not appear to have enervated the courage of the nation."* As the reward of his skill, Marlborough received the colonelcy of the Royal Fusiliers, his commission being dated on the following day, the 26th August. Lord Dartmouth had previously been removed from the command for adhering to the interests of King James.

1690.

The Fusiliers recalled to England.

In the spring of this year the regiment was recalled to England. The civil war had been carried to Ireland, whither William had gone with the army, leaving England bare of troops, while the French were assembling a force in Normandy. To meet this threatened invasion Churchill's brigade was brought home in June. Upon the arrival of the five regiments comprising the brigade, at Gravesend, Hales' (14th) regiment was to march to Dartford, Erith, and Woolwich, Churchill's (3rd Buffs) to Greenwich and Deptford, Colyear's to the Tower Hamlets, the Royal Fusiliers and Fitzpatrick's to Rotherhithe, Southwark, and Lambeth. The Royal Fusiliers went to Southwark. By this time the Fusiliers had shaken off the discordant influences of the turmoil the nation had so recently passed through, and had settled down into the normal condition of a well-disciplined corps. This result had not been arrived at in tranquillity. Considerable change in the command of the regiment had to be effected. The Jacobite element seems to have been entirely removed. Major Soper, who was proclaimed for high treason, had absconded, and Capt. Wilson had succeeded to the Majority, Lieut. Hart succeeding to his Company. In August the Regiment changed quarters; it was sent to Greenwich, Deptford, and Lewisham; Fitzpatrick's Regiment relieving it in Southwark. Immediately afterwards it again changed its quarters, being sent to Salisbury and Wilton.

Quartered in Southwark.

While William, in prosecuting the war in Ireland, was brought to bay before Limerick, Marlborough proposed, as a diversion, the attack of Cork, then accounted strong from the works constructed by the Irish and French, and possessed by a garrison of 4000 men. "He pressed the Queen and Council to trust him with 5000 of the troops who were then lying idle in England, and pawned his reputation that he would take both Cork and Kinsale before winter." Confident of success, Marl-

* Macaulay—*History of England.*

borough persisted until the matter was laid before the King. William approved of the measure, and ordered the Queen to provide him with the necessary forces. The Royal Fusiliers were one of the regiments selected. It was immediately recalled from Salisbury, and without knowing the object of the change, ordered to Southsea Common, the place appointed by Marlborough for the rendezvous of the forces. It arrived at Southsea on the 27th August. On the 29th and 30th, the whole of the troops were embarked, but, owing to adverse winds, they did not sail until the 18th September, when the fleet stood out to sea. They arrived in Cork Harbour on the 21st, and were immediately landed. The train of Artillery consisted of ten demi-culverins, twelve drakes, and two three-pounders. Batteries were at once erected against the works. After a siege of four days, on the 28th the breach in the city wall was ready for assault. Four English regiments, of which the Fusiliers were one, were ordered forward, the Grenadiers leading. To reach the breach they had to pass a bog, called the Rape Marsh, in which they sank to the armpits, but they struggled gallantly through the quagmire, and reached the breach. The close fighting was just about to begin, when a parley was beaten, and Cork surrendered.

Ordered for foreign service.

Land at Cork.

From Cork Marlborough instantly pushed on to Kinsale. The Old Fort was carried by a *coup de main*; batteries were then erected against the stronger works, and again in a few days Kinsale was ready for assault, but like Cork, it declined to meet the storm: as the troops were about to mount the breach it surrendered. The Irish troops retired to Limerick. The Royal Fusiliers were placed in garrison at Kinsale, where they remained during the rest of the year. Though the campaign had not been costly of life by the sword, "the deadly work which, in that age, the moist earth and air of Ireland seldom failed, in the autumnal season, to perform on English soldiers," had stricken down many men; the Fusiliers had 186 sick in hospital, the other regiments suffering in like proportion, and with representatives of the other regiments several of the officers of the Royal Fusiliers were sent over to England to recruit.

Capture of Kinsale.

1691.

In January, the Royal Fusiliers and Fitzpatrick's Regiment received orders to embark for Flanders, where William, freed now from anxiety for Ireland, determined to carry on a vigorous campaign. The transports arrived at Kinsale on the 11th

Embark for Flanders.

when the regiments embarked. After a long delay caused by the still threatened invasion of the French and the great alarm that prevailed in England, where the Militia were assembled and marched down to the Coast, the watchmen being posted at the beacons, the regiments sailed under convoy of the "Nonsuch" and "Milford" frigates. In bearing down Channel they met with a succession of dreadful storms, and had to put into Milford Haven on the 13th March, short of one ship. They sailed again on the 21st, but on the 28th were compelled to put into Plymouth. Eventually they reached Ostend, early in April. The regiment went into quarters in West Flanders, where it was joined by the recruits and men left sick in Ireland. The army assembled at Gemblours, the Royal Fusiliers being placed in Churchill's brigade, together with Bath's (10th), Hodge's (16th), and Fitzpatrick's Regiments. The campaign of this year was not important; on the 20th September there was a sharp rear-guard combat in passing the defiles of Catoire, between Leuse and Cambronne, when both sides suffered. In October, the Fusiliers were encamped at Ninove under Prince Waldeck. The army separated on the 19th October; the Royal Fusiliers were sent to Namur, the other English Regiments going to Louvain and other garrisons in Flanders.

1692.

On the 23rd January, the Earl of Marlborough, who had fallen into disrepute at the Court, was superseded in the command of the Royal Fusiliers, he was succeeded by Lord George Hamilton, a celebrated soldier who afterwards became Earl of Orkney.

During the month of January the French were moving between the Sambre and Meuse, and "in the meantime our parties were continually abroad from Brussels, Namur, Charleroy, Huy, and Liege, who advance as far as Dinant, Thuin, Walcourt, and Beaumont, to observe the enemy's motions; and the necessary measures are taken for the assembling and marching our forces upon the first command." Among their other duties the Fusiliers were engaged in making the "new way, 60 yards broad," to communicate with Liege and Huy.

In May the British forces assembled at Duffel, near Malines. The French had laid siege to Namur with an army of 40,000 men, Luxemburgh with other 60,000

1692—FLANDERS.] *Record of the Royal Regiment of Fusiliers.* 19

covering the siege. The Royal Fusiliers and Castleton's Regiment formed part of the garrison. The siege was conducted with great vigour. The defence was {Nemur beseiged by the French.} equally energetic, much heavy fighting taking place from time to time, wherein both parties suffered heavy losses. The overwhelming force of the French was not, however, to be denied. On the 28th the town capitulated. The garrison retired into the Castle.

The defence of the Castle of Namur and the new fort, called Fort William, and constructed by Coehorn, was a gallant exploit. On the 1st, 2nd, 3rd, 4th, and 5th of June the French assaulted Fort William, and on each occasion were driven off with a loss amounting in the aggregate to not less than 6000 men. The fort, however, was carried by assault on the 13th, when the French turned all their efforts against the Castle. Again the same stubborn fighting was renewed. Once or twice the guns of the Castle drove the French out of their works in Fort William, but with a pertinacity created as much by superior numbers as by courage, they clung to the post. At length a breach was made in the Castle walls, when with magazines nearly empty, with provisions exhausted, and with a force reduced to one-tenth of the besiegers, the garrison was compelled to capitulate. But so hardly had they fought, so severely had they punished their conquerors, that they were {The Castle capitulates.} allowed to march out of the place with arms loaded and matches lighted, with drums beating and colours flying, to Louvain, where the two English regiments joined William's army. They were among the English regiments reviewed by the King in the presence of the Elector of Bavaria on the 29th June.*

William was then encamped at Mele, hoping to be able to raise the siege of Namur, but the great force and skilful manœuvres of Luxemburgh, who covered the siege, had frustrated his every attempt. After the capture of the fortress both armies

---

* We believe that at this time the Company of Miners was entirely separated from the regiment; but it also seems to have been on active service. "MARIE R.—Whereas it hath been represented to us that the arms belonging to the Company of Miners, commanded by Capt. John Pitt, are become unserviceable, Our will and pleasure is therefore that out of the stores remaining within the Office of our Ordnance you cause the said Company of Miners to be supplied with 52 long carbines strapt, 2 partzans, 2 drums, 52 hatchets, 2 officers' tents furnished, the same to be delivered to Capt. Pitt, or whom he may appoint to receive them, taking the usual indenture. Our further pleasure is that you also cause the unserviceable arms now with the said company to be received into our stores, there to remain for our further service.

"By Her Majesty's command,
"NOTTINGHAM."

continued to manœuvre until the 24th July, when William attacked Luxemburgh at Steinkirk. The contemporary account of the action, in which it is impossible to discover the operations of the Fusiliers further than as belonging to the detachment of Churchill's brigade, is as follows:—

<small>Battle of Steinkirk.</small>

"On Sunday, July 24th (Aug. 3, N. S.) our army marched early in the morning, the heavy baggage being ordered to repass the Senne at Hal. There were several defiles to pass, and the ways to be made, which made it a tedious march; but, however, about ten o'clock, the Prince of Wirtemburg with the vanguard, which consisted of four battalions of English foot, two of the Danes, and a detachment of Churchill's brigade, advanced towards the enemy, and fell upon them with so much vigour that he drove them from bridge to bridge, posted himself in the road that fronted the right wing of their army, and erected two batteries of cannon on little eminences, one on the right and the other on the left of the wood. Whilst these batteries were playing upon the enemy the Confederate Army marched up to the head of the defile, about half an English mile from the wood, where it opened in a little plain, not above half a league over, which terminated upon the right of the wood, and upon several rows of high trees planted in order. Upon the right of this plain there was a farm, which soon after the engagement was set on fire by the enemy, to cover (by the smoke) several of their battalions that were ordered this way. From the head of the defile, upon the left of the plain, there was a deep hollow way, with high trees and hedges upon the banks of it, which reached as far as the wood where the vanguard was posted, and there it branched itself into two other deep ways, and going through the wood upon the left to the Danes' attack, and to that of the Guards; and the other upon the right, going along the outside of the wood. Between these two last were posted the regiments of Sir Robert Douglas (Royal Scots), Col. Fitzpatrick, and Col. O'Farrel (21st Regiment).

"When the Confederate Army was come up to the head of these defiles, and just entering into the small plain, they were ordered to halt, except the English Life Guards, and horse, and dragoons, the Lord Cutts's, Lieut.-Gen. Mackay's, Sir Charles Graham's, and the Earl of Angus's regiments; which, being interlined with the horse, were commanded at the same time to the right skirts of the wood; whilst the Prince of Hesse's (6th), Colonel Lowther's, and the Earl of Leven's (25th) Regiments were also intermingled with the left wing of horse, and posted upon the outside of the wood. Things being thus disposed, and the army continuing in their halt, Prince Wirtemberg, after he had commanded for above two hours, began the attack with the Danes upon the right, which was immediately followed by the other four English regiments, which composed the vanguard; and seconded by Cutts's, Mackay's, Angus's, Graham's, Lowther's, the Prince of Hesse's, and Leven's regiments. Never was more terrible, and, at the same time, more regular firing heard, for during the space of two hours it seemed to be continued claps of thunder. The vanguard behaved themselves with so much bravery and resolution that, though they received the charge of several battalions of the enemy's, one after another, yet they drove them beyond one of their batteries of seven pieces of cannon, of which the Danes and the second battalion of English Guards possessed themselves, and which Colonel Wauchop, who commanded the English, would have sent away, had not the French cut off the traces, and carried away the horses. Sir Robert Douglas, with his first battalion, charged several of the enemy's, and beat them from three several hedges, and made himself master of the fourth; when going through a gap to get on the other side he was unfortunately killed upon the spot. All the other regiments behaved themselves with equal bravery: firing muzzle to muzzle through the hedges, they on the one side, and the enemy on the other." *

But their bravery was of little avail; assailed by overpowering numbers, including the Household Brigade—the chivalry of France, who rushed on with the most violent energy to save the shattered infantry—the allies were borne back and compelled to retreat. Slowly and defiantly, turning from time to time upon their pursuers, they left the field of battle; nor were the French disposed to push them hard, for their own sufferings had been vast and terrible; they had felt too keenly the temper of the men over whom they had triumphed. "Though the French did follow us for some time," writes one of the actors, with a grim quaintness that realises the desperate scene, "yet they did not fire a shot; such was the order of our retreat they did not dare venture upon it. The English Grenadiers brought up the rear, and whenever the French moved towards us, they faced to the right about, and presented themselves to the enemy: then the enemy would halt, and so our rear-

Retreat of the British.

* Kennett's History of England, vol. 3, p. 650.

guard then marched on: this halting and facing, and then marching continued for some time, till the night put an end to the enemy's farther motion. And thus the army came back to Halle, on Monday morning about three of the clock."*

The total losses of the Fusiliers in this bloody battle are not exactly known but they were considerable; one officer, Lieut. McDonnell is known to have been killed. It is also believed that two of the officers captured by the French, Lieuts. Groves and Ruthin, belonged to the Royal Fusiliers. The death of Sir Robert Douglas gave the colonelcy of the Royal Scots to Lord George Hamilton, who was succeeded in the command of the Fusiliers by Col. Fitzpatrick.

Col. Fitzpatrick appointed to the Regiment.

From Steinkirk William retreated to Halle. On the 22nd August, the Fusiliers were detached under Lieut.-Gen. Talmash with the Coldstreams, Scots Fusilier Guards, Trelawney's (4th) and Stanley's (16th) Regiments to Bruges, where they were joined by another detachment sent thither under Brigadier Ramsey. For a time, Talmash encamped at Oudenbourg, whence the Coldstreams, Selwyn's, and the Royal Fusiliers were sent under Brig. Ramsey to occupy Dixmude, where they were employed in repairing the works. From Dixmude, in October, the Coldstreams, Trelawney's, and the Fusiliers, occupied the line of the canal of Bruges for a few days before going into winter quarters. The Coldstreams and the Fusiliers then proceeded to Ghent, where they remained during the winter, except for a few days, when they were ordered to the relief of Furnes, suddenly captured by Boufflers on the 4th January, and whence they returned to Ghent.

The Regiment winters in Ghent.

1693.

On the 26th May, the King occupied quarters in a house belonging to the Prince of Taxis, about five miles from Brussels and one from Vilvorde; at the same time there were twenty battalions of foot encamped at Dighem, of which were two battalions of Dutch guards, Churchill's, Trelawney's, the Royal Fusiliers, Erle's and Collingwood's. The Royal Scots, with Selwyn's and Stanley's, were in the neighbouring villages, where they remained for a few days in consequence of the great rains, before they occupied their quarters in the camp. On Sunday, the 27th, Boufflers marched from Tournay to Leuze; next day to Cambronne. The whole

Encamped at Dighem.

*D'Auvergne's Campaign of 1692, p. 45.

French army then commenced to move. The Allies were still in camp at Dighem. Luxemburgh joined Boufflers on the 3rd June, when the combined French armies moved towards Nivelles and Genappe. On the 5th William marched from Dighem, <small>Move to Parck.</small> with all his foot and artillery, and encamped at Parck, near Louvain. Here the Fusiliers were brigaded with the Royal Scots, the Queen Dowager's (2nd), the Prince of Denmark's (3rd), and the Queen's Regiments, under Brig.-Gen. Churchill. On the 7th, Luxemburgh encamped at Walheim, Boufflers at Gemblours. On the 15th, Luxemburgh, who had again joined Boufflers, marched from Gemblours to Judoigne, his left wing being then within half a league of William's camp at Parck. William left his camp on the 19th July, and marched to Tirlemont. The result of these manœuvres was the battle of Landen.

On the evening of the 18th July the French army reached William, then in position at Landen. The day was too far gone to commence the action. The French bivouaced on their ground; the British prepared for the battle the morrow must bring. William's position stretched from the village of Laer on the right. through the village of Neer Winden, to the village of Neer Landen on the left. Ramsey's Brigade occupied Laer, the Germans Neer Winden; Neer Landen being occupied by the Royal Scots, Churchill's, Selwyn's, and Trelawney's English Regiments, together with some Danes. The ground between the villages of Neer Winden and Neer Landen was open: so William ordered an entrenchment to be carried between the two villages, "which was indeed but a slight breastwork, as may easily be judged by the short time they had to make it, and the small number of men that worked at it, to wit, thirty per battalion." The rest of the foot were drawn up in line in this entrenchment to defend it.

Sunrise discovered the French drawn up within gunshot of the British army, <small>Battle of Landen.</small> whose artillery immediately opened upon them. At six o'clock they made their advance. As the first rays of the morning sun gilded the horizon, waving masses of glittering arms surging over the undulating grounds in front indicated the attack. First the village of Laer was assailed. The veteran Ramsey hurled back his assailants with tremendous slaughter. Luxemburgh then sent his impetuous brigades against Neer Winden. They were again repulsed. He then tried the left of the line, but in Neer Landen there were troops as stout and as stedfast as those on the right.

Again were the gallant French thrown back with the rudest violence. During this time the Fusiliers were only spectators of the action. The battle seemed to have been decided without their aid. But Luxemburgh was not yet defeated. He again brought up his army to the attack. In Laer, Ramsey continued to hold out, he could not be forced; in Neer Winden, the French obtained a footing. Then with the entrenchment flanked by the fire of their comrades, it was assailed in front by heavy columns of pikemen and musketeers, consisting of the French brigades of Vermandois, Nice, Roussillon, and Sare, flanked by dragoons, and preceded by a cloud of grenadiers. Colonel Fitzpatrick was at the head of the Fusiliers, directing his men to reserve their fire until the close approach of the assailants. As the French soldiers sprang forward, with their characteristic energy, a close and well-directed volley from the Fusiliers rent chasms in their ranks. The terrible effects of the volleys that now crushed down the assailants were bitterly felt, and not soon forgotten by the French Army;* still the survivors, supported by an immense superiority of numbers, and urged forward by Marshal Villeroy, swept up to the attack. Villeroy, himself, led a chosen body of men to the charge, and forced the right of the entrenchment. The Royal Fusiliers, and the other troops in this part of the field, were attacked in front and flank. A sanguinary, but unequal conflict ensued. Col. Fitzpatrick was carried from the field badly wounded, and with his arm broken. Rank after rank of Frenchmen ascended the breastwork and entered into the conflict. At length the British battalions were overpowered and driven from their ground. But they speedily rallied, and rushing, sword in hand, upon their opponents, again gained the lost ground. A momentry pause ensued; but soon a fresh body of French renewed the fight, when, by superior numbers, the British

The British finally overpowered. regiments were again overpowered. In this conflict, which rivals the fiercest strife that has ever distinguised the two contending parties, the Royal Fusiliers displayed that stern valour which has always characterised British soldiers, their commanding officer, Lieut.-Col. Whalley, fell mortally wounded, Major Wilson was removed bleeding to the rear, yet they disputed the ground with unyielding tenacity until all chance of ultimate success had passed away, when they withdrew from the field,

* See St. Simon's *Memoires*, who speaks of the destroying fire from the entrenchment, that is, from the Royal Fusiliers.

and joining a large body of infantry under Lieut.-Gen. Talmash—their first Lieut.-Colonel—retired by the brook Beck upon Dormal, and thence to Lewe. The enemy attempted to stop their retreat, but the British battalions, promptly facing about to confront their pursuers, the French soon halted, and the retrograde movement was performed with trifling loss.

The casualties of the regiment in this action were very severe. Among the killed was Lieut.-Col. Whalley, a veteran of distinguished merit, who raised one of the companies of the regiment at its formation, and Lieutenants Fairbrother, Cooper, and Blackmore; Captain Ruthwin died of his wounds. Among the wounded were Colonel Fitzpatrick, so badly hurt that, for nearly two years, he was unfit for service, Major Wilson, who seems afterwards to have died of his wounds, Captains Hart, Betesworth, Withers, and Lieutenant Fletcher. The loss of non-commissioned officers and soldiers was very great, but the exact number cannot now be ascertained. <small>Losses of the Regiment.</small>

The regiment was employed in the subsequent movements of the army until the end of the campaign, when it proceeded to Ghent. It was stationed in Ghent during the winter with three battalions of Foot Guards and Selwyn's regiment. The estimates inform us that at the end of this year the establishment of the regiment was thirteen companies, composed of 46 commissioned officers, 104 non-commissioned officers, 780 privates and 69 servants; and that its cost to the country was £16,455 8s. 4d. per annum. <small>Winters in Ghent.</small>

1694.

The military operations in the campaign of this year were insignificant. On the 21st of May the Fusiliers left Ghent and assembled in camp at Bethlem Abbey, near Louvain, and on the 13th June moved to Hertogendall, and afterwards to other places. When the regiment took the field it was reviewed by King William, who complimented it warmly on its martial appearance, and the steadiness with which it performed the manœuvres practised at that period. The regiment served in Brigadier-Gen. Earle's (the second) brigade, but though many severe marches fell to the lot of the troops, no general action was fought. When the winter came the Fusiliers were sent into their old quarters in Ghent. <small>Again winters in Ghent.</small>

1695.

At the end of May, the English forces, which had been encamped at Aersele, Caneghem, and Wonterghem, were ordered to assemble at Aersele under the Prince de Vaudemont. In June, both armies commenced their movements. On the 12th the English left Aersele and marched to Rouslaer. William was then closing on Namur, the capture of which he had determined on. On the 19th Col. Fitzpatrick joined the regiment from England, where he had been since he was wounded at Landen. He was then made a Brigadier-General, the Royal Fusiliers being placed in his brigade. On the 3rd July, William invested Namur, the troops under the Earl of Athlone taking one side of the town, and those of Brandenburg the other, the Sambre dividing the attacks. The fortress mounted 100 guns, and contained a garrison of 12,000 men. The King took up his quarters in the village of Flawen. On the 6th the Fusiliers, with the regiments of Seymour and Columbine, opened the trenches upon the enemy's covered way on the hill of La Bougé. On the 12th the lines were finished and fire opened. By the 18th the trenches had been pushed nearly close to the tower of La Bougé, which William then determined to storm. The attack was to be made in the evening by five battalions of Foot Guards, supported by nine battalions more of English and Scotch, under the command of Brig.-Gen. Fitzpatrick. The following is the contemporary account, as published in the *London Gazette:*

"The disposition of the attack was as follows:—The 1st battalion of the 1st Guards, the battalion of the Coldstreams, and the battalion of Scots Guards for the right attack towards the bottom: the 2nd battalion of the 1st Guards, and one battalion of the Dutch Guards for the left attack by the old tower. At the head of each of these attacks were 120 armed Fusiliers, carrying fascines before them, and 120 grenadiers followed by 100 workmen with tools and gabions. On the right of the body on the right hand were 100 grenadiers carrying fascines before them, followed by 50 workmen; and the same number of grenadiers and workmen on the right of the body on the left hand, betwixt the two attacks. The signal being given at half-past six p.m., the several battalions marched forward in the order before mentioned, with the greatest courage and undauntedness that ever was seen, without taking any notice of the enemy's fire, which was very furious; the Fusiliers in the front carrying their fascines to the very palisades, when, laying them down, they fired upon the enemy, and the grenadiers threw their grenades into the tower and works, while the battalions marched close after them in order with their arms shouldered, till they came so near that they presented over the palisades, drove the enemy from thence, and pursued them through a large place of arms to the bottom of that work.

"The French making fresh fire from the counterscarp, and a redoubt on the other side of a hollow way on our flank, my Lord Cutts with three battalions from our trenches came immediately to sustain our men, viz., Tidcomb (14th), Stanley (16th), and Collingwood, with the first of which he marched to the lowest palisades, and with the Guards again repulsed the enemy, part into the water and the rest where they could best escape.

Brigadier Fitzpatrick marched at the same time with the regiment of Lord George Hamilton (Royal Scots), the Royal Fusiliers, Ingoldsby's (the Royal Welsh), Saunderson's, Lauder's, and Maitland's (25th); the two first of these were sent to relieve the Dutch Guards, and those with the Lord Cutts at the lowest palisades; and the rest were drawn up by the Tower to sustain as the action should require, except the regiment of Lauder, which was posted on the side of the hollow way to prevent being flanked or surprised. In the meantime, Major-General Ramsey ordered all the pikemen to carry fascines, and to dig till a work was made sufficient to resist musket-shot, when he posted the regiments of Ingoldsby, Saunderson, Lauder, and Maitland, and at the point of day drew off the rest of the troops to the first parade. The heat of the action lasted about two hours, during which time we possessed ourselves of the enemy's works, which were defended by a great number of men."

Such was the spirit and energy with which the British soldiers rushed upon their opponents, that when the palisades were broken down and the covered way carried, the French were overpowered and chased from their works, many of them throwing themselves into stone pits to escape the fury of their assailants. William witnessed the whole affair, and so well pleased was he with the conduct of the troops, that as the French were being driven from point to point, he laid his hand upon the shoulder of the Elector of Bavaria, saying, "See my brave English! See my brave English! And, indeed," continues the author, who repeats the expression, with delightful quaintness, "it must be remembered to their immortal honour, that without any shelter, they advanced boldly, and undisturbed amidst showers of great and small shot, bombs and hand-grenades." The Royal Fusiliers lost Lieutenant Dancy of the Grenadiers, killed; Captain Negus wounded with the workmen, and a number (but unrecorded) of private soldiers.

Signal defeat of the French.

The success of the attack on the tower of La Bougé, by enabling the besiegers to carry their trenches to the village of Bougé, towards the St. Nicholas Gate, greatly facilitated the operations of the siege. On the 26th, Fort Pollard was carried; next day the Grenadiers of the army, supported by the Royal Welsh, effected a lodgment in the counterscarp of the place, near St. Nicholas Gate. Batteries were at once erected to breach the works. On the 3rd August, the town surrendered. Its capture is related in the following letter from the camp:—

The town captured.

From the Camp before NAMUR, July 25th (Aug. 4th), 1695.

"On Monday last, the second inst., it being resolved that a lodgment should be made in the counterscarp before the Half-moon, and upon the demi-bastion on our left, near the Maese, the attack was accordingly begun about seven o'clock that evening. It was carried on, on the right by Lord Cutts with 200 English Grenadiers and 250 workmen, sustained by the 1st battalion 1st Guards, and the 1st battalion Coldstreams; on the left by Brigadier Dedem, with a like disposition of equal numbers of the Dutch. By ten o'clock the lodgment on the right was made cannon proof, but on the left the Dutch were not able to maintain themselves in the demi-bastion by reason of the number of grenades the enemy threw upon them; however, they made their lodgment upon the point of that work. Major-General Ramsey and Brigadier Fitzpatrick marched down to relieve the trenches at the usual hour, but by reason of the attack, His Majesty not thinking fit to make any movements till the great firing was abated and the posts a little secured, commanded them to draw up their battalions in reserve till further orders. Some time afterwards the trenches were relieved, and then Major-General Ramsey went to view the new lodgments, and having commanded fresh pioneers, he ordered the lodgment against the counterscarp of the Half-moon to be continued about fifty paces further to our right, along the enemy's palisades, which being done, Brigadier Fitzpatrick visited the head of the lodgment, and placed detachments in the advanced posts under the fire of the enemy, so as to secure the possession of what we had taken. There were killed and wounded on this occasion, of the English about 500 men, and not much less of the Dutch, besides several officers as well of the Guards as of the detached parties. This attack had that good effect, that yesterday, about two p.m., the enemy hung out a white flag, and desired to capitulate for the town, whereupon hostages being exchanged, the capitulation was begun yesterday in the evening, and concluded this day; and in pursuance thereof Colonel Ingoldsby's regiment is gone to take possession of one of the gates of the town, which is to be immediately delivered up."

Siege of the Castle.

With the town in his hands William immediately commenced the siege of the Castle. Besides the batteries already erected between the Sambre and the Maese, others were ordered to be raised, both gun and mortar batteries, as well on the ramparts as in the gardens of the city, to open simultaneously on the Terra Nova and Fort Cohorn. Fire was opened on the 13th August, with a terrible bombardment, "such as was never seen since powder was first invented. The cannon and mortars answered one another in time, and formed a dismal tremendous harmony; clouds of smoke and flashes of sooty flame filled the air, as if hell itself had vomited its kindred brimstone; and the shower of red hot bullets and bombs that poured continually upon the Castle so scared the enemy that none of them durst peep out of their shelters underground, except such as were obliged to be upon duty." On the 18th the French made a sortie with 200 mounted dragoons and 500 grenadiers, but they were beaten back by the Count de Rivera and Lord Cutts, who had just posted the advanced guard to cover the workmen.* On the night of the 30th the

---

* In repulsing this sortie a gallant exploit was performed, but it is difficult now to discover who really performed it. The contemporary narrative is as follows:—"About eleven p.m. of the 18th August, the enemy made a sally with 200 dragoons mounted, and 500 grenadiers. They first made an attack on our right with 160 grenadiers, when the Count de Rivera, visiting the night posts immediately repulsed them; then making an attack on our left, where Lord Cutts had just posted the advanced guard, 100 dragoons came upon Mr. Sutton, a Lieutenant of Colonel Seymour's regiment, who being posted in the plain of Salsine with 37 English Fusiliers, let them come on till they were within a few yards of him, and then firing upon them, retreated softly towards our main body; and the dragoons pressing again upon him, he gave them a second volley, at which time the Spanish and Bavarian horse, who were posted in the plain of Salsine to sustain the infantry, fell in with the enemy, sword in hand, and followed them to the very gates of the Castle, killing several and making some prisoners, so that we went on with our work without interruption. The enemy own to have had 100 dragoons killed and wounded out of 200, and the officer that commanded them was killed." There is no doubt that the men belonged to the Royal Fusiliers, but there is some confusion as to the identity of the officer. In the Life of King William he is said to have been a Lieutenant-Colonel. It is possible that Lieut. Sutton, who was in the regiment in 1687, still remained, but we cannot show that he was really the person.

breaches in the Terra Nova and Fort Cohorn were declared practicable, and the assault was ordered. The storming of the Castle of Namur by the British under Lord Cutts is one of the great deeds of the British army, and as a military exploit has never been surpassed; but in the "dark ages" when it occurred, neither historians nor gossips condescended to give such ample details as would enable us to chronicle the separate deeds of individuals, or even of regiments, and therefore for the exploits of the Royal Fusiliers we must take the exploits of the whole army, and say they were of the glorious band who did these things! The regiment had many men killed and wounded, Captain Grove and Lieut. Rainsford being among the latter.* The capture of Namur ended the campaign, and the army being dismissed, the Royal Fusiliers returned to their quarters in Ghent.

The following list of officers is believed to belong to the end of this year:

List of Officers of the Regiment of Fusiliers commanded by Col. Fitzpatrick:—†

Col. Fitzpatrick.	Capt.-Lieut. Marm. Rawdon.	2nd Lieut. Grove.
Lieut.-Col. Shrimpton.	Lieut. Jackson.	,, Wilson.
Maj. Christ. Worthevale.	,, Spragg.	,, Salter.
Capt. Thomas Hart.	,, Senargus.	,, Copley.
,, Salter.	,, Bayly.	,, Fouks.
,, Seaton.	,, Cook.	,, Johnson.
,, Fitzpatrick.	,, Day.	,, Winne.
,, Withers.	,, Carr.	,, Coghlan.
,, Henry Grove.	,, Rainsford.	,, Brydle.
,, Lucas.	,, Duterme.	,, Stone.
,, Negus.	,, Crompton.	,, Row.
,, Turner.	,, Gion.	,, Fairbrother.
,, Simpson.	,, Dancy.	,, Campion.

1696.

In March the French began to assemble their troops about Dunkirk and Calais for the invasion of England, in concert with the conspirators who had formed a design to assassinate William and restore the Stuarts. Several English regiments were marched to the coast to embark for England to resist the invasion, among which were the Royal Fusiliers, who embarked at Sas Van Ghent, and sailing from thence to Flushing, passed over to England with the forces under the Duke of

The Regiment ordered to England.

---

* Capt. Grove is believed to be the same officer who was captured by the French at Steinkirk.
† Addtl. MS., Brit. Mus., 17918. See also p. 30.

COL. EDWARD FITZPATRICK'S REGIMENT, 1695.

The List of Names is to be found in the British Museum, Add. MSS. 17918. The dates are taken entirely from the Extracts from the Commission Books. It is a great misfortune that we have not been able to recover all the dates of appointments, but imperfect as it is in that respect the list plainly shadows forth the loss of officers, subalterns especially, that the regiment sustained at Landen. It seems that about a dozen lieutenants disappeared from the roll immediately after that action.

RANK IN THE ARMY.

RANK AND NAME.	RANK IN REGIMENT.	Colonel.	Lieut.-Col.	Major.	Captain.	Capt.-Lieut.	Lieut.	Ensign.	REMARKS.
Col. EDWARD FITZPATRICK	1 Aug., 1692	...	...	...	...	...	...	...	Drowned 10th Nov., 1696—succeeded by Sir C. O'Hara, 1st Guards, 26th Nov., 1696.
Lieut.-Col. SHEMPTON	...	...	1 Aug., 1692.	...	...	...	...	...	Left the Regiment as Major, 1st Guards, 1695—Governor of Gibraltar, died 24th Dec., 1707.
Major C. WORTHEVALE	1 Aug., 1693	...	...	...	...	...	23 Aug., 1685	...	Lieut.-Col. of Reg.—Out 25th Dec., 1704.
Capt. THOMAS HART	...	...	...	...	...	...	15 June, 1685.	...	
,, JOHN SALTER	...	...	...	...	...	...	18 June, 1685.	...	
,, PATRICK SEATON	...	...	...	...	...	...	Occurs 1687.	...	
,, EDWD. FITZPATRICK	...	...	...	...	...	...	...	...	
,, HUNT WITHERS	...	...	...	...	...	...	...	...	
,, HENRY GROVE	20 May, 1693	...	...	...	...	1 Aug., 1692	...	...	Major in Colt's Regiment, 24th July, 1695—Lieut. F. Rainsford, 14th Sept., 1695.
,, JAMES LUCAS	1 Aug., 1693	...	...	...	...	20 May, 1693	...	...	In succession to Lieut.-Col. T. Whalley.
,, DANIEL NEGUS	5 April, 1694	...	...	...	...	...	26 Oct., 1688	...	In succession to Capt. William Frowde.
,, RALPH TURNER	12 Dec., 1694.	...	...	...	...	1 Aug., 1693	...	...	Major, 25th Dec., 1704.
,, CHRIST. SIMPSON	1695.	...	...	...	...	...	...	...	
Capt.-Lt. MALM RAWDON	...	...	...	...	...	...	...	...	
Lieut. JOSHUA JACKSON	1 June, 1689	...	...	...	...	...	...	...	Jacques Wybault, 15th Sept., 1695.
,, WILLIAM SPRAGG	1 Dec., 1687.	...	...	...	...	...	...	...	
,, — SEN-AMES	...	...	...	...	...	...	...	...	Out—John Bennett, 30th Aug., 1695.
,, — BAYLY	...	...	...	...	...	...	...	...	
,, JOHN COOKE	...	...	...	...	...	...	...	...	Capt.-Lieut., 10th June, 1703.
,, — DAY	...	...	...	...	...	...	...	...	
,, WILLIAM CARR	...	...	...	...	...	...	...	...	Captain, 14th September, 1695.
,, FRANCIS RAINSFORD	...	...	...	...	...	...	...	...	
,, LOUIS DUTERME	14 May, 1695.	...	...	...	...	...	...	...	
,, JOHN CROMPTON	...	...	...	...	...	...	...	...	
,, — GION	...	...	...	...	...	...	...	...	
,, ROBERT DANCY	19 June, 1685	...	...	...	...	...	...	...	Killed at Namur, 17th July, 1695.
2nd Lieut. GEORGE GROVE	28 Aug., 1693	...	...	...	...	...	...	...	Captain, 25th Dec., 1704, in succession to Lieut.-Col. Worthevale.
,, GEORGE WILSON	20 July, 1692	...	...	...	...	...	...	21 May, 1692.	
,, B. SALTER	1 Aug., 1693.	...	...	...	...	...	...	...	
,, CHARLES COPLEY	...	...	...	...	...	...	...	...	
,, — FOULKS	...	...	...	...	...	...	...	...	
,, JOHN JOHNSON	...	...	...	...	...	...	...	...	
,, — WINNE	...	...	...	...	...	...	...	...	
,, JAMES COGHLAN	1 Aug., 1693	...	...	...	...	...	...	...	Entered as Lieut. to Capt. Withers.
,, THOMAS BRYDLE	1 Aug., 1692	...	...	...	...	...	...	...	Entered as 2nd Lieut. to Major Worthevale.
,, JOHN STONE	1 Mar., 1693.	...	...	...	...	...	...	...	
,, JOHN ROW	1 Aug., 1693.	...	...	...	...	...	...	...	Entered as Lieut. to Capt. Ruthwin.
,, GEO. FAIRBROTHER	1 Aug., 1693.	...	...	...	...	...	...	...	Entered as Lieut. to Capt. W. Frowde.
,, ROBERT CAMPION	1 Aug., 1693.	...	...	...	...	...	...	...	Quarter-Master, 1st Aug., 1692.

Wirtemburg, and landed at Gravesend on the 10th March. But the danger was then over through the plot having been discovered and frustrated. The troops were ordered to return with the first fair wind. They sailed from Gravesend on the 31st March without having landed in England, and again took their place in the army. *Returns to Flanders.*

The campaign of this year was not marked with great events. The regiment served with the Brabant army, commanded by King William; but no fighting took place. The marshals of France had begun to look upon the veterans of Steinkirk and Landen, the captors of Namur, as the most formidable soldiers they had ever met, and too strong and fierce in battle to be lightly engaged. They therefore did not seek battles. William had found that his throne was safe in the keeping of his subjects, and he was tired of slaughter. In the beginning of September, the Fusiliers joined the army of Flanders under the Prince de Vaudemont, and encamping near the village of St. Michael, were employed in constructing works for the protection of Bruges. In October, the regiment left the army and again took up its quarters in Ghent, when Brigadier Fitzpatrick returned to England. In crossing over to Ireland in the packet-boat "William," from Holyhead to Dublin, on the evening of the 10th November, with about eighty other passengers, among whom were several officers, the boat was driven ashore in a violent storm near Sutton in Dublin Bay. Fitzpatrick and all the persons on board were drowned, except the master and a boy. The Brigadier's body was cast ashore on the 19th, and conveyed to Dublin, where it was honourably interred in St. Patrick's Cathedral. The gallant veteran was succeeded in the command of the Fusiliers by Brig.-Gen. Sir Charles O'Hara, whose commission, according to the published Army List, was dated the 12th November. *Colonel Fitzpatrick drowned.*

1697.

Leaving Ghent on the 13th March, the Royal Fusiliers proceeded into quarters in some of the villages between Brussels and Malines, whence two companies were detached to form part of the garrison of Oudenarde; the remainder subsequently encamped behind the forest of Soignies, where the men suffered much from hot weather and the want of clothing, which, though due, had not arrived from England. The regiment served the campaign which terminated on the 10th September by the peace of Ryswick. Its establishment was thirteen companies, containing 46 officers, 104 non-commissioned officers, and 780 privates. The regiment was then ordered to England. After a campaign of six years, the Royal Fusiliers arrived at Gravesend at the close of November. On the 30th, they were ordered forthwith to disembark and march to Southwark. On the 7th December, four companies were ordered into detached quarters, two to Bishop Stortford, one to Hatfield and Broadoak, and the other to Puckeridge and Buntingford. Two companies had been sent to Sandwich; on the 10th December they returned to Southwark. During this month the quarters of the outlying companies were frequently changed, but only for short intervals; for a few days we find detached companies at Hatfield, Barnet, Dunstable, St. Albans, Bushy, Bedford; and detachments from Southwark at Tottenham, Edmonton, and the villages in the neighbourhood, at Stevenage and Hitchin, Baldock and Shefford.

Peace declared; the regiment returns to England.

1698.

The regiment remained in these detached quarters during the spring and early summer of this year. Its actual strength on the 28th March was 546 men. On the 23rd August the Fusiliers were ordered to the Channel Islands; six companies to proceed to Guernsey and seven to Jersey. The detached campanies were all to assemble at Portsmouth, where they embarked.

1699.

Stationed in the Channel Islands.

The regiment remained in Guernsey and Jersey without any change, except reduction to the peace establishment, when it consisted of thirteen companies, composed of forty-one officers, sixty-eight non-commissioned officers, fifty-four servants, and 466 privates, total 629 strong.

1700-1701.

In June, 1700, three companies were sent to New York, these companies had been taken off the establishment on the 25th April, and became Independent companies serving in America. The remainder of the regiment still continued in their quarters in the Channel Islands.

MAJOR-GENERAL SIR C. O'HARA'S REGIMENT, 1702.

The following list is compiled from different sources. The names will be found to be those given in the embarkation returns of the regiment in the expedition to Cadiz; the dates of commissions are obtained from the Commission Books in the War Office, and the "Remarks" from those books and other publications.

RANK AND NAME.	RANK IN REGIMENT.	RANK IN ARMY.						REMARKS.
		Colonel.	Lieut.-Col.	Major.	Captain.	Capt.-Lieut.	Lieut.	Ensign.	
Major-Gen. Sir C. O'HARA	26 Nov., 1696	...	1st April, 1689	...	...	...	...	...	Promoted—succeeded by Hon. James O'Hara, 29th Jan., 1713.
Lt.-Col. C. WORTHEVALE	... 1695	...	...	1 Aug., 1693	...	...	23 Aug., 1685	...	Left the regiment, Dec., 1704—succeeded as to his Company by George Wilson, 25th Dec., 1704.
Major HUNT WITHERS	... 1695	...	...	...	...	...	...	...	Lieut.-Col., 23rd Dec., 1704—succeeded as to his (Colonel's) Company by Thomas Archdale, 27th April, 1708.
Capt. JOHN SALTER	...	...	...	...	...	...	18 June, 1685.	...	
,, FITZPATRICK.	...	...	...	...	...	...	...	...	
,, JAMES LUCAS	1 Aug., 1693	...	...	...	...	20 May, 1693	26 Oct., 1688.	...	Major, 25th Dec., 1704—
,, CHRIST. SIMPSON	... 1695	...	...	...	...	1 Aug., 1693	...	...	
,, RALPH TURNER	12 Dec., 1694.	...	...	...	...	...	...	...	
,, DANIEL NEGUS	5 April, 1694	...	...	...	...	...	...	...	In succession to Capt. W. Frowde.
,, FRANCIS RAINSFORD.	14 Sept., 1695	...	...	...	...	...	Occurs 1694	...	
Capt.-Lt. MARM. RAWDON	... 1695	...	...	...	...	...	...	...	Out, 10th June, 1703—Lieut. John Cooke.
Lieut. JAS. COGHLAN	1 Aug., 1693	...	...	...	...	...	...	...	Capt., 25th March, 1703—
,, B. SALTER	1 Aug., 1693	...	...	...	...	...	...	...	Entered as Lieut. to Major Worthevale.
,, THOS. TALMISH	14 April, 1702	...	...	...	...	...	...	...	Entered as Lieut. to Capt. Simpson.
,, WILLIAM CARR.	...	...	...	...	...	...	...	...	
,, JOHN JOHNSON.	...	...	...	...	...	...	...	...	
,, JOSHUA JACKSON.	1 June, 1689.	...	...	...	...	...	...	...	
,, JACQUES WIBAULT	15 Sept., 1695	...	...	...	...	...	...	...	Entered as Lieut. to Col. Shrimpton. Promoted Capt.-Lieut., 10th June, 1703.
,, JOHN COOKE	...	...	...	...	...	...	...	...	
,, CHARLES COPLEY.	...	...	...	...	...	...	...	...	Became Captain.
,, GEO. FAIRBROTHER.	1 Aug., 1693	...	...	...	...	...	...	...	
,, LOUIS DUTERME	14 May, 1695.	...	...	...	...	...	...	...	
,, JOHN CROMPTON.	1 Aug., 1693.	...	...	...	...	...	...	...	Captain, 10th June, 1703.
,, ROBT. CAMPION	1 Aug., 1692	...	...	...	...	...	...	...	
,, THOMAS BRIDDLE	...	...	...	...	...	...	...	...	
,, JAMES FOX.	...	...	...	...	...	...	...	...	
,, GEORGE WILSON	20 July, 1692	...	...	...	...	...	...	...	Appointed Capt. of Col. Worthevale's Company, 25th Dec., 1704—Robert Carthew, 25th Dec., 1704. Promoted Capt., 15th March, 1703.
,, GERVASE PARKER	17 May, 1697	...	...	...	...	...	...	...	
,, JOHN STONE	1 Mar., 1693.	...	...	...	...	...	...	...	
,, GEORGE GROVES	25 Aug., 1693.	...	...	...	...	...	...	...	
Adjt. LOUIS DUTERME.	...	...	...	...	...	...	...	...	
Qr.-Mast. GREGORY ODIAM	21 April, 1701	...	...	...	...	...	17 May, 1697	...	Capt., 30th Sept., 1707.
Chaplain SAML. HARWARD	10 Mar., 1702.	...	...	...	...	...	...	...	

1702.

The regiment remained in the Channel Islands until May, when it was sent to England. The Royal Fusiliers arrived at Cowes on the 27th, Sir Chas. O'Hara being ordered to place himself and his regiment under the Duke of Ormond. A large force had assembled "for service on board the fleet," to which Sir Charles was appointed Major-General. In this force seven companies of Fusiliers and five of Villier's formed a provisional battalion of 833 strong. The object of the expedition soon became known. The accession of Queen Anne to the British throne had caused a rupture with France and Spain which persisted in recognising the Pretender. In return for the hostility of Spain, England espoused the cause of Charles III., whom the accession of Philip Duke of Anjou had deprived of the Spanish throne. Europe was again in a blaze of war through the alliance of the French and Spanish Bourbons to the exclusion of the House of Austria. The blow which England was about to strike was to be delivered on some of the coast towns of Spain in behalf of Charles. The troops assembled at St. Helen's, where they embarked on board a mighty armada consisting of 203 sail. The disposition of the Royal Fusiliers was as follows:—

Ships' Names.	Companies.	Sergts.	Corps.	Drum.	Sentinels.
FLAMBOROUGH and NEWPORT.	Maj.-Gen. Sir C. O'Hara.				
	Capt.-Lieut. Marm. Rawdon, Lieut. Jas. Coughlan.				
GRAFTON.	Lieut.-Col. Christ. Wortheval.	2	2	1	31
	Lieut. B. Salter, Lieut. T. Talmish.				
POOL.	Major Hunt Withers.				
	Lieut. Wm. Karr, Lieut. John Johnson.				
GRAFTON.	Capt. John Salter.	2	2	1	31
	Lieut. Jos. Jackson, Lieut. Jac. Wibault.				
PHŒNIX and HAWKE.	Capt. Fitzpatrick.	2	2	1	32
	Lieut. John Cooke, Lieut. Chas. Copley.				
WILLIAM.	Capt. J. Lucas.	2	2	1	31
(Transport).	Lieut. Geo. Fairbrother, Lieut. Louis Duterme.				
Do.	Capt. Christ. Simpson.	2	2	1	33
	Lieut. John Crompton, Lieut. Robt. Campion.				
Do.	Capt. Ralph Turner.	3	3	2	32
	Lieut. Thos. Briddle, Lieut. Jas. Fox.				
DUNWICH.	Capt. Dan. Negus.	..	..	..	..
	Lieut. Geo. Wilson, Lieut. Jervis Parker.				
GRAFTON.	Capt. Fras. Rainsford.	2	2	1	32
	Lieut. John Stone, Lieut. Geo. Groves.				
RANLAGH	Louis Duterme, Adjt., G. Odiam, Qr.-Mr., S. Harward, Chaplain.*				

* This list, copied from the embarkation returns, is certainly incomplete in the return of rank and file. The same papers state that the number of Fusiliers ordered to serve on board the fleet was 379 rank and file, but only 308 paraded when all the troops were inspected on the 2nd June.

A landing was effected on the 15th August, near Cadiz, between Rota and Fort St. Catherine. The towns of Rota, Port St. Mary's, and Fort Catherine were captured, when a great deal of plundering ensued, and for some time discipline was at an end. An attempt was made on Fort Matagorda, a portion of the enceinte of Cadiz, but it was found to be too strong, and the army had to retire. The capture of Cadiz being thus found impracticable, the troops re-embarked on the 14th, 15th, and 16th September at Rota, and sailed for England. At sea they learnt that the Spanish galleons under a French convoy had put into Vigo. It was determined to attack them. For this purpose the infantry formed two brigades; the first consisting of the battalion of Guards and the regiments of Churchill, Columbine, and Fox, commanded by the Duke of Ormond and Brigadier Hamilton; the second consisting of the regiments of Bellasis, Seymour, the Royal Fusiliers, and Shannon, commanded by Lord Portmore and Brigadier Lloyd. The troops were landed on the south side of the river above Vigo, when the Grenadiers carried the fort of Rodondella, mounting forty guns at the entrance of the harbour. A passage being thus opened the ships followed in, and the whole of the French and Spanish ships were either captured or destroyed, an immense booty falling into the hands of the British. The sack of the place which followed presented many curious scenes. A quaint catalogue of the plunder is still extant,* enumerating instances of Grenadiers receiving five guineas for a diamond ring, while others were running about with bags of dollars in their hands. The share of the Fusiliers in this plunder is given, under the signature of Major Withers, as "one-ninth part of all the silver and vinelloes." The troops marched from Rodondella to embark on the 17th October, and two days afterwards they sailed for England. Each of H.M.'s ships "Sorlings," "Phœnix," and "Hawke" carried one company of the regiment, while two more companies were conveyed by the "Grafton."†

Capture of Vigo.

Owing to these disgraceful proceedings, an enquiry was ordered into the failure of discipline, the plundering of the town, and the alleged removal of a great quantity of property on board the fleet. Several officers were charged with par-

* Harl. MS., 7052.

† This arrangement only accounts for five companies, while ten appear to have embarked. Coupling this statement with the previous statement that the regiment formed part of a provisional battalion, it would seem that some of the companies continued on board the fleet serving as marines.

ticipating in the plunder, among whom was Sir Charles O'Hara. The trial, however, was futile, Sir Charles being acquitted.

On the return home of the troops on the 7th Nov., three companies of the Fusiliers disembarked at Dover. One company, under Lieutenant Coughlan in the "Newport," was landed at Plymouth, to remain there until further orders. Another, under Lieutenant Copley, was landed at Portsmouth. The three companies at Dover were marched to Deal, and then embarked for Portsmouth, whence they were marched one to Cranbourn, one to Ringwood, and one to Fordingbridge. In December the regiment gave three companies to complete Brigadier-General Gustavus Hamilton's regiment, then serving in the West Indies. It is also said that three companies were sent to garrison Tilbury Fort.

Three companies sent to the West Indies.

1703.

In January, the regiment was stationed at Portsmouth. On the 8th February, it was ordered to march to Reading in two divisions; it arrived there on the 16th and 17th of that month. It left Reading on the 16th March, three companies to Winchester, three to Farnham, and three to Southampton, whence the usual detachment was furnished to Hurst Castle, relieving a company of Lord Portmore's regiment. In April, one company that had been left at Portsmouth, where it had landed from the fleet, after having served as marines, proceeded to Ringwood. From these stations the regiment marched to Portsmouth in August, when it was ordered to be re-embarked for service on board the fleet, but the order was afterwards cancelled, and the regiment returned to Reading.

1704.

On the 7th April, the head quarters left Reading for Portsmouth, where the Fusiliers were to serve in garrison. A portion of the regiment had been left at Taunton, whence two companies were detached, one for Honiton, and the other for Tiverton. On being relieved at Portsmouth by Lord Paston's regiment, the Royal Fusiliers left that garrison early in August for Salisbury, where they were reviewed by their Colonel Sir Charles O'Hara. From Salisbury six companies were sent to Taunton, two to Bridgewater, one to Ilminster, and one to Wellington. In October, the company at Ilminster marched to Chard; in November, one from Taunton went to Langport and South Petherton. In December, Lieutenant-Colonel Worthevale, who had served with the regiment since its establishment, left, and was succeeded by Major Withers. The establishment was this year 408 men.

1705.

In January, the two companies at Bridgewater marched to Sherborn, and the company at Langport and South Petherton to Crookhorne. On the 23rd April, the regiment changed quarters, three companies to Tavistock, one to Kellington, one to Liskeard, one to Saltash, one to Plympton, and one to Brent, whence, on the order of the Governor of Plymouth, the regiment was to march into that fortress. This year the regiment was augmented by two companies, of 2 sergeants, 3 corporals, 2 drummers, and 59 privates each, which, on completion, were to proceed to Plymouth, where they were clothed in August. The officers appointed to the new companies were Captain James O'Hara,* Lieutenants William Cropp and Benjamin Huffum; Captain Alexander O'Hara, Lieutenants James Powell and Wharton Wilson. The other companies were augmented by 1 corporal, 1 drummer, and 19 privates each. The two companies at Sherborn marched to Southampton for the Isle of Wight; they were withdrawn in May and sent to Lymington. During the summer the regiment was employed in escorting prisoners to Farnham and Salisbury. Two other companies were sent to the Isle of Wight and thence to Lymington whence, in November, they marched to join the regiment. During the summer some of the companies had been serving on board the fleet as marines.

Regiment augmented by two companies.

1706.

The war of the Spanish Succession causing England to send an army to Spain, the Royal Fusiliers embarked at Plymouth on the 19th February, with the rest of the troops sent on that service under Sir Charles O'Hara. The regiment was conveyed to Gibraltar with Sir J. Leake's fleet. Its establishment was 834 men; it was commanded by Lieut.-Col. H. Withers, Christopher Simpson being the Major. In the meantime the French had laid siege to Barcelona, the news of which sent the

Sails for Spain.

---

* The future colonel of the regiment. These appointments are so given in the Commission Books.

English forces to succour the place. The troops were at once transferred from the transports to the men-of-war, which sailed immediately for Barcelona, orders being left for Sir George Byng to sail after them with the forces from Ireland. A considerable concentration of troops at Barcelona was now being made, for the French were pushing the siege with vigour. On the 28th March, the Earl of Peterborough had started from Valentia towards Catalonia with 1,500 horse; Lord Donegal had brought up 1,100 men from Girona, and the garrison then consisted of 3,000 English troops, besides Catalans. At this time the Royal Fusiliers were under the command of the Lieutenant-Colonel, for Sir Charles O'Hara, as a Lieutenant-General, had left the regiment at Lisbon, whence he proceeded to Alcantara, and took up a command there on the 16th April, the day the enemy were evacuating the place. After having been detained for six days by contrary winds in the Bay of Altea,

Siege of Barcelona. where Leake had been joined by Byng, the fleet proceeded to Barcelona. On the 7th May, it was joined off Taragona by the Earl of Peterborough at the head of 1,400 troops, and at noon on the 8th anchored in Barcelona Bay. The French had then been besieging the town for thirty-five days. Their army at the beginning of the siege consisted of about 20,000 men, of which they lost by assaults on Fort Monjuich, which Lord Donegal stubbornly defended, and from sorties and the fire of the place, not less than 5,000 men. Before the succours came, Monjuich, in which Lord Donegal was killed, had fallen, the French were getting the upper hand, and the assault on the town hourly looked for. The opportune arrival of the fleet, however, changed the face of affairs. By 8 P.M. the troops had been landed, and posted under arms behind the breaches to repel the threatened attack. But with this reinforce-

The French retire. ment to aid the garrison, the French declined the assault. On the night of the 11th May, they retired, leaving their artillery, provisions, and other stores; and, while defiling through a pass within half a league of Barcelona, were attacked by the Miguelets, who in half an hour cut off 500 of them.

The siege being thus raised, the land forces generally were taken from Barcelona by Sir John Leake, and landed at Valentia; they were afterwards sent on to

The Fusiliers march to Gironne. Carthagena, where the fleet arrived on the 12th June. The Royal Fusiliers, however, marched to Gironne, a fortified town in Catalonia, at the base of a steep mountain, with the River Tar running through the town, where they proceeded to put the neglected fortifications in a state of repair. The regiment passed the remainder of the year in Gironne in a state of comfort and great efficiency. It was then in the hands of veteran officers: Hunt Withers, the Lieutenant-Colonel, had fought through all William's wars, being wounded at Landen; Christopher Simpson, the Major, who had served under Marlborough at Cork and Kinsale, was also of Steinkirk, Landen, and Namur, in the breach of which Capt. Rainsford had been wounded; and others there were, as Odiam, and Parker, Negus, Turner, and Jackson, who had followed William to his victories and shared with him in his defeats. A complete list of officers is given on the following page.

1707.

At the opening of the campaign, Lord Galway, the Commander-in-Chief of the forces in Spain, ordered the Royal Fusiliers from Gironne, and the two battalions of English marines, also quartered in Catalonia, to join the army; but the King of Spain would not suffer them to leave their quarters, and consequently it was in the inaction thus imposed upon them that they heard of the fatal battle of Almanza, fought on the 25th of April, where the British and their allies had been nearly destroyed. Sir Charles O'Hara, now created Lord Tyrawley, had been in command at Almanza, as was also his son, Capt. James O'Hara, of the Fusiliers, who was there wounded. After his grand victory Berwick lost seven weeks in inaction; meanwhile the allies had gained Tortosa and Lerida, which they put in a state of defence. The Castle of Xativa also was occupied by the British, and when the French proceeded to besiege Lerida they discovered that Xativa must be reduced before their operations could be safely started. They attacked the Castle, but, according to their own account, "the English garrison made so obstinate and vigorous a defence that it has, in a great measure, frustrated our operations this campaign. The siege of Lerida is deferred till autumn, and the troops are to march into their summer quarters." The Fusiliers are believed to have occupied Tortosa.*

Siege of Lerida.

But Berwick's hold on Lerida was too strong to be broken. On the 10th September he invested the town. For more than a month the little garrison held the place despite all the efforts of the French. On the 12th October, however, a breach

---

* The commission of Lieut. Charles Parker is dated at Tortosa, May 14th.

SIR CHARLES O'HARA'S REGIMENT, 1706.

The Names and Regimental Appointments are from a MS. List in the War Office; the other matters have been supplied from the Commission Books. It is believed that this list gives the exact roll of officers who proceeded with the Regiment to Spain to serve in the War of the Spanish Succession.

RANK AND NAME.	RANK IN REGIMENT.	RANK IN ARMY.							REMARKS.
		Colonel.	Lieut.-Col.	Major.	Captain.	Capt.-Lieut.	Lieut.	Ensign.	
Col. Sir Charles O'Hara	26 Nov., 1696	…	1 April, 1689.						Promoted Col.—Thomas Archdale, 27th April, 1708.
Lieut.-Col. Hunt Withers	25 Dec., 1704	…							Became Lieut.-Col.; out of regiment 29th Aug., 1707, when Peter Beavoir succeeded his company.
Major Christ'r. Simpson	25 Dec., 1704	…		1695.	1695.	1 Aug, 1693			Became Lieut.-Col.
Capt. Daniel Negus	5 April, 1694								
,, Ralph Turner	12 Dec., 1694						Occurs 1694		
,, Francis Rainsford	14 Sept., 1695						17 May, 1697.		
,, Gervase Parker	15 Mar., 1703						1 Aug., 1693.		Succeeded to Col. Worthevale's company.
,, James Coghlan	25 Mar., 1703						1 Aug., 1692.		Appointed to "a company to be raised and added." Became Col. 1713.
,, Thomas Brydall	10 June, 1703						20 July, 1692.		
,, George Wilson	25 Dec., 1704						15 May, 1703		
,, James O'Hara	24 Mar., 1705								Appointed to "a company to be raised and added."
,, Alexander O'Hara	24 Mar., 1705								
Capt.-Lieut. John Cooke	10 June, 1703								Promoted Capt.
Lieut. John Stone	1 Mar., 1693								Promoted Capt.—30th Sept., 1707—Jas. Fleming, 12th May, 1715.
,, Joshua Jackson	1 June, 1689								
,, Geo. F. Airbrother	1 Aug., 1693								
,, Gregory Odiam	17 May, 1697								Became Capt., served till 1712.
,, Andrew Fitzpatrick	15 Mar., 1703								Made Captain, vice Colonel Christopher Simpson, 29th August, 1707.
,, Richard Baynes	23 Mar., 1702								Became Capt., and served till 1713.
,, Chas. Marsland	8 Nov., 1703								
,, —Gore	25 Oct., 1703								
,, Peter Beavoir	24 April, 1704								
,, John Cutler	15 June, 1704								Lieut. to Col. Worthevale.
,, Sam. Birmingham	11 Nov., 1704								Lieut. to Captain Negus.
2nd Lieut. Richard Hill	16 Oct., 1704								Lieut. to Capt. Alex. O'Hara.
,, Robert Carthew	25 Dec., 1704								Capt., 1st May, 1718.
,, Henry (?Jas.) Powell	25 Mar., 1705								
,, William Cropp	25 Mar., 1705								
,, John Turner	26 April, 1705								Lieut. to Capt. J. O'Hara.
,, Ben. Huffum	12 May, 1705								Lieut. to Capt. A. O'Hara.
,, Wharton Wilson	25 Mar., 1705								
,, Silvester Tucker	4 May, 1705								Promoted Lieut. to Major Christopher Simpson, 20th Sept., 1705, Lieut. T. Stoneman.
,, Thomas Jeffreys	3 May, 1705								
,, Edward Peachey	18 May, 1705								
,, Thomas Stoneman	20 Sept., 1705								Made Captain, 1st June. 1711.
,, Thomas Smith	21 Sept., 1705								
Chaplain Sam. Harward	10 Mar., 1702								Promoted Lieutenant.
Adjutant Roger Hale	26 April, 1705								
Qr.-Master Sam. Burbridge	15 Mar., 1703								
Chirurgeon W. M. Okey	30 July, 1703								

having been effected, the town was carried by assault. The garrison then retreated into the Castle. Here Berwick was held in check for another month. From the 16th October to the 10th November the siege was carried on with unabated vigour. But now the supplies were entirely exhausted, and the garrison reduced to 500 men fit for service. The Castle was therefore compelled to capitulate. As a regiment the Royal Fusiliers were destroyed, but "the very brave and bloody resistance" they and their fellow-soldiers had maintained won for them the most advantageous terms, and the high respect of their opponents. The remnant of the garrison marched out of Lerida on the 12th, with their baggage, two pieces of cannon, and their colours flying. They were conducted to the Confederate army then lying within three leagues of the city, whence they were sent to Barcelona.

The Castle capitulates; the regiment destroyed in the defence.

1708.

As the Fusiliers were no longer of strength sufficient to take their place in the army, the men were drafted into other regiments, the officers and staff in the early summer being sent home to recruit. On the 8th July Lord Tyrawley was ordered to cause the officers and non-commissioned officers lately landed from Spain to march to Taunton Deane. The establishment was fixed at thirteen companies, twenty-five sergeants, thirty-six corporals, twenty-four drummers, and 644 privates. Recruiting for the regiment was vigorously carried on, strong drafts of recruits from various places being sent through London to Taunton Deane. At Marlborough's suggestion " that particular care must be taken that no more men are allowed and mustered than are actually in the service; to which end each regiment* should have a head-quarters assigned to it, with orders to bring the men thither as they are listed, and not to be mustered anywhere else," the Fusiliers were detained at Taunton Deane until the recruiting was completed. In December a change of station took place, four companies remained at Taunton Deane, two were sent to Bridgewater, and one to each of the following places: Wivelscombe, Wellington, Tiverton, Cullumpton, Honiton, and Chard. In these quarters the regiment passed the winter.

Return to England.

Head Quarters at Taunton Deane.

---

* That is, Portmore's, Stewart's, and Tyrawley's; see Marlborough's letter on the recruiting of these regiments in his *Despatches*, June 25th, 1708.

1709.

In March the effective strength of the regiment was twenty-five sergeants, thirty-six corporals, twenty-four drummers, 708 privates. On the 5th April the out-lying companies changed their stations, the company at Honiton going to Kellington, that at Wivelscombe to Tiverton and Crediton, that at Chard to Tavistock. The regiment was again ready for service, and, as the arms of the Confederates had experienced a disaster in the battle of La Gudina on the 7th May, Spain was again chosen as the theatre of its operations.

The regiment returns to Spain.

It was selected to take part in the expedition to Cadiz under Lieut.-General Stanhope, who was also to bring troops from Minorca. With the other reinforcements consisting of the Scots Fusilier Guards, the regiments of Brigadier Whetham, Colonels Gore, Bowles, Lepel, Munden, and Dormer, and the Earl of Rochford's dragoons, the Fusiliers embarked on board the fleet commanded by Admiral Baker, which was to sail for Gibraltar, to meet Byng's squadron from Minorca. Bad weather and contrary winds, however, detained Baker's fleet beating about the Channel, between Dartmouth, Portsmouth, and Torbay, until the 18th August when it sailed. Even then so unfavourable was the weather that the fleet did not reach Lisbon until the 8th October, when the Admiral received letters from General Stanhope then at Gibraltar, who finding himself deceived by false representations and the inadequate efforts of the English Government, had abandoned the enterprise, and was only awaiting the arrival of the reinforcements to return to Barcelona.

Proceeds to Barcelona.

Baker therefore continued his voyage to Gibraltar, and having joined with Byng the whole armament proceeded to Barcelona, where the Admirals arrived only to find the campaign over, and the army sent into quarters. So the Fusiliers were ordered into camp at Tarragona, "Where they will be very well this winter," says Stanhope in a letter to Sunderland, "and I am glad to tell your lordship that they landed much more complete and in better condition than it was reasonable to expect, so that I hope by spring Her Majesty will have in Catalonia a better body of English in the field than there has been yet."

1710—1712.

The history of the Royal Fusiliers for the three years preceding the peace of Utrecht is very obscure. From the time the regiment went into camp at Tarragona we have been able to learn little of it. On the 11th June, 1710, it was reviewed by King Charles with the rest of the English troops in the camp at Balaguer. Whether it participated in the victories of Almenara and Saragossa or not, we do not know, but it was certainly in Spain when these actions were fought.

1713.

On the 29th January, the Hon. James O'Hara succeeded his father in the colonelcy of the Fusiliers. On the 13th February of this year, the regiment was in garrison at Minorca with Phillips's (40th), Whetham's (27th), and Sankey's (39th) regiments. The strength of each of these regiments is given in the estimates as 625 men. See *Commons' Journal*, vol. 17, p. 382.

Proceeds to Minorca.

1714.

During this year the regiment remained at Minorca. Its strength continuing the same, the yearly cost of its maintenance being £13,015 5s. 10d.

Some reorganisation of the regiment, after its chequered career in the late war, seems to have been now effected. The appended list is believed to give the officers then and for some time before serving with the regiment, but its incomplete state is evidence of uncertainty arising from the looseness that had previously prevailed.

List of Officers of His Majesty's Royal Regiment of Fusiliers commanded by Colonel O'Hara, with the dates of their commissions:—*

---

* The list was found at the War Office, in a MS. Army List for 1709. The dates in brackets are not in the original, but have been supplied from the Commission Book. It cannot refer to 1709 alone, for besides that, it gives the Hon. James O'Hara instead of Lord Tyrawley as colonel; it contains appointments extending over three years later, and the regiment is described as *His* Majesty's Royal Regiment of Fusiliers. There can, however, be little doubt, that it gives the names of the men who served during the later period of the war with the regiment in Spain; and, as an explanation of the fact that the majority of the names have no dates attached, we venture to suggest that official irregularity, as well as the exigencies of war, allowed the appointments to stand improperly recorded until they were settled by the Gazette of 1715, the renewal of commissions at the accession of George I., which we give in its place.

Col. James O'Hara [29th Jan., 1712—13].

Lieut.-Col. Gervase Parker [11th Jan., 1715].
Capt. Joshua Jackson [11th Jan., 1715].
,, Richard Baynes [11th Jan., 1715].
,, James Browne [11th Jan., 1715].
,, Robt. Cunningham [24th Dec., 1709].
,, James Fleming [12th May. 1715].
Lieut. Geo. Crofts [7th March, 1707].
,, William Cropp [25th March, 1707].
,, Edward Butler [13th May, 1709].
,, Roger Hale.
,, John Bradshaw [11th Jan., 1715].
,, John Little, 13th May, 1709.
,, Thomas Powell [11th Jan., 1715].
,, John Cooke.
,, John Gumby, 7th April, 1709.
,, Matthew Jones, 20th July, 1708.
,, John Shireman [11th Jan., 1715].
,, Jeffery Gibbon [20th July, 1708].
Adj. John Bradshaw.
Qt.-Mast. Thomas Rogers.

Major Francis Rainsford [11th Jan., 1715].
Capt. Pierse Griffith, 18th Feb., 1710.
,, Richd. Pierson, 31st March, 1711.
,, David Barry, 16th May, 1712.
,, Stephen Pettitot, 14th Nov., 1712.
Capt.-Lieut. Robt. Carthew.
Lieut. Henry Crofton [11th Jan., 1715].
,, And. Fitzpatrick [15th March, 1703].
,, John Marshall [19th Oct., 1709].
,, Jos. Dambon [11th Jan., 17 5],
,, Thomas Hollyland [11th Jan., 1715].
,, Saml. Clutterbuck [11th Jan., 1715].
,, Willm. Rudduck, 14th May, 1710.
,, Geo. Speke Petty, 12th May, 1715.
,, Chas. Parker, 14th May, 1707.
,, Christ. Hamilton [11th Jan., 1715].
,, Chas. Bucknall [11th Jan., 1715].
Chaplain, Smith Stone.
Surgeon, Edward Higgins.

1715.

On the 11th January, as a renewal of commissions on the accession of George I., the following officers were gazetted to the regiment:—

James O'Hara, Esq., Colonel and Captain of a Company.
Gervase Parker, Esq., Lieut.-Col. and Captain of a Company.
Francis Rainsford, Esq., Major and Captain of a Company.
Joshua Jackson, Esq., Captain.
Richard Baynes, Esq.   ,,
James Browne, Esq.   ,,
Robert Cunningham, Esq. ,,
Pierce Griffith, Esq.   ,,
Richard Pierson, Esq.   ,,
George Crofts, Gent., Lieut. to the Colonel's Company.
William Cropp and Edward Butler, Gents., Lieuts. to Capt. Gervase Parker.
Roger Hale and John Bradshaw, Gents., Lieuts. to Francis Rainsford.
John Little and Thos. Powell, Gents., Lieuts. to Capt. J. Jackson.
John Gumby, Gent., Lieut. to Capt. R. Baynes.
Matthew Jones and John Shireman, Gents., Lieuts. to Capt. Browne.
Henry Crofton, Gent., Lieut. to Capt. R. Cunningham.
Andrew Fitzpatrick and John Marshall, Gents., Lieuts. to Capt. G. Odiam.
Thomas Hollyland and Joseph Dambon, Gents., Lieuts. to Capt. P. Griffith.
Saml. Clutterbuck and Wm. Rudduck, Gents,, Lieuts. to Capt. R. Pierson.
Christ. Hamilton and Chas. Bucknall, Gents., Lieuts. to Capt. S. Pettitot.
Stephen Pettitot, to be Captain of a Company.
Charles Parker, Gent., Lieut. to Capt. David Barry.
John Bradshaw, Gent., to be Adjutant.
Thomas Rogers, Gent., to be Quartermaster.
Smith Stone, to be Chaplain.

THE HON. JAMES O'HARA'S REGIMENT, 1715.

The names are taken from a List in the War Office, to which dates of commissions are not attached. It agrees with the Gazette of the 11th Jan., 1715, which gives the renewal of the commissions at the accession of George I., and the fact that, except in a few cases, the dates are wanting seems to shew that during the absence of the regiment in Spain the appointment of officers was so irregularly performed that when the times became settled a ratification of their appointments became necessary. This list may, therefore, be taken to represent the men who served with the regiment at the end of the war of the Spanish Succession.

RANK AND NAME.	RANK IN REGIMENT.	Colonel.	Lieut.-Col.	Major.	Captain.	Capt.-Lieut.	Lieut.	Ensign.	REMARKS.
Col. JAMES O'HARA	29 Jan., 1713				24 Mar, 1705		15 May, 1703.		
Lt.-Col. GERVASE PARKER					15 Mar, 1703		17 May, 1697.		
Major FRANCIS RAINSFORD					14 Sept., 1695.		Occurs 1694		
Capt. JOSHUA JACKSON	Occurs 1708						1 June, 1689.		
,, RICHARD BAYNES							23 Mar., 1702.		
,, JAMES BROWNE									Promoted Capt. at Barcelona vice Peter Beavoir.
,, ROBT. CUNNINGHAM	24 Dec., 1709								Vice Capt. G. Odiann.
,, JAMES FLEMING	12 May, 1715						7 Sept., 1706.		Out—Lieut. Jeff. Gibbon, 15th May, 1718.
,, PIERSE GRIFFITH	18 Feb., 1710.								Succeeded Capt. Chas. Marsland; out—Capt. J. Cochrane, 19th June, 1716.
,, RICHARD PIERSON	31 Mar, 1711								
,, DAVID JOHN BARRY	16 May, 1712								Vice Capt. Cutler; died — Thomas Manle, 25th Feb., 1730.
,, STEPHEN PETTITOT	14 Nov., 1712				16 June, 1705.				Out—Geo. Crofts.
Capt.-Lt. ROBT. CARTHEW	11 Jan., 1715						25 Dec., 1704		Capt.-Lieut., 12th Nov, 1733; Capt., 25th April, 1741.
Lieut. GEO. CROFTS	7 Mar., 1707								Promoted Capt. 1st May, 1718.
,, WILLIAM CROPP	25 Mar., 1705								Capt.-Lieut., 5th April, 1723; Capt. vice W. Cropp, 12th Nov., 1733.
,, EDWARD BUTLER	13 May, 1709								Capt., 9th May, 1722.
,, ROGER HALE	11 Jan., 1715.								
,, JOHN BRADSHAW	13 May, 1709.								
,, JOHN LITTLE	11 Jan., 1715.								
,, THOMAS POWELL	11 Jan., 1715.								
,, JOHN COOKE	7 April, 1709.								
,, JOHN GUMBY	20 July, 1708.								
,, MATTHEW JONES	11 Jan., 1715.								
,, JOHN SHIREMAN	20 July, 1708								Capt., 15th May, 1718.
,, JEFFREY GIBBON	15 Mar., 1703.								
,, AND. FITZPATRICK	19 Oct., 1709						2 Aug., 1709		Capt.-Lieut., 25th April, 1741.
,, JOHN MARSHALL	11 Jan., 1715.								
,, JOSEPH DAMRON	11 Jan., 1715.								
,, THOMAS HOLLYLAND	20 July, 1708								Capt.-Lieut., 9th July, 1729; Capt., 5th April, 1733.
,, SAML. CLUTTERBUCK	14 May, 1710.								
,, WILLIAM RUDDUCK	12 May, 1715								Entered as Lieut. to Capt. Barry.
,, GEO. SPEKE PETTY	14 May, 1707								Entered as Lieut. to Major G. Parker.
,, CHARLES PARKER	11 Jan., 1715.								
,, CHRIST. HAMILTON	11 Jan., 1715.								
,, CHARLES BUCKNALL									
Adjt. JOHN BRADSHAW.									
Qr.-Mr. THOMAS ROGERS.									
Chaplain SMITH STONE.									
Surgeon EDWARD HIGGINS.									

Many of these officers had been serving in their respective grades for years. Capt. Cunningham was promoted captain at Barcelona, 24th Dec., 1709; Capt. Pettitot on the 14th Nov., 1712; Capt. Barry, who is mentioned but not gazetted in the above list, on the 16th May, 1712; Lieut. Chas. Parker, who appears as his lieutenant in the above gazette, was appointed lieutenant at Tortosa, 14th May, 1707.

1716—1717.

The regiment continued at Minorca.

1718.

In the early part of this year the regiment was in garrison at St. Philips' Castle, Minorca, under the command of its colonel, the Hon. James O'Hara. On the 23rd July, Admiral Byng's fleet arrived at Port Mahon, disembarking some new regiments to relieve those in garrison for active service against the Spaniards in Sicily. The Royal Fusiliers and the 39th Regiment were embarked on board the fleet, which, after a stay of a day or two, left Minorca, and on the 31st cast anchor in the Bay of Naples. On the next day the troops were sent off to garrison the citadel and fort of Messina. They arrived off Messina on the 9th August. Next day Byng attacked the Spanish fleet, and defeated it in a sharp action. The exact share of the Fusiliers in the action cannot be determined, for the *London Gazette* does not give details. For the remainder of the year the regiment was occupied in operations in Sicily; it seems to have wintered at Naples. On the 13th July the regiment was transferred from the English to the Irish Establishment.

Service in Sicily.

1719.

On receiving an account of the intention of the Spaniards to attempt a descent on Great Britain, Sir Geo. Byng at once ordered the Royal Fusiliers and Sankey's (39th) Regiment to proceed from Naples to England. They were despatched from Naples in April. Col. O'Hara proceeded from Naples, *via* Paris, by land. The *London Gazette* informs us that on the morning of the 27th May, 1719, Capt. Charles Hardy, in H.M.S. "Defiance," with the "Guernsey," "St. Albans," and "Lynn," having on board Gen. Sankey's Regiment (39th), and two companies of the Royal

[1719—ENGLAND.] *Record of the Royal Regiment of Fusiliers.*

Fusiliers, arrived at Portsmouth. They left Port Mahon on the 18th April. On the arrival of the whole regiment it was to rendezvous at Taunton. Four companies landed at Plymouth, and having received the recruits who were assembled at Plymouth, marched thence to Taunton; the establishment of the regiment was here augmented by two additional companies; it now numbered 857 men. In June two companies were sent back to Plymouth; in July these two companies marched to Bideford, where the regiment embarked for Ireland, then in an unsettled state.* It was stationed at Cork with a detachment of two companies at Youghal, which on the 6th of August were ordered to march to Duncannon Fort, where they spent the rest of the year.

Ordered to England.

Proceeds to Ireland.

The prices of Commissions, rather higher in this regiment than in ordinary line regiments, were this year fixed as follows:—

	£	s.	d.
Colonel and Captain	5000	0	0
Lieut.-Colonel and Captain	2000	0	0
Major and Captain	1500	0	0
Captain	840	0	0
Captain-Lieutenant	380	0	0
Lieutenant	250	0	0
Ensign (2nd Lieutenant)	170	0	0
Adjutant	125	0	0
Quarter-Master	125	0	0

The following list of officers' widows on "the Establishment of Ireland, residing in Great Britain and Ireland, for whom three months' pension is humbly demanded to Lady Day, 1719," is curious, both as an evidence of the *generosity* of the Government, and the death of the several officers in the service of their country:—

	£	s.	d.		£	s.	d.
Johanna Simpson—Major	7	10	0	Eliza Campion—Lieut.	5	0	0
Hannah Cooke—Capt.	6	10	0	Jane Jeffreys ,,	5	0	0
Abigail Bridall ,,	6	10	0	Martha Crompton ,,	5	0	0
Frances Salton ,,	6	10	0	Frances Philpot ,,	5	0	0
Cornelia Turner ,,	6	10	0	Sophia Driborough ,,	5	0	0

* We give here a sad story, which only shews too truly the treatment the army received in these disgraceful days—"About 1718 or 19, the Fusiliers, with another regiment, were put on board Admiral Byng's fleet, after the action off Messina. They were landed and quartered at Devizes, Taunton, and the neighbouring towns, at which time there were four years pay due to them. Although no money was paid for the above period, a commissary, by the connivance of the colonel, attended the regiment occasionally furnishing necessaries to the different officers, and even some times paying their tavern bills, taking numerous assignments on their pay for such goods and disbursements. After some time the officers presented a memorial to their colonel, Lord Tyrawley; he

1720.

By an order dated 9th January, 1719-20, eight companies of the regiment quartered at Cork were sent to Waterford, the two at Duncannon Fort remaining there. In May the stations of the regiment were changed. On the 20th the two companies at Duncannon Fort were relieved by Lord Hinchinbrook's (37th) regiment, and in June the Fusiliers occupied the following places, viz.:—Two companies Clare Castle Barracks, two companies Limerick, three companies Dingle Barracks, two and a half companies Cullen Redoubt, Abbington Redoubt, Silver Mines and Bryan's Bridge, and half company Colecormack Redoubt.

By an order, dated 8th October, the Muster Master-General was commanded to pay to the Regiment of Foot under the command of Col. O'Hara the full pay due to them from 13th July, 1718, the day they commenced on this Establishment, to 31st March last, both days inclusive. Some slight amends for the treatment already mentioned!

1721

Stationed at Cork.

During this year some portion of the regiment had returned to Cork, for on the 30th November an order is issued to the Master General and principal officers of the Ordnance to cause to be delivered to the commanding officer of the regiment two barrels of ball and 1000 flints for the use of the detachment doing duty in the Cove of Cork (Queenstown), to oblige ships coming from abroad to perform quarantine.

referred them to Mr. Ford, the agent, who said he had not had any money from the Treasury for six years. At this they memorialised the colonel anew and also the War Office, and after a course of time were promised to be paid in the following proportions, till the money could be raised to pay them in full:—a captain to have lieutenant's pay; a lieutenant that of ensign, and an ensign one half of his daily pay. But this promise was not kept. In the meantime, the officers paid none of their bills, and kept together in bodies armed to prevent arrest, and finally embarked for Ireland. On their arrival in Ireland, their pay being greatly diminished by the difference of the establishments, it caused the officers more earnestly to solicit for their arrears of pay, and they accordingly filed a bill in chancery against Mr. Ford, who in his answer deposed that Lord Tyrawley had for twenty years charged certain sums against each officer's pay on their first appointment or promotion, viz., to captains, £120; a lieutenant £70, and an ensign £40, some more, some less. On complaint being made of this to my Lord, he pleaded the custom of the army, and said it was not unknown to the King. After many years these particulars were laid before King George II., who paid my informer, then a midshipman, £100, as some compensation for the demand of his father, on account of his pay as lieutenant and adjutant."—MS. R. U. S. Institution.

1722.

The regiment seems to have spent the early portion of the year at Cork, whence it proceeded to Dublin. It was now known as Lord Kilmaine's Regiment, the Hon. James O'Hara having been created in 1721, and during the lifetime of his father, Lord Kilmaine, "in recompense for his eminent military services during Queen Ann's Wars." On the death of his father, June 9th, 1724, he succeeded to the title of Lord Tyrawley, when the regiment was again distinguished by that name.

Col. O'Hara created Lord Kilmaine.

1723.

The regiment was in Dublin where it remained during the summer, when it went to Galway. In September the whole of the officers, with some civilians, were appointed members of a court-martial, that is to say, justices of the peace. The times were seemingly unsettled, and the disturbed state of the country rendered very severe the duties both of the soldiers and magistrates.

While in Dublin the distinction between the first and second lieutenants was abolished.

Rank of second Lieutenant abolished.

"In pursuance of His Majesty's desires unto us, bearing date 23rd Jany., in the 9th year of His Majesty's reign, these are to direct and require you to place on the present and all future establishments of His Majesty's military expenses in His Majesty's Kingdom the youngest lieutenants of the Royal Regiment of Fusiliers, commanded by the Lord Kilmaine, and now on the Establishment of Ireland, at the like allowance of pay as all other Lieutenants do enjoy, the same to commence Dec. 24th, 1721, and likewise to prepare a warrant or warrants, and present the same by our signature for paying the said youngest Lieutenants of the said Regiment as much as the difference between the pay they have already received and that of Lieutenants of Foot here doth amount unto respectively between the said 24th Dec., 1721, and the day to which they were last paid, they being to be paid from henceforth as Lieutenants of Foot in like manner as officers of other regiments on H.M.'s Establishment are paid or payable. And for so doing this shall be your warrant.

"T. BELCHER.

"To M. M.-G. of the Kingdom or his Deputy."

1724.

The regiment remained in Galway, where the officers were again appointed with their civilian coadjutors a court-martial to administer the law both civil and military.

Some insight into the rank and file of the regiment, and the mode of recruiting it is given in the following curious license dated 18th Dec., 1724, for Sergt. Richard

Parsons of the Colonel's Company; Lieut. Geo. Crofts and Corp. William Edwards of Lieut.-Col. Fleming's Company; Sergt. H. Freeman and Drummer W. Duffy of Major Jones's Company; Corp. R. Peyton of Capt. Pettitot's Company; Lieut. John Marshall, Sergeant M. Hanna, Corp. T. Cahill, and Drummer J. Grey of Capt. Croft's Company; Captain Gee and Sergt. H. Browne of his Company; Lieut. Richd. Burchett and Corp. W. Factor of Capt. R. Hale's Company; Corp. T. Mulholland of Captain Proby's Company; Capt. John Aldercron, Sergt. W. Shaw and Corp. E. Saint of his Company; Capt. Thos. Maule, Lieut. Geo. Lukyn, Sergt. W. Whatham, and Drummer W. Rolleston of his Company, of Lord Kilmaine's Royal Regiment of Fusiliers to go into Great Britain to raise recruits for the said regiment, and to be absent out of the kingdom on that service for the space of three months from this date.

1725.

The station of the regiment has not been discovered. Recruiting was again carried on vigorously in Great Britain, many men being absent on that duty. On the 31st March the following are returned absent on leave, and the number is rather astonishing.

Colonel's Company	The Colonel, Chaplain, and ten men absent.
Lieut.-Col. Fleming's Company	The Lieutenant-Colonel and eleven men absent.
Major Jones's Company	The Major, Lieut. Rudduck, and ten men absent.
Capt. Hale's Company	Nine men absent.
Capt. Gee's Company	Nine men absent.
Capt. Maule's Company	Drummer recruiting, nine men absent.
Capt. Aldercron's Company	Lieuts. Parker and Ford, and nine men absent.
Capt. Pettitot's Company	The Captain and nine men absent.
Capt. Smith's Company	Lieuts. Johnson and Everard and ten men absent.
Capt. Cropp's Company	One sergeant recruiting and eight men absent.

1726.

The stations of the regiment for this year have not been discovered. There is little doubt, however, they were in the south of Ireland, and probably in the neighbourhood of Cork.

1727.

The Fusiliers returned to England in the beginning of the year 1727, in obedience to the following order:—

[1727—ENGLAND.] *Record of the Royal Regiment of Fusiliers.*

Ordered to England.

"In pursuance of H.M's commands signified unto us by His Excellency the Lord Lieutenant of the Kingdom in his letter bearing date 22nd Dec. last, these are to direct and enjoin you to cause the regiment of foot under your command to hold themselves in readiness to embark under the directions of Lieut.-General Macartney on board such ships as shall be provided to receive them from Kinsale or Cork. Given, &c., 9th Jan., 1726-27."

Two companies added to the Regiment.

On their arrival, in consequence of the threatened rupture with France and Spain, two additional companies were added to the regiment, a Quarter-Master was also added to the establishment, and each of the existing companies was increased by one sergeant, one corporal, one drummer, and twenty-six privates. In February they were quartered in Marlborough, Caln, Hungerford, Warminster, Troubridge, and Westbury. On the 26th April the two companies at Marlborough were separated; one went to Hooton Basset, and the other to Chippenham; those from Caln to Bradford. In July the companies at Hooton Basset and Chippenham went to Devises, one company going thence to Lavington, Amesbury, and Andover. In September the four companies at Troubridge, Westbury, Devises, and Caln, went to Salisbury and Fisherton; those from Warminster to Basingstoke. On the 20th June the officers of the regiment were re-appointed; the list was as follows:—

Captains.	*Lieutenants.*	*Lieutenants.*
Colonel James *Lord* Tyrawley.	Capt. Lieut. Wm. Davison.	Samuel Clutterbuck.
Lieut.-Col. James Fleming.	Geo. Burston.	Geo. Crofts.
Major Benj. Jones.	Henry Ormsby.	Wm. Rudduck.
Stephen Pettitot.	Stephen Pettitot.	Thos. Griffith.
Wm. Cropp.	John Harris.	Chas. Parker.
Roger Hale.	Richd. Burchett.	John Fleming.
John Aldercron.	Anthony Bligh.	Edwd. Butler.
Thos. Maule.	John Darassus.	Wm. Elwes.
Marcus Smith.	Meredith Everard.	James Clarke.
Lovelace Gilby.	Rupert Pratt.	Edwd. Higgins.
Thos. Bludworth.	Geo. Watkins.	Wm. Kellett.
Augustus Pynyot.	John Marshall.	Philip Craddock.

Chaplain James Cunningham.   Quarter-Master J. Congreve Chillcot.
Adjutant Stephen Pettitot.   Surgeon Edwd. Higgins.

1728.

On the 14th January the regiment assembled at Hounslow Heath, and was reviewed by His Majesty, after which it returned to quarters, three companies at Colnbrook and Longford, five at Uxbridge, and four at Staines and Egham. In March the regiment assembled at Salisbury. In April head quarters removed

LORD TYRAWLEY'S REGIMENT, 1727.

The List of Names is taken from a MS. War Office List, dated 20th June, 1727, and made on the renewal of the Commissions at the Accession of George II.; the dates of regimental rank being taken from the same document, except in some few cases; where slight differences appeared the dates adopted are those given in the Commission Books.

RANK AND NAME.	RANK IN REGIMENT.	RANK IN ARMY.							REMARKS.
		Colonel.	Lieut.-Col.	Major.	Captain.	Capt.-Lieut.	Lieut.	Ensign.	
Col. Lord Tyrawley	29 Jan., 1713	…	…	…	24 Mar., 1705	…	15 May, 1703	…	Made Col. of Pearce's Horse—succeeded by W. Hargraves, 27th Aug., 1739.
Lieut.-Col. Jas. Fleming	4 Aug., 1722		…	…	12 May, 1715	…	7 Sept., 1706	…	Made Col. of Bland's, 36th Foot—Major J. Aldercron, 5th Feb., 1741.
Major Benj. Jones	24 Mar., 1722			…	…	…	…	…	Dead, July, 1733—Capt. Berkeley.
Capt. Stephen Pettitot	16 June, 1705			…	…	…	…	…	Dead—Lieut. T. Maule, 25th Feb., 1730.
,, Lovelace Gilby	25 Dec., 1726			…	8 June, 1710.	…	…	…	Retired.
,, Augustus Pynyot	26 Dec., 1726			…	10 Sept., 1712	…	16 May, 1706	18 Oct., 1703	Major, 3rd Sept., 1733—Lieut. E. Butler, 12th Nov., 1733.
,, William Cropp	1 May, 1718			…	…	…	…	…	Died at Gibraltar.
,, Roger Hale	9 May, 1722			…	…	…	…	…	Made Major of Regiment, 5th Feb., 1741.
,, John Aldercron	4 Aug., 1722			…	…	…	…	…	Out—Thomas Forbes, 20th June, 1727.
,, Thomas Maule	24 Mar., 1723			…	…	…	…	…	Major, 13th Feb., 1741.
,, Marcus Smith	4 Nov., 1724			…	…	…	…	…	Went to Coldstream Guards from h. p.
,, Thos. Budworth	26 Dec., 1726			…	…	…	…	…	Capt.-Lieut., 12th Nov., 1733—Thomas England, gent., 12th Nov., 1733.
Lieut. George Crofts	7 Mar., 1707			…	…	…	…	…	Capt.-Lieut., 9th July, 1729.
,, Saml. Clutterbuck	20 July, 1708			…	…	…	…	…	Capt.-Lieut. 5th April, 1733—Thomas Wilson, gent, 5th April, 1733.
,, Edward Butler	13 May, 1709			…	…	…	…	…	Capt.-Lieut., 25th April, 1741—Francis Smith, gent, 25th April, 1741.
,, John Marshall	19 Oct., 1709			…	…	…	…	…	
,, Richard Burchett	8 Oct., 1717			…	…	…	23 Dec., 1711.	…	Made Capt. in Wolfe's Marines, 1740.
,, Rupert Pratt	13 July, 1718			…	…	…	15 Aug., 1717	…	
,, John Harris	13 April, 1719			…	…	…	…	…	
,, Edward Higgins	15 Aug., 1719.			…	…	…	…	14 May, 1710.	
,, Stephen Pettitot	19 Oct., 1720.			…	…	…	…	…	
2nd Lieut Geo. Burston	1 May, 1721.			…	…	…	…	…	Capt., 18th Dec., 1739.
,, John Darassus	17 Nov., 1721			…	…	…	…	…	Dead.
,, Meredith Everard	7 Sept., 1722			…	…	…	…	…	
,, Henry Ormsby	20 May, 1723.			…	…	…	…	…	
,, Anthony Bligh	4 Nov., 1724.			…	…	…	…	…	
,, James Clarke				…	…	…	…	…	
,, William Elwes	20 Oct., 1726.			…	…	…	…	…	Went to Coldstream Guards, 8th May, 1730.
,, William Kellett	26 Dec., 1726.			…	…	…	…	…	
,, George Watkins	26 Dec., 1726.			…	…	…	…	…	
,, Philip Craddock	26 Dec., 1726.	…		…	…	…	…	…	Capt., 22nd Sept., 1742—J. Market, 22nd Sept., 1742.
,, John Fleming	26 Dec., 1726			…	…	…	…	…	

to Bristol, whence one captain, two lieutenants, and fifty men with the colours went to Bath to remain there as a guard of honour to the Princess Amelia so long as she should remain. The Princess entered Bath on the 9th May, when she was received by the detachment, and at a levee held by her in the afternoon Lord Tyrawley presented the officers of the regiment to her.

<small>Guard of honour at Bath.</small>

At the end of June a subaltern and twenty men were sent from Bristol to Aberystwith and Aberdovy to assist the officers of the customs " in executing several legal processes against owlers and smugglers, and in hindering the exportation of wool and the illegal importation of prohibited goods." At the end of October two companies were sent from Bristol, one to Bedminster and the other to Lanford's Gate to assist the Civil power in repressing the violence and disorder which had spread over the whole country, but more especially over the south-western counties.* The quarters of detachments were afterwards changed to Andover, Devises, Wallingford, Henley, and Basingstoke; whence, in December, two companies were sent to Warminster to aid the civil power against riots in Wiltshire.

1729.

In May the head quarters were changed. The regiment left Bristol and sent eight companies to Exeter, two to Taunton, one to Columpton, and one to Wellington; the detachment being also withdrawn from Aberystwith. In June a captain and one company were sent to Dotreaux Castle and Port Isaac, Cornwall, to aid the civil power in the suppression of smuggling. This detachment also occupied Ross Castle, where it was relieved by other detachments. All these places were then in a particularly disturbed state. At the end of the year the two additional companies were disbanded, and the remaining companies each reduced ten men.

<small>Reduction of the Establishment.</small>

<small>* Smollet draws a doleful picture of the times:—" England was at this period infested with robbers, assassins, and incendiaries, the natural consequences of degeneracy and corruption, and the want of police in the interior government of the kingdom.... The peculiar depravity of the times was visible even in the conduct of those who preyed upon the Commonwealth. Thieves and robbers were now become more desperate and savage than ever they had appeared since mankind was civilized. In the exercise of their rapine they wounded, maimed, and even murdered the unhappy sufferers, through a wanton barbarity. They circulated letters demanding sums of money from certain individuals, on pain of reducing their houses to ashes, and their families to ruin; and even set fire to the house of a rich merchant in Bristol, who had refused to comply with their demand. The same species of villany was practised in different parts of the kingdom; so that the Government was obliged to interpose, and offer a considerable reward for discovering the ruffians concerned in such execrable designs."—*Smollet's History of England;* see also the *London Gazette.*</small>

1730.

The regiment assembled at Exeter in April, and at the end of June marched to Plymouth, where it remained for the year. The establishment was 615 men.

1731.

The possible rupture of the peace of Europe involved in the succession to the Duchy of Parma, caused England to prepare for war. The Royal Fusiliers were one of the regiments ordered for active service. On the 26th August, Sir Charles Wager sailed from Portsmouth with a strong squadron, to support the claims of the Spanish Prince. But there was no war, the prince's claim being placed beyond dispute by the course of domestic events. The regiment, which had embarked but not left England, landed at Portsmouth in November, and having remained ten days at Petersfield, Alresford, and the neighbourhood, proceeded to Marlborough, Caln, Hungerford, Troubridge, Bradford, Hoton-Basset, Chippenham, and Warminster. The head quarters and two companies were at Marlborough; there was one company at each of the other places.

Embark for service, but recalled.

1732—1733.

The establishment of the regiment in 1732 was 615 of all ranks. It continued quartered in the south-western counties of England until it embarked for Gibraltar. The exact time when the Fusiliers were sent to Gibraltar is not quite clear. The *Gentleman's Magazine* tells us that on the 1st December, 1732, Capt. Roger Hale, of Lord Tyrawley's regiment at Gibraltar, died much lamented there; and, although the bare statement is not of itself conclusive, it is believed the regiment had been sent out shortly before that time.

Embark for Gibraltar.

In July, 1733, Capt. Berkeley was promoted Major of the regiment in the room of Major Jones, deceased. The establishment and pay of the regiment were as follow:—

ROYAL REGIMENT OF FUSILIERS,
Consisting of 10 Companies of 50 effective Private Men in each.

Field and Staff Officers.	£ s. d.	per diem. £ s. d.	per annum. £ s. d.
Colonel, as Colonel	0 12 0		
In lieu of his Servants	0 2 0	0 14 0	255 10 0

1733—GIBRALTAR.] Record of the Royal Regiment of Fusiliers.

	£ s. d.	per diem. £ s. d.	per annum. £ s. d.
Lieutenant-Colonel, as Lieutenant-Colonel	..	0 7 0	127 15 0
Major, as Major	..	0 5 0	91 5 0
Chaplain	..	0 6 8	121 13 4
Adjutant	..	0 4 0	73 0 0
Quarter-Master	0 4 0		
In lieu of Servant	0 0 8	0 4 8	85 3 4
Chyrugeon	0 4 0		
His Mate	0 2 6	0 6 6	118 12 6
		2 7 10	872 19 2
One Company.			
Captain	0 8 0		
In lieu of his Servants	0 2 0	0 10 0	182 10 0
Two Lieutenants, each	0 4 0		
In lieu of their Servants	0 1 4	0 9 4	170 6 8
Three Sergeants, each	0 1 6	0 4 6	82 2 6
Three Corporals, each	0 1 0	0 3 0	54 15 0
Two Drummers, each	0 1 0	0 2 0	36 10 0
Fifty effective Private Men, each	0 0 8	1 13 4	608 6 8
		3 2 2	1134 10 10
Allowance to the Widows	..	0 1 4	24 1 8
To the Colonel, for Clothing lost by Deserters	..	0 1 2	21 5 10
To the Captain, for Recruiting	..	0 1 0	18 5 0
To the Agent	..	0 0 6	9 2 6
		3 6 2	1207 10 10
Eight Companies more, each same as above	..	..	9660 6 0
One Company of Grenadiers.			
Captain	0 8 0		
In lieu of Servants	0 2 0	0 10 0	182 10 0
Two Lieutenants, each 4s.	0 8 0		
In lieu of Servants	0 1 4	0 9 4	170 6 8
Three Sergeants, each	0 1 6	0 4 6	82 2 6
Three Corporals, each	0 1 0	0 3 0	54 15 0
Two Drummers, each	0 1 0	0 2 0	36 10 0
Fifty effective Private Men	..	1 13 4	608 6 8
		3 2 2	1134 10 10
Allowance to Widows, Colonel, Captain, and Agent	..	0 4 0	73 0 0
Total for this Regiment	..	£35 9 6	£12,948 7 6

In all, 615 men, officers included.

1734.

A draft made from this and the other regiments in garrison to the amount of 680 men, to form six companies for Jamaica.

1735.

While the regiment was at Gibraltar, the Colonel, Lord Tyrawley, was appointed a Brigadier-General (Dec. 18th).

1736-1738.

The regiment remained at Gibraltar.

1739.

The regiment was twice augmented this year, each time 10 men per company, by which its establishment was increased to 815 men.

On the removal of Lord Tyrawley to the 4th Dragoon Guards Major-Gen. Hargrave, from the 9th Foot, was appointed Colonel.

1740.

The regiment remained at Gibraltar. The following list of officers for 1740 was printed by order of the House of Commons. It shews the old lamentable state of stagnation in the regiment, and is one more evidence of the corrupt selfishness the British army so long suffered from.

	DATE OF PRESENT COMMISSION.	DATE OF FIRST COMMISSION IN THE ARMY.
Major-Gen. W. Hargrave, Colonel	27th Aug., 1739	Ens., 23rd April, 1694.
Lieut.-Col. James Fleming	4th Aug., 1722	Lieut., 7th Sept., 1706.
Major John Aldercron	13th Dec., 1739	Ens., 23rd Feb., 1708-9.
Capt. Marcus Smith	4th Nov., 1724.	
,, Augustus Pynyot	26th Dec., 1726	Ens., 18th Oct., 1703.
,, Samuel Clutterbuck	3rd April, 1733	Capt.-Lieut., 9th July, 1729.
,, Edward Butler	12th Nov., 1733	Lieut., 13th May, 1709.
,, Lord Glencairn	3rd April, 1734	Ens., 10th Jan., 1728-9.
,, Matthew Hewitt	1st Jan., 1735-6	Capt., 5th Mar., 1707-8.
,, John Darassus	13th Dec., 1739	Lieut., 17th Nov., 1721.
Capt.-Lieut. Geo. Crofts	12th Nov., 1733	Ens., 6th Aug., 1706.
Lieut. John Marshall	19th Oct., 1709	Lieut., 2nd Aug., 1709.
,, Richard Burchett	8th Oct., 1717	Lieut., 23rd Dec., 1711.
,, Rupert Pratt	13th July, 1718	Ens., 14th May, 1710.
,, Meredith Everard	7th Sept., 1722.	
,, Henry Ormsby	20th May, 1723.	
,, William Elwes	20th Oct., 1726.	
,, John Fleming	26th Dec., 1726.	
,, Richard Rudyerd	11th April, 1733.	

	Date of Present Commission.	Date of First Commission in the Army.
Lieut. James O'Hara	13th Dec., 1732.	
,, William Burton	1st July, 1734	Ens., 26th Nov., 1717.
,, John Butler	31st Jan., 1735-6.	
,, John Donaldson	10th March, 1737-8.	
,, William Shuttleworth	20th April, 1738.	
,, John Bonamy	7th Feb., 1738-9.	
,, Thomas Fothergill	13th Dec., 1739.	
,, John Heylin	17th Jan., 1739-40.	
,, Congreve Chilcott	18th Jan., 1739-40.	
,, James Smith	19th Jan., 1739-40.	
,, Philip Le Geyt	22nd Mar., 1739-40	Ens., 5th April, 1732.

1741-43.

The regiment remained on the Rock during these years without any more material incident in its career than the appointment of Lieut-Col. Fleming to the command of the 36th Regiment. He was succeeded by Major Aldercron, who was succeeded by Capt. Marcus Smith.

1744-45.

In April, 1744, Hargrave's (7th), Columbine's (10th), Fullers's (29th), and Houghton's (45th), the regiments then stationed at Gibraltar, were ordered to send recruiting parties into Middlesex, London, Westminster, and Southwark. Great difficulty was experienced in recruiting these regiments, so to facilitate it and obtain the requisite number of men, an Act was passed at the beginning of 1745 ordering deserters from regiments on the home stations when captured to be sent off to fill up the vacancies.

1746-48.

The regiment remained at Gibraltar; the establishment being 815.

1749.

The spring reliefs of this year sent the regiment home from Gibraltar. It was not, however, placed on the English Establishment, but sent to Ireland; it landed at Kinsale on the 21st July, and was immediately reduced to the Irish Establishment,

LORD TYRAWLEY'S REGIMENT OF FOOT [1738].

Extracted from a MS. Army List at the War Office. The dates and remarks in brackets [ ] have been supplied from other official sources.

RANK AND NAME.	RANK IN REGIMENT.	Colonel.	Lieut.-Col.	Major.	Captain.	Capt.-Lieut.	Lieut.	Ensign.	REMARKS.
Col. Lord Tyrawley	29 Jan., 1713	…	…	…	24 Mar., 1705	…	15 May, 1703	…	Made Colonel of Pearce's Horse—succeeded by W. Hargraves, 27th Aug., 1739.
Lieut.-Col. Jas. Fleming	4 Aug., 1722	…	…	…	12 May, 1715	…	7 Sept., 1706	…	Made Col. of Bland's—Major J. Aldercron, 5th Feb., 1741.
Major William Cropp	3 Sept., 1733	…	…	…	30 April, 1719	…	25 Mar., 1705	…	Retired—Capt. Marcus Smith, 13th Feb., 1741.
Capt. John Aldercron	4 Aug., 1722	…	…	…	…	…	…	23 Feb., 1709	Made Major—Lieut. J. Darassus, 13th Dec., 1739.
,, Marcus Smith	4 Nov., 1724	…	…	…	…	…	…	…	Made Major—[Lieut. Ventris Scott, 25th April, 1741].
,, Augustus Pynyot	26 Dec, 1726	…	…	…	10 Sept., 1712	…	16 May, 1706 [20 July, 1708]	18 Oct., 1703	Retired—Lieut. J. Fleming, 22nd Sept., 1742.
,, Saml. Clutterbuck	5 April, 1733	…	…	…	…	9 July, 1729	…	…	
,, Edward Butler	12 Nov., 1733	…	…	…	…	5 April, 1733	13 May, 1709	…	Made Major to Pawlett's—Capt.-Lieut. Geo. Crofts, 25th April, 1741.
,, Lord Glencairn	3 April, 1734	…	…	…	…	…	…	10 Jan., 1729	Made Capt.—Lieut. J. Marshall, 25th April, 1741.
,, Matthew Hewitt	1 Jan., 1736	…	…	…	5 Mar., 1708	…	7 Mar., 1707	6 Aug., 1706	Made Capt.—Francis Smith, 25th April, 1741.
Capt.-Lieut. Geo. Crofts	12 Nov., 1733	…	…	…	…	…	2 Aug., 1709	…	
Lieut. John Marshall	19 Oct., 1709	…	…	…	…	…	23 Dec, 1711	…	
,, Richard Burchett	8 Oct., 1717	…	…	…	…	…	15 Aug., 1717	14 May, 1710	Made Capt. in Wolfe's Marines—J. Heylin, 17th Jan., 1740.
,, Rupert Pratt	13 July, 1718	…	…	…	…	…	…	…	Made Capt.—Thomas Fothergill, 13th Dec., 1739.
,, John Harris	13 April, 1719	…	…	…	…	…	…	…	Dead—Ferrier, 28th Sept., 1739.
,, John Darassus	17 Nov., 1721	…	…	…	…	…	…	…	Dead—J. Bonamy, gent., 7th Feb., 1739.
,, Meredith Everard	7 Sept., 1722	…	…	…	…	…	…	…	Dead—T. Wilkinson, 4th June, 1742.
,, Thomas Griffith	17 Dec., 1722	…	…	…	…	…	…	…	
,, Henry Ormsby	20 May, 1723	…	…	…	…	…	…	…	Made Capt.—J. Market, 22nd Sept., 1742.
,, William Elwes	20 Oct., 1726	…	…	…	…	…	…	…	Dead—Roger Kynaston, 28th Sept., 1743.
,, John Fleming	26 Dec., 1726	…	…	…	…	…	…	…	Dead—Jas. Smith, 19th Jan., 1740.
,, Richard Rudyerd	11 April, 1733	…	…	…	…	…	23 Mar., 1728	26 Nov., 1717	
,, James O'Hara	13 Dec., 1732	…	…	…	…	…	…	…	
,, William Burton	1 July, 1734	…	…	…	…	…	…	…	
,, Gervase Parker	20 June, 1735	…	…	…	…	…	3 May, 1709	…	Made Capt. in Moreton's Marines—Congreve Chillcot, 18th Jan., 1740.
,, John Butler	31 Jan., 1736	…	…	…	…	…	…	…	Removed to Invalids—Ensign P. Legeyt, of Invalids, 23rd March, 1740.
,, John Lind	23 July, 1737	…	…	…	…	…	…	…	Made Lieut. in Providence—Lieut. W. Shuttleworth, of Providence, 20th April, 1738.
,, Nicholson Ward	10 Aug., 1737	…	…	…	…	…	5 July, 1737	…	
,, William Bubrard	11 Aug., 1737	…	…	…	…	…	…	…	
,, John Donaldson	10 Mar., 1738	…	…	…	…	…	…	…	

MAJOR-GENERAL HARGRAVE'S REGIMENT OF FOOT [1743].

Extracted from a MS. Army List at the War Office. The dates in brackets [ ] have been supplied from other official sources.

RANK AND NAME.	RANK IN REGIMENT.	RANK IN THE ARMY.							REMARKS.
		Colonel.	Lieut.-Col.	Major.	Captain.	Capt.-Lieut.	Lieut.	Ensign.	
Col. Wm. Hargrave	27 Aug., 1739	15 Nov., 1711	27 April, 1708	31 Aug., 1705	18 Oct., 1703	...	17 July, 1702	23 April, 1694	Dead—succeeded by Col. Mostyn, Capt. 2nd Guards, 26th Jan. 1750.
Lt.-Col. John Aldercron	5 Feb., 1741	...	...	...	4 Aug., 1722	...	...	23 Feb., 1709	Col. of 39th Foot—Marcus Smith, 3rd June, 1752.
Major Marcus Smith	13 Feb., 1741	...	...	...	4 Nov., 1724	...	...	...	Lieut.-Col.—Capt. J. Donaldson, 3rd June, 1752.
Capt. Augustus Pynyot	26 Dec., 1726	...	...	...	10 Sept., 1712	...	16 May, 1706	18 Oct., 1703	Retired—Capt. H. Gore, of Fleming's 36th Foot, 8th May, 1749.
,, Saml. Clutterbuck	5 April, 1733	...	...	...	...	9 July, 1729	[20 July, 1708]	...	Resigns—Lieut. J. Gwilliam, 2nd May, 1751.
,, Edwd. Butler	12 Nov., 1733	...	...	...	...	...	13 May, 1709	...	Retired.
,, Matthew Hewitt	1 Jan., 1736	...	...	...	5 Mar., 1708	...	...	...	Retired—Lieut. J. O'Hara, 9th Oct., 1747.
,, John Darassus	13 Dec., 1739	...	...	...	...	5 April, 1733	17 Nov., 1721.	...	Resigns—Lieut. J. Heylin, 1st Feb., 1751.
,, George Crofts	25 April, 1741	...	...	...	...	...	7 Mar, 1707	6 Aug., 1706	Invalided—Capt.-Lieut. R. Pratt, 3rd June, 1752.
,, John Price	25 Mar., 1742	...	...	...	28 Aug., 1737	12 Nov., 1733	18 Aug., 1708	...	
Capt.-Lt. John Marshall	25 April, 1741	...	...	...	...	26 Aug., 1737	2 Aug., 1709	...	Dead—Lieut. Congreve Chillcot. 3rd June, 1752.
Lieut. Richard Burchett	8 Oct., 1717	...	...	...	...	...	23 Dec., 1711	...	Capt.-Lieut.—Lieut. J. Caldwell, from Irish half-pay, 2nd May, 1751.
,, Rupert Pratt	13 July, 1718	...	...	...	...	...	15 Aug., 1717	14 May, 1710	Capt.-Lieut.—Ensign C. Veaitch, from Irish half-pay, 9th Feb., 1751.
,, Meredith Everard	7 Sept., 1722	...	...	...	...	...	...	...	Dead—Lieut. J. Thompson, from Irish half-pay, 7th April, 1750.
,, William Elwes	20 Oct., 1726	...	...	...	...	...	...	...	Made Captain.
,, John Fleming	26 Dec., 1726	...	...	...	...	...	...	...	Capt.—Jas. Manseargh, 31st Mar., 1748.
,, Richard Rudyerd	11 April, 1733	...	...	...	...	...	...	...	Capt.—Ensign J. Hargrave, of Reads's, 9th Oct., 1747.
,, James O'Hara	13 Dec., 1732	...	...	...	...	...	...	...	
,, William Burton	1 July, 1734	...	...	...	...	...	23 Mar, 1728	...	Dead—Roger Kynaston, 28th Sept., 1743.
,, John Butler	31 Jan., 1736	...	...	...	...	...	3 May, 1709	...	Dead—James Edgar, 25th April, 1745.
,, John Donaldson	10 Mar., 1738	...	...	...	...	...	...	26 Nov., 1717	Capt.—Ensign R. Mercer, 47th Foot, 19th June, 1751.
,, Wm. Shuttleworth	20 April, 1738	...	...	...	...	...	10 Aug., 1737.	...	Dead—2nd Lieut. E. Brice Dobbs, from Irish half-pay, 3rd June, 1752.
,, John Bonamy	7 Feb., 1739	...	...	...	...	...	...	...	Invalided—Robt. Dechair, 13th April, 1745.
,, Thos. Fothergill	13 Dec., 1739	...	...	...	...	...	...	...	Capt.—Chas. Heylin, 9th Feb., 1751.
,, John Heylin	17 Jan., 1740	...	...	...	...	...	...	...	Capt.-Lieut.—Ensign J. Hayro, of Folliot's 18th Foot, 3rd June, 1752.
,, J. Congreve Chillcot	18 Jan., 1740	...	...	...	...	...	...	...	Dead—Capt. T. Spears, 2nd May, 1751.
,, James Smith	19 Jan., 1740	...	...	...	...	...	...	...	Dead—Capt. 42nd Foot—Moses Corbett, 19th April, 1748.
,, Philip Legeyt	23 Mar., 1740	...	...	...	...	...	...	[5 Apl., 1732]	Capt. in Tyrawley's—Matthew Smith, 7th July, 1747.
,, Francis Smith	19 Jan., 1741	...	...	...	...	...	...	...	Capt. in Jeffrey's—Lieut. P. Dromgole, of Independent Company in Providence, 1st Dec., 1745.
,, Thomas Wilkinson	4 June, 1742	...	...	...	...	...	...	...	

by which 7 sergeants, 4 corporals, 6 drummers, and 340 privates were discharged. The regiment was then broken up into detachments. Four companies remained at Kinsale; four companies proceeded to Cork (barracks and town); and two to Bandon, Rosscarberry Barracks and town.

1750.

During the spring reliefs the regiment proceeded to Dublin, the several detachments assembling there from their respective stations on the 23rd and 25th June.

1751.

By Royal Warrant, dated 1st July, 1751, the Royal Fusiliers are authorised to wear the following distinctions:—

Distinctive badges awarded.   In the centre of their colours the ROSE within the GARTER, and the CROWN over it; the WHITE HORSE in the corners of the second colour. On the grenadier caps the Rose within the Garter, and Crown as in the colours. White Horse and motto over it, *nec aspera terrent*. The same device of the Rose within the Garter and Crown on their drums and bells of arms, with the rank of the regiment underneath.

For the first half of the year the regiment remained in Dublin. On the 17th June, Naizon's (13th) Dragoons, 1st Batt. Royal Scots, Fowke's (2nd Queen's), Irwin's (5th), and the Royal Fusiliers were reviewed by Viscount Molesworth, in the Phœnix Park, "and performed their exercises and evolutions to the entire satisfaction of all the Field Officers and numerous spectators who were present." Between the 25th and 29th June the regiment, together with the Royal Scots, marched into country quarters; five companies to Carrackfergus (two of which should march thence to Armagh, Charlemont Barracks); and five companies to Londonderry. They were succeeded in Dublin by the 42nd Highlanders and the 9th Foot.

1752.

The regiment was in "Country Quarters," the head quarters being at Londonderry. On the 8th May the regiment again changed quarters, the five companies from Londonderry, three from Carrickfergus, and two from Charlemont commenced their march to Enniskillen. In June, after the regiment had been inspected, the Fusiliers assembled at Limerick. On the 3rd June Lieut-Colonel Aldercron was promoted Colonel of the 39th Foot; he was succeeded in the regiment by Major Marcus Smith.

1753.

The regiment marched to Waterford from Limerick between the 24th May and 2nd June. To complete the 39th (now under orders for India) the Royal Fusiliers and nine other regiments were called upon to give each fifty volunteers; those from the Fusiliers, the 9th, and the 42nd were obtained on the spot. The drafts assembled at Cork on the 20th Feb., 1754; the volunteers from the Fusiliers being replaced by recruits raised in Ireland. The 39th has the honour of being the first English regiment which served in India. Colonel Aldercron was appointed General and Commander-in-Chief in the East Indies, where he pursued a brilliant career.

1754.

In May the regiment proceeded from Waterford to Cork, relieving Lord Loudon's regiment. The head quarters, under Major Donaldson, and four companies were at Cork Harbour; two companies were at Cork; two, under Captains Heylin and Shuttleworth, were at Ross Carberry; and two, under Captains Chillcot and Smith, at Ichageela. Colonel Mostyn being transferred to the 13th Dragoons, he was succeeded on the 20th August by Colonel Lord Robert Bertie. Later in the year the companies at Ichageela and Rosscarberry were transferred respectively to Macroom and Bandon. On the 10th November, the anniversary of His Majesty's birthday, a *feu-de-joie* of three volleys was fired at the Cove by the four companies, and in the evening the barracks were entirely illuminated. Drink was given to the soldiers and populace to drink His Majesty's health round a large bonfire, the night concluding with all other demonstrations of joy. The following list of officers refers to the close of the year 1754; it immediately precedes the "Army List," which was published by authority for the first time in 1755.

[margin: Lord Robert Bertie appointed Colonel.]

		COMP.				COMP.	
Col. Lord R. Bertie		No. 1	20th Aug. 1754	Lieut. Chas. Heylin		No. 9	9th Feb., 1750-51
Lieut.-Col. Marcus Smith	..	2	3rd June, 1752	,, J. Caldwell	..	3	2nd May, 1751
Major J. Donaldson	..	3	,,	,, Thos. Sheares	..	8	,,
Captain Henry Gore	..	4	8th May, 1749	,, Richard Mercer	..	7	19th June, 1751
,, J. Heylin	..	5	9th Feb. 1750-1	,, John Hay	..	2	3rd June, 1752
,, Thos. Gwillim	..	6	2nd May, 1751	,, Edwd. Brice Dobbs	..	6	,,
,, J. Congreve Chillcot		7	16th Dec. 1752	,, Geo. Bird	..	4	27th Nov. 1752
,, Jas. Edgar	..	8	20th June, 1753	,, J. Cunningham	..	1	16th Dec. 1752
,, Mat. Smith	..	9	28th Aug. 1753	,, Thos. Bourne	..	9	20th June, 1753
,, W. Shuttleworth	..	10	4th Sept. 1754	,, Wm. Colhoun	..	5	28th Aug. 1754
Capt.-Lieut. Moses Corbett		1	,,	,, Geo. Julian	..	3	12th Mar. 1754
Lieut. W. Elwes	..	5	20th Oct. 1726	,, R. Gamble	..	2	4th Sept. 1754
,, Pat. Dromgole	..	10	1st Dec. 1745	Chaplain, Edm. Baxter	..		1738
,, Thos. Hargrave	..	8	9th Oct. 1747	Adjt., Moses Corbet	..		27th Nov. 1752
,, Jas. Harvey	..	7	23rd July, 1748	Surgeon, Geo. Fryer	..		4th Jan. 1749-50
,, Chas. Thompson	..	4	7th April, 1750	Mate, Adam Giles		..	
,, Chas. Veaitch	..	6	9th Feb. 1750-1	Qr.-Master, Thos. Hargrave	..		25th Mar. 1755

1755.

The regiment embarks for England.

The regiment, composed of 3 field officers, 7 captains, 11 lieutenants, 9 ensigns, 4 staff, 20 sergeants, 20 corporals, 10 drummers, and 350 privates, embarked at Cork for England on the 31st March, together with Colonel Jordan's Regiment. They arrived at Bristol on the 9th April. At the close of the year the regiment was sent to Dover Castle.

The regiment had, during the summer, been augmented from 29 men per company to 70, and was placed upon a war footing to meet the exigencies of the impending war with France. Two additional companies were also added, to which James Harvey and Thomas Calcraft were appointed captains; — Blomer, Charles Lind, Francis Kineer, and James Gardner, lieutenants. Towards the end of the year they were detached to form part of the new regiments then being raised.

1756.

On the 2nd March the regiment was inspected in Dover Castle by H.R.H. the Duke of Cumberland. Being relieved by a detachment of the Guards, the Fusiliers left Dover Castle and proceeded to Portsmouth. On the 30th March the *Embarks for service on board the Fleet.* regiment embarked on board Admiral Byng's squadron, the head quarters under Lieut.-Colonel Smith on board the flag ship, except one company reserved for the

"Intrépide," a ship belonging to the squadron, but in a more backward state of preparation than the rest; the marines on board all the ships being disembarked to make room for the Fusiliers. The squadron sailed from Portsmouth on the 5th April, it made the Rock of Lisbon on the 17th, and doubled Cape St. Vincent on the 19th. The destination of the squadron was the relief of Minorca, but negligence and delays had removed every chance of success, for on the 20th the French took possession of Port Mahon. Whether on the embarkation of the regiment it was intended to serve as marines, or to be conveyed by Byng as a reinforcement to the garrison of Gibraltar, is difficult to decide, from the careless and inefficient manner in which the naval and military affairs were then administered. Byng lost his life for conduct more strongly marked by incompetence than cowardice, and Fowke, the Governor of Gibraltar, was dismissed the service for conduct only less infamous than that of Byng. The Admiralty instructions were clear "that the Royal Regiment of Fusiliers, commanded by Lord Robert Bertie, should serve aboard His Majesty's ships in the Mediterranean, and that the said regiment should be landed at Minorca, in case the Governor or Commander-in-Chief of that island should think it necessary for its defence;" but that the War Office orders really meant the same thing it is somewhat difficult to believe. We give them in their chronological order.

"To Lieut.-Gen. Fowke, or in his absence to the Commander-in-Chief in His Majesty's Garrison of Gibraltar.

"WAR OFFICE, March 21st, 1756.

"SIR,—I am commanded to acquaint you that it is His Majesty's pleasure that you receive into your garrison Lord Robert Bertie's regiment to do duty there, and in case you shall apprehend that the French threaten to make any attempt upon His Majesty's Island of Minorca, it is His Majesty's pleasure that you make a detachment out of the troops in your garrison equal to a battalion to be commanded by a lieut.-colonel and major, to be the eldest in your garrison, to be put on board the fleet for Minorca at the disposition of the admiral.

"I am, Sir, your most obedient Servant,
"BARRINGTON."

"WAR OFFICE, March 28th, 1756.

"SIR,—I am commanded to acquaint you that it is His Majesty's pleasure, in case you shall apprehend that the French threaten an attempt on Minorca, that you make a detachment from the troops in your garrison equal to a battalion, commanded by a lieutenant-colonel and a major, for the relief of that place, to be put on board the fleet at the disposition of the admiral; such lieutenant-colonel and major to be the eldest in your garrison.

"BARRINGTON."

"WAR OFFICE, April 1st, 1756.

"SIR,—It is His Majesty's pleasure that you receive into your garrison the women and children belonging to Lord Robert Bertie's regiment.

"BARRINGTON."

These orders from the War Office clearly indicate that by the military authorities the Royal Fusiliers were intended to form a portion of the garrison of Gibraltar. By the very terms of the orders they could not as a battalion be sent to the succour of Minorca, and the Admiralty order to Byng, which is consistent with the arrangement that deprived the fleet of its marines before sailing, simply contradicts them.

Takes part in Byng's action.

The regiment took part in Admiral Byng's engagement on the 20th May, Lord Robert Bertie, Lieutenant-Colonel Smith and the head-quarters being on board the "Ramillies." This engagement, a blunder in itself and ill-conducted, was futile, for the French had already captured Minorca, the capitulation of which allowed the troops to be conveyed to Gibraltar. By the 1st August the whole of the troops had been landed there, making eleven regiments in the garrison, and singularly enough they included the only Fusilier regiments then in the English service. Many of these regiments were however only landed temporarily, and were sent home as speedily as opportunity offered. But the Royal Fusiliers were detained on the Rock for another tour of garrison duty there.

1757—60.

The regiment remained at Gibraltar. In November the following was the state of the regiment:—56 officers, 50 non-commissioned officers, 598 men fit for duty, 38 men sick, 721; total establishment 815.

1763.

The regiment returned to England. It was quartered at Chatham.

1764.

In May the Fusiliers left Chatham and proceeded to London. On the 26th they were reviewed in Hyde Park. After a stay of a few days in London they marched to Gloucester, where they remained the rest of the year.

1765.

In the spring the regiment left Gloucester and marched to Berwick-on-Tweed, where it was stationed during the year.

1766.

From Berwick it proceeded in the spring by march to Edinburgh Castle, and occupied that fortress for the remainder of the year. Its strength was 32 officers, 47 non-commissioned officers, 379 men fit for duty, 27 sick, total, 485; establishment, 529.

1767-68.

In April, 1767, the Fusiliers proceeded to Glasgow and Perth, where they remained during this and the succeeding year. The facings of the regiment were blue, white lace, with a blue stripe.

1769.

The regiment left Perth and proceeded to Fort William. Its strength was this year reduced to 448 men.

1770.

In the spring of this year the regiment returned to Berwick, where its establishment was increased at the general augmentation of the army.

1771.

In the early part of the year the regiment returned to Chatham. In April the Royal Fusiliers and the 61st Regiment embarked at Stokes Bay for Minorca; but the order being countermanded the regiments disembarked at Portsmouth.

1772.

The Royal Fusiliers remained in the South of England, the growing troubles in America keeping them in expectation of service in the discontented colonies.

1773.

The rebellious spirit that was evidently increasing in America, sent the regiment upon active service. The Fusiliers embarked at Portsmouth in March, and proceeded to Canada, the regiment landing in Quebec, where it was put in garrison. Its stay in Quebec was not however long, for after a few months it embarked for Montreal, and proceeded thence to occupy several posts in Lower Canada.

1774.

For some portion of the year the regiment continued to occupy its advanced posts, but before the winter it was recalled to Montreal. The regiment being weak in numbers, recruiting was vigorously carried on in England. The detachment under Major Stopford remained at Chamblé.

1775.

On the 17th May Lieut. Despard arrived at Quebec with a large draft of recruits from England. The outbreak of hostilities immediately sent the regiment to the front. On the advance of the American army, Lieut.-General, Sir Guy Carleton ordered a detachment of the Royal Fusiliers, numbering 150 men, and the 26th regiment from Montreal to St. John's, where they began to fortify their position. These troops were nearly all the regular troops Sir Guy had in Canada, and were manifestly unequal to even the smallest of open operations.

Fort St. John's besieged.

On the 17th September, the American Colonel Montgomery, acting under the orders of General Schuyler, commenced the siege of Fort St. John's. The garrison consisted of 550 men of the Royal Fusiliers and 26th Regiment, under the command of Major Charles Preston, of the 26th. From the first the American prospect of success was discouraging. Montgomery's troops were lacking all organisation, his stores were inadequate, and according to all appearances, the British were determined to hold their post. While despair was creeping upon him the fortunate termination of a vigorous stroke suddenly renewed his hopes of success.

Some Canadians who had attached themselves to the Americans had determined to attack Fort Chamblé, an outpost four miles lower down the Sorel, where a company of the Royal Fusiliers was stationed to keep open the communication between St. John's and Montreal. With considerable skill and secrecy they had carried their artillery on batteaux past the fort of St. John's, and suddenly investing Chamblé, the place, which had been negligently left in a somewhat imperfect state, found itself in no condition whatever for defence, and was compelled to capitulate. Major Stopford proposed that the officers and men of the Royal Fusiliers should not be made prisoners, but should march unmolested with their arms, accoutrements, 24 rounds of ammunition each, drums beating, colours flying, and provisions and carts sufficient to pass by the shortest road to Montreal, or any other place in the province of Quebec, at his option. Major Brown, the American commander, would not however assent to these terms. He stipulated that the officers and men should surrender themselves prisoners of war, and in that case they should be allowed all their baggage, agreeable to their desire.

These terms Major Stopford was compelled to accept. On the 9th October the Americans took possession of the fort, and to their extreme joy found it contained the things they most wanted—an ample supply of the munitions of war. Their greatest acquisition was about six tons of gunpowder and some shot, the possession of which enabled Montgomery immediately to open fire upon St. John's. The garrison of Fort Chamblé, consisting of Major Stopford, Captain Brice (sick), Captain Goodwin* and Lieutenants Hamer, Harrison, and Shuttleworth, one surgeon, and 83 men of the Royal Fusiliers thus became prisoners of war, but were allowed their baggage. The colours of the regiment were unfortunately in the fort, and, being captured, were sent off to Congress as a proud trophy of the valour of their troops. They were the first presents of the kind Congress ever received.

This success immediately called forth new exertions on the part of Montgomery and his despondent followers before Fort St. John's. On the 1st November he opened an incessant fire of artillery upon the place, which the garrison quickly returned, but on the 2nd negociations commenced, and on the 3rd, the garrison

---

* There is no record of Captain Goodwin having served in the Royal Fusiliers. The other officers all belonged the regiment.

having surrendered themselves prisoners, marched out with the honours of war, "as what was due to their fortitude and perseverance." Among the officers captured at St. John's was Lieutenant Cleveland, of the Royal Fusiliers.

The misfortunes of the regiment did not end here. Colonel Prescott with a portion of it remained at Montreal, to which place Montgomery now pushed forward. The artillery of the rebels commanded the navigation of the St. Lawrence; the season was too far advanced to obtain succour, and on the 12th November the city fell into the hands of the Americans. General Carleton escaped, but Colonel Prescot with 11 other officers and 120 soldiers were compelled to surrender prisoners. It was thus that the whole regiment, except Captain Owen's company which was in Quebec, was captured. The prisoners were sent by the Americans to Philadelphia.

<small>Montreal captured.</small>

In the midst of a Canadian winter, Montgomery, flushed by his successes, on the 14th November laid siege to Quebec. The hazardous nature of the enterprise seemed to approach to the very verge of folly, but it was nevertheless a stroke of true military genius. As the forces of the besiegers and the besieged were alike contemptible, and in the aggregate incapable of otherwise exercising an influence upon the campaign, their existence or non-existence as combatant bodies was a matter of small moment, while the possession of Quebec was in the moral sense to each of them a matter of infinite importance. To the Americans the enterprise was especially worth the attempt.

<small>Quebec besieged.</small>

The garrison consisted, as nearly as possible, of the following forces:—

Colonel Maclean's men, Royal Highland Emigrants	170
Captain Owen's Company of the Royal Fusiliers	60
Marines	40
Seamen	450
Militia (about)	800
	1520

This number fluctuated, and was subsequently increased; it is said the garrison on the 1st December was nearly 1800 men bearing arms, the Company of the Royal Fusiliers then numbering 70 men. Of these, scarcely any were worthy of being called regular troops. Colonel Maclean's corps was just being raised, all the troops were of the rawest description, the company of the Royal Fusiliers being composed of three-fourths of recruits, most of them Norfolk men, who had joined last spring. "Indeed," says an eye witness, "the militia was of more importance than you can conceive, and behaved very well."

Montgomery's force was of similar materials, but of smaller proportions. Fortunately for them, just before the siege was laid, they had captured a stock of clothing sent out from England for the Royal troops, and it was in His Majesty's uniform that they commenced operations. The winter was severe, and the troops on both sides having to serve amidst ice and snow, suffered greatly. Their hardships compelled the Americans to attempt a *coup-de-main*. About 5 a.m., of the 31st December, Montgomery led forward his troops in two divisions, one by way of Cape Diamond, and the other by the Guardhouse of St. Roque, to carry the place by assault. He was met by the garrison with determined resolution, and effectually repulsed. Indeed the morale of the besieged troops seems to have been excellent, and such as a vigorous commander would have turned to a better account. " The seamen were under the strictest discipline; Colonel Hamilton and Major Mackenzie headed the brave fellows, who behaved, as they do on all occasions, like British tars. The handful of Fusiliers, commanded by Captain Owen, distinguished themselves, and the Royal Emigrants behaved like veterans. The French Militia showed no backwardness, a handful of them stood to the last at Saut au Matelot; overcome by numbers, they were obliged to retreat to the barrier." [Quebec assaulted.]

In this attempt Montgomery was slain; Arnold, his second in command, was wounded, many of his men were captured, and a considerable number put *hors-de-combat*. The garrison only lost one officer, Lieutenant Anderson, of the navy, who was doing duty as a captain; four privates killed and thirteen wounded, of whom two eventually died. A Council of War, held by the Americans immediately after their repulse, determined that the siege should be converted into a blockade. For this purpose they retired about three miles from the city, and placed themselves in village cantonments.

1776.

Having fortified their posts, the Americans kept up the blockade until the 4th April, when they again opened fire upon Quebec. They continued their siege operations until the 6th May, when the garrison was reinforced by the Grenadiers of the 29th Regiment. Lieutenant-General Carleton marched out of the city to give them battle, whereupon the Americans literally bolted from their lines, leaving behind them all their artillery and stores. The British followed their opponents up the country, recovered Montreal, and drove the Americans out of Canada.

<small>Gallant exploit of Captain Forster, 8th Regiment.</small> One of the feats in this pursuit deserves recording, not less for its gallantry than for its association with the Royal Fusiliers. On the 19th May Captain Forster, with his light company of the 8th Foot, one hundred Canadians and two hundred Indians, but without cannon, having descended from the Lakes, attacked "the Cedars," a fort about 43 miles above Montreal, held by 390 Americans under Colonel Beadle. The audacity of the measure was Captain Forster's real strength, for it so completely cowed the garrison that the fort was surrendered at discretion, the men giving themselves up as prisoners of war. Not knowing what to do with his prisoners, who were threatened with wholesale massacre by the Indians, the Captain agreed to release them in exchange for the men of the 7th and 26th Regiments taken at Fort Chamblé and St. John's, viz.:—2 majors, 9 captains, 20 subalterns, and 443 soldiers. The conditions being accepted, the captains of the American force were sent as hostages to Quebec, the men returning to their homes. Congress, being disgusted with the defence, dishonourably refused for a time to carry out the exchange. It was at length however effected; the liberated men of the Royal Fusiliers left Philadelphia where they had been quartered, and on <small>The regiment liberated; returns to New York.</small> the 2nd December marched into New York, the then head quarters of the regiment, where they were supplied with clothing and again entered upon their regimental duties.

In the spring of this year a detachment of the regiment had been sent from England to Boston, where it remained until the evacuation, when it proceeded to Halifax in Nova Scotia. It proceeded in the autumn to New York, where, as we have already stated, the head quarters of the regiment had been established. The re-formation of the regiment involved great changes in the list of officers; Lieut.-Col. Alured Clarke, from the 54th Regiment, was appointed Lieut.-Col. *vice* Colonel Prescott, who had been promoted to the Colonelcy in succession to Lord Robert Bertie, appointed to the 2nd Life Guards. Colonel Prescott had been serving as a

Major-General, and was cleverly captured by the rebels in July. "I am extremely concerned, my Lord," says Sir W. Howe, in a dispatch to Lord George Germaine, "to close this letter with a circumstance as distressing as it was unexpected. An express is just arrived from Rhode Island with intelligence that a small party of the rebels made a descent there on the night of the 10th inst., surprised Major General Prescott in his quarters, carried him off, and Lieutenant Barrington of the 7th Regiment, with such secrecy and despatch as to frustrate every attempt to rescue them."

From New York the Fusiliers marched to Amboy, where they were placed in the division commanded by Earl Cornwallis.

1777.

The regiment passed the winter and spring at Amboy. At this station, the army was very sickly, dysentery carrying off great numbers daily. On the 23rd June the Fusiliers were at King's Bridge formed in brigade with the 26th, 35th, and 63rd Regiments of Foot and the 17th Light Dragoons, under Major-General Vaughan, the head quarters of the army being still at Amboy. Following the fortune of Lord Cornwallis's division, the regiment moved to Staten Island at the end of June, when the division was withdrawn from the Jerseys. In September the regiment formed part of a force, taken by Sir Henry Clinton, for a raid into the Jerseys, as a diversion in favour of the operations of the army under Sir W. Howe, proceeding to Philadelphia, and that under Lieut.-General Burgoyne against Albany. The 7th, 26th, and 52nd Regiments, with the Anspach and Waldeck Grenadiers and 300 Provincials, all under the command of Brigadier Campbell, were landed at Elizabeth-town Point on the 12th September, whence they proceeded to Newark. In the skirmishes which ensued, extending over three days, with such scattered bodies of rebels as could be collected to dispute Clinton's progress, the Fusiliers had Lieutenant Hamer and one man wounded: the greatest glory that the regiment acquired, besides "the strict attention to discipline," which received the approbation of the General, was its share in the capture of a few hundreds of cattle and sheep. As a diversion the affair had failed, for it had not at all influenced the

Head Quarters at Amboy.

main operations of the American armies. On the 16th, General Campbell marched his brigade to Bergen Point, where the troops re-embarked and returned to Staten Island.

In the beginning of October the Royal Fusiliers formed part of another expedition, sent to capture forts Clinton and Montgomery on the Hudson's River. On the 6th they disembarked at Stoney Point. From this point the troops had to march a distance of twelve miles over the mountains. A portion of them immediately started forward to the attack; the Royal Fusiliers and the Hessian Regiment of Trumbach being detained as the rearguard under Major-General Tryon; who was "to leave a battalion at the Pass of Thunder Hill, to open our communications with the fleet." All the operations were eminently successful. Before they terminated Major-General Tryon was sent, on the 9th, with Emerick's Chasseurs, 50 Jägers, the Royal Fusiliers, the Regiment of Trumbach, and two three-pounders to finish the affair by destroying the rebel settlement called the Continental Village, a post where a barrack for fifteen hundred men had been built and stores gathered. The extreme badness of the weather made it necessary to be as expeditious as possible, and so both the barrack and stores were burnt to the ground, the troops returning to camp in the evening without having suffered any loss.

Stationed at Philadelphia.

In December the regiment which, after the capitulation of Burgoyne at Saratoga, had been sent to Philadelphia, took part in the operations that Sir W. Howe commenced against Washington, who had encamped at White Marsh. In the effort to draw the Americans from their camp, and bring them to battle, the regiment lost one man, missing. The Fusiliers occupied Philadelphia during the winter.

1778.

There is no doubt that the efficiency of the regiments in garrison at Philadelphia was greatly impaired during the occupation. In the first place an inactivity that can only be called disgraceful, permitted 4,000 Americans to remain in an almost helpless condition within twenty-six miles of the British without the slightest molestation. "Nor was this the only, or perhaps the most serious, error committed. Philadelphia became the Capua of the British army. Discipline was totally relaxed. Gaming, if not encouraged, was permitted to a most ruinous extent; and the gross misconduct of very many officers disgusted to such a degree the inhabitants of a town in which, perhaps more than in any other, profligacy was offensive, that feelings very averse to British authority were engendered or increased among a people originally loyal. These bad impressions were never removed or overcome."

The occupation terminated on the 18th June, when the troops crossed the Delaware, in retreat to New York. The acknowledgment of the Independence of the States by France and the alliance of the two countries had put a great strain upon the British commander. It was now absolutely necessary for him to concentrate his troops. New York was selected as his base of operations. The journey across the Jerseys was especially arduous. The excessive heat of the weather imposed great sufferings upon the men, whose retreat was insulted by the enemy, with whom they had to fight several smart skirmishes. In none of these skirmishes do the Royal Fusiliers appear to have suffered any loss. This retreat, so unfortunate so far as the result of the war is concerned, was the only operation in which the regiment was engaged this year. On reaching New York the regiment went into camp, and there remained during the winter. It was augmented by one "additional company," the captaincy of which was given to Lieutenant John Aston Shuttleworth, his commission being dated 10th June.

Return to New York.

1779.

The regiment remained in the lines near New York until summer, when it was employed in the expedition sent into the East Sound under General Tryon with a view to draw Washington from the strong position he occupied in the mountains into Connecticut for the defence of the towns on the coast. The troops embarked at White Stone on the evening of the 3rd July, and at five a.m. of the 5th commenced their disembarkation in the harbour of Newhaven. The first division consisting of the flank companies of the Guards, the Royal Fusiliers, the 54th Regiment, and a detachment of Jägers with four field pieces under Brigadier-General Garth, landed a mile south of West Haven, and began their march making a circuit of seven miles to pass the head of the creek on the western side of the town. As soon as the boats that had landed the first division had returned to the ships, the General landed the 2nd division on the eastern side of the harbour, and

Expedition to the East Sound.

instantly began his march to the ferry from Newhaven East to Brentford. In the meantime Garth pushed forward with his troops and got into Newhaven, but "not without opposition, loss, and fatigue," for the enemy who had collected in force upon advantageous ground, and with heavier artillery than his own, eventually stopped him at the bridge over Neck Creek. In this advance the Royal Fusiliers lost one sergeant, seven men wounded, and two men missing.

On the morning of the 6th, Garth embarked his troops—except the 54th which he sent on board the transports—at the south-east part of the town, and crossing the ferry, joined Tryon on the East Haven side, without one shot being fired to molest his retreat. The public stores, some vessels, and ordnance having been destroyed, and six field-pieces and an armed privateer carried off, the troops embarked at Rock Fort in the afternoon, and anchored on the morning of the 8th off the village of Fairfield. Having burnt this village at the cost of some sharp fighting, in which the Fusiliers suffered no loss, the troops crossed the Sound to Huntingdon in Long Island, and there continued until the 11th; repassing on that day they anchored five miles from the Bay of Newark. The evening fell before the troops were landed, and it was the dawn of next day when the march commenced. The 54th Regiment soon fell in with the rebel outposts, which were driven in, and Drummond Hill and the heights at the end of the village seized. By 9 a.m. Garth's division had passed the bridge and proceeded to the north end of the village, from whence, and especially from the houses, there had been a long continuous fire upon the advanced guard. "The Fusiliers, supported by the light infantry of the Guards, began the attack, and soon cleared the quarters, pushing the main body and 100 cavalry from the northern heights, and taking one piece of their cannon. After many of the saltpans were destroyed, whale-boats carried on board the fleet, and the magazines, stores, and vessels set in flames, with the greatest part of the dwelling-houses, the advanced corps were drawn back, and the troops retired in two columns to the place of our first debarkation, and unassaulted took ship and returned to Huntingdon."*

A further incendiary raid was intended, but on the 13th Tryon received orders to return with the troops and fleet to Whitestone. A disaster had befallen the

---

* General Tryon adds in his dispatch,—"I should do injustice if I closed this report without giving every praise to the troops I had the honour to command."

British army. On the night of the 15th the American General Wayne, with admirable secrecy and courage, had taken the important post of Stoney Point by surprise, and against him the efforts of the British must be turned. In the expedition to Norwalk the Fusiliers had but one man killed, two sergeants, thirteen men wounded, one of whom died of his wounds, and one man missing. And so ended an operation which in a military sense only exposed the feebleness of the generals whose strategy was completely baffled.

The remainder of the year was practically wasted by reason of the inability of the British commanders to bring Washington to action until December, when an attack was made on South Carolina by General Sir Henry Clinton. The troops, among which were the Royal Fusiliers, 400 strong on the day of embarkation, sailed from New York on the 26th December. The ultimate object of the expedition was the siege of Charlestown. The fleet experienced much tempestuous weather, which separated the ships, and wrecked several transports, by which operations were greatly delayed.

1780.

The fleet arrived at Savannah at the end of January; it was the 11th February before it reached the North Edisto, on the coast of South Carolina. On that day, the General, with the Grenadiers and Light Infantry, landed on St. John's Island; next day the rest of the troops disembarked and joined them. The Royal Fusiliers, the 23rd and 33rd Regiments, with the Jägers, occupied Stono Ferry, the Grenadiers being stationed at Gibb's, on John's Island. Preparations for the siege were at once entered into. The passage of the Ashley river under the directions of Captains Elphinstone and Evans, of the Royal Navy, was effected on the 29th March, under cover of the galleys in Charlestown neck, without any molestation from the rebels. On the 30th the army moved towards Charlestown; and in the night of the 1st April, broke ground within 800 yards of the enemy's works, the approaches against the town being pushed forward with the utmost regularity and dispatch. On the 9th, the batteries opened, being aided by the fire of the ships. Henceforth the siege was carried on with some vigour until the 11th May, when the Governor capitulated, and ten American regiments, with three battalions of artillery, and the town and

Charlestown besieged; it capitulates.

county militia, became prisoners of war. During the whole siege the Royal Fusiliers had only lost one man killed and two wounded.

Throughout the remainder of the year the Royal Fusiliers, 23rd, 33rd, part of the 60th, 63rd, 64th, and 71st Regiments, together with some regiments of Hessians, composed the division with which Earl Cornwallis held portions of Carolina and Georgia. The Royal Fusiliers, the 63rd and 64th British regiments, with the Hessian regiments of Ditfour and Cruger remained in garrison in Charlestown. At this time the regiment was not in the highest state of efficiency; it had suffered heavily from disease, and the few men who represented it were almost entirely recruits. It passed the winter in camp at Wynnesborough.

1781.

Early in January, Lord Cornwallis ordered the Royal Fusiliers to proceed to Fort Ninety-Six, to reinforce the garrison, the fort being then besieged by the Americans. The regiment had only 167 rank and file, and 9 officers present and fit for duty. While on its march its destination was changed; a force being detached under Colonel Tarleton to disperse the Americans under Morgan, who was posted at Pacolet with a strong force. The Royal Fusiliers were ordered to join Tarleton. Tarleton's progress was neither rapid nor easy, for the heavy winter rains had rendered the country difficult of passage. This advance was however marked with considerable vigour, possibly more vigour than discrimination.

Action at the Cowpens. On the evening of the 16th January he reached the ground where the Americans had bivouaced during the day, and therefore believing them to be within his grasp, he resumed his march in the early morning of the 17th, coming up with Morgan at a place called "The Cowpens" by eight o'clock. Though his troops were greatly fatigued by their march Tarleton decided at once to commence the attack. From the first his dispositions were faulty, his eagerness having led him forward without due arrangement. The Royal Fusiliers formed part of his first line; the 71st being in the second, or reserve line. "Without the delay of a single moment, and in spite of extreme fatigue, the Legion Infantry and Fusiliers were ordered to form into line. Before the order was executed, and while Major Newmarsh, who commanded the latter corps, was posting his officers, the line, though far from complete, was led to the attack by Tarleton himself. The British advanced with a shout and poured in an incessant fire of musketry." In this advance the recruits of the Fusiliers commenced a promiscuous firing which had to be stopped before the whole line, composed of the light infantry, the Fusiliers, and the Legion Infantry, could advance. Notwithstanding these false steps the attack was eminently successful. The American line, composed mainly of Militia, men who were all expert shots and armed with rifles, in which respect they were much superior to the British, was broken and driven back upon the reserves, principally old troops. The rest of the affair we give in the words of an American writer:—"The American light parties quickly yielded, fell back, and arranged with Pickens. The enemy shouting, rushed forward upon the front line, which retained its station, and poured in a close fire; but continuing to advance with the bayonet on our militia, they retired and gained with haste the second line. Here, with part of two corps, Pickens took post on Howard's right, and the rest fled to their homes, probably with orders to remove them to a greater distance. Tarleton pushed forward, and was received by his adversary with unshaken firmness. The contest became obstinate: and each party, animated by the example of its leader, nobly contended for victory. Our line maintained itself so firmly as to oblige the enemy to order up his reserve. The advance of McArthur re-animated the British line, which again rushed forward, and, outstretching our front, endangered Howard's right. This officer instantly took measures to defend his flank, by directing his light company to charge its front; but mistaking this order the company fell back, upon which the line began to retire, and General Morgan directed it to retreat to the cavalry. This manœuvre being performed with precision, our flank became relieved, and the new position was assumed with promptitude. Considering this retrograde movement the precursor of flight, the British line rushed in with impetuosity and disorder; but, as it drew near, Howard faced about and gave it a close and murderous fire. Stunned by this unexpected shock, the most advanced of the enemy recoiled in confusion. Howard seized the happy moment and followed his advantage with the bayonet. This decisive step gave us the day."*

* This account of the affair at the Cowpens is taken from Lee's *Memoirs of the War in the Southern department of the United States*, and is a fair and modest one, infinitely better than Tarleton's passionate censures of his troops, or Cornwallis's official dispatch, which glosses over the affair. Tarleton, we need scarcely add, was a

Losses of the regiment.   This affair at the Cowpens was the last in which the Royal Fusiliers took part in the war of the American Revolution. In it the regiment was destroyed. Of the nine officers who were present, Captain Helyar and Lieutenant Marshall were killed, Major Newmarsh and Lieutenants Harling and L'Estrange were wounded. Its sufferings in killed and wounded were great, but they have not been detailed. For a second time during this unfortunate war its colours were captured by the enemy, and most of its surviving representatives were in his hands. The fame of the British army was undoubtedly dimmed, but in the midst of all these misfortunes the glories of the British soldier, as represented alike by the private sentinel and the company officer, shone with an untarnished lustre. The system under which they were organised was the parent of their misfortunes. The natural bravery and vigour of the men was the origin of their power on the field of battle; the lack of real military education for the higher leaders, springing from one of the falsest military systems that ever was devised, was their weakness and the source of their disasters.

The few of the Fusiliers who escaped from the Cowpens rejoined Earl Cornwallis's army: they were placed in garrison in South Carolina, where they remained until the return of peace in 1782, by the acknowledgment of the independence of the United States. On the evacuation of South Carolina the regiment proceeded to New York.

1782.

The Fusiliers spent this year in garrison in New York.

1783.

Peace having been declared between Great Britain and the United States the Fusiliers returned to England. A general reduction of the army took place, the regiment being reduced to eight companies.

---

mere raider; in the era of another and a greater war he was the discoverer of the Duke of Wellington's military imcompetence! It is difficult, however, to arrive at the whole truth of this miserable matter. Another writer, himself an actor in the scene, but an open enemy of Tarleton, asserts that the troops were in no degree at fault. As to the Fusiliers and the report that their recruits prematurely commenced the action, he says, "The Fusiliers had served with credit in America from the commencement of the war, and under an excellent officer, General Clarke, had attained the summit of military discipline," and confirms the report that Tarleton hurried them on to the attack before their formation was completed. See Mackenzie's *Strictures on Tarleton's History*.

1784.

This year the regiment was quartered in and near the city of Gloucester, under the command of Major J. Darby; it was chiefly engaged in recruiting its ranks and restoring its discipline.

1785.

On the 12th April the regiment commenced its march from Gloucester to Plymouth, where it stayed during the remainder of the year.

1786.

On the 26th April the Fusiliers left Plymouth, marching to Scotland, where they were quartered as follows:—Three companies at Aberdeen, two at Dundalk, two at Montrose, and one at St. Andrew's. The head-quarters under Major Darby were at Aberdeen.

1787.

On the 12th May six companies under Major John Despard were detached to Fort George. In October the regiment was augmented 22 sergeants and 268 privates, by which an eleventh company was raised. This company was reduced on the 24th December, and the Captain, John Baker, placed on half-pay.

1788.

On the 18th April the battalion marched in three divisions for Dundee. It arrived there on the 3rd, 5th, and 16th of May, and again moved on the 12th in two divisions to Edinburgh; it reached Edinburgh on the 14th and 15th, where it marched for Glasgow, arriving there three days later. On the 25th May, the regiment was augmented to 32 sergeants, 22 drummers, and 600 rank and file, receiving a draft of 100 men from the 35th Regiment, and one of 97 men from the 44th. On the 4th June four companies were detached to the Isle of Man.

On the decease of General Prescott, 26th November, the colonelcy of the Regiment was conferred on Major-General the *Hon.* William Gordon.

Order of Merit established.

In 1788 Lieutenant-Colonel Clarke established an order of merit of two degrees. The badge of the first degree was a silver medal, that of the second a bronze medal. Each medal bore on one side the regimental badge, and the inscription "Military Virtue rewarded—VII. Regiment or Royal Fusiliers;" on the other side two figures representing Victory and Minerva crowning a veteran, and the inscription "Order of merit established MDCCLXXXVIII." These medals were worn round the neck of the recipient, suspended by a blue ribbon two inches wide; the former was given for fourteen years' good character, the latter for seven. A fac-simile of the medal is now to be found in the Royal United Service Institution; the original is in the British Museum.

1789.

The Fusiliers remained quartered at Glasgow and the Isle of Man. On the 9th April Major-General the *Hon.* W. Gordon was transferred to the colonelcy of the 71st Regiment, whereupon H.R.H. Prince Edward, afterwards Duke of Kent, was appointed to the command of the Royal Fusiliers.

1790.

It being necessary to reinforce the garrison of Gibraltar, the Fusiliers were ordered to hold themselves in readiness for foreign service. The six companies at Glasgow marched to Leith, and embarked on board the "Ulysses," man-of-war. They found on their arrival in the Bay of Gibraltar, on the 27th August, that the four companies from the Isle of Man had already preceded them. The whole disembarked on the following day, when the regiment was quartered in the King's Barracks. H.R.H. the Duke of Kent was governor of the fortress and commander of the garrison.

Ordered to Gibraltar.

On this occasion the stay of the regiment was not long, but it was unquestionably one of the most remarkable periods in the life of the regiment. At that time the discipline of the army was greatly relaxed; the military code, it is true, allowed brutal severity to be used in correcting the private soldier; but brutal severity has never been the means of raising and maintaining a brave and highly efficient army, unless it was only resorted to in the last extremity by men who performed their duty with rigid exactness, and were in all respects a pattern for those whom they commanded. So much, however, could not then be said of all ranks in the British Army. Great slackness existed, and when the young Duke of Kent attempted to exact a proper and honourable performance of his duty from each of his subordinates, his measures were received with great and ill-concealed disgust. "His notions of discipline," says the Prince's biographer, "rendered him unpopular with the men. Representations relative to the dissatisfaction prevalent in the Fusiliers were made at home; and the result was that His Royal Highness was ordered to embark with his regiment for America." His enemies—and the Prince had a great many upon the Rock, and they were not of the lowest order—were striving to create discord between him and his Fusiliers; but ere long the tightening hand was felt to be the hand of a benefactor, not of a tyrant, and before the regiment left the Rock his merits were being appreciated, not only by the Royal Fusiliers but by the rest of the garrison.

1791.

Proceeds to Canada.

The regiment did not leave the Rock until May. On the 11th, the officers of the garrison gave the Prince a grand entertainment at the Hotel de l'Europe. On the 27th the regiment embarked, the right wing under His Royal Highness the Duke on board H.M.S. "Ulysses," the left wing under Captain Shuttleworth on board H.M.S. "Resistance," and sailed for Quebec. The change that had come over the minds of the Duke's subordinates is marked with some degree of vigour in the following song, composed especially to be sung at the entertainment already referred to:—

> Ascending Calpé's stately brow,
> We see sweet flowers spontaneous grow;
> As these their mingling scents disclose
> The rocky steeps their horrors lose;
> Regaled we turn our eyes to view
> The distant landscape's purple hue,
> The liquid plain's transparent bound
> And scenes for warlike deeds renown'd.
>   War's rugged paths have also flowers—
> Gay mirth and song and festive hours;
> And from the steep ascent to fame
> The prospect of a glorious name.

> See o'er yon western mountain's shade
> The evening's blushing radiance fade!
> So fades our joy round Calpé's brow,
> *For Royal Edward leaves us now!*
> *'Twas he who taught us how to bear*
> *The soldier's toil, the leader's care;*
> *Yet cheered fatigue with festive hours*
> *And strewed war's rugged path with flowers.*
> Ye breezes waft him safely o'er
> To brave the cold Canadian shore!
> To spread afar his rising fame
> And make his own a glorious name.

It is said that the passage to "the cold Canadian shore" was one of considerable hardships, during which the regiment endured the miseries of a floating prison. Both wings arrived at Quebec on the 27th August, and landed the following day.

1792-3.

During these two years the regiment remained at Quebec under the immediate command of the Duke.

In December, 1793, the Duke applied for an appointment to serve under Sir Charles Grey, who was then engaged in the reduction of the French West India Islands, and was appointed. Lieut. G. S. Smyth of the Fusiliers accompanied him.

1794.

In January H.R.H. quitted Quebec to take up his command.

The Fusiliers did not accompany him; in June two companies were detached to Halifax, Nova Scotia, and in October the remaining eight companies followed, giving detachments to Labhene and Coteau du Lac.

1795.

The regiment remained at Halifax during this year. In September a strong draft of recruits arrived from England, whereupon the regiment was formed into two battalions. The second battalion was raised and formed between June and August, the lieutenants being appointed during that time. But this arrangement only held for a few months.

1796.

The reduction of the second battalion was carried into effect on the 24th April, in accordance with orders from England. The first battalion having been completed to 54 sergeants, 22 drummers, and 1000 rank and file, the remaining men were drafted into the 4th "King's Own" regiment.

The Fusiliers were now again under the orders of their colonel, who, having returned from the West Indies, was appointed commander-in-chief of the force in Nova Scotia, and promoted subsequently to the rank of lieutenant-general. Under his searching eye the regiment was raised to the highest state of efficiency. He taught it to be orderly and well-conducted in quarters, not from the fear of punishment, but by educating the self-respect of every man in the regiment. He raised its military skill in the performance of its duties by a constant but intelligent attention to its drill and field movements; and he liberally rewarded those who were worthy of reward. The following non-commissioned officers at his recommendation received commissions for their general attention to duty and unvaried good conduct during their service in the Fusiliers.

Sergeant Walter Beavan	Ensign Nova Scotia Fencibles	1795
Sergeant Joseph Parker	Qr.-Mas. Royal Fusiliers	1796
Sergeant Christopher Taylor	Lieutenant Royal Fusiliers	
Qr.-Mas. Sergeant John Opinslaw	Ensign in Invalids	
Sergeant James Colledge	Ensign St. John's Island Provincials	
Sergeant James Turner	Ensign 31st Regiment	1797
Sergeant-Major Frederick Plansker	Ensign Fencible Corps	

1797-98.

The regiment continued in Halifax during these years without any more material change or prominent event in its career than the disbanding of one company and the reduction of the remainder by the following order:— *The Establishment reduced.*

"War Office, November 25th, 1797.

"SIR,—His Majesty having thought fit to order, that from the 25th December next inclusive, the recruiting company of the 7th Regiment of Foot under your command, shall be discontinued on the establishment; and also that a reduction of 40 private men shall be made on the establishment of each of the other ten companies. I have the honour to acquaint you therewith; and that in consequence of the said reduction, His Majesty's orders, signified in my letter of the 2nd inst., for restoring one lieutenant per company to the establishment of your regiment are countermanded.

"The commissioned officers who shall be supernumerary to the reduced establishment are to continue to serve with the regiment *en second* in their respective ranks; and in like manner the non-commissioned officers and drummers of the recruiting company are to be continued as supernumeraries, and are to fall into vacancies as they shall occur.

"I have, &c.,
"W. WINDHAM.

"Colonel of the 7th Foot."

"War office, 20th December, 1797.

"SIR,—I have the honour to acquaint you that in consequence of the reduction of the 7th Regiment of Foot under your command to 600 rank and file, there will be only one assistant surgeon borne on the establishment thereof from the 25th inst. inclusive.

"I have, &c.,
"W. WINDHAM."

As a curiosity we give the "List of Necessaries to be provided by Stoppage from the pay of the Soldiers of Regiments of Foot, Militia, and Fencible Infantry."

	Per annum.	
	s.	d.
For two pairs of black cloth gaiters, at 4s. per pair	8	0
For a second pair of breeches	6	6
For one hair leather	0	2¼
Two pairs of shoes, at 6s. per pair	12	0
Mending ditto	4	0
One pair of stockings, or two pairs of socks	1	6
Two shirts, at 5s. 6d. per shirt	11	0
A foraging cap	2	3
A knapsack, at 6s., once in six years	1	0
Pipe clay and whiting	4	4
A clothes brush, at 1s., once in two years	0	6
Three shoe brushes, at 5d. each	1	3
Black ball	2	0
Worsted mitts	0	9
A powdering bag and puff, once every three years, at 1s. 6d.	0	6
Two combs, at 6d. each	1	0
Grease and powder for the hair	3	0
Washing, at 4d. per week	17	4
£3	16	1¼

Ordered by warrant dated 25th May, 1797.

1799.

His Royal Highness Prince Edward having returned to England on account of ill-health, was created on the 23rd April Duke of Kent. At his departure the command of the regiment devolved upon Colonel J. Despard.

1800.

The regiment continued to be stationed in Halifax, still under the command of Colonel Despard.

1801.

In August the Duke of Kent was removed to the 1st Royal Scots; he was succeeded in the colonelcy of the Fusiliers by Lieutenant-General Sir Alured Clarke, the old lieutenant-colonel of the regiment, who had commanded it through the most stirring portions of the American war.

Sir A. Clarke appointed Colonel.

1802.

After having passed eleven years in British North America, the Royal Fusiliers were ordered to the West Indies. The right wing under Lieutenant-Colonel Layard proceeded to the Bermuda; the left wing under Bt. Lieutenant-Colonel Burroes to the Bahamas. The right wing arrived at Bermuda on the 24th October; the left wing at the Bahamas on the first November.

Sergeant-Major John Robertson was promoted ensign 2nd battalion Royals.

1803.

The stations of the regiment remained unchanged. The wing at the Bahamas suffered severely from sickness.

1804.

While the regiment was thus stationed in the West Indies, a second battalion was raised in conformity with the Additional Forces Act. In September the recruiting officers of the regiment were ordered to repair to Wakefield, and there await further instructions. From Wakefield parties were sent to Leeds and the manufacturing towns of the neighbourhood, and in December 150 men from the 15th battalion of Reserve joined at Wakefield, where the 2nd battalion was formed.

Second Battalion formed.

The 1st battalion still remained at Bermuda and the Bahamas.

Qr.-Mas. Sergeant Francis Gillman was promoted quarter-master in the Nova Scotia Fencibles.

1805.

On the 18th and 19th of June, the 2nd battalion marched from Wakefield in two divisions to Chelmsford Barracks. It afterwards proceeded to Winchester.

1806.

On the 14th July, the right wing 1st battalion, under Captain Burton, sailed from Bermuda and anchored in Plymouth Sound on the 24th August. It disembarked on the 29th, and marched September 3rd to Weymouth, where the 2nd battalion was stationed, having been moved at the commencement of the year from Winchester. This wing, marched into Weymouth on the 10th, when Lieutenant-Colonel Parkenham here assumed the command of the 1st battalion, drafting from the 2nd 7 sergeants and 417 rank and file.

On the 16th October the 1st battalion marched for Deal; it arrived on the 3rd November, and while quartered there was joined by the left wing from the Bahamas, under Captain Bernard. The battalion marched in two divisions for Liverpool, November 22nd, and embarked on the 30th for Dublin.

Sergeant-Major Geo. Galbraith, ensign and adjutant 1st Royals.

Qr.-Mas. Sergeant John Hogan, Qr.-Mas. Royal Fusiliers.

1807.

On the 1st January, the 1st battalion landed at the Pigeon House and moved into George Street and the Old Custom House Barracks.

The 2nd battalion being reduced to little more than a depot was ordered to remain in England to recruit. On the 26th June it sent a draft of 119 rank and file to the 1st battalion, which, having been inspected by Major-General Leith and commended both for its appearance and discipline, was ordered for foreign service.

The times were then unsettled and the demand for men great. Napoleon's machinations were alarming the English Government. The audacious attempt to seize the Danish fleet and use it against England was the first move that compelled the ministry to act. An army was at once summoned for service in Denmark, of which the 1st battalion Royal Fusiliers was to form a part, although not yet twelve months at home from a tour of foreign service extending over fifteen years. It embarked at the Pigeon House on the 24th July, landed at Liverpool on the 27th, and on the 29th began its march to Hull. It arrived at Hull on the 6th August, was immediately embarked on board transports, and sailed for Zealand under convoy of H.M.S. "Agamemnon." The battalion disembarked at Zealand on the 21st August, and the following day joined the army under Lord Cathcart investing the city of Copenhagen. _{Service in Denmark.}

Copenhagen capitulated on the 7th September, when the British Grenadiers, with detachments from all the other corps of cavalry and infantry, under the command of Colonel Cameron of the 79th, with two brigades of artillery, marched into the citadel; while Major-General Spencer having embarked his brigade at the Kalk Brandiere, landed at the dockyard, and took possession of each of the line of battle ships and of the arsenal, the Danish Guards withdrawing as the British were ready to replace them: and thus the capital and fleet of the representatives of our old Norse ancestors, the Vikings, of whose kinship we are even yet the most proud, fell into our hands. Of glory in the exploit certainly little was obtained. The losses by sword and bullet were insignificant, but the waste of men must have been considerable.

As soon as the operations were concluded the Royal Fusiliers were sent home. They and the 8th Regiment embarked at the Arsenal on the 14th October, and disembarked on the 18th November at Portsmouth. The Fusiliers occupied Fort Moncton Barracks and Haslar until the 26th December, when they marched to Lewes.

The 2nd battalion still remained at Weymouth.

1808.

The 1st battalion arrived at Lewes on the 1st January, when it received a draft of 372 men from the 2nd battalion, nearly all volunteers from the militia, who by volunteering gave five lieutenants to the regiment. It was no sooner reorganised than it was again ordered for foreign service. On the 18th, 19th, and

20th it marched to Portsmouth, where it embarked on the 21st and two following days. Together with the 8th and 13th Regiments, the Royal Fusiliers sailed under convoy of the "Penelope," "Undaunted," and "Banterer." Leaving the 13th Regiment at Bermuda, the Royal Fusiliers proceeded to Nova Scotia; they arrived in Halifax Harbour April 7th, and disembarked on the 15th.

1st Battalion proceeds to Nova Scotia.

Expedition to Martinique.

In the meantime, the 2nd battalion had been transferred to Tilbury Fort, whence it embarked in May for Ireland, and landed at Monkstown in the middle of June, under the command of Lieutenant-Colonel Sir William Myers, Bart.

The expedition against Martinique requiring a part of the force stationed under Sir George Prevost in Nova Scotia, the Royal Fusiliers were among the regiments selected. With the exception of sickly men and boys unfit for service in the severe climate of the West Indies, the battalion embarked on the 24th November. The convoy sailed on the 6th December under the "Penelope" frigate, with Sir George Prevost and staff. The whole force, viz., the Royal Fusiliers, the Royal Welsh Fusiliers, the 8th Regiment and Artillery, arrived safely at the rendezvous of the expedition, Carlisle Bay, on the 29th December.

1809.

Land at Malgre Tout.

The force remained in Carlisle Bay until the 28th January, when it sailed. At 4 p.m. of the 30th, it landed at Malgre Tout, in the bay Robert, Martinique. The two Fusilier battalions, the Royal and Royal Welsh, forming the 1st brigade, 1st division, moved the same night, marching to De Manceaux's Estate. They arrived there late in consequence of the difficult nature of the country. The troops were given a few hours' repose, during which the remainder of the division arrived; but before daybreak the division resumed its march, proceeding to Papin's, where it halted, except the Royal Fusiliers and the Grenadier company of the 1st West India, who, with the enemy retiring before them, were pushed forward to De Bork's Estate, where they bivouaced. Next morning at daybreak they were joined by the Royal Welsh and the Light Infantry Battalion, when Lieutenant-Colonel Pakenham advanced with the Royal Fusiliers and the Rifle Company of the Royal Welsh, supported by the Light Battalion to the heights of Morne Bruno.

Brigadier General Hoghton, having joined this force with the Royal Welsh, then proceeded to force the heights of Desfourneaux, the Royal Welsh forming the reserve. The column was scarcely in motion before a considerable body of the enemy's regular forces, commanded by General of Brigade, D'Houdelot, was discovered very advantageously posted on the declivity of a hill with the river Monsieur in their front, and one or two field pieces on their left. Having reconnoitred their position, Hoghton determined to attack them. Colonel Pakenham, with the Rifle Company and Grenadiers of the 7th and the Rifle Company of the 23rd, was directed to turn the right, the Light Companies were to turn the left, while Hoghton assailed the front with the Battalion Companies of the 7th and the Grenadiers of the 1st West India. The result was a perfect success; the enemy, driven back from every part of the position, retired in the greatest disorder.

Colonel Pakenham having turned the right flank of the French, pushed forward towards the heights of Surirey, at first supported by the right wing of the 23rd under Lieutenant-Colonel Ellis, and subsequently by the remainder of that regiment, which joined shortly after the action on the river Monsieur. The enemy had collected a considerable force to defend the approaches to these heights, yet Pakenham compelled him, by a very spirited charge, to take refuge under cover of the redoubts, on which next day, the 2nd February, Sir George Prevost commenced his attack. The execution of it was given to Colonel Pakenham, who led forward the Fusiliers, supported by the Light Battalion, but the operation, being made in open daylight on a strongly entrenched position well defended, was both very costly in life, and for the moment not successful. The men displayed their usual headlong bravery and vigour, yet so severe and heavy was the fire of grape from the batteries, that neither their resolute onset nor the free manner in which they sacrificed themselves enabled them to carry the works. But the enemy, notwithstanding his success in this repulse, declining a renewal of the assault, abandoned his position, "with evident marks of disorder," spiked his guns, and retired to Fort Bourbon and the advanced Redoubt Bouillie.

Heights of Surirey attacked.

The cost of these gallant actions was rather heavy for the Royal Fusiliers. On the 1st February the battalion lost Capt. Taylor, acting deputy quarter-master general, and 9 men killed, 2 sergeants, 1 drummer, and 56 men wounded, 4 men missing. On the 2nd the losses were greater, Sergeant Joshua Redshaw and 20 men were killed; Lieutenant-Colonel Pakenham, Capts. Rowe and Cholwich, Sergeant John Henry, 1 drummer, 58 men wounded, and 3 men missing.

On these occasions the following orders were issued by Sir George Beckwith:—

<small>Extracts from General Orders.</small>

"Head Quarters, Preclaire, Martinique, 2nd February, 1809.

"The commander of the forces desires to express his entire approbation of the steady conduct of the troops engaged in the cause of yesterday, and desires that the general officers and soldiers will be pleased to accept his thanks, and to assure them that he will not fail to lay their merit before the King; and he feels fully persuaded that in what is to be done they will manifest a similar superiority over the enemy. Lieutenant-General Sir George Prevost having reported the unremitting exertions of Lieutenant-Colonel the Hon. E. M. Pakenham of the Royal Fusiliers, the commander of the forces feels great pleasure in making this known to the army."

Extract from G.O. "Head Quarters, Preclaire, 3rd February, 1809.

"The great benefits which the advanced corps under Lieutenant-General Sir George Prevost have produced to His Majesty's Service, from the gallant and successful attack made upon Morne Bruno, and afterwards even to the very heights of Surirey on the 1st inst., by the brigade of the army and the light battalion under the command of Brigadier General Hoghton, demand from the commander of the forces a reiteration of his acknowledgments and his assurance to the Brigadier General and to the commanding officers of the Royal Fusiliers, of the Royal Welsh Fusiliers, and of the Light Battalion, and the other officers, non-commissioned officers, and soldiers of those regiments, that he will not fail to lay their meritorious exertions before the King. The exertions of all the corps engaged yesterday were conspicuous, and although the general regrets that the state of the works possessed by the enemy did not admit of their being carried by the bayonet, which rendered it his duty to direct the corps employed to retire, they manifested a spirit and determination which, when tempered by less impetuosity, will shortly lead to the happiest result. Such services in their nature must be attended with loss, and the General is extremely concerned that so many valuable officers have suffered, particularly the Hon. Lieutenant-Colonel Pakenham and Major Campbell commanding the Light Battalion, who were both wounded with several other most valuable and respectable officers."

On the 4th, Pigeon Island, and on the 7th, Fort Edward, were evacuated. On the 19th the batteries were opened on Fort Bourbon, which surrendered on the 24th. The Citadel was taken possession of on the following day by the flank companies of the 1st brigade. The French garrison marched out on the 7th March, and laid down their arms, embarking to be conveyed to France as prisoners of war until exchanged. Three eagles being taken at Fort Bourbon, the three regiments of the 1st brigade each received one,—that awarded to the Royal Fusiliers being the eagle of the 82nd of the line; it is now at Chelsea. The following day the force under Sir George Prevost re-embarked from Fort Royal to return to Halifax. Sir George Beckwith took leave of the army addressing to it the following order:—

<small>Re-embark for Halifax.</small>

"Head Quarters, Preclaire, 8th March, 1809.

"At the close of this short but brilliant campaign, and at the moment on which the army is on the point of separation, the Commander of the forces is led, by every feeling which can actuate the human heart, but in language feeble indeed when compared with the occasion, to renew for the last time his expressions of thanks and affectionate respect to the generals and field-officers, and others of the staff, and to the non-commissioned officers comprising the army, for the eminent services they have rendered their King and country in the course of the late operations, which have terminated in a manner splendid and honourable to all concerned.

"The commander of the forces desires to express his obligations to Lieutenant-General Sir George Prevost for his general exertions, and to the fine and efficient corps led by him from North America, now embarking. The commander of the forces is anxious to renew all these assurances of public and individual consideration to which from their distinguished services they are fully entitled, and he requests as an old soldier that he may live in their remembrance and friendship."

Brevet Lieutenant-Colonel Blakeney received a gold cross for his distinguished conduct during this campaign, and in the course of time we shall find the tardy authorities permit the regiment to bear the word "Martinique" on the colours. The Fusiliers sailed from St. Pierre, Martinique, March 15th, and anchored at St. Kitts on the 17th; they left St. Kitts on the 22nd and arrived at Halifax on the 15th April. The service, from wounds and the effect of climate, had told severely upon the battalion. The death of Captain Taylor gave Lieutenant Robert Cuthbert a company; Volunteer Pike obtained the lieutenancy as a reward for his bravery. Between the 1st and 27th February the battalion had in hospital 135 men, of whom 119 were suffering from gunshot wounds, two from fever, and 15 from fluxes; of these 35 of the gunshot wounds, two fever cases, and two of the fluxes, were discharged cured; three cases of wounds and one of flux were fatal; and at the end of the above period there remained in hospital 81 cases of wounds and 12 of fluxes.

The total losses of the regiment during the operations cannot be arrived at, but inasmuch as Lieutenant Jones of the Royal Montgomery Militia, Charles Barrington of the Cambridgeshire, Edward Penrise, Robert Daniel, William Payne of the Worcestershire, and Thomas Fawcet Wray of the North York, received lieutenancies, it is clear that large numbers of men were raised from the Militia during the year.

On the return of the battalion to Halifax, Lieutenant-Colonel Pakenham, apparently following the idea initiated by Sir Alured Clarke, to do justice to soldiers then serving who were worthy of reward, as well as to stimulate future Fusiliers by distinguishing merit in those whom the regulations or fashion of the service then deemed too insignificant to be noticed in despatches, assembled a board of merit, having Lieutenant-Colonel Blakeney as President, to deliberate on a method of doing so. The board agreed that a BOOK of MERIT should be kept, in which the names and services of worthy non-commissioned officers and soldiers should be recorded. The result of the first meeting was as follows:—

Board of Merit instituted

Proceedings of a Board of Merit, held by order of the Hon. E. M. Pakenham, commanding Royal Fusiliers, Halifax, July 20th, 1809.

President, Lieutenant-Colonel Blakeney; members, Capts. Beatty and Spencer, Lieuts. MacGenis and Moultrie.

Sergeant Thomas Beale of Captain Burton's company, on the evidence of Surgeon Robinson and Lieutenant Robison, for long continued good conduct in a situation of considerable trust, is deemed worthy by the board to be recorded in the book of merit.

Sergeant John Henry of the Light Company, recommended by Captain Cholwich for extraordinary good conduct, particularly so on the 1st February, 1809; distinguished by eminent gallantry, after having received a wound in the right shoulder.

Drummer Thomas Maude of the same company, recommended by Captain Cholwich, supported by the testimony of Privates William Berwick and John Kenna.

Qr.-Mas. Sergeant Timothy Meagher, recommended by Captain Cuthbert for universal good conduct.

Sergeant Thomas Miller, recommended by Captain Cuthbert, for honesty and integrity on all occasions, and coolness and perseverance in the field, supported by the testimony of Privates Patrick Kenny and John Nowlan.

Sergeant Thomas Simpson, recommended by Captain Cuthbert for great steadiness and intrepidity in advancing against the enemy on the 1st February, 1809, at Martinique, and for rendering essential service in encouraging and assisting his comrades in a difficult march in front of the enemy.

Sergeant George Kenny of Captain Burton's Company, recommended by Lieutenant Robison for uniform good conduct in quarters as well as for bravery on the 1st and 17th February, at Martinique.

Privates Mark Ewing, William Vagg, Benjamin Price, James Houghney, for long service and good conduct.

Corporal Dove, for excellent conduct; and Sergeant Joshua Redshaw, of

Captain Despard's Company, for uniform good conduct, and particularly for gallant behaviour in the island of Martinique, on the 1st and 2nd February, on the latter of which days he was killed.

Sergeant Thomas Wilson, of the same company, for gallantry.

Sergeant George Clementson, of Captain Spencer's Company, for gallantry.

Sergeant John Day, of Captain Beatty's Company, for gallantry.

Private William Delaney, of Captain Woolridge's Company, for good conduct.

Private Nathaniel Moss, of the same Company, for gallantry.

Sergeant John Ledsom, of Captain Salmon's Company, for good conduct.

Sergeant William Inchbold, of Captain Bushe's Company, for gallantry.

Sergeant William Harris, of Captain Rowe's Company, for gallantry.

Sergeants Meagher, Henry, and Ledsom were afterwards promoted to commissions, and, as we shall see, were distinguished in the after career of the regiment.

In July the battalion lost its commander, Colonel Pakenham, who proceeded to the Peninsula, and at the close of the year was appointed deputy adjutant-general to the army in Portugal.*

Col. Pakenham proceeds to the Peninsula.

His loss was fully appreciated in the regiment. His anxiety for the corps was ever on the alert to promote its interests, and he departed with the respect, gratitude, and good wishes of all ranks. On his taking leave of the battalion, the officers unanimously requested that he would permit his portrait to be taken, and that he would also accept a sword of 200 guineas value, presenting to him at the same time the following address:—

Col. Pakenham accepts a sword; his portrait to be placed in the Mess Room.

"Halifax, N.S., July 21st, 1809.

"To the Hon. Lieutenant-Colonel Pakenham, commanding Royal Fusiliers.

"The officers of the 1st battalion Royal Fusiliers, having learnt with unfeigned regret your intention of leaving for a time the immediate command of the regiment, avail themselves of this opportunity to assure you of the sincere regard and esteem felt by every member of the corps.

---

* "Lord Wellington to the Commander-in-Chief.

"SIR, "Badajos, 16th November, 1809.

"I have availed myself of the presence of Colonel Pakenham, of the 7th Fusiliers, in this country, to employ him as an assistant in the department of the adjutant-general; and he is now doing the duty of that department, in consequence of the absence of Brig.-General the Hon. C. Stewart, for the recovery of his health. As the office of deputy adjutant-general has never been filled up, and as Colonel Pakenham is the senior of all the officers doing duty in the department, and is well qualified for it, I beg leave to recommend him to be appointed deputy adjutant-general."

"A series of years passed in unremitted exertions for the benefit of the service in general, and for the honour and benefit of the regiment in particular, calls for the most unequivocal expression of our admiration and gratitude; convinced, however, that language can but ill convey an adequate sense of our feelings we refrain from expatiating on merits which speak more forcibly for themselves.

"To the marks of public approbation and private esteem which you already possess, permit us to request that you will allow your portrait to be placed in our mess-room, and, as a further token of our regard, your acceptance of a sword, value 200 guineas, sensible that the motive of these offers will in your mind constitute their worth.

"By request of the officers of the corps,
"(Signed)   EDWARD BLAKENEY.
"Major Royal Fusiliers and Brevet Lieutenant-Colonel."

"To Lieutenant-Colonel Blakeney and Officers of the Royal Fusiliers.

"I have received your letter, caused by my proposed departure, with warmth equal to its tenor, with satisfaction few have a right to experience. Friendship, formed at ease, confirmed in danger, becomes too sacred to need professions. Your cordial zeal, however, anticipated my wishes towards the prosperity of the corps, which your generosity has too much attributed to my past exertions. Let my actions speak a continuance of attachment.

"Your gift and desire of recollection hereafter will serve to me as professional impellents. In leaving the Fusiliers I separate from the best comrades, from the chief source of my soldier's pride; yet it is for the object of duty! Here draw the line! Do you by usual energy continue ripe for service; and it is for me to improve the more honourably to lead you.

"(Signed) E. M. PAKENHAM, Lieutenant-Colonel."

After Lieutenant-Colonel Pakenham's departure the immediate command of the battalion devolved on Lieutenant-Colonel Blakeney. Continuing at Halifax, the battalion took the outpost duty, sending detachments to George's Island, Melville Island, Point Pleasant, York Redoubt, &c.

2nd Batt. sails from Ireland to Portugal.

While the 1st battalion was thus employed in Nova Scotia, the 2nd was in Ireland, preparing for service in the Peninsula. Having been reported fit for duty, and pronounced "one of the most highly regulated bodies of men in His Majesty's Service," it was ordered from Clonmel to Cork, to join the forces then assembling under Lieutenant-General Sir John Craddock (Lord Howden), where it embarked. For some time the fleet was delayed awaiting the coming of some commissariat stores and artillery horses, which were shipped immediately on their arrival. With a fine northerly breeze blowing, the ships weighed anchor on the morning of the 29th March. Before night had closed, the Irish Coast was lost to view. An uneventful voyage carried the troops to the seat of war. The fleet anchored off Alcantara, a suburb of Lisbon, on the evening of the 5th April. The 6th was passed in preparation, and on the 7th, the troops landed. The following was the state of the battalion on landing.

Lieut.-Col. Sir W. Myers, *Bart.*	Lieut. Digby Mackworth.	Lieut. Pitt Hannam.
Major Wm. Disney.	,, W. H. Hammerton.	,, Richd. Johnson.
Capt. Wm. Pilkington.	,, Jas. Anderson.	,, Fred. Gibbons.
,, John Crowder.	,, Geo. Henry.	,, John Healey.
,, James Singer.	,, Richd. Hackett.	,, Henry Beaufoy.
,, Geo. King.	,, Richd. Kirwan.	,, Holt Archer.
,, S. B. Auchmuty.	,, Pat. Burke.	Surg. W. Wallace.
,, T. Oliver Anderdon.	,, H. J. Jones.	Paymaster Thos. Berkeley.
,, Charles Cox.	,, John Ormsby.	Adj. W. E. Page.
,, Hon. Henry Percy.	,, Ed. Morgan.	Asst.-Surg. M. Mahoney.
,, Geo. Prescott.	,, Robt. Muter.	Qr.-Mas. John Hogan.

33 sergeants, 13 drummers, 33 corporals, and 542 privates.

On the 11th, the battalion was conveyed up the Tagus to Villa Franca; on the 15th it marched to Leyria, on the 3rd May it occupied Coimbra. On the 4th May the army was brigaded; the 2nd battalion Fusiliers, the 53rd, and the 1st battalion 10th Portuguese, with one company of the 5th battalion, 60th Rifles, constituted the 5th brigade under Brig.-General Alex. Campbell. The brigade was posted to the right wing of the army.

Sir Arthur Wellesley assumed the command on the 23rd April, while the troops were in Coimbra. No sooner were the brigade arrangements concluded than the army was put in motion. The advanced guard and the cavalry marched on the 7th May, for Oporto, then recently captured by Soult. Campbell's brigade, with the Guards and two other brigades, moved on the 9th by the high road from Coimbra to Oporto, with the whole of the artillery stores attached to them, and halted at Mealhada. In the course of a few days occurred the splendid manœuvres, by which Wellesley crossed the Douro, and on the 12th May drove Soult out of Oporto. In this action Campbell's brigade was not deployed and did not lose a man; indeed it did not arrive at the scene of action while the actual strife continued. Sergeant Cooper,* of the Royal Fusiliers, who was with the battalion, thus describes their efforts:—"The last day's march was really horrible, under a scorching sun and clouds of dust. The road was narrow, and little or no water all the way. We had heavy knapsacks, sore feet, and after marching between twenty and thirty miles, for a finish we ran to get into action, about four miles, to a town opposite Oporto, called Villa Nova: but the enemy were beaten before we arrived and gave us the

Capture of Oporto.

---

* See Cooper's *Seven Campaigns in the Peninsula*, a book to which we owe many obligations. The writer was a native of North Yorkshire, and a volunteer from the North York Militia.

slip by a hasty retreat. We were quartered in a splendid mansion in the highest part of the city. In this palatial edifice our men did justice to a grand dinner, which had been prepared for the French officers."

The capture of Oporto, one of the most daring and brilliant feats of the whole war, compelled Soult to retreat precipitately, abandoning his artillery and ammunition; the Fusiliers being employed in the pursuit. Panic-stricken and impotent, the French army, relinquishing both its guns, stores, and baggage, was chased across the frontier at Orense, where the pursuit terminated. On the 24th the returning troops re-entered Oporto, where they were received with rapturous applause.

From Oporto, on the 14th June, the British retired to Abrantes, where the Royal Fusiliers were encamped until the end of the month, pending the subsequent advance into Spain to succour the Spanish general, Cuesta. While the regiment was at Abrantes it had the misfortune to lose some men, murdered by the Portuguese. On the 18th the brigades were formed into divisions, Campbell's and Colonel Peacock's brigades forming the 4th Division, which for the time remained under the command of Brigadier-General Campbell.

<small>The 4th Division formed.</small>

On the 27th June the British Army broke up its cantonments at Abrantes, and in two columns directed its march upon Placentia, the route of Campbell's division being on the northern bank of the Tagus. On the 18th July Wellesley quitted Placentia; on the 20th the Head Quarters were at Oropesa, where a junction was effected with Cuesta's army. At Oropesa the Royal Fusiliers were quartered in a convent until the 22nd, when the advance continued. These movements resulted in the battle of Talavera. The allied army, taking up a position touching Talavera, a town built close to the river, had the Spaniards on the right in contact with the town; Campbell's division, formed in two lines and with a redoubt on his right flank, touched the Spanish left; the remaining British troops prolonging the line to the left which rested on one of the hills bounding the flat and woody country. The left of the British was attacked on the evening of the 27th July; this attack was easily repulsed, but it was more vigorously renewed when the French came forward, on the 28th, with brilliant ardour. The action again opened on the left, where a stout fight was maintained before the French were repulsed. Then occurred a lull

<small>Battle of Talavera.</small>

until midday, when the attack was changed to the right and the most serious effort made. The Light Company of the Fusiliers, under Captain Percy, was extended in front of the battalion as the French began to move. Covering their front with a cloud of light troops, four dense French columns, supported by 80 guns, bore down upon Campbell's division. The 4th French Corps came forward with great impetuosity, and soon cleared the intersected ground in its front, falling upon Campbell, whom it had deceived by its advance with all its force. After threading its way among the trees and grape-vines, the column came up directly in front of the Light Company of the Fusiliers, and, while deploying, called out "Espanoles," hoping to give the impression that they were Spaniards. Captain Percy was thus deceived; he thought they were Spaniards, and ordered the men not to fire. But he was soon convinced of his mistake by a rattling volley. The Light Company thereupon immediately retired upon the regiment which sprang up; "but," says Sergeant Cooper, who belonged to the Light Company, "our men, being all raw soldiers, staggered for a moment under such a rolling fire. Our Colonel, Sir William Myers, seeing this, sprang from his horse, and snatching one of the colours, cried, 'Come on, Fusiliers!' 'Twas enough. On rushed the Fusiliers and 53rd Regiment, and delivered such a fire that in a few minutes the enemy melted away, leaving six pieces of cannon behind which they had not time to discharge." *The Fusiliers capture six guns.*

Gallantly, but in vain, the French strove to recover their artillery; all their efforts were overcome and the guns secured. The French veterans rallied on their supports, and appeared resolutely bent on another attack, but the steady deportment and invincible resolution of the British Infantry, and the terrible volleys with which they smote every formation, at length broke the French and secured the victory on that part of the field. On the right of the Fusiliers, however, things had not gone well. The Spaniards had fled in terror and left their flank exposed; even for veteran troops assailed by such a sturdy foe the position was dangerous; but for the Fusiliers the danger speedily passed away; the dreadful severity of their fire and the vigour of their attack soon became their safeguard. The slaughter they wrought upon their assailants is thus recorded by an eye-witness:—"Some of the little enclosures in front of the right of the British were choked with French dead; and in one little field more than four hundred bodies were counted."

With the fight that raged in the other parts of the line we need not interfere. The victory that the Fusiliers had initiated was soon everywhere secured. Sir Arthur Wellesley, in his despatch, says, "Brigadier Campbell mentions particularly the conduct of the 97th, the 2nd Battalion of the 7th, and the 2nd Battalion of the 53rd, and was highly satisfied with the manner this part of the position was defended." In his General Order of the 29th, Sir Arthur Wellesley reports that he had "opportunities of noticing the gallantry and discipline, on the 28th, of the 7th and 53rd, and he requests the commanding officers, Lieutenant-Colonel Sir W. Myers and Lieutenant-Colonel Bingham, to accept his particular thanks."

On the 27th, the Fusiliers did not suffer any loss; on the 28th, the battalion lost Lieutenant Beaufoy and six men killed; Lieutenants Kirwan and Muter, severely, Adjutant Page slightly, one sergeant, two drummers, 51 men wounded, and one man missing. The Commanding Officer, Sir W. Myers, received the gold medal for the action, and the regiment bears the word "Talavera" upon its colours. The wounded were conveyed to a large hospital established in the town of Talavera, and, when on the morning of the 3rd August the British departed, they were handed over to the care of the Spanish General, Cuesta, who in a few days deserted them and left them to fall into the hands of the French, who re-entered Talavera on the 5th. The three officers of the Fusiliers being thus made prisoners were sent to Bordeaux, where they were detained until the end of the war. The following is the list of officers who served with the 2nd battalion at Talavera:—

Lieut.-Col. Sir W. Myers, *Bart.*	Lieut. Hamerton.	Lieut. Muter.
Capt. Pilkington.	,, Anderson.	,, Hannam.
,, Crowder.	,, Henry.	,, Johnson.
,, Singer.	,, Kirwan.	,, Gibbons.
,, King.	,, Burke.	,, Healey.
,, Cox.	,, Ormsby.	,, Beaufoy.
Lieut. Mackworth.	,, Morgan.	,, Archer.
Adjutant Page.	Paymaster Berkeley.	Asst.-Surg. Mahoney.
Qr.-Mas. Hogan.	Surgeon Wallace.	,, Walters.

Retreat to Portugal. From Talavera the allied armies retreated towards Portugal. For a time the head-quarters of the British were at Jaraicejo, whence Wellesley hoped to re-commence offensive operations, but the utter defeat of the Spaniards at Almonacid, and above all the base neglect of the Spanish government to provide food for the army, compelled him to continue his retreat. Leaving Jaraicejo on the

20th August, he marched by Truxillo upon Merida. During this retreat, and while halted for a few days at Delatoza, the Fusiliers suffered heavily from sickness and disease, but they were not engaged in actual conflict with the enemy. The retreat being concluded the English troops were distributed in Badajos, Elvas, Campo Mayor, and other places on both banks of the Guadiana. On the 3rd September, the battalion encamped in the olive grounds near Badajos and afterwards on some high grounds eight or nine miles from that city. In this camp, called Nuestra Senora de Tobo, the battalion remained until the 6th October; on the 7th it moved to Olivenza and was quartered in the bomb proof barracks. The sufferings of the troops increased during the winter, "the pestilent fever of the Guadiana assailing bodies already predisposed to disease made frightful ravages. Dysentery, that scourge of armies, raged; and in a short time about 5000 men died in the hospitals."

1810.

The head quarters of the 1st battalion were still at Halifax, where the battalion had been brought up to its full strength and to the highest pitch of discipline and efficiency. In accordance with its anticipations the exigencies of the time did not allow it to remain in Nova Scotia. The demand for men in the Peninsula, increased by the mortality already alluded to, together with the failure of that most mismanaged affair, the Walcheren expedition, brought the battalion to Europe. Having been placed under orders for service in Portugal, it embarked at Halifax on the 24th and 25th June, on which occasion Lieutenant-General Sir George Prevost issued the following order:— *1st Battalion embarks for Portugal.*

"Halifax, June 27th, 1810.

"Morning Orders.—On the departure of the Royal Fusiliers, the lieutenant-general commanding acknowledges with pride and pleasure another instance in British Soldiers of the union of regularity and good conduct in quarters with patience and valour in the field of battle.

"Lieutenant-General Sir George Prevost has that opinion of the commanding officer, the officers, non-commissioned officers, and privates of this already distinguished corps, which induces him to pronounce his confidence that the Royal Fusiliers will maintain their reputation on whatever service they may be employed, and that when called on to face the enemy of their country they will again add to their fame and exalt the glory of the British Army.

"(Signed) A. PILKINGTON, Dep. Adj. Gen."

STATES OF THE 1st BATTALION ROYAL FUSILIERS 1784—1810.

Date.	Station.	Colonel.	Lieut.-Col.	Major.	Captains.	Lieutenants.	Staff.	Sergeants.	Drummers.	Present Fit for Duty.	Sick in Quarters.	Sick in Hospital.	On Command.	Recruiting.	On Furlough.	Total.
Jan. 1st, 1784	At Sea	...	...	...	1	6	3	14	18	156	8	...	60	...	...	224
Jan. 1st, 1785	Gloucester	...	...	1	2	5	4	7	12	172	17	.	6	46	19	260
Jan. 1st, 1786	Plymouth Dock	...	...	1	3	8	4	9	8	266	15	...	...	48	18	347
Jan. 1st, 1787	Aberdeen	...	...	...	4	9	3	11	7	261	24	11	27	17	7	347
Jan. 1st, 1788	Fort George	...	...	...	6	9	4	12	7	300	11	...	13	38	4	366
Jan. 1st, 1789	Edinburgh Castle	...	...	1	3	10	4	18	11	327	27	13	...	15	12	384
Jan. 1st, 1790	Glasgow	...	...	1	2	7	3	12	7	217	11	...	138	9	3	378
Jan. 1st, 1791	Gibraltar	1	...	...	4	12	3	27	13	392	6	33	...	...	...	431
Jan. 1st, 1792	Quebec	1	...	...	4	14	4	21	11	344	37	...	...	4	...	385
Jan. 1st, 1793	Quebec	1	...	1	6	12	4	21	11	325	24	...	...	3	...	352
Jan. 1st, 1794	Quebec	...	1	1	4	9	4	19	8	312	27	...	5	11	5	360
Jan. 1st, 1795	Halifax	1	...	1	5	11	4	27	13	326	13	...	4	10	1	354
Jan. 1st, 1796	Halifax	1	...	1	2	12	4	42	21	777	60	...	4	4	5	850
Jan. 1st, 1797	Halifax	1	1	2	4	22	6	57	25	888	111	...	...	5	3	1007
Jan. 1st, 1798	Halifax	1	...	1	6	23	6	51	22	852	86	..	...	3	2	943
Jan. 1st, 1799	Halifax	...	...	1	1	5	16	1	51	21	546	44	...	...	3	7	600
Jan. 1st, 1800	Halifax	...	...	1	1	3	11	4	43	21	564	22	..	2	10	2	600
Jan. 1st, 1801	Halifax	...	...	...	1	1	4	13	3	47	21	555	29	...	...	3	13	600
Jan. 1st, 1802	Halifax	...	...	...	1	1	4	13	5	43	16	518	56	...	..	3	23	600
Jan. 1st, 1803	Bermuda	...	1	...	3	7	2	16	12	241	13	12	...	1	3	270
Jan. 1st, 1804	Bermuda	...	...	...	4	6	3	17	12	277	3	12	...	1	2	295
Jan. 1st, 1805	Bermuda	...	...	...	4	4	...	18	12	262	15	5	...	1	2	285
Jan. 1st, 1806	Bermuda	...	...	...	5	1	3	18	12	256	13	1	...	1	1	272
Jan. 1st, 1807	Dublin	...	...	...	7	9	5	33	20	721	...	5	1	13	9	749
Jan. 1st, 1808	Lewes	...	...	1	8	16	6	40	18	701	7	28	...	...	...	736
Jan. 1st, 1809	Barbadoes	...	1	2	7	19	4	48	14	886	...	...	90	...	...	976
Jan. 1st, 1810	Halifax	...	...	2	4	17	5	45	21	814	...	52	79	...	...	945

The battalion sailed for Lisbon June 28th, in H.M.S., "Swiftsure," "Milan," "Martin," and "Ferret," the head quarters being in the "Swiftsure." The transport "Ariel" conveyed the women and baggage. The battalion arrived in the Tagus on the 27th July, and disembarked on the 31st, at Lisbon, 51 sergeants 22 drummers, and 905 privates, every man being present in the ranks. The battalion was stationed in barracks at Campo d'Ourique while preparing for the field. The following is the list of officers who disembarked with the battalion.

Bt. Lieut.-Col. Blakeney.	Lieut. Cotton.	Lieut. Mullins.
Major Nooth.	,, Wylly.	,, Moses.
Captain Wooldridge.	,, Moultrie.	,, Baldwin.
,, Despard.	,, Mair.	,, Wilkinson.
,, Cholwich.	,, Drawwater.	Paymaster Armstrong.
,, Spencer.	,, Wemyss.	Adjutant Cotton.
,, Salmon.	,, St. Pol.	Surgeon Robinson.
Lieut. Magennis.	,, English.	Assist. Surgeon Armstrong.
,, Prevost.	,, S. B. Johnstone.	Qr.-Master Crawford.

On the 9th August, having received the necessary equipment, the battalion marched to join the army, then near Almeida, which was besieged by the French under Massena. Halting for a few days at Thomar it was reviewed by General Leith before the Portuguese General Miranda. Its efficiency called forth the praise of both the reviewing officers. On the 26th it started for Villa Cortez, but in consequence of the surrender of Almeida on the 25th, it returned to Ponte de Murcella. Here the Battalion and the 79th Regiment were formed into a brigade and placed in the 1st Division (Sir Brent Spencer's), stationed at Mealhada de Sorda. ^{1st Battalion joins the Army.}

On the 22nd February, while the Head Quarters of the Army were at Viseu, ^{2nd Batt.} Major-General Cole's Brigade, consisting of the 3rd Battalion of the 27th, 97th, and 40th Regiments, was added to Brigadier-General Campbell's Division, the Head Quarters of which were at Guarda. Cole succeeded to the command. To each of the Brigades of the Division was also added a Company of the 5th Battalion of the 60th Rifles. In the beginning of May, Wellington advanced towards the frontier to check the advance of the French on Ciudad Rodrigo. With his Head Quarters at Celorico, his Divisions were pushed along the valley of the Mondego, the 2nd Battalion Fusiliers being quartered at Cea. In June, during one of the reconnaissances in front of Rodrigo, while the French were besieging the place, Captain Percy was taken prisoner. After the fall of Rodrigo and Almeida, and the third invasion of Portugal by Massena, the British Army retired. In September, Guarda was occupied by the French, and the Allies were in motion to cross the

Mondego. On the 20th, the 3rd, 4th, and Light Divisions passed that river at Pena Corva, Olivarez, and other places, and were distributed, the Light Division at Mortagoa, the 3rd and 4th Divisions in the villages between the Sierra de Busaco and Mortagoa. These movements were the prelude to the battle of Busaco. The 4th Division had a few days previously been stationed at the convent of Busaco, but before the day of battle it closed a little to its left, covering a path leading to Mealhada, where the Cavalry held the flat ground. In these positions Wellington awaited the attack of the French. On the morning of the 27th September Massena assailed the British. The details of this memorable action only slightly include the services of the Royal Fusiliers, for the storm of war burst upon the right and centre of the British line, and there the action was virtually decided. British troops posted in a strong position were not to be forced, and with a loss of 5000 of his bravest troops Massena had to retire. The loss of the 2nd Battalion of the Fusiliers was only one man killed, and Lieutenant Mair and 22 men wounded. The officers present in the action were:—

Commanding Brigade—Lieut.-Col. *Hon.* E. M. Pakenham.
1st Battalion—Bt. Lieut.-Col. E. Blakeney; Major Nooth.
Captains Wooldridge, Despard, Beatty, Cholwich, King, Singer, and Crowder.
Lieuts. Magennis, Prevost, Wylly, Moultrie, Mair, St. Pol, English, Johnstone, Mullins, Hamerton, Moses, Baldwin, Anderson, Morgan, Ormsby, Jones, Lester, Seaton, Fraser, and Delgairnes.
Adjutant Cotton; Paymaster Armstrong; Qr.-Master Crawford.
Surgeon Robinson; Assist.-Surgeons Armstrong and Mahoney.
2nd Battalion—Lieut.-Col. Sir W. Myers, *Bart.*; Major Burton.
Captains Prescott, Preston, Tarleton, and Erck.
Lieuts. Henry, Archer, Hackett, Hannam, Johnstone, Healey, Payne, Irwin, Logan, Wray, Fowler, Hartley, Green, Wallace, and Pyke.
Adjutant Jas. Hay; Paymaster Berkeley; Qr.-Master Hogan.
Surgeon Williamson; Assist.-Surgeon Deugan.

After his unsuccessful attempt to force the British position, Massena manœuvred to turn Wellington's left, when the army fell back to the lines of Torres Vedras. The 4th Division was posted in the Valley of Zibreira to guard the lines from thence to Torres Vedras. The Head Quarters of Campbell's brigade occupied Ribaldiera, where the 2nd Battalion of the Fusiliers was quartered. On the 10th October, while stationed here, the 1st Battalion was brigaded with the 61st Regiment and the Brunswick Oels, the 79th being removed to another brigade. This arrangement only endured until the 21st November, when the "Fusilier Brigade" was formed, consisting of the two Battalions of the Royal Fusiliers, and the 1st Battalion of the Royal Welsh, then lately arrived from America. The command of the brigade was given to Colonel Pakenham. Sir W. Myers, as Senior Lieutenant-Colonel, assumed the command of the 1st Battalion, and Brevet Lieutenant-Colonel Blakeney that of the 2nd. The brigade formed the left of the 4th Division. While occupying these lines, on the 13th October, the 9th Company of the 2nd Battalion greatly distinguished itself by dispersing, at the point of the bayonet, a reconnoitring party of French, who had seized the village of Burlada, a point between the two armies. By the middle of November Massena discovered that he could no longer hold his line of investment. On the night of the 14th the French Army broke up from its encampment, and returned to cantonments extending from Santarem to Thomar. On the 20th the Fusiliers proceeded to Azambuja.

Fusilier Brigade formed.

1811.

On the 24th January, the Fusiliers left Azambuja, and moved to the village of Averias de Cima. The command of the brigade was there changed, in consequence of Colonel Pakenham having been placed at the head of the adjutant general's department. He was succeeded by Major-General Houston. In these quarters the brigade continued without further change until March, the French at Santarem still obstinately keeping up the blockade, though at a terrible cost to themselves.

Massena commenced his retreat from Santarem on the night of the 5th March. The 4th division entered upon the pursuit next morning, marching to Galegoa. The division took part in the attack at Pombal on the evening of the 10th, and again on the 12th, on the 6th French corps in the defile between Pombal and Redinha; but its active interference was scarcely required, for so roughly were the French handled by the 3rd and Light Divisions that they declined to await the onset of the other British troops, and fled to Condeixa. Napier, describing this attack as "a most splendid spectacle of war," says "the woods seemed alive with troops; and in a few minutes thirty thousand men, forming three gorgeous lines of battle, were stretched across the plains, but bending in a gentle curve, and moving majestically onward, while horsemen

Massena retreats from Santarem.

and guns, springing forward simultaneously from the centre and from the left wing, charged under a general volley from the French battalions: the latter were instantly hidden by the smoke, and when that cleared away no enemy was to be seen."

On the 13th, the enemy was again attacked and driven from Condeixa. On the 14th he was brought to action at Casal Nova, where the Light Division attacked, but it was found that he could only be dislodged by movements on his flanks. "Accordingly," says Wellington in his despatch, "I moved the 4th division under Major-General Cole upon Panella, in order to secure the passage of the river Esla, and the communication with Espinhel, near which place Major-General Nightingale had been in observation of the 2nd Corps since the 10th." During the action, Regnier, seeing the approach of the 4th division, hastily abandoned Panella; and Cole having effected a junction with Nightingale, passed the Deuca, when Marmont fearing lest they should gain his rear, set fire to the town of Miranda de Corvo, and passed the Ceira that night.

The 4th Division proceeds to Beresford.

The 4th division was then detached to the Alentejo to reinforce the army under Beresford. It marched by Espinal, Thomar, where it arrived on the 16th, and was quartered for two days in the ruined convents, Aripinda, and crossed the Tagus by a bridge of boats at Gouveo on the evening of the 19th, continuing through Portalegre. Having arrived at Arronches, on receipt of the news of the surrender of Badajos, Beresford's instructions were to relieve Campo Mayor, then held by Portuguese Militia, and besiege Olivenza and Badajos. Campo Mayor had however surrendered, but on the approach of the British it was forthwith evacuated by the French. On arriving at Campo Mayor the 4th division was quartered there. On the 8th April, the division left Campo Mayor to take part in the siege of Olivenza. Operations commenced on the night of the 12th, by seizing a lunette which the enemy had left unoccupied in front of the San Francisco gate. On the 15th the place surrendered at discretion. The loss of the Fusiliers in the operation consisted of two men, one belonging to the 1st battalion was wounded; and the other belonging to the 2nd battalion was killed.

From Olivenza Beresford led his troops, who were suffering greatly from the severity of their labours, and "were barefooted and exhausted," to Badajos, the siege of which was immediately commenced. The place was invested on the 5th May. The siege failed for want of proper materials, whereupon it was turned into a blockade, which was broken by Soult, who advanced from Seville. Beresford took up a position at Albuera, where Soult attacked him on the 16th May. Hearing of Soult's approach Beresford raised the blockade, holding, however, his position until the last moment. The Royal Fusiliers continued at their post before the place throughout the night of the 15th, and only commenced their march to join the covering army at 2 a.m. of the 16th. The right brigade was indeed left at Badajos. "About midnight," says Sergeant Cooper, "we were suddenly ordered to march, weary and jaded as we were, having been on picket duty near the city walls for 36 hours. After marching till daylight appeared, we halted and put off our great coats." The brigade, having traversed a distance of 20 miles, reached the army at 9 a.m., as the enemy were crossing the small rivulet which runs in front of the village of Albuera, on the left of the position. The Fusilier brigade, commanded by Lieutenant-Colonel Sir W. Myers of the Royal Fusiliers, was at once ordered to form in an oblique line behind the right with their own right thrown back. The 1st battalion of the Royal Fusiliers was commanded by Major J. W. Nooth, and the 2nd by Lieutenant-Colonel Blakeney.

By the time the deployment was finished the success of the action was more than doubtful. The Spaniards had been driven from the heights that commanded the combined lines; the first brigade had been pushed back by sheer force, and the retreat it is said had sounded. Cole, anxious for the order to advance, was importuned by Sir W. Myers to issue the orders on his own responsibility, and at last succeeded in obtaining his end. Turning then to his people, he exclaimed, "It will be a proud day for the Fusiliers," and called them forward. Their advance we will describe in the words of Sergeant Cooper, who participated in it:—" The day was now apparently lost, for large masses of the enemy had gained the highest part of the battlefield, and were compactly ranged in three heavy columns, with numerous cavalry and artillery, ready to roll up our whole line. The aspect of that hill covered with troops was no jest, as we had no reserve to bring up. At this crisis the words 'Fall in, Fusiliers,' aroused us, and we formed line. Having arrived at the foot of the hill, we began to climb its slope with panting breath,

Advance of the Fusiliers

while the roll and thunder of furious battle increased. Under this tremendous fire of the enemy our thin line staggers; men are knocked about like skittles, but not a step backward is taken. Here our Colonel and all the field officers of the brigade fell killed or wounded, but no confusion ensued. The orders were, 'Close up! Close in! Fire away! Forward!' We are close up to the enemy's column; they break and rush down the other side of the hill, in the greatest mob-like confusion." As the brigade commenced its march, Sir W. Myers's charger was shot under him, and he advanced on foot until another charger was brought, which he had scarcely mounted when the fatal shot struck him, passing from under the hip upward in an oblique direction through the intestines.

The charge of the Fusiliers at Albuera, perhaps the most magnificent effort ever accomplished even by British soldiery, has been described by Napier in one of the finest passages that has appeared in the page of military history, and to it as worthy of the effort we turn.

Napier's description of the charge of the Fusiliers.

"The 4th Division had only two brigades in the field, the one Portuguese under General Hervey, the other commanded by Sir William Myers, and composed of the 7th and 23rd British Regiments, was called the Fusilier Brigade. General Cole directed the Portuguese to move between Lumley's Dragoons and the hill, where they were immediately charged by some French Horsemen, but beat them off with great loss; meanwhile he led the Fusiliers in person up the height.

"At this time six guns were in the enemy's possession, the whole of Werle's reserves were coming forward to reinforce the front column of the French, and the remnant of Houghton's Brigade could no longer maintain its ground; the field was heaped with carcasses, the Lancers were riding furiously about the captured artillery on the upper part of the hill, and on the lower slopes a Spanish and an English Regiment, in mutual error, were exchanging volleys; behind all, General Hamilton's Portuguese, in withdrawing from the heights above the bridge, appeared to be in retreat. The conduct of a few brave men soon changed this state of affairs. Colonel Robert Arbuthnot, pushing between the double fire of the mistaken troops, arrested that mischief, while Cole, with the Fusiliers flanked by a battalion of the Lusitanian Legion under Colonel Hawkshaw, mounted the hill, dispersed the Lancers, recovered the captured guns, and appeared on the right of Houghton's Brigade exactly as Abercrombie passed it on the left.

"Such a gallant line, issuing from the midst of the smoke, and rapidly separating itself from the confused and broken multitude, startled the enemy's heavy masses, which were increasing and pressing onwards as to an assured victory; they wavered, hesitated, and then vomiting forth a storm of fire, hastily endeavoured to enlarge their front, while a fearful discharge of grape from all their artillery whistled through the British ranks. Myers was killed; Cole and the three Colonels, Ellis, Blakeney, and Hawkshaw, fell wounded; and the Fusilier Battalions, struck by the iron tempest, reeled and staggered like sinking ships. Suddenly and sternly recovering, they closed on their terrible enemies, and then was seen with what a strength and majesty the British soldier fights. In vain did Soult, by voice and gesture, animate his Frenchmen; in vain did the hardiest veterans, extricating themselves from the crowded columns, sacrifice their lives for the mass to open out on such a fair field; in vain did the mass itself bear up, and, fiercely striving, fire indiscriminately upon friends and foes, while the Horsemen, hovering upon the flank, threatened to charge the advancing line. Nothing could stop that astonishing infantry. No sudden burst of undisciplined valour, no nervous enthusiasm weakened the stability of their order; their flashing eyes were bent on the dark columns in their front; their measured tread shook the ground; their dreadful volleys swept away the head of every formation; their deafening shouts overpowered the dissonant cries that broke from all parts of the tumultuous crowd, as, foot by foot, and with a horrid carnage, it was driven by the incessant vigour of the attack to the farthest edge of the hill. In vain did the French reserves, joining with the struggling multitude, endeavour to sustain the fight; their efforts only increased the irremediable confusion, and the mighty mass, giving way like a loosened cliff, went headlong down the ascent. The rain flowed after in streams discoloured with blood, and fifteen hundred unwounded men, the remnant of six thousand unconquerable British soldiers, stood triumphant on the fatal hill!"

The losses of the Fusiliers were of course tremendous, but their glory was more than commensurate with their sufferings. Their colour staves were shattered to pieces and their colours rent to rags; their Battalions were broken up into fragments, some of their Companies were represented by units, but they had brought back the lost colour of the "Buffs," they had secured the victory, and the army admitted that "the Fusiliers exceeded everything that the usual word *gallantry* can convey." In the exhibition of "an example of steadiness and heroic gallantry which history cannot surpass," they found a soldier's consolation for the loss of the comrades who had fallen to win them their fame. _{Recover the colour of the "Buffs."}

Sir William Myers was borne off the field in a dying state to Valverde, where, in the 27th year of his age, he expired next day. His last great fight was fought—his work of glory done! His corpse was borne to the grave, under an olive tree, in a grove in the neighbourhood of Valverde, by six of his own Fusiliers. Beside him and the undermentioned officers the 1st Battalion had 2 sergeants, 63 men killed; 14 sergeants and 263 men wounded; the 2nd Battalion had 1 sergeant, 46 men killed; 16 sergeants, 1 drummer, and 269 men wounded. When the 2nd Battalion mustered after the battle it numbered about 80 men; it went into action 435 strong. The 1st Battalion was some hundreds stronger.

Officers who served with the Fusiliers at Albuera:—

Commanding Brigade—Lieut.-Col. Sir W. Myers (killed).

First Battalion.	Second Battalion.
Major Nooth.	Bt. Lieut.-Col. Blakeney (severely wounded).
Captain Wooldridge.	Captain Despard, *Acting Major*.
,, Cholwich (slightly wounded).	,, Erck (killed).
,, King.	,, Orr (wounded).
,, Singer (slightly wounded).	,, Fernie.
,, Crowder (slightly wounded).	,, Tarleton (wounded).
Lieut. Prevost (died of wounds).	,, Magennis (left arm amputated).
,, Wylly.	Lieut. Healey (arm amputated).
,, Moultrie (killed).	,, Penrise.

FIRST BATTALION.	SECOND BATTALION.
Lieut. Mair.	Lieut. Payne.
,, Wemyss (severely wounded).	,, Archer (killed).
,, St. Pol.	,, Pyke.
,, S. B. Johnstone (killed).	,, Irwin (killed).
,, Mullins (severely wounded).	,, Wray (wounded).
,, Mackworth.	,, Wallace.
,, Moses (slightly wounded).	,, Hartley.
,, Baldwin.	,, Hutchison.
,, Anderson.	,, Lorentz (wounded).
,, Devey.	,, Geo. Seaton (wounded).
,, Henry (slightly wounded).	,, Dalgairns.
,, Ormsby.	,, Frazer (wounded).
,, Jones (killed).	,, Holden (wounded).
,, Morgan (severely wounded).	,, Orr (wounded).
,, Hannam.	,, Green.
,, R. Johnson (slightly wounded).	,, Lester (wounded).
,, Gibbons (severely wounded).	
Adjutant Hay.	Acting Adjutant Meagher (wounded).
Paymaster Armstrong.	Paymaster Berkeley.
Qr.-Master Hogan.	Qr.-Master Crawford.
Assist. Surgeon Armstrong.	Surgeon Williamson.
,, Mahoney.	Assist. Surgeon Deugan.
	,, Sweeny.

Major Blakeney was promoted to the Lieutenant-Colonelcy; Captain Wooldridge succeeded to the Majority; Major Nooth received a Brevet Lieutenant-Colonelcy; and Captain Despard, who succeeded to the command of the 2nd Battalion on Lieutenant-Colonel Blakeney being wounded, was promoted to a Majority. A gold clasp was sent to the relatives of Sir W. Myers. Colonel Blakeney also received a gold clasp; Major Nooth and Captain Despard gold medals. In addition to these promotions Sergeant-Major Timothy Meagher was promoted Lieutenant in the Regiment; Sergeant-Major William Johnstone, Ensign 57th Regiment; Quarter-Master Sergeant Arthur Bryne, Ensign and Adjutant 27th Regiment; and Sergeant William Gough, for the recapture of the Regimental Colour of the "Buffs," Ensign 2nd West India Regiment.

After the battle the Brigade was attached to the 2nd Division, commanded by Major-General Stewart, who forwarded the following letter to Marshal Beresford, marking his estimation of the conduct of the Fusiliers. The Brigade was then quartered in Almendralejo.

"Almendralejo, 26th May, 1811.

General Stewart's report of the bravery of the Fusiliers.

"Sir,—As you have been so kind as to permit me to transmit to you the names of the officers of the 2nd Division who commanded Corps on the 16th instant, it may not be deemed irregular if, during the absence of Major-General Cole, I forward to you the names of the officers of the Fusilier Brigade who were similarly situated.

"The remains of that gallant Brigade having been attached to the 2nd Division immediately after the action of Albuera, and the Major-General in command of the 4th Division having been obliged to leave the field from a wound, I am induced to lay before you, for such favourable report upon the subject as you may deem expedient to the Commander of the Forces, the enclosed returns which have been put in my possession by the officers now in command of the Fusilier Brigade, and who commanded the same in action after the successive incapacity from wounds of his four senior officers. *I am apprehensive lest by further delay the exertions of that Brigade be not sufficiently known.* From the circumstance of the Fusilier Brigade having been joined with my 3rd Brigade in the hard-fought defence of our centre position for above three hours, from the severe loss sustained by the Fusiliers on the spot, and from the testimony of the surrounding Allied Army, I feel myself authorised in stating that the conduct of the Fusilier Brigade, on the 16th instant, was admirable, and such as effectually secured the victory of that day.

"It is a duty, moreover, which I owe to the brave soldiers under my temporary command, to report that the 2nd Division is indebted to the Royal Fusiliers for the re-capture of a six-pounder, and of a Regimental Colour of the 'Buffs,' both of which had been lost in the too successful attack of the enemy's cavalry in the beginning of that day.

"I am, &c.,
"WILLIAM STEWART, Major-General.
"To Marshal Beresford."

To the universal praise of the army, Wellington added his condolence to Lady Myers on the death of her son.

"Elvas, May 20th, 1811.

"Madam,—I cannot allow the dispatches which I am now sending to England to go away without writing a few lines to condole with your ladyship upon the severe loss of which they convey the intelligence. Although the mind of the wife and mother of soldiers must be in some degree prepared to receive intelligence of this description, it cannot be expected that you should not be severely afflicted by the loss you have sustained; and I do not address your ladyship with the hope that anything I can write will have the immediate effect of alleviating your sorrow. It must, however, be some consolation to you hereafter to know that your son fell in an action in which, if possible, the British troops surpassed all their former deeds, and at the head of the Fusilier Brigade, to which a great part of the final success of the day was to be attributed. *Wellington's letter of condolence to Lady Myers.*

"As an officer he had already been highly distinguished, and if Providence had prolonged his life he promised to become one of the brightest ornaments to his profession, and to increase the military reputation of his family, and to be an honour to his country. I could not deny myself the melancholy satisfaction of communicating to you my sense of your late son's merits, in hope that at some future period the occasion and mode of his death, as well as this evidence of my favourable opinion of him, under whose command he had served for some time, may alleviate your affliction.

"I have the honour to be, Madam,
"Your Ladyship's most obedient, humble Servant,
"WELLINGTON."

The severe losses of the two Battalions having reduced them below the strength of a single battalion, on the 22nd May Lord Wellington informed the Earl of Liverpool of his intention to form the two Battalions into one, and to send the officers and non-commissioned officers of the 2nd Battalion home to recruit. It is singular that from the same country, and almost exactly a century before the ravages of war had necessitated a similar step. The intention was carried into effect next month.

"26th June, 1811.

2nd Batt. drafted into the 1st, and staff sent home to recruit.

"G.O.—The Commander of the Forces having received orders to draft the 2nd Battalion of the Royal Fusiliers into the 1st Battalion, the following arrangement is to be made for that purpose. All the private men in the 2nd Battalion in Portugal and Spain are to be drafted into the 1st Battalion, and to be distributed into companies in the 1st Battalion. The transfer is to be made as soon as it may be convenient, and the officers commanding companies in the 2nd Battalion are to draw pay for their men up to the 24th instant, and are to account in the usual manner with the officers commanding Companies in the 1st Battalion, to whose companies their men will be transferred under this order. When the transfer shall be completed the officers, non-commissioned officers, and staff of the 2nd Battalion are to proceed to Lisbon, preparatory to their embarkation for England.

"The Commander of the Forces begs the 2nd Battalion of the Fusiliers will accept his thanks for their services since they have been in the Peninsula. They have on every occasion supported the high character of the Royal Fusiliers, and the Commander of the Forces hopes soon to have this Battalion under his command again in renewed strength."

2nd Batt. reorganised and sent to Jersey.

The Staff of the Battalion consequently returned to England in July. Large numbers of recruits had been obtained from the Militia, and from these, which were with the depôt at Maidstone, the Battalion was at once placed again on a war footing, for recruits from the Militia in those days were perfectly trained soldiers, as far as barrack yard training can be perfect. In November the 2nd Battalion was sent to Jersey, where it continued during the remainder of the Peninsula war.

After the retreat of Soult the siege of Badajos was resumed. The Fusiliers were sent back to form part of the besieging army. The operations of this siege were again weakly conducted, for want of means rather than for want of men. The duties of the Fusiliers though arduous, were not particularly dangerous. Between the 30th May and the 5th June, the regiment lost two men wounded; between the 6th and 10th it had other two men wounded. By this time two assaults on Fort San Christoval had failed, Soult was known to be ready to advance to relieve the place, and so on the 10th the stores were removed and the attack again turned into a blockade. A concentration of the enemy's forces having taken place, on the 14th the allies withdrew into the woods behind the Caya, about Torre Mouro, where they awaited the attack of the enemy. On the 19th, the French relieving troops entered Badajos. Wellington now prepared for battle; but, as the French declined to venture an attack after their recent and terrible experience at Albuera, the allied army broke up from the Caya in July. The

Royal Fusiliers moved towards the northern frontier of Portugal, halting for Return to the Northern Frontier of Portugal. a fortnight at Aldea de Santa Margarita, whence they afterwards marched to Aldea del Bispo. There they were joined by a draft of seven subalterns and 300 men, under Lieutenant Barrington, from the depôt at Maidstone. This draft left the depôt, and embarked on the 18th July, at Portsmorth, its departure being precipitated by the urgent need to fill up the losses of Albuera. It was detained by contrary winds at Spithead and Falmouth until the 7th August, but it reached Lisbon in safety on the 20th, and thence proceeded to Head Quarters.

Meanwhile Wellington blockaded Ciudad Rodrigo, to relieve which Marmont was advancing with 60,000 men. On the 25th September, he attempted to force the blockade by assailing Generals Colville and Alten in position at El Bodon. Although the Fusiliers were moved up to support Colville and Alten, the gallantry of the 5th and 77th Regiments especially rendered their interference unnecessary. Lieutenant Cameron, who was then marching with the draft to join the army, thus describes the affair. "As we approached Guinaldo we heard a heavy cannonade, and saw columns of our troops on the heights near the village. An officer was sent forward to report our arrival, who, on his return, informed us that the French army under Marmont had advanced with a convoy to relieve Rodrigo. The convoy had entered the town the day before, and the enemy's cavalry and artillery were now advancing towards us. A brigade of the 3rd division (5th, 94th, and 77th Regiments) was pressed very hard by the enemy's cavalry, and the Fusilier brigade had just marched forward to support them as we arrived. The position consisted of a semi-circular range of hills, about a mile and a half in extent, with a small battery on each flank. The heights retired on the left to low ground covered with wood; on the right was the Agueda and high mountains. We were placed at the battery on the right of the position, until the regiment returned. The enemy advanced within cannon-shot of us, they then halted for their infantry, and our troops retired to their position. The Fusilier brigade occupied the battery on the left when we first joined them. Our officers and men were immediately told off to different companies."

Wellington was, however, compelled to retreat; next day he fell back behind

Fuente Guinaldo, his retreat being covered by a body of cavalry, and by the Fusiliers occupying the battery on the left of the position, where they remained all day. The whole French army was gathering in the plain below, and so near that the different regiments could be distinguished by the British. About 11 p.m. Wellington withdrew his rear guard. The Fusiliers were ordered to fall in, and were marched off in the greatest silence, leaving good fires burning. The brigade still formed the rear guard. The whole column moved upon a narrow road; and the night being very dark, progress was slow. At 9 a.m. of the 27th, the brigade passed through Aldea de Ponte, taking up a position in rear of it. The enemy appeared in pursuit shortly afterwards, a body of his Cavalry advancing to the position where the Royal Fusiliers were posted in column. On their approach, the Light Company was sent out to line the road. It opened fire on the Cavalry, which retired after a few shots. At 2 p.m. a strong column of Infantry attempted to get possession of a hill on the left of the Fusiliers which commanded the position. At this moment Wellington arrived, and at once ordered the Royal Fusiliers to deploy and charge the French down the hill, their attack being supported by a Portuguese regiment in column on each flank. This charge was so vigorously made that the French, who had advanced well up the hill, were driven back, and though they afterwards attempted to turn the brigade by a wood, which was distant about musket-shot from the right, while their Cavalry advanced to the foot of the hills, the Artillery sufficed to baffle the effort. Then the English General taking the offensive, directed the 23rd Royal Welsh and the Caçadores, supported by six companies of the Royal Fusiliers, to turn the French left and seize the opposite hills. This stroke succeeded, and Aldea de Ponte was again occupied by the allies. Wellington, who had been much exposed to fire in these operations, then rode to another part of the position where the remaining four companies of the battalion were also engaged with the French, but scarcely had he departed, when the enemy from the Forcalhos road joined those near Aldea de Ponte, and at six o'clock, renewing their attack, re-took the village. Pakenham with his Fusiliers immediately recovered it, but the French were very numerous, the country rugged and so wooded, that he could not tell what was passing on the flanks; whereupon knowing that the chosen ground of battle was behind the Coa, he abandoned Aldea

Affair of Aldea de Ponte.

de Ponte, and regained his original position. In the night the allies retreated, and on the morning of the 28th occupied a new and very strong position in front of the Coa, the right resting on the Sierra de Meras, the centre covered by the village of Soita, and the left at Rendo on the Coa. The Royal Fusiliers were at Albugal.

In this affair, where the troops "conducted themselves remarkably well," the Royal Fusiliers lost 9 men killed, 1 sergeant and 28 men wounded. The casualties among the officers are given in the following list of officers who were present in the action:— [*Losses at Aldea de Ponte.*]

Commanding Brigade—Colonel E. M. Pakenham.

Lieut.-Colonel Blakeney.	Lieut. Moses.	Lieut. Hutchison.
Major Wooldridge.	,, Baldwin.	,, Lester.
,, Despard.	,, Anderson.	,, Robt. Johnson.
Captain Cholwich.	,, Wilkinson.	,, Russel, *Hon.* F.
,, King.	,, Devey.	,, Knowles.
,, Singer.	,, Henry.	,, Seaton (severely wounded).
,, Crowder.	,, Hannam.	,, Bell.
,, Preston.	,, R. Johnson.	,, Cameron.
,, Wylly (severely wounded).	,, Pyke.	Adjutant Hay.
,, Mair.	,, Barrington (slightly wounded).	Qr.-Master Hogan.
,, Drawater.	,, Payne.	Assist.-Surgeon Armstrong.
Lieut. St. Pol.	,, Wallace (slightly wounded).	,, Mahoney.

These operations closed the campaign for the winter. The Battalion marched through Villa Mayor to Alameda, where it remained for a few days; on the 4th October it marched to Aldea del Bispo, and from thence, on the 16th, it moved into cantonments, being quartered at Villa de Ciervo, where it stayed, except one change of quarters for five days, during the remainder of the year. The Fusilier Brigade was then under the command of Major-General Bowes, who joined on march from the south of Portugal. It would seem from some expressions in Wellington's despatches that at some periods of the year the Regiment was far from healthy. In August as many as 700 of the men were in hospital from wounds and sickness, but this number included the Albuera men. It is, however, notorious that the Regiment suffered the greatest hardships and privations in its marches against Olivenza and Badajos. All ranks were absolutely barefooted, and their clothing an aggregate of rags and tatters. Nor did the health of the Regiment improve much during the winter. Speaking of the stay in Villa de Ciervo, Lieutenant Cameron says, "When in cantonments we were billeted on the inhabitants, the [*Quartered at Villa de Ciervo.*]

officers in the best houses or cottages, according to seniority, and the soldiers in the remainder. We had chimneys built, and oil-paper or sheepskin answered for glass in the windows. General Cole lived in the curé's house at Villa de Ciervo. Our biscuit and rum came on mules from Oporto, and we were often without rations of these articles. The officers messed two or three together, generally the officers of a Company, it being impossible to have a general mess. Being now in winter quarters every exertion was made in drilling and proficiency for the next campaign. Our Volunteers were from different Militia Regiments, and most of them very young soldiers. They were kept so close at it that with scanty food and a cold wet season they were very sickly. Out of 400 men, nearly 300 died or were invalided within the first year of our arrival."

1812.

Siege of Rodrigo.

For some time during the winter the 4th, with the other divisions of the army, had been preparing materials for the siege of Rodrigo, for which the 1st, 3rd, 4th, and Light Divisions were destined. On the 8th January the Light Division crossed the Agueda, and opened the siege by their brilliant capture of the redoubt of San Francisco. The first turn of duty under fire fell to the 4th Division on the 10th, when "it relieved the trenches, and 1000 men laboured, but in great peril, for the besieged had a superabundance of ammunition, and did not spare it. In the night the communication from the parallel to the batteries was opened, and on the 11th the 3rd Division undertook the siege." In this service the Battalion lost one man killed and two wounded. Its turn for trench duty occurred again on the 14th, when the enemy made a vigorous sortie, overturned some gabions, and even penetrated into the parallel. In repulsing them the Royal Fusiliers had three men wounded. Their turn for trenches occurred again on the 19th, when the assault was delivered, and thus acting as guard of the trenches they escaped actual participation in the assault. In the performance of their duties, however, they lost one man killed and three wounded; and it is one of the incomprehensible things of the British Military Regulations that the Regiment shall not be allowed to wear the badge "Ciudad Rodrigo" upon its colours.

After the capture of Rodrigo the Royal Fusiliers remained in the village of Cileces el Chico, where they were detained several days by the swelling of the Agueda from heavy rains. They subsequently retired and on the 17th February occupied Alameda, a village in front of Fuentes d'Onor, until ordered to march to the province of Estremadura, to take part in the projected siege of Badajos. Leaving these cantonments on the 27th February the Battalion commenced its march, and crossing the Guadiana, on the 15th March, it formed part of the investing force which took up its position before Badajos on the next day.

The operations of the siege with their attendant losses commenced immediately. Between the 18th and 22nd, the period occupied in completing the batteries and approaches, the Battalion lost two men killed and six men wounded, besides Captain Cuthbert, who, on the 19th, was mortally wounded while acting as aide-de-camp to Picton in repulsing a sortie made by the enemy from the gate of La Trinidad; between the 23rd and 26th it had two men killed and twelve wounded; and between the 31st March and 2nd April it had four men killed and six wounded. On the 6th, the breaches having been reported practicable, Wellington determined to give the assault, and for that purpose issued the following instructions:— *Third Siege of Badajos.*

"The fort of Badajos to be attacked at ten o'clock this night. The attack must be made on three points, the castle, the face of the bastion of La Trinidad, and the flank of the bastion of Santa Maria. The attack of the castle to be by escalade; that of the two bastions by the storm of the breaches.

"The 4th Division, with the exception of the covering party in the trenches, must make the attack on the face of the bastion of La Trinidad, and the Light Division on the flank of the bastion of Santa Maria. These two Divisions must parade in close column of Divisions at nine o'clock. The Light Division with the left in front, the 4th Division with its advanced guard with the left in front, the remainder with the right in front. The 4th Division must be on the left of the little stream near the picket of the 4th Division, and the Light Division must have the river on their right.

"The advance of both Divisions must consist of 500 men from each, attended by twelve ladders; and the men of the storming party should carry sacks filled with light materials to be thrown into the ditch to enable the troops to descend into it. Care must be taken that these bags are not thrown into the covered way.

"The advance of the Light Division must precede that of the 4th Division, and both must keep as near the inundation as they possibly can.

"The advance of both Divisions must be formed into firing parties and storming parties. The firing parties must be spread along the crest of the glacis to keep down the fire of the enemy; while the men of the storming party, who carry bags, will enter the covered way at the *place d'armes* under the breached face of the bastion of La Trinidad; those attached to the 4th Division on its right, those to the Light Division on its left, looking from the trenches on the camp.

"The storming party of the advance of the Light Division will then descend into the ditch, and, turning to its left, storm the breach in the flank of the bastion of Santa Maria; while the storming party of the Light Division will likewise descend into the ditch and storm the breach in the face of the bastion of La Trinidad. The firing parties are to follow in rear of their respective storming parties.

"The heads of the two Divisions will follow their advanced guards, keeping nearly together, but they will not advance beyond the shelter afforded by the quarries on the left of the road till they shall have seen the heads of the advanced guards ascend the breaches; they will then move forward to the storm in double quick time."

The assault of La Trinidad. Beyond these orders it was arranged that Captain Mair should lead the attack on La Trinidad; Captain Cholwich taking that on the breach in the curtain connecting the bastions of La Trinidad and Santa Maria. The assault was compelled to be prematurely made owing to the enemy having discovered, by a lighted carcass, the assembly of the troops for the attack of the castle. At once all the Divisions rushed forward to execute their task. The Light and 4th Divisions were not perceived by the enemy till they reached the covered way, when the advanced guards of the two Divisions descended without difficulty into the ditch, protected by the fire of the troops extended along the glacis. The stormers then rushed on to the assault with the utmost intrepidity. No sooner had they descended into the ditch than they were stopped for a moment by the explosion of a heap of powder and shells, which carried death and destruction through their ranks. "Suddenly," says one of them, "an explosion took place at the foot of the breaches, and a burst of light disclosed the whole scene—the earth seemed to rock under us—what a sight! The ramparts crowded with the enemy, the French soldiers standing on the parapets, the 4th Division advancing rapidly in column of companies on a half-circle to our right, while the short-lived glare from the barrels of powder and combustibles flying into the air, gave to friends and foes a look as if both bodies of troops were laughing at each other. A tremendous fire now opened upon us, and for an instant we were stationary."

Undismayed by this terrible havoc the troops raised a shout and then pushed on for the breach. The ditch, however, was intersected by a cunette of which they were ignorant; "a deep cut made in the bottom of the ditch as far as the counter-guard of the Trinidad, was filled with water from the inundation; into this watery snare the head of the 4th division fell, and it is said that more than a hundred of the Fusiliers, the men of Albuera, were there smothered." Among them was Captain Cholwich who was leading.*

For three dreadful hours the troops struggled to gain a footing in the breach, but struggled in vain. Of themselves the breaches had been rendered impassable. They had been covered with loose planks, studded with sharp iron spikes, and covered with *chevaux-de-frise* formed of sword blades, and at the head of them there stood with a stern valour that would not yield, numbers of French soldiers, whose musketry and grape swept down every living thing that dared to approach them. In the attempt to carry La Trinidad the Royal Fusiliers suffered severely, as the following table of losses will show:

Officers who served at the siege of Badajos with casualties at the assault:—

Lt.-Col. Blakeney (severely wounded).	Lieut. Anderson.	Lieut. Wallace.
Major Singer (killed).	,, Devey (severely wounded).	,, Lester (severely wounded).
Capt. Cholwich (killed).	,, Henry (severely wounded).	,, Knowles (slightly wounded.)
,. King.	,, Hannam.	,, Russel (severely wounded).
,, Wylly.	,, Johnson.	,, George (severely wounded).
,, Mair (severely wounded).	,, Pyke (killed).	Adjutant Hay.
,, Hamerton.	,, Barrington (severely wounded)	Qr.-Master Hogan.
Lieut. St. Pol. (died of wounds).†	,, Wray (killed).	Surgeon Armstrong.
,, Moses (severely wounded).	,, Hartley (slightly wounded).	Assist.-Surgeon Mahoney.
,, Baldwin (slightly wounded).	,, Fowler (killed).	,, Williams.

Besides these the battalion had 2 sergeants and 42 men killed; 11 sergeants and 108 men wounded. Lieutenant-Colonel Blakeney was mentioned in the despatches, and he and Captain Mair received gold medals.

*"Major Singer and Captain Cholwich, of the Royal Fusiliers, and I had sat together for several hours upon an eminence observing the effect produced by our breaching batteries upon the curtain of La Trinidad, which was soon reduced to a heap of ruins. The assault was expected to take place that evening. On our parting, Major Singer shaking my hand said, ' To-morrow I shall be a lieutenant-colonel, or in the kingdom of heaven!' Picton's division being in possession of the castle, and General Walker's Brigade having entered by escalade the bastion of San Vincente, close to the Guadiana, on the opposite side of the town, the enemy abandoned the breaches, to visit which I set out at dawn of day. Meeting some men of the Fusiliers, I inquired for Major Singer. 'We are throwing the last shovelfuls of earth upon his grave;' the brink of which where he fell was marked with his blood. 'Is Captain Cholwich safe.' 'In the act of climbing over that palisade (intersecting the inundation) he was wounded, fell into the water and was seen no more.' "—Captain Cooke's *Memoirs*.

† Captain St. Pol, son of Louis Philippe, Duke of Orleans, to whom he bore a striking resemblance, died of the wounds he received during the assult, after having had his leg amputated. He was the friend and *protégé* of the duke of Kent, who, on hearing of his death, expressed the consolation that he derived from the reflection, that his " noble and heroic conduct had so justly secured to him the esteem and attachment of those who were acquainted with him." Captain St Pol. had only a few weeks before been gazetted captain, and he died ignorant of the fact. He led the Light Company at the assault.

Return to the line of the Agueda.

Badajos having fallen, on the 12th April the army left the province of Estremadura, and returned to the line of the Agueda, crossing the Tagus at Villa Velha on the 20th, and from thence proceeding to its old cantonments. The Royal Fusiliers were quartered at Valongas, where they remained undisturbed until the 5th June, when the army prepared to move forward. The battalion was still very weak; in May its strength had been reduced by sickness and losses to 14 officers and 300 men, but by the beginning of June it rose to 18 officers and 400 men. On the 5th June, says Lieutenant-Cameron, "we marched from our cantonments through Mala, Alameda, and Fuentes d'Onor, and on the 11th bivouaced near Ciudad Rodrigo, where the whole army was assembled, except Hill's corps, which remained in the Alemtejo." On the 13th, the weather having become favourable, Wellington opened the campaign by a march from the Agueda to the Tormes. On the 16th he reached the Rio Valmusa, within 6 miles of Salamanca. The siege of the forts was then commenced by the 6th division; and meantime sundry skirmishes took place, in one of which, the attack of the village of Villares on the 22nd, the Royal Fusiliers had one man wounded. With the object of relieving the forts, Marmont brought up his whole army, and a series of manœuvres ensued. In July, Wellington following Marmont, who had crossed the Douro, left Sir Stapleton Cotton with the 4th and Light Division, and Anson's Cavalry on the river Trabancos. Meanwhile Marmont gathered together his army and returned to his old position at Tordesillas and Pollos, and on the 18th

Affair at Castrejon.

attacked Cotton in Castrejon. A sharp, confused outpost fight, mainly waged by the Artillery of both armies, took place, in which the Royal Fusiliers, although they did not bear as prominent a part as the 3rd Battalion 27th, and 40th Regiments, who routed the enemy with the bayonet, had one man killed, Lieutenant Nantes (who commanded a company) and fourteen men wounded, and three men missing.

Such an evidence of the strength and proximity of the French army as the skirmish at Castrejon afforded could not be neglected. Wellington immediately ordered a retreat of Cotton's force upon the main body. The troops retired in admirable order to Torrecilla de la Orden, having the enemy's whole Cavalry on their flank or in their rear, and thence to the Guarena, passing that river in front of the enemy, and so retiring until they effected their junctions with the army. Wellington then withdrew to his former position in front of Salamanca where he gave battle to Marmont. On the 21st July, the army marched to the banks of the Tormes about a league above Salamanca, keeping between the enemy and the city. The French having crossed at Huerta and Alba de Tormes, "we forded at Aldea Lengua" says Lieutenant Cameron, "having the 3rd Division and some Spanish troops on the right bank. Our division advanced to a wood on the heights of Nuestra Senora de la Pena. It was now dark and the enemy was near us. We remained here during the night. I was attached to the Light Company, and we were on outlying picket. It was one of the most tremendous nights of thunder, lightning, wind, and rain I ever witnessed, which the soldiers considered an omen of battle next day."

The battle of Salamanca commenced early in the morning by skirmishes for points of position in the line of battle. Marmont took possession of the ridge of Calvarissa de Ariba, the height on which stood the old chapel of Nuestra Senora de la Pena, and also, after a sharp conflict, one of the two solitary hills called the Arapiles, the other being occupied by the British. This position was a *point d'appui* which threatened Wellington with serious inconvenience; he therefore extended his right to the low ground, sending the Light Companies of the Guards and the Grenadier and 2nd Company of the Fusiliers, under Captain John Crowder, to drive the French out of the village of Arapiles. This service was performed by the Fusiliers, under the eyes of Lord Wellington, with such vigour and resolution that he demanded to know the name of the officer commanding, who, for his skill and bravery, was mentioned in his lordship's despatch, and rewarded with the rank of brevet-major. The Light Companies of the Guards then marched into the village, the 4th Division being placed in support.

Battle of Salamanca, July 22nd.

Captain Crowder drives the French from the village of Arapiles.

The serious fighting did not commence until afternoon. Marmont resorting to manœuvre, in an unlucky moment, separated his left wing from the centre in an attempt to gain the Ciudad Rodrigo road. The vastness of the error was at once manifest to Wellington, who, seizing the happy moment, hurled his full strength upon his adversary. The 4th Division under Lieutenant-General Cole, and the Cavalry under Sir Stapleton Cotton, were ordered to attack in front, Pack's

Portuguese Brigade having to assail the Arapiles. The attacks of the British Divisions were eminently successful, and for a time all went well. As the British columns advanced they deployed into line, marching over heavy ploughed ground, through the storm of grape that smote them with deadly effect. This forward movement was splendidly maintained, sweeping all before it. The Fusiliers were in the front line; they stormed and carried a height upon which the French had thrown 30 guns into battery, and of these they captured 18. But at the very point of the destruction of their foes, the failure of Pack's Portuguese Brigade left them outflanked and compelled to act on the defensive. When the Portuguese retired, the enemy's cavalry, which were very numerous at this point, threatened both the flanks and rear of the Fusiliers, while his Infantry advanced in front. "We were at this moment," says Lieutenant Cameron, "ordered by Colonel Beatty to retire and form square, a most hazardous movement when the enemy's Infantry were advancing, and within thirty yards of us. The order was only partially heard and obeyed on the right, while on the left we kept up a hot fire on the enemy, who were advancing up-hill, and within a few yards of us. The Companies on our right having retired in succession we found ourselves alone, but the ground the enemy were ascending was so steep that we got off without loss and joined the rest. Luckily while we were forming square to receive the cavalry, the 6th Division came up and received the charge intended for us."

The tardy movements of the 6th Division had for a moment placed the victory in jeopardy; the guns that had been captured had to be abandoned; but the soldierly devotion of the 4th Division so far redeemed the time as to allow the 6th to come into action and restore the fight to its former success.* Thus succoured,

---

* A correspondent writing to England the details of this affair gives the salient points in a manner which, dividing the praise and blame with unmistakeable clearness, compels us to use his own words :—

"Salamanca, 31st August, 1812.

"I yesterday went over the field of battle, accompanied by an officer who was present in the action. The position the French took up was strong ground, rising for a mile in their rear. It appears that three Divisions of the army maintained all the fighting, and did the business. The 4th Division formed the first line, and, marching in line, charged and drove the enemy from their first position, followed them up, forced them from their second position and took eighteen guns. The 6th Division, which should have supported this gallant band, slowly advanced in column; so that the French, perceiving the situation of the 4th Division, attacked them with much superior numbers, and they were forced to give way. The enemy re-took their guns and then retired on the right, but were closely followed by the 4th Division. The 6th Division marching in ordinary time, under a heavy fire, at length deployed at the bottom of a hill of easy ascent, and then began to fire regular volleys.

the Fusiliers again formed line and dashed at the heights; and the corresponding efforts of the other troops being successful, the enemy broke, and fled through the woods towards the Tormes.

By this time the night was far spent; it had passed ten o'clock, "and the whole French army vanished as it were in the darkness." At daybreak of the 23rd the Royal Fusiliers, with the other troops who had carried the last hill, crossed the Tormes, and commenced the pursuit. They came up with the French rearguard posted on the hill of La Serna, who, on being charged by the Cavalry, made a short fight and then broke and fled, being no longer capable of offering sustained resistance. The pursuit was continued as far as Peneranda, the French retiring to Valladolid. The 4th Division arrived at Valladolid on the 30th; it then discontinued the pursuit, and on the 1st August took the road to Cuellar.

<small>Pursuit of the French.</small>

In this battle the Battalion was commanded by Major J. W. Beatty, who received the Gold Medal. Captain Crowder was thus mentioned in the despatch:—
"I must also mention Lieutenant-Colonel Woodford, commanding the Light Battalion of the Brigade of Guards, who, supported by two Companies of the Fusiliers under Captain Crowder, maintained the village of Arapiles against all the efforts of the enemy, previous to the attack upon their position by our troops." The Battalion entered the field 19 officers and about 390 rank and file, and lost one-half its force. During the first advance the officers carrying the colours were both wounded; Lieutenant Cameron then seized one of the colours and he escaped. Prescott, the Captain of the Grenadiers, was killed and his subaltern wounded, when Cameron, though serving with the Light Company, took up the command and held it for the remainder of the day.

Officers who served at Salamanca, with casualties:—

Commanding Battalion—Major J. W. Beatty.

Major King.	Lieut. Henry (severely wounded).	Lieut. Cameron.
Capt. Crowder.	,, Hannam (severely wounded).	,, Knowles (severely wounded).

In consequence they suffered very severely. After the first volley a charge had been made by the 6th Division in support of the 4th, which vigorously charged the enemy, hill after hill, for upwards of half-a-mile; by the rapidity of the motion the predicament would have been avoided which the tardy, precise movement entailed on the Division. Notwithstanding the gallant ardour of the 4th, which pursued the enemy at all points, their loss was nothing in comparison to the 6th, who were tactically exposed to a destructive fire."—*Military Panorama, vol. 2, p. 257.*

Officers who served at Salamanca, with casualties—*continued* :—

Capt. Prescott (killed).
,, Hamerton (severely wounded).
,, English.
Lieut. Baldwin.
,, Anderson.
,, Johnson (severely wounded).
,, Hartley (severely wounded).
,, Nantes (severely wounded).
,, Wallace (severely wounded).
,, Hutchison (severely wounded).
Lieut. Bell.
Adjutant Hay (severely wounded).
Surgeon Williamson.
Assist.-Surgeon Mahoney.
,, Williams.

	Officers.	Sergeants.	Rank and File.
Killed	1	2	17
Wounded	10	6	162

Total :—20 killed ; 178 wounded.

Entry into Madrid.

The victory of Salamanca resulted in the capture of Madrid, the only *promenade militaire* of the whole war, into which the Fusiliers marched with the rest of the army on the 12th August, amidst the joyful acclamation of the people, who recognized and did honour to the men who had freed them from the yoke of a hated conqueror. It was a proud moment when the British Regiments marched into the Spanish capital. The act was the mark of their military prowess, the testimony of bravery that had carried them through the shock of battle to the reward of victory; the emblem of freedom given to a nation. Received as the deliverers of Spain the troops remained for some days stationed in Madrid; on the 18th August they moved thence to the Escurial, and were quartered in the buildings adjoining the Royal Palace until the 6th October, when they marched to Valdemoro and Campo, where the Battalion was quartered for a fortnight.

From these positions the concentration of the French armies caused the British to retire. From its first commencement the retreat was one of great hardship. At 10 a.m. of the 31st October the Battalion reached Madrid. "The baggage and servants having been sent off while I was on picket," says Lieutenant Cameron, "of course my rations were carried off too, and I had nothing to eat on this march which lasted twenty-four hours. During our halt without the walls of Madrid, which was only for two hours, Lieutenant Bell and I, being both very hungry, ran into the town. We did not lose any time in admiring the fine streets and buildings, although we had not been in Madrid before, but made straight for the market-place, where we bought as much bread and cheese as we could easily convey with us. Our load was much lightened by the time we got back to the camp, having made good use of our time on the way." That night the army bivouaced in rear of Madrid, and continued its march next morning before daylight. The troops received supplies of biscuit at Madrid, but they got no more until they reached Alba de Tormes, so that they were some days without bread. Before the troops reached the line of the Tormes they had endured incredible hardship. All the regiments suffered both from hunger and the concurrent difficulties attending a march through a destitute country during the most inclement weather; many of them suffered also from the shell and sabres of their resolute pursuers, but amongst these the Royal Fusiliers are not included. The Agueda having been reached, the 4th Division moved to San Joa de Pesquiera, which it reached on the 3rd December.

While at San Joa de Pesquiera, where the battalion remained until the following year, every man's kit was completed. The intolerable burden imposed upon the soldier elicited the remark "that the government should have sent us out a new backbone to bear the extra weight." The following is a list of articles served out to each man, with their weights:—

Equipment of a Fusilier.

1 fusee and bayonet .... 14 lbs.	2 pair of shoes .... 3 lbs.
1 pouch and 60 rounds of ball ...... 6 ,,	1 pair of trousers .... 2 ,,
1 canteen and belt .... 1 ,,	1 pair of gaiters .... $0\frac{1}{4}$,,
1 mess tin .... 1 ,,	2 pairs of stockings .... 1 ,,
1 knapsack and belts .... 3 ,,	4 brushes, buttonstick and comb ...... 3 ,,
1 blanket .... 4 ,,	2 cross belts .... 1 ,,
1 great coat .... 4 ,,	Pen, ink, and paper .... $0\frac{1}{4}$,,
1 dress coat .... 3 ,,	Pipe clay, chalk, &c. .... 1 ,,
1 white jacket .... $0\frac{1}{2}$,,	2 tent pegs .... $0\frac{1}{4}$,,
2 shirts and 3 breasts .... $2\frac{1}{2}$,,	53 lbs

EXTRA WEIGHT FOR MARCHING.

Three days' bread .... 3 lbs.
2 days' beef .... 2 ,,
Water in canteen .... 3 ,, —— Total 61 lbs.

Besides this weight the orderly sergeant of each company had to carry the orderly book, whose weight was perhaps two pounds, and in turn the regimental colours.

On the re-arrangement of the recruiting districts in the summer of 1812, Captain Robinson was appointed superintending officer of the Maidstone district; and Lieutenant Daniel, of the Marlborough subdivision of the Gloucester district. Volunteer Richard Montgomery was appointed ensign in the 36th Regiment for his services up to the battle of Salamanca.

1813.

During the last campaign the numerical strength of the battalion had been well kept up by drafts from the 2nd Battalion; and for the opening of this campaign, although there were nearly 300 men in hospital from wounds, another draft from England, consisting of 16 sergeants, and 311 rank and file, received in the early days of January, raised the Fusiliers to a superb battalion of 1200 strong.

On the 7th January, the battalion moved from San Joa de Pesquiera to Arvidiza where it remained until the next month. It was in Arvidiza that the 20th Regiment joined the brigade. In February, the brigade moved to Castle Melhor, on the right bank of the Coa. There the Fusiliers remained until the 18th May, when they took the field with the army, which then broke up from its cantonments. The 4th Division passed the Douro on the 20th May, to assemble at the points of rendezvous, Braganza and Miranda de Douro. On the 25th, the 1st, 3rd, 4th, 6th, and 7th Divisions were encamped with their right on Miranda. Hence with an audacity that confounded his opponents, Wellington marched straight upon Salamanca, which he reached on the 25th, driving the French before him as he entered the town. The French retired by the road of Babilla Fuente, whereupon his lordship continued to press forward until the 19th June, when he arrived at the little river Bayas, where he found a division of French Infantry posted. "I found the enemy's rearguard," says the despatch, "in a strong position on the left of the river, having his right covered by Subijana, and his left by the heights in front of Pobes. We turned the enemy's left with the Light Division, whilst the 4th Division under Lieutenant-General Sir Lowry Cole attacked them in front." In this operation the Fusilier brigade and the 20th Regiment were ordered forward, the Royal Fusiliers to attack the village of Montevite. The French were completely surprised, for in the rough broken country, abounding with trees, the foliage enabled the assailants to creep into the position unperceived; a few musket-shots sufficed to drive the French completely out of their camp, leaving their cooking utensils and dinner on the fires, and also abandoning some arms and accoutrements. The three regiments then took up the pursuit. Some skirmishing ensued, which forced the French across the Zadora. The Royal Fusiliers lost three men wounded.

Next day the Fusiliers halted in the position on the Bayas to enable the army, which was somewhat straggled, owing to the length of its march, to concentrate. On the 21st the troops moved down into the valley of the Zadora to give battle to the French, then in position in front of Vittoria. The 2nd Division, with the British Cavalry and some Spanish and Portuguese troops, was to attack the French left; their centre was to be assailed by the 3rd, 4th, and 5th Divisions under the personal command of the Duke of Wellington; their right by General Graham. The first operation was to be on the flanks, which having been turned, the centre was to be assailed. As the attack developed the centre divisions formed line, the Fusiliers moving down from Montevite by Olabarre into position opposite the bridge of Nanclares, where the division was well covered by rugged ground and woods. To meet Hill's overpowering assault the French weakened their centre; Picton's division was then hurled upon them, and that stout soldier, pushing his eager troops through them with a vigour that could not be resisted, the complete defeat of the French began. "The 4th Division pushed back the left centre of the French, and were fighting successfully, performing prodigies of valour, among crags and broken ground." With his flanks thus turned, and his centre assailed with the rudest violence, it only remained for King Joseph to make a retreat as rapidly and orderly as circumstances would allow. The last stand of the French was made in the hills between the villages of Ali and Armentia, where a terrible cannonade and musketry checked the 3rd Division, which still continued to lead the attack. "Again the battle became stationary, and the French Generals had commenced drawing off their Infantry in succession from the right wing, when suddenly the 4th Division rushing forward carried the hill on the French left, and the heights were at once abandoned." The impetuous vigour of the division in this onset was its safety, for its task was not devoid of danger. "At this period of the action," notes one of the combatants, "it was absolutely necessary to strain every nerve to win it before nightfall. The 4th Division, on our right, shot forward against a sugarloaf hill,

Battle of Vittoria.

and broke a French division, who retired up it in a confused mass, firing over each others heads without danger to themselves, owing to the steepness of the ascent." It was this blow that decided the fate of Spain; it drove the French into ignominious retreat.

Then commenced a fight which ended in the destruction of the once grand French Army, and left Spain all but free from their dishonouring presence. From the commencement of the retreat the Fusiliers took up the pursuit. For its steady deportment on the actual battlefield, across which, for a distance of four miles, the Battalion had advanced in line, dressed and preserved with all the regularity of a parade movement, it won loud praise; but the stern discipline of the Regiment, that mighty power that led it up the heights of Albuera, won greater praise when it carried the Fusiliers through the heaps of treasure with which the wreck of the plunder of Spain had strewed their path, without a single man leaving the ranks, and carried them on in restless pursuit of the rapidly dissolving army they had so completely defeated. But when the halt was sounded a wild indulgence ensued. Speaking of the scene, Lieutenant Cameron says, "Our men had been half starved for weeks, and had eaten nothing this day, for the action lasted till 9 p.m. They now formed themselves in the midst of cattle and sheep, wine and biscuit, which the French Army had left. They sat up cooking, eating, and drinking the whole night. Next day the weather became wet, and numbers were left on the road from weakness and dysentery."

Losses of the Battalion.

With singularly good fortune the Royal Fusiliers emerged from this, one of the most decisive battles of the world, with an utterly insignificant loss. The casualties consisted in two men killed and two wounded. Lieutenant-Colonel Blakeney, who had recovered from the wound he had received at Badajos, had rejoined, and was again in command of the Regiment. He received a gold clasp for his services, and on the colours of the Royal Fusiliers is inscribed the word "Vittoria," in commemoration of their share in the glories of the day.

List of officers who served with the Battalion at Vittoria:—

Lieut.-Colonel Blakeney.	Lieut. Burke.	Lieut. Cameron.
Major Despard.	,, R. Johnson.	,, Knowles.
Captain Crowder.	,, Loggan.	,, Bell.
,, Fernie.	,, Payne.	,, King.

List of officers who served with the Battalion at Vittoria—*Continued* :—

Captain Orr.	Lieut. Hutchison.	Lieut. Russell.
,, Tarleton.	,, Fraser.	,, Garrett.
,, Hamerton.	,, Orr.	Adjutant Hay.
,, Morgan.	,, Delgairnes.	Qr.-Master Hogan.
Lieut. Anderson.	,, Lorentz.	Surgeon Williamson.
,, Wilkinson.	,, Nunn.	Assist.-Surgeon Mahoney.
,, Henry.	,, L'Estrange.	

From Vittoria the Fusiliers followed the French to Pampeluna. They were employed in the blockade of that fortress until the 25th, when they formed part of the force detached to Logrono to intercept General Clausel who was there with a division of the French Army, which had not joined in the battle of Vittoria. This expedition was one of the greatest severity, and so harassed the men that many fell out. Clausel, however, by what Wellington describes as "some extraordinary forced marches," escaped by the pass of Jaca. On the 5th July the Royal Fusiliers returned to Pampeluna, where they remained for a few days, cantoned in the village of Burlada, within range of the guns of the place. Subsequently they proceeded to the Pyrenees, the 4th Division taking post at Viscayret, in the valley of Urroz, to support the troops in the pass of Roncesvalles, the Battalion being at Espinal, two miles in advance. On the 24th one wing of the Regiment was ordered on picket on the top of the mountain Mendeschari, westward of Roncesvalles, to secure the pass, the remainder of the Battalion being sent there during the succeeding night. Soult, now again in command of the French, determined to assail the pass. On the 25th the Marshal burst upon the British by attacking Byng's post, when some severe skirmishing took place. Lieutenant-General Cole then moved up to his support. As both sides gathered strength the fighting became closer and more severe. Major-General Ross's Brigade of the 4th Division, opposed to Reillé's advanced guard on the summit of the Lindouz, "on a narrow ridge that would not admit of a larger front than that required for two companies skirmishing," was severely engaged all the afternoon, the companies being relieved as the fight was more stubbornly pressed by the enemy. In these struggles, in which the Brigade was greatly distinguished, but more especially the 20th Regiment, the Royal Fusiliers had Lieutenant Knowles and six men killed; one sergeant and 23 men wounded.

Finding himself greatly outnumbered, and in an advanced and exposed position, Cole determined, as soon as night should set in, to retreat to the main body of the army. Though his post had not been forced, and though his hardy soldiers still held the great chain of mountains, yet his flanks were in danger of being turned. Under these circumstances he wisely retired. Ross's Brigade was left to cover the retreat, which being for four or five miles downhill, and flanked by the Lindouz, "was uneasy and unfavourable." The march was at once both difficult and dangerous, and "will ever be remembered by the Fusiliers who were present to have been one of the most anxious and fatiguing ever experienced." It is thus described by Sergeant Cooper who performed it:—" The order to retire came along the chain of skirmishers in a whisper. While making this movement we came to an open space in a wood, where a number of our badly wounded were lying, wrapped in their blankets. They heard the rustle of our feet, and one of them asked, What Regiment is that? The Seventh! we answered, and passed on, for the retreat was so suddenly and quietly ordered that we were obliged to leave them on the ground. We got no bread this day, and our rum was purposely spilt to prevent drunkenness. This night's march was horrible, for our path lay among rocks and bushes, and was so narrow that only one man could pass at a time; consequently our progress was exceedingly tedious, stopping, as we did, five or ten minutes every two or three yards. This was made much worse by the pitchy darkness. Many were swearing, grumbling, stumbling, and tumbling. No wonder, we were worn out with fatigue and ravenous with hunger. However, I kept up, though my gaiter strap and one of my shoe ties were broken. I called the roll of the Company when we halted, and was surprised to find every man present. About noon next day we were favoured with some biscuit, and were preparing to cook when the enemy debouched from a wood in front and began to drive in our pickets. Of course the cooking was stopped, and we retired to a new position."

Thus fighting and retiring, Cole joined Picton, and the two divisions took up a position in the neighbourhood of Zubiri to cover Pampeluna. In other places the fight had gone ill; the pass of Maya was forced, and the roads were opened for Soult to pour his forces into Spain, and to execute his promise of driving the English beyond the Ebro.

On the 28th Soult again attacked the British. Picton turned to bay on the heights of Mont Escava and San Christoval, thus screening Pampeluna by sealing the mouths of the Lanz and Zubiri valleys. The 4th Division was posted on a hill near Zabaldica, commanding the road to Huarte. The troops were then suffering great privations from the rain and fog of the mountains on which they were posted without any shelter, from the arduous nature of their services which kept them constantly on the move, and also from the scanty supplies that reached them; but at no time during the whole Peninsula Campaign were they more ready or eager for the fight or more resolute in the presence of the foe. Major-General Ross's Brigade was on the left of the Division and in front of the village of Villalba, the Royal Fusiliers being on the left of the Division at a small ruined chapel near the highroad from Ostiz.

About mid-day Clausel's Division, in the valley of the Lanz, fell upon Cole's left, but after some hard fighting was driven back; his second division, seeing the turn of the fight, threw itself headlong into the fray. "One column darting out of the village of Sauroren, silently, sternly, and without firing a shot, worked up to the chapel under a tempest of bullets, which swept away whole ranks without abating the speed and power of the mass. The 7th Caçadores shrunk abashed, and that part of the position was won. Soon, however, they rallied upon General Ross's brigade, and the whole running forward, charged the French with a loud shout and dashed them down the hill. Heavily stricken they were, yet undismayed, and recovering their ranks again, they ascended in the same manner to be again broken and overturned. But the other columns of attack were now bearing upwards through the smoke and flame with which the skirmishers had covered the face of the mountains, and the 10th Portuguese regiment, fighting on the right of Ross's brigade, yielded to their fury; a heavy body crowned the heights, and, wheeling against the exposed flank of Ross, forced that gallant officer also to go back. His ground was instantly occupied by the enemies with whom he had been engaged in front, and the fight raged close and desperate on the crest of the position, charge succeeded charge, and each side yielded and recovered by turns; yet this astonishing effort of French valour was of little avail." The inability of the Portuguese to withstand the severe shock of the French was the cause of the serious loss to the Fusiliers, who, so long as they could keep the enemy in their front were but, comparatively, little harmed. But with their flank exposed, their position became critical, and it was in the encounters maintained at that time that the "bludgeon work", of which Wellington spoke, occurred. Four times the Royal Fusiliers rushed on the raging host of assailants with the bayonet, and on each of these occasions it was only the fiercest use of that weapon that could give them victory. Everywhere the fighting was hand to hand, and of the most desperate nature. The ground was covered with old stone walls and rocks, so that there could be no regularity in the charges or movements on either side. The troops were engaged and mingled with each other in separate parties. The two halves of the battalion were separated from each other by a narrow ravine; the right half-battalion being commanded by Colonel Blakeney, the left by Major Crowder. In passing from one to the other Captain Tarleton was captured before the very eyes of the regiment. "Some of them," says Sergeant Cooper," seized the Captain of the 9th Company, and endeavoured to pull off his epaulettes; this he resented with a blow of his left fist, however, he was led off a prisoner." It was in one of these encounters that Lieutenant the *Hon.* F. Russell felled two French Grenadiers with the pole of the colour he carried; and it was in recognition of the gallantry with which these combats were maintained that Wellington wrote in his despatch,—"In the course of this contest the gallant 4th Division, which has so frequently been distinguished in this army, surpassed their former good conduct. Every regiment charged with the bayonet; and the 40th, the 7th, 20th, and 23rd four different times. Their officers set them the example, and Major General Ross had two horses shot under him." He finishes his eulogium by declaring that "upon the whole I never saw the troops behave so well. It was impossible to describe the enthusiastic bravery of the 4th Division."

The losses of the battalion.

The losses of the Royal Fusiliers, who were the greatest sufferers, were terrible: they are given below. When the battalion came out of action not a single Captain remained in command of his company.

List of officers who served with the battalion at the first combat of Sauroren, with the casualties:—

Commanding Battalion—Lieut.-Colonel Blakeney.

Major Despard (died of wounds).	Lieut. Loggan (severely wounded).	Lieut. Cameron.
Bt. Major Crowder (slightly wounded).	,, Payne.	,, Haggup.
Capt. Fernie (killed).	,, Hartley.	,, King (slightly wounded).
,, Orr (severely wounded).	,, Hutchison.	,, Hon. F. Russell.
,, Tarleton (missing).	,, Fraser (died of wounds).*	,, Garrett (severely wounded).
,, Wemyss (died of wounds).*	,, Orr.	,, Adjutant Hay.
,, Hamerton (severely wounded).	,, Delgairnes.	,, Qr.-Master Hogan.
Lieut. Anderson.	,, Lorentz.	Surgeon Mahoney.
,, Wilkinson.	,, Nunn (slightly wounded).	Assist.-Surgeon Williams.
,, Johnson.	,, L'Estrange.	,, Fisher.

	Officers.	Sergeants.	Rank and File.
Killed	4	3	40
Wounded	7	11	148

Total 213.

On the 29th all was quiet; both sides spent the day in collecting the wounded and burying the dead. The Royal Fusiliers remained in Villalba for the day. During the remainder of the operations known as the battles of the Pyrenees the critical position of the army and the vigour of the French Commander gave them little rest. On the morning of the 2nd August, the 4th, 7th, and Light Divisions advanced to drive the enemy from the Puerto de Echallar. To participate in the combat of Echallar the 4th Division marched from Yanzi; it was to attack the enemy's front, but the fighting fell on the 7th Division, which arrived sooner than the others. This Division advanced before the others could co-operate, with a regularity and gallantry, which, writes Wellington, "I have seldom seen equalled, and actually drove two Divisions of the enemy from the formidable heights, notwithstanding the resistance offered." In this service, which left "no enemy in the field within this part of the Spanish Frontier," the Fusiliers suffered no loss. In that matter fortune for once protected them, for they were already more than sufficiently shattered, as well by the bullet as by the hardships of war. For nine days the Division had been occupied in almost constant marching and fighting, and was much cut up and exhausted in consequence; it alone lost 104 officers killed and wounded.

---

* Captain Wemyss and Lieutenant Fraser died in the village of Sauroren a few days after the action. A coffin was made of some old furniture, and the Captain was buried in a garden beside the Lieutenant.

After the combat of Echallar the two commanders sank into quietude, the one to re-organize his army, the other to give his troops rest. In the middle of August the 4th Division occupied Lesaca, where, by the repose it had obtained, it soon recovered its health and efficiency. The next great operation in the war which Wellington had to achieve was the capture of San Sebastian, which Graham had once unsuccessfully assaulted. On the 30th August the 4th Division marched to the Crown Mountain to support the Spaniards posted on the heights of San Martino. On the 31st the French crossed the Bidassoa at the ford of Andarra, and attacked the Spaniards on San Martino. A sharp fight ensued, but they were repulsed. "During this action we were on a steep hill, just above the combatants, and could see, at the same time, the battle at our feet and the storming of San Sebastian at a short distance to our left. The night of the 31st was very stormy. I was posted on outlying picket, near the scene of action, on the declivity of the Crown Mountain, where the water ran over us as if we had been in the bed of a torrent."*

Volunteers for the storming of San Sebastian.

While Soult was struggling to win his way across the Bidassoa, and drive the Spaniards from San Marcial, Graham was wresting by assault from his tenacious grasp the fortress of San Sebastian. To the Volunteers called forth by Wellington, "men who could shew other troops how to mount a breach," the Royal Fusiliers had the honour to furnish their quota. The 200 men of the 4th Division were commanded by Major Rose of the 20th Regiment; those furnished by the Royal Fusiliers were as follow :—

	Comp.		Comp.
Lieutenant Joseph Hutchison.		Private John Briggs	No. 5.
Sergeant James Levers	No. 2.	,, Patrick Donovan	No. 6.
Corporal John Styles	No. 9 (severely wounded).†	,, John Gilchrist	No. 7 (severely wounded).
Private Benjamin Walker	No. 1 (severely wounded).	,, Wm. Goldesborough.	No. 7.
,, Phenis Walker	No. 1.	,, Thomas Dutton	No. 8.
,, William Woodward	No. 2.	,, William Neale	No. 9.
,, Abraham Ainsworth.	No. 2.	,, John Maloney	No. 9.
,, Isaac Davis	No. 3 (severely wounded).	,, James Thompson	No. 10 (slightly wounded).
,, James Morris	No. 3 (severely wounded).	,, Richard Bramley	No. 10.
,, Oliver Brown	No. 4.		

* Lieutenant Cameron's *Journal*.

† "In a few minutes ten sergeants and old Styles volunteered as stormers. We assembled at the colours and drew lots. The first sergeant who drew got the prize, went and fell wounded (?). Old Styles also drew a prize; he marched with the stormers next morning and fell severely wounded by a musket ball through the knee joint, in the breach. The old veteran was taken to hospital and told that his leg must be amputated next

This list is not quite complete; one sergeant, one corporal, and twenty privates were called for and furnished by the Battalion. There was on these occasions no lack of candidates for a position in the "ranks of death." Lieutenant Hutchison claimed the command by reason of seniority, and on that ground only obtained it. When let loose the Volunteers "went like a whirlwind" into the breach, but their task was serious, and the effort demanded of them, the fiercest that courage could supply. The French stood manfully to their posts. The most desperate fighting ensued, and it was not until after great loss that the place was won; and then it fell more from an accidental explosion, which destroyed the curtain and opened a way, than the might of the stormers, "although their courage had been pushed to the verge of madness."

On the 3rd September the Battalion returned to the camp near Lesaca; on the 10th it moved thence to Yansi, where it stayed until the 6th October, when it started to take part in the operations connected with the passage of the Bidassoa. On the 7th the Division was posted on the heights of Santa Barbara as the reserve of the Light Division, which carried "La Rhune," in the affair known as the "Second Combat of Vera." The Battalion did not lose any men. After the passage of the Bidassoa the Royal Fusiliers were encamped for nearly a month near the Bridge of Lesaca and heights of Liran, where drafts amounting to nearly 200 non-commissioned officers and men were received from the 2nd Battalion.

In the battle of Nivelle, on the 10th November, the Battalion took part with *Battle of Nivelle.* the 4th Division in the capture of the village of Sarre. The Division moved at daylight, and remained in column about 200 yards off the enemy's redoubt in front of Sarre. It afterwards moved forward to support the 3rd and 7th Divisions in their attack of St. Pee. In these operations, beyond Captain Cotton, who, while acting as Brigade Major, was so severely wounded that he died of his wounds, the Battalion suffered no loss. On the 11th it took up its quarters in a large deserted chateau at Ascain.

---

morning. But when the doctors came Jack said that he and his leg should not be parted. The medical men left him, and his leg mended in a contracted state; and when strong he joined in France. He was a cripple, but did his duty as before, and was present afterwards in the battles of Orthes and Toulouse." Poor old Styles loved drink too well, and had at different times suffered the severest punishments on account of it.—Sergeant Cooper's *Campaigns.*

Battle of the Nive.

On the 8th December the Division was moved up to assist in forcing the passage of the Nive, but for the time it remained in rear of the Light Division. On the 10th the 4th Division was sent up to support the Light Division in repelling an attack successfully made by the French on the Portuguese. The affair was a bloody one, but the Light Division needed no help; it proved more than equal to the effort, and the 4th Division was halted on an open heathy ridge of a hill, about a mile behind the church of Arcangues. From this point Cole sent Ross's Brigade down into the basin, on the left of the 52nd Regiment, to cover Arbonne, he being prepared to march with the remainder of the Division if the French attempted any further movement in force. For that day, however, the fighting was over and the Division was not engaged. The battered condition of the veterans, whose hardy valour had led them victorious from the early struggle at Talavera, up the bloody heights of Albuera, and through the fiery breach of Badajos to the plains of France, was well depicted when the Royal Fusiliers unfurled their colours on these memorable days. Lieutenant Nantes, his arm in a sling from the compound fracture it had received at Salamanca, carried the Regimental Colour; while the King's Colour was borne by Lieutenant Healey, in the only hand that remained to him after the terrible night that gave Badajos to the British, and to the immortal fame of those who won it. In the combat of the 12th the Division was manœuvred to seize such an opportunity as might present itself, but it was not seriously engaged.

The series of combats known as the battle of the Nive terminated the operations of the year. After them the Fusiliers, now under the command of Major Beatty in the absence of Lieutenant-Colonel Blakeney, who was on leave in England for the first time since the Battalion joined the army, quietly kept the field with the Division until the end of the year, when the Battalion was stationed at Arcangues.

1814.

On the 6th January the 3rd and 4th Divisions were ordered to drive the French from La Bastide. The enemy retired upon the Bidouze, and the affair terminated in a slight skirmish. The Allies then resumed their old position on the right of the Nive. The advance of the British commenced on the 13th February; the passage of the Gaves was effected, the 4th and 7th Divisions occupying the Bastide de

Clerence on the right of the Joyeuse. On the 23rd Beresford, who with the 4th and 7th Divisions was in observation on the lower Bidouze, attacked the French in their fortified posts at Hastingues and Oeyergave, on the left of the Gave de Pau, and compelled them to retire within the *tete de pont* at Peyrehorade. These operations terminated in the battle of Orthes on the 27th.

The 4th and 7th Divisions, still under Beresford's command, were stationed on the ridge of St. Boes, standing on the highroad with the colours unfurled and much exposed. At the opening of the action Ross's Brigade, composed of the 7th, 20th, and 23rd Regiments, supported by Portuguese, assailed the village of St. Boes. The Fusiliers were thrown forward as light troops to commence the action and cover the advance of the columns of attack. The village was vigorously held by a strong force of French, and for three hours the assault continued with carnage and wavering fortune, until at length, the Portuguese being broken, Ross's right flank was exposed, was rudely assailed, and he was compelled to retreat. The moment was inauspicious; it seemed to indicate the victory of the French. Ross was wounded, and his regiments severely handled; but succour was at hand, the 52nd Regiment was hurled on the flank of the French, and their violent onset opened the way for the 4th Division to carry St. Boes. Cole then advanced the 4th Division to attack the French right wing, but in the endeavour to debouch from the village he was checked, and was obliged to content himself with keeping possession of St. Boes. The losses of the Fusiliers were rather severe, but they earned for the Regiment the badge "Orthes," which is borne on the colours.

List of Officers who served with the Royal Fusiliers at Orthes, with casualties.

Commanding battalion—Major J. W. Beatty.

Major King.
" S. B. Auchmuty.
Capt. Orr.
" Robison.
" Morgan.
" Devey
" Henry.
" Hackett.
Lieut. Burke (severely wounded).
" Hannam.

Lieut. Healey.
" Daniel.
" Hartley.
" Nantes (severely wounded).
" Wallace.
" Seaton.
" Orr.
" Lorentz (severely wounded).
" Nunn.
" L'Estrange.

Lieut. Cameron (severely wounded).
" Stuart.
Adjutant Hay.
Paymaster Brennan.
Qr.-Master Hogan.
Surgeon Mahoney.
Assist.-Surgeon Sweeney.
" Fisher.

	Officers.	Sergeants.	Drummers.	Rank and File.
Killed	0	1	0	5
Wounded	4	4	0	52

Total, 66.

Lieutenant Cameron carried one of the colours, and was wounded by a musket ball in the leg as the regiment stood on the highroad. After the battle some French partizans got in rear of the English army, and carried off several parties on the way to join. Lieutenant Burke, who had been wounded, was thus captured with some others at a village where they were quartered.

The Royal Fusiliers formed part of the force detached, under Beresford, on the 8th March, towards Bordeaux, which city they entered on the 12th amid the acclamations of the inhabitants, who then declared for the Bourbons. The Division afterwards returned to the army, and on the 10th April took part in the battle of Toulouse.

<small>Battle of Toulouse.</small> The 4th and 6th Divisions, on the right of the Ers, were to cross the river at the bridge of the Croix d'Orade, the 4th Division leading, with which Beresford immediately carried Mont Blanc. He then moved up the Ers in the same order, over most difficult ground, in a direction parallel to the enemy's fortified position, and as soon as he reached the point at which he turned it, he formed line and moved to the attack. He then assailed and carried the heights on the enemy's right, and the redoubt which covered and protected that flank, lodging his troops on the same height with the enemy. These operations were mainly conducive to the success of the battle, but in them the Royal Fusiliers had not taken a very prominent part. "The 4th Division," says Wellington in his despatch, "although exposed on their march to a galling fire, were not so much engaged as the 6th, and did not suffer so much, but they conducted themselves with their usual gallantry." The Royal Fusiliers only lost one man killed and three wounded. Major S. B. Auchmuty, commanding the Light Companies of the Brigade, received the gold medal and the rank of Lieutenant-Colonel. The regiment bears the word "Toulouse" upon its colours.

The battle of Toulouse ended the Peninsula war: that mighty struggle which the British troops had maintained for six years, and out of which they had come with a glory not surpassed even by their immortal ancestors, whose feats of arms are at once the admiration and astonishment of the world. At the close of these campaigns, when the reputation of the Royal Fusiliers was advanced to such a towering height, justice to an individual, whose long and unwearied exertions in their behalf, from the commencement of their services to the termination of the war, requires that his name should be recorded in their history, and set forth as a watchword of strict attention to duty and zealous endeavour for the credit and interest of the corps to which he belonged.

<small>Complimentary mention of Lieutenant and Adjutant Hay.</small>

"In recording the name of Lieutenant and Adjutant James Hay, his commanding officer and brother officers who have served with him, will with pleasure bear testimony to his zeal and constant anxiety for the fulfilment of the arduous duties which his situation required during so many long and fatiguing campaigns, in which on all occasions he manifested the same promptitude and ready wish to second the views of his commanding officer as he had evinced at the commencement. The most severe marches never relaxed his performance of duty, nor was he ever absent but from wounds from his corps. It is impossible to convey here fully an adequate idea of his rigorous exactitude, but those officers who have served with him will always be ready to testify to it; and such exemplary conduct ought to stimulate the soldier and urge him to the performance of his own duty in the above manner; the continuance of which will merit the approbation, esteem, and reward of his commanding officer, and also entitle him to the distinction of a good soldier."

On the 26th April the Battalion moved from cantonments into quarters in Condom, where it remained until the end of May, leading a life of ease and pleasure. "We had no duty to perform and passed our time very comfortably. There were many respectable families in the town and neighbourhood, who were very hospitable, asking us frequently to their evening parties. Our men were well fed, and had plenty of wine cheap; but they behaved well, and were on the best of terms with the inhabitants." In return for the hospitality they had received, on the eve of departure the officers of the Fusilier Brigade determined to give a ball and supper to their friends. All arrangements were elaborately made, a large empty house was converted into a ball room; the arms of the brigade were arranged in stars and different figures on the walls; a supper consisting of "the greatest delicacies of the season" was provided. The night before the ball was to take place, an order came for the Brigade to march to Bordeaux. For a moment hope fled and bitter disappointment attended the cruel mandate. But on second thoughts neither hosts nor guests were inclined to miss the opportunity for such an enjoyable *réunion*. The guests were therefore hastily summoned, and "we danced and entertained our friends till four o'clock in the morning, when the soldiers came to take down their arms. The Brigade marched at five, and we never saw the place nor our friends again." From the 6th to the 11th June the Battalion remained in camp at Bordeaux; it moved thence to Pouilhac, marching through Clerac and Chateau Margaux.

R

Record of the Royal Regiment of Fusiliers.

REGISTER OF STATIONS AND MARCHES OF THE 1st BATTALION IN THE PENINSULA.*

DATE.	FROM	TO	ENG. MILES	CAMP OR QRS.	REMARKS.
1810.—July 31	Disembarked	at Lisbon	...	Q.	51 Sergeants, 22 Drummers, and 905 Men.
Aug. 9	Lisbon	Villa Franca	...	,,	1st Battalion marches to join the Army.
,, 12	Villa Franca	Azambuja	12	,,	
,, 13	Azambuja	Santarem	16	,,	
,, 15	Santarem	Torres Novas	16	,,	
,, 16	Torres Novas	Thomar	16	,,	Reviewed by Gen. Leith.
,, 22	Thomar	Cabacas	18	,,	
,, 23	Cabacas	Espinal	20	,,	
,, 24	Espinal	Foz d'Arouce	16	,,	
,, 25	Foz d'Arouce	Murcella	16	,,	1st Battalion brigaded with the 79th.
,, 26	Murcella	Gallices	20	,,	
,, 27	Gallices	Penache	16	,,	
,, 28	Penache	Villa Cortes	20	,,	
,, 29	Villa Cortes	San Jago Falgosa	16	,,	
,, 30	San Jago Falgosa	Gallices	16	,,	
Sept. 3	Gallices	Ponte Murcella	20	,,	
,, 19	Ponte Murcella	Santa Andrida	12	,,	
,, 20	Santa Andrida	Ponte de Morte	16	C.	Cross the Mondego; retreat to Torres Vedras.
,, 21	Ponte de Morte	Busaco	16	,,	
,, 27	...	...	...	...	Battle of Busaco.
,, 29	Busaco	...	16	,,	Changed position. "Major-Gen. Cole's division will march off at 12 p.m. through the village of Varsus, and close up near to the Mealhada Road, at Lameiro de San Pedro.
,, 30	...	Coimbra	12	,,	
Oct. 1	Coimbra	Pombal	25	,,	
,, 2	Pombal	Condeixa	13	,,	
,, 3	Condeixa	Leiria	25	,,	
,, 4	Leiria	Ponte Carvalles	28	,,	
,, 6	Ponte Carvalles	Rio Mayor	17	,,	
,, 7	Rio Mayor	Brigada	16	...	
,, 8	Brigada	Sombral	14	Q.	
,, 10	Sombral	Caxarias	6	,,	1st Batt. brigaded with 61st and Brunswick Oels.
,, 13	Caxarias	Caxarias	...	...	Affair at Burlada.
Nov. 18	Caxarias	Sombral	6	,,	Commanding Battalion, Col. Blakeney.
,, 19	Sombral	Alenquer	12	,,	
,, 20	Alenquer	Azambuja	16	,,	
,, 21	Azambuja	Azambuja	...	...	Fusilier Brigade formed.
1811.—Jan. 24	Azambuja	Averias da Cima	6	,,	Commanding Battalion, Sir W. Myers, Bart.
Mar. 5	Averias da Cima	Santarem	20	,,	The French retreat from Santarem; the pursuit commenced by the British.
,, 7	Santarem	Galegoa	16	,,	
,, 8	Galegoa	Thomar	16	,,	
,, 10	Thomar	Caxarias	15	C.	
,, 11	Caxarias	Redinha	24	Q.	
,, 12	Redinha	Pombal	18	,,	Affair between Pombal and Redinha.
,, 13	Pombal	Espinal	20	,,	
,, 15	Espinal	A wood	14	C.	The Division sent to join Beresford.
,, 16	A wood	Thomar	28	Q.	
,, 18	Thomar	...	...	...	
,, 19	...	Gouveo	16	C.	Cross the Tagus.
,, 20	Gouveo	Alpalhao	13	,,	
,, 22	Alpalhao	Portalegre	12	Q.	
,, 24	Portalegre	Arronches	16	,,	
,, 25	Arronches	Campo Mayor	13	,,	Quartered in Campo Mayor.
April 1	Campo Mayor	Elvas	12	,,	
,, 4	Elvas	Juramenha	12	C.	
,, 7	Juramenha	Villa Real	6	,,	
,, 8	Villa Real	Olivenca	6	,,	
,, 15	Olivenca	Valverde	6	,,	Olivenca surrendered.

* This Register is copied from the MS. Record of the Services of the Regiment. It seems to have been compiled from contemporary documents, and is a highly valuable evidence of the services of the Battalion in the Peninsula; but there is ample internal evidence to prove that it is neither absolutely correct nor complete. Such, however, as it is, we give it without any attempt at emendation. The remarks alone are added.

Register of Stations and Marches of the 1st Battalion in the Peninsula—Continued.

Date.	From	To	Eng. Miles	Camp or Qrs.	Remarks.
1811.—April 16	Valverde	Almendral	12	Q.	
,, 17	Almendral	Santa Marta	14	,,	
,, 20	Santa Marta	Latorne	12	,,	
,, 21	Latorne	Almendral	2	,,	
,, 24	Almendral	Valverde	12	,,	
,, 25	Valverde	Talavera Real	24	,,	
,, 26	Talavera Real	Merida	24	,,	
May 6	Merida	Talavera Real	24	,,	
,, 7	Talavera Real	Badajos	13	C.	
,, 16	Badajos	Albuera	20	,,	Battle of Albuera; commanding Battalion, Major Nooth.
,, 19	Albuera	...	2	,,	
,, 21	...	Solano	14	,,	
,, 23	Solano	Almendralejo	6	Q.	
June 11	Almendralejo	Solano	6	C.	Second siege of Badajos.
,, 13	Solano	...	10	,,	
,, 14	...	Albuera	7	,,	
,, 16	Albuera	Badajos	19	,,	The Infantry under Lieut.-Gen. Hill, 2nd and 4th Divisions, and Major-Gen. Alten's Brigade of Light Infantry, fell back to the rivulet on the ridge of the pine forest between Valverde and Badajos.
,, 17	Badajos	Elvas	14	,,	
,, 18	...	Elvas	2	Q.	
,, 19	Elvas	Torre de Moro	7	C.	
,, 24	...	...	...	...	2nd Battalion broken up; staff ordered home to recruit; 7 sergeants and 534 men transferred to 1st Battalion.
July 21	Torre de Moro	Elvas	7	,,	
,, 24	Elvas	Alcar Ovissas	16	,,	
,, 25	Alcar Ovissas	Estremos	7	Q.	
,, 31	Estremos	Frontinha	16	C.	
Aug. 1	Frontinha	Craito	20	,,	
,, 2	Craito	Alpalhao	16	,,	
,, 3	Alpalhao	Niza	12	,,	
,, 4	Niza	Sarnadas	12	,,	
,, 5	Sarnadas	Castel Branco	16	Q.	
,, 8	Castel Branco	Escaltao da Cima	16	,,	
,, 9	Escaltao da Cima	Peragoa	12	,,	
,, 11	Peragoa	Aldea Santa Margarita	12	,,	
,, 27	Aldea Santa Margarita	Pedragoa	12	,,	
,, 28	Pedragoa	Parado	9	,,	
Sept. 2	Parado	Aldea de Bispo	12	,,	Commanding Battalion, Col. Blakeney.
,, 18	Aldea de Bispo	Alamanda	12	,,	Draft received of 5 sergeants, 2 drummers, and 327 privates.
,, 20	Alamanda	Castanhina	16	,,	
,, 23	Castanhina	Almadilla	16	,,	
,, 24	Almadilla	Fuente Guinaldo	14	C.	
,, 27	Fuente Guinaldo	Aldea de Ponte	12	C.	Affair at Aldea de Ponte
,, 28	Aldea de Ponte	Albugal	16	Q.	
Oct. 1	Albugal	Villa Mayor	16	,,	
,, 2	Villa Mayor	Alamanda	12	,,	
,, 4	Alamanda	Aldea de Bispo	12	,,	
,, 16	Aldea de Bispo	Villa de Cervo	4	,,	Major-Gen. Bowes commanding Brigade.
Nov. 24	Villa de Cervo	Campillo	20	,,	
,, 29	Campillo	Villa de Cervo	20	,,	
1812.—Jan. 8	Villa de Cervo	Cilices el Chico	12	,,	Siege and capture of Rodrigo.
Feb. 10	Cilices el Chico	Carpio	20	,,	
,, 17	Carpio	Alameda	12	,,	
,, 27	Alameda	Nave d'Aver	12	,,	Start for the Siege of Badajos.
,, 28	Nave d'Aver	Scito	16	,,	
,, 29	Scito	Urguira	10	,,	
Mar. 1	Urguira	Cataneus S. Antonia	16	,,	
,, 2	Cataneus S. Antonia	Teraboa	8	,,	

REGISTER OF STATIONS AND MARCHES OF THE 1ST BATTALION IN THE PENINSULA—*Continued.*

Date.	From	To	Eng. Miles	Camp or Qrs.	Remarks.
1812.—Mar. 3	Teraboa	Alpedrinha	16	,,	
,, 4	Alpedrinha	Alcaines	12	,,	
,, 5	Alcaines	Castel Branco	8	,,	
,, 7	Castel Branco	Carpedoncea	12	,,	
,, 8	Carpedoncea	Niza	28	,,	
,, 9	Niza	Alpalhao	12	,,	
,, 10	Alpalhao	Portalegre	12	,,	
,, 14	Portalegre	Monte Forte	16	,,	
,, 15	Monte Forte	Elvas	16	,,	
,, 16	Elvas	Badajos	20	C.	Third siege of Badajos.
April 6	...	...	...	...	Capture of Badajos.
,, 12	Badajos	Campo Mayor	12	Q.	Commanding Battalion, Captain King. Return to the line of the Agueda.
,, 13	Campo Mayor	Arronches	13	C.	
,, 14	Arronches	Portalegre	20	Q.	
,, 15	Portalegre	Castel d'Vide	16	,,	
,, 16	Castel d'Vide	Povodos Medos	12	,,	
,, 19	Povodos Medos	Sarnados	28	C.	
,, 20	Sarnados	Castel Branco	12	Q.	
,, 21	Castel Branco	Escaillas Baxa	8	,,	
,, 22	Escaillas Baxa	Pedrogoa	16	,,	
,, 23	Pedrogoa	Castaneira	16	,,	
,, 24	Castaneira	Sabugal	12	C.	
,, 26	Sabugal	Richoso	20	Q.	
,, 27	Richoso	Safardao	12	,,	
,, 28	Safardao	Alvarea	16	,,	
,, 29	Alvarea	Marialva	12	,,	
,, 30	Marialva	Sedavim	20	,,	
May 1	Sedavim	Penella	8	,,	
,, 2	Penella	Valenza	4	,,	Quartered in Valenza.
June 5	Valenza	Meda	16	,,	
,, 7	Meda	Povo del Rey	12	,,	
,, 8	Povo del Rey	Canvalhal	12	,,	
,, 9	Canvalhal	Fuentes d'Onor	16	,,	
,, 10	Fuentes d'Onor	Villa de Porca	12	C.	
,, 11	Villa de Porca	Ciudad Rodrigo	8	,,	Rendezvous of the whole Army. Opening of the campaign.
,, 13	Ciudad Rodrigo	Barara	16	,,	
,, 14	Barara	Cabrillas	16	,,	
June 15	Cabrillas	San Munoz	16	C.	
,, 16	San Munoz	Banks of the Tormes	12	,,	Siege of Forts at Salamanca.
,, 22	...	...	...	...	Affair at Villares.
,, 29	Banks of the Tormes	Orbada	16	,,	
July 1	Orbada	Orlegas	16	,,	
,, 2	Orlegas	Medina del Campo	20	,,	
,, 10	Medina del Campo	Rueda	8	,,	Commanding Battalion, Major J. W. Beatty.
,, 18	...	...	...	,,	Affair at Castrejon.
,, 20	Rueda	Salamanca	8	,,	
,, 22	...	...	...	...	Battle of Salamanca.
,, 24	Salamanca	Alba de Tormes	12	,,	
,, 25	Alba de Tormes	La Nava	16	,,	
,, 27	La Nava	Castellana	16	,,	
,, 28	Castellana	San Vincente	12	,,	
,, 29	San Vincente	Hornillos	16	,,	
,, 30	Hornillos	Aldea Mayor	12	,,	
,, 31	Aldea Mayor	...	14	,,	"Two days' march through a pine wood on the banks of the Caya."
Aug. 1	...	...	20	,,	
,, 2	...	Cuellar	16	,,	
,, 8	Cuellar	Segovia	12	,,	
,, 9	Segovia	Guadacima	20	,,	
,, 11	Guadacima	Galapage	16	,,	
,, 12	Galapage	Madrid	12	...	Triumphal entry into Madrid.
,, 17	Madrid	Galapage	12	,,	

REGISTER OF STATIONS AND MARCHES OF THE 1ST BATTALION IN THE PENINSULA—*Continued.*

Date.		From	To	Eng. Miles	Camp or Qrs.	Remarks.
1812.—Sept.	18	Galapage	El Escurial	14	Q.	Quartered in the Palace.
Oct.	6	El Escurial	Maravinda	16	,,	
,,	7	Maravinda	Montoles	12	,,	
,,	8	Montoles	Valdemoro	12	,,	Quartered in Val de Moro
,,	21	Valdemoro	Ciempozuelos	4	,,	
,,	27	Ciempozuelos	Serenada	4	,,	
,,	28	Serenada	Puente Largo	6	C.	
,,	29	Puente Largo	Anavar de Tajo	10	,,	
,,	31	Anavar de Tajo	Madrid	32	,,	
Nov.	1	Madrid	Galapage	12	,,	Retreat to Portugal.
,,	2	Galapage	Guardacima	16	,,	
,,	3	Guardacima	Villa Castaña	18	,,	
,,	4	Villa Castaña	Ballegos	16	,,	
,,	5	Ballegos	Fronteria	16	,,	
,,	6	Fronteria	Peneranda	12	,,	
,,	7	Peneranda	Heights of Tormes	20	,,	
,,	8	Heights of Tormes	Alba de Tormes	8	,,	
,,	10	Alba de Tormes	Arapiles	4	,,	
,,	14	Arapiles	Caravansa d'Ariba	6	,,	
,,	15	Caravansa d'Ariba	...	16	,,	
,,	16	...	...	20	,,	
,,	17	...	...	16	,,	
,,	18	...	...	12	,,	
,,	19	...	Villa de Agua	8	Q.	
,,	27	Villa de Agua	Val de Mula	8	,,	
,,	28	Val de Mula	Aginal	12	,,	
,,	29	Aginal	Santa Fina	16	,,	
Dec.	1	Santa Fina	Barrera	12	,,	
,,	2	Barrera	Sedavim	16	Q.	
,,	3	Sedavim	S. Joa de Pesquera	12	,,	Winter Quarters of the Fusiliers. Drafts received up to 25th December, amounting to 16 sergeants and 311 privates.
1813.—Jan.	7	S. Joa de Pesquera	Arvediza	2	,,	
Feb.	28	Arvediza	S. Joa de Pesquera	2	,,	
Mar.	1	S. Joa de Pesquera	Sedavim	12	,,	
,,	2	Sedavim	Maxagata	8	,,	
,,	3	Maxagata	Castel Melhor	8	,,	
May	18	Castel Melhor	Villa Nova	8	C.	
,,	20	Villa Nova	Torre de Moncorvo	8	,,	
,,	22	Torre de Moncorvo	Legosa	16	,,	
,,	23	Legosa	Villa Velha	16	,,	
,,	24	Villa Velha	Sindim	8	,,	
,,	25	Sindim	Miranda	12	,,	Rendezvous of the Army.
,,	28	Miranda	Brandelonas	8	,,	
,,	29	Brandelonas	Muga	8	,,	
,,	31	Muga	Aluendra	8	,,	
June	1	Aluendra	Mollacilloso	14	,,	
,,	2	Mollacilloso	Villa de Don Diego	12	,,	
,,	4	Villa de Don Diego	Santa Celerea	12	,,	
,,	5	Santa Celerea	Castomonte	9	,,	
,,	6	Castomonte	Ampudia	9	,,	
,,	7	Ampudia	Palencia	12	,,	
,,	8	Palencia	Tamora	12	,,	
,,	9	Tamora	Pina dos Campos	2	,,	
,,	10	Pina dos Campos	Santadillo	10	,,	
,,	11	Santadillo	Villa Sardino	9	,,	
,,	12	Villa Sardino	Santa Marta	12	,,	
,,	14	Santa Marta	Quinta Mayor	20	,,	
,,	15	Quinta Mayor	Ponte de Arena	18	,,	
,,	16	Ponte de Arena	Medina del Pomar	9	,,	
,,	17	Medina del Pomar	Olea	9	,,	
,,	18	Olea	Villa del Monte	20	,,	
,,	19	Villa del Monte	Montevite	8	,,	Affair at Montevite.
,,	21	Montevite	Vittoria	8	,,	Battle of Vittoria. Col. Blakeney commanding.

REGISTER OF STATIONS AND MARCHES OF THE 1ST BATTALION IN THE PENINSULA—*Continued.*

Date.	From	To	Eng. Miles	Camp or Qrs.	Remarks.
1813.—June 22	Vittoria	San Romana	20	C.	Pursuit of the French.
,, 23	San Romana	Escerri	10	,,	
,, 24	Escerri	Toloso	12	,,	
,, 25	Toloso	Pampeluna	6	,,	Blockade of Pampeluna.
,, 26	Pampeluna	Tiebas	10	,,	Advance to intercept Clausel.
,, 27	Tiebas	Taffala	20	,,	
,, 28	Taffala	Galapienza	16	,,	
,, 30	Galapienza	Aybar	4	Q.	Three days' halt in Quarters.
July 2	Aybar	Monte Real	10	,,	
,, 3	Monte Real	...	8	C.	
,, 5	...	Burlada	4	,,	
,, 18	Burlada	Libiri	10	,,	
,, 19	Libiri	Villa Real	6	,,	
,, 23	Villa Real	Espinal	2	Q.	
,, 25	Espinal	Roncesvalles	8	C.	Combat of Roncesvalles.
,, 25	Roncesvalles	Espinal	8	,,	
,, 26	Espinal	Libiri	8	,,	
,, 27	Libiri	Villalba	8	,,	
,, 28	...	...	...	...	Combat of Sauroren.
,, 30	Villalba	...	10	,,	
Aug. 1	...	...	12	,,	
,, 2	...	Echalar	14	,,	Combat of Echalar.
,, 7	Echalar	Lezaca	10	,,	
,, 30	Lezaca	Yrun	10	,,	
Sept. 3	Yrun	Lezaca	10	,,	
,, 10	Lezaca	Yansi	6	,,	
Oct. 6	Yansi	Vera	6	,,	
,, 13	Change of	Encampment	4	,,	Drafts received this year, amounting to 9 sergeants and 170 privates.
Nov. 10	Vera	...	6	,,	Battle of the Nivelle.
,, 11	...	Wood of St Pé	12	,,	
,, 17	Wood of St. Pé	Sarre	12	Q.	
,, 19	Sarre	Olette	12	,,	Draft received of 1 sergeant and 15 men.
1814.—Dec. 8	Olette	Wood of St. Pé	24	C.	
,, 9	Change of	Position	4	,,	Battle of the Nive, 9th to 13th December.
,, 13	Wood of St. Pé	Villa Franque	10	,,	
,, 14	Villa Franque	Ustaritz	6	,,	
,, 15	Ustaritz	Arcangues	6	Q.	
Jan. 3	Arcangues	...	4	C.	
,, 4	...	Ustaritz	6	,,	
,, 5	Ustaritz	...	8	,,	
,, 6	...	...	6	,,	
,, 7	...	Heraritz	16	Q.	
Feb. 15	Heraritz	...	9	C.	
,, 16	...	Castel Cherauner	9	,,	
,, 17	Castel Cherauner	Bedashe	6	,,	
,, 24	Bedashe	...	12	,,	
,, 25	...	...	12	,,	
,, 26	...	...	12	,,	
,, 27	...	Orthes	16	,,	Battle of Orthes.
,, 28	Orthes	...	24	,,	
Mar. 1	...	...	16	,,	
,, 2	...	Grenade	9	Q.	
,, 8	Grenade	Mont de Marsan	16	,,	
,, 9	Mont de Marsan	Roquefort	14	C.	Expedition to Bordeaux.
,, 10	Roquefort	Captieux	16	Q.	
,, 11	Captieux	Bazas	20	,,	
,, 12	Bazas	Langon	12	,,	
,, 15	Langon	Bazas	12	,,	
,, 16	Bazas	Captieux	16	C.	
Mar. 17	Captieux	Roquefort	20	C.	
,, 18	Roquefort	La Viqnan	24	,,	
,, 19	La Viqnan	Tasco	24	...	
,, 20	Tasco	Rebatais	26	...	

REGISTER OF STATIONS AND MARCHES OF THE 1ST BATTALION IN THE PENINSULA—*Continued*.

Date.	From	To	Eng. Miles	Camp or Qrs.	Remarks.
1814.—May 21	Rebatais	Gourdozan	20	C.	
,, 22	Gourdozan	Biero	14	,,	
,, 23	Biero	Lunaze	24	...	
,, 24	Lunaze	Lombaz	16	Q.	
,, 25	Lombaz	Sant Lees	14	C.	
,, 26	Sant Lees	...	12	,,	
,, 27	...	Brax	16	,,	
,, 28	Brax	St. Martin	14	Q.	
April 3	St. Martin	St. Jorny	24	,,	
,, 7	St. Jorny	Bruguienes	3	,,	
,, 8	Bruguienes	St. Genies	8	,,	
,, 10	St. Genies	Toulouse	10	C.	Battle of Toulouse.
,, 12	Toulouse	Bastide de Beaufres	16	,,	
,, 17	Bastide de Beaufres	St. Felix	16	,,	
,, 20	St. Felix	Lanta	20	,,	
,, 21	Lanta	St. Martin	16	Q.	
,, 22	St. Martin	Lisle Jourdain	20	,,	
,, 23	Lisle Jourdain	...	16	C.	
,, 24	...	Auch	12	,,	
,, 25	Auch	...	16	,,	
,, 26	...	Condom	14	Q.	
May 31	Condom	Nerac	12	,,	Draft received amounting to 2 sergeants and 59 men.
June 1	Nerac	Castel Jaloux	20	C.	
,, 6	...	Bordeaux.			
,, 12	...	Pouilhac.			
,, 14	...	Embarked.			
,, 18	Sailed for England	...	...	...	Strength of the Regiment—56 sergeants, 18 drummers, and 812 men.

In April the Duc de Berri, who had been staying in Jersey, was accompanied thence to France by a guard of honour consisting of 200 men selected from the 2nd Battalion under the command of Lieutenant-Colonel Nooth. "It is highly flattering," says a contemporary, "to that excellent regiment that General Don should have paid it the compliment of assigning this memorable duty to a detachment from it." *Guard of Honour to the Duc de Berri.*

On the 12th June the battalion moved to Pouilhac for embarkation. It was under orders for Ireland, to be disembarked at Cork; the only regiments to be sent to England being the Guards, the 43rd, and 52nd Regiments. This arrangement was, however, soon altered, at the instance of Earl Bathurst, Secretary of State for War, who ordered that, in addition to these regiments, the Royal Fusiliers, the Royal Welsh Fusiliers, and the 51st Regiment should be sent to Plymouth. The Royal Fusiliers embarked at Pouilhac on the 14th June on board several small transport brigs, which conveyed the Battalion down the Garonne to H.M.S. "Clarence" in Verdun Roads. In this ship, which received the whole Battalion, *Embark at Pouilhac.*

the Fusiliers sailed for England on the 18th June, and arrived at Plymouth on the 28th; where, after an absence of seven eventful and exciting years from their native country, to which they had given both the glory and advantages of constant victory, they were greeted with the acclamations of their admiring countrymen, who assembled in crowds to testify their welcome to the gallant troops who had won such imperishable honour. Indeed so great was the enthusiasm that, if we may literally accept the statement of an eye-witness, scraps of the colours "were craved for with outstretched hands, to be honoured with a place in the fair bosoms of the ladies of Devonshire."

Joins the 2nd Batt. at Portsmouth.

From Plymouth the Battalion was removed to Totness in Devonshire, where it remained until the 6th July. On that and the two following days it removed to Portsmouth in three Divisions, and, on the 18th, 19th, and 20th, joined the 2nd Battalion, which had been brought from Jersey, where it had been stationed since November, 1811. The two Battalions remained in garrison in Portsmouth until the 3rd October, when the 1st Battalion received an order from the War Office to immediately transfer all absentees to the 2nd Battalion, and to complete its establishment from that Battalion up to 1000 rank and file, preparatory to embarkation for

Ordered to America.

service in America. Next day the 1st, 2nd, 3rd and 4th Companies, and the staff under Lieutenant-Colonel Blakeney embarked on board the "Ceylon" transport, and on the 5th, the remainder of the Battalion, on board the transports "Lady Banks," "Isabella," and "Fame." These ships sailed on the 6th, and anchored on the 8th, in Plymouth Sound, where the Fusiliers were joined by the 43rd Light Infantry, the whole being under the command of Major-General Lambert. Bad weather prevented the immediate departure of the fleet, which only weighed anchor and stood out to sea on the 26th. After a six weeks' voyage the first sight of land was obtained between the islands of Martinique and Dominico; the ships then steered northwards, making the coast of Louisiana on the 31st December.

1815.

Reach Cat Island, mouth of the Mississippi.

On the morning of the 1st January the fleet anchored near Cat Island at the mouth of the Mississippi. The object of the expedition was to reinforce the troops then engaged in operations against New Orleans. As the ships could not reach that place, on the morning of the 2nd the troops were transferred to boats, to be rowed eighty miles up the river for disembarkation. During the progress, on the 4th, the Fusiliers lost a sergeant and sixteen men drowned by the swamping of a boat. With this exception the Battalion reached the camp without any noticeable incident. It disembarked on the left bank of the river on the 5th and 6th, and at once marched to join the army in position. On the 7th January the 1st Brigade, consisting of the Royal Fusiliers and the 43rd Light Infantry (the two corps mustering under arms upwards of 1700 bayonets) were reviewed within cannon shot of the enemy. A more foolish measure was possibly never perpetrated, for beside giving extra time to the Americans to complete their works, it exposed the increased strength of the British. But with the infatuation that marked the operations from first to last the greatest display of pomp was resorted to. The music played, the sun shone brilliantly, and every member of the two regiments was in the highest spirits at the chance of being led forward to attack and carry, as they did not doubt, the place that had for some time baffled even their old Peninsula comrades.

The American position was defended by a line of entrenchments extending from the river to an impenetrable wood. It was skilfully chosen and well manned, but as a fortification it deserves little notice. In this line the principal work was a battery near the river, called the "Crescent" battery. Opposite it the British had thrown up a redoubt whence the attack of the Crescent battery was to be made. The attack was ordered for the 8th. The light companies of the Royal Fusiliers and 93rd Regiment and a Company of the 43rd were to storm the battery, the battalion companies of the Fusiliers and the remainder of the 43rd forming the reserve. The signal for commencing the attack was a rocket, but no sooner was the signal given than the assault may be said to have failed, for instead of the attack being made with order consistent with pre-arrangement, the most lamentable confusion everywhere prevailed, and a series of feeble and disjointed but bloody onsets measured the strength of the British. In the first place the ladders were not properly placed; in the next government and direction, responsibility and capacity, seemed to have deserted the assailants. In one word, it looked, as an eye-witness has stated, "as if folly stalked abroad in the English camp." Officers were running about to seek orders, some of the troops were fighting their way across the lines, certain of destruction for they were without support, and lost to view in the dense mist which surrounded everything; others were standing for orders to push on, but these orders never came.

<small>Attack of the Crescent Battery.</small> With a gallant rush the light companies assailed the Crescent battery, but without the means of passing the ditch and scaling the parapet, their attack was greatly weakened. Yet they pressed on, and at last entered the place through an embrasure the moment after the gun had been fired. Such progress, additionally impeded by the deadly rifles of scores of Kentucky riflemen, was costly and precious. Yet the assailants carried the battery, but they could not hold it, for they, too, were without support, and out of the three companies of 240 men nearly 180 were down, killed, or wounded. The only three officers who escaped from this assault not seriously wounded were Lieut. Hutchison of the Royal Fusiliers, who had three bullets through his cap; Lieut. Lorentz of the same regiment, who was slightly wounded and had the back of his white shoulder belt cut in two by a musket ball; and Lieut. Steele of the 43rd, who was the only one who escaped without a scar or mark of any kind. These were unfortunately not the only casualties in this dreadful affair, at the other points of attack things were worse in every respect. "I hastened to the redoubt," says an artillery-officer, "which had been appointed as a place of rendezvous and *point d'appui*, during the action, and communicated to Col. Dickson the confirmation of our complete repulse on the right. Scarcely had this painful truth been told when an officer and some men of the 7th Fusiliers entered the <small>Death of Major King</small> redoubt bearing in their arms Major King, whom they fondly believed might still live. No sooner had they placed their burden on the earth than it was apparent that all hope had fled; poor King was dead, and his sorrowing friends gave me the painful intelligence that the gallant Pakenham was also numbered with the slain." *

The attack had failed, although gallantry enough had been expended in it to render it the most brilliant success. But it was not gallantry so much as combined efforts that were wanted. When the mist cleared away " we caught a view of the 7th and 43rd Regiments in echelon on our right, near the wood, the Royal Fusiliers being within about 300 yards of the enemy's lines, and the 43rd deploying into line 200 yards in echelon, behind the Fusiliers. These two regiments were every

* Benson Hill's *Recollections*, vol. 2, p. 12.

now and then enveloped by the clouds of smoke that hung over their heads and floated on their flanks, for the echo from the cannonade and musketry was so tremendous in the forest that the vibration seemed as if the earth was cracking and tumbling to pieces, or as if the heavens were rent asunder by the most terrific peals of thunder that ever rumbled; it was the most awful and the grandest mixture of sounds to be conceived, the woods seemed to crack to an interminable distance. Each cannon report was answered one hundred-fold, and produced an intermingled roar, surpassing strange." Such a scene as this need not be dwelt upon. While Lieut. Hutchison and the light company with their gallant comrades had carried the Crescent battery, which they had to relinquish for want of support, the regiment, though kept standing within grape-shot range, was compelled to remain idle spectators of the dreadful events. Thus were two of the most formidable of the Peninsula regiments kept, as one of the combatants remarks, "like two 74's becalmed," while their help was grievously needed. Of the animus of the regiments we may quote other testimony. "While formed within grape range we were lost in amazement at not being led on to the attack, being kept as quiet spectators of the onslaught. Lieut. Augustus D'Este, of the Royal Fusiliers, was aide-de-camp to General Lambert."*

Thus were the British defeated, and badly defeated before New Orleans; and their defeat arose from the simple circumstance that the officers commanding were unequal to their task. The matter need no longer be glossed over to exonerate the British soldiers and company officers, for they did their work well; the failure was with their superiors, as it has too often been. The Fusiliers had to mourn the loss of their revered colonel, Pakenham, and to add to the depth of their mourning, they had lost him, not in victory, but in disaster. The total loss of the battalion on this occasion was Major King and Capt. Henry, 1 sergeant and 23 men killed; Capt. Page, Lieuts. Mullins and Higgins severely, Lieut. Lorentz slightly, 6 sergeants and 62 men wounded.

After this repulse the British Commander determined to withdraw his troops. With his retreat the Americans did not interfere. Their experience had taught them that in the open field great odds were of no advantage against the veteran

The British troops withdrawn.

* Capt. Cooke's *Narrative*, p. 239.

troops whom good fortune had allowed them to humiliate; and that in close fight they were certain to be worsted. They had not forgotten how Hallen's company of Riflemen had dealt with them, and with a military knowledge that does them infinite credit, having accomplished their end in stopping the advance of the British, they preferred to leave them to withdraw at their leisure. By the 19th January the British were finally withdrawn from the Delta of the Mississippi, and having embarked, were landed on Isle Dauphin, north of Mobile Bay, West Florida, on the 9th Feb. Fort Bowyer commanding the entrance to Mobile Bay was then captured and garrisoned by two companies of Fusiliers. This step was preliminary to an attack on Mobile, but further operations were stopped by the Treaty of Peace, which was signed in Paris.

They land on Isle Dauphin.

The evacuation of the American territory commenced on the 20th February, when two companies of the Fusiliers, under the command of Lieut.-Col. Beatty, were embarked on board of H.M.S. "Norge" and proceeded to England. It was not until the 8th April that the remainder of the battalion embarked, the head quarters and four companies on board H.M.S. "Diomede," the rest under the command of Capt. Mullins on board the "Ceylon" transport. On that day the fleet sailed for the Havanna, where they were to complete their provisions for crossing the Atlantic. They arrived at the Havanna on the 21st, but from some neglect the "Ceylon" could not make the harbour, she was obliged to bear up and proceed through the Gulf of Florida, and eventually to Halifax, Nova Scotia, which she indeed reached in safety, but with her people suffering so much from the want of fresh supplies, that most of the soldiers were affected with scurvy. The "Diomede" anchored at Spithead on the 31st May, next day she sailed for the Downs, and anchored off Deal, where the Fusiliers disembarked and were quartered in Deal Barracks until the 16th June, when they marched to Ramsgate, and there embarked on board small craft to reinforce the army in the Netherlands. The Fusiliers landed at Ostend on the 18th, the very day the French were finally defeated at Waterloo, and proceeded in boats up the canal to Bruges. Next day they proceeded to Ghent, and were stationed there until the 24th, when they started in charge of treasure to join the army on march to Paris. Their route lay through Grammont, Ath, Bavay, Le Cateau, Chapelette, Peronne, Brachi, Tilloy, Gournay,

Return to England.

Sent to Ostend.

Pont St. Maxence, La Chapelle; on the 6th July they joined the army at St. Denis.

The Fusiliers then proceeded with the rest of the army to Paris; the 2nd, 3rd, 4th, and 7th companies from the "Ceylon," joined on the 27th July, during the encampment in Paris. The two companies from the "Norge" joined head quarters on the 7th September.

From Paris the battalion marched to Passy, crossing the Seine at the bridge of Neuilly, and passing through the town and forest of St. Germaine, the men were there quartered in temporary barracks, the officers being quartered on the inhabitants. On the 30th November the general order was issued detailing the troops to remain in France as the army of occupation, when the 1st Battalion Royal Fusiliers, the Royal Welsh Fusiliers, and the 1st Battalion 43rd Light Infantry were formed into the Seventh Brigade of Infantry, under the command of Major-General Sir James Kempt, and ordered to Paris. On the 10th the battalion returned to Paris and occupied the *abattoir du Route*, which was fitted up as a barrack. [Enter Paris.]

With the prospects of a lasting peace that the completeness of the victory at Waterloo offered, Great Britain determined to reduce her military establishment; and, in consequence, the 2nd Battalion of the Royal Fusiliers was one of the battalions ordered to be disbanded. The order was to be carried into effect on the 24th December. The officers were retained on full pay for absorption, the best men were to be transferred to the 1st Battalion, and the remainder discharged. A recruiting company was, however, added to the establishment of the 1st Battalion; it consisted of one captain, two lieutenants, eight sergeants, and eight corporals. On the 2nd December the 2nd Battalion transferred its men fit for service to the 1st, and was disbanded at Dover. [2nd Batt. disbanded at Dover.]

1816.

On the 16th January the Brigade evacuated Paris; it marched to Louvres (Head Quarters) and the following villages:—Chenneriere, Roissy, Gousainville, and Thilloy. From these stations it proceeded to various cantonments until the 31st July, when it occupied the following villages in the Pas de Calais:—Ayette, Douchy, Achiel le Petit, Courcelles, Achiel le Grand, Brisancourt, Bievilliers, [Leaves Paris for Louvres.]

Behagnies, Grevilliers, Sapignies, Favereuil, Ervilliers, Gomiecourt, Briqnoy, with the Head Quarters at Amblains-Ville.

<small>Band Contest at Arras.</small>

The band of the regiment, with five others, viz., the bands of the Royal Welsh Fusiliers, the 43rd Light Infantry, and the three Danish Regiments, was invited to Arras on the 25th August, the anniversary of St. Louis, by the prefect of the department, the mayor and corporation of the city, to compete for a gold medal. The judges declared in favour of the Fusiliers, and Mr. Ledsam, the bandmaster, was invested in due form with the trophy of the band's victory.

On the 27th September the Regiment left its cantonments, and marched to camp at Bourlon, near Cambrai. The following letter was here received and put into regimental orders :—

"Horse Guards, 28th September, 1816.

<small>Badges for Martinique and Albuera granted.</small>

"SIR,—I have the honour to acquaint you that His Royal Highness the Prince Regent has been pleased, in the name and on behalf of His Majesty, to approve of permission being granted to the 7th or Royal Fusiliers Regiment of Foot to wear on its colours and appointments, in addition to any other badges or devices which may have been heretofore granted to the Regiment, the words 'MARTINIQUE' and 'ALBUERA,' in consideration of the distinguished services of that Corps in the attack and reduction of Martinique in the month of February, 1809, and in the battle of Albuera on the 16th May, 1811.

"I have the honour to be, Sir,
"Your most obedient, humble Servant,
"R. DARLING, D.A.G.

"To Colonel Sir Edward Blakeney, K.C.B.,
"or Officer commanding Royal Fusiliers, France."

On the 5th October a detachment joined from England under Lieutenant Creser. On the 18th the Regiment marched from its camp to the glacis of Cambrai, where it remained for the night with the 43rd Light Infantry. Next day it continued its march on the highroad to Valenciennes with the other part of the division, consisting of the Brigade of Guards, and Major-General Lambert's Brigade, the 27th, 40th, and 1st Battalion of Rifles; near Denain the division turned off the main road and encamped at L'Ourche, about two miles from the 2nd and 3rd Divisions. On the 22nd October the Army of Occupation, consisting of the British, Saxon, and Danish <small>Reviewed at Denain.</small> Contingents was reviewed by the Dukes of Kent and Cambridge, the manœuvres, which represented a sham battle on the plains of Denain, being directed by the Duke of Wellington in person. After this review the Regiment returned to its former cantonments.

1817.

On the 2nd January an order from the Horse Guards was received for discontinuing the recruiting company from the 25th December, 1816. This reduction was followed on the 31st by another order, dated 21st of the same month, for placing the ten junior lieutenants on half-pay.

Establishment reduced.

On the 5th February, an order was received for sending one captain, two lieutenants, and five sergeants to Valenciennes to be instructed in a sword exercise approved by H.R.H. the Commander-in-Chief. On the 21st February an order was received, dated 5th February, reducing the establishment to 45 sergeants, 22 drummers, 40 corporals, and 760 privates, from the 25th December, 1816, in consequence of which, 14 sergeants, 13 corporals, 1 drummer, being supernumerary to the establishment, were sent to England.

On the 13th April the regiment marched from cantonments near Bapaume to Cambrai, *en route* to Valenciennes, where it arrived on the following day with the 23rd and 43rd, the other two regiments of the Brigade, which with the 2nd Brigade (57th and 91st Regiments), composed the garrison of the place.

The Regiment was present at a review, on the 6th September, of the British and Danish Contingents, by the King of Prussia, near the village of Prouvy. On the 10th the Regiment marched to Cambrai and encamped on the glacis, where the whole of the Infantry comprising the 1st Division, under Lieutenant-General Sir Lowry Cole, G.C.B., was assembled. The Regiment was present at the divisional review, by Lieutenant-General Lord Hill, near Cambrai, and also at Douchy, when the Duke of Wellington reviewed the British, Saxon, and Danish Contingents. After this review the Fusiliers returned to Valenciennes.

Reviewed by the King of Prussia.

1818.

The spring and summer of this year were spent at Valenciennes, relieved from the usual tedium only by a review of the troops, near Valenciennes, by the Grand Duke Michael of Russia. On the 17th August the Regiment moved from Valenciennes to Cambrai. On the 12th October the establishment was again reduced, and on the 26th the Regiment commenced its march for Calais, where it arrived on the 31st,

Moves from Valenciennes; arrives at Dover.

and embarked the following day for Dover. It landed at Dover on the 2nd November, and occupied the Castle barracks, where the regimental depôt joined next day. The departure of the Brigade was thus referred to in Brigade Orders:—

"Calais, 1st November, 1818.

"It having been a source of great satisfaction to Major-General Sir James Kempt to be placed during the last three years in command of a brigade composed of such distinguished regiments as the Fusiliers, the Royal Welsh Fusiliers, and the 43rd Light Infantry, it is with feelings of great regret that he parts from them on the breaking up of this army. During that long period he has had everything to commend, but nothing to blame. In all his reports he has had occasion to speak in terms of the highest praise of the excellent discipline that prevails in these regiments; of the spirit with which both officers and men are animated; of the great ability displayed by Colonel Sir Edward Blakeney, Lieutenant-Colonel Patrickson, and Lieutenant-Colonel Pearson in their respective commands; and, if the brigade had been called into active service, Sir James Kempt has a perfect conviction that the regiments composing it would have been as exemplary for heroism and gallantry in the field as they have been for regularity and good conduct in quarters, each nobly supporting the fame and reputation they had so justly acquired in the Peninsula. For many of the officers Sir James Kempt has a personal regard, and he can never cease to take a deep interest in their welfare.

"(Signed)   C. YORKE, *Brigade Major.*"

Embarks for Ireland.

The stay of the Regiment in Dover was short; it marched thence to Deal on the 13th November, and embarked for Ireland on board the "Albury" and "Wyton" transports, sailing on the 18th and arriving in the Cove of Cork on the 22nd. It disembarked in two divisions and marched to Fermoy on the 26th and 27th, thence on the 1st and 2nd December for Dublin, arriving there on the 9th and 10th. The first five Companies occupied the Royal Barracks; the remainder Richmond Barracks, until the 18th December, when seven companies were sent to George Street Barracks.

1819.

On the 21st January the Regiment was inspected by His Excellency, the Commander of the Forces, General Sir George Beckwith, G.C.B. On the 17th May the whole Regiment took up quarters in the Royal Barracks. A recruiting party was detached on the 1st November to Glasgow. While in the Royal Barracks the Regiment received the following letter from the Adjutant-General of the Forces:—

"Horse Guards, 2nd December, 1819.

Peninsula Badges granted.

"SIR,—I have the honour to acquaint you that His Royal Highness the Prince Regent, in the name and on behalf of His Majesty, has been pleased to approve of the Royal Fusiliers being permitted to wear on its colours and appointments, in addition to any other badges and appointments which may heretofore have been granted to the regiment, the words 'TALAVERA,' 'BADAJOS,' 'SALAMANCA,' 'VITTORIA,' 'PYRENEES,' 'ORTHES,' and 'TOULOUSE,' in commemoration of the distinguished gallantry displayed by the regiment in those actions."

1820.

The Regiment remained in Dublin, where it was inspected by Sir Colquhoun Grant, until August, on the 1st, 2nd, and 3rd of which it marched for Londonderry, arriving there and at neighbouring cantonments on the 10th, 11th, and 12th, where it was inspected by Lieutenant-General Sir David Baird, and again by Major-General Sir Sidney Beckwith, obtaining the approbation of these officers. The recruiting party still continued at Glasgow, another having been sent to Leeds. In November the Regiment embarked at Belfast for Scotland, and landing at Port Patrick, marched from thence to Edinburgh and Glasgow.

Embarks for Scotland.

1821.

At Edinburgh, on the 1st June, the Regiment received a complete set of new arms from the ordnance stores at the Castle. Towards the end of June it was somewhat suddenly ordered to leave Edinburgh for the North of England, when the following order was issued:—

"Adjutant-General's Office, Edinburgh, June 26th, 1821.

"G. O.—In consequence of orders having been received for the march of the Royal Fusiliers to England, Major-General Sir Thomas Bradford cannot permit that distinguished corps to depart from under his command without expressing the warmest approbation of their uniform good conduct and regularity in quarters, as well as high state of discipline in the field, and excellent interior economy and good order. The Major-General requests Colonel Sir Edward Blakeney to convey these his sentiments to the officers, non-commissioned officers, and soldiers of the Royal Fusiliers."

Complimented on its behaviour in quarters.

Leaving Scotland in July the Regiment proceeded to Newcastle-upon-Tyne, head quarters and five companies; Carlisle, two companies under Brevet Lieutenant-Colonel Wylly; Tynemouth, two companies under Captain Robison; and Sunderland, one company under Captain Ford; and in August the establishment was reduced to 650 officers and men.

1822.

On the 29th April the Regiment marched from Newcastle and outquarters to Chatham and Sheerness (four companies under the command of Lieut.-Col. Auchmuty), arriving there on the 22nd May. The three companies at Chatham marched thence to Windsor on the 26th July, the four companies at Sheerness having preceded them at the same station, and thence to Brighton. By the end of July the whole Regiment had assembled at Brighton, where it had the honour of performing the King's duty during the residence of King George IV. at the Pavilion.

<small>Stationed at Brighton.</small>

1823.

In May the Regiment returned from Brighton to Windsor, and was quartered in Windsor Barracks, except two companies stationed, one at Brighton, and the other at Reading. On the 20th October a route was received for Portsmouth, for immediate embarkation for Gibraltar; the troops started, but next day the order was countermanded, and they returned to their former quarters. In December the Regiment left Windsor for Chatham, sending detachments to Landguard Fort, Harwich, and Reading.

1824.

In consequence of the Act for raising six additional regiments of infantry, several applications were made to Sir Edward Blakeney for non-commissioned officers and privates to be transferred to, and promoted in, these new corps; the following were recommended:—

<small>Non-commissioned officers promoted to new regiments.</small>

> To 94th Regiment, Colour-Sergeant John Vagg, as Quarter-Master Sergeant.
> ,,   Sergeant Joseph Rodgers, as Sergeant.
> ,,   ,, John Stroud, ,,
> ,,   Corporal George Cliffe, ,,
> To 96th Regiment, Colour-Sergeant Molloy, as Sergeant Major.
> To 97th Regiment, Lance-Sergeant Richard M'Graith, as Sergeant.
> ,,   Lance-Corporal John Thomas, ,,
> To 98th Regiment, Sergeant Thomas Rorke, as Colour-Sergeant.
> ,,   Corporal John Henderson, as Sergeant.
> ,,   Private Edward Jones, ,,
> To 99th Regiment, Colour-Sergeant Thomas Berry, as Sergeant-Major.
> ,,   Sergeant Edward Lamb, as Colour-Sergeant.
> ,,   Corporal William Leigh, as Sergeant.
> ,,   Private Hugh Crozier, ,,
> ,,   ,, William Sexton, ,,
> ,,   ,, Thomas Kidman, ,,
> ,,   ,, John Groom, ,,

In July the companies at Landguard Fort and Harwich returned to head quarters. On the 9th September the troops in garrison were reviewed by H.R.H.

the Duke of Clarence, when the brigade was highly complimented. Next day the Regiment was reviewed by H.R.H. the Duke and the Adjutant-General, after which the following garrison order was issued:—

"Chatham, 11th September, 1824.

"Garrison Order.—The Commandant has received the commands of H.R.H. the Duke of Clarence to express to the Queen's Royals, Royal Fusiliers, and Royal Marines, whom he has reviewed, the satisfaction he has received in witnessing the progress they have made in the new evolutions, which could only have been accomplished in so short a time by the ability and attention of their officers, and the soldierlike conduct of the men."

On the 29th November the Regiment commenced its march from Chatham to Manchester, which it reached on the 16th December. *Proceeds to Manchester.*

1825.

On the 31st March an order was received in Manchester for the augmentation of the Regiment, as specified below:— *Establishment increased*

Augmented	Field Officers.	Captains.	Lieutenants.	Staff.	Sergeants.	Corporals.	Drummers.	Privates.	Total.
From	4	8	16	5	30	24	12	551	650
To	4	10	20	5	42	36	14	704	835

Recruiting parties were immediately sent to the different villages about this populous city, and were very successful.

In April detachments were sent to Chester and Liverpool. On the 15th May the Regiment was ordered to march to Portsmouth. During the march the route was changed to Winchester, for the purpose of assembling the Regiment for a few days. While at Winchester, Col. Sir Edw. Blakeney, having been promoted to the rank of major-general, issued the following address to the Regiment:— *Sir E. Blakeney promoted.*

"The period having arrived when Sir Edward Blakeney, by his promotion, is obliged to relinquish the command of the Royal Fusiliers, a corps in which he has had the honour and happiness to serve for so many years, he cannot do so without expressing to his gallant companions the high sense he entertains of their uniform good conduct whilst under his command; and the attention they have at all times paid to the duties which the service required, for which he begs the officers, non-commissioned officers, and privates, to accept his best thanks.

"In quitting a regiment whose welfare and prosperity he has so much at heart, he assures them that no time can efface or circumstances diminish the unbounded attachment he feels towards them; and his best and gallant friends will ever possess his warmest wishes for a long continuance of honour, prosperity, and happiness.

"(Signed)
"E. BLAKENEY, Maj. Gen."

This address was thus answered:—

"SIR,

The Regiment's reply.

"We have to advert to a period, which on our own account we have anticipated with feelings of deep regret, for the loss we are about to sustain; but, Sir, on yours with sincere pleasure, as affording to you an opportunity, in a more elevated rank, of displaying fully those qualities from which we have derived so much benefit.

"Through a long series of years you have been at our head, both in the field and in quarters. The gallantry and judgment evinced in the former were a certain guarantee for the subsequent kind, steady, and considerate disposition which manifested itself in the latter—a system combining lenity with authority, added to a persevering and constant attention to the welfare and interest of those under your command, and the good of the service, the success attending which has been unanimity and confidence; and if we refrain from expatiating more fully on the sense we entertain of the many obligations we have experienced, let it be attributed not to a want of feeling as to their importance, but to a consciousness of our own inadequacy to express on this occasion the heartfelt impression all have of the many tests of your increasing care and fervent solicitude for our well-being.

"With the warmest feelings of respect and esteem, we beg, Sir, to offer the most affectionate wishes of our hearts for your future welfare, and the acceptance of a piece of plate as a very faint testimony of our united regard.

"By request of the officers of the corps,
"(Signed)
"J. H. MAIR,
"Major Royal Fusiliers."

While the regiment was thus assembled at Winchester, previous to embarking for the Ionian Islands, it was inspected by its old Commanding Officer, Major-Gen. Sir Edward Blakeney, K.C.B. Sir Edward was succeeded in the command by Lord Frederick Fitzclarence.

Adoption of the Depôt Company system.

The Royal Fusiliers were the first regiment to adopt the six service and four depôt company system. The headquarters with the service companies, under Major Mair, marched to Gosport, and embarked on board the transports, "Princess Royal" (head quarters), "Borodino," and "Diadem." The depôt companies under Major Disney remained at Winchester.

The headquarters' ship and the "Diadem" touched at Gibraltar, where the Fusiliers were received in the kindest manner by their old comrades in arms, the Royal Welsh and the 43rd Light Infantry, and sailed thence to Corfu, which they reached on the 22nd July. The troops were disembarked the following day and quartered in the Citadel Barracks. The "Borodino" did not arrive till the 19th

August. On arrival at Corfu the regiment sent a detachment to Vido, and the customary working parties to the public works and fortifications.

1826.

In March Quarter-Master Simpson was appointed Ensign and Adjutant of the 95th Regiment, stationed at Malta; Quarter-Master Sergeant Ledsam succeeding him in the regiment.

The following non-commissioned officers were transferred to the 95th Regiment. *Non-commissioned officers promoted in the 95th Regiment.*

Colour-Sergeant Anthony Ellis as Sergeant-Major.
Sergeant Edward Keith as Quarter-Master Sergeant.
Corporal Timothy Kilfoyle as Sergeant.

On the 3rd May Lieut.-Col. Fitzclarence joined from England, and Major Mair in handing over the command stated in orders that, "it is a source of no slight gratification and pride at this moment to be enabled to state that it has not been found necessary since in this command to hold a single regimental court-martial, or inflict corporal punishment on a soldier of the Fusiliers."

On the 26th November the regiment was inspected by Major-Gen. the Hon. F. C. Ponsonby, who expressed his entire approbation of the soldier-like and steady conduct of the men. It was during this year that the sergeants' mess and library were instituted by Lord Fred. Fitzclarence.

1827.

The regiment still continued at Corfu and the neighbouring islands, performing the ordinary duties of the station until the 19th December, when the head quarters of the regiment, four companies, colours and band, were ordered to embark for the island of Santa Maura. They embarked on board the "Onyx," under the command of *Removed to Santa Maura.* Major Bell, on the 21st, previous to which the following garrison order was issued:—

"The soldier-like conduct which the regiment has maintained, the excellent example it has shewn at the head of this garrison, entitles it in every respect to the Major-General's notice and marked approbation; and he feels confident that the same good spirit, regularity, and discipline, which have characterised the officers and soldiers in all their respective duties here, will equally distinguish the several detachments now that the public service requires the temporary separation of the corps. The Major-General desires Major Bell will accept his acknowledgments for the steady and effective manner in which the detail and duties of the regiment have been conducted."

The head quarters of the regiment landed on the 23rd.

1828.

On the 10th April the head quarters embarked at Santa Maura on board H.M.S. "Revenge" for Malta, and arrived in harbour on the 20th, when the order was received for the regiment to return immediately to the Ionian Islands. It sailed from Malta on the 23rd, and disembarked at Cephalonia on the 30th. On the same day the detachments from Cerigo and Ithaca joined head quarters. On the 22nd September the regiment embarked on board H.M.S. "Wellesley" for Malta, and landed at Fort Manoel on the 26th. After performing quarantine the regiment marched to Floriana Barracks.

1829.

Lady Fitzclarence presents new colours. On the 9th April the regiment received a new stand of colours, presented by Lady Augusta Fitzclarence. The regiment was drawn up on the Floriana parade, where her ladyship in the presence of His Excellency Major-General the Hon. F. C. Ponsonby, and the officers of the garrison, presented the colours. After the ceremony was finished, His Excellency and the visitors inspected the Floriana barracks, which the men had decorated for the occasion, when the regiment sat down to a dinner given to them by their commanding officer. The old colours, which had been thus replaced, were those which the regiment had fought under throughout the Peninsula Campaigns; they were deposited by Sir Edward Blakeney in the great hall of the Royal Hospital, Kilmainham.

On the 18th December the regiment changed quarters from Floriana Barracks to the Cottonera district, when detachments were sent out to Forts Ricasoli and San Salvadore.

1830.

On the 16th May, the anniversary of Albuera, Lord F. Fitzclarence presented a handsome silver cup with regimental badge in the centre to Colour-Sergeant Parkinson, an old sergeant who had served in that action.

The regiment continued in these stations without change until the 29th June, when the detachment at Fort Ricasoli, Captain the *Hon.* George Liddell's Company, was relieved by Captain Lord Viscount Falkland's. During this year,

Lord Frederick Fitzclarence established a fund, raised by subscriptions among the officers and soldiers, to pay towards the support of a soldier's family, he being at the time in hospital. The commanding officer also shewed his interest in the regiment and welfare of the men by establishing branch schools where they might spend their otherwise idle moments in acquiring sound and useful instruction, and, being employed, escape the temptations which everywhere beset the indolent. *Fund raised for the families of sick soldiers*

Sergeant-Major Thomas Gilley was appointed Adjutant, with the rank of Lieutenant *vice* Hay promoted. The old and gallant Peninsula Adjutant, Lieutenant James Hay, after a series of years of hard service, was promoted to a company in the 52nd Light Infantry.

1831.

On the 24th March the regiment was inspected by Major-General the Hon. F. C. Ponsonby, on which occasion Major Lord William Thynne received His Excellency's commands to express to the regiment his entire approbation of their appearance and interior economy. On the 7th July the troops in garrison were reviewed by the Prince de Joinville on the Floriana Parade. The regiment lost this year another of its old Peninsula officers, Lieutenant M. Orr, who was promoted to a company in the Connaught Rangers.

During the summer there was a severe outbreak of cholera at Hull, where the depôt companies were stationed, to which many of the men fell victims. In September the depôt was moved to Manchester, and in November proceeded to Portsmouth. In the night of the 28th December an order arrived for the depôt to proceed to Bristol, then the scene of a most serious riot. The bugles at once roused the men from their sleep, and one hour from the order reaching the barracks, the depôt was on the march to embark on board a steamship for Southampton, whence they moved by forced marches to Bristol, which they reached on the 1st January, 1832. The gaol, Bishop's Palace, and other public buildings, were then in flames, but the riots had really been quelled on the preceding day. The men were stationed in various public buildings and stores, in order to prevent any fresh outbreak. *Depôt Companies.*

1832.

Lord F. Fitzclarence retires.

The regiment still continued at Malta without any variation in its duties or experiences until August, when it lost its zealous commanding officer, Lord Frederick Fitzclarence, who retired on half-pay on being appointed to the staff of the adjutant-general's department. Major Farquharson was promoted and assumed the command. In September another and important change took place in the staff of the regiment. Field-Marshal Sir Alured Clarke, the veteran who had led the regiment through the war of the American Revolution, died, and was succeeded "to the great delight of every individual in the regiment" by Sir Edward Blakeney.

Sir E. Blakeney appointed Colonel.

During the existence of the 2nd Battalion, and while it was quartered at Winchester, Sir Alured presented to it a small piece of plate as a token of regard for his old corps. On the reduction of the battalion the officers returned it to his keeping, but, at the death of the Field-Marshal, his relatives, in the most handsome manner, re-presented it to the Royal Fusilier mess. Two pairs of the colours of the Fusiliers were also presented by the Marshal's relatives, and delivered to his successor, Major-General Sir E. Blakeney; and one pair embroidered by the Princesses of England for H.R.H. the Duke of Kent, when colonel-commanding the Fusiliers, was given to Lord Frederick Fitzclarence: these colours have been preserved with the greatest care by Lady Augusta Fitzclarence, and are now (1875) in her possession at Etal House, Northumberland.

On the 18th December the detachments stationed at Forts Manoel, Tigne, and Goza, were relieved by the 94th Regiment, and the next day the Fusiliers were removed to the Floriana district. The depôt returned to Portsmouth from Bristol in July, when cholera again broke out amongst the men. The total losses of the depôt from this terrible disease at Portsmouth and at Hull the year before were no less than 86 men.

Depôt suffers from cholera.

1833.

No change took place in the stations or duties of the regiment until the 20th December, when it moved to the Cottonera district; three companies with head quarters occupying Isola Barracks, two companies at San Francisco de Paolo and one at San Salvadore. The command of the regiment was now assumed by Lieutenant-Colonel Farquharson.

In the same month the depôt companies embarked at Portsmouth for Ireland where they arrived in January, 1834; they returned to England in January, 1835, and landed at Portsmouth.

1834.

The regiment remained in the Cottonera district until the 10th December, when it removed to Lower St. Elmo barracks, and occupied the right wing of them. Red beading was added to the trousers of all ranks this year.

1835.

On the 23rd February the troops in garrison were reviewed by Marshal Marmont. On the 20th September the regiment received orders to hold itself in readiness to embark for England. It changed its quarters on the 23rd December, removing to the left wing of Lower St. Elmo barracks, and furnishing detachments to Forts Ricasoli and Tigne.

Garrison reviewed by Marshal Marmont.

1836.

On the 21st January, Nos. 1 and 2 Companies, under Captain Hope, embarked on board the "Sovereign" transport for England, and sailed on the 23rd. The head quarters and remaining companies did not embark until the 8th March, and sailed in the "Moira" transport next morning. The first division arrived at Spithead on the 11th March, disembarked at Gosport, and joined the depôt under Major Lord William Thynne in Forton barracks. The head quarters, under Colonel Farquharson, arrived at Spithead on the 26th April, disembarked on the 28th, and joined the remainder of the regiment in the Forehouse barracks. Five companies had to be sent to the Marine barracks, there not being sufficient accommodation at the Forehouse barracks.

Return to England.

STATIONS OF THE DEPÔT SINCE SEPARATED FROM THE SERVICE COMPANIES ON THEIR EMBARKATION FOR THE IONIAN ISLANDS IN JUNE, 1825.

	STATIONS.	DATE OF ARRIVAL.	DEPARTURE.	REMARKS.
ENGLAND.	Winchester.	June, 1825.	6th July, 1825.	
	Portsmouth.	7th July, 1825.	22nd August, 1825.	
	Dover.	27th August, 1825.	6th June, 1826.	
	Chester.	27th June, 1826.	17th March, 1828.	Detachment to Liverpool.
	Sunderland.	29th March, 1828.	8th October, 1828.	
	Hull.	10th October, 1828.	10th September, 1831.	
	Portsmouth.	15th September, 1831.	13th October, 1831.	
	Winchester.	14th October, 1831.	21st November, 1831.	
	Portsmouth.	22nd November, 1831.	28th December, 1831.	
	Bristol.	1st January, 1832.	9th July, 1832.	
	Portsmouth.	14th July, 1832.	18th June, 1833.	
	Gosport.	19th June, 1833.	9th August, 1833.	
	Portsmouth.	10th August, 1833.	2nd November, 1833.	
IRELAND.	Newbridge.	8th February, 1834.	6th May, 1834.	
	Naas.	7th May, 1834.	4th July, 1834.	
	Drogheda.	7th July, 1834.	4th March, 1835.	Detachment to Cavan.
	Dublin.	5th March, 1835.		
	Gosport.			

On the 16th June the regiment commenced its march to Winchester, and was quartered in Winchester barracks until the end of July, when it marched to Windsor. On the 3rd August His Majesty sent for the commanding officer and adjutant, with the records of the services of the Royal Fusiliers, which were read to His Majesty by Lieutenant-Colonel Farquharson. On Monday, August 8th, the King inspected the regiment in complete heavy marching order, in the quadrangle of the Castle, and was most graciously pleased to express his thorough approbation. Next day the regiment gave a guard of honour to attend on their Majesties in the Home Park at a review of the 2nd Life Guards, after which it marched up to the Castle, where the colours were received by the King with due honours, and handed

The King inspects the records of the Regiment.

by the Lieutenants to the Adjutant-General and Quartermaster-General to be lodged in St. George's Hall. They were guarded by sergeants during the dinner given on the occasion to the officers of the Life Guards, 7th Hussars, and Fusiliers.

While on duty at Windsor, where they were frequently inspected by the King, His Majesty presented to the mess of the regiment a superb silver vase bearing the following inscription :— {Silver vase presented by His Majesty King William IV.}

"The gracious gift of King William the Fourth, July, 1836."
"His Majesty remembers with satisfaction that he became a member of the mess of the Royal Fusiliers at Plymouth in the year 1786, and he has directed his son, Colonel Lord Frederick Fitzclarence, who had the advantage of commanding the regiment for some years, to present this piece of plate as a mark of His Majesty's approbation, and of his high sense of the gallant and admirable services, and of the exemplary discipline and gentlemanly conduct which have uniformly distinguished the Royal Fusiliers."

His Majesty's birthday was kept by the troops on the 22nd August, whereupon the following order was issued by the King himself at the Palace to the commanding officers and adjutants of the Life Guards and Fusiliers.

"Windsor, August 18th, 1836.
"Royal Orders.—A guard of honour, consisting of 1 captain, 2 subalterns, and 60 rank and file of the 2nd Life Guards, with a standard, to be in the quadrangle at half-past twelve o'clock to escort their Majesties to the ground on which the Royal Fusiliers will fire a *feu-de-joie*, which guard having returned with their Majesties to the Castle will lodge their standard in the Castle with military honours, after which they will pass the King by single files and proceed to their barracks. The remaining part of the Life Guards that will not be on duty on that day will parade in the north front with the Queen's Hussars to keep the ground.
"The Royal Fusiliers will be formed at a quarter before one o'clock in the north front, ready to receive their Majesties, and, after having given a royal salute, the Royal Artillery will fire a royal salute from the battery on the north terrace, immediately after which the Royal Fusiliers will fire a *feu-de-joie*. At its conclusion the Royal Artillery will fire another royal salute, after which the Royal Fusiliers will march past in slow and quick time, then reform, and conclude with a royal salute. The Royal Fusiliers will then proceed through the Little Park, and deliver their colours in the grand quadrangle with military honours. They will then pass by the King in columns of sections, and proceed to their barracks. The band of the Life Guards is to be in the gallery of St. George's Hall to play during the entertainment; the band of the Royal Fusiliers to be in the Waterloo Room gallery near the great staircase, to play before dinner, and when their Majesties return to the grand reception room, to play alternately with the Queen's band during the evening. The guards and band will mount at six o'clock on Monday evening."

After the *feu-de-joie* the regiment advanced in line and halted close to the Queen's carriage; it then formed three sides of a square, when the King was graciously pleased to confer upon its gallant old leader, Sir Edw. Blakeney, the honour of the Grand Cross of Hanover, for his distinguished services while lieutenant-colonel of the Fusiliers. Sir Edward had the honour of kissing their Majesties' hands in the Park. The regiment afterwards marched to the Quadrangle of the Castle, and lodged its colours in due form in St. George's Hall. {Sir E. Blakeney appointed G. C. H.}

During the stay of the regiment at Windsor it received the marked attention of the King, who took, as will have been already seen, much more than an ordinary interest in it. The band was frequently called to the Castle, and their Majesties expressed themselves highly pleased with its performance. The sojourn of the regiment in these pleasant quarters was, however, interrupted on the 28th August, by an order to march to the North of England, where trouble was expected from the disturbed state of the country, and the suffering endured by the poor. In taking leave of the regiment previous to its departure, Major-General Blakeney thus addressed it, pointing out at once both the merit and reward of order and discipline. The Major-General "trusts that the Royal Fusiliers will ever remember that it is principally by being in this most efficient state that such magnificent and flattering attention has been paid them by their most gracious and beloved Sovereign."

The Regiment moved to Lancashire.

The first division, consisting of four companies under Captain Baker, marched on the 29th; the second, consisting of head quarters and four companies under Lieut.-Col. Farquharson, on the following day. On the 9th and 10th September the divisions arrived at Congleton, when orders were received to distribute eight companies at the following places:—

    Nos. 1 and 8 Companies, with Head Quarters, at Bolton.
      ,, 3 ,, 7   ,,   Blackburn.
      ,, 5 ,, 10   ,,   Wigan.
      ,,   4   ,,   Rochdale.
      ,,   9   ,,   Haydock Lodge.

On the 6th November, No. 7 Company was suddenly ordered from Blackburn to Preston, in consequence of disturbances. Next day a detachment, which had been left at Weedon under Major Stuart, was sent to Newcastle-under-Lyme; whence it proceeded at the end of the month to Liverpool.

1837.

Changing its quarters in these districts with the change in the political atmosphere, the regiment continued to perform its duty. It was inspected at Bolton on the 10th October by Major-General Sir R. D. Jackson, K.C.B., commanding the Northern District. On the 25th and 26th October, the head quarters, Wigan, and Haydock Lodge detachments marched to Liverpool, and embarked on board the

"Juno" and "Herald" steamers for Dublin, where they disembarked on the 29th, *Proceeds to Ireland* and marched to the Royal Barracks, occupying the Palatine Square. On the 27th November Lieut.-General Sir Edward Blakeney, K.C.B., commanding the forces in Ireland, inspected the regiment in the Royal Square.

1838.

On the 12th January the regiment gave forty volunteers to complete the 65th Regiment, ordered to Canada. The Fusiliers continued in Dublin throughout the year, performing the ordinary garrison duty. In December, an order having been received to the effect that regiments of infantry should be completed to their full establishment, recruiting parties were sent to Kendal, Leicester, Brighton, Glasgow, Blandford, Doncaster, and Ashburne.

1839.

In April the regiment marched to Kilkenny, sending detachments to Carlow, Carrick-on-Suir, Castle Comer, New Ross, Newtown-Barry, and Callen. On the 21st July the regiment was ordered to be held in readiness to proceed to Cork for embarkation for Gibraltar, but on the 31st the order was countermanded, Lieut.-Col. Farquharson being further ordered to proceed with 300 rank and file of the Fusiliers, 200 of the 84th Regiment, and a squadron of the Scots Greys, the whole under Lieut.-Col. Farquharson, to Coonogue, County Carlow, to aid the civil power. The detachment returned on the 8th to Kilkenny; on the 10th the regiment started for Cork.

Under the new order the establishment of the regiment was as follows:—

	Cl.	Lt.-Cl.	Maj.	Capt.	Lt.	Pay.	Adjt.	Qr.-M.	Sur.	A.S.	Sergt.	Corp.	Drum.	Priv.
Service Companies	1	1	1	6	12	1	1	1	1	1	31	24	10	456
Depot Companies	0	0	1	4	8	0	0	0	0	0	16	16	4	304
Total	1	1	2	10	20	1	1	1	1	1	47	40	14	760

The Service companies embarked on the 6th Nov., on board H.M.S. "Apollo," at the Cove of Cork, sailed on the 11th, and arrived at Gibraltar on the 22nd. The *Embarks for Gibraltar.* following morning the regiment disembarked at the New Mole and marched into the south and casemate barracks, where it remained until the embarkation of the 82nd Regiment, when it removed into the Town Range and King's Bastion.

1840.

On the 7th July the Fusiliers formed part of the forces reviewed by His Serene Highness Prince Ernest of Saxe Gotha. On the 11th Nov., the regiment was inspected by Sir Alex. Woodford, K.C.B., who expressed himself highly satisfied.

1841.

This year was passed on the Rock without any event worthy of being recorded. The regiment was inspected on the 4th Nov., when its strength was as follows:—

	F. O.	Cap.	Lt.	Staff.	Sergt.	Corp.	Drum.	Priv.
Effectives	2	6	11	5	34	24	10	544
Wanting	0	0	1	0	0	0	0	32
Establishment	2	6	12	5	34	24	10	576

1842.

The chief event in this year was the change in the chief command at Gibraltar. Sir Alexander Woodford made his last inspection of the Fusiliers on the 5th October, when he remarked that "the Fusiliers had been twice under his command in the last sixteen years, that he had always found them in perfect order, and he trusted they would ever maintain their high state of discipline and good conduct."

Sir Alexander's successor in the command was the veteran Sir R. T. Wilson, who on his arrival ordered a parade of the regiment in review order, and on that occasion issued the following very flattering encomium:—

Sir Robert Wilson compliments the Regiment.

"Gibraltar, Nov. 15th, 1842.

"Garrison Order.—The Commander-in-Chief would, indeed, have been greatly disappointed if, in reviewing H.M.'s 7th Royal Fusiliers, he had not found the characteristic qualities which in former times he had much occasion to admire, and which have rendered this regiment so long and so highly distinguished in the ranks of Her Majesty's service.

"Lieut.-Col. Farquharson, his officers, non-commissioned officers, and privates are entitled to the Commander-in-Chief's most favourable commendation, for their proficiency and the spirited energy with which they executed their movements of yesterday, and also for the general order which prevails throughout the corps, in strict conformity to the regulations of the service."

1843.

In March the regiment changed its quarters, when the following order was issued:—

"Head Quarters, Gibraltar, 13th March, 1843.

The Fusiliers construct the roads on Windmill Hill.

"Garrison Orders.—The Seventh Royal Fusiliers being about to quit their barracks at Windmill Hill, the Governor authorises Lieut.-Colonel Farquharson, with the view of commemorating the voluntary, exemplary, and beneficial labours of his corps during their occupation, to put up at a suitable spot on the Esplanade, a tablet with the following inscription:—

A.D. 1842.
THE ROADS WERE MADE AND SURFACE LEVELLED
OF THIS HERETOFORE RUGGED HILL, BY THE VOLUNTARY LABOURS OF
HER MAJESTY'S SEVENTH ROYAL FUSILIERS.

Sic fuit,	Thus has been,
Sic semper erit,	Thus ever will be,
Miles Britannicus,	The British soldier,
Bello fortis,	In war brave,
Pace, bonus et utilis.	In peace orderly and useful.

On the 21st April the Regiment was paraded in review order, by order of His Excellency the Governor, for the inspection of Prince Napoleon Bonaparte, son to Jerome, late King of Westphalia. Little did the Regiment then think that at the instigation of that Prince it would next take the field against a European enemy in alliance with the legions over whom it had obtained all its victories!

Inspected by Prince Napoleon.

1844.

The early part of the year was passed in an uneventful manner. On the 20th June Lieutenant and Adjutant Dobbie died after a severe and lingering illness. His death was felt by the whole Regiment, for "his mild, conciliating, and amiable conduct had gained him the love and respect of all the soldiers, and the highest esteem of his brother officers." On the occasion of his interment the Governor-General was pleased to state in orders—"The death of this officer deprives his corps and the service of one of its estimable members, raised by the claims of meritorious conduct to the station which he occupied. He undeviatingly discharged all his duties so as to acquire general respect and regard."

In December the Regiment was ordered to proceed to the West Indies. It embarked on the 19th on board H.M.S. "Resistance," arrived in Carlisle Bay on the 17th January, 1845, and disembarked on the 18th and 23rd, relieving the 46th Regiment in the garrison of St. Ann's.

Proceeds to the West Indies.

1845.

On the 17th May three companies embarked on board the "Princess Royal" for British Guiana, being stationed, two companies in Demerara and one in Berbice. On the 23rd May Lieutenant-Colonel Farquharson, having obtained leave of absence after an uninterrupted command of the Regiment for twelve years, proceeded to England, expressing his sincere thanks to the Regiment for its exemplary conduct. In August one of the companies at Berbice was sent under Lieutenant the Hon. W. Monck to Mahaica for change of air, in consequence of the prevalence of fever.

1846.

A detachment sent to St. Lucia.

On the 9th January a detachment consisting of 2 lieutenants, 6 sergeants, 7 corporals, 1 drummer, and 142 privates, under the command of Captain the Hon. C. L. Hare, embarked on board H.M.S. "Hyacinth" for St. Lucia. The Head Quarters, consisting of 1 captain, 2 lieutenants, 2 staff, 14 sergeants, 6 corporals, 6 drummers, and 149 privates, under Major Wilbraham, embarked for St. Vincent on the 29th January and disembarked on the 31st. The three companies detached at British Guiana embarked on the 20th March, under Captain Stuart, and disembarked at Barbadoes on the 25th. On the 4th April one of these companies, under Lieutenant J. P. Young, embarked at Barbadoes to reinforce the Head Quarters at St. Vincent. On the 26th September Major Yea arrived at St. Vincent, and assumed the command of the Regiment.

Shako hats were taken into wear by the Regiment on the 20th August of this year.

1847.

Head Quarters to Barbadoes.

On the 16th February the Head Quarters, under Colonel Farquharson, embarked at St. Vincent for Barbadoes. On the Fusiliers leaving St. Vincent the House of Assembly passed the following resolution complimenting the Regiment:—

"Saint Vincent, House of Assembly, 20th March, 1847.

"SIR,—Pursuant to a Resolution of the Honorable the House of Assembly of this Island, I have the pleasing duty and the honour to communicate to you the high sense entertained by the House of the honourable and gentlemanly bearing of the Officers, and the orderly and correct deportment of the Non-Commissioned Officers and Privates of the Right Wing of Her Majesty's Seventh Royal Fusiliers, under your command, whilst in Garrison in this Island.

"The departure of the Regiment from the Island during the recess alone prevented the presentation of an address to this effect.

"I have the honour to be, Sir,

"Your most obedient, humble Servant,

"Colonel Farquharson, *Commanding Fusiliers*. (Signed) C. D. STEWART, *Speaker*."

In April the detachment from St. Lucia, under Lieutenant Porter, joined Head Quarters. On the 24th October a detachment consisting of 1 sergeant and 25 men, under Lieutenant Porter, proceeded to Tobago to be employed as artificers in re-erecting the buildings destroyed by a hurricane on the 11th October. It returned on the 5th February, 1848.

1848.

On the 10th March the Regiment embarked on board the "Herefordshire" for North America; it arrived at Halifax, Nova Scotia, on the 31st, and disembarked on the 1st and 7th April, relieving the 46th Regiment. At the disembarkation the Regiment looked admirable, more especially after having spent more than three years in West Indian service, two of which had been spent in detachment, and at those stations of worst repute, Berbice, Demerara, and St. Lucia. It had been, however, most fortunate in the matter of health, having lost little more than fifty men during the whole time. At Halifax the Regiment occupied the South Barracks. It is worthy of remark that although the Regiment had no Indian service it had been nearly thirty-eight years absent from Nova Scotia, having last occupied that station in 1810, from whence it embarked for Portugal.

Embarks for Halifax, N.S.

On the 17th April 1 sergeant and 20 men, under Lieutenant Miller, marched to Annapolis; and on the same day a small party proceeded to Windsor. In April Captain Cochrane's Company proceeded to Cape Breton, and No. 5 Company, under Lieutenant Young, to Prince Edward's Island.

1849.

On the 29th January the establishment was ordered to be increased to 47 sergeants, 17 drummers, and 770 rank and file. In June the detachments from Prince Edward's Island, Cape Breton, and Annapolis rejoined Head Quarters.

Establishment increased.

1850.

On the 1st April the establishment was ordered to be reduced to 47 sergeants, 16 drummers, and 750 rank and file: on the same day, 3 sergeants, 3 corporals, and 29 privates were transferred to the Royal Canadian Rifles.

Embarks for England.
On the 29th May the regiment embarked on board the "Bombay" for England. It arrived at Spithead 24th July, disembarked at Portsmouth next day, and proceeded to Winchester, where it joined the depot, consisting of 12 officers and 330 men, who had proceeded from Cork on board the steamer "Royal William" to Portsmouth, where they landed on the 7th March, proceeding the same day to Winchester.

Col. Farquharson retires; succeeded by Major L. W. Yea.
On the 9th August Colonel Farquharson retired, being succeeded by Major Lacy Walter Yea. On the 3rd and 5th September two companies were detached to Weymouth under Captain Wallace. New accoutrements, viz., pouch belt, pouch, and frog-waistbelt were issued to the regiment November 1st.

1851.

The regiment left Winchester, moving into garrison at Portsmouth on the 28th and 29th January, and occupied the Clarence barracks. Twice during the summer the regiment gave guards of honour to receive Her Majesty on her visits to Portsmouth. The companies from Weymouth returned to head quarters on the 1st and 2nd September.

New colours presented by Lady Fitzclarence.
On the 29th September the regiment was drawn up in the Lieutenant-Governor's field, and a new stand of colours were presented by Lady Augusta Fitzclarence, the old colours, which were also presented by her ladyship at Malta, being deposited in the garrison chapel at Portsmouth.

1852.

On the 10th and 12th August the regiment embarked on board the steamship "Foyle," and was conveyed to Plymouth, where it disembarked on the 11th and 13th, and marched to the Citadel barracks. On the 9th October it was inspected by Major-General Sir John Rolt, K.C.B. On the 20th, 21st, and 22nd, the regiment moved from the Citadel barracks, Plymouth, to Devonport, and there occupied George's Square, Mount Wise, and Granby barracks, relieving the 35th Regiment. Detachments were also sent to Dartmoor and Pendennis Castle, the former under command of Captain Mills, the latter of Lieutenant Whitehead. On the 13th November, Lieutenant-Colonel Yea, Captain the Hon. C. L. Hare, and Lieutenant C. E. Watson, together with one sergeant, one corporal, and six privates, proceeded to London to attend the funeral of the Duke of Wellington.

Funeral of the Duke of Wellington.

1853.

On the 12th February Corporal Joseph Penton, Privates Patrick Carlin and George Driver, proceeding to Dartmoor prison, were overtaken by a snowstorm on the open moor, from the severity of which they all lost their lives. In commemoration of their attention to their duty as soldiers, a marble tablet, with the following inscription, was placed in the Parish Church of Princetown, where they were buried:—

Three men lost in a snow-storm.

"Sacred to the memory of Corporal Joseph Penton, Privates Patrick Carlin and George Driver of the 7th Royal Fusiliers, who lost their lives in a snow-storm on the neighbouring moor, on the 12th February, 1853, when in the execution of their duty.

"This tablet is erected in token of his admiration of their ardour as soldiers (in braving the danger in preference to disobeying orders) by their commanding officer, Lieutenant-Colonel Lacy Yea, of the 7th Royal Fusiliers."

The private soldiers erected at their own expense a slate tablet which, bearing the following inscription, is fixed to the wall near their graves:—

"In memory of three valiant soldiers of the 7th Royal Fusiliers, who died on Dartmoor in a snowdrift, on the 12th February, 1853, Corporal Joseph Penton, aged 20; Patrick Carlin, aged 23; George Driver, aged 27."

The detachment from Pendennis Castle, under the command of Lieutenant D. S. Miller, rejoined head quarters at Devonport on the 3rd May; that from Dartmoor, under Captain W. R. Brown, at Plymouth Citadel on the 12th May.

On the 12th, 13th, and 14th May, the regiment moved from George Square, Mount Wise, and Granby barracks, Devonport, to Plymouth Citadel, relieving the 35th Regiment. On the 15th July the regiment proceeded by railway from Plymouth to Windsor, and marched the same evening into the camp at Chobham, where it was brigaded with the 88th and 35th Regiments, under the command of

In camp at Chobham.

Major-General Sir Richard England, K.C.B., forming part of the division under Lieutenant-General Lord Seaton, G.C.B. The regiment participated in all exercises and reviews which took place in that camp between the 15th July and the 13th August, when it marched to Windsor and proceeded by railway to Manchester, where the regiment was quartered in Salford barracks. On the 15th August a guard of honour, consisting of 1 field officer, 1 captain, 2 lieutenants, and 100 rank and file, with the band and the Queen's colour, proceeded to Holyhead to attend Her Majesty on her visit to Ireland.

1854.

Ordered for service in Turkey.

When the war-note sounded through England, calling her troops to resist the aggressions of the Czar, the Royal Fusiliers were one of the regiments first summoned to prepare for the contest. It was immediately ordered to be recruited to a war-strength. The regiment was then at Manchester, and its recruits were to be obtained from the northern counties: the recruiting parties in Yorkshire being most successful. During the early spring the regiment was raised to its establishment, and drilled into one of the smartest and most solid battalions in the service. It was, however, on account of the delay caused by recruiting, not one of the first to proceed to the East, for it did not leave Manchester until Tuesday, April 4th, when the head quarters, with 8 companies, consisting of 3 field officers, 8 captains, 14 lieutenants, 5 staff, 46 sergeants, 15 drummers, 850 rank and file, and 25 women, under the command of Lieutenant-Colonel Lacy Yea, proceeded by the London and North Western Railway to Southampton for embarkation on board the "Orinoco." As was the case with every regiment that proceeded to the seat of war, its departure from the town where it had been stationed was the signal for that outburst of enthusiasm which a free people will always give to its soldiery—its brothers—who depart to fight for the freedom of the oppressed. As the troops marched through the streets they were accompanied by thousands of people, who cheered them with the most fervid vehemence.

Embarks at Southampton for Scutari.

On its arrival at Southampton on the same evening the regiment was at once embarked, and sent on its journey. The ship touched at Gibraltar, Malta, and Scutari, where the troops disembarked on the 22nd. Here the Regiment was brigaded with the 23rd Royal Welsh, and the 33rd Regiment under Brig.-Gen. R. Airey; and with the 19th, 77th, 88th, and 2nd Battalion Rifle Brigade formed the Light Division under Lieut-Gen. Sir Geo. Browne, K.C.B. Although they were all great in history, and bore on their colours the names of England's proudest victories and most heroic struggles, yet none of these regiments, except the Rifles, formed part of the famous legion of the Peninsula whose name they bore, and whose successes they were so soon to emulate. The stay of the Fusiliers at Scutari was not long, nor marked by great events. On the 16th May Sir Geo. Brown inspected the division, and its splendid appearance satisfied even his rigid notions of military perfection. A move was by this time in contemplation, and preparations were being made for it, but things were not in readiness. On the 25th the Regiment was supplied with Minié rifles, except the sergeants; and at last "Old Brown Bess" was discarded. Next day the division was to have left for Varna, but its departure was obliged to be postponed, because the Commissariat would not have provisions enough ready to start for two or three days to come. By the 28th, however, the preparations had been completed, and next morning at daybreak, the division paraded for embarkation, "as steady and solid as ever, with long lines of bullock carts and buffalo arabas drawn up between them, and commenced their march, winding slowly along over the sandy slopes which led to the sea."

Joyous, indeed, were the troops, as, amidst the cheers of thousands of their comrades who had come to witness their departure they stepped into the boats, and were taken off to the ships that were to carry them away, to at once encounter the troops of the Czar. The Royal Fusiliers, 950 strong and 12 horses, embarked on board the 'Megæra;' and before the evening fell she and her sister transports, bearing the rest of the division, had entered the Black Sea, and were speeding on their way. The Regiment disembarked at Varna on the 1st of June, and went into camp "on a plain, covered with scrub and sweet-briar," about half a mile from the town. This, however, was only a temporary encampment, for on the 5th the division moved off to the camp at Aladyn. Before this move, however, the Regiment lost Capt. Wallace, who was killed by a fall from his horse: his death cast a great sorrow over the Regiment.

It was while in camp at Aladyn, that the Regiment was drilled in the use of the Minié rifle. On the 19th the Division was inspected by Gen. Canrobert; it marched past in open columns. The French General particularly expressed his admiration at the steady marching and soldier-like appearance of the Royal Fusiliers. The Division remained here whiling away the time between drills and field sports until the 30th June, when it quitted the camp and marched to Devna, about eight-and-a-half miles further off. Here the Division and the Cavalry Brigade were reviewed by Omar Pasha on the 3rd July, and elicited both from him and the French officers present as spectators, the warmest expression of praise for their gallant bearing and superb discipline. And well and truly was their praise bestowed, for than the British troops who assembled here, never was a finer body of soldiery enrolled. In the allied armies they had no peers; and in their stately bearing and gallant array, the practised eye of the veteran Turkish General at once detected the conquerors of his foes. But, in this "Valley of Death," as the soldiers mournfully soon came to call it, the health and strength that should have been employed to carry them through the Russian hosts, were insidiously sapped by disease. On the 23rd July cholera broke out with great virulence, and in only a few days the troops were so reduced in physique as to ill-fit them for the active duties that were awaiting them. Fortunately, however, the Royal Fusiliers were not the heaviest sufferers in the Brigade, the Royal Welsh having that lamentable distinction. On the 24th the Division struck its camp and marched to Monastir, in the hope of shaking off its unwelcome visitor. It was in the midst of this misery that a draft of 2 sergeants and 100 rank and file under Lieut. H. M. Jones joined from the depôt at Winchester. Among the sufferers of the Fusiliers was Quar.-Mast Hogan, who was seized with cholera on the 26th and died the same night.

Notwithstanding these losses and sufferings, the troops were kept in these unhealthy neighbourhoods until it had been determined to invade the Crimea, and there bring the Russians to action. For this purpose, on the 26th August, the Royal Fusiliers marched from Monastir to Varna. The change immediately raised the spirits of the men, "who sang songs much of the way," but, though it might separate them from the fatal spot where so many of their comrades were slumbering, it could not so soon restore to them their lost strength. The distance was only 26 miles, yet they were three days in performing it, even when divested of their packs, which were carried for them by mules and horses. Many of the privates died on the way, and one officer, Lieut. Molesworth, was invalided, he died at Malta on the 5th October of fever contracted here. Their departure from the fatal spot was saddened by the memory of its fatality. " Through the Valley of Devna, 'the Valley of Death,' the men marched in mournful silence, for it was the place where they had left so many of their comrades, and where they had suffered so much." The Regiment arrived at Varna on the 29th and 30th, and embarked on board the steamers "Victoria" and "Emperor," two companies being afterwards put on board H.M.S. " Fury." Seven days they remained on shipboard before starting, and on the 13th anchored in Kalamita Bay. On the next morning they were to invade the Crimea, the Light Division to land first. The strength of the Regiment on landing was 2 field-officers, 8 captains, 9 lieutenants, 50 sergeants, and 732 rank and file. It fell to the good fortune of the Royal Fusiliers to be the first of the English to take possession; No. 1 Company, under Capt. R. W. Aldworth, first touched the enemy's soil. They were immediately followed by some riflemen, and thus irregularly the Rifles and Fusiliers scrambled ashore. In less than an hour the whole of the Light Division was on the beach. Among the first to land were Sir Geo. Browne and Brig.-Gen. Airey. They immediately pushed into the country to reconnoitre, followed by a picket of Fusiliers and Riflemen. During their reconnaissance they crossed a picket of Cossacks, and were in danger of being cut off. Stealthily the Cossacks crept forward, intent on carrying off the prize that seemed so easily within their reach, and not noticing the soldiers who were watching the steps of their General, the Cossacks were about to pounce upon their prey, who was within 100 yards of them, when a volley from the Fusiliers crashed in amongst them, and then turning their horses they flew like the wind towards Sebastopol.

By eleven the Rifles and Fusiliers had been inspected, and were marching from the left of the line along the front of the yet unformed regiments towards the right. They ascended the slope of the hill over the cliff, marching straight inland. In this position, which was five or six miles from the point of debarkation the division took post, and remained stationary during the four following days, which were consumed in disembarking the cavalry and stores of the army, and making preparations for the march upon Sebastopol.

On the 19th, the allies commenced their march towards Sebastopol in contiguous columns of divisions, the English taking the left of the force, the French on the right, with their right resting on the sea. The first sight of the enemy was obtained at the Bouljanak. The village of that name was in flames and the Russians occupied the road leading through it to Sebastopol. The army halted; the cavalry were thrown out to feel the enemy, and the 1st Brigade of the Light Division (Royal Fusiliers, 23rd and 33rd Regiments) was deployed and took up a position in support. Nothing more serious than a short artillery duel ensued, in which both sides had a few men wounded, when the enemy retired and the British bivouaced for the night.

<small>Affair of the Bouljanak.</small>

Next morning, the 20th September, the march was resumed about eight o'clock, and about eleven the Allies came in sight of the formidable position held by the Russians on the heights above the Alma. At the foot of this position ran the little river, from the bank of which rose the hills in a slope that formed a natural glacis for the battery of 32-pounders that crowned the summit. To carry this position the troops were formed in battle array, and at half-past twelve the French opened the action with their artillery. Their duty was to turn the left flank of the Russian army posted on the heights; the duty of the English was to carry the batteries and drive off the main body of the Russians who held them.

<small>Battle of the Alma.</small>

When the English attack opened the Light Division was the centre division of the army; the 2nd Division was on its right, supported by the 3rd; the 1st Division was on its left, supported by the 4th. The divisional distances for deployment had not been well kept, the Light Division had "failed to take ground enough to the left; and when the deployment was complete, Sir George Brown had the grief of seeing his right regiment (the 7th Fusiliers) overlapped by the left—nay even by the centre of Pennefather's brigade. The fault was not retrieved; it was fruitful of confusion." When the Light Division advanced the Royal Fusiliers had to march through the 95th Regiment, and in the operation carried the 95th from its proper brigade, and brought it into action with the Light Division; but it cleared the front of the Fusiliers, and enabled Lieut.-Col. Yea to operate with his full strength.*

* See Kinglake's *Invasion of the Crimea*, vol. 2, p. 255.

For a time the British were lying idle under the fire of the Russian guns, awaiting the success of the French attack; but, as the shot began to carry casualties into the ranks, it is said that Lord Raglan became impatient and ordered the advance. Yea, " a man of onward, fiery, robust nature, not likely to suffer his cherished regiment to stand helplessly under the muzzles pointed down on him and his people," led the regiment across the Alma, but his course, sadly impeded by the vineyards surrounded by loose stone walls and the full-grown vines, for a moment was checked by the high bank on the Russian side of the river. At length, discovering a place of ascent, he pushed his horse to the top of the bank, shouting to the regiment, "Never mind forming! Come on men, Come on anyhow!" Up on the bank, immediately responsive to the call, rose the colours of the regiment, carried by Lieuts. Coney and H. M. Jones; indeed it is said that Lieut. Jones was actually the first man on the bank. Scarcely a moment elapsed before they were both badly hit, for they were almost under the very muzzles of the Russian skirmishers. Smitten heavily by the tremendous showers of grape with which the Russians swept the crest of the ridge, the Fusiliers followed, promptly responding to the call of their chief, and the lead of the colours, and fell into such order as the desperate nature of their position would allow. Then the Russian skirmishers fell back upon their battalions, and the ground between the guns and the gathering Fusiliers was void of men. During the first period of the advance one of the wounded officers carrying the colours was unable to take post in the line, and the eager Fusiliers went forward to the attack with a colour absent, but it was never lost; it was only missing for a moment before it was brought to the front and borne forward with the regiment.* The other regiments pressing forward as eagerly, in a few moments the brigade was calling to be led on to the attack.

Then the Russians pushed forward columns of infantry to stop the rush on the batteries; "and no sooner had the Royal Fusiliers found themselves ready to advance than their path was stopped by a column of the Kazan Regiment of Infantry, containing not less than 1500 veteran soldiers, who, placing themselves

The Fusiliers engage the Kazan Regiment.

---

* This statement is made in contradiction of a statement made by Dr. Russell, in his letter to the *Times*, to the effect that a colour was lost. Colonel Hibbert, the authority for the contradiction, remembers perfectly that in the confusion of the first formation both the wounded officers were not instantaneously relieved, but both colours were in front by the time the regiment was making its general advance.

between the Fusiliers and the battery, accepted such battle as the Englishmen were prepared to give. They were both Fusilier Regiments, and both were highly honoured in their country, for the English Regiment were the Royal Fusiliers, and the Russian the Regiment of the Grand Duke Michael. They both accepted their task with a stern devotion, and the fight they made for the mastery was one of the most terrible in the whole affair. At a distance of fifty yards from the ragged chain of men that Lacy Yea held command over—for in the confusion soldiers of other regiments had become mixed with the Fusiliers—the Kazan column halted and opened its fire. To this the Royal Fusiliers responded with cheerful alacrity, and as much regularity as their disjointed condition would allow, yet although the shots of individual soldiers and small knots of men had not, of course, the crushing power which would have been exerted by the fire of the 7th Fusiliers when formed and drawn up in line, still the well-handled rifles of our men soon began to carry havoc into the dark-grey oblong mass of living beings which served them for their easy target. And though seemingly the front rank of the compact mass yearned to move forward, there was always occurring in the interior some sudden death, or some trouble with a wounded man, which seemed not only to breed difficulty in the way of an advance, but also to make the column rock, and then begin to look spotted and faulty. The distance was such as to allow a good deal of shooting at particular men. Once Yea himself found that he was singled out to be killed, and was covered by a musket or rifle, but the marksman was so fastidious about his aim that, before he touched the trigger, a quick-eyed English corporal found time to intervene and save his Colonel's life, by shooting the careful Russian in the midst of his studies. 'Thank you, my man,' said Lacy Yea, 'if I live through this you shall be a sergeant to-night.' Whilst this long fight went on, it sometimes happened that the fire or impatience of one or other of the Fusiliers would carry a man into close quarters with the column.

Death of Capt. Monck Of those who were stirred by sudden impulses of this kind, Monck was one. He sprang forward, they say, from his place on the left of the Fusiliers, and saying, 'Come on 8th Company!' rushed up to the enemy's massed battalion, ran his sword through a man in the front rank, and struck another with his fist. He was then shot dead by a musket fired from the second rank of the column. Personal experiences of this kind were incidents varying the tenor of the fight; but it was by musket or rifle ball, at a distance of some fifty yards, that the real strife between the two corps was waged."*

Thus the close and deadly fight lasted during the time that the other regiments of the Light Division were occupied in carrying the battery, and it continued in all its stubbornness while those regiments, broken and doubly decimated, were swept back in retreat by the ponderous columns of infantry who assailed them when the guns could no longer be used. "When the storming battalions came down the regiment was fighting still. When the despondency of the French army was at its worst, when the head of Canrobert's division was pushed down the hill by the 'column of the eight battalions,' when along the whole line of the allies there was no other regiment fighting, Lacy Yea and his people were still at their work. When Evans, having crossed the river, was leading his three battalions to the site of the Causeway Batteries, it was the 7th Fusiliers that stood fighting alone on his left; and nearly at the very time when disaster befel the centre of the Brigade of Guards, Lacy Yea and his Fusiliers were gathering at least the reward of their soldierly virtue."

The resolute stand made by the Royal Fusiliers was unquestionably one of the causes of the success of the action. After the first strife for victory, when the broken regiments which had stormed the batteries had retired for re-formation, and before the supports could be brought into action, the field of battle would have been clear and in possession of the Russians had not the Fusiliers, holding before them the immense Russian column, formed a *point d'appui*, upon which the 1st and 3rd Divisions could continue the attack. Within a very short time the regiment lost one-third of its men, yet the Royal Fusiliers steadfastly maintained their ground, and briskly plied their fire, until the once proud Kazan battalions melted away and left them free to continue their course. In the confusion, as we have stated, many of the men became detached from the regiment and fought with other corps; and in doing so one of these men, Corporal Pye, particularly distinguished himself. He had joined the Royal Welsh, and, accompanying that regiment into the battery, he

* Kinglake's *Invasion*, vol. 2, p. 414. The incident of the corporal saving Colonel Yea's life is not in all its details literally correct. Colonel Aldworth states that the remark attributed to Colonel Yea was indeed made by him to Corporal Pye, not, however, for the reason stated, but assisting at the capture of a gun with Captain Bell, of the Royal Welsh Fusiliers.

assisted Captain Bell, of the 23rd, to seize the only gun that was captured in position on that day. As could only be the case, from the desperate nature of their service, the Royal Fusiliers were heavy sufferers. Captain the Hon. W. Monck, Colour-Sergeant J. Pursell, and Sergeant T. Everett, with 38 rank and file were killed. Captains the Hon. G. L. Hare* severely, C. E. Watson severely, W. H. D. Fitzgerald severely; Lieutenants F. E. Appleyard slightly, D. Persse severely, P. G. Coney severely, the Hon. A. C. H. Crofton slightly, G. W. W. Carpenter slightly, H. M. Jones severely, H. R. Hibbert, and Lieutenant and Adjutant J. St. Clair Hobson slightly; 14 sergeants and 151 men were wounded; two men missing.

<small>Sir E. Blakeney's congratulations.</small>

It is not only proper but gratifying here to insert the following extract relating to the Battle of the Alma, from a letter written by Sir E. Blakeney to Colonel Yea, the testimony of the leader of the men of Albuera to the worth of the men of Alma.

"Monkstrevor, Oct. 13th, 1854.

"My very dear and gallant Friend,

"I cannot find words to express how proud I am at the intrepid conduct of my gallant—and not to be surpassed—regiment. Pray assure all how my heart beat on reading the account of their very valiant conduct. You led them, my good friend, in true Fusilier style, and you may very well say how well they maintained the character of former days. You have one and all my heartiest congratulations on the occasion, and may you all soon recover from the hardships you have gone through.

"Our regimental loss has been great indeed, and you must be much distressed by it, but gallant deeds must have their casualties, although very distressing. I hope the wounded are going on well.

"Believe me always to remain, my dear Yea,

"Your most sincere friend,

"(Signed) "E. BLAKENEY."

<small>March on Sebastopol.</small>

After the Battle of the Alma the Royal Fusiliers proceeded with the Light Division in the march on Sebastopol. We need not enter into the details of that curious operation, but go at once to the hour when the troops settled into their positions to take part in the siege of Sebastopol, an operation the nature and demands of which we do not hesitate to say were but most imperfectly appreciated by the chiefs of both armies. On the 25th the army marched on Balaclava, halting for the night at the village of Traktir; Captain Rose's company (No. 3) of the Fusiliers being sent on outlying picket on the Woronzoff Road. Next day Balaclava was reached, the heights taken possession of by the 1st Brigade Light Division, which, with the co-operation of the fleet, attacked the forts. After a very

---

* He died of his wounds on board the "Andes," September 22nd.

slight resistance, the forts surrendered. On the 28th the army moved up to the front and commenced operations against Sebastopol, the Light Division taking the extreme right of the position.

When at the opening of the bombardment volunteers from regiments of the Light Division were called for to act as sharpshooters to keep down the fire from the batteries, by picking off the enemy's gunners, the following men of the Royal Fusiliers came forward:—Sergeant Charles Sutton; Privates Charles Blacker, Frederick Blacker, John Cronin, William Paynes, William White, William Allen, William Barrack, William Johnson, Andrew Styles, Jesse Hargreaves; they were engaged for some time on this dangerous service. *Volunteer sharpshooters organised.*

The Fusiliers took their turn of duty from the opening of the siege. The first bombardment opened on the 17th October, on which day the regiment was on outlying picket, and had Corporal W. Linegar killed and Corporal Charles Blacker wounded. Thenceforward, in the terrible struggle that was commencing, the regiment furnished men for duty every day. On the 26th, the day of the great sortie after Balaclava, three companies of the Fusiliers, and one of the 2nd Battalion Rifle Brigade, under Major Sir T. Troubridge, were on picket in a small battery, separated by a deep ravine from the enemy. Sir Thomas at once opened a smart flank fire upon the wily Russ, punishing him smartly, and losing in turn three men wounded. The regiment continued to be constantly occupied in its turn in this wasting duty until the terrible morning of the 5th November, when the advance of the Russians called it suddenly into one of the most deadly encounters that has a place in the annals of war. On the first opening of the Battle of Inkerman, such portions of the 7th, 23rd, and 33rd regiments as were not then in the trenches were engaged, under Brigadier Codrington, to cover the left of our 2nd Division, and to occupy the sloping ground towards Sebastopol. They opposed the centre column of the attacking force. The Royal Fusiliers, under Colonel Yea, acted in skirmishing order on the right flank of the enemy, and they and their comrades of the Light Division were, "as usual, foremost in the fray." The reserve, under Sir Thomas Troubridge, was posted in the 5-gun battery. A picquet of the regiment, numbering forty of all ranks, under Lieutenant Butts, 77th Regiment, who was temporarily attached to the Royal Fusiliers, was on duty in the ravine at the White House, and *Opening of the bombardment.* *Battle of Inkerman.*

suffered severely, twenty-seven being killed or wounded, and seven being taken prisoners. Lieutenant Butts was himself captured, but after a very gallant encounter managed to make his escape before the close of the action.

To describe the efforts of the soldiers in the scenes that followed is merely to relate a succession of hand-to-hand combats, where tactics and the science of war were ignored, and where men grappled with their foe and struggled for a victory that could only be obtained by courage and endurance all but superhuman. The representatives of the Light Division materially assisted in checking the rushes of the Russian infantry, but, as they were exposed, perhaps more than any other division, to the hostile cannonade, their loss was fearfully great. In resisting the swarming hordes of Russians the Fusiliers everywhere found themselves pressed with desperate vigour. In the field they could only gain ground by an incessant slaughter of their foes, pushing back, at the point of the bayonet, the sturdy soldiers who assailed them with a vehemence that was even destroying them in victory. Nor was their fate in the battery happier or easier. There Sir Thomas Troubridge was shot down, with both his legs shattered to splinters above the ankles, and many men lost. On the damp hill sides of Inkerman, the few wearied soldiers who represented the British army, and struggled for its supremacy, covered themselves with a glory that shines transcendently brilliant besides the proudest deed of arms that history can relate; but they gained it at a terrible cost. Of the Fusiliers who took part in the combat, eight men: Corporal R. Palmer; Privates J. Burnes, J. Broadman, G. Humphries, J. King, W. Dyer, J. Roach, and H. Wood, were killed on the spot; five Officers, Major Sir Thomas Troubridge severely, Captain R. Y. Shipley severely, Lieutenant H. W. P. Butler severely, Captain E. H. Rose slightly, Ensign L. J. F. Jones slightly; Sergeants W. Richards slightly, J. Serjeant severely; one drummer, forty-six rank and file wounded, and 6 men missing.

Sir J. Troubridge wounded.

With the battle of Inkerman may be said to have commenced the unprecedented miseries endured by the English army as it kept watch and ward over the Russian garrison of Sebastopol. That battle had proved that nothing but the heroic bravery of the soldiers individually could redeem the great fault of holding a position that in a military sense, was perfectly untenable; but, fortunately for England, the utter impotence of her army organisation was a thing that the English soldier could not admit into his consideration; and for old England's sake the gallant fellows willingly held on. Well for them would it have been if their worst foes had been the Russian soldiery. A few days more of that dreary storm-racked November proved to them that their sufferings in battle were as naught. On the 14th November the dreadful hurricane, that plunged the whole British army into ineffable distress, swept over them; two of the Royal Fusiliers were starved to death while performing their duty; and before the gale had died away the regiment found itself shelterless, and robbed by the pitiless blast of the stores and necessaries that a tardy government was only then beginning to send to it. The hardships that the winter introduced were such as no other army ever supported while continuing to hold its supremacy over one superior in numbers; but at that time its supremacy was a potent and glorious thing, it was the prestige that followed from the deeds on the Alma, at Balaclava, and at Inkerman, a mighty power and able to protect those whom it covered from insult in the moment of their helplessness. But still this prestige could not subdue hunger and starvation, nor could it ward off fever and death; it could enable men to stand boldly and prevent the coming of men who should have met them in arms; yet, as it was not food and raiment, it left the British army to perish miserably amid the horrors of an almost Arctic winter.

On the 21st, the regiment received a draft of two sergeants, two corporals, and ninety-eight men, under the command of Ensign G. H. Waller. Their advent to the region of desolate misery is thus described by the *Times*' correspondent:—
"Greatly astonished did they seem as they were invited to walk ankle deep in the mud through arabas, Turks, camels, Frenchmen, Crim Tartars, Greeks, and Bulgarians, along the principal thoroughfare of Balaclava, out to their camps. Like young bears they had their troubles all before them, and the brilliancy of their uniforms, which has just renewed our notions as to what a red coat ought to be, was fading fast when they were last seen before the coating of liquid filth which the natives of Balaclava seem to consider as the normal paving of their thoroughfare."

The severity alike of the season and the duties told heavily upon the army. Sickness was rampant, the prevalent diseases being fever, dysentery, and diarrhœa; "and in the Light Division, on which a large share of the labour of the army falls, there were 350 men on the sick list" at the end of November. This dreadful state

The regiment suffers from sickness.

of suffering and loss continued without relaxation. So great had been the deficiency of officers since November, that one subaltern, Ensign Butts, from the 77th, and two, Lieutenants Clayton and Byron, of the 34th Regiments, were ordered to do duty with the Fusiliers, and in consequence were attached to the regiment. On the 20th December the Russians made an attack on Gordon's Battery and the advanced works, occupied at the time by eight companies of the Light Division, *i.e.*, two of the 23rd, 33rd, and 34th Regiments, and two companies of the Fusiliers, under Lieutenant Byron, of the 34th Regiment. Quietly and stealthily, in the dark and lowering morning, the Russians came on, taking by surprise the troops, who were aroused from sleep to find themselves pressed by the foe; they bayoneted the sentry, who had been badly posted, being too near the works to give sufficient alarm, and entered the trench, wounding five privates of the Fusiliers, and carrying off the officer, Lieutenant Byron, before they were ejected by the 34th Regiment.

1855.

Establishment increased.

On the 5th January the regiment was ordered to be raised to sixteen companies; four to form the depot at Winchester, and four to form a reserve depot at Malta, from which strong drafts could be quickly sent to the front.

With the advent of January the weather grew rapidly worse, frost, snow, and sleet succeeded each other, and the health of the army diminished proportionally. At this period the effective strength of the regiment was not more than 230 men, and on every day it had to supply its quota for the trenches. Its labours and sufferings were almost past endurance,* but they could not then be remedied. For the first amelioration of their dreadful condition, the Fusiliers had to thank the indomitable will of their stern yet thoughtful commander; but his iron determination could not relieve them from their misery before February. As soon as the stores began to arrive, Lacy Yea remembered his Fusiliers, and insisted upon having the supplies. His efforts bore the following fruit:—"There are a good many wooden huts now

---

* "January 10th.—Very hard frost again last night, the thermometer down to 18 degrees Fahrenheit, which, after the wet of yesterday, has made the ground like a sheet of ice. A man of the 7th Fusiliers committed suicide this morning, when on sentry, by blowing his brains out with his firelock. He told a comrade shortly before that he was determined to put an end to himself, as he could not stand the hard work and severity of the weather any longer. He had been sixteen years in the regiment, and bore a good character."

(Feb. 2) erected at the front; almost every regiment has one or two as its field hospital; and two regiments of the Light Division, the 7th Fusiliers and the 77th Regiment, have each got five huts completed, independent of their hospital. These two regiments are indebted, I believe, for their present efficient state to the rigid discipline that has invariably been maintained by their respective lieutenant-colonels. From the first these officers have never allowed the hardship of the campaign to interfere with their regular course of duty, and have never relaxed their discipline one iota more than was absolutely necessary; and the consequence is that, although they have suffered more from losses in action than almost any other regiment in the army, from the brilliant and prominent parts they took in the battles of Alma and Inkerman, yet they are, I firmly believe, at the present moment in a more efficient state than any other regiment who landed with the army in the Crimea in September last."

The weary winter having exhausted its fierceness by March, and the health of the troops being greatly redeemed by the supplies that indignant England poured into the Crimea when it was almost too late, activity returned, and the proper business of the siege was resumed. During the months of January and February, and early parts of March, the regiment continued its wearisome work with uneventful regularity. On the 22nd of March, however, the tranquillity was very rudely interrupted by a sortie of the Russians to check the advance of the French towards the Mamelon. *Sortie of the 22nd March.* The attack extended from the French to the English trenches, where detachments of the 77th and 97th Regiments were on guard. Having thus occupied the attention of this part of the front, another body of Russians advanced against the mortar battery on the left of the right attack, where the detachments of the Royal Fusiliers and 34th Regiments were on duty. From the first the Russians pressed on with great vigour and determination, the attack becoming general along the line. "The gallant old Fusiliers had to run the gauntlet of a large body of the enemy, whom they drove back *à la fourchette*." Lieut.-Col. Tylden of the Royal Engineers was then in the battery, he promptly made the detachments "stand to their arms, and led them with the greatest determination and steadiness against the enemy, who were speedily ejected from the works, and fairly pitched over the parapet with little or no firing on our part." Both detachments, however, suffered rather severely, for

Death of Captain C. Browne.

the combat was rudely and stubbornly fought out. The courage displayed by Capt. Cavendish Browne, of the Royal Fusiliers, was most conspicuous. He was severely wounded at the commencement of the attack, but while the enemy were pressing on with savage energy he refused to go to the rear, although nearly fainting with loss of blood. He continued to lead his Fusiliers on with unflinching resolution, encouraging them with voice and gesture to the front, when he was shot dead. When his body was found it lay far in advance of our line, with three balls in his chest. On his death the command devolved on Lieutenant Lord R. H. Browne, under whom the works were cleared, and the Russians finally driven off.

Besides Captain Browne the regiment lost Lieutenant J. MacHenry, severely, Corporal Matthew Hudson, severely, and seven men wounded. Lieutenant-Colonel Tylden spoke in high terms of the conduct of the troops on this occasion. Among those who most distinguished themselves where many were distinguished, was Sergeant C. Fisher, whose conduct was recognised in the following Order:—

Col.-Sergt. Fisher distinguishes himself.

"24th March, 1855.

"Regimental Order.—The officer in temporary command feels it a duty as well to the individual as to the regiment to notice the gallant, energetic, and zealous conduct of Colour-Sergeant Charles Fisher, on the night of the 22nd instant; noticed not only by those belonging to the 7th Fusiliers but by officers and men of other regiments at the advanced works."

From this time the progress of affairs grew more lively; skirmishes, resulting from endeavours to establish rifle pits, being of constant occurrence. Between the 26th March and the 5th April the regiment had several casualties; on the latter day a sharp affair took place, which is thus described by the *Times'* correspondent:— "There was very heavy firing from half-past ten to half-past eleven o'clock, which was heralded in by some brisk volleys, and we hear that our working parties in the advanced trench happened to meet a working party of the Russians, and that a regular hand-to-hand fight with pickaxes, spades, bills, hatchets, and musket stocks, took place betwixt the two parties, in which the Russians had the best at one time, and we gained the ground at another time, till at last the Island courage did its work, and our men drove the enemy up towards our own lines. The fight was renewed in front of the trenches. The covering parties came out on both sides to the aid of their comrades, and at last the Russians were repulsed after a severe struggle." In this affair the Fusiliers had Private James Stokes killed; Lieutenant

L. J. F. Jones, slightly; Corporals E. Finnegan, C. Marriot, J. Stannard, and five men, wounded.

In April Her Majesty was graciously pleased to confer a medal with gratuity "for distinguished conduct in the field" at the battles of Alma and Inkerman on the following non-commissioned officers and privates:— *Distinguished Conduct Medals granted.*

Colour Sergeant Charles Fisher	.. gratuity of £15	Private Thomas Taylor	.. gratuity of	£5
Corporal James Button	.. ,, 10	,, Jesse Hargreaves	.. ,,	5
,, Joseph Horsnell	.. ,, 10	,, Thomas Burke	.. ,,	5
,, Matthew Hudson	.. ,, 10	,, Hugh Sweeny	.. ,,	5
,, Henry Spence	.. ,, 10	,, John Ryan	.. ,,	5
Private William Allen	.. ,, 5	,, James Spilbury	.. ,,	5
,, James McCabe	.. ,, 5	,, William Paterson	.. ,,	5

The second bombardment of Sebastopol commenced on the 9th April, and with it a succession of increasing losses to each regiment that visited the trenches. By the 18th the strength of the bombardment was spent, the Infantry of both armies being again called into operation in the struggles for positions along the front, or the destruction of works already erected. On the night of the 9th of May the Royal Fusiliers and their old comrades the 34th were again involved in one of these conflicts. The enemy made two serious assaults upon our advanced parallel of the right attack. They were perceived within 50 yards of our most advanced works, when a heavy fire commenced on both sides. The affair was merely a matter of musketry, which "having rolled incessantly for a quarter-of-an-hour, began to cease at intervals along the line. Here and there it stopped for a moment altogether; again it burst forth. Then came a British cheer which thrilled through every heart. 'Our fellows have driven them back; bravo!' A Russian yell, a fresh burst of musketry, more cheering, a rolling volley subsiding into spattering flashes and broken fire, a ringing hurrah from the front followed; and then the Russian bugles sounding the 'retreat,' and our own bugles the 'cease firing,' and the attack after half-an-hour's duration was over. The enemy were retiring to their earthworks." In the affair the Royal Fusiliers had five men wounded; in his despatch Lord Raglan says, "Captain Turner of the Royal Fusiliers and Captain Jordan of the 34th are reported to have done their duty in the most gallant style." The enemy opened a powerful fire on our trenches on the following night, and exposed his columns to a heavy musketry

Second bombardment opened.

fire from the troops on duty; but he neither offered to reach the parapets nor to come even near to them.

<small>Attack of the Quarries.</small> The first serious attack upon the enemy's permanent works took place on the night of the 7th June, when the French assaulted the Mamelon and the English the Quarries. About 5 p.m., 150 rank and file of the Royal Fusiliers, under Major Mills, with a similar party of the 88th, were ordered to assail the Quarries from the right of the zigzag approach on the left of our advanced trench; the 47th and 49th Regiments starting from the left of this approach. The first rush carried the works at an easy cost, when a large working party, including 200 Fusiliers, under Captain Appleyard, entered the place and effected a lodgment. Meanwhile the Russians were preparing to re-capture the place. At dark the attempt was made. Then came the struggle, one of the most determined of the whole war. During the night, repeated attacks, six in all, were made upon the place; and each of these attacks was a fierce hand-to-hand fight, where men strove for the destruction of their opponents with unyielding violence. "During one of these attacks, shortly before dusk, the ammunition on both sides having fallen short, and English and Russians both wishing to keep a few rounds in reserve in case of a sudden attempt being made by either party, the fight was kept up for a short time with stones, of which numbers were lying on the ground, until the pouches were replenished, when the strife was more sternly renewed, with continual success on our part." Never in the long and bloody struggle did the Muscovite Infantry more fiercely strive for victory; never did the men who were so soon to be reproached for failure more signally establish their superiority over their stubborn enemies. On every occasion of bitter conflict during the long course of this blood-stained night did the British soldier hurl back the Russ with a destroying violence. "More than once there was a fierce hand-to-hand fight in the position itself, and our fellows had frequently to dash out in front and take their assailants in flank. The most murderous sortie of the enemy took place about three in the morning; then the whole ravine was lighted up with a blaze of fire, and a storm of shot was thrown in from the screened battery, and every other spot within range. With a larger body in reserve, it was not doubtful that our men could have been into the Redan in a twinkling. This was asserted freely both by

officers and privates, and the latter expressed their opinion in no complimentary manner. They were near enough up to it to see that it was scarcely defended, and one officer lost his life almost within its limits."

Among those who were mentioned in despatches for their gallantry on this occasion was Lieutenant H. M. Jones, of the Royal Fusiliers. The regiment had Major F. Mills, Captain W. W. Turner, Lieutenants H. M. Jones, L. J. F. Jones, and G. H. Waller, all slightly wounded; Colour-Sergeant W. K. Dobbie, Corporal Geo. Parker, Privates Thomas Latimer, Thomas Hargreaves, James Gilvey, William Cook, Benj. Jagger, Thomas Wilson, Wm. Thompson, James Ward, John Brown, and Joseph Horsnell, killed; Sergeants Henry Martin, John Stocks, Jonathan Richmond, all slightly; Corporal John Ross dangerously (since dead), and 70 men wounded; eight men missing. For this success Major Mills was promoted Brevet Lieutenant-Colonel, and Captain Turner Brevet Major. On the 9th the regiment had Captain J. H. Cooper slightly and one man wounded; on the 10th it had Corporal G. W. Henty slightly wounded.

Losses of the Fusiliers.

At this period events were thickening; the crisis of the siege seemed to be at hand. All foresaw that the assault could not be long delayed, and it is no exaggeration to say that every man in the allied army was longing for the time when it should come. At last the thing that had been so long craved for appeared to be about to arrive; it seemed that the guns of the attack were getting a mastery over the guns of the defence: at last the frowning earthworks, that for months had seemed to swell as if by the very weight of shot they had swallowed up in resisting the effort to destroy them, were so battered and ruined that nothing but musketry, and last of all the bayonets of the stubborn defenders, prevented the Allies from rushing into the place.

In a few days it became known that the attempt was to be made, and that it was to be made on the 18th June, the fortieth anniversary of Wellington's greatest battle. Confident in their prowess the soldiers looked upon the day as most auspicious; and in their confidence they fondly believed that ere the sun set on that day their banners would wave over the blood-stained ruins of the fortress, and the war would be virtually terminated. Alas, vain confidence! how soon were they to be deceived! The arrangements having been made, the right assailing column,

Assault of the 18th June.

that representing the Light Division, and furnished by the 7th, 23rd, 33rd, and 34th Regiments under Colonel Yea, was to advance against the left face of the Redan at day-break. The rest of the story we all know too well. From the first period of the onset the weakness of the arrangement, which left them to scramble wildly over the parapet of the trench, clearly foreshadowed the failure of the attack. With columns far too weak, and without any efficient support, the men were sent forward. "The moment they came out of the trench," says Russell, "the enemy began to direct on the whole front a deliberate and well-aimed *mitraille*, which increased the want of order and unsteadiness caused by the mode of their advance. Poor Colonel Yea saw the consequences too clearly. Having in vain tried to obviate the evil caused by the broken formation and confusion of his men, who were falling fast around him, he exclaimed, 'This will never do! Where's the bugler to call them back?' But, alas! at that critical moment no bugler was to be found. The gallant officer, by voice and gesture, tried to form and compose his men, but the thunder of the enemy's guns close at hand, and the gloom frustrated his efforts; and as he rushed along the troubled mass of troops, endeavouring to put them into order for

Death of Col. Yea

a rush at the batteries, a charge of their deadly missiles passed, and the noble soldier fell dead in advance of his men, struck at once in the head and stomach by grape shot. A fine young officer, Hobson, the Adjutant of the 7th, fell along with his chief mortally wounded." Another, Lieutenant Fitzclarence, was smitten down mutilated past recovery. He had a leg and finger amputated in camp on the 18th, and seemed to be progressing rapidly almost up to his death of bronchitis; he died in camp, July 25th.

From the very outset the assault had failed, and it had failed in a manner that harrows the heart of the English soldier to think of. In no case had the storming columns succeeded in reaching the works of the place. Nor was this want of success due to lack of bravery and determination. "The admirable conduct of Capt. Turner, of the 7th Foot," was noticed by Codrington, and mentioned in Raglan's dispatch; Lieut. William Hope with four men braved the whole fire of the place to rescue his comrade, Lieut. Hobson, whom he found wounded to death in the old agricultural ditch running towards the Redan; and of the Fusiliers who were struck down, all of them were men who had held the Quarries, and many of them men who had scaled the heights of Alma, and held with such grim tenacity the gory slopes of Inkerman. The fact is, the assailants were simply decimated before they had time to form, and the thing that was so yearned for had not been accomplished—the fire of the place had not been subdued nor even damaged!

Heavy as was the suffering of the Light Division, the loss that pained all most was the death of the Colonel of the Royal Fusiliers.* His portrait has been worthily painted by Russell, and the portrait must not be omitted from the Record of the Services of the Royal Fusiliers. "Under occasional brusqueness of manner he concealed a most kind heart, and a more thorough soldier, one more devoted to his men, to the service, and to his country, never fell in battle than Lacy Yea. I have reason to know that he felt his great services and his arduous exertions had not been rewarded as he had a right to expect. At the Alma he never went back a step, and there were tears in his eyes on that eventful afternoon, as he exclaimed to me, when the men had formed upon the slope of the hill after the retreat of the enemy, 'There, look there! That's all that remains of my poor Fusiliers! A colour's missing, but thank God no Russians have it.' Throughout the winter his attention to his regiment was exemplary. His men were the first who had hospital huts. When other regiments were in need of every comfort, and almost of every necessity, the Fusiliers by the care of their Colonel, had everything that could be procured by exertion and foresight. He never missed a turn of duty in the trenches, except for a short time, when his medical attendant had to use all his efforts to induce him to go on board ship to save his life." Though Colonel Yea was the only officer killed upon the field, this tale of death did not end with him; Lieut. Hobson died of his wounds; Lieut. the Hon. E. Fitzclarence underwent amputation of the left leg, and as stated above, he died on the 25th July; Major Pack was severely wounded; Capt. F. Appleyard, slightly; Lieuts. L. J. F. Jones, severely, C. Malan, severely, Lord R. H. Browne, slightly; G. H. Waller, slightly; W. L. L. G. Wright, slightly; and Lieut. N. D. Robinson returned as missing, but only slightly wounded; Sergts.

Losses of the Regiment.

* Its effect upon the rugged veterans he had both ruled and led was noticed by Russell, when he watched the wounded being carried in during the armistice, and is thus described:—"I saw in one place two of our men, apart from the rest, with melancholy faces. 'What are you waiting here for?' said I. 'To go out for the Colonel Sir,' was the reply. 'What Colonel?' 'Why Colonel Yea, to be sure, Sir,' said the good fellow, who was evidently surprised that there could be any other Colonel in the world. And indeed the Light division felt his loss."

David Miller, Michael Bergin, Frank Williamson, Corpl. A. K. Bramham, and 15 men were killed; Sergt.-Major W. Bacon, slightly; Corpls. Henry Oaks, Wm. Buck, Matthew Hughes, severely; Sam. Flack, Henry Edwards, Andrew Nutley, slightly; and 50 men wounded.

Colonel Yea's body was found near the abattis, on the right of the Redan. His head was greatly swollen and his features nearly indistinguishable. He was buried on the 20th, his funeral being attended by the whole of his brigade.

Thus ended the first assault on Sebastopol, if an operation can be called an assault which was never extended as a whole beyond the effort to get the assaulting columns into the open from the trenches, and ready for a rush. It was a grievous and bitter disappointment to the English army, for it was the first proof they had received in the Crimea that they were not invincible. It was a sense of painful chagrin for the men who had stormed the heights of Alma and had held the blood-reeking slopes of Inkerman in defiance of all the superior numbers that a subtle and skilful foe could hurl against them, to find that there were positions where the soldiery whom they knew themselves able to conquer could hold them at bay, or force them back with a rudely consuming slaughter. But it was now found to be a fact that there were such positions—a fact, however, which British soldiers could not possibly understand!

On the 7th July Brevet Lieutenant-Colonel Heyland, Lieutenants C. E. Hope, J. Gardiner, O. Colt, and W. P. Browne joined Head Quarters; and on the 12th a draft arrived under Lieutenant F. G. Beauchamp, consisting of Lieutenant H. Plumer, 4 sergeants, 2 drummers, and 82 rank and file.

The bombardment re-opens. The repulse of the 18th initiated another bombardment. The story of "subduing the fire" was again the prevalent one. In the meantime the narrow and intricate trenches had to be manned and held as before, the daily lists of casualties had to be made out, and the siege had to be pushed forward in the tardy manner that had so long characterised it. The old struggles in resisting sorties were again revived; the old encounters of pickets were again the fashion. The losses of the Light Division in these affairs and in the trench duties had already become serious. Writing on the 23rd July the correspondent of the *Daily News* says, most of the Regiments of that Division were greatly reduced in strength; and that some of them had scarcely sufficient officers left to carry on the duty. In this crippled state matters progressed with very little variation from the usual dull turn of trench duty and its accompanying losses until the night of the 2nd August, when the pickets had a smart brush with the Russians at the picket house on the Woronzoff Road. The enemy, whose design was to destroy our abattis, and so open the road, crept up in force, and with terrific yells. After firing a volley, which smote some of the picket, they made a rush at the post, and commenced tearing away the obstacle. The order "Reserves to the front" resounded that instant through Gordon's battery; and parties of the 7th and 77th bounded out with a Hurrah! louder and deeper than that of the enemy. The Russians, in the meantime, had been doing their work with vigour; they had torn down part of the stockade, and were carrying off some of our *chevaux de frise* for their own use, when they were attacked by the Fusiliers and their old comrades of the 77th, and their further progress put an end to by a spirited charge which drove them back into their lines with severe loss. With this little episode breaking the current of events the Fusiliers were relegated to the monotonous trenches, to suffer and endure each day more and more until the final assault should take place. Affair at the Picket House.

In the sortie which took place early on the morning of the 1st September on the advanced trenches of the right attack the Royal Fusiliers had Sergeant Henry Martin and two men severely wounded. On the night of the 3rd September the Russians again made a sortie on the advanced works, when they were repulsed with great loss. The firing was kept up for about twenty minutes, and "while it lasted it was one of the hottest affairs we have yet experienced." Again the 7th and 77th were together; the latter regiment suffered severely, but the Fusiliers had only one man killed. In this affair Captain Hibbert, who was wounded, greatly distinguished himself. Sorties on the 1st and 3rd September.

On the morning of the 5th September the Allies commenced the last bombardment of Sebastopol. Next day the Fusiliers had three men wounded, on the succeeding day they had two men killed. On the 8th they were summoned to again assail the Redan!

We need not go into the details of the plan of attack. As on the 18th of June, they were defective. The French were to attack the Malakoff, the capture of which Second assault of the Redan.

was to be followed by the English assault of the Redan. As soon as the French had made good their footing in the Malakoff, a tricolour was run up to announce the triumph; immediately afterwards a blue and white chequered flag, the flag of the Light Division, the signal appointed for the advance of the English, was displayed from the Eight-gun Battery of the English right attack. The stormers were then ordered forward. The covering party, 100 men of the 2nd Battalion Rifle Brigade, under Capt. Fyers, kept up a vigorous and deadly fire into the embrasures: but the thick rope mantlets, with which Russian ingenuity had long ago completely protected their gunners, saved the Russian artillerymen, and enabled them to pour down their grape, which continued to fly thick and fast over the death space the English had to cross. As the Light Division rushed out into the open, they were swept by the guns of the Barrack Battery, and by several pieces on the proper right of the Redan, heavily loaded with grape. The division made straight for the salient of the Redan, crossed the ditch, and scrambled into the work. At the first rush the stormers took possession of the Redan, and, the Russians flying before them, could have kept it had they been properly supported. But the opportune moment was lost, for in the assault of a breach manned by vigorous defenders the golden opportunity did not exceed a moment, and indecision lost it. Instead of hurling forward the supports, "who crowded the trenches in the rear till the enemy had time to bring up his overpowering reserves and clear the Redan of our men," the rapidly wasting few who first gained possession were left to themselves; and bravely but vainly facing the gathering masses who surged down upon them, they were swept back into the open, to retreat or stand idle and impotent under fresh storms of grape from the guns they had once captured.

In the midst of the confusion, arising in a great measure from the intricacy of the trenches, and the fatal want of space for the formation of troops, orders were sent to the supports to go forward. In a moment the confusion increased, for misunderstanding was added to it. The orders were given to the wrong regiments. The Second Brigade of the Light Division, which had been told off as the proper reserve, was sent forward. Three of the officers and some of the men had already been wounded in the trenches, but no sooner were they in the open, than the pitiless storm burst upon them with a fury that staggered them. "Evident, however, as was the blunder, the gallant 'Fighting 7th,' led by Major Turner, and the 23rd, under Colonel Lysons, advanced to the renewed attack. The other regiments, who should have preceded, followed in a state of beautiful pell-mell, and, under a fire of grape and canister, before which the bravest columns of veterans would have staggered, our young levies were led on to regain the ground which had been lost through mismanagement before." It was not, however, in human nature to make headway against such an iron storm; the men turned and sought cover under the parapet. Two young lieutenants of the Fusiliers, Wright and Colt, were killed; Major Turner received a ball through his scalp—one of the narrowest escapes of that day; and Lieut. H. M. Jones* was knocked down by the fragments of a shell. The assault was over, supports could not be sent up, and the English had failed!

<small>The Royal Fusiliers led on by Major Turner.</small>

The loss sustained by the Fusiliers was heavy, in addition to Lieuts. Colt and Wright, Sergt. A. Seddon, Corpls. W. Hargrave, and 11 men were killed; Lieut.-Col. Heyland, Capts. J. F. Hickie, H. R. Hibbert, Lieut. H. M. Jones, Sergt.-Major W. Bacon, Sergts. J. McCann, G. Whittle, W. H. Farrow, J. S. Wood, F. Holmes, J. Graham, W. Jowett, Corps. G. W. Henty, T. Settle, J. Gumby, and 39 men severely; Bt.-Major W. W. Turner, Sergts. T. Going, R. Holmes, J. Munro, Corps. T. Brooker, and 17 men slightly; Sergts. W. Fraser, John Stocks, and 7 men missing.

Capt. Hibbert's bravery in the affair, and especially in the sortie on the 3rd of September, was thus acknowledged by the Commander-in-Chief:—

<small>Captain Hibbert promoted for gallantry.</small>

"Before Sebastopol, 18th Nov., 1855.

" SIR,—I have great pleasure in forwarding to you an extract of a letter from General Yorke, dated Horse Guards, 3rd Nov., 1855, of which the following are the terms:—

' The Field Marshal has desired me most especially to notice on this occasion the conduct of Capt. Hibbert, of the Royal Fusiliers, on the night of the 3rd September, which you brought to his Lordship's knowledge in your private communication of the 8th September. This officer received a wound when in the advanced sap of considerable severity, which made it necessary to convey him to the rear; but as soon as the wound had been attended to he returned to the advanced sap, upon which a very heavy fire was directed at the time. and remained in command of that part of the trench until the usual hour of relief.

' Capt. Hibbert was again severely wounded in the attack of the Redan on the 8th September.

* "Under the head of 'dangerously' we are sorry to find once more the name of Lieut. H. M. Jones, 'Alma Jones,' of the 7th Fusiliers, who has been hit no less than seven or eight times at the Alma, in the trenches, and the affairs of the 7th and 18th June. He has within the last few days obtained his company, and we may trust he may be as fortunate as heretofore in getting over the injury he has sustained."—*Globe Correspondent.*

'The Field Marshal has great pleasure in recommending this officer for the brevet rank of major, but he requests that you will be good enough to desire that his meritorious conduct on the occasion alluded to, may be recorded in the Regimental Record Book.

'I have the honour to be, Sir,

'Your most obedient servant,

'CODRINGTON, General Commanding.

'The Officer Commanding Royal Fusiliers.'"

Draft joins.

On the 9th September a draft under Lieut. J. E. Elwes, consisting of 2 Sergeants, 2 Corporals, and 125 Privates, arrived at Balaclava and joined Head Quarters. For service they had come too late. Sebastopol was then only a deserted town of burning and blood-stained ruins, shattered to splinters, and crumbling into horrid wreck. In the night the stubborn Russ who so long a time had so valiantly defended it had abandoned it to flames and destruction, retreating to the north side. Practically from this moment the war was at an end; and the twelve months of struggling that we had passed through, with all its glory, its suffering, and its bitter memories of every kind, had been rewarded with success, and of that success not a little was earned by "the gallant Fusiliers." Of that glorious Light Division, which from the beginning of the war was "put at everything," the Royal Fusiliers had been the leading regiment, and in all the infantry fights of the whole campaign it had taken a conspicuous and distinguished part. In constancy, in endurance, in bravery and in strength it had not been surpassed; in toil, in exposure, and in suffering it had not been equalled!

Henceforward the story of the sojourn in the Crimea until the evacuation is one of little event. On the 15th September Capt. C. E. Watson joined from the depôt and took command of the regiment; he was succeeded on the 6th November by Col. W. H. C. Wellesley, who joined from England, and assumed the command. On the 15th November, occurred the great explosion in the French Siege Park, only a few hundred yards in the rear of the camp of the regiment, when 250,000 pounds of powder ignited. From this calamity the Light Division suffered severely, not less than 10 men being killed and 69 wounded, of whom 1 man killed and 12 wounded belonged to the Royal Fusiliers.

Explosion in the French Siege Park.

On this occasion Lieut. W. Hope gave an instance of cool and determined courage, the record of which should not be omitted. An old windmill, not very far in rear of the French Siege Park, was stored with large quantities of powder. Its roof, covered with wooden shingles, had been completely shattered by the explosion; some of the shingles were beginning to catch fire, the contents of the mill were in imminent danger of being ignited, and a further loss of life apparently about to occur. At this time Gen. Van Straubenzee, commanding the right brigade, Light Division rode up and called for volunteers to place wet blankets on the top of the windmill, to avert, if possible, the impending disaster. Lieut. Hope, with twenty-five men of the regiment, undertook the perilous duty, and succeeding in carrying out the General's intentions, prevented a fresh calamity resulting from the accident which had already produced such a terrible effect. Their gallant conduct was thus noticed in the *Gazette*:—" At the great explosion of the French siege train, Nov. 15th, 1855, Lieutenant Hope was conspicuous for his coolness and activity when in charge of a fatigue party, to cover the mill with wet blankets. The roof had been blown off, and 160 tons of gunpowder were exposed to the fire, burning rockets, &c. He mounted the mill, and by his courage and example saved the magazine, which was momentarily expected to explode, and preserved the lives of probably hundreds of the Light Divison. His conduct received the marked encomiums of the authorities. Colonel Sir J. St. George, commanding the siege train, also wished his thanks to be expressed to this officer for his zealous assistance in the performance of an important service at a critical time."

<small>Gallantry of volunteers led by Lieutenant Hope.</small>

1856.

The Regiment passed the winter in strong contrast to the preceding one. Health and plenty reigned, the duties were light, the constant strain of the trenches was no longer felt, and the men began to assume their old appearance, the regiments their old smart efficiency. Peace was proclaimed on the 2nd April, and with it, of course, commenced preparations for the evacuation.

On the 24th May an inspection of the British army took place on the Balaclava plain, in honour of Her Majesty's birthday; the occasion being also seized to distribute the medals given "for valour and discipline" by the Emperor of the French to the non-commissioned officers and soldiers of the British army. Those given to the Light Division were presented by Lord William Paulet; the following men of the Royal Fusiliers being among the recipients:—

<small>Medals distributed.</small>

"Sergt.-Major JOSEPH BELL; landed in the Crimea 14th September, 1854; engaged at Alma and Inkerman, sortie 26th October, 1854, and both assaults on the Redan.

"Colour-Sergt. JOHN WATTS; landed in the Crimea 14th September, 1854; was engaged at the Alma, and brought the company out of action; engaged with the enemy in the sortie of the 26th October; and also at Inkerman, when he brought the company out of action; at the taking of the Quarries, and both assaults of the Redan; and was never absent from his regiment.

"Sergt. JOHN LAW, Sergt. THOMAS POULTON, Corporal PATRICK HANLON, and Corporal WILLIAM MARSHALL (wounded 18th June) were each of them engaged both at Alma and Inkerman, the two assaults on the Redan, in all trench duties, and were never absent from the regiment.

"Private MICHAEL EDWARDS served at Alma and Inkerman, at both assaults of the Redan, and the capture of the Quarries; especially mentioned by the officer commanding the regiment on the last occasion; never missed a day's duty in the trenches.

"Sergt.-Major WILLIAM BACON wounded in the attack on the Redan on the 18th June, and again desperately in the attack on the 8th September.

"Sergt. WILLIAM WHITE, present at the battles of Alma and Inkerman, and in the trenches; left the Crimea in May, 1855."

The following officers, non-commissioned officers, and private soldiers, received the Cross of the Legion of Honour from the Emperor of the French:—

Lieut.-Col. Arthur R. Pack.
Col. Sir Thomas Troubridge, Bart.
Bt. Lieut.-Col. William W. Turner.
Bt.-Major Hugh R. Hibbert.
Capt. Frederick E. Appleyard.

Capt. Henry M. Jones.
Lieut. George H. Waller.
Sergt.-Major Joseph Bell.
Private Thomas Paynes.

The following officers and soldiers received the Sardinian medal:—

Lieut.-Col. Reginald Y. Shipley.
Bt.-Major Hugh R. Hibbert.
Lieut. William Hope.

Private William Barrack.
Private John M'Guire.

The following officers and men received the Victoria Cross:—

"Lieut. WILLIAM HOPE.—After the troops had retired on the 18th June, 1855, Lieut. Hope being informed by the late Sergt.-Major W. Bacon, who was himself wounded, that Lieut. and Adjt. Hobson was lying outside the trenches badly wounded, he went out to look for him, and found him lying in the old agricultural ditch running towards the left flank of the Redan. He then returned and got four men to bring him in. Finding, however, that Lieut. Hobson could not be removed without a stretcher, he then ran back across the open to Egerton's Pit, where he procured one, and carried it to where Lieut. Hobson was lying. All this was done under a heavy fire from the Russian batteries.

"Capt. HENRY MITCHELL JONES—for conspicuous gallantry during the Crimean War, especially during the assault and defence of the Quarries.

"Asst.-Surgeon THOMAS EGERTON HALE, M.D.—for remaining with Lieut. H. M. Jones who was dangerously wounded in the 5th parallel on the 8th September, 1855, when all the men in the immediate neighbourhood had retired, except Lieut. W. Hope and Dr. Hale; and for endeavouring to rally the men in conjunction with Lieut. Hope; secondly, for having on the 8th September, after the regiments had retired into the trenches, cleared the most advanced sap of the wounded, and carried into the sap, under a heavy fire, several wounded men from the open ground, being assisted by Sergt. Charles Fisher, 7th Fusiliers.

"Private MATTHEW HUGHES was noticed by Colonel Campbell, 90th Light Infantry, on the 7th June, 1855, at the storming of the Quarries, twice going for ammunition across the open ground under a heavy fire; he also went to the front and brought in Private John Hampton who was lying severely wounded; and on the 18th June he volunteered to bring in Lieut. Hobson who was lying severely wounded, and, in the act of doing so, was severely wounded himself.

"Private WILLIAM NORMAN.—On the night of the 19th December, 1854, he was placed on single sentry, some distance in front of the advanced sentries of an outlying picket in the White House Ravine, a post of much danger and requiring great vigilance; the Russian picket was posted about 300 yards in his front; three Russian soldiers advanced under cover of the brushwood, for the purpose of reconnoitring. Private Norman, single handed, took two of them prisoners without alarming the Russian picket."

The loss of the Royal Fusiliers, from the time of their arrival at Constantinople in April, 1854, to their return to England, amounted to 14 officers and 559 non-commissioned officers and men. This severe loss is the faithful record of the severity of their services. As has been shewn they had been "put at" everything—they were the first to land, the last to fix their bayonets for a death grapple with the foe; they had been engaged in almost every action and sortie that had taken place, and during the winter they had furnished more men for the trenches than any other regiment in the Division. For a time the detail of their daily duties was rigidly kept, and its fulness speaks more eloquently than the most vivid of general descriptions; it is unfortunate for the regiment that it was not continued to the end of the war.

DETAIL OF DUTIES PERFORMED BY THE ROYAL FUSILIERS AT THE SIEGE OF SEBASTOPOL.

Date.	F. O.	Capts.	Lieuts.	Sergts.	Divisions.	Duty.	Remarks.
1854, Oct. 4	...	1	1	...	No. 3	Outlying p.	The Royal Fusiliers were divided into six Divisions.
5	...	1	1	...	4	do.	
7	...	...	1	...	5	do.	
8	...	...	1	...	6	do.	
,,	...	...	2	3	70 r. & f.	Working party.	
9	...	1	1	...	No. 1	Outlying p.	
10	...	...	1	...	2	do.	
,,	...	...	1	3	200 r. & f.	Working party.	
13	1	1	2	..	3, 4, 5, 6	Outlying p.	
14	...	...	1	...	3, 4	do.	
15	...	...	2	...	2, 5	do.	
16	...	1	1	...	1, 3, 4, 5	do.	Lieut. Cooper joined from Scutari.
17	...	1	...	...	3, 4, 5, 6	do.	Lieut. Tryon joined from Scutari.
18	...	1	1	...	3, 4, 5	do.	
19	...	1	...	...	2, 6	do.	
20	...	1	...	...	1	do.	Ensign L. J. F. Jones joined.
,,	1	1	2	...	3, 4, 5	Working party.	
21	1	2	1	...	2, 3, 4, 5, 6	Trench guard.	
22	...	1	...	...	1	Outlying p.	
23	...	1	1	...	3, 4, 5	do.	
24	...	1	1	...	2, 6	French guard.	
25	...	1	...	...	1, 3	do.	
,,	...	1	1	...	4, 5	Outlying p.	
26	1	1	...	...	4, 2, 6	do.	Major Sir T. Troubridge commanding picket of 3 companies of Fusiliers and 1 of Rifles.
27	1	2	2	...	1, 2, 3, 5, 6	Trench guard.	
29	...	1	1	...	1, 2, 3, 4	Picket.	
30	...	1	1	...	5, 6	Trench guard.	
31	...	1	1	...	1, 2	Outlying p.	
Nov. 1	...	...	2	...	3, 4	Trenches.	
,,	...	1	...	...	5	Picket.	
2	...	2	2	...	6, 1, 2	do.	
3	...	1	2	...	3, 4, 5	Trenches.	
5	2	4	6	...	450 r & f.	5 Gun Battery.	Battle of Inkerman.
6	do.	do.	do.	...	do.	do.	Strength of Regiment, 1 F. O., 1 Capt., 5 Subs., Rank and file.
8	...	1	1	...	2	Picket.	
,,	...	...	2	...	3, 4, 5, 6, 1	Trenches.	Captain Aldworth invalided.
10	...	1	...	...	3, 4, 5, 6	Picket.	Major Sir T. Troubridge, Capt. Shipley, and Lieut. W. Butler invalided to England.
11	...	...	1	...	1, 2	Trenches.	
12	...	...	2	...	3, 4, 5, 6	do.	
13	...	1	...	...	1, 2	Picket.	
15	...	...	1	...	5, 6	Trenches.	
16	...	...	1	...	1, 2	do.	
17	...	1	...	...	3	Picket.	
,,	1	...	3	...	4, 5, 6, 1, 2	Trenches.	
19	1	1	3	...	4, 5, 6, 1, 2	do.	
20	...	1	...	...	3	Picket.	
21	...	...	3	...	4, 5, 6, 1, 2	Trenches.	Ensign G. H. Waller joined in command of a draft of 2 Sergeants and 100 Rank and file. Of this draft, Lieut. Waller and 6 privates only returned to England.
22	...	...	2	..	3, 4, 5, 1, 2	do.	
,,	...	...	1	...	6	do.	
23	...	...	2	...	1, 2, 3, 4, 5	do.	
24	...	1	...	...	5	Picket.	
25	...	...	2	...	1, 2, 3, 4, 6	Trenches.	
26	...	1	...	...	5	Picket.	

Detail of Duties Performed by the Royal Fusiliers at the Siege of Sebastopol.—*Continued*.

Date.	F. O.	Capts.	Lieuts.	Sergts.	Divisions.	Duty.	Remarks.
1854, Nov. 27	1	...	3	...	6, 1, 2, 3, 4	Trenches.	
28	...	...	1	...	5	do.	
,,	...	1	2	...	6, 1, 2, 3, 4	Picket.	
29	...	1	...	...	5	do.	
30	...	...	3	...	6, 1, 2, 3, 4	Trenches.	
Dec. 2	The whole Regiment.				...	do.	
3	...	1	...	...	5	Picket.	
4	...	...	4	...	6, 1, 2, 3, 4	Trenches.	
5	The whole Regiment.				...	do.	
6	...	...	1	...	6, 1	Picket.	Reliefs in the Trenches every 12 hours; effective strength about 250 Rank and file.
,,	...	...	1	...	2, 3, 4, 5	Trenches.	
8	1	1	1	...	2, 3, 4, 5	do.	
,,	...	1	...	...	6, 1	Picket.	
9	...	...	1	...	2, 3, 4, 5	do.	
10	...	...	1	...	6, 1, 4	Trenches.	
11	...	...	1	...	5, 2, 3	do.	
12	...	1	1	...	1, 2, 3, 5, 6	do.	
13	...	...	1	...	4	do.	
14	...	1	..	...	3, 5	Picket.	
,,	...	...	1	...	2, 4	Trenches.	
15	...	...	1	...	6, 1, 2, 3	do.	
16	...	...	1	...	4	Picket.	
,,	...	1	1	...	1, 5, 6	Trenches.	
17	...	...	1	...	1, 2, 3	do.	Lieuts. Byron and Clayton, 34th Regiment, attached to do duty with the Royal Fusiliers.
18	...	...	1	...	1, 2, 4	do.	
,,	...	1	...	...	5, 6	Picket.	
19	1	...	1	...	3, 4	Trenches.	
20	...	1	1	...	5, 1, 2	do.	
,,	...	...	1	...	6	Picket.	
21	...	...	1	...	3, 5	Trenches.	In Gordon's Battery.
,,	...	...	1	...	4	Picket.	
22	...	1	..	...	4, 5	do.	
23	...	...	1	...	6, 1, 2	Trenches.	
24	...	...	1	...	3, 4	do.	
25	...	1	2	...	5, 6, 1, 2, 3	do.	
26	1	...	2	...	4, 5, 6, 1, 2	do.	
27	...	1	1	...	3, 4, 5	do.	
28	...	...	1	...	6, 1, 2	do.	Ensign Disney joined.
29	...	1	...	...	3, 4, 5	Picket.	
,,	...	...	1	...	6, 1, 2	Trenches.	
30	1	...	1	...	3	do.	Effective strength about 230 men.
31	The whole Regiment.				...	do.	
1855, Jan. 1	...	1	2	...	4, 5, 6, 1, 2	do.	
2	...	..	1	...	3	do.	
3	...	...	1	...	4, 5, 6	do.	
,,	...	1	...	...	1, 2	Picket.	
4	...	1	1	...	4, 5, 6	Trenches.	
5	...	...	1	...	1, 2	do.	
6	...	1	1	...	1, 2, 3, 4	do.	
,,	...	1	...	...	5, 6	Picket.	
7	...	1	2	...	2, 4, 5	Trenches.	
8	...	...	1	...	6, 1	do.	
,,	...	...	1	...	2	Picket.	
9	1	1	1	...	1, 4, 5, 6	Trenches.	
,,	...	...	1	...	3	Picket.	
10	...	1	1	...	2, 4, 5	Trenches.	
11	...	...	1	...	3, 6	do.	
,,	...	1	...	...	1, 2	Picket.	
12	...	1	1	...	5	Trenches.	

DETAIL OF DUTIES PERFORMED BY THE ROYAL FUSILIERS AT THE SIEGE OF SEBASTOPOL.—*Continued.*

Date.	F. O.	Capts.	Lieuts.	Sergts.	Companies.	Duty.	Remarks.
1855, Jan. 12	...	1	1	...	4	Picket.	
13	...	1	...	...	5	Trenches.	
14	...	...	1	...	3	do.	
,,	...	1	...	...	4, 6	Picket.	
15	...	...	1	...	2, 3	Trenches.	
16	...	1	1	...	4, 5, 6, 2	do.	
,,	...	...	1	...	1	Picket.	
17	...	1	1	...	3, 4, 5, 6	Trenches.	
18	...	1	...	...	1, 2	Picket.	
,,	...	1	1	...	3, 4, 5	Trenches.	Captain the *Hon.* C. Brown joined from Scutari.
19	...	1	...	...	4, 6	do.	
20	...	1	1	...	1, 2, 4, 6	do.	
,,	...	1	...	...	3, 5	Picket.	
21	...	...	1	...	1, 2	Advanced works.	
22	...	1	2	...	3, 4, 5, 6	Trenches.	Effective strength 250 men.
23	...	2	3	3	136 r. & f.	do.	
24	...	...	1	2	95		
25	...	...	1	1	50	Picket.	
26	...	1	1	2	85	Trenches.	
27	...	1	1	2	100	Picket.	
28	...	2	2	5	263	Trenches.	
30	...	1	1	2	100	do.	Relief at 5 A.M.
,,	1	1	1	3	124	do.	,, at 5 P.M.
31	...	...	1	1	50	Picket.	
Feb. 1	1	2	2	5	205	Trenches.	
3	...	1	2	5	190	do.	
,,	...	...	1	1	50	Picket.	
5	...	1	1	5	190	Trenches.	
,,	...	...	1	1	50	Picket.	
7	...	2	2	5	200	Trenches.	
8	...	...	1	1	50	Picket.	
,,	...	1	1	2	90	Trenches.	
9	...	1	2	3	120	do.	
10	...	1	...	1	50	Picket.	
11	...	1	2	4	200	Trenches.	
13	1	2	3	4	200	do.	
,,	...	...	1	1	50	Picket.	
15	...	2	2	4	190	Trenches.	
,,	...	1	...	1	50	Picket.	
17	...	2	2	4	160	Trenches.	Lieut. Robinson joined.
18	...	...	1	1	50	Picket.	
19	...	2	2	4	200	Trenches.	
20	...	...	1	1	25	Working party.	
,,	...	...	1	1	50	Picket.	
21	...	1	2	4	184	Trenches.	
23	...	...	2	1	50	Picket.	
,,	...	2	2	4	158	Trenches.	
25	...	1	2	4	152	do.	
,,	...	1	...	1	50	Picket.	
,,	...	1	2	3	120	Working party.	
26	...	...	...	...	...	...	Joined from depôt, Major Pack, 1 Captain, 1 Lieutenant, 2 Sergeants, and 101 Rank and file.
27	...	1	1	2	78	Picket.	
,,	...	...	1	1	50	Trenches.	
28	...	1	1	1	50	Picket.	
Mar. 1	...	1	3	3	188	Trenches.	
2	...	...	2	1	50	Picket.	
3	...	2	2	5	208	Trenches.	
5	...	1	...	1	50	Picket.	
,,	...	...	1	2	77	Trenches.	
6	...	1	...	1	50	Picket.	

Detail of Duties Performed by the Royal Fusiliers at the Siege of Sebastopol.—*Continued*.

Date.	F. O.	Capts.	Lieuts.	Sergts.	Rk. & File.	Duty.	Remarks.
1855, Mar. 7	...	...	4	4	200	Trenches.	
8	...	1	...	1	50	Picket.	
9	...	2	...	2	90	Trenches.	
,,	...	...	2	1	50	Picket.	
10	..	...	2	1	50	do.	
11	...	2	1	4	158	Trenches.	
12	...	1	1	2	100	Picket.	
,,	...	2	...	2	100	Covering party.	
13	...	2	2	4	202	Trenches.	
14	...	1	...	1	50	Picket.	
,,	...	1	1	1	48	Working party.	
15	...	2	2	4	172	Trenches.	
,,	...	...	1	1	50	Picket.	
16	...	1	...	2	58	Trenches.	
18	...	2	2	4	200	do.	
20	...	1	2	3	140	do.	Lieutenant Lord R. H. Browne joined.
22	...	1	2	3	135	do.	Captain Browne killed in repulsing sortie.
24	...	2	2	4	200	do.	
26	...	1	2	3	140	do.	
29	...	2	3	6	300	do.	
31	1	...	1	1	50	Working party.	
April 2	...	2	2	5	237	Trenches.	
,,	...	...	1	1	50	Working party.	
4	...	...	2	2	61	Trenches.	
5	1	2	3	5	223	do.	Sortie.
7	...	1	1	2	88	do.	
8	...	2	2	4	180	do.	
9	...	...	1	1	38	do.	Second bombardment commenced.
10	1	1	1	2	80	Advanced trench.	
11	...	1	3	5	224	do.	
13	...	1	3	3	109	do.	
14	1	2	2	4	196	Trenches.	
16	...	1	1	2	90	do.	
17	...	2	1	4	184	do.	
19	...	1	1	2	104	do.	
21	...	1	2	2	100	do.	
23	1	2	1	4	200	do.	
24	...	1	2	3	125	do.	
25	...	...	1	1	44	Working party.	
26	...	1	1	4	159	Advanced trench.	
27	...	1	1	2	79	do.	
28	...	1	1	4	163	do.	
30	...	2	2	6	260	do.	
,,	...	...	2	2	70	Working party.	
May 3	...	1	2	3	163	Reserve.	
,,	...	1	1	2	100	Working party.	
4	...	...	1	1	33	Advanced trench.	
6	1	1	2	5	215	do.	
8	...	1	1	2	65	do.	
9	1	2	4	7	310	do.	Sortie, 5 men wounded.
12	...	1	1	2	98	Trenches.	
,,	..	1	1	4	198	Reserve.	
14	...	...	1	1	44	Trenches.	
15	...	1	1	3	148	do.	
,,	...	1	...	2	59	Reserve.	
,,	...	...	1	1	44	Working party.	
17	...	1	...	2	59	Reserve.	
18	...	...	1	1	59	Advanced works.	
,,	...	1	1	3	134	Trenches.	
,,	...	...	1	1	59	Reserve.	
20	...	1	...	2	73	Advanced works.	
,,	...	...	1	1	45	Reserve.	

The Regiment remained in the Crimea, performing duty in Sebastopol, until after the peace was signed. It embarked for England in the s.s. *Imperatriz*, and arrived at Portsmouth on the 27th June, being sent thence to the newly-formed camp at Aldershot. On the 14th July the Royal Fusiliers were inspected by Her Majesty the Queen. By command of Her Majesty the band was in attendance at the Pavilion. Her Majesty was pleased personally to compliment it upon its performance. She was also most graciously pleased to address the troops in these words:—

Her Majesty the Queen addresses the Regiment.

"Officers, non-commissioned officers, and soldiers,—I wish personally to convey through you to the Regiments assembled here this day my hearty welcome on their return to England in health and full efficiency. Say to them that I have watched anxiously over the difficulties and hardships they have so nobly borne; that I have mourned with deep sorrow for the brave men who have fallen for their country; and that I have felt proud of that valour which, with their gallant allies, they have displayed in every field. I thank God that your dangers are over, whilst the glory of your deeds remains. But I know that should your services be again required, you will be animated with the same devotion which in the Crimea has rendered you invincible."

While at Aldershot the Regiment was rapidly recruited, and speedily shook off the rough and ready habit of soldiering that it had acquired in the trenches. The four depôt companies had joined from Malta under Captain Aldworth, and the four from Pembroke Dock under Captain Coney. Before the end of the year it had again returned to the parade smartness that had distinguished it before the commencement of the war. With the establishment of peace the strength of the Regiment was reduced to 12 companies, composed of 900 rank and file.

This year double-breasted tunics were issued to the army in the place of the old coatee, which, with its wings, was abolished. A new and broader sash was also given to the officers to be worn from the left shoulder. A waist-belt with slings for the sword was also substituted for the old shoulder-belt.

The officers of the Royal Fusiliers having unanimously voted a testimonial to Quarter-Master Thomas Murphy, in appreciation of his very valuable services whilst Hospital Sergeant, on the 25th December a silver breakfast service, bearing the following inscription, was presented to him:—

PRESENTED TO
THOMAS MURPHY, ESQ.,
ROYAL FUSILIERS,
By his brother officers, as a token of their affectionate esteem, and in appreciation of his services during the campaigns of 1854-55-56.

1857.

On the 20th March, 1857, Colonel Wellesley having retired from the service, Major R. W. Aldworth was promoted to the Lieutenant-Colonelcy, and assumed the command of the Royal Fusiliers.

On the 28th April the Regiment left Aldershot by railway for Portsmouth. The Head Quarters, with 3, 4, 5, 6, and 7 Companies, were in the Coleworth and Cambridge Barracks; Nos. 1 and 8 Companies, under Bt.-Major Appleyard, at Haslar Barracks; and No. 2 Company, under Captain H. M. Jones, was at Browndown Fort. On the 27th May, the depôt, four companies under Captain Marten, joined Head Quarters from Pembroke. On the 7th June, No. 4 Company, under Captain Lord Richard H. Browne, proceeded on detachment to Tipner Fort. In consequence of orders having been received on the 14th June for the Royal Fusiliers to prepare for service in India, the Regiment was raised to a strength of 1100 rank and file, formed into ten service and one depôt Companies. At the same time the whole Regiment moved into the Anglesea Barracks.

Although the Regiment had barely been in England for twelve months, the demands of the Indian Mutiny were inexorable in their call for its services abroad. For the first time in its long career the Regiment started to serve in the great Empire of the East. On the 14th July, Captain Marten's and Bt.-Major Appleyard's Companies embarked on board the "Sir George Seymour," under Lieutenant-Colonel R. Y. Shipley, for Kurrachee. The remainder of the Regiment embarked in three detachments: on the 20th July, the Head Quarters, under Lieutenent-Colonel R. W. Aldworth, with Bt.-Major Hibbert and Captain Lord R. H. Browne's Companies, on board the "Owen Glendower;" two companies under Major Watson on board the "Seringapatam;" and three companies on board the "Ramilies," under Major Tryon. No. 1 Company proceeded to Gravesend, under Lieutenant C. G. O'Brien, and embarked on board the "Castle Eden." *The Regiment embarks for India.*

Before leaving England a subscription was raised by the present and past officers of the Regiment, and the friends of those officers who had been killed in *Monument erected in Winchester Cathedral.*

the war, to erect a monument* to the memory of their deceased comrades and friends. The monument, representing an angel in an attitude of grief, sitting beneath the colours of the Regiment, was erected in the south Transept of Winchester Cathedral. It bears the following inscription:—

ALMA. INKERMAN. SEBASTOPOL.
Sacred to the Memory of
Colonel Lacy W. Yea; Lieutenant-Colonel Frederick Mills;
Captain *Hon.* W. Monck, Captain *Hon.* J. C. Hare, Captain A. Wallace,
Captain *Hon.* C. Browne;
Lieutenant J. Molesworth, Lieutenant and Adjutant J. St. Clair Hobson, Lieutenant *Hon.* E. Fitzclarence,
Lieutenant O. Colt;
Lieutenant W. L. L. G. Wright, Lieutenant F. C. Beauchamp;
Qr.-Master J. Hogan; Asst.-Surgeon J. P. Langham;
and 559 Non-commissioned Officers and Private Soldiers of the
7th Royal Fusiliers,
Who fell in action or died of wounds or disease during the campaign in the Crimea,
A. D. 1854 and 1855.
"Not once or twice in our rough Island story,
The path of duty was the path of Glory."
This monument was erected by their brother officers and soldiers.

Arrives at Kurrachee. On the 23rd November the "Ramilies," next day the "Owen Glendower;" on the 1st December the "Seringapatam," on the 13th the "Castle Eden," and on the 18th the "Sir George Seymour," arrived at Kurrachee. The great demand for troops in the Punjaub gave the Regiment no time to delay its advance. It was pushed on as speedily as possible to the front; the women, children, and heavy baggage being left at Kurrachee. The right wing, under Lieutenant-Colonel Aldworth, marched on the 14th December for Kotree; it arrived there on the 24th, and embarked on board the river steamer on the 29th. The left wing, with the exception of No. 10 Company, which was left at Kurrachee for the protection of the town until the arrival of fresh troops, marched on the 26th December, and reached Kotree on the 6th January, 1858.

The 2nd Battalion raised. In September, Poulett G. H. Somerset C.B., late Lieutenant-Colonel in the Coldstream Guards, was authorised to raise 1000 rank and file to form a 2nd

---

* In the Parish Church of Leeds there is a monument erected to the memory of Leeds men who fell in the Crimea. Of the Fusiliers who served the Eastern Campaign many were natives of Leeds, and the names of some of those who fell are properly inscribed on the monument, but unfortunately the want of full information did not allow a correct list to be obtained, and later inquiries, which the existence of the monument started, have shown that many names have been omitted.

Battalion of the Royal Fusiliers. Recruiting was commenced on the 23rd September, and the levy was completed by the 21st January, 1858. The men were raised principally in Somerset, Surrey, Lancashire, Durham, and Gloucestershire. The establishment was fixed by War Office letter, dated 21st November, as follows:—

Lt.Cl.	Majs.	Caps.	Lts.	Ens.	Staff.	Sergts.	Corpls.	Drums.	Privates.
1	2	12	14	10	6	56	50	24	950.

Major Gilley, who in 1830 was promoted from sergeant-major to be adjutant, was made junior major of the battalion.

The battalion was incorporated at Preston about the 27th October; it remained at Preston during the rest of the year. *Incorporated at Preston.*

In this year single-breasted tunics were supplied to the Regiment instead of double-breasted ones, and plumes were substituted for the white ball worn on the shako.

1858.

The right wing of the 1st Battalion arrived at Moultan, January 27th; it was immediately forwarded to Meean Meer in bullock carts. On the 12th January the left wing, which had been joined by the company from Kurrachee, embarked from Kotree on board river steamers for Moultan, where it arrived in February, and was also sent in bullock carts to Meean Meer. On the 8th February one company was sent on detachment to the Fort of Lahore, and one to the Artillery lines; these companies and their successors being relieved monthly. On the 2nd March the Regiment was inspected by Major-General Windham, C.B. Captain P. G. Coney, who, as a subaltern, had carried one of the colours of the Regiment at the Alma, died here of fever, April 30th, deeply regretted by his brother officers, by whom a monument was erected to his memory at Meean Meer. *Capt. Coney's death.*

On the 20th September, a force consisting of the right wing 1st Battalion, under the command of Major Watson, a squadron of the 7th Dragoon Guards, and a troop of Horse Artillery, the whole under the command of Lieutenant-Colonel Blount, C.B., left Meean Meer for Dera Ishmael Khan, where they arrived in October. While on the march the detachment was attacked by cholera; the Fusiliers lost eight men.

On the 2nd February the 2nd Battalion left Preston for Aldershot, where it arrived next day. The establishment was reduced by War Office order, 19th April, 1858, to the following strength:—

Lt.-Cl.	Majs.	Capts.	Lts.	Ens.	Staff.	Sergts.	Corpls.	Drums.	Privates.
1	2	12	14	10	6	54	48	24	902.

2nd Battalion embarks for Gibraltar.

The Battalion was placed under orders for foreign service by Horse Guards letter, dated 9th April. The first Division, consisting of Nos. 7, 8, 9, and 10 Companies, embarked on board H.M.S. "Urgent," at Portsmouth, for Gibraltar, on the 22nd May, and arrived on the 27th, landing on the 29th. The 2nd Division, consisting of Head Quarters and Nos. 1, 2, 3, 4, 5, and 6 Companies, embarked at Portsmouth, in H.M.S. "Vulcan," on the 27th May, and arrived at Gibraltar on the 4th June, landing next day. The Battalion was inspected at Gibraltar by Major-General Rumley on the 21st June; and again by the same officer on the 22nd November.

1859.

In February the Royal Fusiliers were inspected by the Viceroy, Viscount Canning, Governor General of India, and by His Excellency the Commander-in-Chief, Lord Clyde, and received the highest commendation.

The Head Quarters and left wing 1st Battalion, consisting of

F. O.	Capts.	Subs.	Staff.	Sergts.	Drums.	R. and F.
3	3	6	5	29	8	660.

left Meean Meer on the 9th April, and arrived on the 21st at Jhelum, on the right bank of the river Jhelum, where four companies of the right wing joined Head Quarters on the 29th from Dera Ishmael Khan, having left one company, under Captain G. H. Waller, behind to garrison the Fort. The accommodation at Jhelum having been originally intended for native troops only, there were no barracks. The Royal Fusiliers were therefore put into two hospital buildings, a gun shed which had been converted into temporary barracks, and several private bungalows taken for the purpose by the Government. Still the accommodation was not sufficient; the left wing therefore left for Rawul Pindee on the 3rd May. It arrived there on the 8th. The Battalion remained tolerably healthy during the ensuing hot weather. On the 28th October the left wing left Rawul Pindee for Peshawur, arriving there on the 5th November. On the 25th October the Head Quarters left Jhelum, and arrived at Peshawur on the 8th November. On the 15th, the Battalion was inspected by Major-General Sir Sydney Cotton, K.C.B., who expressed himself perfectly satisfied with its drill and discipline.

The establishment of the 2nd Battalion was augmented from the 1st April as follows:—

Lt.-Cl.	Majs.	Capts.	Lts.	Ens.	Staff.	Sergts.	Corpls.	Drums.	Privates.
1	2	12	14	10	6	56	50	25	900.

The Battalion still remained at Gibraltar.

1860.

On the 21st March the company stationed at Dera Ishmael Khan, under Captain G. H. Waller, joined Head Quarters: the following letter from Brig. General Chamberlain records the excellence of its conduct:—

"Dera Ishmael Khan, 20th February, 1860.
"Sir,
"The company of the Royal Fusiliers having been relieved, and being about to return to regimental Head Quarters, I consider it my duty to bring to the notice of the Major-General commanding the division, that its conduct, during the year it has been detached at this station, has been most exemplary, and such as to reflect the greatest credit upon Captain Waller and all ranks.
"The men have been sober, steady, respectful, and well-behaved; and all classes of natives speak of them in the highest terms; in short I may say that they have upheld the honour of Her Majesty's uniform. It affords me much pleasure to be able to make this report, and I have to beg that Major-General Sir Sidney Cotton, K.C.B., will allow its conduct to be communicated to the officer commanding H.M's. 7th Royal Fusiliers.
"I have the honour to be, Sir,
"Your obedient Servant,
"NEVILE CHAMBERLAIN, Brigadier-General,
"Commanding Punjaub Irregular Force."

On the 18th April, and again on the 13th and 14th November, the 1st Battalion was inspected by Major-General Sir Sydney Cotton, K.C.B., commanding the Peshawur division, who expressed himself perfectly satisfied with its efficiency. At the conclusion of the rifle practice this year, the best shot of the Peshawur Division, consisting of five of H.M.'s Infantry Regiments was Private J. Groom, Royal Fusiliers.

The 2nd Battalion remained at Gibraltar without change.

1861.

On the 18th February a detachment, consisting of one captain, two lieutenant, one assistant-surgeon, 10 sergeants, 10 corporals, 2 drummers and 192 privates, under the command of Major Watson, marched to the Fort of Attock to be there stationed. On the 12th April the Head Quarters and eight companies marched from Peshawur to Nowshera to be there stationed. Owing however to the sickness which prevailed in Nowshera, in September and October two companies, which afterwards increased to a wing, under the command of Lieutenant-Colonel Shipley, were sent to Peshawur. The Head Quarters of the Battalion followed on the 29th. On the 9th December the Battalion was inspected by Major-General Sir Sydney Cotton.

The 2nd Battalion remained at Gibraltar; it was inspected by Major-General Franklyn, C.B., at the Windmill Hill Barracks, on the 9th April, and by Major-General Sir Robert Walpole, K.C.B., on the 31st October.

1862.

On the 1st January 65 men volunteered from the 1st Battalion 6th Regiment. On the 15th Lieutenant-Colonel Aldworth having proceeded to England on private affairs, Lieutenant-Colonel Shipley assumed the command. On the 17th, His Excellency the Commander-in-Chief, Sir Hugh Rose, K.C.B., arrived at Peshawur; the whole of the troops were drawn up for grand guard mounting, the Royal Fusiliers performing the part of guards. His Excellency expressed himself very pleased at the steadiness with which the battalion marched past. On the 23rd the Royal Fusiliers were inspected by His Excellency. After marching past in slow and quick time the Battalion was put through some manœuvres by Lieutenant-Colonel Shipley, after which each captain was called out to drill the Battalion. The Battalion was then formed in quarter columns, when Sir Hugh Rose addressed it, as follows:—

Sir Hugh Rose's remarks to the Battalion.

"I am happy to hear such a good account of the discipline and steadiness of the Royal Fusiliers from Sir Sydney Cotton, commanding the Peshawur Division, which is confirmed by what I have seen to day. Nothing could have been better than the marching past, the manual and platoon exercises, and general working of the Battalion. It was evident to all that each man had done his best." Sir Hugh then alluded to the glorious deeds performed by the Regiment under the great Duke in the Peninsula, adding that "he felt sure that were the Regiment to be again called upon to face an enemy, it would distinguish itself as much as in those days." His Excellency further said, that he was happy to have met such a distinguished regiment, and he hoped that each man would endeavour by his good conduct to keep up that high character whether in war or in peace.

On the 7th February the whole Battalion marched from Peshawur to Nowshera; two companies being subsequently sent to Fort Attock. On the 27th the Head Quarters and left wing commenced their march to Ferozpore, where they arrived on the 29th March. The right wing, except three companies left at Meean Meer, marched to Ferozpore, arriving there on the same day as the left wing. On the 12th August, cholera broke out in the Battalion, both at Ferozpore and Meean Meer, cases continuing till about the 20th September, during which time 16 men and three women died. On the 10th December the Battalion was inspected at Ferozpore by Major-General A. S. Cunyngham, C.B., commanding the Lahore Division, who stated at the close of the inspection, that during the eight years he had performed the duties of a Major-General, he had seen no Regiment in such good order as the Royal Fusiliers.

The 2nd Battalion remained at Gibraltar. By order, dated 14th June, its establishment was reduced by 50 privates; the total strength to be 1026, divided into 10 service and 2 depôt companies.

1863.

On the 17th February the three companies on detachment at Meean Meer were relieved by three companies from Head Quarters. On the 19th March the Battalion was inspected by Major-General Cunyngham, who again expressed himself highly satisfied with its excellent state and efficiency. By command of His Excellency the Commander-in-Chief, a regimental order was issued, expressing his "great satisfaction with the extremely favourable reports he had received of the Battalion from the Inspecting-General, and offering his best thanks to Colonel R. Y. Shipley for the excellent state of the Regiment."

The health of the Battalion continued excellent during the hot season; no epidemic having broken out, as in the previous year. In September the Battalion was ordered to be held in readiness to proceed as escort to the Viceroy and Governor-General in his visit to Sealkote, Peshawur, and his return to Lahore. On the 21st October, the Battalion, under Colonel Shipley, marched to Meean Meer, and whilst there Nos. 1 and 2 Companies were detached with part of the camp of the Governor-General to meet His Excellency at Pathancote. On the 5th November the remainder of the Battalion marched for the Peshawur frontier to take part in the campaign against the frontier tribes. Reaching the Umbeyla Pass on the 5th December, the Fusiliers were attached to the 1st Brigade, the whole force being under the command of Major-General Garvock.

On the 14th the troops advanced to attack the enemy's position. On the 15th the Royal Fusiliers formed up in front of the breastwork. The 1st Brigade, under the command of Colonel Turner, C.B. (who had served with the Royal Fusiliers in the Crimea), consisting of the Hazara mountain train guns, the Royal Fusiliers, 3rd, 23rd, and 32nd Punjaub Infantry, and the 5th Goorkhas, advanced by the right of our advanced pickets; the 2nd Brigade, under Brig. Wilde, C.B. on the left. On reaching the crest of the hill, facing the "Conical Hill" which the enemy had fortified and was holding in strength, the Royal Fusiliers formed up in line, when the brigades advanced and carried the position. The 1st Brigade pursued the enemy for some distance, and having captured and burnt the village of Lalloo, bivouaced for the night.

N.W. Frontier; affair at Umbeyla. On the 16th the 1st Brigade, after a long march, reached the valley of Umbeyla, and found the enemy had retreated to the hills on the opposite side, abandoning the village of Umbeyla, which the troops destroyed. The 23rd and 32nd Native Infantry deployed into line, supported by four companies of the Royal Fusiliers (the other four companies forming the rear-guard of the brigade), and advanced to drive the enemy from his position at the foot of the hills. The left being threatened two companies of the Fusiliers were sent to protect it. On nearing the foot of the hills a heavy fire was opened by the enemy; at the same time a body of fanatics armed with tulwars rushed down sword in hand. Their rush caused temporary confusion in the ranks of the Sepoys, but, seeing themselves supported by two companies of the Fusiliers, they again advanced, and the enemy was driven back with great loss. Then finding himself under the fire of Artillery he retired to the top of the hills. The day being too far advanced to make any further attack, the troops took up their position for the night, during which the enemy surrendered unconditionally. The town of Mutkah, the stronghold of the fanatics, was destroyed by the corps of Guides, in conjunction with the Boneyhr tribe who now acted as our allies, though at the commencement of the campaign they had been our determined opponents; and the force being broken up the Royal Fusiliers returned to Ferozpore. For this service Colonel Shipley was appointed a Companion of the Bath.

The establishment of the 2nd Battalion was reduced by War Office order, June 4th, by 100 private soldiers. The Battalion embarked on board H.M. troopship "Orontes" at Gibraltar for Malta on the 9th September. It arrived at Malta on the 13th, and disembarked next day. 2nd Battalion Gibraltar to Malta.

1864.

At the half-yearly inspection the Battalion received the compliments both of the Inspecting-General and the Commander-in-Chief on its efficiency and continued good conduct. The health of the Fusiliers remained excellent during the hot season; no epidemic of any kind having broken out. The battalion still continued to occupy Ferozpore. 1st Battalion Ferozpore.

The 2nd Battalion remained at Malta.

1865.

On the 15th February the Exhibition of the Products of Regimental Workshops was opened at Meean Meer, to which the Royal Fusiliers were amongst the largest contributors, and obtained special praise for the superiority of the boots exhibited.

At the rifle matches, which took place at Meean Meer during the time of the exhibition, Private James Cosgrove won the Adjutant-General's Prize; Private M. Haggerty, one of the Head Quarter Staff Prizes; Private D. Fox, one of the Ferozpore Brigade Staff Prizes; and Privates J. Reading and J. Ankers, each one of the Peshawur Division and Brigade Staff Prizes. The Royal Fusiliers carried off in prizes the sum of 209 rupees, the largest amount gained by any Regiment Shooting matches at MeeanMeer.

attending the meeting. In June Sir William Mansfield, the Commander-in-Chief in India, communicated the expression of his very great pleasure in receiving the report of the inspection of the Battalion, and signified that he had transmitted the report to H.R.H. the Field Marshal Commanding-in-Chief, with remarks of his cordial approval.

Colonel Shipley, C.B., exchanging to half-pay, Lieutenant-Colonel H. R. Hibbert obtained command of the Royal Fusiliers, and was also appointed to the command of the station. During the hot season the Battalion remained in cantonments. The health of the men was generally good, sickness amongst them being comparatively little. On the 29th December Ensign Parnell died at Morar, Gwalior.

The Battalion commenced its march from Ferozpore on the 1st November for Saugor, where the Head Quarters arrived on the 11th January, 1866, having marched 662 miles.

2nd Battalion Malta to Canada. The 2nd Battalion embarked on board H.M.'s troopship "Himalaya" at Malta for Canada, on the 29th April; it arrived at Quebec on the 13th May, and disembarked on the 15th.

1866.

1st Battalion Saugor. Three companies under Captain R. C. Clifford were detached to Nowgong, a small station about 100 miles from Saugor. On the 21st March and 23rd October the Battalion was inspected at Saugor by Brigadier-General W. W. Turner, C.B.

The 2nd Battalion was inspected by Major-General the *Hon.* James Lindsay at Quebec on the 23rd May, 1866.

In consequence of the Fenian raid into Canada, the Battalion, in pursuance of orders received by telegram, left Quebec on the 3rd June on field service. It proceeded to Montreal on the 7th, and thence to West Farnham, leaving West Farnham on the 9th. It went to St. Armand, and joined the field force under Colonel Elrington, Rifle Brigade, detaching three companies on outpost duty to Pigeon Hill. The contemptible efforts of a band of brigands were promptly subdued. The Battalion returned to Quebec on the 19th June. On the 25th September one company, with the regimental baggage, left Quebec for

Brantford, Canada West. Next day three companies left Quebec to join the camp at Niagara Falls; they afterwards proceeded to Brantford on the 8th October: the Head Quarters and six companies having left Quebec on the 4th, arrived at Brantford on the 7th. The Battalion was inspected at Brantford by Major-General Napier, C.B., on the 20th October.

1867.

The 1st Battalion remained at Saugor with the detachment at Nowgong without any noteworthy event.

On the 23rd July the 2nd Battalion received orders to proceed to Quebec next day *en route* to England. It left Brantford on the 24th, arrived at Quebec on the 27th, and embarked on board the hired troopship, "Belgian," sailing on the 28th, and arriving at Spithead on the 8th August. The Battalion disembarked next day, and was quartered at Forts Grange, Rowner and Gomer, Gosport, until it moved from Gosport on the 24th October to Liverpool. On the 10th December the Head Quarters and the right wing moved from Liverpool to Bury. <small>2nd Battalion embarks for England.</small>

1868.

On the 28th February the three companies detached at Nowgong rejoined Head Quarters at Saugor. On the 8th March a draft consisting of 81 recruits, under the command of Lieutenant G. B. Meares, landed at Calcutta. Lieutenant-General Sir Richard Airey, G.C.B., was appointed Colonel of the Royal Fusiliers on the 1st May, in the room of the veteran who had fought with it in the Peninsula, Sir S. B. Auchmuty, deceased. Another draft, consisting of two officers, one sergeant, five corporals, one drummer, and 124 privates, under the command of Captain H. Kerr, landed at Bombay on the 3rd November, and joined the Battalion at Saugor on the 3rd December. <small>Death of Sir S. B. Auchmuty.</small>

Captain Beauchamp's Company was detached from Bury to Warrington on the 1st February in aid of the civil power. <small>2nd Battalion.</small>

The Battalion having fallen considerably below the establishment, by reason of a large number of men having claimed their discharge on the completion of the first period of their engagement, 210 recruits, raised chiefly in the Liverpool and Bristol recruiting districts, joined the Battalion. Captain Beauchamp's Company moved from Warrington on the 6th April to Newton, where it remained until the 8th May, when it proceeded to Liverpool. Captain Sparkes's Company moved from Liverpool to St. Helen's in aid of the civil power; it remained there until the 9th May, when it joined Head Quarters at Bury. Two companies under Captains Herbert and Cole proceeded from Bury to Bradford on the 21st May.

The Battalion was inspected by Major-General Sir John Garvock, K.C.B., at Bury, on the 1st June. Sealskin instead of lambskin caps were taken into wear at Bury on the 14th June.

1869.

1st Battalion Saugor, suffers from cholera.

On the 20th April Ensign Morgan died at Saugor of small-pox: a monument was erected to his memory by the officers of the battalion. In May cholera broke out and continued to September; the battalion lost by it 27 men, six women, and eight children. The hot season was unusually unhealthy, the troops suffering severely from fever and ague. The mortality in the Royal Fusiliers during the year amounted to one officer, 71 men, six women, and 21 children. Before leaving Saugor a monument to the memory of their deceased comrades, and bearing the following inscription, was erected by the men of the Regiment:—

"Sacred to the memory of one hundred and thirty-four non-commissioned officers and privates, eight women and thirty-three children, who died whilst the Regiment was stationed at Saugor from January, 1866, to December, 1869."

The sergeants also erected a monument to the memory of the sergeants who had died during the same time.

Moves from Saugor to Aden.

On the 2nd December the Head Quarters, with Bt.-Major Blackall's, Captains Clifford's, Surman's, Harbord's, Kerr's, Vandaleur's, and Harrison's Companies, marched from Saugor for Aden.

The three companies of Captains Plummer, E. Waller, and Brevet-Major Cochrane, V.C., remained in garrison at Saugor, under the command of Major

G. F. Herbert. The Head Quarters reached Jubbulpore on the 15th December, and Nagpore on the 28th. From Nagpore the Battalion, comprising 19 officers and 538 men proceeded by rail to Bombay.

The Head Quarters and four companies from Bury, the two companies from Bradford, and the four from the North Fort, Liverpool, embarked on the 10th April at the North Landing Stage, Liverpool, on board H.M.S. "Urgent" for Portsmouth. Arriving at Portsmouth on the 13th, the Battalion disembarked next day, and proceeded by train to Aldershot, joining the 1st Infantry Brigade in the South Camp, under the command of Major-General Lysons, C.B. *2nd Battalion Bury to Aldershot.*

A detachment, consisting of 1 field officer, 2 captains, 4 subalterns, 1 surgeon, and 150 non-commissioned officers and men, proceeded to Windsor on the 21st June, reinforced by 1 captain, 1 subaltern, and 82 rank and file, band and Queen's colour on the 25th June, and encamped in the Home Park till the 29th June, when the whole returned to Aldershot. The Battalion proceeded with a flying column, under the command of Major-General Carey, C.B., to Woolmer Forest on the 12th August, and returned to Aldershot on the 14th. The Battalion was inspected by Major-General Lysons, C.B., at Aldershot on the 4th October.

1870.

The Battalion embarked on the 5th January on board the troopships "Euphrates," and (two companies) "Earl Canning." The Head Quarters disembarked at Aden on the 15th, relieving the 82nd Regiment, which proceeded to England. On the 28th January the detachment under Major Herbert marched from Saugor to Poona, where it was stationed during the hot season. *1st Battalion*

On the 2nd February the whole of the troops in garrison were formed upon the brigade parade, when Major-General Sir E. Russell, K.C.S.I., presented gratuities, which had been awarded in the Royal Fusiliers, to

Sergeant PATRICK HANLON; Private MICHAEL MALONEY.

The depôt Battalions in England having been broken up, the depôt companies, under the command of Captain A. Bennett, left Shorncliffe on the 9th March, and proceeded to Portland to be attached to the 2nd Battalion. By order, dated 1st July, two companies were broken up, the men being distributed among the remaining companies at Head Quarters.

On the 2nd June, Private James Ganley was presented with a medal and gratuity "for long service and good conduct."

On the 21st November, the detachment embarked at Bombay on board the "Euphrates," and reached Aden on the 30th. The Head Quarters, being relieved by the 3rd Battalion Rifle Brigade, embarked on board the "Euphrates," and reached Suez on the 9th December. The Battalion was conveyed across the isthmus by rail to Alexandria, where it embarked on board the "Serapis" and sailed for England on the 12th December, reaching Malta on the 16th, and Portsmouth on the 27th. It disembarked on the 28th, and occupied the Anglesea barracks.

2nd Battalion.

The Battalion left Aldershot on the 1st and 2nd March, six companies going to Portland and four to Weymouth. On the 1st April the establishment was fixed as follows:—

Comps.	Lt.-Cl.	Majs.	Capts.	Lts.	Ens.	Staff.	Sergts.	Corps.	Drums.	Privates.
10	1	2	10	10	4	5	48	21	40	460

This arrangement held only for a short time, the number of private soldiers being raised to 760. The valise equipment was supplied to the Battalion at Portland, and taken into wear on the 28th May.

1871.

1st Battalion

The depôt companies joined Head Quarters from the 2nd Battalion on the 4th January. From the date of landing in England the establishment of the Battalion was reduced to

Lt.-Cl.	Majs.	Capts.	Lts.	Ens.	Staff.	Sergts.	Corps.	Drums.	Privates.
1	2	10	10	4	3	49	40	21	560.

In February Miss Yea, sister of the late Colonel Lacy Yea, who commanded the regiment in the Crimea, presented to the officers' mess two handsome silver epergnes, bearing the following inscription:—

Presented to the 1st Battalion Royal Fusiliers,
By MISS YEA,
In memory of her brother,
COLONEL LACY WALTER YEA,
Who was killed when in command of the storming party in the attack on the Redan (Crimea)
on the 18th June, 1855.

Colonel Sir Thomas Troubridge, Bart, A.D.C. to Her Majesty, died in London on the 2nd October, 1871, and left by will a portrait of himself for presentation to the officers of his old Regiment.

In February Snider rifles were issued to the Battalion, the valise equipment substituted for knapsacks, and racoon skin caps were supplied instead of shakos.

On the 6th February Captain Edmund Waller died, deeply regretted by his brother officers, by whom a window was erected to his memory in Tachbroke Church.

In March of this year, a medal for the North-West Frontier, with clasp for Umbeyla, was issued to the officers and men of the Battalion who took part in that campaign. Medal for the N.W. Frontier issued.

On the 23rd August the following soldiers were presented with medals and gratuities "for long service and good conduct:"—

Sergeant JAMES OSMOTHERLEY; Private WILLIAM WILLIS;
Private JAMES MAUGAN; Private ROBERT CHICK;
Private JAMES LINEHAM.

Colonel Hibbert retired on temporary half-pay October 28th, he was succeeded by Major G. H. Waller. On taking leave of the Battalion Colonel Hibbert issued the following order, the expression of feelings associated with the Battalion during a life of toil and danger.

"Portsmouth, 28th October, 1871.

"Col. Hibbert wishes to express to all ranks of the 1st Battalion 7th Royal Fusiliers his great regret at leaving the regiment which has been his home for so many years. He now takes leave of his old companions; and, in wishing them every future success, feels much pride in knowing that he hands over to his successor a command which, for discipline and appearance, and what is still more valuable perfect good feeling amongst officers and men that cannot be surpassed by any Regiment in Her Majesty's army."

The Battalion remained at Weymouth and Portland until the 30th December, when the Head Quarters and eight companies embarked at Portland on board H.M.S. "Simoon" for Ireland. 2nd Battalion.

1872.

The Battalion having received orders to take part in the Autumn manœuvres on Salisbury Plain, marched from Portsmouth on Saturday, August 10th, and 1st Battalion proceeded to Blandford, where it remained some days in standing camp, and formed, with the 2nd Battalion Royal Welsh and the 3rd Lancashire Militia, the 1st Brigade 1st Division of the Southern army. The manœuvres commenced on the 31st August, the Southern Force being opposed to a force which had marched from Aldershot, called the Northern Army. For a fortnight the two armies were moving against each other, the one with the object of gaining, the other with the object of defending London. On the 13th September the manœuvres were closed by a grand review and march past on Beacon Hill, near Amesbury, H.R.H. the Duke of Cambridge being present. On the following day the Battalion marched for Aldershot, where it was brigaded with the 88th, 90th, and 95th Regiments, under the command of Major-General W. Parke, C.B.

On the 19th October Quarter-Master Sergeant William Ames was promoted to quarter-master in the Battalion for long and faithful discharge of duty.

On the 23rd November the following non-commissioned officers were presented with medals and gratuities "for long service and good conduct:"—

Sergeant-Instructor CHARLES EMERY; Sergeant GEORGE GILES.

In December Mrs Cholmeley Dering presented to the officers' mess a portrait of her brother, the late Colonel Yea.

2nd Battalion Fermoy.

The Head Quarters arrived at Kingstown on the 1st January; they disembarked next day and proceeded by rail to the Curragh. The two companies left at Weymouth embarked on the 1st on board the steamer, "Lady Eglington" for Dublin; they arrived there on the 4th, disembarked and proceeded to the Curragh. The battalion left the Curragh on the 18th for Fermoy. The following detachments were furnished from Fermoy during February for election duty in the county Kerry.

2nd. 1 officer and 24 rank and file to Dingle—rejoined in February.
2nd. 3 officers and 75 rank and file to Cahirciveen—reinforced on the
5th. by 1 officer and 49 rank and file—rejoined 14th February.
5th. 3 officers and 172 rank and file to Killarney—rejoined 12th February.
5th. 2 officers and 68 rank and file to Castle Island—reinforced on the
7th. by 1 officer and 30 rank and file—rejoined 12th February.
6th. 1 officer and 40 rank and file to Killorglin—rejoined 11th February.

One company proceeded by march from Fermoy to Michelstown on the 6th March for detachment duty. Two companies proceeded by rail from Fermoy to

Carlisle Fort, Queenstown Harbour, on the 7th, to be employed in the garrison works. This detachment was reinforced by four companies on the 18th May. The detachment at Michelstown rejoined Head Quarters at Fermoy on the 19th July. One company proceeded on detachment from Fermoy to Charles Fort, Kinsale, on the 29th July; it rejoined Head Quarters on the 17th October. In August, the Head Quarters left Fermoy and proceeded to Cork, a detachment being left at Fermoy, and others sent to Youghal and Carlisle Fort, Cork Harbour. Proceeds to Cork.

1873.

At the reorganisation of the army the regiments of the line being associated in brigade with the Auxiliary Forces, and the country being divided into sub-districts, at the Head Quarters of which the brigade depôts were to be located, both battalions of the Royal Fusiliers were placed in the 49th sub-district, together with the 1st and 2nd Battalions Royal Tower Hamlets Militia, and seven corps of Rifle Volunteers, three belonging to Middlesex, two to the Tower Hamlets, and two to Kent, the Head Quarters of the brigade being at Woolwich. Col. R. Y. Shipley, late of the Royal Fusiliers, was appointed to command the brigade. 1st Battalion Aldershot.

The establishment of the 1st Battalion being altered to eight service and two depôt companies, on the 31st May two companies proceeded to Woolwich, under Major Herbert, two companies of the 2nd Battalion also proceeded to Woolwich, and these four companies formed the Regimental depôt. Brigade depôt formed.

In June, the Shah of Persia visited England; in his honour Her Majesty the Queen ordered a grand review to be held in Windsor Great Park on the 24th June. For this purpose the 1st Battalion Royal Fusiliers was ordered to proceed to Windsor for the day, to return by train in the evening. The troops on the ground, amounting to 7000, consisted of two batteries of Horse Artillery, two Field Batteries, the three regiments of Horse Guards, 6th Dragoon Guards, 7th and 13th Hussars. Of Infantry there were six battalions of the Guards, divided into two brigades, 1st Battalion Royal Fusiliers, 2nd Battalion 16th Regiment, 93rd Highlanders, and 1st Battalion Rifle Brigade, under command of Major-Gen. Parke, C.B. The troops were formed in line of double company columns, facing the saluting point. General Lord Strathnairn, G.C.B., G.C.S.I., was in command of the whole; Prince Edward of Saxe Weimar commanded the Infantry.

Review in honour of the Shah of Persia.

At five o'clock the Royal procession arrived from the Castle, headed by an escort of the 2nd Dragoons (Scots Greys). Her Majesty drove in a carriage, accompanied by H.R.H. the Princess of Wales. The Shah rode on horseback, accompanied by the Prince of Wales, the Dukes of Edinburgh and Cambridge, and attended by a numerous staff. When their Majesties reached the saluting point, the line presented arms, the bands playing the National Anthem; after which the Royal procession passed along from right to left of the line, the bands then playing the Persian Anthem, and so returned to the saluting point. The Regiments then marched past, the Cavalry in columns of troops, the Infantry in double company columns. The Cavalry then passed at the trot; the Infantry marched past in line of quarter columns; after which the Cavalry cantered past. The troops then went through a variety of manœuvres, after which the Queen, followed by the Royal procession, left the ground, and the Regiments returned to their quarters.

The 1st Battalion left Aldershot on the 28th August, and proceeded by rail to Dover, occupying the South front barrack. On the 6th September, the battalion moved into the Citadel Barracks, vacated by the 2nd Battalion 9th Regiment.

On the 5th August, the following non-commissioned officers and privates were presented with medals, and some of them with gratuities "for long service and good conduct:"—

Armourer-Sergt. William Conners,
Sergt. Robert Holt,
Private Henry Purch, without gratuities.

Private Frederick Hester,
Private Edward Siffleet,
Private Thomas Davies,
Private Thomas Foy, with gratuities of £5 each.

2nd Battalion.

On the 31st August, orders were received to complete the 2nd Battalion for foreign service; three sergeants, two corporals, two drummers, and 130 privates were accordingly transferred from the 1st September. They embarked on the 6th, in H.M.S. "Tamar," for Cork, to join the 2nd Battalion. At the same time six sergeants, two corporals, two drummers, and 154 privates were transferred from the 2nd Battalion, as being too young or otherwise unfit for service in India.

The battalion remained at Cork with detachments at Youghal, Carlisle Fort, and Spike Island, until placed under orders for India. In June, the two depôt companies, under Captains Sparkes and Paddon, proceeded on board H.M.S. "Simoom," from Cork to Woolwich, to join the brigade depôt. Prior to proceeding on leave of absence, pending his retirement from the service, Col. J. H. Cooper, commanding the 2nd Battalion, thus bade adieu to the battalion :—

> "In saying 'Good bye' to the 2nd Battalion 7th Royal Fusiliers, which I have had the honour to command for so many years, I wish to express my thanks to the officers, non-commissioned officers, and men for the manner in which they have always supported me. On every occasion I have found a willing obedience and high sense of duty among all ranks; and the good order the battalion is in, expressed in the reports of every General in whose command it has served, is due to this sense of duty.
>
> "It is with deep regret that I leave a Regiment where so many happy days have been passed, and where I have such valued friends. Although we must now part my heart will always be with the old corps whose career I shall continue to watch with as much interest as if I was still one of them.
>
> (Signed) "JOSHUA COOPER, Colonel."

Major G. F. Herbert succeeded to the command. The battalion consisting of

Lt.-Col.	Majors.	Capts.	Lieuts.	Sub.-Lts.	Staff.	Sergts.	Corpls.	Drummers.	Privates.
1	2	4	8	5	2	43	37	15	741

embarked on board the Indian troop ship "Serapis," at Queenstown, on the 30th September, and sailed on the 1st October for Bombay. The battalion arrived at Bombay on the 1st November, disembarked, and proceeded by rail the following day to Poona, where it occupied the Ghorporie lines. It proceeded to the camp of exercise, Chinchwud, on the 6th December, and formed part of the Reserve Brigade attached to the 2nd Division. At the expiration of the period of exercise, the battalion returned to Poona by route march on the 24th December.

The Government having decided to send an expedition to the Gold Coast, under the command of Major-General Sir Garnet Wolseley, C.B., K.C.M.G., to punish the King of Ashanti, several of the officers volunteered for active service, and the services of Lieut. and Adjt. G. Barton, Lieut. F. W. Douglass, and Surgeon Atkins having been accepted, these officers embarked during the autumn for the seat of war.

A pair of old colours that had belonged to the Regiment about the beginning of the present century, and which had passed into the possession of Col. R. Walker, who was formerly in the Regiment, was restored to the Fusiliers by the surviving relatives, through Mr. L. W. Adamson, of Whitley House, Northumberland. The ceremony took place at the Citadel, Dover, November 15th, when the colours were received on a full parade of the battalion, with every mark of respect. Mr. Adamson, in restoring them, made a very effective speech, and handed them over to the safe keeping of the 1st Battalion Royal Fusiliers.

1874.

1st Battalion

The 1st Battalion remained at Dover during this year. In March the Ashanti War having been successfully concluded, Lieut. and Adjt. G. Barton, Lieut. F. W. Douglass, and Surgeon Atkins returned to England. Lieut. and Adjt. G. Barton was promoted to a half-pay company, in recognition of his services during this campaign.

May 13th, H.I.M. the Emperor of Russia landed at Dover, the Royal Fusiliers took part in his reception, on which occasion the whole of the troops in the garrison were assembled.

The battalion was inspected by Major-General Sir A. Horsford, K.C.B., commanding the South-Eastern District, on the 15th July.

September 28th, medals for long service and good conduct were presented to the following non-commissioned officers and men :—

Sergeant H. F. Lloyd,
Sergeant E. May,
Private W. Blakeney,
Private J. Reddy, with gratuities of £5 each.

Private J. Newbrook,
Private J. Sealey,
Private J. Pease, without gratuities.

Martini-Henry rifle supplied.

On the 19th October, the battalion was armed with the Martini-Henry Rifle, which had been approved of, to replace the Snider, which was shortly afterwards returned into store.

1875.

Ashanti Medal.

In March of this year a medal for Ashanti, with clasp for Coomassie, was issued to the officers who had taken part in that campaign.

March 24th, Lieut. F. W. Douglass was promoted to a half-pay company, in recognition of his services during the Ashanti War.

On the 15th June the 1st Battalion was inspected by Major-General Parke, C.B., commanding the S.E. District. On the 24th June it proceeded by rail from Dover to Aldershot to take part in the summer drills and encamped in the "Guards Enclosure," forming with the 3rd Batt. Grenadier Guards and the 1st Battalion Scots Fusilier Guards the 1st Brigade, 1st Division, of the 1st Army Corps; the Brigade being under the command of Colonel Lord Abinger, Scots Fusilier Guards.

Summer Drills.

On the 28th June the 1st Army Corps marched to Kingsley, Sleaford, and Woolmer, the 1st Brigade encamping at the first-named place. The Army Corps subsequently moved to Frensham and thence to Aldershot, where it remained manœuvring at times against the 2nd Army Corps until the termination of the summer drills, which were brought to a conclusion by a march past of the whole force, numbering nearly 20,000 regular troops. On this occasion each Army Corps marched past by divisions in line of double company quarter columns. The weather throughout the whole period had been very unfavourable. Rain fell constantly during the time that the troops were under canvas, and although the men were on several occasions wet through for a considerable period, their health was not in any way affected by it.

On the 27th July the 1st Battalion moved by train to Colchester Camp in the Eastern District, under command of Major-General Sir E. Greathed, K.C.B., and was brigaded with the 18th Royal Irish and 96th Regiments.

1st Battalion moves to Colchester.

LISTS OF OFFICERS OF THE ROYAL REGIMENT OF FUSILIERS.

In the following lists the Colonels of the Regiment are given separately and in chronological order. That method has been adopted to suit the later arrangement, which makes the Colonel of a Regiment an honorary rather than an active officer. The early Colonels of the Regiment were, however, the actual commanders of the Regiment, the Lieutenant-Colonels occupying the positions of the present senior Majors; yet, notwithstanding this, it has been determined to introduce them in the chronological, and not in the alphabetical, list.

As regards medals and distinctions, it will be seen that in some cases services are denoted by numbers, in others by the name of the action in which the recipient participated. That distinction arises from the fact that of the war of the French Revolution the actions were numbered, and the clasps referred to in the Army List by the numbers in the official key, while in later cases the clearer and better plan of giving the actual name of the action has been followed. To explain the services of those who fought in the wars of the French Revolution, I shall, therefore, give the list of battles and actions for which medals were granted under the General Order of the 1st June, 1847.

1. Maida . . . . . 4th July, 1806.
2. Roleia . . . . 17th Aug., 1808.
3. Vimiera . . . . 21st Aug., 1808.
4. Sahagun and . . . . Dec., 1808.
   Benevente . . . . Jan., 1809.
5. Corunna . . . 16th Jan., 1809.
6. Martinique . . . . Feb., 1809.
7. Talavera . . 27th and 28th July, 1809.
8. Guadaloupe . . . Jan. and Feb., 1810.
9. Busaco . . . . 27th Sept., 1810.
10. Barossa . . . . 5th Mar., 1811.
11. Fuentes d'Onor . . . 5th May, 1811.
12. Albuera . . . . 16th May, 1811.
13. Java . . . Aug. and Sept., 1811.
14. Ciudad Rodrigo . Jan. and Feb., 1812.
15. Badajos . . . Mar. and April, 1812.
16. Salamanca . . . 22nd July, 1812.
17. Fort Detroit, America . . Aug., 1812.
18. Vittoria . . . . 21st June, 1813.
19. Pyrenees . . 28th July to 2nd Aug., 1813.
20. San Sebastian . . Aug. and Sept., 1813.
21. Chateauguay, America . 26th Oct., 1813.
22. Nivelle . . . . 10th Nov., 1813.
23. Chrystler's Farm, America . 11th Nov., 1813.
24. Nive . . . 9th to 13th Dec., 1813.
25. Orthes . . . . 27th Feb., 1814.
26. Toulouse . . . . 10th April, 1814.
27. Egypt . . . . . . 1801.

It must be further stated that 𝔚 before a name denotes the medal for Waterloo; 𝔙.𝔊. the Victoria Cross. Wherever in the list no Regiment is given with the date of appointment, it must be understood that the appointment has taken place in the Royal Regiment of Fusiliers.

SUCCESSION OF COLONELS OF THE ROYAL FUSILIERS.

GEORGE LEGGE, *Lord Dartmouth*, aptd. Col., 11th June, 1685; deprived of the command, 1689; imprisoned in the Tower for corresponding with King James II.; died there in bed suddenly of apoplexy, 21st Oct., 1691, and was interred in a vault in the Trinity Chapel, Minories.

Entered the Royal Navy in 1665, and served during the first Dutch War as lieutenant; on the 7th December, 1670, he was appointed Lieut.-General of the Ordnance; served in the second Dutch War as captain in the attack on the Smyrna Fleet and the battle of Solebay; greatly distinguished himself in command of the Royal Catherine in Rupert's attack on Van Tromp, 28th May, 1673, and in the succeeding actions of that war, at the conclusion of which he was appointed Governor of Portsmouth, Master of the Horse, and Gentleman of the Bedchamber to the Duke of York. In 1683 he was sent to destroy the fortress of Tangier and withdraw the garrison, an operation which he performed with the most signal success. Appointed Constable of the Tower, Feb., 1685. His career during the reign of James II. has been sketched in the early services of the regiment. "The crime of having been personally the friend of James was deemed a sufficient ground to induce at least a suspicion of treason. He was arrested and committed prisoner to the Tower, where grief or indignation, at the treatment he experienced, is supposed to have accelerated that end which his enemies ought ever to have lamented, because superior worth existed not among them."

JOHN CHURCHILL, *Duke of Marlborough*; Ens., 14th Sept., 1667, 1st Foot Guards; Capt., 1672, Duke of Monmouth's Foot; Lieut.-Col., 1673, Sir Chas. Littleton's Regt.; aptd. Col. of an English Regt. in the service of France, 3rd April, 1674; aptd. Col. of a Regt. of Dragoons, 1680; aptd. Col., 3rd Troop of Life Guards, 18th Dec., 1682; aptd. Col., 1st Royal Dragoons, 19th Nov., 1683; Lieut.-Gen., 1685; aptd. Col., Royal Fusiliers, 26th Aug., 1689; deprived of his command, 21st Jan., 1692; aptd. Gen. of Foot, and Commander-in-Chief of the Forces in Holland, 1st June, 1700; Col., 1st Foot Guards, 25th April, 1704; dismissed from all his employments, 31st Dec., 1711; reaptd. Col., 1st Foot Guards, 26th Sept., 1714; died at Windsor Lodge, 16th June, 1722.

Entered the 1st Foot Guards, and served at Tangier; in 1672 he served with the French Army, and distinguished himself at the siege of Nimeguen, and in 1673 at the siege of Maestricht, where he was wounded. Served the following campaign with the French Army on the Rhine in command of an English regiment. Proceeded to Flanders in 1678 in command of a brigade of infantry, but returned to England at the Peace of Nimeguen. Served during Monmouth's rebellion, and for his conduct at Sedgemoor was rewarded with the Colonelcy of the 3rd Troop of Life Guards. Commanded the English at the battle of Walcourt, and at the capture of Cork and Kinsale, 1690; and on the accession of Queen Anne was appointed Capt.-General and Commander of the Allied Forces acting against the French. The succession of victories achieved in that war are perhaps unequalled in the career of any other general. He took Venloo, Ruremonde, Stevenswaert, and Liege 1702; forced Bonn, Huy and Limburg, 1703; forced the intrenchments at Schellenberg, and won the decisive battle of Blenheim, 1704; relieved Liege, re-took Huy, and forced the French lines at Helixem and Neer Hespen in 1705; won the battle of Ramilies, 23rd May, 1706, and laid the French power in Flanders at his feet; won the battle of Oudenarde in 1708; captured Lisle, conquered at Malplaquet, took Mons, Douay, Bethune, Aire, St. Venant, Bouchain, and in ten campaigns proved himself invincible, and, as has been said of him,

"The bravest leader of the bravest host!
A veteran chief that in the bloody field
For forty rolling years, untaught to yield,
Thro' half the severed globe obtained renown,
And with its brightest gems adorned the British crown."

GEORGE HAMILTON, *Earl of Orkney*, K.T., Lieut.-Col., 1688; Col., 1st March, 1690; aptd. Col. of the Royal Fusiliers, 23rd Jan., 1692; aptd. Col. of the Royal Scots, 1st Aug., 1692; Major-Gen., March, 1702; Lieut.-Gen., Feb., 1703; Gen., 1711; Field-Marshal, Jan., 1736; died, 29th Jan., 1737.

Served in the Royal Scots under Charles II. and James II.; adhered to the Protestant cause, and took service under William III.; distinguished himself at the battle of the Boyne, present at the siege of Athlone, wounded at the battle of Aghrim and siege of Limerick. Distinguished himself at the head of the Royal Fusiliers at Steinkirk; present with the Royal Scots at Landen; and as Brigadier at the capture of Namur. Served under Marlborough at Stevenswaert, Schellenberg, Blenheim, Siege and capture of Huy, Ramilies, Siege of Menin, Oudenarde, covering the Siege of Lisle, forcing the passage of the Scheldt, Malplaquet, Siege of Douay, and siege of Bouchain. Promoted Governor of Edinburgh Castle and Governor of Virginia, March, 1705.

EDWARD FITZPATRICK, Capt., 3rd Buffs; aptd. Col. of a Regt. of Foot, 1688; aptd. Col. Royal Fusiliers, 1st Aug., 1692; Brigadier Gen., 1694; drowned in Dublin Bay, during his passage to Ireland, 10th Nov., 1696.

Served with the Buffs in Holland; embraced the cause of the Prince of Orange at the Revolution, who promoted him to a regiment afterwards disbanded. Served with his regiment at Walcourt, and at the sieges of Cork and Kinsale; returned with it to Flanders, present at Steinkirk. Severely wounded at the head of the Royal Fusiliers at Landen, and commanded the brigade in which they served at the siege of Namur.

Sir CHARLES O'HARA, *Lord Tyrawley*, Capt. and Lieut. Col. 1st Foot Guards, 1st April, 1689; Col., 12th Nov., 1696, Royal Fusiliers; Maj. Gen., 1702; Lieut. Gen., 1704; resigned the Colonelcy of the Royal Fusiliers, 27th Jan., 1713; Gen. Nov., 1714; died in Dublin, 8th June, 1724.

Served in the English Brigade in the Dutch service in the reign of Charles II., and commanded a company in the Earl of Ossory's regiment. Served under King William in Flanders, and commanded a brigade in the expedition to Cadiz and Vigo, 1702. Served in the war of the Spanish Succession, and commanded the left wing of the allied army at Almanza in 1707, where he was wounded. On the breaking out of the rebellion of 1715, he raised a regiment of foot in Ireland, which was disbanded in 1718. He was for several years Commander-in-Chief in Ireland, Governor of Minorca and of the Royal Hospital of Kilmainham.

JAMES O'HARA, *Lord Tyrawley*, Lieut., 15th May, 1703, Royal Fusiliers; Capt., 24th Mar., 1705, Royal Fusiliers; aptd. Col. of the Royal Fusiliers, 29th Jan., 1713; Brig. Gen., 23rd Nov., 1735; Maj. Gen., 2nd July, 1739; aptd. Col. 4th Drag. Guards, 26th Aug., 1739; Lieut. Gen., 31st March, 1743; aptd. Col. 2nd Troop of Horse Grenadier Guards, 1st April, 1743; aptd. Col. 3rd Troop of Life Guards, April, 1745; aptd. Col. 10th Foot, 26th Dec., 1746; aptd. Col. 14th Light Dragoons, 24th July, 1749; to 3rd Dragoons, 8th July, 1752; to Coldstream Guards, 8th April, 1755; General, 7th March, 1761; Field Marshal, 10th June, 1763; died at Twickenham, 13th July, 1773.

Proceeded with the Royal Fusiliers to the relief of Barcelona, and was afterwards placed on the staff of the army in Spain; wounded at Almanza, where it is said he was instrumental in saving Lord Galway's life. Served afterwards with the Fusiliers in Minorca. Appointed Governor of Portsmouth and afterwards of Minorca, and was also employed as Envoy and Ambassador to the Courts of Portugal and Russia.

WILLIAM HARGRAVE, Ens., 23rd April, 1694; aptd. to 36th Regt., 1700; Lieut., 17th July, 1702, 36th Regt.; Capt., 18th Oct., 1703, 36th Regt.; Major, 31st Aug., 1705, 36th Regt.; Bt. Lieut. Col., 27th April, 1708; Col., 15th Nov., 1711; aptd. to 31st Regt., 1st Jan., 1730; aptd. to 9th Regt., 27th Jan., 1737; aptd. to Royal Fusiliers, 27th Aug., 1739; died 26th January, 1751.

Served with the 36th Regt. in the expedition to Cadiz and Vigo; served also with that Regiment in the war of the Spanish Succession, present with it at the relief of Barcelona, 1705, and at the battle of Almanza, 1707. Served with the 36th in the rebellion of 1715, present at the battle of Dumblaine.

JOHN MOSTYN, Ens., Feb., 1732, 31st Regt.; Lieut., 1734, 31st Regt.; Capt., Dec., 1736, 31st Regt.; aptd. Capt. Lieut. Coldstream Guards, 2nd Sept., 1742; Capt. and Lieut. Col., 2nd April, 1743; Col., 3rd April, 1747; aptd. Col. Royal Fusiliers, 26th Jan., 1751; aptd. to 13th Light Dragoons, 8th July, 1754; Maj. Gen., 8th Feb., 1757; aptd. Col. 5th Royal Irish Dragoons, 18th Oct., 1758;

Lieut. Gen., 8th April, 1759; aptd. Col. 7th Dragoons, 18th Aug., 1760; aptd. to 1st Dragoon Guards, 13th May, 1763; General, 25th May, 1772; died April, 1779.

<small>Served with the Coldstream Guards in Flanders, wounded at Fontenoy. Served with the British Cavalry in Germany during the Seven Years' War; distinguished himself at Minden and Warburg.</small>

Lord ROBERT BERTIE, Ens., 9th July, 1737, Coldstream Guards; Lieut., 13th Feb., 1742, Coldstream Guards; Capt. and Lieut.-Col., 11th April, 1744, Coldstream Guards; Col., 4th Mar, 1752; aptd Col. Royal Fusiliers, 20th Aug., 1754; Major-Gen., 15th May, 1758; Lieut.-Gen., 18th Dec., 1760; aptd. Col. 2nd Life Guards, 2nd Oct., 1776; Gen., 29th Aug, 1777; died at his house in Mortimer Street, London, 10th March, 1782.

<small>Served with the Coldstreams at Fontenoy, wounded; accompanied the Royal Fusiliers to the Mediterranean and served in Admiral Byng's action off Minorca.</small>

RICHARD PRESCOTT, Major, 20th Dec., 1756, Royal Fusiliers; aptd. to 50th Regt., 11th Dec., 1759; Bt. Lieut.-Col., 22nd Jan, 1761; Lieut.-Col., 22nd May, 1761, 50th Regt.; aptd. to Royal Fusiliers, 19th Nov., 1761; Col., 22nd June, 1772; aptd. Col. of the Royal Fusiliers, 12th Nov., 1776; Maj.-Gen., 29th Aug., 1777; Lieut.-Gen., 26th Nov., 1782; died in Queen Anne Street West, Cavendish Square, 21st Nov., 1788.

<small>Served with the 50th in Germany during the Seven Years' War, served first in command of the Fusiliers, and afterwards as a Major-General in America during the Revolutionary War; captured at Rhode Island.</small>

Hon. WILLIAM GORDON, Capt., , 1759, 16th Light Dragoons; Major 84th Regt.; Lieut.-Col., 11th Oct., 1762, 105th Regt.; disbanded 1763; Col., 29th Aug., 1777; aptd. Col. 81st Regt., 19th Dec., 1777; regt. disbanded 1783; Maj.-Gen., 19th Oct., 1781; aptd. Col. Com. 60th Regt., 3rd Oct., 1787; aptd. Col. Royal Fusiliers, 20th Oct., 1788; aptd. Col. 71st Regt., 9th April, 1789; Lieut.-Gen., 12th Oct., 1793; Gen., 1st Jan., 1798; aptd. Col. 21st Regt., 6th Aug., 1803; died at Maryculter House, near Aberdeen, 25th May, 1816.

H.R.H. PRINCE EDWARD, *Duke of Kent*, K.G., G.C.B., Col., 30th May, 1786,

Hanoverian Guards; aptd. Col. Royal Fusiliers, 9th April, 1789; Major-Gen., 2nd Oct., 1793; Lieut.-Gen., 12th Jan., 1796; aptd. Col. of the Royal Scots, 21st Aug., 1801; Gen., 10th May, 1799; Field-Marshal, 5th Sept., 1805; died at Sidmouth, 23rd Jan., 1820.

Commanded the 2nd Queen's at Gibraltar, served in Canada and the West Indies, present at the capture of Martinique, St. Lucie, and Guadaloupe, 1794. Commanded the forces in Nova Scotia; Governor of Gibraltar, 1802.

Sir ALURED CLARKE, *G.C.B.*, Ens., 20th March, 1759, 50th Regt.; Lieut., 10th May, 1760, 50th Regt.; Capt., 7th Jan., 1767, 5th Regt.; Major, 28th Nov., 1771, 54th Regt.; Lieut.-Col., 20th Sept., 1775, 54th Regt.; aptd. to 7th, 10th March, 1777; Major-Gen., 28th April, 1790; aptd. Col. 5th Regt., 25th Oct., 1794; Lieut.-Gen., 27th Jan., 1797; aptd. Col. of the Royal Fusiliers, 21st Aug., 1801; Gen., 29th April, 1802; Field-Marshal, 22nd July, 1830; died at the Vicarage, Llangollen, 16th Sept., 1832.

Served with the 50th in Germany during the Seven Years' War, and through the American War with the Royal Fusiliers. Invested with the command of the army that captured the Cape of Good Hope in 1795, but arrived only during the unexpected struggle with the Dutch, and served afterwards in the East Indies.

Sir EDWARD BLAKENEY, *G.C.B.*, *G.C.H.*, Cornet, 28th Feb., 1794, 8th Light Dragoons; Lieut., 24th Sept., 1794, 121st Regt.; Capt., 24th Dec., 1794, late 99th Regt.; exchd. to 17th Regt., 8th March, 1798; Major, 17th Sept., 1801, 17th Regt.; placed on h. p. of it, 1802; aptd. to 47th Regt., 9th July, 1803; exchd. to 7th, 24th MAR., 1804; Bt. Lieut.-Col., 25th April, 1808; Lieut.-Col., 20th JUNE, 1811; Col., 4th June, 1814; Major-Gen., 27th May, 1825; aptd. Col. of the 7th, 20th SEPT., 1832; Lieut.-Gen., 28th June, 1838; Gen., 20th June, 1854; aptd. Col. 1st Foot, 21st Dec., 1854; Field-Marshal, 9th Nov., 1862; Col.-in-Chief of the Rifle Brigade, 28th Aug., 1865; aptd. Gov. of Chelsea Hospital; died at Chelsea, 2nd Aug., 1868. *Gold Medal for* 6, 12, 15, 18, 19. *Silver Medal for* 9, 14, 22, 24.

Accompanied the expedition under Major-Gen. White, to the West Indies, present at the capture of Demerara, Berbice, and Essiquibo, 1796; in the course of this service he was three times taken prisoner by Privateers, and suffered severe hardship. In 1799 he accompanied the expedition to Holland, present in the actions of the 10th and 19th Sept., and of the 2nd and 6th Oct. Expedition to Copenhagen in 1807; joined Lord Cathcart's expedition, and was present at the capture of the **Danish Fleet** and surrender of Copenhagen.

Served at the capture of Martinique, 1809. In 1810 he sailed for Lisbon in command of the Fusiliers; severely wounded through the thigh at Albuera; affair of Aldea de Ponte; severely wounded through the arm at the assault of Badajoz, combat of Pampeluna, and the various minor affairs. Proceeded with the Regiment to New Orleans, present at the assault of the lines before that place. Present also at the capture of Paris, and with the army of occupation.

Sir SAMUEL BENJAMIN AUCHMUTY, *G.C.B.*, Ens., 15th Oct., 1797, 60th Regt.; Lieut., 13th Mar., 1800, 68th Regt.; Capt., 14th Nov., 1805, 68th Regt.; exchd. to 70th Regt., 5th July, 1806; exchd. to 7th, 22nd Oct., 1807; Bt.-Major, 26th Aug., 1813; Major, 28th Oct., 1813; Bt. Lieut.-Col., 12th April, 1814; exchd to h. p. of 8th Gar. Batt., 1st Aug., 1822; Col., 6th May, 1831; Major-Gen., 23rd Nov., 1841; aptd. Col. 65th Regt., 31st Jan., 1851; Lieut.-Gen., 11th Nov., 1851; aptd. Col. 7th Fusiliers, 18th JAN., 1855; Gen., 19th June, 1860; died at Pau, Basses Pyrenees, 30th April, 1868. *Gold Medal for* 25, 26; *Silver Medal for* 7, 9, 11, 18, 19.

Served several years in the West Indies; present at the storming of Morne Fortunee, St. Lucia. In 1809, accompanied the 2nd Batt. Royal Fusiliers to Portugal; present at Oporto and Talavera, as Major of Brigade to Sir Alex. Campbell; at Busaco, the retreat of the army to and subsequent advance from the lines of Torres Vedras; and battle of Fuentes d'Onor, as deputy Asst. Adjt. Gen. to the 6th Division. On return to the Peninsula from sick leave, was appointed extra Aide-de Camp to Sir Lowry Cole; with the 4th Division at Vittoria and the Pyrenees, at the latter promoted Brevet Major. Succeeding to the Regimental Majority, he commanded the Light Companies of Major-Gen. Ross's Brigade, served with them at Orthes and Toulouse, at the latter promoted Brevet Lieut.-Col.

Sir RICHARD AIREY, *G.C.B.*, Ens., 15th Mar., 1821, 34th Regt.; Lieut., 4th Dec., 1823, 34th Regt.; Capt., 22nd Oct., 1825, h. p. Comp.; exchd. to 34th Regt., 11th June, 1826; Major, 9th May, 1834, 34th Regt.; Lieut.-Col., 10th Feb., 1838, 34th Regt.; Col., 11th Nov., 1851; Maj.-Gen., 12th Dec., 1854; Lieut.-Gen., 24th Oct., 1862; aptd. Col. 17th Regt., 20th July, 1860; aptd. Col. 7th Fusiliers, 1st May, 1868; Gen., 9th April, 1871.

Served throughout the Eastern campaign of 1854-5—first in command of a brigade, and afterwards from the disembarkation in the Crimea as Qt.-Mast. Gen., present at the battles of the Alma, Balaclava, and Inkerman, and siege of Sebastopol. (Medal with four clasps, K.C.B., Commander of the Legion of Honour, Commander of 1st Class of the Military Order of Savoy, 2nd Class of the Medjidie and Turkish Medal.)

Alphabetical List of Officers of the Royal Fusiliers.

NAME.	ENSIGN, &c.	LIEUTENANT.	CAPTAIN.	HIGHER RANKS AND REMARKS.
A'BECKETT, Reginald Broadhurst	30th DEC., 1862;	29th SEPT., 1865;	…	Retired 25th Sept, 1869.
ABERCROMBIE, George	…	29th JULY, 1781; exchd. to h. p. of 81st Regt., 15th March, 1786;	…	Died 1805.
ACHMUTY, Charles	28th Aug., 1808, 1st Dragoons, K.G.L.	17th AUG., 1809;	…	Died 10th Sept. 1810.
ADAMS, James	…	…	11th JUNE, 1685;	Promoted to Col., and aptd. Governor of …, Jan., 1692.
ADDERLEY, George	…	28th FEB., 1805;	9th July, 1803, 3rd Batt. of Reserve; regt. disbanded, 1805;	Retired 3rd March, 1808.
ADDERLEY, Ralph	…	7th Nov., 1759; exchd. to h. p, 3rd Feb, 1769.	…	
ADLAM, Wm. John Erasmus *Silver Medal for Salamanca.*	Lieut., 14th May, 1803, Sussex Militia;	21st JAN., 1808; aptd. Cornet, Royal Horse Guards, 10th Jan., 1811;	…	Retired 16th July, 1812; aptd. Captain in the Ayrshire Militia, 11th Feb., 1814; died 20th Aug., 1828.
AFFLECK, Sir Gilbert, *Bart.*	5th Nov., 1778, 23rd Regt.;	19th SEPT., 1779;	30th April, 1781, 63rd Regt.; aptd. to 98th Regt.;	Retired 1794; aptd. Cornet Rutlandshire Fencible Cavalry, Feb., 1795; Lieut., 20th May, 1795; Capt., 28th June, 1803, Rutland Militia; died in Dean Street, South Audley Street, 17th July, 1808.
ALDERCRON, John Embarked with the 39th for Madras in 1754; served in Bengal, at the relief of Trichinopoly, and at the reduction of Wandewash; commanded the first British regiment that ever served in India, *Primus in Indis*.	23rd Feb, 1709.	…	4th AUG., 17??, Regt.; aptd. to 7th, 20th June, 1727;	Major, 13th Dec., 1739; Lieut. Col., 5th Feb., 1741; Major-Gen., 16th May, 1758; Col., 14th March, 1752, 39th Regt.; Lieut.-Gen., 18th Dec., 1760; died 31st Aug., 1766.
ALDWORTH, Richard William *Medal for the Crimea. Turkish Medal.*	19th Aug., 1844, 60th Regt.; Served the Eastern Campaign of siege of Sebastopol and sortie of 26th October.	22nd OCT., 1847; 1854 up to the 8th Nov., including	7th JUNE, 1854; the battles of Alma and Inkerman,	Major, 27th MAY, 1856; Lieut. Col. 20th MAR., 1857; Col., 20th March, 1863; retired 29th May, 1863.
ALLAN, George	17th April, 1817, h. p. of 60th Regt.; exchd. to 18th Hussars, 25th Jan, 1821; placed on h. p. of it, 10th Nov., 1821;	17th JULY, 1823;	1st Oct., 1825, unatt.: exchd. to 5th Foot, 25th Sept., 1826;	Major, 1st Oct., 1829, 5th Foot; exchd. to h. p. unatt., 6th June, 1834; Bt. Lieut. Col., 23rd Nov., 1841; exchd. to 88th Regt., 12th May, 1843; retired same day.
ANDERDON, Thomas Oliver *Silver Medal for 7, 9.*	April, 1804, 69th Regt.; exchd. to 9th L. D., 1804;	19th July, 1804, 53rd Regt.; placed on h. p. of it, 1804; exchd. to 1st Drags., 26th July, 1805;	10th April, 1806, 1st Drags.; exchd. to 7th, 15th DEC., 1808;	Retired 8th Aug., 1811; called to the Bar and became Q.C.; died in St. James's Square, Bath, 16th April, 1859.
ANDERSON, Henry Archibald Landed with the 2nd Batt. in the Peninsula, 1809; present at the capture of Oporto.	16th JULY, 1873.	28th AUG., 1807;	1st SEPT., 1813; placed on h. p. of the Regt., 25th Feb., 1816, exchd. to Ceylon Rifles, 8th June, 1820; 1st July, 1795, 4th West India Regt.; aptd. to 31st Regt., 25th May, 1796;	Major, 2nd May, 1834, Ceylon Rifles; Lieut. Col., 29th April, 1842, Ceylon Rifles; retired on f. p. of the Regt.; died in Glasgow, 3rd June, 1845.
ANDERSON, James Served in the Peninsula from 1809 to the end of the war, including the battles of Talavera, Busaco, first siege of Badajoz, Albuera, Salamanca, Vittoria, capture of Oporto, the battles of Toulouse, the combat of Pampeluna, and all the minor affairs.	From Lieut. North York Militia.	31st March, 1791, 51st Regt.;		
ANDERSON, Paul Went to Gibraltar in 1792, and Toulon; from thence to Corsica, Fort, and siege of Calvi. Appointed the storming Morne Chabot, St. taking of Morne Fortunee, in repulsing the enemy's sortie, and final Holland, present at the first landing battle of Fonke's Hill, and the reduction of the place; served during present at the landing and battle of taking of Wexford; expedition to right arm, the full use of which he 2nd October; expedition to Egypt, was the favoured friend of Sir John 1806; Walcheren expedition, 1809; whose death he was present. his Peninsula campaign, and at	31st March, 1788, 51st Regt.; after remaining there for two years where he was present at the storming Brigade Major to Sir John Moore in Lucia, where he received a severe contusion in the side; also at the reduction of the place; served during action of Fonke's Hill, and the retaking of Wexford; expedition to 2nd October; expedition to Egypt, of which he received a shot in the 1806; Walcheren expedition, 1809; never recovered; expedition to Sicily, his Peninsula campaign, and at	embarked with the 51st Regt. for the West Indies, and employed in reduction of the Convention Redoubt, Moselle action of the 10th September and the 13th and 21st March, at the latter Moore, with whom he served during		Major, 25th June, 1801, 9th Foot; placed on h. p. of it; exchd. to 7th, Nov., 1802; exchd. to h. p. of Corsican Rangers, April, 1803; exchd. to 40th Regt., 5th Oct., 1804; Lieut. Col., 17th Oct., 1805; exchd. to h. p. of 4th Foot, 30th Oct., 1806; exchd. to 60th Regt., 14th Jan., 1808; Col., 4th June, 1813; placed on h. p. of the Regt., 25th Feb., 1817; Maj. Gen., 12th Aug., 1819; aptd. Lieut. Governor of Gravesend and Tilbury Fort, 13th Dec., 1827; aptd. Governor of Pendennis Castle, 23rd July, 1832; Lieut. Gen., 10th Jan., 1837; aptd. Col. of the 78th Regt., 9th Feb., 1837; Gen., 11th Nov., 1851; died at Bath, 17th Dec, 1851.

Alphabetical List of Officers of the Royal Fusiliers.

NAME.	ENSIGN, &c.	LIEUTENANT.	CAPTAIN.	HIGHER RANKS AND REMARKS.
ANDRÉ, John Served during the war of the	25th Jan., 1771, 23rd Regt.; his American Revolution until	24th Sept., 1771; death.	18th Jan., 1777, 26th Regt.; aptd. to 54th Regt., 9th Sept., 1779;	Hanged, by order of Washington, as a spy, 2nd Oct., 1780, aged 29.
ANDRÉ, *Sir* William Lewis, *Bart.*	…	5th July, 1777;	5th Nov., 1778, 44th Regt., aptd. to 26th Regt., 6th Sept., 1779; exchd. to h. p. of it; 2nd Feb., 1791;	Capt. Loyal Essex Fencible Cavalry; died at Dean's Leaze, Hants, 11th Nov., 1802.
ᛞᚷ ANGLESEY, Henry William *Marquis of*, K.G., G.C.B., G.C.H. *Gold Medal for Sahagun and Benevente.* Raised the 80th Regt. in 1793 among his father's tenantry, in Staffordshire ; joined the Duke of York in Flanders, 1794, in command of his Regt.; in the retreat had temporary expedition to Holland 1799; commanded the cavalry in the action of enemy's cavalry having been defeated the 2nd Oct., late in the evening, the charged by the cavalry under Lord Artillery on the beach, and being Paget, were driven with loss nearly to Egmont-op-Zee; in the retreat he protected the rear with his cavalry, which several guns fell into the hands of the enemy; with one squadron he Gen. Simon, six times his own command in 1808 proceeded to the Peninsula in numbers, retaking the British, and 1809 proceeded to the Peninsula in command of two brigades of cavalry; vente; commanded a division in the J. Moore he brought up the rear; attacked and defeated the enemy at Walcheren expedition, 1809; commanded the cavalry in the campaign in protecting the infantry in the of 1815; engaged in frequent charges right thigh by a cannon shot—leg close of Waterloo was struck on the amputated.	…	7th Mar., 1793;	25th Mar., 1793, 23rd Regt.;	Major, 29th May, 1793, 65th Regt.; Lieut.-Col., 12th Sept., 1793, 80th Regt.; exchd. to 16th L. D., 16th June, 1795; Col., 3rd May, 1796; exchd. to 7th L. D., 6th April, 1797; aptd. Col. of the Regt. 16th May, 1801; Maj.-Gen., 29th April, 1802; Lieut.-Gen., 25th April, 1808; Gen. 12th Aug., 1819; aptd. Mast. Gen. of the Ordnance, 1st April, 1827, which he held to 28th April, 1828; aptd. Col. of the Royal Horse Guards, 20th Dec., 1842; reaptd. Mast. Gen. of the Ordnance, 8th July, 1846, which he held to April, 1852; Field Marshal, 9th Nov., 1846; died at Uxbridge House, Burlington Street, London, 29th April, 1854.
ANGUS, John	1st March, 1864, 79th Regt.;	8th Feb., 1868, 79th Regt.; exchd. to 7th, 27th Aug., 1873.		
ANSTRUTHER, *Sir* Philip, *Bart.*	14th Aug., 1767, 6th Foot;	26th Jan., 1770;	19th Feb., 1777;	Retired Feb., 1780; died at Elie House, Fifeshire, 5th Jan., 1808.
ANTRIM, Hugh Seymour, *Earl of*	25th June, 1829, 43rd Regt.; retired on h. p. of 39th Regt., 9th Dec., 1831; aptd. to 60th Regt., 21st June, 1833;	26th July, 1833;	…	Retired 22nd Jan., 1836; died at Glenarm Castle, co. Antrim, 18th July, 1855.
APPLEYARD, Fredk. Ernest, C.B. *Medal for Pegu*; *Medal for the Crimea*; *Legion of Honour*; 5th Class of the Medjidie Served with the 80th Regt. in the capture of the great Dagon Pagoda; Burmese war of 1852, present at the sent at Alma (wounded), Inkerman, ture of the great Dagon Pagoda; with the storming party at the capture of the Redan, 18th June, (wounded). 1854-5 with the Royal Fusiliers, present at the of the Quarries 7th June, and assault 14th Aug., 1872.	14th June, 1850, 80th Regt.;	12th Oct., 1852, 80th Regt.; aptd. to 81st Regt., 27th May, 1853; aptd. to 7th, 17th June, 1853;	29th Dec., 1854;	Bt. Major, 26th Dec., 1856; Major, 31st Aug., 1858; exchd. to a Depot Batt., 24th Dec., 1858; exchd. to 85th Regt., 5th Feb., 1861; Lieut. Col., 6th Mar., 1867, 85th Regt.; Col., 6th Mar., 1872.
APPLEYARD, Richard Locke	…	14th Aug., 1874;	before Rangoon, 12th–14th April; Served the Eastern campaign of operations also at the Capture of Prome. on the 5th April and 9th May, defence	
ARABIN, John	…	16th Aug., 1750;	19th June, 1751; 27th April, 1708.	Regt.;
ARCHDALE, Thomas	…	…	…	
ARCHER, Holt Landed with the 2nd Batt. in the Peninsula; present at the capture of	From Lieut., Armagh Militia ;	3rd Nov., 1808; Oporto, and battles of Talavera and 17th Jan., 1766 ; exchd. to h. p., 15th July, 1767; aptd. to 13th Regt., 22nd July, 1767	Busaco.	Killed at Albuera, 16th May, 1811.
ARDESOIF, Thomas	…	…	…	Died in London, Aug., 1774.
ARNOTT, Archibald James	6th July, 1855, 55th Regt.;	19th Dec., 1856, 55th Regt.; aptd. to 7th, 2nd Feb., 1858;	…	Retired Feb., 1861.
Re-entered the army	29th July, 1862, Royal Newfoundland Comps.; aptd. to Royal Canadian Rifles, 2nd Dec., 1862;	22nd Feb., 1868, Royal Canadian Rifles; Regt. reduced, placed on h. p. of it;	…	Retired Nov., 1872.
ASHBURNHAM, *Hon.* John Expedition to Copenhagen in 1807.	…	20th Feb., 1806; aptd. Ens. Coldstream Guards, 1st Jan., 1807;	…	Supposed to have been drowned on his passage from Portugal, Sept., 1809.
ASHTON, Arthur	8th Feb., 1858; aptd. to 4th D. G., 25th May, 1860;	…	…	Retired 13th Dec., 1861.
ATWICK, Richard	…	20th Oct., 1762; aptd. to 3rd Foot, 1763; placed on h. p. of it, 1763;	…	Died or retired, 1785.

Alphabetical List of Officers of the Royal Fusiliers.

NAME.	ENSIGN, &c.	LIEUTENANT.	CAPTAIN.	HIGHER RANKS AND REMARKS.
AUCHMUTY, Sir Saml. Benj., G.C.B. *Silver Medal for* 7, 9, 11, 18, 19. (*Gold Medal for* 25, 26.) Served several years in the West Indies; present at the storming of 1809, accompanied the 2nd Batt. Royal Fusiliers to Portugal; present Brigade to Sir Alex. Campbell; at Busaco, the retreat of the army to lines of Torres Vedras; and battle of Fuentes d'Onor, as deputy Asst. return to the Peninsula from sick Adjt. Gen. to the 6th Division. On 4th Division at Vittoria and the leave, was appointed extra Aide-de-Regimental Majority, he commanded Camp to Sir Lowry Cole; with the Orthes and Toulouse, at the latter Brevet Major. Succeeding to the AVARNE, Jonas Jeffrey Ross's Brigade, served with them at the Light Companies of Maj. Gen. promoted Brevet Lieut.-Colonel.	15th Oct., 1797, 60th Regt.;	13th March, 1800, 68th Regt.; Morne Fortunee, St. Lucia. In at Oporto and Talavera, as Major of and subsequent advance from the	14th Nov., 1805, 68th Regt.; exchd. to 70th Regt., 5th July, 1806; exchd. to 7th, 22nd OCT., 1807;	Bt. Major, 26th Aug, 1813; Major, 28th OCT., 1813; Bt. Lieut. Col., 12th April, 1814; exchd. to h. p. of 8th Gar. Batt., 1st Aug., 1822; Col., 6th May, 1831; Maj. Gen., 23rd Nov., 1841; aptd. Lieut. Col., 65th Regt., 31st Jan., 1851; aptd. Col. 7th Regt., 11th Nov., 1851; aptd. Col. 7th Regt., 18th JAN., 1855; Gen., 19th June, 1860; died at Pau, Basses Pyrenees, 30th April, 1868. Died 1795.
AYLMER, *Hon.* Matthew	21st JUNE, 1864;	23rd JUNE, 1869;	...	Retired 27th April, 1870.
BACKHOUSE, Peter	...	4th May, 1814;	...	Retired April, 1815;
Re-entered the army	5th Aug., 1815, 53rd Regt.; exchd. to 17th L.D., 16th Nov., 1815; exchd. to h. p. of 8th Hussars, 2nd Oct., 1823;			Died 15th Nov., 1858.
BAGNALL, Charles from Lieut. 2nd Warwick Mil.	8th July, 1856, 53rd Regt.	9th Jan., 1857, 53rd Regt.; exchd. to 7th, 24th MAY, 1861;	...	Killed by a fall from his horse at Meean Meer, 3rd April, 1862.
BAILLIE, James William	18th Dec., 1760, 25th Regt.;	19th April, 1762, 25th Regt.; placed on h. p. of it, 1763; aptd. to 7th, 29th MAY, 1765;	3rd JUNE, 1774.	Bt. Major, 19th March, 1783; retired 3rd March, 1784; aptd. Fort Major of Fort George, N.B., same day; died at Cradle-hall, near Inverness, 15th Aug., 1805.
BAILLIE, Thomas Maubourg	29th JULY, 1862; removed to 52nd Regt., 5th Oct., 1862;	2nd June, 1865, 52nd Regt.;	3rd June, 1868, 52nd Regt.	Major, 10th June, 1871, 52nd Regt.
BAYLY,	...	Occurs as Lieut. to Capt. Salter's Company, 1695;	...	Out of the Regiment prior to 1702.
BAINBRIGGE, *Sir* Philip, K.C.B. *Silver Medal for* 14, 15, 16, 18, 19, 20, 24, 26. Served in the Peninsula in the Q. M. General's department from at the lines of Torres Vedras, part part of the siege of Olivenca, siege of Badajoz, affairs of the Guarena, Ciudad Rodrigo, last siege of Burgos, part of the siege of San Villa Muriel, retreat from Sebastian, actions at Bidart, Bussussary, and Villa Franque, Garris, Tarbes, and Vic Bigorre.	30th June, 1800, 20th Regt.	13th Nov., 1800, 20th Regt.; placed on h. p. of it, 1803; aptd. to 7th, 1803;	17th Oct., 1805, 18th Foot; exchd. to 93rd Regt., 4th June, 1807;	Major and Asst. Q. M. Gen., 15th OCT., 1812; Bt. Lieut. Col., 21st Jan., 1817; Lieut. Col., 2nd Aug., 1827, staff; Col., 10th Jan., 1837; aptd. Dep. Q. M. Gen. in Ireland, 23rd Nov., 1841; Maj. Gen., 9th Nov., 1846; aptd. Col. of the 20th Regt., 31st March, 1854; Lieut. Gen., 20th June, 1854; Gen., 24th Aug., 1861; died at Titchfield, Hants, 20th Dec., 1862.
BAKER, John	...	...	on h. p., 24th Dec., 1787.	
BAKER, Thomas Richard	9th Dec., 1819, 14th L. D.;	1st April, 1824, 14th L. D.;	18th Feb., 1826, unatt.; exchd. to 7th, 8th Nov., 1827;	Major, 31st AUG., 1838; retired 19th Jan., 1844; died at Wellington, New South Wales, 22nd Dec., 1854.
BALDWIN, Anthony *Silver Medal for* 9, 12, 14, 15, 16. Served with the Fusiliers at the capture of Martinique; landed with wounded in the breast by a spent musket ball in the breach of Badajoz. BALFOUR, William	Lieut., 1st Nov., 1803, North York Militia;	27th AUG., 1807; the 1st Batt. in the Peninsula; 2nd Sept., 1836, unatt.; exchd. to 7th, 16th SEPT., 1836; exchd. to h. p. unatt., 26th July, 1838; aptd. to 79th Regt., 26th July, 1839;	3rd JUNE, 1813; placed on h. p. of the Regt., 25th Feb., 1816;	Died at Ipswich, 18th Jan., 1851. Retired 14th Oct., 1842.
BAMFORD, John	1st July, 1798, 5th Drags. appointed to 18th L. D., 12th April, 1799;	17th May, 1803, 18th L. D., exchd. to 7th, 1st JAN. 1805; exchd. to h. p. of Scotch Brigade, 20th June, 1805;	...	Aptd. Adjt. of the London and Westminster Yeomanry, 4th July, 1805; died at Collin Deep, Hendon, 13th March, 1846.

Alphabetical List of Officers of the Royal Fusiliers.

NAME.	ENSIGN, &c.	LIEUTENANT.	CAPTAIN.	HIGHER RANKS AND REMARKS.
BARNARD, Henry John	30th Mar., 1855;	9th Sept., 1855;	...	Retired 11th Feb., 1862.
BARON, Peter Served with the Fencibles in Ireland during the Rebellion.	From Capt. Loyal Durham Fencibles.	14th Sept., 1804; exchd. to 18th Regt., 5th Mar., 1807; exchd. to h. p. of 10th Gar. Batt., 18th June, 1807;	...	Name removed from Army List, 1811.
BARR, William Lamb *Medal for India.*	17th Nov., 1857, 53rd Regt.;	11th May, 1858, 53rd Regt.; exchd. to 48th Regt., 2nd April, 1860, exchd. to 7th, 7th July, 1863;	1st April, 1870; placed on h. p. 20th June, 1870.	
Served with the 53rd Regt., the Indian campaign of 1858-9, including the passage of the Goomtee, and occupation of Sultanpore, Nov. 25th, action of Toolsepore, and minor affairs.				
BARRINGTON, Charles Landed in command of a detachment at Lisbon, 20th Aug., 1811; storming of Badajoz.	From Lieut., Cambridge Militia;	9th April, 1809; slightly wounded in the affair at	14th Aug., 1813, 60th Regt.;	Retired 23rd Dec., 1824.
BARRINGTON, William Served with the Fusiliers during Prescott; taken prisoner at Rhode Island.	...	22nd Feb., 1775; and later as aide-de-camp to General	6th June, 1777, 70th Regt.;	Retired 2nd Sept., 1779.
BARRY, David John	...	...	...	
BARTER, Richard *Medal for Central India. Medal for Oude.*	28th April, 1846, 75th Regt.;	3rd April, 1849, 75th Regt.;	16th May, 1712;	Out of the Regt., 19th June, 1716.
Served as Adjt., 75th Regt., Campaign of 1857-8; present at battle of Budlee-ke-Serai (severely wounded), siege, storm, and capture of Delhi, including the six days fighting in the streets, where he commanded the remnant of his Regt. for nearly twenty-four hours, all senior to him having been killed or disabled. Served with Greathed's column in pursuit, present at the action of Bolundshure, affairs of Allyghur and Akerabad, and battle of Agra. With Sir Hope Grant's column at Canoge, during the advance) on Cawnpore; crossed into Oude, and present at Maharajgunge and skirmish near the garrison, and at the relief of Luck-Alumbagh. With the Alumbagh now by Lord Clyde. Present with nunow, constantly engaged in repelling the Ressalahs of irregular cavalry in the occupation of Bignour, (Medal, Advance into Oude, occupation advance into Rohilcund, and re-out-posts and camp before Luck-Medal with two clasps and a repulse of the enemy's attacks. (after the relief of the fortified now, under Sir J. Outram, and two clasps, and a year's service). year's service.)		17th April, 1858, 24th Regt., exchd. to 7th, 11th Aug., 1858; transferred to Bengal Staff Corps, 17th Nov., 1863;	Major, 28th April, 1866, Bengal Staff Corps; Lieut. Col., 28th April, 1872, Bengal Staff Corps; aptd. Commandant 15th Bengal N. I., 5th Feb., 1862.	
BARTHOLOMEW, J. B.	From Ensign, Royal Cumberland Militia;	28th April, 1808; exchd. to 62nd Regt., 8th June, 1809;	...	Superseded 23rd Aug., 1810.
BARTON, Daniel	...	19th Dec., 1826;	12th July, 1833; exchd. to h. p. of 68th Regt., 8th Mar., 1839; exchd. to 85th Regt., 31st March, 1843;	Retired 31st March, 1843.
BARTON, Geoffry *Medal for Ashanti.* Served in the Ashanti war;	3rd Oct., 1862; wounded in an affair of the 3rd February.	14th Feb., 1865;	1st April, 1874, h. p. company; aptd. to 23rd Royal Welsh Fusiliers, 4th Nov., 1874; re-aptd. to 7th, 7th Aug., 1875.	
BARTON, Hugh Massey	5th April, 1864, 67th Regt. aptd. to 7th, same day;	29th May, 1869; exchd. to 37th Regt., 30th Oct., 1869; exchd. to 17th Lancers, 9th Aug., 1871;	...	Retired 14th Feb., 1872.
BAYNES, Richard	...	23rd Mar., 1702;	...	Supposed to have died a Maj. Gen. 11th June, 1727.
BEATTY, John Walwyn, C.B. *Gold Medal for 16, 25, 26.* Served with the Fusiliers at the affair also with them at New Orleans, and with the army of occupation in France.	3rd June, 1795, 2nd Regt.; Capture of Martinique; landed with them in the Peninsula, and	14th June, 1796, 2nd Regt.;	19th Aug., 1804; served during the whole war;	Major, 2nd Jan., 1812; Bt. Lieut. Col., 12th April, 1814; retired 26th June, 1823; died at Windsor Barracks, 2nd July, 1823.
BEAUCHAMP, Francis G.	7th Nov., 1854;	9th March, 1855;		Died before Sebastopol, 2nd Oct., 1855, of inflammation of the throat.
BEAUCHAMP, Fitzmaurice Served with the force under Brig. Chamberlain, attached to the and May, 1860, and was present at the forcing of the Burrura Pass, *Silver Medal for 16, 18, 22,* 14th March, 1811, 16th L. D.; 24, 25, 26. Served in the Peninsula with the 16th Light Dragoons.	16th Oct., 1855;	26th Jan., 1858; 24th (Mushie) Sikhs against the taking of Mukeen, and other minor 19th Feb., 1812, 16th L. D.;	24th Jan., 1865. Mahsood Wuzeerees during April affairs. Medal and clasp. 6th July, 1820, 19th Lancers; disbanded, placed on h. p. of it, 10th Nov., 1821; aptd. to 7th, 29th Jan., 1824;	Major, 13th Aug., 1825, unatt.; aptd. to 49th Regt., 8th June, 1826; Lieut. Col., 5th Aug., 1828, unatt.; exchd. to Gren. Guards, 2nd July, 1829; exchd. to h. p. unatt., 9th Mar., 1832; Col., 23rd Nov., 1841; exchd. to 49th Regt., 17th Nov., 1843; retired same day; died in Dublin, 10th Aug., 1850.

Alphabetical List of Officers of the Royal Fusiliers.

NAME.	ENSIGN, &c.	LIEUTENANT.	CAPTAIN.	HIGHER RANKS AND REMARKS.
BEAUCLERK, Aubrey Fred.	…	7th Aug., 1835, Scots Fus. Guards; aptd. to 7th, 28th Aug., 1838.	19th Jan., 1844;	Retired 24th Dec., 1847.
BEAUFOY, John Henry	Nov., 1807, 46th Regt.;	17th Dec., 1807;	…	Killed at Talavera, 28th July, 1809.
BEAVOIR, Peter	…	24th April, 1704;	29th Aug., 1707;	Out of the Regt., 24th Dec., 1709.
BEAVER, Peter	14th Mar., 1777, 25th Regt.;	22nd July, 1778, 25th Regt.;	1783, 25th Regt.; placed on h. p. of it; aptd. to 7th, 27th June, 1795; placed on h. p. of it, 31st Oct., 1795; aptd. to 27th Regt., 17th May, 1800;	Aptd. Major of the Hants Fencible Cavalry, 13th April, 1795; Bt. Major, 1st Jan., 1800; Bt. Lieut. Col, 1st Jan., 1801; retired April, 1803.
BECKETT, John Robert	16th Jan., 1866, 37th Regt.;	16th Dec., 1868, 37th Regt.; exchd. to 7th, 30th Oct., 1869;	…	…
BECKMAN, *Sir* Martin In March, 1686, knighted by James France. In 1692, he was on board Sir Cloudesley Shovel's fleet before H.		in several expeditions to the coast of Dunkirk; in July, 1694, he was employed 16th May, 1811;	1685; engaged in the attack on Havre. 20th June, 1822;	Out of the Regt. prior to 1695; died (? in London) June, 1702.
BELL, Edward Wells *Silver Medal* for 16, 18, 22, 24. Joined the Fusiliers in the Peninsula and Aldea de Ponte, advance on Portugal. In 1814, he embarked at Paris, and remained until its		insula in 1811, and served there Salamanca, affairs of San Christoval and Rueda, advance to and retreat from Madrid, advance from with the Royal Fusiliers to join the army force before New Orleans, present at the assault. Joined the withdrawal.		Major, 19th Dec., 1826; Lieut. Col, 29th June, 1830, unatt.; Col, 9th Nov., 1846; Maj. Gen., 20th June, 1854; aptd. Col., 66th Regt., 26th Dec., 1859; Lieut. Gen., 27th Dec., 1860; Gen. 12th July, 1868; died at Kempsey, Worcester, 9th Oct., 1870.
BELL, John	25th Mar., 1782, 18th Regt.;	Regt.; placed on h. p. of it, 1783; aptd. to 7th, 25th Sept., 1787; exchd. to 41st Regt., 25th Dec., 1787; placed on h.-p. of 101st, 9th April, 1788;	…	Died or retired 1810.
BELL, Montague Wigley	12th July, 1845, 66th Regt.;	9th April, 1847, 66th Regt.; aptd. to 7th, 18th Aug., 1847; exchd. to 97th Regt., 2nd Aug., 1850; aptd. to 28th Regt., 21st Feb., 1851;	…	Died before Sebastopol, 7th Jan., 1855.
BELLAIRS, Edmund Hooke Wilson	16th Nov., 1841, 60th Regt.;	16th Aug., 1842;	…	Retired 29th Dec., 1848; aptd. an Exon of the Yeomen of the Guard, 1848; retired 1852.
BENNETT, Adrian *Medal for the Crimea; 5th Class of the Medjidie; Medal for the N. W. Frontier.* Served the Eastern campaign of Sebastopol and sortie on the 26th Oct. Eusofzye Field Force, present at at Umbeyla, and destruction of the Conical on, and storming of the village at the foot of the submission of the hill tribes next day.	5th Nov., 1854;	9th Mar., 1855; 1854-5 with the Fusiliers, including Served also in the Indian N. W. the defence of the Sungahs at the Frontier war of 1863, with the attack Hill, and destruction of Lalloo on the 15th Dec.; also in the action Bonair Pass, which ended in the complete rout of the enemy, and	1st May, 1858; Alma, Inkerman, siege of Sebastopol, Umbeyla Pass, and at the attack	Major, 28th Oct., 1871.
BENNETT, John	…	30th Aug., 1695; defended Gibraltar in 1704-5; aptd.	Gov. thereof, 1710.	Out of the Regt. prior to 1702.
BENNETT, Robert Served with the Regt. in Flanders;	present at the capture of Namur; 1st Oct., 1794, 5th Foot;	5th Sept., 1795, 5th Foot; exchd. to h. p. of Scotch Brigade, Nov.,1800; exchd. to 7th, 20th June, 1805; retired on h. p. of Waggon Train, 14th Aug., 1806;	…	Name removed from Army List, 1810.
BENTINCK, *Lord* Frederick, C.B. Served in 1799 with the combined Light Dragoon regiment; present battle of Marengo and blockade of went to Spain in September, and	1st Feb., 1798, 32nd Regt.; Russian and Austrian army in at the battle of Novi, siege of Genoa; served in Sicily, 1806; returned home in January, 1808;	1st May, 1798, 24th L. D.; Italy, as volunteer in an Austrian Alexandria, &c.; in 1800 at the Walcheren expedition, 1809.	19th Oct., 1799, 24th L. D.; aptd. to 52nd Regt., 25th May, 1803;	Major, March, 1804, 45th Regt.; Lieut. Col, 21st April, 1804; re-aptd. to 45th Regt., 5th May, 1804; exchd. to 1st Foot Guards, 31st Jan., 1805; Col, 4th June, 1813; aptd. Lieut. Col., Grenadier Guards, 26th July, 1814; Major Gen., 12th Aug., 1819; aptd. Col. 58th Regt., 6th Sept., 1826; died at Rome, 11th Feb., 1828.

Alphabetical List of Officers of the Royal Fusiliers.

NAME.	ENSIGN, &c.	LIEUTENANT.	CAPTAIN.	HIGHER RANKS AND REMARKS.
BERESFORD, *Sir* Geo. De La Poer, *Bart.*	8th Mar., 1827, 88th Regt.	14th Feb., 1828 ;	19th Feb., 1836, unattached ; aptd. to 7th D. G. 19th March, 1852 ;	Bt. Major, 9th Nov, 1846 ; retired 19th March, 1852 ; died in Glasgow, 11th Feb., 1873.
BERKELEY	...	...	...	Major, July, 1733.
BERNAL-OSBORNE, Ralph	8th June, 1830, 71st Regt. ;	21st June, 1833 ;	27th July, 1838 ;	Retired 14th Dec., 1841 ; Secretary to the Admiralty from Dec., 1852, to March, 1858 ; M.P. for Wycombe, July, 1841 ; for Middlesex, Aug., 1847 ; for Dover, March 1857 ; Defeated at Dover, 1859 ; returned for Liskeard, Aug., 1859 ; resigned his seat, June, 1865 ; returned for Nottingham, May, 1866 ; for Waterford, 1870.
BERNARD, William Served with the Fusiliers at the capture of Copenhagen, and with the 70th, at the capture of Guadaloupe.	...	11th Mar., 1795 ;	25th June, 1803 ; exchd. to 70th Regt. 22nd Oct., 1807; aptd. to 1st Vet. Batt. Mar., 1816 ; reduced 24th May, 1816 ; placed on retired f. p. of it; aptd. to 5th Vet. Batt. 1st Nov., 1819 ; disbanded 1821, placed on retired f. p. of it ;	Bt. Major 4th June, 1814 ; died 17th Dec., 1843.
BEETLES, Henry Beckett	1st June, 1838, 34th Regt.	30th Dec., 1841 ; exchd. to 3rd West India, 7th April, 1843 ;	...	Retired 1st Sept, 1848.
BEST, *Hon.* John Charles	21st June, 1827, 20th Regt. ; exchd. to 17th Regt. 29th Nov., 1827 ;	29th Oct., 1829 ;	15th Aug., 1834, unattached; exchd. to 50th Regt., 22nd Aug., 1834 ;	Drowned at Norfolk Island by the upsetting of a boat, 13th Feb., 1840.
BEST, Richard Mordesley *Medal for the Punjaub,* Served with the 10th Foot in the operations before Mooltan, and wounded in the leg, at the battle of Goojerat.	20th April, 1832, 64th Regt.	16th Jan., 1835 ;	7th June, 1839 ; aptd. to 57th Regt., 14th Jan., 1842 ; exchd. to 10th Foot, 11th Dec., 1844 ;	Bt. Major 11th Nov., 1851 ; Major 8th Jan., 1858, 10th Foot ; Bt. Lieut. Col., 26th Oct., 1858 ; exchd. to 86th Regt. 19th Mar., 1861 ; Col. 5th Feb., 1863, Lieut. Col. 20th Feb., 1863, 86th Regt. ; exchd. to 79th Regt. 13th Sept., 1864 ; aptd. Brig. Gen. at Madras, 4th Aug., 1870 ;
BETESWORTH, Richard Wounded at Landen.	19th June, 1685 ;	...	1st Aug., 1692 ;	
BIBBY, Thomas	12th June, 1767, 24th Regt. ;	28th Jan, 1775, 24th Regt. ;	18th Sept., 1780, 80th Regt. ; aptd. to 7th, 19th Jan., 1781 ; placed on h. p., 1783 ;	Died or retired 1810.
BIRD, George	...	27th Nov., 1752 ;	27th Dec., 1755, 58th Regt. ; aptd. to 123rd Regt. ; placed on h. p. of it, 1763 ;	Died or retired 1772.
BIRMINGHAM, John	15th Aug., 1775, 63rd Regt. ;	7th Oct., 1777, 63rd Regt. ; exchd. to h. p. of 101st Regt., 1785 ; aptd. to 7th, 1st May, 1793 ;	28th July, 1795 ; placed on h. p. of the Regt. ; aptd. to f. p. of it, 17th May, 1796 ;	Retired 25th Sept., 1800.
BIRMINGHAM, Samuel	...	11th Nov., 1704.		
BERTWHISTLE, John *Medal for Goojerat.*	11th Dec., 1847, 32nd Regt. ; Served at the second siege operations before Mooltan, wounded, including the storm and capture of fort and garrison of Cheniote.	3rd Sept., 1849, 32nd Regt. ; also at the surrender of the city, and surrender of the for tress;	28th June, 1857, 32nd Regt.;	Major, 25th Sept., 1860, 32nd Regt. ; exchd. to 7th, 5th March, 1861 ; retired 11th April, 1862.
BISHTON, Thomas	21st June, 1839, 6th Foot ;	7th Oct., 1842 ;	...	Retired 20th Dec., 1842.
BISSETT, John	7th Nov., 1805, 14th Foot ;	23rd April, 1807, 14th Regt. ; exchd. to 90th Regt., 16th July, 1807 ; exchd. to 7th, 5th April, 1809 ; exchd. to h. p. of 90th Regt., 11th July, 1811 ;	...	Died at Nantes, 12th Sept., 1825.

Alphabetical List of Officers of the Royal Fusiliers.

NAME.	ENSIGN, &C.	LIEUTENANT.	CAPTAIN.	HIGHER RANKS AND REMARKS.
Black, John Lewis *Medal for the Sutlej.* Slightly wounded at Waterloo; Sobraon.	22nd April, 1813, 49th Regt.; present at Buddiwal, Alliwal, and	10th Mar., 1814, 49th Regt.; placed on h. p. of it, 1814; exchd. to 1st Foot, 23rd Feb., 1815; placed on h. p. of it, 1816; exchd. to Rifle Brigade, 18th July, 1816; placed on h. p. of it, 25th Dec., 1818; exchd. to 7th, 16th March, 1820;	16th June, 1825, 53rd Regt.	Bt. Major, 28th June, 1838; Major, 26th July, 1844, 53rd Regt.; exchd. to h. p., unatt., 3rd Dec., 1847; Bt. Lieut. Col., 11th Nov., 1851; exchd. to 14th L. D., 30th Dec., 1853; retired same day; died in Lansdowne Crescent, Bath, 3rd Feb., 1859.
Blackall, Robert (*Medal for China.*) Served with the 49th Regt. in China; present at the first taking of Chusan	19th Jan., 1838, 49th Regt.;	6th May, 1840, 49th Regt.; exchd. to 22nd Regt., 10th May, 1844;	15th March, 1853, 22nd Regt.; exchd. to 75th Regt., 13th Sept. 1854; exchd. to 7th, 10th Dec., 1858;	Bt. Major, 11th Mar., 1865; Bt. Lieut. Col., 3rd July, 1872; retired on f. p. of the Regt.
Blackmore,	...	Occurs as Lieut., 1693;	...	Killed at Landen, 19th July, 1693.
Blakeney, Sir Edward, G.C.B., G.C.H. *Gold Medal for* 6, 12, 15, 18, 19. *Silver Medal for* 9, 14, 22, 24. Accompanied the expedition, under course of this service he was three times taken prisoner by Privateers, the 10th and 19th Sept., and of the 2nd and 6th Oct. Expedition to Fleet and surrender of Copenhagen. In 1810 he sailed for Lisbon in command of the Fusiliers; severely wounded through the arm at the assault of the lines before that place.	28th Feb., 1794, 8th L. D.;	24th Sept., 1794, 121st Regt.;	24th Dec., 1794, late 99th Regt.; exchd. to 17th Foot, 8th Mar., 1798;	Major, 17th Sept., 1801, 17th Foot, placed on h. p. of it, 1802; aptd. to 47th Regt., 9th July, 1803; exchd. to 7th, 24th March, 1804; Bt. Lieut. Col., 25th April, 1808; Lieut. Col., 20th June, 1811; Col., 4th June, 1814; Maj. Gen., 27th May, 1825; aptd. Col. of the 7th, 20th Sept., 1832; Lieut. Gen., 28th June, 1838; Gen., 20th June, 1854; aptd. Col. 1st Foot, 21st Dec., 1854; Field Marshal, 9th Nov., 1862; Col.-in-Chief of the Rifle Brigade, 28th Aug., 1865; aptd. Gov. of Chelsea Hospital; died 2nd Aug., 1868.
Maj. Gen. White, to the West Indies, Berbice, and Essiquibo, 1796; in the 1799 he accompanied the expedition Copenhagen in 1807; joined Lord Served at the capture of Martinique, Albuera; affair of Aldea de Ponte; Pampeluna, and the various minor Present also at the capture of Paris, and with the army of occupation.				
Blaney, Cadwallader Davies, Lord	7th June, 1821, 4th Foot; exchd. to Rifle Brigade, 5th July, 1821;	27th Jan., 1825, Rifle Brigade; exchd. to 7th, 9th Nov., 1825;	8th April, 1826, unatt.; exchd. to 80th Regt., 7th June, 1827;	Retired 11th June, 1830.
Blewer, Benjamin.	...	4th Nov., 1724.	...	...
Bligh, Anthony	...	Oct., 1755.	...	...
Blomer	...	...	...	...
Bloomfield, Henry Keane Present at the storming of Cambray, and capture of Paris.	30th Sept., 1813, 59th Regt.	7th Aug., 1817, 59th Regt.; aptd. to 7th, 21st Nov., 1822; aptd. to 11th Foot, 27th Feb., 1823;	1st April, 1824, 11th Foot;	Bt. Major, 28th Jan., 1838; Major, 26th Feb., 1841, 11th Foot; Lieut. Col., 27th June, 1845, 11th Foot; Col., 20th June, 1854; retired on h. p. of the Regt., 1st April, 1859; Major Gen., 1st April, 1860; Lieut. Gen., 13th Aug., 1868; aptd. Col. 64th Regt., 20th Jan., 1867; died 11th Feb., 1870.
Bludworth, Thomas	...	...	26th Dec., 1726; placed on h. p. of the Regt.; exchd. to Coldstream Guards, 25th Dec., 1729; retired Jan., 1789;	Became Groom of the Bedchamber to the Prince of Wales, 1740.
Blundell, John	From Ens. 1st West York Militia;	5th May, 1808; exchd. to 60th Regt., 2nd Aug., 1810; exchd. to 4th Garr. Batt., 24th Jan., 1811; aptd. to 101st Regt., 11th June, 1812;	...	Killed in a duel near Newport, Isle of Wight, 11th July, 1813; for particulars, see *Sporting Magazine*, vol. 42, 1813, pp. 179 and 229.
Bolam, Chas. Godfrey	9th Feb., 1858;	...	...	Retired 9th April, 1861.
Bonamy, John	...	7th Feb., 1739;	...	Died 1752.
Bourke, James	...	1st Oct., 1794, 4th Batt. Irish Brigade; exchd. to 7th, 24th Dec., 1797; exchd. to h. p. of the Regt., 1800; exchd. back to f. p., 28th July, 1801;	...	Retired 1st Aug., 1801.

Alphabetical List of Officers of the Royal Fusiliers.

NAME.	ENSIGN, &c.	LIEUTENANT.	CAPTAIN.	HIGHER RANKS AND REMARKS.
BOURKE, Joseph Deane	9th Oct., 1817, 9th Foot;	24th Dec., 1818, h. p. of Grenadier Guards; exchd. to 7th, 21st Dec., 1820; placed on h. p. of it, 1821; exchd. back to f. p., 4th July, 1822; 20th JUNE, 1763;	…	Died 7th June, 1824.
BOURNE, Thomas	…	…	22nd Nov., 1756, 76th Regt.; placed on h. p. of it, 1763;	Died 12th Jan., 1813.
BOWEN, Lewis	…	10th May, 1811; exchd. to 4th Gar. Batt., 7th May, 1812; exchd. to 36th Regt., 3rd June, 1813; placed on h. p. of it, 1814; aptd. to f. p. of it, 13th July, 1815; exchd. to 89th Regt., 18th July, 1816; placed on h. p. of it, 25th Jan., 1817; aptd. to 94th Regt., 9th Feb., 1818;	…	Retired 10th Feb., 1818.
BOWES, George Crawley	13th Oct., 1825, 16th Foot;	27th July, 1826;	9th Nov., 1830;	Retired 23rd Feb., 1838.
BOWYER, Sir William, *Bart.*	10th May, 1758, Coldstream Guards;	23rd Dec., 1763, Coldstream Guards; exchd. to 7th, 4th OCT., 1765;	…	Retired 1768; died at Lower Seymour Street, London, 11th April, 1799.
BOWYER, William	31st Aug., 1793, 55th Regt.;	31st Jan., 1794, 55th Regt.; placed on h. p. of 95th Regt., exchd. to 7th, 24th AUG., 1795;	25th July, 1798, 59th Regt.;	Bt. Major, 15th May, 1806; retired 7th Oct., 1809.
BOWYER, William	66th Regt.;	5th July, 1797, 66th Regt.; exchd. to h. p. of 4th Batt. Irish Brigade, 18th July, 1799; exchd. to 7th, 30th OCT., 1800;	23rd Feb., 1803, 24th Regt.;	Major, 5th June, 1806, 8th West India; died at Barbadoes, 12th June, 1808.
BOYLE, *Hon.* Henry Charles	20th Sept., 1833, 24th Regt.;	17th FEB., 1837;	…	Retired 18th May, 1841; died at Florence, 6th April, 1846.
Boys, John	11th JAN., 1715.	…	19th June, 1685.	Left the Regt. between 1687 and 1695.
BRADSHAW, John	31st May, 1833, 60th Regt.;	…	…	Retired 16th Nov., 1841.
BRANDLING, Ralph Thos.	24th Nov., 1869, 1st D. G.;	6th MAY, 1836;	…	Retired 27th Feb., 1875.
BRANSON, Chas. Bilderbeck Mead	…	28th Oct., 1871, 1st D. G.; aptd. to 7th, 1st Feb., 1873;	…	
BRICE, Arthur Hill Served with the Regiment during the American War; taken prisoner at Fort Chambly.	27th Aug., 1756, 10th Foot;	19th Oct., 1758, 10th Foot;	13th Feb., 1762, 121st Regt.; placed on h. p. of it, 1763; exchd. to 7th, 28th Nov., 1766;	Bt. Major, 29th Aug., 1777; retired 1777; died in High Street, Marylebone, 8th May, 1817.
BRICE, Edward	…	7th JAN., 1771;	28th Nov., 1771, 24th Regt.;	Retired 7th July, 1775.
BRIDGES, Edward	4th JUNE, 1858;	11th APRIL, 1862; exchd. to 48th Regt., 7th July, 1863;	…	Retired 6th March, 1867.
BRINE, James *Silver Medal* for 12, 19, 22, 24.	…	31st Oct., 1805, 39th Regt.;	3rd March, 1808, 39th Regt.; placed on h. p. of it, 24th Oct., 1821; exchd. to 7th, 25th JAN., 1824;	Bt. Major, 27th May, 1825; Major, 19th Sept., 1826, unatt.; retired Sept., 1827; died at Sidmouth, Devonshire, 9th July, 1859.
BRISBANE, Thomas	…	Capt. Lieut., 7th Nov., 1759;	27th April, 1803, 27th Regt.; exchd. to 15th L.D., 9th July, 1803;	Retired 21st March, 1762.
BROADHURST, John	24th July, 1800, 16th L. D.;	3rd DEC., 1802;	…	Retired 11th May, 1809.
BROOK, Thomas	…	12th Dec., 1746.	…	
BROWN, Anthony	…	168.	…	
BROWNE, *Hon.* Cavendish The courage displayed by Captain Cavendish Browne, of the 7th, was nearly fainting from loss of blood. When his body was found, it lay far	5th Nov., 1847, 85th Regt.;	25th SEPT., 1849; most conspicuous. Severely wounded He led on his men, encouraging them balls in the chest.—*Times Correspondent.*	4th AUG., 1854; at the commencement of the attack, by voice and gesture, to the front.	Killed before Sebastopol on the night of the 22nd March, 1855, whilst leading a detachment of the Fusiliers against a sortie of the enemy.

Alphabetical List of Officers of the Royal Fusiliers.

NAME.	ENSIGN, &C.	LIEUTENANT.	CAPTAIN.	HIGHER RANKS AND REMARKS.
BROWNE, *Hon.* James Lyon *Medal for the Crimea.* Served the campaign of 1854-5 with Sebastopol	14th Jan., 1842, 64th Regt.; the 21st Fusiliers, including the	8th Nov., 1844, 64th Regt.; battles in the Crimea and siege of	22nd Dec, 1848, 64th Regt.; exchd. to 7th, 16th FEB., 1849; exchd. to 21st Regt., 17th JAN., 1851; Commission renewed 11th JAN., 1715.	Major, 29th Dec., 1854, 21st Regt.; Lieut. Col., 18th March, 1856, 21st Regt.; placed on h. p. of the Regt., 10th Nov., 1856.
BROWNE, James	...	...	...	Died 1792.
BROWNE, John Hamilton	11th Feb., 1777, 44th Regt.;	9th JUNE, 1778;	15th March, 1784, 74th Regt.; Regt. reduced same year; placed on h. p.; aptd. to 52nd Regt., 6th Jan., 1790; 13th JULY, 1855;	
BROWNE, *Lord* Richard Howe *Medal for the Crimea, 5th class of the Medjidie.* Served with the Fusiliers in the Crimea from the 20th March, 1855, the 7th June, assaults of the Quarries on by the bursting of a shell in Sebastopol.	23rd Nov., 1852, 43rd Regt.; aptd. to 7th, 9th Aug., 1854; including the siege and fall of Sebastopol, sorties on the 22nd March and the 18th June (severely wounded) and 8th Sept., was slightly wounded 9th May, defence of the Quarries on			Major, 29th MAY, 1863; exchd. to 96th Regt., 8th Sept., 1863; retired, 21st Feb., 1865.
BROWNE, Valentine J. A.	30th JUNE, 1863;	...	...	Retired, 9th June, 1865.
BROWNE, William Henry	20th Oct., 1861, 101st Regt.;	17th July, 1866, 101st Regt.; exchd.to7th, 17th FEB., 1869;	...	Aptd. to Bengal Staff Corps, June, 1872.
BROWNE, William Lloyd	15th Nov., 1855;	1st MAY, 1858; exchd. to 12th Lancers, 11th June, 1859; aptd. to 5th Lancers, 10th July, 1860;	11th March, 1862, 5th Lancers;	Major, 12th Oct., 1868, 5th Lancers.
BROWNE, William Pryce *Medal for Sebastopol.* Served at the siege of Sebastopol.	9th MARCH, 1855;	19th AUG., 1855;	2nd DEC., 1862;	Retired, 18th Dec., 1867; died at Blackheath, 4th Oct., 1874.
BROWNE, William R.	from the 7th July, 1855. 29th Sept., 1837, 61st Regt.;	5th MARCH, 1841;	27th MARCH, 1846;	Retired 12th Jan., 1855.
BROWNLOW, Frederick	9th Nov., 1815, 23rd Regt.;	13th JUNE, 1816; placed on h. p. of the Regt., 25th Mar, 1817; exchd. to 43rd Regt., 15th Jan., 1818; exchd. back to 7th, 14th May, 1818;	21st June, 1821, Ceylon Rifles; exchd. to 72nd Regt., 4th July, 1822;	Major, 26th AUG., 1824, 72nd Regt.; exchd. to h. p. unatt., 10th Nov., 1825; exchd. to 7th D. G, 10th Oct., 1834; retired on the 17th of same month.
BROWNLOW, John	...	9th SEPT., 1813; placed on h. p. of the Regt., 25th Feb., 1816; exchd. back to f. p. of it, 9th July, 1818; exchd. back to h. p. of it, April, 1819;	...	Retired January, 1828.
BRYDLE, Thomas	1st AUG., 1692;	...	10th JUNE, 1703;	Died in the service.
BUCKINGHAMSHIRE, Robert, *Earl of*	...	...	25th July, 1778, 30th Regt.;	Major, 15th AUG., 1783, 18th L. D.; died in Hamilton Place, London, 4th Feb., 1816, in consequence of a fall from his horse some time before.
BUCKNALL, Charles	...	8th MAY, 1776;	...	Aptd. Fort Major of the Castle of Edinburgh; died there 10th March, 1729.
BULKELEY, James Served with the Fusiliers in Ireland during the Rebellion.	27th May, 1776, 22nd Regt.; America during the Revolutionary	11th JAN., 1715;		
BULKELEY, Thomas Dangerously wounded at Moodkee.	...	18th JAN., 1777; war, and with the Fencibles in	21st May, 1778, 43rd Regt.; placed on h. p. of it, 1783; aptd. to f. p. of it, 25th Sept., 1787;	Retired 24th Sept., 1789; Lieut. Col. Northampton Fencibles, 25th Oct, 1794.
BUNYON, Charles Spencer	1st Aug., 1826, 28rd Regt.;	5th MAY, 1814; placed on h. p. of the Regt., 25th Feb., 1816; aptd. to 31st Regt., 8th April, 1825;	22nd Mar, 1840, 31st Regt.;	Major, 31st Dec., 1845, 31st Regt.; retired 21st Jan., 1848.
		16th July, 1829, 30th Regt.; placed on h. p. of it, same day; exchd. to 90th Regt., 4th Oct., 1831; aptd. to 7th, 7th SEPT., 1832; exchd. to h. p. unatt., 16th Sept., 1836.		

Alphabetical List of Officers of the Royal Fusiliers.

NAME.	ENSIGN, &c.	LIEUTENANT.	CAPTAIN.	HIGHER RANKS AND REMARKS.
BURCHETT, Richard	...	...	...	Died late in 1750 or early in 1751.
BURGOYNE, Sir John, Bart	...	26th May, 1759;	4th March, 1761, 85th Regt.;	Major, 13th Feb., 1762, 52nd Regt.; Lieut. Col., 19th Dec., 1764, 58th Regt.; to 14th L. D., 15th July, 1773; Col., 29th Aug., 1777; aptd. Col. 23rd L. D., 24th Sept., 1781; Maj. Gen., 20th Nov., 1782; died in the East Indies, 1785.
BURKE, James	19th June, 1806, 67th Regt.;	3rd Feb., 1807;	...	Retired 30th May, 1810.
BURKE, John	13th Feb., 1805, 81st Regt.; aptd. to 103rd Regt., 1810;	16th Jan., 1811;	...	Retired 16th July, 1812.
BURKE, Patrick John	From Ens. Galway Militia;	28th Oct., 1807;	17th March, 1815; placed on h. p. of the Regt., 25th Feb., 1816;	Died at Newtown Leixlip, 30th June, 1835.
BURNETT-STUART, Eustace Robert	9th June, 1865;	27th April, 1870; exchd. to 79th Regt., 27th Aug., 1873.	...	
BURRARD, William	...	11th Aug., 1737; exchd. to Indept. Comp., 20th April, 1738.	...	
BURROES, James	...	24th July, 1775;	18th Sept., 1780;	Bt. Major, 1st March, 1794; Major, 16th April, 1755; Bt. Lieut. Col., 1st Jan., 1798; exchd. to 47th Regt., 24th March, 1804; retired Aug., 1804.
BURROES, Thomas	Feb., 1793, Indept. Comp.	13th Nov., 1793;	11th Oct., 1794, 112th Regt.; to 38th Regt., 1st Sept., 1795;	Major, 2nd Aug., 1804, 38th Regt.; retired 8th Feb., 1807.
BURSTON, George	...	1st May, 1721.		
BURTON, Robt. Haly Served as a Private in the 30th Regt. two years, as Corporal three years, as Sergeant four years; aptd. 12th April, 1786; served with the Staff in Regiments for fifteen years in hagen, in Nova Scotia, and at the Canada, and afterwards as Major of Mas. Gen. at the head of the Staff in America, and five in the West Indies. capture of Martinique.		31st Dec., 1794;	23rd Dec., 1799; Asst. Adjt. and Qr. Mas. 60th Regt. Served with the Fusiliers as Dep. Qr. in Bermuda, at the siege of Copen-	Major, 18th May, 1809; Bt. Lieut. Col., 26th Aug., 1813, 13th Vet. Battt.; made 7th , 1815; reduced 24th May, 1816; placed on retired f. p. of it; aptd. to 6th Vet. Battt., 1st Nov., 1819; retired on f. p. of it, 15th June, 1820; retired August, 1826; aptd. Barrack Master at Dorchester; died at Dorchester, 25th Sept., 1831.
BURTON, William	26th Nov., 1717, Regt.; aptd. to 7th, 23rd Mar., 1728;	1st July, 1734;	...	Died 1743.
BUSBY, John	3rd Oct., 1846, 18th Foot; exchd. to 13th Foot, 30th Dec., 1845;	24th Dec., 1847; exchd. back to 13th Foot, 3rd Mar., 1848;	1st April, 1853, 13th Foot;	Retired 1st July, 1853.
BUSHE, Richard Served with the Fusiliers at Copenhagen and served with it during the siege. Commanded the two flank companies at Barossa, where he was so much liked by the ladies of mortally wounded. "He was so chivalrous, and so particularly by the ladies of that his death was deeply lamented, Cadiz."	1st Feb., 1800, 64th Regt.;	30th July, 1800, 64th Regt.; Joined the 20th Portuguese at Cadiz,	4th July, 1803, 60th Regt.; aptd. to 7th, 6th Sept., 1804;	Major, 16th Feb., 1809, Portuguese service; died of wounds at La Isla, Cadiz, 20th April, 1811.
BUTLER, Edward	13th May, 1709;	11th Jan., 1715; Capt. Lieut., 5th April, 1733;	12th Nov., 1733;	Retired Sept., 1742.
BUTLER, Henry Wm. Paget	17th Sept., 1850, 4th Foot;	9th July, 1852;	29th Dec., 1854; exchd. to 85th Regt., 26th Feb., 1856; exchd. to 3rd Foot, 19th Aug., 1856; placed on h. p. of it, 10th Nov., 1856;	Retired 15th June, 1855.
BUTLER, Lord James	7th Nov., 1834, 85th Regt.;	16th Sept., 1838;	3rd June, 1842;	Retired 28th April, 1846.
BUTLER, John	...	3rd May, 1709; aptd. to 7th, 31st Jan., 1736;	...	Died 1745.

Alphabetical List of Officers of the Royal Fusiliers.

NAME.	ENSIGN, &c.	LIEUTENANT.	CAPTAIN.	HIGHER RANKS AND REMARKS.
BUTLER, Lindsey Holland	13th JULY, 1855 ;	21st DEC., 1855 ;	18th DEC., 1867.	Retired 13th Aug., 1858.
BUTLER, Robt. Fowler	10th FEB., 1858 ;	11th FEB., 1862 ;		
BUTLER, Thomas	9th May, 1834, 60th Regt. ;	7th APRIL, 1837 ;		Retired 28th July, 1840.
BYRON, Edmund J. S.	18th Aug., 1790, 26th Regt. ;	11th MAY, 1791 ;	18th APRIL, 1795 ;	Retired 9th March, 1803.
CADOGAN, *Hon.* Edward	July, 1807, 61st Regt. ;	28th OCT., 1807 ;		Retired 17th Jan., 1811.
CALCOTT, George Berkeley	27th Sept., 1775, 29th Regt. ;	24th Nov., 1775 ;		Died at St. Lucia, 1779.
Silver Medal for 3, 5, 14, 15, 16, 18, 19, 22, 24, 26. Served the campaign of 1808-9 with cheren in 1809. Subsequently in the capture of Paris.	10th Sept., 1807, 43rd Regt. ; the 43rd, including the retreat under Sir John Moore; expedition to Walcheren in 1809.	6th April, 1809, 43rd Regt. ; Peninsula. Present at the expedition to New Orleans.	16th Oct., 1778, 49th Regt. ; 26th Oct., 1815, 43rd Regt. ; placed on h. p. of it, 25th Mar., 1817 ; exchd. to 7th, 11th DEC, 1817 ; exchd. to h. p. of it, 4th Dec., 1823 ; aptd. to 36th Regt, 31st Jan., 1845 ;	Bt. Major, 10th Jan., 1837 ; retired 31st Jan., 1845 ; died at St. John's House, Blackheath, 29th Aug., 1868.
CALCRAFT, Thomas	...	...	8th Nov., 1755 ; aptd. to 50th Regt.	Major, Lieut. Col., 12th Jan., 1760, 91st Regt.; aptd. to 50th Regt., 29th Jan., 1762; Col., 25th May, 1772; Maj. Gen, 29th Aug., 1777 ; aptd. Col. 65th Regt., 6th Jan., 1779.
CALDWELL, John Served with the Fusiliers in Gibraltar and Minorca ; and with the 8th Regt. during the American war.	...	2nd May, 1751 ;	20th DEC, 1755 ;	Major, 18th July, 1766 ; Lieut. Col., 27th Oct., 1772, 8th Regt. ; aptd. Lieut. Col. Commt. of British Militia in Canada, 1775.
CALVERT, *Sir* Harry, *Bart.*	29th April, 1819, 31st Regt. ;	30th SEPR., 1819 ;	6th June, 1822, 72nd Regt. ; exchd. to h. p. of 52nd Regt., 5th July, 1822 ; exchd. to Grenadier Guards, 26th Feb., 1824 ;	Major, 13th Nov., 1827, unatt. ; retired July, 1830.
CAMPBELL, Colin	26th Feb., 1772, 1st Foot ;	3rd JUNE, 1774 ;	3rd Aug., 1804, 5th Regt.; exchd. to h. p. of York Rangers, 9th June, 1805 ;	Retired 14th Oct., 1778.
CAMPBELL, Donald	...	29th JULY, 1795 ;		Omitted from Army List of 1820, he not having drawn his h. p. for seven years previously.
CAMPBELL, John	25th Jan., 1771, 37th Regt. ;	9th MAY, 1774 ;		Retired 1776.
CAMPBELL, John Thomas *Medal for Sebastopol.* Served the Eastern campaign of 1855, including the expedition to Kertch and siege of Sebastopol.	19th Aug., 1851, 72nd Regt. ;	6th June, 1854, 72nd Regt. ;	29th July, 1856, 72nd Regt. ; placed on h. p. of it, Nov., 1856; aptd. to 7th, 23rd OCT., 1857 ; exchd. to Canadian Rifles, 18th July, 1862 ;	Major, 4th April, 1865, Canadian Rifles ; Lieut. Col., 7th Nov., 1868, Canadian Rifles ; placed on h. p. of it, Oct., 1869.
CAMPBELL, Robert Preston Aide-de-camp to Sir Fred. Adam ; a French howitzer; accompanied Sir Lockhart's *Life of Scott*, vol. 5, p. 64.	fired the last shot at Waterloo from Walter Scott over the field. See	26th MAY, 1814 ; placed on h. p. of the Regt., 25th Feb, 1816 ; aptd. to 61st Regt., 2nd Jan., 1823 ; exchd. to h. p. 60th Regt., 23rd Sept., 1819 ;	27th March, 1823, Ceylon Rifles ;	Died at Kandy, 18th June, 1825.
CAMERON, Donald Served with the Fusiliers in the Ponfe, San Marcial, near San Sebastian, Aug. 31st; wounded at Orthestion. The author of the Journal of Peninsula from Aug., 1811, to the Afterwards present at the attack on Paris, and with the army of occupathe Peninsular War.		7th MAY, 1811 ; aptd. to 10th Foot, 9th May, 1851 ;		Aptd. Capt. in the Renfrew Militia, 30th May, 1820 ; died 3rd Aug., 1870.
Silver Medal for 16, 18, 19, 22, 24, 25).	23rd, Feb., 1844, 55th Regt. ; exchd. to 11th Foot, 26th Sept., 1845 ;	11th APRIL, 1851; aptd. to 10th Foot, 9th May, 1851 ;	of Fuente Guinaldo and Aldea de New Orleans ; at the capture of	
CAMERON, Geo. John Arnolds				Retired 13th Feb., 1852.
CAMERON, John	27th Aug., 1794, Loyal Sheffield Regt. ; aptd. to 64th Regt., 6th April, 1796 ;	1st April, 1797, 64th Regt. ;	7th SEPT., 1804 ; aptd. to 2nd Gar. Batt., 25th Feb., 1805 ; placed on h. p. of it ; aptd. to 8th Vet. Batt., 24th Feb., 1820 ; disbanded, 1821 ; placed on retired f. p. of it.	Bt. Major, 4th June, 1814 ; died at Perth, 29th April, 1829.
CAMPION, Robert	...	1st AUG., 1693 ;	...	Died in the service.
CARNEGIE, Charles	22nd Nov., 1850, 23rd Regt. ;	25th March, 1853, 23rd Regt. ; aptd. to 7th, 11th OCT., 1853 ; aptd. to 27th Regt., 23rd Dec., 1853 ;	...	Retired 7th Sept., 1855.

Alphabetical List of Officers of the Royal Fusiliers.

NAME.	ENSIGN, &c.	LIEUTENANT.	CAPTAIN.	HIGHER RANKS AND REMARKS.
CARPENTER, G. W. Wallace *Medal for the Crimea. Turkish Medal.* Served in the Eastern Campaign of 1854; wounded at the Alma.	17th June, 1851, 41st Regt.;	27th Jan., 1854;	12th Jan., 1855;	Major, 13th May, 1859; exchd. to 32nd Regt., 5th March, 1861; retired 22nd Jan., 1864.
CARR, William.				
CARTER, Harry Lee	14th April, 1843, 69th Regt.; aptd. to 6th D. G., 2nd Aug., 1844;	1st May, 1846, 6th D. G.; exchd. to 7th, 22nd OCT., 1847;	...	Retired 29th Dec., 1848; aptd. Paymaster of the Oxford Militia, 21st Nov., 1855; aptd. to 13th Foot, 25th Aug., 1858; exchd. to Military Train, 19th Feb., 1859; placed on h. p. of it; died 3rd Oct., 1862.
CARTER, John, *K.H.* Served in the East Indies during the Maharatta Campaign; and as France. Served with the 72nd Regt. at the Cape of Good Hope.	June, 1796, 84th Regt.;	2nd July, 1796, 84th Regt.; Capt. of Grenadiers of the 84th, was	31st Dec., 1806, 84th Regt.; present at the taking of the Isle of	Major, 20th Jan., 1814, 84th Regt.; exchd. to 72nd Regt., 12th Sept, 1816; exchd. to 7th, 27th March, 1823; Lieut.-Col. 3rd March, 1825, unatt.; aptd. to 2nd West India, 2nd June, 1825; exchd. to 1st Foot, 30th April, 1827; Col. 28th June, 1838; exchd. to 79th Regt., 29th Oct., 1841; exchd. to h. p. unatt., 14th June, 1842; died at Springfield Villa, Exeter, 6th Aug., 1845.
CARTER, Willoughby Harcourt	4th Oct., 1839, 98th Regt.;	2nd July, 1841, 98th Regt.; exchd. to 64th Regt., 20th Dec., 1842;	2nd June, 1848, 64th Regt.; exchd. to 21st Regt., 22nd Dec., 1848; exchd. to 7th, 17th JAN., 1851.	Retired 24th Feb., 1854.
CARTHEW, Robert	...	25th Dec., 1704;	Capt. Lieut., 11th Jan., 1715.	
CARTWRIGHT, John Theodore	2nd Feb., 1855, Cape M. Rifles;	5th Sept., 1856, Cape M. Rifles;	25th Feb., 1861, Cape M. Rifles; exchd. to 7th, 21st JULY, 1863.	Retired 18th April, 1868.
CAVENDISH, *Hon.* Hen. Fred. Compton *Silver Medal for 4, 5.* Served in the Peninsula from July, 1808, to Jan., 1809; wounded de-camp to Lord William Bentinck; commanded three squadrons of the	...	26th MAY, 1808; aptd. to 10th L. D., 22nd June, 1808; exchd. to 24th L. D., 26th July, 1810; through the wrist at the Battle of Household Brigade at the funeral of	6th June, 1811, 103rd Regt.; exchd. to h. p. of 25th Regt., 1812; Corunna, where he served as Aide-the Duke of Wellington.	Major 2nd April, 1818, 75th Regt.; exchd. to 9th Lancers, 24th Sept., 1818; Lieut.-Col., 12th July, 1821, 1st D. G.; Lieut.-Col. and Col., 10th Jan., 1837, 1st D. G.; Major-Gen., 9th Nov., 1846; Lieut.-Gen., 20th June, 1854; aptd. Col. 2nd D. G., 2nd June, 1853; Gen., 9th Nov., 1862; died in Burlington Gardens, 5th April, 1873.
CHAPPELLE, John	...	86th Regt., 16th April, 1797.		
CHARD, William Wheaton	30th DEC., 1859;	2nd DEC., 1862;	28th OCT., 1871.	
CHARLTON, Henry	29th DEC., 1843, 1st Foot;	28th April, 1846;		Died at Southampton, 9th Aug., 1847.
CHEEK, Thomas	...	...	1685;	Retired 9th June, 1687.
CHICHESTER, *Hon.* Adolphus William	...	9th June, 1841, Gren. Guards; exchd. to 7th, 31st MARCH, 1843; aptd. to 45th Regt., 11th Aug., 1843;	...	Retired 7th Feb., 1845; died at Boulogne, 24th Aug., 1855.
CHICHESTER, *Lord* Arthur	...	9th JUNE, 1825;	...	Died at the Mauritius, 21st July (? 25th June), 1840.
CHICHESTER, *Lord* Hamilton Francis	...	7th DEC., 1826;	6th Dec., 1827, unatt.; exchd. to 87th, 1st May, 1828; 28th DEC., 1832; retired on h. p. of 9th Foot, 13th April, 1838; exchd. to 2nd Foot, 11th Feb., 1848;	Bt. Major, 9th Nov., 1846; retired 11th Feb., 1848; died at Malta, 1st Jan., 1854.
CHICHESTER, *Lord* Spencer A.	29th Aug., 1822, 43rd Regt.;	4th Nov., 1824;		
CHILLCOTT, John Congreve	...	18th JAN., 1740; Capt. Lieut., 3rd JUNE, 1752;	16th DEC., 1752; exchd. to h. p. as Qr. Mas., 25th Mar., 1755. 1st July, 1795, West India Regt.	Died at Richmond, 27th May, 1825.
CHITTER, Robert	...	JUNE, 1795;		
CHIVERS, Michael	13th June, 1685.			
CHOLWICH, William Served with the Fusiliers at the 1st Batt. in the Peninsula.	30th Nov., 1796, 41st Regt.; capture of Martinique, and with the	1st July, 1798, 41st Regt.; placed on h. p. of it; aptd. to 81st Regt., 9th July, 1803;	21st AUG., 1804;	Killed at the assault of Badajoz, April, 1812.

Alphabetical List of Officers of the Royal Fusiliers.

NAME.	ENSIGN, &c.	LIEUTENANT.	CAPTAIN.	HIGHER RANKS AND REMARKS.
CHRISTIE, Thomas	...	14th Aug., 1800, 69th Regt.; aptd. to 7th, 21st Aug., 1800;	3rd April, 1801, 5th Regt.; exchd. to 70th Regt., 14th May, 1801; exchd. to h. p., 17th Feb., 1803;	Omitted from List of 1840, he not having drawn his h. p. for two years previously.
CHURCH, Edward	...	...	...	Retired 25th Aug., 1807.
CHURCHILL, Charles	...	19th Sept., 1804; aptd. to 68th Regt., 16th May, 1805; exchd. to 93rd Regt., 6th Feb., 1806;	...	...
CLARINA, E. C. H., Lord *Medal for the Crimea*; *Legion of Honour*; *5th Class of the Medjidie*; *Medal for India*.	8th Oct., 1847, 68th Regt.; Served with the 95th in the Crimea from the 22nd Nov., 1854, including the siege and capture of Kotah, siege and capture of Pouree (mentioned in Dispatches).	25th Nov., 1760; 21st Nov., 1851; exchd. to 31st Regt., 30th July, 1852; Served also in the Indian Mutiny Kota-ke-Serai, general action resulting in the capture of Gwalior, siege	2nd April, 1772, 19th Regt.; 14th Jan., 1853, 31st Regt.; exchd. to 95th Regt., 30th June, 1854;	Died or retired 1779. Bt. Major, 1855; Major, 17th Nov., 1857, 95th Regt.; Bt. Lieut. Col., 20th July, 1858; Col., 3rd April, 1865; Lieut. Col., 1st April, 1873, 97th Regt.
CLARKE, Sir Alured, G.C.B. Served with the 54th and the Fusiliers during the war of the American Revolution; served in the East Indies; was invested with the command of the army that captured the Cape of Good Hope, but arrived only during the unexpected struggle with the Dutch.	20th March, 1759, 50th Regt.;	10th May, 1760, 50th Regt.;	7th Jan., 1767, 5th Foot;	Major, 28th Nov., 1771, 54th Regt.; Lieut. Col., 20th Sept., 1775, 54th Regt.; aptd. to 7th, 10th Mar., 1777, Major Gen., 28th April, 1790; aptd. Col. 5th Regt., 25th Oct., 1794; Lieut. Gen., 27th Jan., 1797; aptd. Col. Royal Fusiliers, 21st Aug., 1801; Gen., 29th April, 1802; Field Marshal, 22nd July, 1830; died at the Vicarage, Llangollen, 16th Sept., 1832.
CLARKE, Frederick	1st July, 1797, 27th L. D.;	24th Jan., 1801, 27th L. D., made 24th L. D., 1804;	23rd Aug., 1804;	Died at York, 18th Dec., 1804.
CLARKE, James	...	26th Sept., 1726.	...	...
CLARKE, John Hen. C.	21st Aug., 1866;	27th Oct., 1871.	...	...
CLAYHILLS, James Menzies *Medal for the Crimea*; *Turkish Medal*.	23rd Nov., 1852, 93rd Regt.; Served with the 93rd Highlanders including the battle of Balaclava, assault of the Redan, Sept. 8th.	13th Aug., 1854, 93rd Regt.; the Eastern campaign of 1854-5, siege and fall of Sebastopol, and	31st Aug., 1855, 93rd Regt.; placed on h. p., Nov., 1856; aptd. to 7th, 23rd Oct., 1857;	Major, 20th June, 1865: retired on h. p., 28th Oct., 1871.
CLEATHER, William H.	...	1805; aptd. to 4th Ceylon Regt., 21st March, 1805;	10th Jan., 1811, 4th Ceylon Regt.;	Died 1820.
CLEAVELAND, Samuel	2nd Nov., 1762, 95th Regt.; placed on h. p. of it, 1763; aptd. to 13th Foot, 12th July, 1770;	26th March, 1773;	...	Retired 5th July, 1777; aptd. Major in the Lymington Volunteers, 13th Nov., 1805; Lieut.-Col. Lymington Volunteers; died at Lymington, April 1816.
CLIFFE, Loftus Anthony Served with the Fusiliers during the early part of the American War.	...	18th April, 1816; placed on h. p. of the Regt., 25th March, 1817;	...	Retired June, 1825.
CLIFFE, Walter Sailed with the 28th Foot as a Cape Fear, May 1st, 1775, viz.,—attack Plains, and taking of Rhode Island; Fairfield, Newark, and the manded the Forces in Georgia and returned to England. Appointed Dep. Adj.-Gen. to the Expedition of Bengal as Adj.-Gen. of the King's Alured to Madras. Served also in	22nd Dec., 1776, 28th Regt.; Volunteer to America, in Oct. 1775; on Charlestown, Battle of Brooklyn, carried the colours of the 28th at Siege of Charlestown. From May, East Florida. Continued in America	9th June, 1778; served with the Light Company of landing on York Island, action at Brandywine. Present with the 1780, to July, 1782, served as Brigade Major to Sir A. Clarke, who commanded for the reduction of the Cape of Good troops in the East Indies.	31st Dec., 1782; that regiment from the landing at MacEwan's Pass, Battle of White Fusiliers at Monmouth, Newhaven, New York, Nov., 1783, when he Hope, and then accompanied Sir	Bt. Major 1st Mar., 1794; Bt. Lieut.-Col. 31st Mar., 1795; Major 7th Feb., 1798; Col. 29th April, 1802; exchd. to h. p. of 9th Foot, 30th Nov., 1802; Maj.-Gen., 25th Oct., 1809; Lieut.-Gen. 4th June, 1814; died at Taunton, 13th July, 1816.
CLIFFORD, Richard Cormick *Medal for the Punjaub*. Served with the 10th Regt. in the Punjaub Campaign; present at the Battle of Goojerat.	17th Oct., 1845, 10th Regt.;	1st Jan., 1847, 10th Reg.;	30th July, 1857, 10th Regt.; exchd. to 48th Regt., 21st Dec., 1860; exchd. to 7th, 17th Dec., 1862;	Major, 1st April, 1870; placed on h. p. 6th May, 1870.
CLUTTERBUCK, Samuel	...	11th Jan., 1715; Capt. Lieut., 9th July, 1729;	3rd April, 1733;	Retired 2nd May, 1751.
COANE, James	11th Dec., 1805, 95th Rifles;	7th Jan., 1807;	...	Died 1807.
COANE, Henry	1803, 78th Regt.;	31st March, 1803, 78th Regt.;	8th Feb., 1810; aptd. to 73rd, 8th March, 1810;	Retired 3rd Feb., 1820.
COBB, Robert	...	...	...	...
COCHRANE, James	...	1st Oct., 1755;	19th June, 1716.	Died or retired 1757.

Alphabetical List of Officers of the Royal Fusiliers.

NAME.	ENSIGN, &c.	LIEUTENANT.	CAPTAIN.	HIGHER RANKS AND REMARKS.
COCHRANE, Hon. Basil Commanded the 36th Regt. in the Peninsula.	…	29th July, 1795;	17th Sept., 1799, 4th Regt.; placed on h. p. of it, 1802; aptd. to 72nd Regt., 25th May, 1803;	Major, 10th March, 1804, 96th Regt.; Lieut.-Col., 9th Oct., 1806, 36th Regt.; Col., 4th June, 1814; died on passage from Dublin to Liverpool, 14th May, 1816.
COCHRANE, Hon. Charles Served with great distinction during the American War; defeated the rebels at Sagg Harbour, Feb. 1st, 1779; on the 3rd Oct., 1781, he left New York with dispatches for Earl Cornwallis; went in a small vessel to the Cape of Virginia, thence in an open boat he made his way through the whole of the French fleet, reached Yorktown on the 10th, and delivered his dispatches to Lord Cornwallis.	…	21st April, 1768;	6th May, 1774, 4th Regt.; to 1st Foot Guards, 21st Nov., 1778;	Aide-de-camp to Lord Cornwallis; killed (head shot off by a cannon ball) at Yorktown, Virginia, 17th Oct., 1781.
COCHRANE, Charles Stewart	8th April, 1836, 60th Regt.;	17th Aug., 1838;		Died at Kurrachee, 27th Aug., 1850.
C. COCHRANE, Hugh Stewart *Medal for Central India.*	13th April, 1849, 86th Regt.;	15th Oct., 1852, 86th Regt.;	12th Jan., 1844; exchd. to 64th Regt., 16th Feb., 1849. 24th Aug., 1858, 16th Regt.; exchd. to 7th, 21st March, 1859;	Bt. Major, 19th Jan., 1864; Major, 28th Oct., 1871; Bt. Lieut.-Col., 7th Jan., 1874.
COCKBURN, James *Medal for North-west Frontier.* Chandairee (slightly wounded); under a tremendous fire from the top of the Palace; siege, storm, and capture of Koonch; various actions before Calpee, 15–21st, May, 1858; battle and city and fortress of Gowlowlee; capture of the city and fortress of Gwalior; Sir Robert Napier, in pursuit of the jungles of Central India (twice commanded Irregular Cavalry, under mentioned in dispatches, and Victoria Cross); served as Major of Force during the North-west Frontier Brigade with the Eusofyze Field War of 1863.	Served as Adjt. of the 86th the Hugh Rose; present at the storming Battle of Betwa (three horses shot fort, he planted the British flag on Battle of Gowlowlee; capture of the	25th March, 1791, 19th L. D.; 31st July, 1787, 69th Regt.;	19th Sept., 1795; aptd. to 2nd Drags., 30th Dec, 1795;	Major, 7th Sept., 1797, 81st Regt.; exchd. to 24th L. D., 3rd Oct., 1798; retired, 24th Aug., 1800.
COCKS, John Somers	26th July, 1855;	1st April, 1856;	…	Died 4th Dec., 1856.
CODD, Garlike Philip Robert	1st April, 1813, 67th Regt.;	27th May, 1813; aptd. to 85th Regt., 22nd July, 1813;	…	Killed at Bladensburg, 24th Aug., 1814.
COGHLAN, James	…	1st Aug., 1693;	25th March, 1703.	
COGHLAN, John	… 23rd Regt.;	18th Jan., 1777;	…	Retired 5th Nov., 1777.
COLE, Fras. Burton Owen *Medal for N.W. Frontier.* Served under Brig. Chamberlain, storming of the Burrura Pass, capture and burning their stronghold Mahsood Wuzeerees during keen, and various minor affairs.	24th April, 1855, 20th Regt.; aptd. to 7th, 4th May, 1855; attached to 1st Coke's Rifles, against	16th Oct., 1855;	29th May, 1863; March, April, and May, 1860, present at the	Retired 6th Sept., 1863.
COLHOUN, William	…	28th Aug., 1754;		Died or retired 1756.
COLT, John Hamilton	6th Feb., 1806, 41st Regt.;	20th Nov., 1806; exchd. to 3rd Drags., 15th Jan., 1807;		Retired 1809; died 10th Sept., 1840.
COLT, Oliver	25th Aug., 1854, 5th Foot; aptd. to 7th, 2nd Feb., 1855;	27th July, 1855;		Killed in the attack on the Redan, Sebastopol, 8th Sept., 1855.
COLTMAN, Thomas	10th May, 1827, 66th Regt.; retired on h. p. unatt., 21st May, 1829;	29th June, 1830; aptd. to 10th Hussars, 19th Nov., 1830;		Retired 16th Aug., 1831.
COLVIN, William Butterworth	17th Nov., 1857;	16th Aug., 1859;	7th Nov., 1862.	
CONDUIT, Robert	…	26th Dec., 1726.		
CONEY, Philip George *Medal for the Crimea.* Severely wounded at the Alma.	9th July, 1852, 1st Foot;	3rd March, 1854;	1st June, 1855;	Died at Meean Meer, 30th April, 1858.
CONNOR, Aug. S. W.	13th Feb., 1867, Ceylon Rifles; exchd. to 7th, 9th Feb., 1870;	28th Oct., 1871;		Transferred to Bombay Staff Corps, 2nd Nov., 1872.
CONNOR, W. Shewbridge	20th April, 1809, 61st Regt.;	28th Feb., 1811;		Death in List of March, 1814; but no date.
CONOLLY, William	31st Jan., 1865, 36th Regt.; aptd. to 7th, 30th June, 1865.	7th Feb., 1871;		
CONYNGHAM, John	…	16th Dec., 1752; Capt.-Lieut., 26th May, 1759;	15th Oct., 1759; exchd. to h. p. 121st Regt., 28th Nov., 1766.	
COOK, William	…	Occurs 1720;	…	Out of Regt., 5th April, 1720.
COOK, John	…	Capt.-Lieut., 10th June, 1703.	…	
COOK, John	11th Jan., 1715;	…	…	
COOK, William From Qr.-Mas. Sergt. Grenadier Guards.	15th April, 1856;	…	…	Died in the Service. Retired 31st July, 1857.

Alphabetical List of Officers of the Royal Fusiliers.

NAME.	ENSIGN, &c.	LIEUTENANT.	CAPTAIN.	HIGHER RANKS AND REMARKS.
COOPE, William Jesser; *Turkish Medal for Sebastopol*; *Turkish Medal*. Served at the siege and fall of Sebastopol, at the capture of Kinburn.	17th Feb., 1854, 57th Regt.;	15th Sept., 1854, 57th Regt.; Quarries, assault of the Redan, June 18th, also at the bombardment and capture of Kinburn.	26th Feb., 1856, 57th Regt.; placed on h. p. of it 7th Nov., 1856; aptd. to 7th, 23rd OCT., 1857; exchd. to 64th Regt., 3rd March, 1863; retired on h. p. of it, 27th Feb., 1867; aptd. to 17th Lancers, 1st April, 1868;	Retired 1st April, 1868; aptd. Capt. in the 2nd Middlesex Militia, 19th March, 1872.
COOPER		...	24th FEB., 1854;	Killed at Landen, 19th July, 1693.
COOPER, Joshua Harry *Medal for Crimea*; *5th Class Medjidie*; *Turkish Medal*. Served the Eastern Campaign of Inkerman, and Siege of Sebastopol; appointed aide-de-camp to Col. Yee, present also at the attack on the Quarries, 7th June (wounded on the 8th), and assault on the Redan, 18th June.		16th Sept., 1851, 11th Foot;	1854-5 with the Fusiliers, including he Sortie of the 26th Oct., the battle pol; appointed aide-de-camp to Col. Yee, present also at the attack on the 8th), and assault on the Redan, 18th June.	Major 11th April, 1862; Lieut.-Col., 21st June, 1864; Col. 21st June, 1869; retired 6th Sept., 1873.
COPLEY, Charles	...	9th April, 1748; Capt. Lieut., 4th Sept., 1754;	22nd JAN., 1755;	Major, 19th Nov., 1761; retired 18th July, 1766.
CORBET, Moses. Appointed Lieutenant Governor of Jersey; taken prisoner by the French office for signing the capitulation of the island, May, 1781.			Jan. 6th, 1781; dismissed from his when they landed in that island, office for signing the capitulation of it.	
CORKORAN, Lewis Henry	29th May, 1867, 31st Regt.; aptd. to 52nd Regt., 21st Aug., 1867;	3rd APRIL, 1869;		Retired 14th Aug., 1872.
CORNWALL, Henry			1685;	Major, aptd. Col. 9th Regt., 1685.
CORRANCE, John	24th SEPT., 1743.			
COTTON, Thomas D'Avenant. Served at Copenhagen and at the capture of Martinique; proceeded acting as Brigade Major of the 2nd Salamanca and the Pyrenees. Whilst the enemy's entrenchments before Anhoue, on the 10th December.		11th APRIL, 1805; with the 1st Batt. to the Peninsula in Division, he was mortally wounded	30th AUG., 1810; 1810, particularly distinguished at in carrying a redoubt on the left of	Died at Anhoue, near Bayonne, of wounds received there, 1813.
COURTENAY, Charles S.	24th April, 1855;	3rd OCT., 1855;		Retired 20th April, 1860.
COURTENAY, George		18th APRIL, 1805;		Retired 23rd March, 1806.
COVENTRY, Corbet John	9th APRIL, 1861;			Retired 6th Feb., 1863.
COX, Charles. *Silver Medal for Talavera.*	17th APRIL, 1803, 21st L. D.; h. p. of it, 1804;	16th May, 1805, 2nd Foot;	14th April, 1808, 4th Gar. Batt.; aptd. to 7th, 2nd JUNE, 1808; re-aptd. to 2nd Foot, 7th June, 1810; exchd. to h. p. of 41st Regt., 9th Nov., 1815;	Died at Naples, 13th Oct., 1866.
CRADDOCK, Philip		26th DEC., 1726; placed on h. p. of it; aptd. to 26th Regt., 29th Oct., 1730.		
CRESER, Richard	10th Jan., 1811, 100th Regt., exchd. to 55th Regt., 1st Aug., 1811;	3rd JUNE, 1813; placed on h.p of the Regt., 25th March, 1817;		Aptd. Paymaster of the 21st Regt., 14th Jan., 1819; retired on h. p. of 27th Regt., 17th Nov., 1825; died 18th Sept., 1857.
CRESSWELL, Edmund	From Ens. Shropshire Militia;	21st JULY, 1808;		Retired 16th Nov., 1809.
CREWE, Kinder		4th JUNE, 1812; exchd. to h. p. of the Regt., 6th June, 1816; aptd. to 4th Vet. Batt. 24th Aug., 1820; disbanded 1821; placed on retired f. p. of it; aptd. to 2nd Vet. Batt., 25th Dec., 1821; reduced 1826; placed on retired f. p. of it.		Died June, 1847.
CRICHTON, Archd. Edwd.	21st AUG., 1869;	28th OCT., 1871; transferred to 70th Regt., 1st Feb., 1873.		
CROFTON, Hon. Alfred H. *Medal for the Crimea*. Slightly wounded at the Alma.	...	26th Aug., 1853, Grenadier Guards; aptd. to 7th, 3rd MARCH, 1854;		Retired 31st Aug., 1855.
CROFTON, Henry	...	11th JAN., 1715;	6th Feb., 1719, Regt.	
CROFTON, Hon. Wm. Gorges. Served with the Coldstreams in the 18th Oct., 1812.	...	6th AUG., 1803; aptd. to Coldstream Guards, 7th Dec., 1803;	Lieut. and Capt., 10th March, 1808, Coldstream Guards;	Killed before Bayonne during the sortie 14th April, 1814.
CROFTS, George	6th Aug, 1706, ... Regt.;	Capt. Lieut., 11th JAN., 1715;	25th APRIL, 1741;	Retired 9th Feb., 1750-1.
CROFTS, George		7th MARCH, 1707; Capt. Lieut., 12th Nov, 1733;	25th APRIL, 1741;	Retired 1751.

Alphabetical List of Officers of the Royal Fusiliers.

NAME.	ENSIGN, &C.	LIEUTENANT.	CAPTAIN.	HIGHER RANKS AND REMARKS.
CROMPTON, John	...	Occurs 1695 ;	...	Died in the service.
Served in Flanders and in the expedition to Cadiz and Vigo, 1702.				
CROPPE, William	25th MARCH, 1705 ;	Aptd. to Col. Parker's Compy., 11th Jan., 1715 ;	30th April, 1719 ;	Major, 3rd SEPT., 1733 ; died in England, 20th July, 1740.
CROSBIE, William	16th July, 1757, 38th Regt. ;	8th Sept., 1759, 38th Regt. ; General to the army in North	9th May, 1769, 38th Regt. ;	Major, 20th Sept., 1778, 38th Regt. ; exchd. to 7th, 29th OCT., 1778 ; Lieut. Col, 18th Sept., 1780 ; aptd. to 22nd Regt., 24th April, 1781 ; Col., 18th Nov., 1790 ; aptd. Col. of the 89th Regt., 3rd Dec., 1793 ; Maj. Gen., 3rd Oct., 1794 ; aptd. Col. of the 22nd Regt., 23rd Dec., 1795 ; died at Portsmouth, 16th June, 1798.
Served with the 38th in the Leeward Islands ; aptd. Barrack-Master		America, Nov., 1780.		
CROSBIE, Pierce	29th MAY, 1863 ;	1st MAY, 1866 ;	...	Retired 10th May, 1871.
CROTTY, Andrew	15th Sept., 1758, 44th Regt. ;	16th Aug., 1760, 44th Regt. ; placed on h. p. of it, 1763 ; aptd. to 7th, 1st MAY, 1765 ;	...	Retired 20th Feb., 1767.
CROTTY, Henry	...	29th JULY, 1795 ;	...	Retired July, 1799 ;
CROWDER, John, K.H.	From Lieut. West Riding Yeomanry ;	16th JUNE, 1803 ;	5th Nov., 1806 ;	Bt. Major, 17th Aug., 1812 ; Major, 9th SEPT., 1813 ; exchd. to h. p. of 23rd Regt., 25th May, 1815 ; Bt. Lieut. Col., 27th May, 1825 ; died at Cheltenham, 27th Aug., 1888.
Served at Copenhagen ; subsequently in the Peninsula, present at Talavera, Busaco, Albuera (wounded), Salamanca he commanded a detachment of two companies in support of the village of Araplies ; mentioned in dispatches for gallantry on that occasion.				
CUNNINGHAM, Robert	15th Mar., 1810, 16th L. D. ;	27th Dec., 1810, 57th Regt. ; exchd. to 14th L. D., 7th Mar., 1811 ;	24th DEC., 1709.	Major, 24th Oct., 1821, 55th Regt.; exchd. to h. p. of Spanish Staff, 27th July, 1822 ; aptd. to 20th Regt., 12th Dec., 1826 ; Lieut.-Col., 23rd Nov., 1841 ; Maj. unatt. ; Col., 11th Nov., 1851 ; aptd. Col. of the 16th Lancers, 9th April, 1859 ; Lieut. Gen., 14th May, 1859 ; Gen., 12th Jan., 1866.
CUST, Hon. Sir Edward, K.C.H. Silver Medal for 11, 16, 18, 19, 22, 24.			9th Dec., 1813, 60th Regt. ; placed on h. p. of it, 1814 ; reaptd. to f. p. of it, 8th Feb., 1816 ;	
Joined the army in the Peninsula end of 1813 ; present with the 16th Light Dragoons at Fuentes d'Onor, Ciudad Rodrigo and siege of Badajoz, prior to the advance from Portugal in 1811, and continued with it to the and afterwards with the 14th Light and generally in all the affairs of that period until he quitted the army on of the Annals of the Wars of the 18th and 19th Centuries, a standard work of military history.				
CUTHBERT, Robert	...	22nd AUG., 1804 ;	3rd FEB., 1809 ;	Died of wounds received in repulsing a sortie from Badajoz, April, 1812.
Served with the Fusiliers at the capture of Martinique.				
CUTHBERT, Robert H.	...	2nd Nov., 1826 ; aptd. to 2nd Foot, 21st May, 1829 ;	...	Retired 4th Dec., 1835.
CUTLER, John	7th Sept., 1809, 17th Foot ;	15th JUNE, 1812 ;	Occurs 1712 ;	Out of the Regt. before Nov., 1712.
DALGAIRNES, William Silver Medal for 9, 12, 18, 19.		5th JULY, 1810 ; aptd. to 55th Regt., 8th Dec., 1813 ; exchd. to h. p. of it, 24th July, 1817 ;	...	Died at the Rosaire, Guernsey, 26th Feb., 1869.
Served with the Regt. in the Peninsula, including the occupation of the Massena, capture of Olivenza and first siege of Badajoz, pursuit of Pampeluna ; after which he went to investment of Holland with Sir J. Graham's army as Adjutant of the 55th Regt. ; wounded at the storming of Bergen op Zoom, and taken prisoner.				
DALY, William	15th Oct., 1861 ;	12th APRIL, 1864.	...	
DAMBON, Joseph	11th JAN., 1715 ;		6th SEPT., 1873 ;	
DANIEL, John	16th Dec., 1795, 86th Regt. ;	20th Jan., 1796, 86th Regt. ;	24th DEC., 1802 ; placed on h. p. of the Regt. ; aptd. to 30th Regt., 9th July, 1803 ;	Major, 28th Feb., 1805, 99th Regt. ; Bt. Lieut. Col., 1st Jan., 1812 ; Lieut. Col., 16th June, 1812, 99th Regt., afterwards made 98th ; disbanded 1818 ; aptd. to 54th Regt., 17th June, 1819 ; placed on h. p., 14th Sept., 1820 ; Inspectg. Field Officer, Recruiting District, 14th Sept., 1820 ; aptd. to 49th Regt., 19th June, 1823 ; Col., 22nd July, 1830 ; retired 22nd Nov., 1836.
DANIEL, Robert	From Lieut. Worcestershire Militia ;	11th APRIL, 1809 ; exchd. to h. p. of the Regt., 19th March, 1818 ;	...	Died 9th March, 1842.
DANSY, Robert	...	19th JUNE, 1685 ;	13th DEC., 1739 ;	Killed at Namur, 17th July, 1695.
DARASSUS, John	...	17th Nov., 1721 ;	12th Dec., 1774, 17th Regt. ;	Retired 16th Dec., 1752.
DARBY, William John	6th May, 1762, 17th Regt. ;	24th Nov., 1769, 17th Regt. ;		Major, 10th Aug., 1780 ; Lieut. Col., 13th Regt., 1789, 44th Regt. ; retired 26th

Alphabetical List of Officers of the Royal Fusiliers.

NAME.	ENSIGN, &c.	LIEUTENANT.	CAPTAIN.	HIGHER RANKS AND REMARKS.
DAUBENY, Alfred Goodlad *Medal for the Crimea; Turkish Medal.*	23rd Nov., 1852, 90th Regt.; Served with the 90th in the Crimea ture of the Quarries, siege and fall of Sebastopol, attack of the Redan on the 10th June; formed one of the storming party on the 8th Sept.	8th Sept., 1854, 90th Regt.; from Dec. 5, 1854, including the capture of the Quarries, siege and fall of Sebastopol, attack of the Redan on storming party on the 8th Sept.	30th Nov., 1855, 90th Regt.: placed on h. p. of it; aptd. to 7th, 23rd OCT., 1857;	Major, 23rd JUNE, 1869.
DAUNT, Arthur Hildesley	Lieut. 2nd Durham Militia, 27th Nov., 1871;	12th Nov., 1873.		
DAUVERGNE, James	…	6th JULY, 1747.	…	…
DAVENPORT, Sharrington	…	11th FEB., 1756; Capt. Lieut., 18th JULY, 1766;	…	Died 3rd March, 1767.
DAVIDSON, William	…	Capt. Lieut., 20th JUNE, 1727.	…	…
DAVIE, Francis	Royal Marines;	7th May, 1793, Royal Marines; aptd. to 7th, 29th JULY, 1795; reaptd. to Royal Marines, 13th Feb, 1795;	…	…
DAVIS, Charles Winter	3rd Sept., 1812, Newfoundland Fencibles;	24th Feb., 1814, Newfoundland Fencibles; exchd. to 8th Foot, 11th April, 1815; placed on h. p. of the Regt., 25th Feb., 1816; exchd. to 7th, 20th APRIL, 1820; exchd. to h. p. of 30th Regt., 17th Sept., 1829; aptd. to 17th Regt., 16th Nov., 1849;	…	Retired 16th Nov., 1849.
DAVISON, Hugh Percy	25th Oct., 1805, 27th Regt.;	11th Nov., 1806, 27th Regt.;	26th Nov., 1807, 7th West India; exchd. to 7th, 28th JAN., 1808; exchd. to 18th L. D., 26th May, 1808; exchd. to 17th L.D., 17th Dec., 1812;	Major, 19th March, 1814, 67th Regt.; Lieut. Col. 24th Aug., 1815, 67th Regt.; exchd. to h. p. of 5th West India Regt., 5th Feb., 1818; Col., 10th Jan., 1837; Maj. Gen., 9th Nov., 1846; died at Stanley Hall, Shropshire, 5th July, 1849.
DAWSON, Richard	…	21st APRIL, 1808; exchd. to 1st Drags., 30th June, 1808;	…	Retired Dec., 1810.
DAWSON, William	18th Aug., 1799, 35th Regt.;	21st Mar., 1800, 35th Regt.; placed on h. p. of it, 1802; re-aptd. to f. p. of it, 25th Mar., 1803; to 1st Drags., 20th Mar., 1806; exchd. to 7th, 30th JUNE, 1808.	…	
DAWKINS, Clinton Fras. Berens	31st Dec., 1844, 60th Regt.;	5th Nov., 1847; aptd. to 35th Regt., 10th April, 1849;	…	Retired 30th Jan., 1852.
DAY		Occurs 1695.		
DAY, Elisha	17th Feb., 1804, Wagon Train;	15th Aug., 1805, Wagon Train; aptd. to 7th, 14th AUG., 1806;	…	Retired 21st Dec. 1809.
DE BRAKELL, M. A. Jacob D'ESTE, *Sir* Aug, Fred., K.C.H. Served with the Fusiliers in America, 1815; present at New Orleans.	1st April, 1806, 60th Regt.;	31st JULY, 1806; 26th SEPT., 1811;	14th March, 1815, York Chasseurs; aptd. to 12th Foot, 6th July, 1815;	Retired 26th April, 1810. Major, 11th July, 1822, 11th Foot; exchd. to 4th D. G., 24th Oct., 1822; Lieut. Col., 1st July, 1824, unatt.; Col., 28th June, 1838; exchd. to 69th Regt., 10th Nov., 1848; retired same day.
DE LANIER, Henry				
DE MONTMORENCY, Raymond Elmeric	17th Nov., 1840, 26th Regt.;	12th JAN., 1844; aptd. to 50th Regt., 23rd Feb., 1844;	…	Died in London 2nd June, 1848.
DEAN, Thomas	1794, 58th Regt.;	20th JUNE, 1794;	1st July, 1795, 39th Regt.; aptd. to West India Regt., 1st Sept., 1795; aptd. to 53rd Regt., 2nd Nov., 1796; exchd. to 64th Regt., 25th July, 1802;	Bt. Major, 25th April, 1808; Major, 25th June, 1808, 1st Foot; Bt. Lieut. Col., 4th June, 1814; Lieut. Col., 29th June, 1815, 1st Foot; retired 23rd Nov., 1815.
DECHAIR, Robert	…	18th APRIL, 1745;	…	Retired 12th March, 1754.

Alphabetical List of Officers of the Royal Fusiliers.

NAME.	ENSIGN, &c.	LIEUTENANT.	CAPTAIN.	HIGHER RANKS AND REMARKS.
DESPARD, John Served with the 12th Foot in Germany, present at Warburg and Fellinghausen, and to the end of the Seven Years' War. In March, 1773, embarked with the Fusiliers for Quebec; in the following year was raised a sufficient number of recruits sent to England on the recruiting service; in March, 1775, having ordered to complete the regiment, he embarked at Gravesend, and arrived at St. John's with a sufficient number of Fusiliers took post at St. John's with a few days afterwards, the Fusiliers were retired with the prisoners, the Fusiliers were retired with the prisoners, and the 26th Regt. The siege continued and strengthening the post until reduced to three days' allowance, and exchanged with the regiment, and America with the regiment under Prince Edward.	21st April, 1760, 12th Foot;	12th May, 1762, 12th Foot; placed on h. p. of it, 1763; exchd. to 7th, 1st Sept. 1768;	5th Oct., 1777, th Regt.; aptd. to 7th, 7th Oct., 1777;	Bt. Major, 19th Feb., 1783; Major, 13th June, 1789; Lieut. Col., 13th July, 1791; Col., 21st Aug., 1795; Maj. Gen., 18th June, 1798; Lieut. Gen., 30th Oct., 1805; aptd. Col. 12th Vet. Batt., 25th June, 1808; aptd. Col. 5th West India Regt., 29th Dec., 1809; Gen., 4th June, 1814; died at Oswestry, 3rd Sept., 1829.
			Quebec on the 17th May. A few days after the rebels having employed in constructing a redoubt at Ticonderoga, &c. The rebels having constructed by a detachment of the allowance of provisions—and being 150 men, and were besieged that redoubt and another three weeks the troops on two-thirds 5th Nov., 1775. In Dec., 1776, he was they were compelled to surrender the war; and again returned to Light Infantry. Served throughout		
DESPARD, William *Gold Medal for Albuera.* Served with the regiment at the capture of Martinique.	...	4th Sept., 1754;	21st March, 1762; exchd. to to h. p. of 72nd Regt., 1763; 14th May, 1804;	
DEVENISH, Francis	11th June, 1685; aptd. to Col. St. Clair's Compy., 1st May, 1686.	27th May, 1795;		Bt. Major, 20th June, 1811; Major, 15th Aug., 1811; died of wounds received in the Pyrenees, 28th July, 1813.
DEVEREUX, Hon. George (Hereford *Viscount*)	...	19th Nov., 1761; exchd. to h. p. 8th Jan., 1768;	...	Died at Nanteribba Hall, Montgomeryshire, 31st Dec., 1804.
DEVEY, Henry Fryer Served with the Regt. in the Peninsula, present at Albuera and Badajos.	...	30th Aug., 1807;	28th Oct., 1813; placed on h. p. of the Regiment, 25th Aug., 1814;	Died at Handsworth, near Birmingham, 13th June, 1840.
DICKINSON, Douglas John *Medal for Ghuznee.* Served with the Queen's Royals in Afghanistan and Beloochistan, throughout the campaign of 1838-9, present at the assault and capture of the fortresses of Ghuznee and Kelhat (leg broken by a musket shot);	30th June, 1837, 2nd Foot;	30th Jan., 1839, 2nd Foot; aptd. to 7th, 15th Dec., 1840; retired on h. p. of 2nd Foot, 27th Feb., 1846;	...	Aptd. Adjt. Brecknock Militia, 7th Feb., 1846; aptd. Major of it, 13th Nov., 1852; Lieut. Col., 30th Aug., 1860; died at Jersey, 22nd March, 1865.
DIGBY, George	25th March, 1758, 53rd Regt.;	22nd June, 1761;	...	Retired 1768.
DIGBY, William Henry	...	14th April, 1791;	...	Died 1819.
⊞ DISNEY, Brabazon	16th Sept., 1811, 11th L. D.;	5th Aug., 1813, 11th L. D.; exchd. to 23rd L. D., 15th Sept., 1814;	30th Oct., 1793, Regt.; aptd. to 121st Regt., 16th June, 1795; reduced but retained on f. p. of it; 8th April, 1816, 67th Regt.; placed on h. p. of it, 25th July, 1817; exchd. to 7th, 22nd April, 1819;	Major, 3rd March, 1825; Lieut. Col., 31st Aug., 1830, unatt.; died in Dublin, 15th Mar., 1833.
DISNEY, Edgar John	25th Aug., 1854;	12th Jan., 1855;	26th Jan., 1858; exchd. to 24th Regt., 11th Aug., 1858;	Retired 21st Oct., 1859; aptd. Capt. Essex Rifle Militia, 6th May, 1862.
DISNEY, Frederick	...	19th June, 1758;	19th Feb., 1766, 21st Regt.;	Bt. Major, 10th Nov., 1780; retired 1783; died at Lincoln, 13th June, 1788.
DISNEY, William Henry	8th July, 1795, 10th Foot;	12th Sept., 1795, 10th Foot;	24th Dec., 1802, 60th Regt.; aptd. to 47th Regt., 17th Sept., 1803;	Major, 27th Nov., 1806, 6th Gar. Batt.; aptd. to 7th, 28th Jan., 1808; died 11th April, 1809.
DIVE, Hugh John Hector	Lieut. 1st West York Mil., 6th June, 1870.	12th Nov., 1873.	...	
DIXON, Henry *Medal for the Crimea.* Served the Eastern campaign of 1854-5, including the battles of Alma and Inkerman, and siege of Sebastopol.	6th Feb., 1847, 41st Regt.;	29th Dec., 1848;	...	Aptd. Paymaster of the Regt., 29th Oct., 1852; aptd. to 1st Drags., 5th Feb., 1856; Hon. Major, 29th Oct., 1862; retired on h. p. of the Regt., 28th May, 1870.
DOBBIE, David	...	28th Dec., 1838;	...	Died at Gibraltar, 20th June, 1844.
DOBBS, Edward Brice	...	3rd June, 1752; 8th May, 1758;	26th May, 1759;	Retired 25th May, 1772; was twice Mayor of Carrickfergus.
DOLMAN, John	...	23rd Dec., 1813; placed on h. p. of the Regt., 25th Feb., 1816; exchd. to 83rd Regt., 4th April, 1816; exchd. to 40th Regt., 7th Nov., 1816; placed on h. p. of it, 25th Mar., 1817; exchd. to 86th Regt., 4th May, 1820;		Died at Barbadoes, 7th Jan., 1828.

Alphabetical List of Officers of the Royal Fusiliers.

NAME.	ENSIGN, &c.	LIEUTENANT.	CAPTAIN.	HIGHER RANKS AND REMARKS.
DOMVILLE, Charles	...	13th April, 1791 ;	17th March, 1795 ;	Major, 16th Sept., 1795 ; died at Halifax, Nova Scotia, Feb., 1798.
DONALD, Colin George	21st Sept., 1874.			
DONALDSON, John	...	10th March, 1738 ;	12th Dec., 1746 ;	Major, 3rd June, 1752 ; Lieut. Col. 25th Dec., 1755 ; died or retired 1758.
DONDE, Peter	27th Aug., 1756, 53rd Regt. ;	11th Aug., 1759 ;	25th Dec., 1770 ;	Retired 19th Feb., 1777.
DONELIAN, Ralph		24th April, 1755 ; aptd. to 92nd Regt., 29th Jan., 1760 ; placed on h. p. of it, 1763.		
DONKIN, Geo. David	15th Aug., 1834, 52nd Regt. ;	1st Dec., 1837 ;	...	Retired 21st Sept., 1841 ; died at Wyfold Court, Oxfordshire, 23rd Jan., 1857.
DOUGLASS, Fras. Wingfield *Medal for Ashantii.*	4th Dec., 1863 ;	16th Oct., 1867 ;	24th Mar., 1875, unatt.	
DOWBIGGIN, Montagu Hamilton *Medal for the Crimea ; Legion of Honour ; 5th Class of the Medjidie.* Served the Eastern campaign of Sebastopol.	30th June, 1848, 71st Regt. ; 1854-5, including the battles of Alma	16th Sept., 1851 ; aptd. to 4th Regt., 5th Dec., 1851 ; and Inkerman, and siege of	29th Dec., 1854, 4th Foot ;	Bt. Major, 17th July, 1855 ; Major, 1st Feb, 1856, unatt. ; aptd. to a Depôt Batt., 1st Oct., 1856 ; exchd. to 99th Regt., 22nd July, 1859 ; Lieut. Col., 3rd March, 1863, 99th Regt. ; placed on h. p. of it, 10th Dec., 1863 ; aptd. to 7th, 20th June, 1865 ; retired same day ; died in Portland Place, Brighton, 3rd Feb., 1866.
DOWSON, Chas. Sutherland *Medal for the Punjaub.* Served with the 29th throughout the Punjaub campaign of 1848-9, including the affair of Ramnuggur, battles of Chillianwallah and Goojerat.	3rd June, 1842, 90th Regt. ; aptd. to 25th Regt., 13th Oct., 1843 ;	27th May, 1846, 29th Regt. ; aptd. Qr. Mas. of it, 10th Dec., 1847 ; aptd. Lieut., 8th Foot, 11th Oct., 1853 ; the passage of the Chenab, and	23rd Oct., 1857 ;	Major, 1st April, 1866, unatt. ; aptd. to 3rd Foot, 3rd June, 1868 ; Lieut. Col., 1st April, 1870, unatt. ; placed on h. p., 2nd Aug., 1870.
DRAWATER, Augustus Chas. *Silver Medal for 6, 9.* Served with the Fusiliers in the expedition to Copenhagen in 1807 ; and subsequently in the Peninsula.	1st May, 1805, 45th Regt. ; Landed with the 1st Batt. at Lisbon ;	20th March, 1806 ; the capture of Martinique in 1809 ; present at Aldea de Ponte.	15th Aug., 1811 ; exchd. to 70th Regt., 2nd July, 1812 ; exchd. to 62nd Regt., 16th Mar., 1815 ; placed on h. p. of it, 25th Mar., 1817 ; exchd. to 26th Regt., 23rd July, 1818 ; exchd. to h. p. of 104th Regt., 30th Sept., 1819 ; aptd. Paymaster of the 64th Regt., 11th Nov., 1819 ; aptd. Paymaster 4th D. G., 29th Dec., 1825 ; retired on h. p. of the Regt., 9th April, 1847 ;	Died at Bathwick Hill, Bath, 12th Sept., 1857.
DROMGOLE, Patrick	Indept. Comp. ;	1st Dec., 1745 ; Capt. Lieut., 2nd Oct., 1755 ;	29th July, 1757 ;	Died or retired 1759.
DRYBOROUGH, John	...	13th Aug., 1708 ;	...	Died in the service.
DYER, John	...	28th June, 1783 ; placed on h. p. of it, 1788 ; re-aptd. to Regt., 3rd Mar., 1784 ;	...	Retired 1791.
DYER, *Sir* John Swinnerton, *Bt.* Committed suicide in a moment of despondency, increased by the absence of his son then serving in Egypt as aide-de-camp to Sir R. Abercrombie.	...	7th Nov., 1759, 72nd Regt. ;	28th July, 1762, 72nd Regt. ; placed on h. p. of it, 1763 ; aptd. to 7th, 8th Aug., 1764 ; exchd. to Coldstream Guards, 4th Oct., 1765 ; Capt. Lieut. and Lieut. Col., 21st Nov., 1777, Coldstream Guards ;	Aptd. Capt. and Lieut. Col., 1st Foot Guards, 14th May, 1778 ; Col., 20th Nov., 1782 ; retired 1790 ; shot himself 21st March, 1801.
DYER, *Sir* Thos. Richard, *Bart.* Served with the Brigade of Guards expedition to the Helder, 1799 ; the	25th Dec., 1781, 100th Regt. ; the campaign in Flanders, 1793 ; campaign in Egypt, 1800-1.	28th June, 1783, 3rd Regt. ; aptd. to 7th, 3rd March, 1784 ; placed on h. p. of it ;	14th April, 1791, 14th Regt. ; aptd. to Gren. Guards, 27th April, 1793 ;	Bt. Major, 1st Jan., 1798 ; Capt. and Lieut. Col., 23rd Oct., 1799, Gren. Guards ; exchd. to 14th Regt., 1st Oct., 1807 ; exchd. to Royal York Rangers, 31st March, 1808 ; Col., 25th Oct., 1809 ; Maj. Gen., 1st Jan., 1812 ; Lieut. Gen., 27th May, 1825 ; died in Clarges Street, Piccadilly, 12th April, 1838.

Alphabetical List of Officers of the Royal Fusiliers.

NAME.	ENSIGN, &c.	LIEUTENANT.	CAPTAIN.	HIGHER RANKS AND REMARKS.
DUCKWORTH, Geo. Henry	1801, 39th Regt. ;	25th June, 1801, 68th Regt. ; to 11th Regt., 25th Aug., 1801 ;	17th Aug., 1803, 60th Regt. ; aptd. to 55th Regt., 6th July, 1804 ; aptd. to 7th, FEB., 1805 ; aptd. to 59th Regt., 14th Nov., 1805 ;	Major, 25th July, 1806, York Light Infty. ; exchd. to 67th Regt., 2nd Oct., 1806 ; Lieut. Col., 14th Jan., 1808, 1st West India ; exchd. to 48th Regt., 16th June, 1808 ; killed at Albuera, 16th May, 1811.
DUFFE, William	...	14th DEC., 1770 ;	9th April, 1777, 26th Regt. ;	Major, 4th Jan., 1786, 26th Regt. ; retired 19th March, 1793.
DU JARDIN, Benj. Stephens	5th July, 1855, Ceylon Rifles ;	23rd April, 1858, Ceylon Rifles ;	21st July, 1871, Ceylon Rifles ; placed on h. p. of the Regt., 1873 ; aptd. to 7th, 25th Feb., 1874 ;	
DUNDAS, William	...	25th AUG., 1756 ;	...	Died or retired 1759.
DUNDEE, Edward	...	3rd AUG., 1815 ; placed on h. p. of the Regt., 25th Feb., 1816 ; exchd. to 86th Regt., 11th April, 1816 ; exchd. to 47th Regt., 8th Jan., 1818 ; 14th May, 1695.	8th Oct., 1829, 47th Regt. ;	Died at Malta, 1st June, 1840.
DUTERME, Louis Served as Adjt. of the Regiment in the expedition to Cadiz and Vigo.				
DUTTON, William Holmes	...	4th MAY, 1815 ; placed on h. p. of the Regt., 25th Feb., 1816 ; exchd. to 71st Regt., 6th June, 1816 ; placed on h. p. of it, 1816 ; exchd. to 85th Regt., 6th Nov., 1817 ; aptd. to 4th Foot, 19th Nov., 1818 ;	15th Aug., 1822, 4th Foot ;	Major, 20th March, 1827, 4th Foot ; exchd. to h. p., unatt., 5th July, 1827 ; Bt. Lieut. Col., 23rd Nov., 1841 ; Col. 20th June, 1854 ; Maj. Gen. 26th Oct., 1858 ; died in London, 7th Jan., 1863.
EARDLEY, Hon. William	...	24th AUG., 1792 ;	3rd Nov., 1793, Indep. Comp. ;	Major, 12th March, 1794, 82nd Regt. ; Bt. Lieut. Col., 16th Sept., 1795 ; died at Fladong's Hotel, Oxford Street, 17th Sept., 1805.
EDGAR, James	...	25th APRIL, 1745 ; Capt. Lieut., 16th DEC., 1752 ;	20th JUNE, 1753 ;	Died or retired 1762.
EDGAR, Richard	26th June, 1779, 56th Regt. ; 11th July, 1843, 4th L. D. ;	24th Sept., 1787 ;	...	Retired May, 1794.
EDGELL, Geo. Rashleigh		20th DEC., 1844 ;	8th APRIL, 1853 ;	Retired 13th Dec., 1853 ; Major 2nd Somerset Militia, 4th Mar., 1871.
EDWARDS, Timothy	20th Dec., 1760, 14th Regt. ;	28th OCT., 1761 ;	...	Retired 1765.
ELLIOTT, George Augustus	15th Mar., 1855, 33rd Regt. ;	16th Oct., 1855, 33rd Regt. ; aptd. to 25th, 12th Dec., 1859 ;	22nd Dec., 1863, 25th Regt. ; exchd. to 7th Fus., 1st MAR., 1864 ;	Out of the Regt., April, 1868.
ELLIOTT, John	20th June, 1780, 50th Regt. ;	20th SEPT., 1780 ;	29th April, 1782, 74th Regt. ; aptd. to 36th Regt., 28th Feb., 1783 ;	Retired 4th Dec., 1784.
ELLWOOD, Charles	22nd April, 1802, 47th Regt. ;	6th July, 1804, 47th Regt. ;	11th July, 1805, 99th Regt. ; exchd. to 5th Gar. Batt., 31st Mar., 1808 ; exchd. to 7th, 11th JUNE, 1812 ;	Retired 3rd June, 1813.
ELWES, John Emilius	12th JAN., 1855 ;	19th JUNE, 1855 ;	...	Retired 12th June, 1860 ; died at Clifton, Bristol, 16th Jan., 1865.
ELWES, William	...	20th OCT., 1726 ;	...	Died or retired 1754.
ENGLAND, Thomas	...	12th Nov., 1733.		
ENGLISH, Hamilton *Silver Medal for 6, 9, 16.*	16th May, 1805, 93rd Regt. ;	3rd April, 1806, 90th Regt. ; aptd. to 7th, 11th SEPT., 1806 ;	14th MAY, 1812 ;	Retired 18th Oct., 1821.
ENGLISH, Thomas	26th July, 1800, 64th Regt. ;	25th July, 1803, 7th West India ; aptd. to 7th, 14th JULY, 1804 ;	...	Died or retired 1804.
ERCK, Gaspar	8th Sept., 1802, 24th Regt. ;	7th April, 1804, 24th Regt. ;	25th APRIL, 1809 ;	Killed at Albuera, 16th May, 1811.

Alphabetical List of Officers of the Royal Fusiliers.

NAME.	ENSIGN, &c.	LIEUTENANT.	CAPTAIN.	HIGHER RANKS AND REMARKS.
ERSKINE, *Sir* James, *Bart.* Served the campaigns of 1793-4 in Flanders; present at Cateau, April 26th, 1794; on the plains of Cysoing, 10th May, and in the reserve in the actions of the 17th and 18th of that month; at the battle of Tournay, and Bergen; commanded a district in the actions near Boxtel; present at the siege of Scotland until the 18th April, 1809, when he left England for Portugal in but returned from severe indisposition on the 20th Sept., 1809.	26th Feb., 1788, 26th Regt.;	9th JAN., 1793;	8th March, 1793, Indept. Comp.; aptd. to 37th Regt., 1st Nov., 1793;	Major, 19th May, 1794; Lieut. Col., 22nd Aug., 1794, 133rd Regt.; reduced, but retained on f. p. of it; aptd. to 15th L. D., 27th Feb., 1796; Col., 1st Jan., 1800; aptd. to 2nd D. G., 10th Feb., 1803; Maj. Gen., 25th April, 1808; Lieut. Gen., 4th June, 1813; died in London, 3rd March, 1825.
ERSKINE, John	27th Sept., 1808, 94th Regt.;	18th Jan., 1810, 94th Regt.; exchd. to 7th, 10th Nov., 1813;	...	Retired 13th Jan, 1814; died 23rd Nov., 1824.
EVERARD, Meredith	...	7th SEPT., 1722;	...	Died 1750.
EWING, George	...	20th FEB., 1767;	...	Retired 6th Jan., 1771.
EYRE, Walpole G.	12th Aug., 1825, 11th Foot; aptd. to 36th Regt., 29th Dec., 1825;	23rd Nov., 1828, 36th Regt.; aptd. to 7th, 21st MAY, 1829;	...	Retired 1st Dec, 1837.
FAIRBROTHER, George FAIRBROTHER	...	1st Aug, 1693;	Occurs 1708.	Killed at Landen, 19th July, 1693.
FALKLAND, Lucius Cary, *Viscd.*, G.C.H.	19th April, 1821, 22nd Regt.; placed on h. p. of it, 1821; aptd. to 63rd Regt., 13th Dec., 1821; aptd. to 71st Regt., 20th Dec., 1821;	6th JAN., 1825;	19th DEC., 1826;	Retired 9th Nov., 1830; aptd. Capt. of the Yeomen of the Guard, 1846; Governor of Nova Scotia from 1840 to 1846; Gov. of Bombay from Feb., 1848, to Dec., 1853.
FANE	...			
FARQUHARSON, Frederick	17th Sept., 1813, 101st Regt.;	MAY, 1807; exchd. to h. p. Royal Wagon Train, 26th May, 1807. 25th May, 1814, 101st Regt.; placed on h. p. of it, 1816; exchd. to 75th Regt., 12th Dec., 1816; placed on h. p. of it, 25th Mar., 1817; exchd. to 10th Regt., 28th Aug., 1817; exchd. back to 75th Regt., 29th April, 1818;	23rd Sept., 1819, 75th Regt.; placed on h. p. of it, 1821; exchd. to 7th, 22nd AUG., 1822;	Major, 29th JUNE, 1830; Lieut. Col., 7th SEPT., 1832; Col., 9th Nov., 1846; retired 9th Aug., 1850; died at 11, Cranbury Place, Southampton, 7th April, 1856.
FAWCETT, Morris James	31st AUG., 1858;	18th AUG., 1863;	...	Retired 30th March, 1867; aptd. Adjt. Cumberland Militia, same day.
FENWICK, William	...	3rd MAY, 1815; placed on h. p. of the Regt., 25th Feb., 1816; exchd. to 58th Regt., 1st Jan., 1824;	21st July, 1825, unatt.; exchd. to 23rd Regt., 17th Nov., 1825;	Major, 24th March, 1837, 23rd Regt.; died at Brompton, Middlesex, 11th Sept., 1837.
FERGUSON, William Dick	3rd April, 1817, h. p. of 60th Regt.; exchd. to 57th Regt., 26th Aug., 1823;	8th APRIL, 1825;	...	Retired 28th Aug., 1828; died at Danavourd House, 1836.
FERNIE, Andrew	...	27th AUG., 1804;	26th APRIL, 1809 ;	Killed at Sauroren, 28th July, 1813.
FERRIER, Richard	...	28th SEPT., 1743.		
FERRIES, Richard	1st Oct., 1794, 6th Irish Brigade;	1st Dec., 1797, 6th Batt. Irish Brigade; aptd. to 7th, 24th DEC., 1797;	...	Retired Dec., 1802.
FIELDING, Wm. Rob., *Viscount*	...	4th MAR., 1777;	2nd Aug., 1778, 75th Regt.; aptd. to 3rd D. G., 4th May, 1779;	Major, 6th March, 1782, 19th L. D.; Lieut. Col., 31st Dec. 1782, 22nd Drags.; reduced, placed on h. p. of it, 1783; Col., 12th Mar., 1793; aptd. Col. 22nd L. D., 24th Feb., 1794; Maj. Gen., 26th Feb., 1795; died in Newcastle, 8th Aug., 1798.
FINLEY, Robert	...	2nd JUNE, 1796 ; exchd. to h. p. of the Regt., July, 1801.	...	
FITZCLARENCE, *Hon.* Edward	3rd Nov., 1854, 62nd Regt.; aptd. to 7th, 4th NOV., 1854;	12th JAN., 1855;	...	Died of wounds received in the assault of the Redan, 18th June, 1855.

Alphabetical List of Officers of the Royal Fusiliers.

NAME.	ENSIGN, &c.	LIEUTENANT.	CAPTAIN.	HIGHER RANKS AND REMARKS.
FITZCLARENCE, *Lord* Frederick, G.C.H.	12th May, 1814, Coldstream Guards;	...	23rd Feb., 1820, Cape Corps Infty.; aptd. to 11th Foot, 9th Aug., 1820;	Major, 10th Jan., 1822, 11th Regt.; Lieut. Col., 1st April, 1824, 11th Regt.; aptd. to 7th, 2nd June, 1825; Col., 6th May, 1831; exchd. to h. p., unatt., 24th Aug., 1832; Maj. Gen., 23rd Nov., 1841; aptd. Col. 36th Regt., 23rd July, 1851; Lieut. Gen., 11th Nov., 1851; died at Poorunder, Bombay, 30th Oct., 1854.
FITZCLARENCE, *Hon.* Fred. Chas. Geo.	22nd April, 1842, 73rd Regt.;	23rd May, 1845; aptd. to 10th Hussars, 8th Aug., 1845; 15th Aug., 1811; aptd. to 15th Hussars, 23rd Jan., 1813; aptd. to 10th Hussars, 25th Mar., 1813; exchd. to 22nd L. D., 12th Nov., 1814;	12th April, 1850, 10th Hussars;	Retired 22nd May, 1857.
FITZCLARENCE, Henry	...	...	...	Died in India, 1817.
FITZGERALD, Edwd. Thos., K.H. Slightly wounded at Waterloo.	13th June, 1804, 20th L. D.; where he served on the staff of the Qr. Mas. General.	June, 1806;	23rd Aug., 1806, 101st Regt.; aptd. to 25th Regt., 13th Sept., 1810; exchd. to 12th Regt., 3rd April, 1817; placed on h. p. of the Regt., 25th Jan., 1818;	Bt. Major, 21st June, 1817; Bt. Lieut. Col., 22nd July, 1830; diedat Turlough Park, Castlebar, 19th Sept., 1845.
FITZGERALD, John	6th June, 1778, 37th Regt.;	29th April, 1782;	...	Retired 15th June, 1791; died at Geraldine, Queen's County, 1834.
FITZGERALD, Thos. Geo.	11th May, 1800, 1st Foot Guards;	...	17th Dec., 1802, 1st Foot Guards; placed on h. p. of the Regt., 1802; aptd. to 61st Regt., 9th July, 1803;	Major, 20th Aug., 1806, 101st Regt.; exchd. to 8th Gar. Batt., 8th Oct., 1807; placed on h. p. of it, 1810; Bt. Lieut. Col., 4th June, 1813; exchd. to 7th, 1st Aug., 1822; exchd. to 72nd Regt., 27th Mar., 1823; retired 26th Aug., 1824; died at Turlough Park, Mayo, 5th June, 1850.
FITZGERALD, W. H. Dominic *Medal for the Crimea.* Severely wounded (shot through both legs) at the Alma.	8th Oct., 1844, 72nd Regt.;	27th Mar., 1846;	24th Feb., 1854; exchd. to h. p, unatt., 1st June, 1855;	Bt. Major, 2nd Nov., 1855; Major, 19th Dec., 1856, unatt.; Bt. Lieut. Col., 2nd April, 1865; retired Oct., 1872.
FITZPATRICK, Andrew	...	15th March, 1703.	Occurs 1695.	
FITZPATRICK, Edward	...	12th May, 1729.	...	
FITZROY, *Lord* Frederick	18th Oct., 1792, 66th Regt.;	1st Oct., 1794, 66th Regt.;	16th Sept., 1795; aptd. to 62nd Regt., 20th Jan., 1796;	Retired 1797.
FITZSIMMONS, Thomas	...	29th July, 1795; exchd. to h. p. of 52nd Regt., Feb., 1803;	...	Aptd. Town Adjt. of Cape Breton, July, 1799; died or retired in 1807.
FITZWILLIAM, Charles	From Capt. h. p. 52nd Regt.;	...	15th June, 1685.	
FISHER, Thomas Forrest	...	24th Jan., 1805;	19th Mar., 1807, 5th Gar. Batt.; exchd. to 6th D. G., 2nd April, 1807;	Bt. Major, 20th Feb., 1812; Bt. Lieut. Col., 9th Mar., 1815; died at Blackwell, 13th Sept., 1818.
FLEETWOOD, Henry	12th June, 1685;	2nd Oct., 1688;	...	
FLEMING, Arthur Cecil Crewe	11th Oct., 1839, 1st D. G.;	16th Nov., 1841;	12th May, 1715;	Retired 28th Jan., 1842.
FLEMING, James Commanded the 36th Regt. in Scotland during the rebellion of 1745-6.	...	7th Sept., 1706;	...	Major, ; Lieut. Col., 4th Aug., 1722; aptd. Col. 36th Regt., 9th Jan., 1741; Maj. Gen., 20th Sept., 1747; Lieut. Gen. ; died at Gibraltar, March, 1751.
FLEMING, John	...	26th Dec., 1726;	22nd Sept., 1742.	
FLETCHER Wounded at Landen.	...	...	...	
FLOOD, Douglas	1st Apl., 1856;	24th May, 1859;	...	Retired 1st Dec., 1863.
Lieut. Wexford Militia, 16th Dec., 1854.				
FOLLETT, Hardinge Gifford	29th Feb., 1856, 87th Regt.; aptd. to 7th, same day.	13th Aug., 1858;	...	Died at Taplow, 15th July, 1861.

Alphabetical List of Officers of the Royal Fusiliers.

NAME.	ENSIGN, &c.	LIEUTENANT.	CAPTAIN.	HIGHER RANKS AND REMARKS.
FORBES, Thomas	...	3rd Oct., 1688 ;	20th June, 1727.	
FORBES, William	9th Sept., 1819, 52nd Regt. ;	8th April, 1825 ;	10th June, 1826, unatt. ;	Died or retired 1833.
FORBES, William	...	4th Nov., 1724.		
FORD, Edward	...	15th Aug, 1775 ;		Retired 23rd Feb., 1784.
FORD, James	...			
FORD, Harry Geo. Wakelyn	21st Nov., 1865, 11th Regt. ; aptd. to 7th, 2nd March, 1866 ; exchd. to Ceylon Rifles, 9th Feb., 1870 ;	28th Oct., 1871, Ceylon Rifles ; placed on h. p. of the Regt., June, 1873 ; aptd. to 56th Regt., 18th Oct., 1873 ;		
FORD, Matthew William	1803, 8th West India Regt. ;	24th Aug., 1804, 70th Regt. ;	23rd April, 1812, 70th Regt. ; exchd. to 7th, 2nd July, 1812 ; exchd. to 1st Foot, 27th June, 1822 ; exchd. to h. p. of 24th L. D., 14th Nov., 1822 ; exchd. to Paymaster 16th Foot, 15th May, 1823 ;	Cashiered Oct., 1837.
FORMAN, Edw. Rowland	15th Oct., 1841, 60th Regt. ;	29th Dec., 1843 ; exchd. to 88th Regt., 23rd July, 1844 ;	18th June, 1852, 88th Regt. ; aptd. to Rifle Brigade, 28th Jan., 1853 ;	Killed at the attack on the Redan, 18th June, 1855.
FORTESQUE, *Hon. John Wm.*	14th July, 1837, 29th Regt. ;	7th June, 1839 ;	...	Retired 16th Aug., 1842 ; aptd. Major in the East Devon Militia, 24th April, 1846 ; Lieut. Col., 23rd Sept., 1853 ; retired 12th July, 1856 ; died at Camacha, Madeira, 25th Sept., 1859.
FORSTER, John *Medal for Sebastopol ; Turkish Medal ; Medal for India.* charge against a band of fanatic	25th Aug., 1843, 43rd Regt. ; Served with the 6th D. G. in the Crimea from the 26th July, 1855, to bineers before Delhi ; accompanied Gazees, and was wounded in seven	3rd Sept., 1847 ; exchd. to 6th D. G., 22nd Oct., 1847 ; the fall of Sebastopol. Second in Gen. Shower's column when Penny places, losing a portion of one hand	2nd Nov., 1850, 6th D. G. ; command of a wing of the Carawas killed, on this occasion he led a (Brevet of Major).	Bt. Major, 20th July, 1858 ; Major, 18th Feb., 1859, unatt. ; aptd. to 6th Regt., 28th Jan., 1862 ; retired same day.
FORSTER, William Frederick	22nd April, 1779, 65th Regt. ;	1st Dec., 1779, 90th Regt. ; aptd. to 7th, 8th Mar., 1793 ;	4th July, 1793, Indept. Comp. ;	Col. 30th Oct., 1794, Somersetshire Fencible Infantry.
FOSTER, Francis John	3rd Aug., 1855 ;	28th Nov., 1856 ;	...	Died at Biggleswade, 30th Oct., 1860.
FOSTER, Trevor John	11th Sept., 1872.			
FOTHERGILL, Thomas		13th Dec, 1739 ;		Invalided 18th April, 1745.
FOUKS (? James, see Fox)	Occurs 1695.			
FOWLER, Richard	...	14th Sept., 1809 ;	16th June, 1685 ;	
FOWLER, Robert J.	...	Occurs 1702 ;		Killed at Badajoz, April, 1812.
FOX, James Served with the Regt. in the expedition to Cadiz and Vigo, 1702.				
FRAMPTON, William John	12th Dec., 1856 ;	18th Sept., 1859 ; exchd. to 59th Regt., 4th Feb., 1862 ;	29th Sept., 1865, 59th Regt. ;	
FRANCE, Henry Hugh Atherton	12th Sept., 1865, 6th D.G. ; aptd. to 15th Regt., 28th Dec., 1866 ; aptd. to 7th, 13th Feb., 1867 ;			Retired 10th Nov., 1869.
FRANKLIN, Geo. J.	9th Oct., 1855 ;	21st June, 1810 ;		Retired 22nd May, 1857.
FRASER, James Baillie Present at Busaco ; shot through the thigh at Albuera, when all the wounded ; returned with the staff of men and officers of his company present at Vittoria		the 2nd Batt. to England, and was employed in recruiting at Leicester.	except four, were either killed or In 1812 he again returned to Spain ;	Died at Sauroren from wounds received on the 28th July, 1813.
FREEMAN, John	...	8th Jan., 1768.	28th Mar., 1752 ;	Retired 4th Sept., 1754.
FREEMAN, John	placed on h. p. of it, 1763 ;			
FREEMAN, William	...	...	19th June, 1685 ;	Retired 1st May, 1686.
FREER, Charles Thomas	29th Nov., 1827, 65th Regt., ;	26th Oct., 1830, 65th Regt. ; retired on h. p., unatt., 3rd Feb., 1832 ; aptd. to 7th, 15th Feb., 1833 ;	...	Retired 17th Feb., 1837 ; aptd. Capt. in the Leicestershire Yeomanry, 3rd June, 1846 ; Major, 13th May, 1863.
FROUDE, William	21st June, 1685 ;	...	Occurs as Capt, 1693.	Left the Regt. 5th April, 1694 ; he was alive and a Col. (?) in 1713.

Alphabetical List of Officers of the Royal Fusiliers.

NAME.	ENSIGN, &C.	LIEUTENANT.	CAPTAIN.	HIGHER RANKS AND REMARKS.
GAGE, Henry	...	25th March, 1777;	14th April, 1779, 26th Regt.;	Major 17th Feb., 1783, 93rd Regt.; reduced 1783; placed on h. p. of it; Bt. Lieut. Col. 1st March, 1794; Col. 1st Jan., 1798; Maj. Gen. 1st Jan., 1805; died in Arlington Street, 29th Jan., 1808.
GAGE, James Stirling	...	24th Oct., 1811; placed on h. p. of the Regt. 25th Mar., 1817; exchd. back to f. p. of it 19th March, 1818.	6th Jan., 1825;	Retired 26th Feb., 1830; died at Streeve Hill, 7th Nov., 1836.
GAGE, John	...	1st March, 1783; placed on h. p. 1783; aptd. to f. p. 23rd Feb., 1784;	25th June, 1788, 45th Regt.; placed on h. p. of it same day; exchd. to First Guards, 16th Dec, 1789;	Left the Guards, 23rd June, 1794.
GALL, Charles D. M.	9th Aug., 1873, 1st Foot; aptd. to 7th 24th Sept., 1873.			
GALLWEY, Payne, Sir W. Bart.	29th July, 1824, 88th Regt;	22nd Sept., 1825, 88th Regt.;	21st Dec., 1832, 88th Regt.;	Major, 1st Nov., 1839, 88th Regt.; exchd. to 7th, 20th March, 1840; retired 3rd June, 1842.
GAMBLE, Arthur	...	1st Aug., 1716.		
GAMBLE, Robert	...	4th Sept., 1754.		
GARDNER, Anthony	18th May, 1855, 1st Foot;	12th May, 1857, 1st Foot; aptd. to 7th 2nd Feb., 1858; exchd. to 22nd Reg, 13th April, 1858.	10th June, 1862, 22nd Regt.;	Retired July, 1867.
GARDNER, James		5th Oct., 1755; aptd. to Regt.		
GARDNER, James Anthony *Medal for Sebastopol.*	29th March, 1855; Served at the Siege of Sebastopol	9th Sept., 1855; from the 7th July, 1855.		Retired 21st Sept., 1860.
GARLICK, Theophilus		11th June, 1685.		
GARRETT, Sir Robt., K.C.B.; K.H. *Silver Medal for 11, 16, 18, 19; Medal for Sebastopol.* Served in the Peninsula with the divisions were engaged from Fuentes D'Onor in May, 1811, until the end received two wounds at the attack of the forts at Salamanca, on which with some artillery devolved upon him, he being the only surviving wounded in the Pyrenees. Served with the 46th Regt. at the Siege of	6th March, 1811, 2nd Foot; 6th Division in 1811, and with the 4th Division in 1812 and 13, present in of 1813, when he was sent to England occasion the command of the Light officer of the column he attacked Sebastopol.	3rd Sept., 1812, 2nd Gar. Batt.; exchd. to 7th, 2nd Oct., 1812; all the actions in which these two for the recovery of his wounds. He Company of the Queen's (2nd) Regt. with; and he was again severely	7th July, 1814, 97th Regt.;	Major 19th Sept., 1826, unatt.; exchd. to 46th Regt. 7th Feb., 1834; Bt. Lieut. Col., 23rd Nov., 1841; Lieut. Col., 16th May, 1845, 46th Regt.; Col., 20th June, 1854; Major. Gen., 26th Oct., 1858; aptd. Col. of the 4th West India Regt. 1st April, 1862; Lieut. Gen., 10th Mar., 1866; aptd. Col. 43rd Regt., 14th Jan., 1866; died at 40, Pall Mall, 13th June, 1869.
GARFORTH, Francis Served with the R.N.B. Fusiliers at the capture of Guadaloupe.	2nd Dec., 1777, 63rd Regt.;	19th Sept., 1779;	1st May, 1782, 22nd Regt.; placed on h. p. of it, 1783; exchd. to 21st Regt., 27th Aug., 1785.	Died in Guadaloupe, 1794.
GATACRE, Edwd. Lloyd	7th Feb., 1858;	23rd Aug., 1861;		Retired 11th March, 1862.
GEDDES, William Lorraine	6th Feb., 1858;	29th Jan., 1861; exchd. to 53rd Regt., 24th April, 1861;	20th July, 1866, 53rd Regt.	
GEE, W.			Occurs 1724.	
GEE, Joseph *Silver Medal for Salamanca.*	30th Mar., 1809, 98th Regt.;	8th Nov., 1810; exchd. to Cornet Royal Horse Guards, 14th Mar., 1813;		Retired February, 1814.
GEORGE, John *Silver Medal for 11, 15.* Present at the defence of Cadiz, in four places at Badajoz; present at	28th Feb, 1810, 44th Reg.; and lines of Torres Vedras; wounded New Orleans, 1815.	7th Nov., 1811; placed on h. p. of the Regt., 25th Mar., 1817; exchd. to 21st Regt, 26th Nov., 1818;	8th April, 1825, Royal African Corps; aptd. to 66th Regt., 8th June, 1826; exchd. to h. p., unatt, 6th Dec. 1827; 15th May, 1718.	Appointed Chamberlain at the Royal Hospital at Kilmainham.
GIBBONS, Geoffry	20th July, 1708;	13th Aug., 1708;		
GIBBONS, Frederick Served with the 1st batt. in the Peninsula, wounded at Albuera.	4th March, 1806, 37th Regt.;	21st Aug., 1806, 16th Foot; exchd. to 7th, 1st Sept., 1808;	7th Nov., 1813, 56th Regt.; placed on h. p. of it, 6th Sept., 1817; exchd. to 91st Regt., 21 Jan., 1819; aptd. to 95th Regt, 1st Dec., 1823.	Retired 18th Dec., 1828.

Alphabetical List of Officers of the Royal Fusiliers.

NAME.	ENSIGN, &c.	LIEUTENANT.	CAPTAIN.	HIGHER RANKS AND REMARKS.
GIBBS, Edward	11th Sept., 1760, 3rd Foot;	25th March, 1763, 3rd Foot; placed on h. p. of it, 1763; aptd. to 7th, 18th DEC., 1766; 27th JULY, 1838; exchd. to 6th D. G., 1st Feb, 1889;	...	Retired 26th Jan., 1770.
GIFFORD, Robert Francis, *Lord*	4th Dec., 1835, 52nd Regt. ;	...	...	Retired 13th July, 1841, died at Ampney Park, Gloucestershire, 13th May, 1872.
GILBY, Lovelace	...	...	25th DEC., 1726.	
GILLEY, Thomas	...	9th Nov., 1830 ;	3rd Nov. 1854, unatt. ; aptd. Adjt. of Depôt Batt. ; aptd. to 7th, 23rd OCT., 1857.	Aptd. Paymaster of the Regt., 11th May, 1838 ; retired on h. p. of it, 29th Oct., 1852 ; aptd. to 78th Regt., 10th Dec., 1852 ; Bt. Major, 26th Dec., 1856 ; retired 31st Aug., 1858 ; died at Castle Connell, 28th Mar. 1869.
GILLILIAN, William	26th July, 1864, 76th Regt. ;	21st Mar., 1868, 76th Regt., exchd. to 7th, 7th Nov., 1868.	...	Retired 8th June, 1872.
GION GLEGG, Berkenhead	12th JUNE, 1867 ;	Occurs 1695. 28th Ocr., 1871 ;	...	Retired 9th Sept., 1874.
GLENCAIRN, William, *Earl of*	10th Jan., 1729, 3rd Regt. ;	3rd APRIL, 1734.	3rd APRIL, 1734 ;	Left the Regt. April, 1741; aptd. Governor of Dumbarton Castle 12th March, 1734 ; Col., 19th Feb, 1762 ; died 9th Sept., 1775.
GLENTWORTH, Edmund Henry *Lord*	...	12th APRIL, 1827 ;	24th JAN., 1834 ;	Retired 20th June, 1834 ; died in Manchester Square, 16th Feb., 1844.
GLOVER, George Grenville	20th Nov., 1827, 82nd Regt. ;	26th FEB, 1830 ;	31st AUG., 1838 ;	Retired 12th July, 1839 ; aptd., Capt. in the 2nd Norfolk Militia 23rd Nov., 1852 ; Major, 16th March, 1860 ; Hon. Lieut. Col.
GLYNN, Robt. Carr	13th Dec., 1851, 85th Regt. ;	18th Feb, 1853, 85th Regt. ;	30th Nov., 1855, 85th Regt. ; exchd. to 7th, 26th FEB. 1856 ; placed on h. p. of the Regt., Nov., 1856 ; exchd. back to f. p. of it, 31st July, 1857 ;	Retired 18th July, 1862 ; died 9th April, 1867.
GODFREY, John	...	5th APRIL, 1720.		
GORDON, William	18th July, 1809, 1st Foot ;	21st DEC., 1809 ; re-aptd. to 1st Foot, 1st March, 1810 ;	...	Died or retired Jan., 1815.
GORE, Henry (*Lord Annaly*)	...	...	36th Regt. ; aptd. to 7th, 8th MAY, 1749 ;	Major, 30th DEC., 1755 ; Lient. Col., 7th April, 1759, 13th Drags. ; retired ; aptd. Col. of the Battle Axe Guards, 6th Feb., 1764 ; M.P. for Longford ; died in Dublin, 5th June, 1793.
GORE	...			
GORE, Sir Ralph, *Bart.*	...	25th OCT., 1703. 13th MAY, 1795 ;	26th Aug., 1796, 100th Regt. ; made 92nd Regt. ; aptd. to 9th Regt., 8th Aug., 1799 ;	Major, 7th Jan., 1803. h. p. late York Fusiliers ; Bt. Lieut. Col., 25th July, 1810 ; retired 1826 ; died 20th March, 1842.
GOSSIP, William	...	28th APRIL, 1782 ;	24th June, 1783, 60th Regt. ; placed on h. p. of it, 1783 ;	Retired June, 1825 ; died at York, 21st Aug., 1833.
GRAHAM, Henry Alex.	28th May, 1829, 17th Foot; aptd. to 75th Regt., 25th June, 1829 ;	15th June, 1832, 75th Regt. ; aptd. to 7th, 26th FEB. 1836 ; retired on h. p. of 20th Regt, 9th June, 1837 ; aptd. to 95th Regt., 17th Feb, 1838 ;	...	Retired 13th July, 1888.
GRANT, James Murray	21st July, 1781, 71st Regt. ;	aptd. to 7th, Regt. ; 1783 ;	1783, 74th Regt. ; Regt. reduced same year, placed on h. p. of it; aptd. to 39th Regt., 24th Sept, 1803 ; to h. p. p. of 3rd Foot Guards, 1804.	Bt. Major, 1st March, 1794 ; died at York, 25th Aug., 1817.
GRANT, John Burgoyne	...	16th OCT., 1778 ;	3rd May, 1782, 64th Regt. ;	Died or retired 1785.

Alphabetical List of Officers of the Royal Fusiliers.

NAME.	ENSIGN, &c.	LIEUTENANT.	CAPTAIN.	HIGHER RANKS AND REMARKS.
GRANT, Patrick J. John	14th April, 1846, 3rd West India Regt.;	28th April, 1848, 96th Regt.;	15th April, 1856, 96th Regt.	Major, 8th Sept., 1863; retired 13th Oct., 1868; died in London, 13th Aug., 1874.
GRANT, William Lewis	7th April, 1837, 60th Regt.;	28th July, 1840;	23rd May, 1845;	Retired 21st June, 1850; aptd. Lieut. Col. Tower Hamlets Militia, 23rd Dec., 1852; aptd. an Exon. of the Yeomen of the Guard, 1852.
GRAVES, W. E. Hely *Medal for the N.W. Frontier.* Served in the N.W. Frontier war with the Eusafzie Field Force; present at the defence of the Conical Hill, and at the attack on and destruction of Lalloo, 15th Dec.; also action at Umbeyla Pass, Dec. 16th, and conclusion of the village at the foot of the war.	11th April, 1862;	23rd June, 1865; exchd. to 64th Regt., 11th April, 1868; sent at the defence of the Sungahs at Umbeyla and destruction of 25th June, 1812, 89th Regt.;	the Umbeyla Pass, storming of the village at the foot of the Bonair	Retired 17th March, 1869; aptd. Lieut. in the 1st Royal Cheshire Militia, 19th May, 1871; Capt., 24th May, 1873, 1st Royal Cheshire Militia
GREAVES, Richard Served the American campaign;		16th July, 1812; placed on h. p. of it, 25th Mar, 1817; exchd. back to f. p. of it, 14th Jan., 1819;	28th Oct., 1824, 34th Regt.;	Major, 8th May, 1828, 34th Regt.; exchd. to h. p. unatt., 2nd Jan., 1837; Bt. Lieut. Col., 29th Sept., 1837; Col., 11th Nov., 1851; Maj.-Gen., 9th Nov., 1856; Lieut. Gen., 8th June, 1863; Col., 40th Regt., 15th Dec., 1861; Gen., 25th Oct., 1871; died at 69, Chester Square, London, 22nd May, 1872.
GREEN, Richard	…	31st Oct., 1747;	…	Retired 2nd May, 1751.
GREEN, William	…	28th Dec., 1809;	…	Retired Nov., 1811.
GREGORY, Arthur Chaplain	…	6th Jan., 1771;	…	Died July, 1775.
GRENVILLE, Christopher	…	13th Aug., 1708.		
GREVILLE, Geo. Henry Macartney Served with the Coldstreams in the Peninsula from 25th June, 1811, to 1st Nov., 1812, when he returned to England on promotion in the 2nd battalion.	4th Dec., 1806, Cape Corps;	8th Sept., 1808, Colds. Guards;	24th Sept., 1812, Colds. Guards; exchd. to 7th, 23rd Sept., 1813; exchd. to 25th L. D., 18th Nov., 1813; disbanded 24th Nov., 1819, placed on h. p. of it; exchd. to 3rd L. D., 27th April, 1820; placed on h. p. of the Regt., 25th Dec., 1821; aptd. to 16th Lancers, 26th May, 1822;	Major, 13th Nov., 1827, unatt.; exchd. to 38th Regt., 26th Nov., 1830; died at Berhampore, 25th Sept., 1834.
GREY, Thomas	…	11th May, 1791;	20th Nov., 1793, Indep. Comp.	
GREY, *Hon.* William	…	28th Dec., 1791;	30th April, 1794, 21st Regt.;	
GRIFFITH, Edwd. Wynne	2nd Feb., 1858;	21st Sept., 1860; exchd. to 1st Drags., 3rd March, 1863;	24th March, 1869, 1st Drags.;	Major, 15th Aug., 1798, 7th West India Regt.; Lieut. Col., 31st March, 1803, 6th Vet. Batt.; aptd. to 7th Vet. Batt., 1st Aug., 1811; placed on retired f. p. of it, 1814; died in Upper Berkeley Street, 10th Aug., 1817.
GRIFFITH, Pierce	…	20th June, 1727.	18th Feb., 1710.	Retired 8th June, 1870.
GRIFFITH, Thomas	16th Jan., 1835, 6th D. G.;	5th Oct., 1838, 6th D. G.; exchd. to 7th, 1st Feb., 1839;	…	Retired 20th Dec., 1844; died at Seafield, Howth, Co. Dublin, 20th Nov., 1852.
GROGAN, George	2nd Dec., 1862;	20th June, 1865;	…	
GROUBE, Thomas *Medal for the N.W. Frontier.* Served with the Fusiliers in the beyla Pass, and at the attack on and storming of the Conical Hill and destruction of the village at the foot of the Bonair Pass, Dec. 16th, which ended 25th Aug., 1863;	N.W. Frontier war of 1863 with the	Eusafzye Field Force; present at the struction of Lalloo, Dec. 15th; also in the complete rout of the enemy and	defence of the Sungahs at the Um-in the action at Umbeyla, and destruction submission of the Hill tribes next day.	
GROVE, George Served with the Fusiliers in the campaigns in Flanders under William.				"Col. Geo. Grove to be Governor of Dartmouth Castle, 23rd Oct., 1727;" Col., 5th Aug., 1715, 19th Foot; died 13th Oct., 1729.
GROVE, Henry Served with the Fusiliers in Flanders; wounded at the assault of the paigns of 1702-10; commanded it at Oudenarde; taken prisoner at the	1st Dec., 1688;	Capt. Lieut., 1st Aug., 1692; Terra Nova, Namur, 20th Aug., 1695; siege of Ghent; present at the siege	20th May, 1693; served with the 10th in the cam-of Tournay and battle of Malplaquet.	Major, 24th July, 1695, Regt.; Lieut. Col., 10th Foot, 23rd June, 1715; died 20th Nov., 1736.

Alphabetical List of Officers of the Royal Fusiliers.

NAME.	ENSIGN, &c.	LIEUTENANT.	CAPTAIN.	HIGHER RANKS AND REMARKS.
GUARD, William	6th Nov., 1824, 62nd Regt. ;	31st Oct., 1826, 62nd Regt. ;	10th Jan., 1828, 62nd Regt. ; exchd. to 7th, 1st MARCH, 1833 ; exchd. to h. p. of Sub-Inspector of Militia, 29th March, 1842 ;	Bt. Major, 23rd Nov., 1841 ; retired 26th April, 1844.
GUMBY, John	7th APRIL, 1709 ;	11th JAN., 1715.		
GURNEY, Charles	21st SEPT., 1855 ;	28th AUG., 1857 ;		Died at Cadiz from the effects of a fall from a horse, 6th June, 1864.
GUYON, Gardiner F.	31st Jan., 1865, 49th Regt. ;	16th May, 1868, 49th Regt. ; exchd. to 7th, 7th Nov., 1868.		
GWILLIAM, Thomas	… …	4th JULY, 1746 ;	2nd MAY, 1751 ;	Major, 1st MAY, 1759 ; Lieut. Col. 1761, 50th Regt. ; retired 29th Jan., 1762.
GWYDIR, Peter, Lord	July, 1807, 2nd West India Regt. ;	AUG., 1807 ; placed on h. p. of 4th Regt., 9th Oct., 1807;	…	Died at Brighton, 29th June, 1820.
HACKET, Richard Silver Medal for 7, 12, 18, 19, 22, 24.	From Lieut. North Down Militia ; Served with the Fusiliers in America,	26th OCT., 1807; present at New Orleans.	17th DEC., 1813 ; aptd. to 9th Foot, 14th Aug., 1817 ; exchd. to h. p. of 14th Foot, 6th Aug., 1818 ;	Aptd. Capt. of Invalids at Kilmainham Hospital ; died in Corfu, 13th July, 1848.
HACON, Charles	… …	27th OCT., 1688.		Promoted to a Regiment, 1st May, 1686.
HAGGERSTONE, Edward	… …	1st MAY, 1687.		Deprived of his command, 11th Dec., 1688 ; took service under King James in Ireland, and was killed there.
HAGGERSTONE, Sir Thos., Bart.	… …	… …	1st MAY, 1687 ;	
HAGGERSTONE, Thomas	… …	… …		Died at Gibraltar, 1st Dec., 1732.
HALE, Roger	… …	11th JAN., 1715 ;	9th MAY, 1722 ;	Retired 11th June, 1801 ; entered the profession of the law ; aptd. Judge of the Supreme Court of Nova Scotia, 1811 ; Chief Justice of the same Court, 1835 ; died at Halifax, Nova Scotia, 16th July, 1860.
HALIBURTON, Sir Brenton, Kt.	… …	28th JAN., 1795 ;	27th Jan., 1798, 81st Regt. ; exchd. to 7th, 31st MAY, 1798 ;	
HALL, Herbert Byng, K.S.F.	10th DEC., 1824, 39th Regt. ;	15th Dec., 1825, 39th Regt. ; aptd. to 7th, 26th JAN., 1826;	7th SEPT., 1832 ; exchd. to 62nd Regt., 1st March, 1833 ;	Retired 20th Sept., 1833 ; joined the British Legion of Spain ; Major, 18th July, 1835.
HALL, Savage	21st Jan., 1853, 89th Regt. ;	8th Dec., 1854, 89th Regt. ;	9th Jan., 1857, 89th Regt. ; placed on h. p., 16th Jan., 1857; aptd. to 7th, 31st DEC., 1857.	Retired.
HALL, Richard Spencer	25th MAY, 1860 ;	29th MAY, 1863 ; transferred to Coldstream Guards, 1st Dec., 1863 ;	18th JAN., 1867, Coldstream Guards ;	Aptd. Aide-de-camp to Maj. Gen. Hardinge, Bengal Staff, 22nd Oct., 1873.
HALL, Thomas	41st Regt. ;	17th MAY, 1803 ;	20th DEC., 1777, 72nd Regt. ; aptd. to Invalid Compy. at Plymouth, 28th Jan., 1784 ;	Retired 20th March, 1806.
HAMER, Ibbetson	Royal Marines ; placed on h. p. of them ;	27th OCTOBER, 1772 ;	…	Died at York, Dec., 1789.
HAMERTON, W. Meadows Silver Medal for 7, 9, 14, 15, 16, 18, 19. Accompanied the Fusiliers to the Torres Vedras, severely wounded at he was again severely wounded.	Dec., 1806, 61st Regt. ; aptd. to 95th Rifles, Jan., 1807 ; Peninsula in Feb., 1809 ; present at Salamanca, Roncesvalles, heights of Present at the capture of Paris.	19th MARCH, 1807 ; the capture of Oporto, in the lines of Pampeluna, and the Pyrenees, where	16th JAN., 1812 ; exchd. to h. p. of 67th Regt., 22nd April, 1819 ; aptd. to 97th Regt., 30th Nov., 1849 ;	Bt. Major, 21st Jan., 1819 ; Bt. Lieut. Col., 10th Jan., 1837 ; retired 30th Nov., 1849.
HAMILTON, Chichester	12th April, 1827, 59th Regt. ; aptd. to 65th Regt., 27th April, 1827 ;	11th JAN., 1715. 13th DEC., 1827 ;	6th MAY, 1836 ;	Retired 30th Dec., 1836.
HAMILTON, Gerard Baillie	… …			
HAMMILL, Robert	3rd DEC., 1803, Nova Scotia Fencibles ;	22nd Feb, 1806, Nova Scotia Fencibles ;	29th July, 1811, Nova Scotia Fencibles ; exchd. to 7th, 6th MAY, 1813 ; placed on h. p. of the Regt., 25th Feb., 1816 ; exchd. to 18th Foot, 19th June, 1817 ;	Bt. Major, 22nd July, 1830 ; Major, 22nd Oct., 1839, 18th Foot ; died at Chusan, 7th Feb., 1841.

Alphabetical List of Officers of the Royal Fusiliers.

NAME.	ENSIGN, &c.	LIEUTENANT.	CAPTAIN.	HIGHER RANKS AND REMARKS.
HANNAM, Pitt. Landed with the 2nd batt. in the Peninsula, 1809, present at the affair of Aldea del Ponte, severely wounded at Salamanca, Orthes, and Toulouse.	From Lieut., 2nd Royal Lancashire Militia;	20th April, 1808; exchd. to h. p. of the Regt., 14th Jan., 1819;	...	Died 11th Nov., 1828.
HARBORD, Richard	22nd Dec., 1846, 36th Regt.;	11th April, 1851, 36th Regt.;	2nd Feb., 1858; placed on h. p. of the Regt.	Major, 1st April, 1870, unatt.; aptd. Garrison Instructor at Cork, 11th July, 1870.
HARDING, Henry Magnan	31st July, 1857;	5th Jan., 1791;	16th April, 1795;	Retired 17th Dec., 1858.
HARDYMAN, Frederick, C.B.	13th June, 1783, Regt.; exchd. to 18th Foot, 9th May, 1789;			Major, 16th July, 1803, 1st Foot; Bt. Lieut. Col., 6th July, 1804; Lieut. Col. 31st Oct., 1805, 17th Foot; Col., 4th June, 1813; Major Gen., 12th Aug., 1819; died in Bengal, 28th Nov., 1821.
HARE, Hon. Charles Luke. "He was severely wounded just as we were on the point of entering the battery, which, as you will see in the papers, caused such havoc among our poor fellows. Shot through the ear, he was picked up, and next day embarked on board the 'Andes,' together with myself and other fellow-sufferers. He died next morning."	18th March, 1836, 18th Foot;	7th Dec., 1838;	23rd Aug., 1844;	Died on board the "Andes" (of wounds received at the Alma), 23rd Sept., 1854.
HARGRAVE, Thomas	...	9th Oct., 1747;	...	Aptd. Qr. Mast., 25th March, 1755.
HARLING, William	...	18th Aug., 1778;	...	Retired April, 1787.
HARRIOT, George. Served with the Regiment during the American War; wounded at the Cowpens.				
HARRIOTT, George. Bronze Star for Maharajpore. Served the campaign in Affghanistan under Lord Keane, including the siege and capture of Ghuznee, and the action of Maharajpore.	11th April, 1834, 16th Lancers;	8th July, 1836, 16th Lancers; aptd. to 7th, 13th Aug., 1847;	...	Retired 22nd Oct., 1847.
HARRIS, George. Seeking for more active service, and arrived in Holland but the day before the action which terminated his life.	Indept. Comp.; than Halifax presented, he exchanged into the 5th Foot, then on active service.	17th April, 1795; exchd. to 5th Regt., 25th July, 1799; 13th April, 1719;	...	Killed at the passage of the Helder, 19th Sept., 1799.
HARRIS, John	...	...	Marines. 1740, Wolfe's	
ℳ HARRIS, Sir Thos. Noel, K.H. Re-entered the army Silver Medal for 11, 14, 15. Served the Waterloo campaign as Major of Brigade to Sir Hussey Vivian in 1813-14, in which the Prussians under England the first intelligence of the all the actions during the campaigns surrender of Paris, 1814; served at the battle of Leipsic.	5th Feb., 1801, 87th Regt.; March, 1811, 13th L. D.; lost an arm on the 18th. Served in Blucher were engaged; brought to	24th Dec., 1802, 96th Regt.; aptd. to 25th Regt., 23rd Nov., 1804; aptd. to 18th L. D., 4th April, 1805; 15th Aug., 1811, 18th L. D.;	27th Aug., 1807, 18th L. D.; exchd. to 7th, 26th May, 1808; exchd. to 1st Drags, 15th Dec., 1808; 9th June, 1814, York Chasseurs; placed on h. p. of 36th Regt., 1814; aptd. to 1st D. G., 8th Sept., 1815; placed on h. p. of it, 25th March, 1816;	Retired 5th Jan., 1809; Bt. Major, 14th March, 1817; Bt. Lieut. Col., 13th Feb., 1823; Major, 16th July, 1830, unatt.; retired 1834; died at Updown Eastry, Kent, 23rd March, 1860.
HARRISON, Arthur John	10th March, 1857;	20th April, 1860;	16th March, 1867.	Retired.
HARRISON, Horace Sibbald	27th July, 1855, 30th Regt.;	22nd May, 1857, 30th Regt.; aptd. to 7th, 2nd Feb., 1858.	...	
HARRISON, John. Served with the 51st Regt. in Germany during the Seven Years' War; with the Fusiliers in America during the Revolutionary War; taken prisoner at Fort Chambly.	21st May, 1761, 51st Regt.;	31st March, 1763, 51st Regt.; placed on h. p. of it, 1763; exchd. to 7th, 4th Feb., 1767;	25th March, 1777;	Retired 1781.
HARRISON, Joseph John Crofton. Re-entered the army	1st Dec., 1808, 53rd Regt.;	21st May, ..., 1812; aptd. to 3rd D. G., 23rd July, 1812; Lieut. 27th May, 1813, 3rd D. G., placed on h. p. of it, 1814; aptd. to 6th Drags., 13th May, 1815; placed on h. p. of it, 25th March, 1816;	...	Retired Feb., 1812; Died or retired 1839.
HARROW, Henry Edward	20th July, 1855, 59th Regt.	11th Aug., 1858, 59th Regt.; exchd. to 7th, 4th Feb., 1862;	...	Retired 14th Feb, 1865.
HART, Thomas. Served with the Regt. in Flanders; wounded at Landen.		15th June, 1685;	Occurs Capt. 1692.	
HARTLEY, Thomas. Present at Busaco, Albuera, Badajoz (severely wounded), Salamanca (slightly wounded), Salamanca, Orthes, and Toulouse.	12th May, 1807, 23rd Regt.;	3rd Dec., 1807, 23rd Regt.; exchd. to 7th, 3rd Aug., 1808;	...	Retired 1814.

Alphabetical List of Officers of the Royal Fusiliers.

NAME.	ENSIGN, &C.	LIEUTENANT.	CAPTAIN.	HIGHER RANKS AND REMARKS.
HARTRICK, William	16th Nov., 1855, 1st West India Regt. ;	14th July, 1857, 1st West India Regt. ; exchd. to 1st Foot, 4th Dec., 1857 ; aptd. to 7th, 2nd Feb., 1858 ; retired on h. p., May, 1868 ;	…	Died in Dumbartonshire, 14th Nov., 1873.
HARVEY, Edwd. Frederick	21st June, 1786, 33rd Regt. ;	5th Sept., 1787 ;	…	Retired 28th Jan., 1789.
HARVEY, George Lake	30th July, 1858, 1st Drags. ;	21st Sept., 1860, 1st Drags. ; exchd. to 7th, 18th Feb., 1862 ;	…	Died 22nd June, 1865.
HARVEY, James	…	23rd July, 1748 ; Capt. Lieut., 22nd Jan., 1755 ;	15th Oct., 1755 ;	Retired 1761.
HAUTENVILLE, Alex. Jeffray	18th July, 1865, 17th Regt. ; aptd. to 7th, 8th Aug., 1865 ;	26th Jan., 1804 ;	…	Retired 18th March, 1805.
HAWKES, Robert Tomkyns	…	…	…	Aptd. Lieut. Bengal Staff Corps, 24th Sept., 1868.
HAWTHORNE, Robt. Stewart	…	28th Oct., 1761, Regt. ; placed on h. p. of it, 1763 ; exchd. to 7th, 15th July, 1767.	…	
HAY, Alexander	…	28th Oct., 1760, 49th Regt. ; to 7th, 2nd June, 1762 ;	…	Retired March, 1777.
HAY, James *Silver Medal for 7, 9, 12, 14, 15, 16, 18, 19, 22, 24, 26.*	Served as Adjutant during the whole Peninsula War, and was never absent from his Regiment except for the recovery of his wounds.	3rd May, 1810 ;	31st Aug., 1839, 52nd Regt. ;	Retired 8th Oct., 18 ; aptd. a Providore at Kilmainham Hospital ; died at the Institution, 2nd July, 1854.
HAY, John	18th Regt. ;	3rd June, 1752 ;	…	Died or retired 1755.
HAY, *Hon.* Samuel	6th Oct., 1825, 16th Foot ; aptd. to 7th, 22nd Oct., 1825 ;	7th Mar., 1826 ;	2nd Nov., 1830 ; exchd. to h. p., unatt., 4th Dec., 1832 ; exchd. to 25th Regt., 22nd Oct., 1833 ;	Retired 25th Oct., 1833 ; died at Clyffe Hall, Wilts, 25th Nov., 1848.
HAYES, Patrick	1st Oct., 1796, 6th Batt. Irish Brigade ;	18th Jan., 1798, 6th Batt. Irish Brigade ; placed on h. p. of it, same year ; exchd. to 7th, 18th July, 1799 ;	…	Died 1804.
HAYTER, Charles James	11th March, 1859 ;	…	…	Retired 29th July, 1862.
HEALEY, John *Silver Medal for 7, 9, 12, 25, 26.*	4th June, 1808, 99th Regt. ; Landed with the 2nd batt. at Lisbon, 5th April, 1809 ; lost an arm at Albuera.	8th Sept., 1808 ;	26th June, 1823 ; exchd. to h. p. of 39th Regt., 25th Jan., 1824 ;	Died at Morris Grange, near Richmond Yorkshire, 15th Dec., 1868.
HEATHCOTE, Henry	9th July, 1805, 30th Regt. ; aptd. to 42nd Regt., 3rd June, 1806 ;	28th Aug., 1806 ;	19th Oct., 1809, 60th Regt. ; aptd. to 10th Foot, 23rd Nov., 1809 ; aptd. a Sub-Inspector of Militia in the Ionian Islands, 20th May, 1819 ;	Major, 31st March, 1825, 27th Regt. ; exchd. to 88th Regt., 6th Oct., 1825 ; died at Newcastle, Staffordshire, 5th May, 1829.
HELYAR, Charles	26th Oct., 1775, 32nd Regt. ;	8th May, 1776 ;	1st Feb., 1780 ;	Killed at the Cowpens, 17th Jan., 1781.
HELYAR, John	1779, 1st Foot ;	26th Feb., 1780 ;	…	Retired 28th Jan., 1784.
HENRY, George	From Lieut. Armagh Militia	25th Oct., 1807 ;	9th Sept., 1813 ;	Killed at New Orleans, 8th Jan., 1815.
HERBERT, Dennis Served on the continent under Lord Moira and the Duke of York ; engaged during the Carib war in St. Vincents ; at Port au Prince in St. Domingo ; and at Fort Irois during the three months' siege ; present at Copenhagen in 1807.	Jan., 1794, 40th Regt. ;	4th Sept., 1794, 40th Regt. ;	21st Feb., 1799, 10th West India Regt. ;	Major, 30th Jan., 1800, Royal Tarbert Fencibles ; aptd. to 7th, 15th Aug., 1804 ; Lieut. Col. and Inspecting Field Officer of Militia in Nova Scotia, 28th Jan., 1808 ; Col., 4th June, 1814 ; placed on h. p., 17th March, 1817 ; Maj. Gen, 27th May, 1825 ; Lieut. Gen., 28th Jan., 1838 ; Gen., 20th June, 1854 ; died 1861.
HERBERT, Geo. Flower *Medal for Sebastopol. Turkish Medal.* and 8th Sept. ; wounded during the throwing up an intrenchment in the HERON-MAXWELL, W. H. Stopford	15th Oct., 1850, 31st Regt. ; Served with the 31st Regt. in the including the siege and fall of Sebastopol, and attacks of the 18th June employed as an Assist. Engineer in eight gun battery, right attack.	10th Dec., 1852, 31st Regt. ; Crimea from the 22nd May, 1855, intopol, and attacks of the 18th June employed as an Assist. Engineer in 3rd Aug., 1874.	9th Sept., 1855, 31st Regt. ; placed on h. p. of it, Nov., 1855 ; aptd. to 7th, 23rd Oct., 1857 ;	Major, 14th Oct., 1868 ; Lieut. Col., 6th Sept., 1873.

Alphabetical List of Officers of the Royal Fusiliers.

NAME.	ENSIGN, &c.	LIEUTENANT.	CAPTAIN.	HIGHER RANKS AND REMARKS.
HERVEY, Frederick A.	...	26th July, 1799 ;	11th June, 1801 ; aptd. to 20th Regt., 14th Feb., 1805 ;	Retired 1809.
HERVEY, Stephen	...	15th Aug., 1775 ;	...	Retired 8th May, 1776.
HESKETH, Thomas	... 1765, 28th Regt. ;	21st March, 1766 ;	27th Oct., 1772 ;	Retired 1777.
HEWITT, Matthew	...	...	5th March, 1708, Regt. ; aptd. to 7th, 1st Jan., 1736 ;	Retired 9th Oct., 1747.
HEYLAND, John Rowley *Medal for Sebastopol ; Sardinian Medal; Turkish Medal; 5th Class of the Medjidie.*	8th Jan., 1824, Ceylon Rifles ;	7th Jan., 1826, unatt.; exchd. to 87th Regt., 2nd Feb., 1826 ; placed on h. p. of it, Sept., 1827 ; aptd. to 6th Foot, 1st Nov., 1827 ; aptd. to 61st Regt., 20th Dec., 1827 ;	12th April, 1831, unatt.; exchd. to 35th Regt., 22nd Feb., 1833 ; exchd. to h. p. unatt., 23rd June, 1848 ; aptd. to 7th, 29th Dec., 1854 ;	Bt. Major, 9th Nov., 1846 ; Bt. Lieut. Col., 20th June, 1854 ; Major, 21st Dec., 1855, unatt. ; aptd. to Military Train, 20th Feb., 1857 ; retired 30th Mar., 1858 ; aptd. Barrack Master at Jersey.
HEYLIN, Charles	...	9th Feb., 1751 ;	...	Died or retired 1757.
HEYLIN, John	...	17th Jan., 1739—40 ;	9th Feb., 1751 ;	Died or retired 1759.
HIBBERT, Francis	12th Dec., 1857, Regt. ;	12th Nov., 1858, 24th Regt.; placed on h. p. of it ; aptd. to 35th Bengal N. I., 1863 ; re-aptd. to 24th Regt., 1st Dec., 1863 ;	1st April, 1870, unatt.; aptd. to 7th, 17th Aug., 1870.	...
HIBBERT, Hugh Robert *Medal for the Crimea ; Legion of Honour; Sardinian Medal; 5th Class of the Medjidie ; Turkish Medal.*	28th Sept., 1847, 39th Regt.; Served the campaign of 1854-5 siege of Sebastopol, including sortie severely wounded.	16th Aug., 1854 ; with the Fusiliers; present at the of 26th Oct. assaults of the Redan	22nd Dec., 1854 ; Alma (wounded) and Inkerman, on the 18th June and 8th Sept.	Bt. Major, 2nd Nov., 1855, Major, 23rd Oct., 1857 ; Lieut. Col., 1st Dec., 1863 ; Col., 1st Dec., 1868 ; retired on h. p. of the Regt., 28th Oct., 1871 ; aptd. Lieut. Col. of the 9th Brigade Depôt, Feb., 1874.
HICKIE, James Francis *Medal for Sebastopol ; Turkish Medal.*	21st April, 1853, 59th Regt.; Served with the Regiment in the on the 18th June, severely wounded	12th Jan., 1855 ; Crimea from the 17th June, 1855, at the attack on the 8th Sept.	3rd Aug., 1855 ; present at the assault on the Redan	Major, 1st Dec., 1863 ; Lieut. Col., 29th May, 1869, unatt. ; aptd. to 6th D. G., 6th July, 1870 ; retired same day.
HIGGINS, Edward	...	15th Aug., 1719.	...	Died at Presteign, Radnorshire, 1st May, 1835.
HIGGINS, Matthew	19th June, 1811, 48th Regt. ;	13th Dec., 1812, 4th Gar. Batt. ; exchd. to 7th, 3rd Dec., 1812 ; placed on h. p. of the Regt., 25th March, 1817 ; exchd. back to f. p. of it, 16th Dec., 1819 ;	3rd Mar., 1825 ; exchd. to 27th Regt., 21st April, 1825 ; exchd. to h. p, unatt., 28th Sept., 1832 ;	
HILL, John	10th June, 1772, 13th Regt. ;	5th Dec., 1774 ;	...	Died Feb., 1775.
HILL, Richard	16th Oct., 1704.			
HILL, John Lee	17th March, 1761, 13th Foot;	14th March, 1764 ;	29th Nov., 1765, 27th Regt.	
HILL, Rowland	15th Feb., 1861 ;	15th Mar., 1864 ; exchd. to 39th Regt., 9th Dec., 1864.		
HOARE, William Tesse	12th Jan., 1844, 59th Regt. ;	1st May, 1846, 59th Regt. ; exchd. to 7th, 28th May, 1847;	6th June, 1854 ; exchd. to 15th Foot, 15th Sept., 1854 ;	Retired 15th Dec., 1854.
HOBART, Beauchamp Robert	7th July, 1869 ; aptd. to 66th Regt., 18th Aug., 1869;	28th Oct., 1871, 66th Regt.	...	...
HOBART, Geo. Vere	10th Sept., 1784, 35th Regt. ;	1st Oct., 1789 ;	July, 1791, Indept. Compy. ;	Retired ; aptd. Lieut. Gov. of Grenada ; died there 5th Nov., 1802.
HOBSON	...	May, 1795.	...	
HOBSON, James St. Clair	16th Jan., 1847, 30th Regt. ;	10th Mar., 1854 ;	...	Killed in the attack on the Redan, 18th June, 1855.
HOLBOURNE, Francis	...	7th April, 1808 ; aptd. Ensign 3rd Foot Guards, 22nd June, 1809 ;	...	Died of wounds received in the sortie from Bayonne, April 14th, 1814.
HOLDEN, John Fish	...	12th July, 1810 ;	...	Retired 9th April, 1812.
HOLLAND, Fredl. Byam Braham	...	29th July, 1795 ; exchd. to h. p. of 6th Regt. Irish Brigade, 25th July, 1799 ; aptd. to 69th Regt., 21st Aug., 1800 ; exchd. to h. p. of 46th Regt., 1803 ;	...	Died at Quebec, 14th Sept., 1836.

Alphabetical List of Officers of the Royal Fusiliers.

NAME.	ENSIGN, &c.	LIEUTENANT.	CAPTAIN.	HIGHER RANKS AND REMARKS.
HOLLAND, John Frederick	...	24th June, 1795; exchd. to h. p. of Irish Brigade, 1799;	...	Aptd. Barrack Master at Prince Edward's Island, 1802.
HOLLYLAND, Thomas	...	11th Jan., 1715.	...	
HOLMES, William Prescod	1st Mar., 1864;	18th Dec., 1867; exchd. to 101st Regt., 17th Feb, 1869.	...	
HOLYOAKE, Geo. Wm. Henry	5th Feb., 1858;	16th July, 1861;	...	Retired 30th Dec., 1862.
HOME, Walter	28th Sept., 1757, 4th Regt.;	9th Jan., 1760, 4th Regt.; exchd. to 7th, 12th June, 1760;	25th May, 1772;	Major, 28th April, 1782, 42nd Regt.; retired 16th March, 1791.
HOPE, *Hon.* Alexander	...	8th April, 1826;	...	Died on board the "Lady Mary Pelham," on passage from Corfu to England, 24th Oct., 1827.
HOPE, Charles Errol *Medal for Sebastopol; Turkish Medal.* Served with the Fusiliers in the topol, and assault of the Redan on	25th Aug., 1854, 10th Foot; aptd. to 7th, 16th Jan., 1855; Crimea from the 7th July, 1855, the 8th Sept.	26th July, 1855; including the siege and fall of Sebas-	17th Nov., 1863; exchd. to 25th Regt., 1st Mar., 1864;	Aptd. Adjt. of the 46th Middlesex Rifle Vols., 14th June, 1873.
HOPE, William	4th Nov., 1824, 45th Regt.; aptd. to 81st Regt., 16th Dec., 1824;	27th Oct., 1825, 96th Regt.;	14th Feb., 1828, 96th Regt.; aptd. to 7th, 2nd April, 1829; exchd. to h. p., unatt., 23rd May, 1845; exchd. to 89th Regt., 23rd Jan., 1846;	Bt. Major, 23rd Nov., 1841; retired 23rd January, 1846; aptd. Clerk to the Council of the Cape of Good Hope, 1846; afterwards Auditor General; died at Cape Town, 3rd Oct., 1850.
V.C. HOPE, William *Medal for the Crimea.*	5th Jan., 1855; Served at the siege of Sebastopol ries, 7th June, and assault of the	23rd March, 1855; from the 31st May, 1855, including Redan on the 18th June.	... the attack and capture of the Quar-	Retired 3rd March, 1857.
HOPSON, Wm. Hopson	4th July, 1839, Ceylon Rifles;	28th Dec., 1841;	24th Dec., 1847; exchd. to 26th Regt., 1st Dec., 1848;	Major, 5th Sept., 1856, 26th Regt.; retired 8th Jan., 1858; died at Surbiton, 12th April, 1866.
HORTON, Samuel	...	8th Dec., 1802;	16th Jan., 1806; exchd. to 56th Regt., 25th May, 1808.	
HOSACK, John	17th Nov., 1863; aptd. to 14th Regt., 4th Dec., 1863;	6th July, 1867, 14th Regt.	...	
HOWARD, William	...	17th Dec., 1756;	...	Retired 1759.
HOWE, Hayfield Graham	...	24th June, 1795;	...	Died 1806.
HUFFUM, Benjamin	12th May, 1705.			
HUGGUP, Robert	...	11th May, 1811; exchd. to h. p. of the Regt., 10th Dec., 1818;	14th July, 1804;	Died 7th Feb., 1831.
HUGHES, Dillon	21st July, 1800, 46th Regt.;	30th June, 1801, 46th Regt.; placed on h. p. of it, 1802; aptd. to 18th Foot, 9th July, 1803; exchd. to 7th, 5th March, 1807;	...	Died 1810.
HUGHES, Wm. Carlyon	...	14th March, 1771;	12th Jan., 1779, 60th Regt.; re-aptd. to 7th, 19th Oct., 1780;	Bt. Major, 1st March, 1794; Major, 20th June, 1795; Lieut. Col., 22nd July, 1795, 87th Regt.; Col., 28th April, 1802; died 1808.
HULME, William Served in the Pindaree campaign, Dec., 1817; he again commanded	27th Sept., 1803, Nova Scotia Fencibles; and commanded the flank companies them when the Fort of Fulnair was	26th June, 1805, 1st Foot; in the general action of the 21st stormed, 27th Feb., 1818.	26th Aug., 1813, 1st Foot; placed on h. p. of it, 25th June, 1817; exchd. back to f. p. of it, 25th Aug., 1820; exchd. to 7th, 27th June, 1822; aptd. to 96th Regt., 29th Jan., 1824;	Bt. Major, 23rd Dec., 1817; Major, 9th March, 1834, 96th Regt.; Bt. Lieut. Col., 10th Jan., 1837; Lieut. Col., 18th Aug., 1848, 96th Regt.; retired 15th June, 1849.
HULME, William Browne	...	11th Oct., 1796; retired on h. p. of Irish Brigade, 26th Aug., 1800; aptd. to Staff Corps, 3rd Oct., 1805;	31st May, 1809, half pay of Staff Corps;	Died 8th Nov., 1841.

Alphabetical List of Officers of the Royal Fusiliers.

NAME.	ENSIGN, &c.	LIEUTENANT.	CAPTAIN.	HIGHER RANKS AND REMARKS.
HUNT, Arthur	10th Oct., 1846, 54th Regt.;	30th Sept., 1850, 54th Regt.; exchd. to 7th, 22nd APRIL, 1853;	...	Retired 3rd March, 1854.
HUNT, John Edwd.	31st Jan., 1805, 59th Regt.	26th Feb., 1806, 26th Regt.; exchd. to 4th Gar. Batt., 8th Aug., 1811; exchd. to 7th, 7th May, 1812; exchd. to 94th Regt., 10th Nov., 1813; exchd. to h. p. of 47th Regt., 23rd Feb., 1815;	...	Died in Dublin, 15th July, 1827.
HUNTER, David	6th June, 1788, 14th Regt.;	24th Jan., 1791, Indept. Compy., placed on h. p. of it; exchd. to 16th Regt., 11th May, 1791;	2nd April, 1793, Indept. Compy., aptd. to 93rd Regt., 30th Oct., 1793;	Major, APRIL, 1795; Lieut. Col, 17th April, 1795, Angus Fencibles; placed on h. p., 1802; Col., 29th April, 1802; Major Gen., 25th Oct., 1809; Lieut. Gen., 4th June, 1814; Gen., 10th Jan., 1837; died in London, 11th March, 1846.
HUNTER, Geo. Orby	...	11th FEB., 1785;	...	Retired July, 1790.
HURLOCK, Henry Francis	31st Dec., 1864, 87th Regt.;	14th Sept., 1866, 87th Regt.; exchd. to 7th, 16th JULY, 1868;	...	Retired 29th May, 1869.
HUTCHINS, John	...	20th JUNE, 1759;	...	Died or Retired, 1761.
HUTCHINSON, Fred. Sydney	14th Aug., 1828, 71st Regt.;	28th DEC., 1832;	9th JUNE, 1838;	Retired 7th June, 1839; aptd. Major in the East York Militia, 1st Feb., 1855.
HUTCHISON, Joseph	Peninsula, present at Albuera, the Pyrenees.	26th APRIL, 1810; present at Aldea de Ponte, severely wounded at Salamanca, Vittoria, led	8th APRIL, 1825;	Major, 7th SEPT., 1832; retired 6th May, 1836, died 11th April, 1839.
INGLIS, Raymond ; *Turkish Medal for Sebastopol; Turkish Medal.* Served in the Crimea with the 18th 18th June, 1855.	22nd Nov., 1843, 2nd Foot; Royal Irish from the 30th Dec., 1854,	11th Feb., 1848, 2nd Foot; including the siege of Sebastopol,	15th March, 1850, 2nd Foot; exchd. to 18th Foot, 24th March, 1854; assault and capture of the cemetery,	Bt. Major, 6th June, 1856; Major, 19th Sept., 1856, unatt.; aptd. to a Depôt Batt., 18th Aug., 1858; exchd. to 7th, 24th DEC., 1858; retired 13th May, 1859.
IRWIN, Edward Present with the 2nd Batt. at Busaco.	...	1st DEC., 1808;	...	Killed at Albuera, 16th May, 1811.
JACKSON, Joshua Served with the regiment through- out the campaigns in Flanders and	...	1st JUNE, 1689; the war of the Spanish Succession. 15th MAY, 1718.	Occurs 1708.	
JANSEN, Bryan	3rd MAY, 1705.			
JEFFREYS, Thomas	...			
JENNER, Robert Fred. Lascelles	4th April, 1845, 41st Regt.;	7th July, 1846, 41st Regt.;	27th Dec., 1850, 41st Regt.; exchd. to 7th, 9th SEPT., 1851; exchd. to h. p. of the Regt., 31st July, 1857;	Retired 25th March, 1853.
JERVOIS, Edwyn Stanhope	13th July, 1849, Ceylon Rifles; aptd. to 10th Foot, 9th May, 1851;	28th MARCH, 1854;	16th Nov., 1855;	Apt. Commandant of the Convalescent Establishment at Yarmouth.
JODRELL, Thomas	...	11th MAY, 1804;	22nd May, 1806, Nova Scotia Fencibles; aptd. to 24th Regt., 12th July, 1806; aptd. to 35th Regt., 25th July, 1806.	
JOHNSON, Benjamin	...	30th AUG., 1756;	28th Oct., 1760, 97th Regt.; placed on h. p. of it, 1763; aptd. to 18th Regt., 8th Oct., 1767;	Died in Ireland, 29th Aug., 1775.
JOHNSON, Godschall	...	21st FEB., 1805; aptd. to 9th L. D., Feb., 1805; aptd. to 16th L. D., 13th June, 1805;	...	Retired 1806.
JOHNSON, Guy	...	9th AUG., 1718;	...	
JOHNSON, John	Occurs 1695.			Out of the Regt., 26th Sept., 1726.
JOHNSON, Richard Landed with the 2nd Batt. at Lisbon, 5th April, 1809; present at Ponte, Salamanca (severely wounded),	From Lieut. Armagh Militia; 28th JULY, 1808; Talavera, Busaco, Albuera (slightly wounded), Vittoria, Pyrenees			Retired June, 1814.

Alphabetical List of Officers of the Royal Fusiliers.

NAME.	ENSIGN, &c.	LIEUTENANT.	CAPTAIN.	HIGHER RANKS AND REMARKS.
JOHNSTONE, James *Silver Medal for* 14, 15, 22, 25.	29th Dec., 1808, 50th Regt.;	30th Aug., 1810, 50th Regt.;	10th June, 1813, 60th Regt.; exchd. to 7th, 16th DEC., 1813; placed on h. p. of the Regt., 25th Feb., 1816;	Died at Torquay, 17th Dec., 1852.
JOHNSTON, Richard	14th Nov., 1770, Scots Greys		19th Aug., 1778, 13th Foot;	Died or retired 1782.
JOHNSTON, Robert Joined the Regt. in the Peninsula in 1811, present at the affair of Aldea de Ponte.	From Lieut. North Devon Militia;	26th FEB., 1772; aptd. to 13th Foot, 5th DEC., 1774; 13th DEC., 1810;	…	Retired 27th Aug., 1812.
JOHNSTON, Stephen B. Landed with the 1st Batt. at Lisbon, 27th July, 1810, present at Busaco.	1st Oct., 1794, 65th Regt.; exchd. to h. p. of 79th Regt., 21st June, 1797; aptd. to 88th Regt, 20th Feb., 1806;	8th JAN., 1807;	…	Killed at Albuera, 16th May, 1811.
JONES, Benjamin	…	15th OCT., 1778;	17th Nov., 1719;	Major, 20th June, 1727; died July, 1733.
JONES, Geo. Wm. Dyall	…	…	…	Retired 24th Aug., 1792.
JONES, Henry Ireson Landed with the 2nd Batt. in the Peninsula.	44th Regt.;	29th OCT., 1807;	…	Superseded Oct., 1811; died March, 1812, at Elvas of wounds received at Albuera, 16th May, 1811.
V. C. JONES, Henry Mitchell *Medal for the Crimea; Knight of the Legion of Honour; Turkish Medal.*	18th April, 1849, 18th Foot; exchd. to 60th Regt., 9th Sept., 1850;	17th MAR., 1854;	19th AUG., 1855;	Retired 28th Aug., 1857.
JONES, Lewis John Fillis *Medal for the Crimea; 5th Class of the Medjidie; Turkish Medal; Medal for India.* present at the battle of Inkerman April (wounded), and 9th May, captured. on the 18th June (very severely wounded in all the actions at Cawnpore, under subjugation of Oude (Brevet of Major).	Served the Eastern campaign of Sebastopol, including sortie on 9th assault on the Redan, 8th Sept., and 14th JULY, 1854; the first Ensign ever aptd. to the Regt.; Served with the Royal Fusiliers in (wounded), siege of Sebastopol, 5th ture of the Quarries, 7th June wounded). Served in the 88th Regt. Gen. Wyndham, also as at the action of	1854-55, present at the battle of Alma May, attack and capture of the gerously wounded. 8th DEC., 1854; the Crimea from the 20th Oct., 1854, cluding sorties of the 26th Oct., 5th (wounded), and assault of the Redan during the Indian Mutiny; present Bhognapore, capture of Calpee, and	(severely wounded) and siege of Quarries, 7th June (wounded), and 27th MAY, 1856; placed on h. p. of the Regt., Nov., 1856; exchd. to 88th Regt., 17th July, 1857; exchd. to 8th Foot, 31st Jan., 1860; aptd. Adjt. of a Depôt Batt., 10th June, 1861;	Bt. Major, 16th April, 1861; Major, 29th June, 1866, 4th Depôt Batt.; placed on h. p.; retired 21st Jan., 1872.
JONES, Matthew	…	20th JULY, 1708.	…	Superseded Nov., 1805.
JONES, William	Aug., 1804, 81st Regt.;	7th SEPT., 1804;	…	Superseded Jan., 1812.
JONES, Watkin H.	Lieut. Royal Montgomery Mil., 20th Aug., 1803;	6th APRIL, 1809;	…	
JULIAN, George	…	12th MARCH, 1754;	…	Died or retired, 1756.
KAYE, Robert	16th Nov., 1839, 70th Regt.; aptd. to Qr. Mas. of it, 2nd Sept., 1840; reverted to formerrank, 29th Oct., 1841;	27th SEPT., 1844;	…	Died in Manchester, 1st April, 1851.
KEANE, *Hon.* John Arbuthnot	11th Sept., 1835, 81st Regt.;	17th SEPT., 1839; aptd. to 33rd Regt., 15th Dec., 1840;	20th Nov., 1846, 56th Regt.; aptd. to 91st Regt, 8th Jan., 1847; aptd. to Rifle Brigade, 15th Jan., 1847;	Retired 9th June, 1848.
KEANE, William Paer	…	23rd APRIL, 1812; placed on h. p. of the Regt., 1817; aptd. to 21st Regt., 25th Sept., 1817	…	Died in the West Indies, 11th Jan., 1823.
KEATS, W. McGeachy	14th Oct., 1842, 75th Regt.;	21st April, 1846, 75th Regt.; exchd. to 84th Regt., 26th Nov., 1847;	6th Nov., 1857; aptmt. cancelled, 11th Dec., 1857; 26th Sept., 1857, 84th Regt.;	Retired 21st Feb, 1860.
KEIGHTLEY, Robt. H. H.	2nd April, 1841, 93rd Regt.; exchd. to 76th Regt., 21st May, 1841;	11th Nov., 1845, 76th Regt.; aptd. to 7th, 17th DEC., 1852;	…	Retired 28th March, 1854.
KELLETT, William	…	26th DEC., 1726; exchd. to Coldstream Guards, 8th May, 1730;	9th Feb., 1740—1, Coldstream Guards;	Died of wounds received on 11th May, 1745, at Fontenoy.
KEMPSON, Carteret Houstoun	4th APRIL, 1856;	22nd APRIL, 1859; exchd. to 1st Drags., 18th Feb, 1862;	…	Retired 31st March, 1863.
KEMPTHORNE, Rupert	…	17th JUNE, 1685.	…	

Alphabetical List of Officers of the Royal Fusiliers.

NAME.	ENSIGN, &c.	LIEUTENANT.	CAPTAIN.	HIGHER RANKS AND REMARKS.
KENNEDY, Thomas Entered the Militia in 1795; joined the 36th Regt. as Captain with him. In Oct., 1802, the officers serving with temporary rank were reduced to h. p.; on the war again breaking out, he offered to resign his h. p. Captaincy for an Ensigncy with the Fusiliers. Served at Copenhagen in 1807, and on his return to England he was accepted, and was aptd. to the Fusiliers. In 1808 he was sent to Spain to organise the Spanish troops.	From Capt., temp. rank, 36th Regt.; upwards of 100 men having volunteered to serve with permanent rank, and the offer being accepted, he was aptd. to the Sicilian Regt. and removed to the 96th. In	4th Dec., 1805;	18th Feb., 1808, Sicilian Regt.; aptd. to 96th Regt., 3rd Mar, 1808; to h. p. of it, July, 1811;	Died at Guernsey, 18th Dec., 1849.
KEOGH, Peter	24th April, 1797, 14th L. D.;	23rd May, 1800, 14th L. D.;	14th Nov., 1805, 14th L. D.; exchd. to 7th, 21st June, 1810; aptd. to 7th Vet. Batt, 17th April, 1811; reduced, 1814, placed on retired f. p. of it; aptd. to 5th Vet. Batt, 25th May, 1815; reduced 24th May, 1816, placed on retired f. p. of it; aptd. to 1st Vet. Batt., 1st Nov., 1819; disbanded 1821, placed on retired f. p. of it;	Died in Dublin 1830.
KERR, Henry *Medal for N. W. Frontier.* Served with the Fusiliers in the Frontier war of 1863, with the Eusafzye Field force; present at the destruction of Lalloo on the 15th Dec.; also ended in the complete rout of the bastopol, from the 24th Nov. to the end fence of the Sungrahs, at the Umbeyla in the action at Umbeyla and destruction enemy and submission of the hill of the war. Also in the Indian N.W. Pass, and at the attack at the foot of the tion of the village at the foot of the tribes on the 17th.	26th Jan., 1855;	27th July, 1855;	11th April, 1862.	
KEYSER, Fred. Charles	28th May, 1858;	4th March, 1862,	18th April, 1868.	
KING, Edward Hammond	16th May, 1851, Newfoundland Vet. Comp.; aptd. to 94th Regt., 31st Oct., 1851; aptd. to Ceylon Rifles, 3rd March, 1854; aptd. to 27th Regt., 7th April, 1854;	2nd Feb., 1855; aptd. Paymaster 59th Regt., 10th Aug., 1855; reverted to Lieut. 83rd Regt., 28th Aug., 1857;	...	Retired 16th Oct., 1857.
KING, Fielder	7th Nov., 1793, Indept. Comp.;	1st Mar., 1794, 84th Regt.;	8th March, 1794, 84th Regt.;	Major, 18th Sept., 1794, 84th Regt.; reduced 1795; retained on f. p. of it; aptd. to 98th Regt., 17th May, 1796; Lieut. Col., 2nd Mar., 1797, 98th Regt.; altered to 91st, 1798; aptd. Lieut. Col. Comm. Cape Regt., 25th June, 1801; placed on h. p. of it, 1802; aptd. to 47th Regt., 9th July, 1803; aptd. to 7th, Jan., 1804; retired April, 1804.
KING, George *Gold Medal for Badajoz.* *Silver Medal for 9, 18, 19.* of Aldea de Ponte, Badajoz, Salamanca, Orthes, and Toulouse.	25th Jan., 1801, 29th L. D.; Landed with the 2nd Batt. at Lisbon, 5th April, 1809; present at 11th July, 1840, 2nd Foot;	18th Feb., 1802, 25th L. D.; 29th April, 1842, 2nd Foot; aptd. to 7th, 27th Feb., 1846; exchd. to 59th Regt., 28th May, 1847;	18th April, 1805; Talavera, Busaco, Albuera, the affair 29th April, 1853, 59th Regt.;	Major, 14th May, 1812; killed at New Orleans, 8th Jan., 1815.
KING, John				Retired 15th June, 1860.
KING, John Duncan Served the Walcheren expedition, 1809, present at the siege of Flushing; served in the Peninsula; at Aldea de Ponte; Fuente Guinaldo; affair at action of Osma; severely wounded in the right shoulder in the Pyrenees, 28th July, 1813.	28th Aug., 1806, 71st Regt.;	18th Feb., 1808, 71st Regt.; exchd. to 1st Foot, 28th July, 1808; exchd. to 7th, 13th June, 1811; exchd. to h. p. of 8th Foot, 20th April, 1820; exchd. to 75th Regt., 14th May, 1829;	16th March, 1830, 75th Regt.; exchd. to h. p, unatt., 28th Dec., 1830;	Aptd. a Military Knight of Windsor; died there, 21st Aug., 1863.
KING, Robert	...	31st Aug., 1807,	...	Not in Army List of 1810.
KINNEER, Francis	...	2nd Oct., 1755; Capt. Lieut., 21st March, 1762;	14th March, 1764;	Major, 7th Oct., 1777, 63rd Regt.; retired 10th Aug., 1778.
KIRK, Charles Edmondson *Medal for the Crimea.* Served the Eastern campaign of 1854-5, including the battles of Alma	5th Nov., 1847, 68th Regt.;	2nd Jan., 1852; aptd. to 1st Foot, 28th May, 1852; present at the siege of Sebastopol, and Inkerman,	15th May, 1855, 1st Foot;	Retired 9th Jan., 1857; died in Bath, 29th July, 1857.

Alphabetical List of Officers of the Royal Fusiliers.

NAME.	ENSIGN, &C.	LIEUTENANT.	CAPTAIN.	HIGHER RANKS AND REMARKS.
KIRWAN, Andrew Hyacinth	...	5th Aug., 1813; placed on h. p. of the Regt., 25th Feb., 1816; exchd. to 66th Regt., 4th July, 1822;	29th Oct., 1825, 66th Regt.; exchd. to h. p., unatt., 25th Nov., 1828; exchd. to 95th Regt., 25th May, 1855; 23rd Oct., 1860, 25th Regt.;	Bt. Major, 28th June, 1838; Bt. Lieut. Col., 11th Nov., 1851; retired 25th May, 1855; died at No. 3, Promenade Terrace, Cheltenham, 3rd Aug., 1872.
KIRWAN, George	10th Aug., 1855;	3rd March, 1857; exchd. to 25th Regt., 1st May, 1857;	...	Retired 2nd Aug., 1871.
KIRWAN, John T. Macan	23rd June, 1869;	28th Oct., 1871;	...	Retired 29th Oct., 1873.
KIRWAN, Richard *Silver Medal for Talavera. Severely wounded at Talavera.*	From Lieut. Galway Militia; Captured by the French after that action, and detained as a prisoner until the end of the war.	27th Oct., 1807;	16th March, 1815; placed on h. p. of the Regt., 25th Feb., 1816; exchd. to 6th Foot, 31st May, 1821; placed on h. p. of it, Oct., 1821; exchd. to 94th, 9th Dec., 1824; exchd. to h. p., unatt., 24th July, 1828;	Died at Brighton, 6th Jan., 1853.
KIRWAN, Richd. Andrew Hyacinth	5th July, 1831, 5th Foot;	26th Sept., 1834;	...	Retired 28th Aug., 1838.
KNOWLES, Robert *Present at the affair of Aldea de Ponte, Badajos (slightly wounded),*	16th Oct., 1807;	8th May, 1811; Salamanca (severely wounded),	Vittoria.	Killed in the affair of Roncesvalles, 25th July, 1813.
KNOX, Richard	24th June, 1802, h. p. of 2nd D. G.; exchd. to 25th L. D., 24th May, 1804;	1st Nov., 1871, 18th Hussars. 7th Dec., 1804; exchd. to 18th L. D., 30th Jan., 1805;	...	Died 4th July, 1844.
KNUDSON, St. George	18th Sept., 1780, 16th Regt.;	25th Feb., 1783, 104th Regt.; aptd. to 7th,	1st Mar., 1783, 94th Regt., placed on h. p. of it same year;	Died or retired 1816.
KORTRIGHT, John		1783;		
KYNASTON, Roger	24th Sept., 1743;	30th April, 1748;	...	Died, Nov., 1752.
KYNASTON, Thomas	...	13th March, 1805;	...	Retired 17th Dec., 1807.
LAKE, Warwick, *Viscount*	...	27th July, 1815; placed on h. p. of the Regt., 25th Feb., 1816;	...	Retired Oct., 1833; died in Park Street, Grosvenor Square, 24th June, 1848.
LAMONT, Archibald	...	24th Oct., 1761, 114th Regt.; aptd. to 7th, 20th Mar., 1764;	...	Died or retired 1765.
LAMONT, John	...	26th Aug., 1759, 105th Regt.; exchd. to 7th, 2nd April, 1762.	...	...
LAMPHIER, Joseph	From Ens. 1st West York Militia;	1st Sept., 1807; aptd. to 2nd Gar. Batt. 25th Aug., 1808; placed on h. p. of it, 6th Dec., 1814;	...	Died 5th Nov., 1838.
LANE, Charles Leveson	16th Mar., 1860, 1st Drags.	8th Aug., 1862, 1st Drags.; exchd. to 7th, 3rd March, 1863;	...	Retired 16th Oct., 1867.
LANE, William	...	11th Oct., 1779;	...	Retired 26th Jan., 1785.
LANGFORD, C. W. W., *Lord*	5th Aug., 1842, 85th Regt.;	16th Feb., 1844;	...	Retired 27th Feb., 1846; died at Castletown, Co. Dublin, 19th July, 1854.
LANGHORNE, Alfred R. M.	1st May, 1866;	10th May, 1871; exchd. to 52nd Regt., 28th Oct., 1871.	...	Retired 10th July, 1866; aptd. Capt. 2nd Somerset Militia, 29th Mar, 1867.
LANGWORTHY, Vincent Upton	3rd Feb., 1858;	31st Oct., 1860; exchd. to 100th Regt., 20th Feb, 1863; exch. cancelled, 30th June, 1863; exchd. to 73rd Regt., 6th Feb, 1866;	...	
LA TOUCHE, CECIL	1st April, 1824, 11th Foot;	13th Aug., 1825;	29th June, 1830;	Retired 12th July, 1833; died at Glen Southwell, Co. Dublin, Jan., 1835.
LAYARD, Anthony Lewis *Landed with the Fusiliers in throughout the war, returning with*	23rd Jan., 1769, 70th Regt.; Canada in 1773; present at the siege it to] England at the peace of 1783.	4th April, 1771; of Quebec. Served with the Regt. Commanded the Regiment in Halifax	9th June, 1778; at New York, Charlestown, and in 1798, and afterwards in Bermuda.	Major, 13th July, 1791; Bt. Lieut. Col., 13th April, 1795; Col., 29th April, 1802; retired on h. p. of 54th Regt., Jan., 1804; Major Gen., 25th Oct., 1809; aptd. Col. 2nd Vet. Batt., 22nd Feb., 1810; Lieut. Gen., 4th June, 1814; died 1823.

Alphabetical List of Officers of the Royal Fusiliers.

NAME.	ENSIGN, &c.	LIEUTENANT.	CAPTAIN.	HIGHER RANKS AND REMARKS.
LAYARD, Brownlow Villiers	30th May, 1794, 80th Regt.;	16th April, 1795;	12th Jan., 1805, 23rd Regt.	Retired 16th June, 1803.
LEAHY, John Thomas *Gold Medal for Badajoz.*	...	24th Oct., 1799, 4th Foot; aptd. to 69th Regt., 14th Jan., 1802;	...	Bt. Major, 27th April, 1812; Major, 17th June, 1813, 23rd Regt.; placed on h. p. of the Regt., 25th Dec., 1814; exchd. to 7th, 25th May, 1815; placed on h. p. of the Regt., 25th Feb., 1816; exchd. to 21st Regt., 22nd April, 1819; Lieut. Col., 24th Aug., 1821, 21st Regt.; retired 4th Dec., 1835; died at Sydney, Australia, from the effects of an accidental fall, 1839.
LEESON, Aug. Johnnes	14th Aug., 1850, 31st Regt.;	21st May, 1852, 31st Regt.; exchd. to 7th, 30th July, 1852; exchd. to 12th Foot, 24th Feb., 1854;	13th April, 1858, 12th Foot;	Retired 16th May, 1865.
LESTER, Thomas Young Served with the Regt. throughout the Peninsula War; wounded both at Albuera and Badajoz.	...	30th May, 1810; placed on h. p. of the Regt., 25th Oct., 1821;	...	Died 28th Feb., 1829.
L'ESTRANGE, Alured Henry	...	4th April, 1811;	...	Retired 16th Oct., 1817; died 1820.
L'ESTRANGE, Thomas Served throughout the Peninsula War.	26th Oct., 1775, 54th Regt.;	11th Aug., 1778; the Cowpens.	23rd April, 1788; exchd. to 4th Gar. Batt., 25th Sept., 1807; aptd. to 1st Gar. Batt., 14th April, 1808;	Bt. Major, 3rd May, 1796; Bt. Lieut. Col., 29th April, 1802; Col., 4th June, 1811; Inspecting Field Officer of the Newry Recruiting District; Maj. Gen., 4th June, 1814; Lieut. Gen., 22nd July, 1830; died at Highgate, 8th Mar., 1845.
L'ESTRANGE, Torriano Francis Served throughout the war of the American Revolution; wounded at	20th Oct., 1814, 5th Foot; placed on h. p. of it, 25th Feb., 1816; exchd. to 34th Regt., 22nd Aug., 1816;	16th Oct., 1817; exchd. to h. p. of Coldstream Guards, 16th Nov., 1820;	...	Aptd. Capt. Royal Cumberland Militia, 15th Jan., 1853; died at Warwick House, New Wandsworth, 13th Dec., 1867.
Le Geyt, Philip	5th April, 1732, Regt.;	22nd Mar., 1740;	9th April, 1748, Regt.;	Retired March, 1753.
Le Maistre, Francis	...	28th Oct., 1760, 98th Regt.; placed on h. p. of it, 1763; aptd. to 7th, 18th July, 1766;	6th May, 1776, Regt.; to 8th Foot, 5th Nov., 1776;	Died or retired 1781.
Lennox, *Lord* Frederick	3rd Sept., 1818, 91st Regt.; aptd. to 62nd Regt., 21st Jan., 1819;	24th June, 1824;	24th Sept., 1825, unatt.; re-aptd. to 7th, 19th Sept., 1826;	Retired 25th June, 1829; died at Chichester, 19th Oct., 1829.
Lennox, James Fitzmaurice	27th Oct., 1803, 6th Foot;	16th Jan., 1804;	8th July, 1859, 98th Regt.; exchd. to 7th, 11th Feb., 1860; exchd. to 48th Regt., 17th Dec., 1862;	Retired June, 1806.
Lewes, Wm. Langmead	23rd Mar., 1855, 50th Regt.;	2nd Oct., 1855, 50th Regt.; exchd. to 98th Regt., 8th July, 1856;		Retired 14th Mar., 1868; aptd. Adjt. 2nd Administrative Batt. Worcestershire Rifle Volunteers, 3rd Dec., 1868.
Lewis, Gwynne Orton	27th May, 1853, 25th Regt.;	23rd Oct., 1855, 25th Regt.; exchd. to 7th, 1st May, 1857; Feb., 1807;	...	Retired 15th March, 1864; died at Lyttleton, New Zealand, 6th Nov., 1871.
Ley, William	...	26th June, 1823;	...	Retired 28th May, 1807.
Liddell, *Hon.* George	...	4th Oct., 1755.	18th July, 1826;	Retired 24th Jan., 1834.
Lind, Charles	...	23rd July, 1737;		
Lind, John	...		18th Jan., 1740, Moreton's Marines.	
Lindsay, John	29th Aug., 1826, 23rd Regt.	15th Sept., 1829, 30th Regt.; exchd. to 7th, 17th Sept., 1829;	...	Retired 11th Jan., 1833.
Lindsay, Robt., *Marquis of*	...	1776;	...	
Little, John	...	11th Jan., 1715.	...	Retired 5th Nov., 1777; died 18th July, 1779.
Little, Henry Alexander *Medal for the N.W. Frontier.* Served with the 17th Regt. in the Crimea, subsequent to the fall of Sebastopol, from the 26th Nov., 1855, till the evacuation in June, 1856. Served as Adjt. 1st Batt. Royal Fusiliers in the N.W. Frontier War of 1863 with the Eusafzye Field Force; present at the Umbeyla Pass and at the destruction of Laloo on the 15th Dec.; also in the action at Umbeyla and destruction of the village at the foot of the Bonair Pass on the 16th Dec., which ended in the complete rout of the enemy, and the submission of the hill tribes next day.	16th Mar., 1855, 17th Regt.;	29th May, 1857, 17th Regt.; aptd. to 7th, 23rd Oct., 1857;	14th Oct., 1868; exchd. to Bengal Staff Corps, 9th Aug., 1871; the storming of the Conical Hill, and	Bt. Major, 31st March, 1869, Bengal Staff Corps.

Alphabetical List of Officers of the Royal Fusiliers.

NAME.	ENSIGN, &C.	LIEUTENANT.	CAPTAIN.	HIGHER RANKS AND REMARKS.
LIVESAY, John	20th JUNE, 1685;	…	…	Deprived of his command for disloyalty to James II., 1688.
LLOYD, Edw. Wm. Cadwallader From Lieut. Royal North Lincoln Militia.	1st APRIL, 1856;	24th DEC., 1858;	1st April, 1870, unatt.;	Retired Nov., 1872.
LLOYD, James John	16th April, 1841, 1st Foot; exchd. to 13th L. D., 8th Nov., 1842;	19th MAY, 1846, 13th L. D.; exchd. to 93rd Regt., 7th July, 1846; exchd. to Canadian Fencibles, 5th May, 1848; aptd. to 7th, 27th APRIL, 1849;	…	Retired 9th Nov., 1849.
LLOYD, Thomas	…	22nd NOV., 1775;	31st Jan., 1778, 10th Regt.; aptd. to 80th Regt., 1783.	
LOFT, James Wallis	…	…	…	Retired Dec., 1833.
LOGAN, George *Silver Medal for 9, 16, 18, 19. Wounded in the Pyrenees, 28th July, 1813.*	8th May, 1806, 47th Regt.;	16th MAR., 1815; placed on h.p. of the Regt., 25th Feb., 1816; 14th Jan., 1808, 47th Regt.; exchd. to 7th, 5th APRIL, 1809;	21st APRIL, 1814; placed on h. p. of the Regt., 25th Feb., 1816; exchd. to 92nd Regt., 9th Dec., 1819;	Retired 13th June, 1822; aptd. a Military Knight of Windsor; died there, 1st March, 1860.
LONGDON, James Duncan	31st March, 1843, 18th Foot;	3rd Nov., 1846, 13th Foot; exchd. to 7th, 3rd MAR., 1848;	…	Retired 22nd Feb., 1850.
LONGFORD, Wm. Lyggon, *Earl of*, K.C.B. *Medal for the Crimea; Knight of the Legion of Honour; Commander 2nd Class St. Maurice and St. Lazarus; Turkish Medal; 3rd Class of the Medjidie.*	25th Aug., 1837, 52nd Regt.; Served the Eastern campaign of 1854-5 as Assist. Adjt. Gen., including the battles of Alma, Balaclava, and Inkerman, and as Assist. Adjt. Gen. up to the 24th June, 1855, after which as Adjt. Gen., including the battles of siege and fall of Sebastopol.	31st AUG., 1888;	26th JAN., 1844;	Major, 6th July, 1852, unatt.; Lieut. Col. 12th Dec., 1854; Col., 17th July, 1855; Maj. Gen., 6th March, 1868.
LONSDALE, Edgar	29th Nov., 1859, 49th Regt.;	21st Oct., 1862, 49th Regt.;	10th Aug., 1870, 49th Regt.; exchd. to 7th, 15th JAN., 1873; retired on temp. h. p., 21st July, 1875.	
LORENTZ, Charles, *Baron von Silver Medal for 12, 18, 19, 22, 24, 25.*	1st Oct., 1807, 60th Regt.;	8th Oct., 1809, 60th Regt.; exchd. to 7th, 2nd AUG., 1810; exchd. to h. p. of 1st Foot Guards, 21st Dec., 1820;	…	Retired 1821; died at Moira House, Addiscombe, 6th Feb., 1873.
LOVERIDGE, Edwd. Henry	4th FEB., 1858;	…	…	Superseded, having broken his arrest and deserted, 15th Oct., 1861.
LOWE	Qr. Mast., 1st Aug, 1695.			
LOWE, *Sir* Hudson, K.C.B., G.C.M.G. Served at the capture of Minorca, present at the attack of the Martello Tower, storming of the Convention Redoubt, and sieges of Bastia and Calvi; served in the expedition to Egypt and present at the principal occurrences of that campaign; accompanied the expedition to the Bay of Naples, and commanded the first line of the advance. Present at the attack and capitulation of Ischia; and subsequently at the attack and capitulation of Zante and Cephalonia.	25th Sept., 1787, 50th Regt.;	16th Nov., 1791, 50th Regt.;	6th Sept., 1795, 50th Regt.;	Major, 5th July, 1800, Corsican Rangers; placed on h. p. of it, 1802; exchd. to 7th, 19th April, 1803; aptd. Major Commnd. Corsican Rangers, 15th Oct., 1803; Lieut. Col. Commnd. Corsican Rangers, 25th June, 1804; Maj. Gen., 4th June, 1814; local rank of Lieut. Gen. at St. Helena, 9th Nov., 1815; aptd. Col. 93rd Regt., 4th June, 1822; Lieut. Gen., 22nd July, 1830; aptd. Col. 56th Regt., 24th July, 1832; of the 50th Regt., 17th Nov., 1842; died at Charlotte Cottage, Sloane Street, 10th Jan., 1844.
LOWE, Hudson	17th Jan., 1834, 30th Regt.; exchd. to 60th Regt., 7th Feb, 1834;	22nd JULY, 1836;	…	Retired 15th Sept., 1837.
LOWICK, Robert	…	Occurs 1685;	…	Deprived of his command for adhering to James II.; took service under that King in Ireland, and rose to the rank of Major; executed for high treason in 1696.

Alphabetical List of Officers of the Royal Fusiliers.

NAME.	ENSIGN, &c.	LIEUTENANT.	CAPTAIN.	HIGHER RANKS AND REMARKS.
LUCAS, James Served with the Regiment in the Company in the expedition to Cadiz	Low Countries and commanded a	26th OCT., 1688; Capt. Lieut., 20th May, 1693;	1st AUG., 1693.	
LUKYN, George		Occurs 1724.		
LYON, James	... Regt.;	27th Sept., 1762, Regt.; placed on h. p. of it, 1763; exchd. to 7th, 3rd FEB., 1769;	31st OCT., 1770, 35th Regt.;	Died of wounds received at Bunker's Hill on the 17th June, 1775.
McADAM, Jas. Kennedy	11th JAN., 1855;	19th JUNE, 1855;	24th May, 1859;	Retired 29th May, 1863; aptd. Major Ayrshire Vol. Rifles, 26th May, 1873.
MACBEAN, Frederick, K.H. *Silver Medal for* 2, 3, 5, 18, 19. Served the Walcheren expedition, 1809; in the Peninsula from Oct., 1812, to Nov., 1813; campaign in Upper Canada in 1815.	9th June, 1803, 6th Foot;	6th March, 1805, 6th Foot;	7th Jan., 1813, 6th Foot; placed on h. p. of it, 1816; exchd. back to f. p. of it, 16th May, 1816; exchd. to h. p. of 7th, 31st May, 1821; exchd. to f. p. of the Regt., 4th DEC., 1823;	Major, 18th July, 1826, unatt.; exchd. to 84th Regt., 6th Aug., 1829; Lieut. Col., 2nd Nov., 1838, 84th Regt.; retired 10th Dec., 1847; died 15th March, 1865.
McCUDDEN, Lionel A. T.	16th MAR., 1867;	28th OCT., 1871;	...	Transferred to Bombay Staff Corps, 30th Nov., 1870.
McDONALD, James	Regt.; placed on h. p. of 84th Regt.;	30th OCT., 1793;	29th JULY, 1795; reduced 1796, but retained on f. p. of 2nd Batt.; aptd. to 43rd Regt., 2nd Feb., 1797;	Died at St. Pierre, Martinique, Oct., 1798.
McDONNELL, H.	...	29th DEC., 1804;	...	Killed at Steinkirk, 24th July, 1692.
MACDONNELL,	...			Died or retired 1807.
McDOUALL, Patrick	26th Jan., 1785, 52nd Regt.;	24th SEPT., 1787;	13th April, 1791, Indept. Comp.; disbanded 1791; placed on h. p. of it; aptd. to 79th Regt., 18th Jan., 1794;	Major, 30th Jan., 1794, 79th Regt.; Bt. Lieut. Col., 3rd May, 1796; Lieut. Col., 1st Nov., 1796, 79th Regt.; died May, 1801, of wounds received at Rosetta, Egypt.
MACHENRY, John *Medal for Sebastopol.* Served with the Fusiliers at the siege of Sebastopol from Jan., 1855, on the 22nd March.	2nd April, 1847, 11th Foot;	18th April, 1851, 11th Foot; exchd. to 7th, 16th JUNE, 1854; and was severely wounded in a sortie	21st DEC., 1855; placed on h. p. of the Regt., to Nov., 1856; to 77th Regt.	Retired Jan., 1858.
MACKAY, George	25th March, 1836, 62nd Regt.;	23rd March, 1838, 62nd Regt.; aptd. to 7th, 4th AUG., 1843; 15th Dec., 1837, 4th Foot; exchd. to 7th, 15th JUNE, 1838;	...	Retired 14th Feb., 1845; aptd. Capt. in the Argyll Militia, 24th Jan., 1855.
MACLAINE, Murdock	29th Nov., 1833, 91st Regt.;	1798.	...	Retired 12th June 1840.
McKINNON, D.				
McKINNON, William	13th June, 1781, 60th Regt.;	28th May, 1783, 60th Regt.; placed on h. p. of it, 1783; exchd. to 7th, 9th FEB., 1797; exchd. to h. p. of Irish Brig., 1799; exchd. to 60th Regt., 18th Sept., 1800;	...	Died or retired 1806.
M'LEAN, Hector	...	14th June, 1775, 84th Regt.; placed on h. p. of it, 1783; to 5th Regt., 8th June, 1798; exchd. to 7th, 25th JULY, 1799;	6th Aug., 1803, York Rangers;	Aptd. Town Major of Halifax.
MACMANUS, Roger	...			Cashiered 21st Feb., 1718.
MACHELL, Richard Wounded at the capture of Martinique and shot through the body at Badajoz.	30th June, 1804, 31st Regt.;	22nd JAN., 1805;	2nd Jan., 1808, 3rd West India Regt.; exchd. to 30th Regt., 27th Oct., 1808;	Died at Prince of Wales Island, East Indies, 17th Nov., 1822.
MACKWORTH, *Sir* Digby, *Bart.* K.H. *Silver Medal for* 7, 9, 12, 15, 22, 24, 25, 26. Served six campaigns in the Peninsula and France. Was Aide-de-Camp to General Lord Hill in the Peninsula and France, and when his lordship was Commander of the Forces in Great Britain. Received the Guelphic Order and the thanks of H.M. William IV. for assisting in putting down the riots in Bristol and the Forest of Dean.		9th JULY, 1807;	16th JULY, 1812; exchd. to 13th L. D., 31st Dec., 1818; exchd. to h. p. of 8th Hussars, 23rd Oct., 1823;	Bt. Major, 21st Jan., 1819; Major, 13th Aug., 1830, unatt.; Bt. Lieut. Col., 10th Jan., 1837; died at Glen Uske, 22nd Sept., 1852.

Alphabetical List of Officers of the Royal Fusiliers.

NAME.	ENSIGN, &c.	LIEUTENANT.	CAPTAIN.	HIGHER RANKS AND REMARKS.
MAGENNIS, Henry Arthur *Silver Medal for* 22, 25, 26. Served with the Fusiliers in the expedition to America, present at New Orleans.	1st Oct., 1812, Royal Horse Gds. ;	4th March, 1813 ; placed on h. p. of the Regt., 25th March, 1817 ;	9th Sept., 1819, 37th Regt. ; aptd. to 28th Regt, 19th Oct., 1820 ; aptd. to 82nd Regt, 30th Sept., 1824 ;	Major, 20th Nov., 1827, unatt. ; exchd. to 93rd Regt, 22nd Feb, 1831 ; aptd. to 87th Regt, 25th Feb, 1831 ; Bt. Lieut. Col., 23rd Nov., 1841 ; Lieut. Col., 18th April, 1845, 87th Regt. ; exchd. to 27th Regt., 23rd Mar., 1849 ; aptd. Inspecting Field Officer of the York Recruiting District, 1st April, 1852 ; died at York, 14th Nov., 1852.
MAGENNIS, Richard *Silver Medal for* 6, 9, 12.	... Served with the 1st Batt. at the it in the Peninsula, lost his left arm	8th Dec., 1804 ; capture of Martinique ; landed with at Albuera.	28th Feb., 1811 ; placed on h. p. of the Regt., 20th Aug., 1812 ;	Bt. Major. ; retired 1822.
MAINWARING, Rowland	...	31st July, 1761, Indept. Comp. at Guadaloupe ; placed on h. P., 1763 ; aptd. to 7th, 2nd Oct., 1765 ;	19th Sept., 1771, 1st Foot ;	Retired 1778 ; aptd. Capt. Staffordshire Militia, 1st March, 1780 ; Barrack Master at Northampton, 1791-98 ; died 1815.
MAIR, Cornelius Cuyler Philip	...	7th April, 1814 ; placed on h. p. of the Regt., 1816 ; exchd. to 64th Regt., 4th June, 1818 ;	17th Nov., 1825, 99th Regt. ;	Major, 22nd May, 1829, 99th Regt. ; exchd. to h. p., unatt., 5th April, 1839 ; Bt. Lieut. Col., 23rd Nov., 1841 ; exchd. to 34th Regt., 13th Dec., 1842 ; retired same day ; died at Bognor, Sussex, 13th Oct., 1868.
MAIR, John Hastings, K.H. *Gold Medal for Badajoz.* Served at the capture of Copenhagen, 1807 ; at the capture of Martinique, 1809 ; proceeded with the 1st Batt. to the Peninsula, present at Busaco (severely wounded), Albuera, Aldea de Ponte, siege of Rodrigo, and Badajoz (severely wounded). Served with the Army of Occupation in France.	27th Nov., 1805, 23rd Regt. ;	19th Feb., 1806 ;	17th July, 1811 ;	Major, 30th Dec., 1824 ; Lieut. Col., 19th Dec., 1826, unatt. ; aptd. Lieut. Gov. of Grenada, 1835 ; died there, 21st March, 1836.
MAITLAND, Thomas	7th July, 1777, 55th Regt. ; 1st Sept., 1797, 22nd L. D. ; placed on h. p. of it, 1802 ; aptd. to 3rd Batt. of Reserve, 9th July, 1803 ;	20th Aug., 1803, 3rd Batt. of Reserve ; aptd. to 59th Regt., 4th Aug., 1804 ; aptd. to 13th L. D., 19th Dec., 1805 ;	5th Nov., 1818, 13th L. D. ; exchd. to 7th, 31st Dec., 1818 ;	Retired Nov., 1778.
MAJOR, John		1778 ;		Retired 27th May, 1819 ; died of cholera in London, 11th Aug., 1833.
MALAN, Charles H. *Medal for Sebastopol ; Turkish Medal.*	6th Nov., 1854 ; Served with the Royal Fusiliers in including the siege and fall of Sebastopol, from the 12th June, 1855, four places at the assault of the Redan on the 18th June.	9th Mar., 1855 ; and was severely wounded in	4th June, 1858 ; exchd. to 75th Regt., 10th Dec., 1858 ;	Major, 14th Oct., 1868, 75th Regt. ; retired 17th July, 1872.
MALCOLM, George P.	13th Aug., 1830, 2nd Foot ; aptd. to Rifle Brigade, 31st Aug., 1830 ;	12th July, 1833 ; exchd. to 50th Regt., 28th Mar, 1834 ;	...	Died 1837.
MALLOCK, Thos. J. Raymond	17th July, 1863 ;	21st Aug., 1866.		
MANNING, Robt. Barlow	17th July, 1863, 64th Regt. ;	22nd Feb., 1868, 64th Regt. ; exchd. to 7th, 11th April, 1868.		
MANSEL - PLEYDELL, Henry Bingham Morton	Lieut., 7th Mar, 1871, Dorset Militia ;	2nd Dec., 1874, 49th Regt. ; transferred to 7th, 27th Feb., 1875.		
MANSERGH, James		31st March, 1748,	4th Sept., 1754.	
MANSFIELD, James	29th March, 1833, 92nd Regt. ;	18th March, 1836 ;	...	Retired 7th Dec., 1838.
MANSFIELD, William, *Earl of*	...	1798 ;	...	Died at Leamington, 18th Feb., 1840.
MARKET, John	...	22nd Sept., 1742.	...	
MARKHAM, David	...	13th May, 1785 ;	25th Dec., 1787, 76th Regt. ;	Major, 20th Feb., 1793, 20th Regt. ; Lieut. Col., 26th March, 1794, 20th Regt. ; killed in action with the Maroons in Jamaica, 25th March, 1795.
MARSHALL, John	...	2nd Aug., 1709, Regt. ; aptd. to 7th, 19th Oct., 1709 ; aptd. to Capt. Odiam's Comp., 11th Jan., 1715 ;	Capt. Lieut., 25th April, 1741 ;	Died 1752.
MARSHALL, Matthew	27th Aug., 1776, 37th Regt. ;	7th Nov., 1778 ;	...	Killed at the Cowpens, 17th Jan., 1781.
MARSLAND, Charles	...	8th Nov., 1703 ;	...	Out of the Regt., 16th May, 1712.

Alphabetical List of Officers of the Royal Fusiliers.

NAME.	ENSIGN, &c.	LIEUTENANT.	CAPTAIN.	HIGHER RANKS AND REMARKS.
MARTEN, Thos. Wright *Medal for Sebastopol; Turkish Medal; Medal for N.W. Frontier.* Served with the Royal Fusiliers at the Umbeyla Pass, and commanded at the action at complete rout of the enemy and submission of the hill tribes next day.	6th July, 1849, Ceylon Rifles; Served with the Royal Fusiliers on the 18th June and 8th Sept., on across the ditch of that work, and in the Indian N.W. Frontier war of 1863 with the Eusafzye Field Force; present at the defence of the Sungahs cal Hill and destruction of Lalloo, Dec. 16th, which ended in the com-	13th Dec., 1853; Sebastopol from the 17th June, 1855, the last of which he succeeded to the subsequently brought it out of action attack on and storming of the Coni- village at the foot of the Bonair Pass,	19th June, 1855; including the assaults of the Redan command of the Regiment, led it —mentioned in dispatches. Served present at the defence of the Sungahs	Major, 2nd Dec., 1862; Lieut. Col., 20th June, 1865; Col., 20th June, 1870; placed on h. p. of the Regt., 28th Dec., 1870.
MARTIN, Charles	20th Dec., 1776, 37th Regt.;	28th April, 1778;	14th Sept., 1779, 26th Regt.;	Major, 8th Aug., 1783, 99th Regt.; re-duced, placed on h. p. of it; Lieut. Col., 1st March, 1794; aptd. Capt, 7th Gar. Batt., 25th Dec., 1802; reduced, placed on f. p. of it; died 1827.
MASKELYNE, Wm. Vivash *Medal for the Crimea.* Present at the siege and fall of Sebastopol and capture of Kinburn.	8th June, 1854, 20th Regt.;	29th Dec., 1854, 20th Regt.;	30th Sept., 1855, 20th Regt.; placed on h. p. of it, Nov., 1856; aptd. to 7th, 6th Nov., 1857;	Died at Gibraltar, 17th Sept., 1859.
MAUDE, Robert Henry	30th Aug., 1860;	1st Dec., 1863;	6th Sept., 1873;	
MAULE, Thomas	...	...	20th June, 1727; aptd. to Regt., 2nd Dec., 1730;	Died 1734.
MAUNSELL, Chas. Cullen	23rd Feb., 1849, 90th Regt.;	28th May, 1852; exchd. to 54th Regt., 22nd April, 1853;	17th July, 1857, 54th Regt.;	Retired 19th Nov., 1858.
MAUNSELL, Richard	24th April, 1835, 45th Regt.;	9th March, 1839;	...	Retired 5th March, 1841; aptd. Capt. in the Antrim Militia, 16th Dec., 1854; aptd. Adjt. 1st Surrey Rifles, 22nd May, 1866.
MAXWELL, *Sir* John Shaw Heron, *Bt.*	24th Oct., 1788, 68th Regt.;	15th June, 1791;	10th March, 1794, 23rd L. D.;	Major, 11th March, 1795, 23rd L. D.; Lieut. Col., 1st Jan., 1797, 23rd L. D.; reduced, placed on h. p. of it, 1803; Col., 30th Oct, 1805; Major Gen., 4th June, 1811; Lieut. Gen., 12th Aug., 1819; died at Springwell, Co. Dumfries, 29th Jan., 1830;
MAYNE, Taylor Lambard *Medal for the Punjaub.* Present at Ramnugger, passage of the Chenab; battles of Chillianwallah and Goojerat; pursuit of the enemy across the Jhelum, and of the Affghans over the Indus and through the Khyber Pass.	6th Aug., 1841, 25th Regt.;	20th Dec., 1842; aptd. to 14th L. D., 13th Aug., 1847;	2nd Oct., 1855, 3rd Drags.; placed on h. p. of the Regt., Nov., 1856; aptd. to 2nd D. G., 17th June, 1857; re-aptd. to 3rd L. D., 9th Oct., 1857; aptd. to 8th Hussars, 6th Nov., 1857	Major, 6th Aug., 1858, unatt.; aptd. to 3rd D. G., 20th Feb., 1863; Lieut. Col., 5th July, 1864, unatt.; died 5th May, 1872.
MEADE, Thomas Roche, K.H. *Silver Medal for Fuentes d'Onor.* Served in the Peninsula from Sept., 1813; present at the action of Has-had his horse killed and left arm dis-ment of Antwerp.	3rd Aug., 1809, 92nd Regt.; 1810, to Oct., 1811; served on the staff of General Count Walmoden, Hanover; at the defence of Rostock, present at Merxem and bombard-	23rd Oct., 1811; exchd. to 73rd Regt., 26th Nov., 1812;	17th Feb., 1814, 60th Regt.; exchd. to 21st Regt., 27th Nov., 1816;	Bt. Major, 10th Jan., 1837; Major, 28th Dec., 1838, 21st Regt.; exchd. to h. p. unatt., 31st May, 1839; aptd. Dep. Asst. Adjt. Gen., same day; died in Trevor Square, Brompton, 16th Nov., 1849.
MEAGHEN, Timothy Served with the 1st batt. at the with it to the Peninsula; wounded batt.; promoted Lieut. and returned	From Sergt. of the Regt.; capture of Martinique; proceeded at Albuera as Acting Adjutant, 2nd home with the staff of that batt.	17th July, 1811; exchd. to 43rd Regt., 14th May, 1818; placed on h. p. of it, 25th Dec., 1818;	...	Died 1820.
MEARE, Abraham	...	19th April, 1718;	...	
MEARES, Geo. Brooke *Medal for the N.W. Frontier.* Served with the Fusiliers in the Conical Hill, and destruction of Bonair Pass on the 16th Dec, which	3rd June, 1859; N.W. Frontier War of 1863, present Lalloo on the 15th Dec., also in the ended in the complete rout of the Lieut. North York Militia, 1st January, 1804;	17th Nov., 1863; at the defence of the Sungahs at the action of Umbeyla and destruction enemy and submission of the hill 10th March, 1808; aptd Cornet 2nd Life Guards, 4th July, 1809, Lieut., 23rd Sept., 1812, 2nd Life Guards;	3rd July, 1872. Umbeyla Pass, at the storming of the of the village at the foot of the tribes. 24th Mar., 1817, h. p. of 18th Foot; exchd. back to 2nd Life Guards, 23rd June, 1817; exchd. to 60th Regt., 12th Dec., 1818; placed on h. p. of it same day;	Retired July, 1829.
MEARES, Richard *Silver Medal for* 18, 26,				

Alphabetical List of Officers of the Royal Fusiliers.

NAME.	ENSIGN, &c.	LIEUTENANT.	CAPTAIN.	HIGHER RANKS AND REMARKS.
MERCER, Richard	47th Regt.;	19th June, 1751;	21st Sept., 1756, 66th Regt.; aptd. to 5th Drags., 17th March, 1761;	
MERVIN, Henry	…	…	…	Death in army list of Dec., 1833, but no date given.
MEYRICK, Herbert	27th April, 1870;	18th Oct., 1814; placed on h. p. of the Regt., 25th Jan., 1816;		
MILDMAY, Sir Henry Bouverie Paulet St. John, *Bart.*	20th Nov., 1828, 10th Foot;	28th Oct., 1871, 10th Regt.; 8th June, 1880;	7th April, 1837, unatt.; exchd. to 95th Regt. same day; aptd. to 2nd D. G., 27th Jan., 1838; exchd. to h. p. of 60th Regt., 25th April, 1848;	Retired 1859; aptd. Major in the Hants Yeomanry, 9th Oct., 1859; Lieut. Col., 3rd March, 1862; Lieut. Col. Commd., 16th June, 1868.
MILLER, Dugald Stewart	27th Sept., 1842, 69th Regt.;	8th Aug., 1845;	13th Dec., 1853;	Retired 24th Feb., 1854; aptd. Adjt. North York Militia, 30th March, 1855; retired 26th Nov., 1874; died at Richmond, Yorkshire, 27th Feb., 1875;
MILLER, Oliver	…	16th Jan., 1806; aptd. to 74th Regt., 20th Feb., 1806;	…	Retired 1807.
MILLS, Frederick	25th Jan., 1839, 84th Regt.;	1st April, 1842;	21st June, 1850;	Major, 29th Dec., 1854; Bt. Lieut. Col., 17th July, 1855; died at Southsea, Portsmouth, 18th Aug., 1855, a few days after landing from the Crimea.
MINCHIN, Hugh Dillon Massy	11th Feb., 1875.			
MITFORD, William	…	28th Jan., 1784;	…	Died at the Hotwells, Bristol, 22nd Dec., 1790.
MOLE, Frederick		11th June, 1685.		
MOLESWORTH, James	14th March, 1851, 49th Regt.;	8th April, 1853;		
MONCK, *Hon.* William	28th Aug., 1840, 84th Regt.;	29th April, 1842, 84th Regt.; aptd. to 7th, 24th May, 1844;	7th March, 1851;	Died at Malta, 5th Oct., 1854, of fever, contracted at Varna.
MONCKTON, Henry H. Served during the Irish rebellion; was afterwards ten months with Lord W. Bentinck with the Austrian army in Italy.	10th March, 1795, 95th Regt.; aptd. to 14th Regt., 1795;	29th April, 1795;	20th April, 1796, 24th L. D.;	Killed at the Alma, 20th Sept., 1854. Major 24th July, 1802, 24th L. D.; placed on h. p. of them, 1803; exchd. to 3rd Foot, 15th May, 1806; exchd. to 8th L. D., Jan., 1807; Lieut. Col., 18th June, 1807, 72nd Regt.; Col., 4th June, 1814; Maj. Gen., 9th July, 1821; Lieut. Gen., 11th Nov., 1851; died at Clifton, 29th June, 1854.
MONRO, Hector Wm. Bower	9th Dec., 1813, 59th Regt.;	3rd May, 1814; placed on h. p. of the Regt., 1816; exchd. to 94th Regt., 28th Nov., 1816; placed on h. p. of it, 1817; exchd. to 32nd Regt., 19th June, 1817; exchd. to h. p. of 65th Regt., 29th May, 1823;	…	Died at Ewell Castle, Surrey, 20th March, 1842.
MONTAGUE, Geo. Wroughton	3rd April, 1806, 43rd Regt.;	30th April, 1807;	28th June, 1810, 82nd Regt.;	Major, 10th Dec., 1818, 82nd Regt.; exchd. to 56th Regt., 12th April, 1821; Lieut. Col., 19th May, 1825, unatt.; aptd. to Coldstream Guards, 10th Jan., 1837; retired same day.
MONTFORD, Lewis	8th Feb., 1806, 82nd Regt.;	2nd Oct., 1806; exchd. to 47th Regt., 5th April, 1809;	…	Killed in a duel at Gibraltar, by Lieut. Heaviside, 30th Regt., 1810.
MONTGOMERY, Alex. Nixon	1st June, 1855;	16th Nov., 1855;	19th July, 1864; retired on h. p. of the Regt., 17th Aug., 1870.	
MOORE, Henry	4th Oct., 1839, 87th Regt.;	27th May, 1842, 41st Regt.; aptd. to 7th, 11th Aug., 1843;	…	Retired 14th Feb., 1845.
MOORE, Thos. Ottiwell	6th Feb., 1863; transferred to 20th Regt., 30th June, 1863.			

Alphabetical List of Officers of the Royal Fusiliers.

NAME.	ENSIGN, &c.	LIEUTENANT.	CAPTAIN.	HIGHER RANKS AND REMARKS.
MOORSOM, Wm. Scarth	22nd Mar., 1821, 31st Regt.; placed on h. p. of it, Oct., 1821; aptd. to 69th Regt., 7th Nov., 1822; exchd. to 79th Regt., 27th Feb., 1823; 14th Regt.;	12th Feb., 1825;	28th Jan., 1826, unatt.; aptd. to 52nd Regt., 8th April, 1826;	Retired 2nd March, 1832.
MORDEN, Charles William	19th Feb., 1777;		9th Nov., 1778, 46th Regt.; exchd. to h. p., 23rd May, 1786.	
MORGAN, Anthony		4th Oct., 1757, 70th Regt.; aptd. to 96th Regt., 1760;	21st June, 1762, 96th Regt.; placed on h. p., 1763; aptd. to 7th, 15th Aug., 1775;	Left the Regiment in 1777.
MORGAN, Arthur Henry	6th July, 1864;			Died at Saugor, East Indies, 20th April, 1869.
MORGAN, Edward *Silver Medal for 7, 9, 12, 18, 22, 24, 25, 26.*	22nd Oct., 1807, 7th Gar. Batt.; Embarked with the Fusiliers at Halifax for Portugal, March, 1810; severely wounded in the knee at Albuera, and disabled for nearly twelve months. In April, 1813, he re-joined the Regt. in the Peninsula, and served to the end of the war. Present also at the attack of New Orleans, Jan., 1815.	4th Feb., 1808;	5th March, 1812; exchd. to h. p. of 75th Regt., 22nd Aug., 1822;	Lieut. Col. Commd. Merioneth Militia, 20th Oct., 1852; died at Golden Grove, Flint, 11th May, 1861.
MORGAN, Sir John, Bt.			1685;	Appointed Governor of Chester, 28th May, 1689; aptd. Col. of the 23rd Royal Welsh Fusiliers, 20th April, 1692; died Jan., 1693.
MORETON, Hon. Howard	1st May, 1855;	31st Aug., 1855;	…	Died at Tortworth Court, Gloucestershire, 27th Nov., 1856.
MORETON, Hon. W. Percy *Medal for N. W. Frontier.*	31st Dec., 1859;	30th Dec., 1862;	…	Retired 29th Sept., 1865.
MORPHEW, Charles John		Jan., 1805;	…	Retired March, 1805.
MORRISON, Richard Fielding *Medal for the Crimea; Turkish Medal.* Re-entered the army Served with the 19th Regt. the Sebastopol up to the 28th Oct., 1854.	12th Jan., 1849, 60th Regt.; 3rd Foot;	16th July, 1852, 3rd Foot; exchd. to 19th Regt., 12th Oct., 1852;	29th Dec., 1854, 19th Regt.; exchd. to 51st Regt., 17th Aug., 1855;	Retired 17th Nov., 1857.
	30th Mar., 1858, 16th Lancers; Eastern campaign of 1854, including	24th Dec., 1853, 16th Lancers; the battle of the Alma, and siege of	10th July, 1863, 16th Lancers; exchd. to 7th, 9th Oct., 1863; exchd. to 5th D. G., 29th Mar., 1864;	Retired on h. p. of the Regt., 8th Aug., 1868.
MORRICE, John	…	23rd May, 1805; aptd. to 9th Gar. Batt., 2nd Dec., 1806; made 103rd Regt., 1808;	30th April, 1812, 103rd Regt.; exchd. to 73rd Regt., 18th April, 1813; exchd. to h. p. of York Rangers, 20th June, 1815;	Died in Edinburgh, 30th Aug., 1836.
MORRIS, Apollos	…	8th May, 1758;	3rd Sept., 1761, 27th Regt.;	Major, 28th Nov., 1771, 27th Regt.; retired 1st Sept., 1775.
MORRITT, John	14th June, 1821, 78th Regt.; aptd. to 64th Regt., 12th July, 1821;	24th Feb., 1825; exchd. to h. p. of 64th Regt., 15th Sept., 1825;	…	Died 11th Sept., 1827.
MORSHEAD, William T.	14th Dec., 1820, 51st Regt.;	23rd June, 1825;	26th Feb., 1830;	Retired 16th Feb., 1838; aptd. Capt. in the 2nd Cornwall Militia, 5th May, 1853; resigned 13th Jan., 1855.
MOSES, Thomas *Silver Medal for 9, 12, 14, 15.* Served with the 1st batt. at the it in the Peninsula; slightly wounded Ponte; severely wounded at Badajos.	From Lieut. Royal Westmoreland Militia; capture of Martinique; landed with at Albuera; present at Aldea de	26th Aug., 1807;	20th Aug., 1812; placed on h. p. of the Regt., 25th Mar., 1817; aptd. to 9th Vet. Batt., 24th Feb., 1820; disbanded 1821; placed on retired f. p. of it;	Retired July, 1831.
MORTIMER, Chas. L.	1st Sept., 1869;	28th Oct., 1871;	…	
MOSLEY, Godfrey Goodman *Medal for the Crimea.* Served the Eastern campaign of 1854 with the 20th Regt., including Alma, Inkerman, and siege of Sebastopol.	1st May, 1846, 59th Regt.;	11th May, 1849, 59th Regt.; exchd. to 7th, 19th April, 1850;	…	Aptd. Paymaster of the 20th Regt., 11th Oct., 1853; aptd. to 7th, 11th Nov., 1857; placed on h. p. as Lieut. of the Regt., 19th Nov., 1858; aptd. to 75th Regt., 29th May, 1861; retired same day.
MOSTYN, Edw. Alf.	10th Nov., 1869;	28th Oct., 1871.		

Alphabetical List of Officers of the Royal Fusiliers.

NAME.	ENSIGN, &c.	LIEUTENANT.	CAPTAIN.	HIGHER RANKS AND REMARKS.
MOULTRIE, Thomas Served with the 1st batt. at the capture of Martinique, and landed at the Arenberg, Lord Ventry	8th Nov., 1804, 6th Foot;	5th Dec., 1805; with it in the Peninsula.	...	Killed at Albuera, 16th May, 1811.
MULLINS, Thos. T. Landed with the 1st batt. at Albuera (severely wounded).	...	5th Feb., 1807; bon, July, 1810; present at Busaco,	8th Aug., 1811; exchd. to h. p. of 43rd Regt., 11th Dec.,1817;	Died at Burnham House, Dingle, 20th Jan., 1868.
MUNN, Henry Oldman	4th Aug., 1854, 13th Hussars;	3rd July, 1855, 13th Hussars;	16th April, 1858, 13th Hussars; exchd. to 7th, 3rd Oct., 1862;	Died at Canterbury, 18th July, 1864.
MURE, Chas. Reginald *Medal for Kaffir War, 1851-52; Medal for Sebastopol; 5th Class of the Medjidie.*	16th Aug., 1850, 43rd Regt.; Served the Kaffir War of 1851-3 as A. D. C. to Maj. Gen. Markham 1855.	19th July, 1853, 43rd Regt.; with the 43rd Regt.; in the Crimea from the 29th July to the 20th Sept.	8th Aug., 1856; placed on h. p. of the Regt., Nov., 1856; exchd. back to 43rd, 10th April, 1857;	Killed at the Gate Pah, New Zealand, 30th April, 1864.
MURRAY, Hon. David Henry	20th March, 1827, unatt.; exchd. to 9th Foot, March, 1828; exchd. to 42nd Regt., 26th April, 1828;	9th Nov., 1830; aptd. to 60th Regt., 23rd Nov., 1832;	15th May, 1835, unatt.; exchd. to 25th Regt., 24th July,1835; exchd. to Scots Fus. Guards, 23rd March, 1838;	Bt. Major, 9th Nov., 1846; retired 4th Feb., 1848.
MURRAY, F. Johnston	21st Sept., 1860;	1st Dec., 1863;	...	Retired 5th April, 1864.
MURRAY, Walter	28th May, 1833, 55th Regt.;	10th July, 1835, 55th Regt.; exchd. to 20th Regt., 9th Jan., 1836; aptd. to 7th, 9th June, 1837; aptd. to 21st Regt., 28th Dec., 1838;	...	Retired 25th Sept., 1841.
MURTON, George	From Capt. Cambridge Militia;	25th Aug., 1807;	27th May, 1819; placed on h. p. of the Regt., 25th Oct., 1821; aptd. to Canadian Rifles, 16th July, 1841;	Aptd. Paymaster of the Regt., 26th Mar., 1812; placed on h. p. of it, 25th Feb., 1816; died in Drummond Street, Euston Square, 12th March, 1838. Bt. Major, 10th Jan., 1837; Major, 18th Dec., 1845, Canadian Rifles; Lieut. Col., 9th Feb., 1849, Canadian Rifles; retired 22nd Oct., 1850; died at Toronto, Canada, 26th Oct., 1874.
MUTER, Robert *Silver Medal for Talavera.* Present at the passage of the Douro and capture of Oporto; dangerously wounded at Talavera, 28th July, 1809; taken prisoner whilst in hospital, and detained at Bordeaux until the peace of 1814; present at the attack upon New Orleans, 8th Jan., 1815; commanded the right advance on the night the army retired.	5th March, 1807, 83rd Regt.;	3rd March, 1808;		
MYERS, *Sir Wm. James, Bart.* Served with the Coldstream Guards in Egypt; wounded on landing at Aboukir Bay, 8th March, 1801; proceeded to the Peninsula in command of the 2nd Batt. Royal Fusiliers; commanded the Fusilier Brigade at Albuera.			18th Dec., 1794, Indept. Comp.; aptd. to Coldstream Guards, 11th Jan., 1800; present at Talavera and Busaco;	Major, 6th May, 1802, 15th Foot; Lieut. Col., 1802, 62nd Regt.; placed on h. p. of it, 1802; aptd. to 7th, 15th Aug., 1804; mortally wounded at Albuera, 16th May, 1811.
NANTES, Richard *Silver Medal for 14, 16, 24, 25, 26.* Served with the Fusiliers in the affair at the Guarena, and at the battles of Salamanca and Toulouse; places; he was again slightly was slightly wounded at the Guarena; most severely at Salamanca, accidentally hurt by one of his own men, his right arm being broken in two and carried off the field in the operations of the Nive.	...	19th Oct., 1809; exchd. to h. p. of 55th Regt., January, 1815;	...	Aptd. a Military Knight of Windsor; died there, 4th April, 1871.
NAPIER, Alexander	20th Jan., 1790, 19th Regt.;	11th May, 1791;	12th Feb., 1794, 100th Regt.;	Major, 12th Mar., 1796, 92nd Regt.; Lieut. Col., 5th April, 1801, 92nd Regt.; died 1809.
NEAME, Chas. Covell	20th May, 1842, 47th Regt.;	14th Feb., 1845; aptd. to 8th Foot, 30th April, 1847; exchd. to h. p. of 13th Foot, 27th May, 1856.	...	
NEGUS, Daniel Served with the Regiment in the Low Countries, wounded at the storming of Namur; commanded a company in the expedition to Cadiz and Vigo in 1702.	...	...	5th April, 1694.	
NEVILLE, George Henry *Medal for the Punjaub.* Served with the 29th throughout the Punjaub campaign of 1848-9, including the passage of the Chenab (wounded), and Goojerat.	19th Feb., 1847, 29th Regt.;	30th Nov., 1849, 29th Regt.; aptd. to 12th Foot, 12th July, 1850; exchd. to 7th, 24th Feb., 1854;	2nd March, 1855;	Retired 13th July, 1855.
NEWMARSH, Timothy Served with the Fusiliers in Gibraltar and Minorca in 1756, and in at the Cowpens where he commanded the Regiment.	...	30th Dec., 1755;	18th July, 1766; the Revolutionary war. Wounded	Major, 10th Aug., 1780, 60th Regt.; retired 1783; died at Brownberries, near Leeds, 16th May, 1802.

Alphabetical List of Officers of the Royal Fusiliers.

NAME.	ENSIGN, &c.	LIEUTENANT.	CAPTAIN.	HIGHER RANKS AND REMARKS.
NEWTON, Henry	3rd Foot ;	31st DEC., 1782 ; placed on h. p., 1783 ; exchd. to 2nd D. G., 11th Feb., 1790 ;	...	Retired 31st July, 1790.
NEWTON, William Henry, K.H. Served in the West Indies in the campaign of 1810, under Sir George Beckwith; served on the coast of America, in 1814, under Sir J. C. Sherbrook; joined the army in Belgium in June, 1815, and was present at the taking of Landrecy by the Prussians.	20th June, 1800, 18th L. D. ;	25th Dec., 1800, 60th Regt. ; aptd. to 7th, 1st AUG., 1801 ; removed to h. p. of 15th Foot, Dec., 1802; aptd. to 1st Foot, 23rd Aug., 1804 ;	25th June, 1808, 64th Regt. ; exchd. to 62nd Regt. 29th June, 1815 ; placed on h. p. of it, 25th May, 1817 ; aptd. to 75th Regt., 8th April, 1825 ;	Bt. Major, 27th May, 1825 ; Major, 11th May, 1826, unatt. ; Bt. Lieut. Col., 28th June, 1838 ; aptd. to Canadian Rifles, 16th July, 1841 ; Lieut. Col., 18th Dec., 1845, Canadian Rifles ; retired 9th Feb., 1849.
NEWTON, William Henry	...	13th SEPT., 1804 ;	4th DEC., 1806, 6th Gar. Batt. ; reduced 1814 ; placed on h. p. of it ;	Died 7th Jan., 1842.
NISBETT, Francis	29th Dec., 1814, 3rd Foot; aptd. to 18th Hussars, 19th Oct., 1815 ;	26th Nov., 1818, 18th Hussars ; placed on h. p. of it, 25th Dec., 1822 ; aptd. to 7th, 23rd Nov., 1832 ; retired on h. p. of the Regt., 12th April, 1833 ;	...	Retired Dec., 1833.
NOBLE, Mungo	...	20th Sept., 1777, 21st Regt. ;	9th July, 1781, 60th Regt. ; exchd. to 10th Foot, 18th July, 1781 ; aptd. to 7th Regt., 29th APRIL, 1782 ; placed on h. p., 1783 ; exchd. to 14th L. D., 31st May, 1792;	Major, 1st Nov., 1793, 38th Regt. ; Lieut. Col., 2nd Dec., 1794, 84th Regt. ; aptd. to 67th Regt., 18th Mar., 1795 ; died on board the *Ambuscade*, on passage to Jamaica, 1801.
NOOTH, Henry. *Silver Medal for Corunna.* Served with the Fusiliers in the expedition, under Sir David Baird, Corunna. Accompanied the 14th to NOOTH, Henry Stephen	...	expedition against Copenhagen, 1807, with the 2nd Batt. 14th Regt. in the and was in the retreat of Sir John Moore's army, and at the battle of Waldcheren, present at the siege of Flushing. From Ens. Dorset Militia ;	22nd AUG., 1804 ; aptd. to 14th Foot, 2nd June, 1808 ; exchd. to h. p. of it, 26th March, 1818 ; 14th May, 1812 ; exchd. to 6th D. G., 15th Aug., 1816 ; 29th Jan., 1824, 6th D. G. ; exchd. to h. p. of it, 13th May, 1824 ;	Bt. Major, 4th June, 1814 ; Bt. Lieut. Col., 10th Jan., 1837 ; died at Albemarle Villas, Stoke, Devonport, 28th Aug., 1861. Died at Cliftonville, Brighton, 13th June, 1871.
NOOTH, John Mervin, C.B. *Gold Medal for* 6, 12. Served with the 1st Batt. at Albuera, after which he returned capture of Martinique; landed with it home in command of the staff of the	...	6th JULY, 1796 ; at Lisbon, July, 1810, present at 2nd Batt., which he re-raised and	6th SEPT., 1798 ; Busaco, commanded the 1st Batt. at commanded to the end of the war.	Major, 30th DEC., 1806 ; Bt. Lieut. Col., 20th June, 1811 ; Lieut. Col., 2nd JAN., 1812 ; placed on h. p. of the Regt., 25th Feb., 1816 ; exchd. to 21st Regt., 6th June, 1816 ; died at Demerara, 23rd Aug., 1821.
NORMAN, Richard	25th Nov., 1824, 90th Regt. ;	1st Nov., 1827 ;	20th JUNE, 1834 ; 10th Aug., 1799, 17th Regt. ; exchd. to 34th Regt., Sept., 1799 ; exchd. to 22nd Regt., 23rd Jan., 1800 ; aptd. to York Hussars, 11th April, 1800 ; placed on h. p. of the Regt., 1802 ; aptd. to 8th L. D., 25th May, 1803 ;	Retired 27th July, 1838.
NOWELL, Charles	...	24th AUG., 1795 ;		Died or retired 1804.
NUGENT, *Sir George, Bt.*, G.C.B. Joined the Fusiliers at New York in Sept., 1777, and was employed in the expedition up Hudson River under Sir Henry Clinton for the relief of Gen. Burgoyne's army, present at the capture of Forts Montgomery and Clinton; he then proceeded with his regiment to Philadelphia and remained till the evacuation of that place by the British in June, 1778. Served with the 57th Regt. from April, 1778, to the end of the war. Served with the Coldstream Guards on the continent in 1793, present at the siege of Valenciennes, battle of St. Amand and action at Lincelles. Raised the 85th Regt. in 1794, and accompanied it to Walcheren, and in October joined the Duke of York at Thél-on-the-Waal. Served afterwards during the rebellion in Ireland, and later as commander-in-chief in the East Indies. Appointed Lieut. Governor of Jamaica, 1st April, 1801.	5th July, 1773, 39th Regt. ;	23rd Nov., 1775 ;	28th April, 1778, 57th Regt. ;	Major, 3rd May, 1782, 57th Regt. ; Lieut. Col., 8th Sept., 1783, 97th Regt. ; aptd. to 13th Regt., 20th Dec., 1787 ; aptd. to 4th D. G., 16th June, 1789 ; aptd. to Coldstream Guards, 6th Oct., 1790 ; Col., 28th Dec., 1793 ; aptd. Col. 85th Regt., 1st March, 1794 ; Maj. Gen., 3rd May, 1796 ; Lieut. Gen., 25th Sept., 1803 ; aptd. Col. 62nd Regt., 27th Dec., 1805 ; Gen., 4th June, 1813 ; Col. 6th Regt., 26th May, 1806 ; Field Marshal, 9th Nov., 1846 ; died at his residence, Westhorpe House, Little Marlow, March 11th, 1849.

Alphabetical List of Officers of the Royal Fusiliers.

NAME.	ENSIGN, &c.	LIEUTENANT.	CAPTAIN.	HIGHER RANKS AND REMARKS.
NUNN, John Loftus	89th Regt.;	17th JAN., 1811; exchd. to Cornet h. p. of 18th Hussars, 17th July, 1823; exchd. to 66th Regt., 30th April, 1827;	27th April, 1832, unatt.:	Died at the Cove, Jan., 1840.
Served with the regiment during the Peninsula War; severely wounded at the Pyrenees.				
O'BRIEN, Charles Wm.	10th JULY, 1866;	1st Nov., 1871;	...	Retired 19th June, 1872; aptd. Capt. Armagh Militia, 30th April, 1873.
O'BRIEN, Cornelius Geo.	19th JULY, 1855;	16th Nov., 1855;	29th MAY, 1863; exchd. to Cape Mounted Rifles, 21st July, 1863;	Died at Newtonards, 21st Dec., 1867.
O'BRIEN, Donough	12th Sept., 1822, 65th Regt.; placed on h. p. of it, 10th April, 1823; aptd. to 96th Regt., 29th Jan., 1824;	2nd JULY, 1829; aptd. to 72nd Regt., 29th Oct., 1829;	31st Oct., 1840, 72nd Regt.; exchd. to 86th Regt., 13th June, 1845;	Bt. Major 11th Nov., 1851; died at Colaba, 22nd Jan., 1855.
O'BRIEN, Morgan	Lieut., 5th July, 1809, North York Militia;	22nd MARCH, 1810;	...	Died 1811.
O'DONNELL, Hugh	...	JAN., 1795.		
O'HARA, Alexander	...	...	24th MARCH, 1705.	
O'HARA, Edward, C.B. *Gold Medal for Guadaloupe.*	...	12th OCT., 1796;	6th AUG., 1803, York Rangers; aptd. to 1st Foot, 20th Feb., 1805; exchd. to 46th Regt., 25th Sept., 1806;	Major, 12th April, 1807, York Light Infantry, 12th April, 1807, York Light Infantry; Bt. Lieut. Col., 4th June, 1813; Lieut. Col., 15th June, 1815, York Light Infantry; placed on h. p. of it, 1816; exchd. to 63rd Regt., 19th Dec., 1816; exchd. to 2nd West India Regt., 2nd May, 1822; retired 16th same month; died in London, 24th June, 1833.
Served in the West Indies, present at the capture of Guadaloupe in 1810; had also the command and civil administration of St. Lucia.				
O'HARA, James, *Lord Tyrawley*		15th MAY, 1703;	24th MARCH, 1705; staff of his father.	Col., 29th JAN., 1713; aptd. Col. of the 4th D. G., 26th Aug., 1739.
Served with the regiment in Spain during the war of the Spanish Succession; present at Almanza on the 13th Dec., 1732;				
O'HARA, James			9th OCT., 1747;	Retired 28th Aug., 1753.
O'MALLEY, *Sir* Wm., *Bart.*	28th Dec., 1832, 97th Regt.; aptd. to 3rd D. G., 27th Dec., 1833; aptd. to 14th Foot, 21st Nov., 1834;	2nd Oct., 1835, 45th Regt.; exchd. to 7th, 5th FEB., 1836;	12th JULY, 1839;	Retired 12th Jan., 1844; aptd. Barrack Master at Fethard; Lieut. Col. North Mayo Militia, 1855.
OAKES, Henry Ferdinand	6th MAY, 1860;	29th MAY, 1863;	28th OCT., 1871; exchd. to 49th Regt., 15th Jan., 1873. 30th SEPT., 1707;	Out of the Regt., 12th May, 1715.
ODIAM, Gregory		17th MAY, 1697; succession.		
OGILVIE, James, C.B.		23rd AUG., 1800;	25th March, 1802, 4th Foot; exchd. to 8th Foot, 13th May, 1802;	Major, 4th June, 1807, 8th Foot; Bt. Lieut. Col., 4th June, 1813; Lieut. Col., 28th Feb., 1814, 8th Foot; placed on h. p. of it, 25th Feb., 1816; exchd. to 20th Regt., 21st Dec., 1820; exchd. to h. p., unatt., 12th Jan., 1826; Col., 22nd July, 1830; Major Gen, 23rd Nov., 1841; died at Banff, 2nd July, 1845.
Served with the Regt. at Cadiz and Expedition to Hanover, 1805; 1813, to the peace; served in Upper Canada from March, 8th Regt. at the surprise of the American Corps at Gages (severely wounded), at the defeat of the American Corps at Gages (severely wounded), at the siege of Fort Erie, and various other affairs.				
OGILVIE, John Mitchell	5th Oct., 1820, 87th Regt.; exchd. to 27th Regt., 9th Nov., 1820; placed on h. p. of it, 1821; aptd. to 28th Regt., 7th April, 1825;	27th OCT., 1825;	...	Died at Chester Castle, 23rd Jan., 1828.
OGLE, Thomas	...	20th Nov., 1793;	30th SEPT., 1795; aptd. to 58th Regt., 20th Feb., 1796;	Major, 3rd April, 1800, 58th Regt.; killed at Aboukir, 8th March, 1801.
ORBY, Thomas	11th JUNE, 1685; aptd. to Lord Dartmouth's Company, 1st May, 1686.			
ORD, Thomas	...	27th OCT., 1777;	1778, 28th Regt.;	Retired same year.
ORMSBY, Henry	...	20th MAY, 1723.		

Alphabetical List of Officers of the Royal Fusiliers.

NAME.	ENSIGN, &c.	LIEUTENANT.	CAPTAIN.	HIGHER RANKS AND REMARKS.
ORMSBY, H. M.	...	31st JAN., 1805; aptd. to 4th Vet. Batt., 4th Sept., 1806; aptd. to 12th Vet. Batt., 25th June, 1808; to h. p. of 71st Regt., 1810; 29th OCT., 1807;	...	Not in 1817 List.
ORMSBY, John. *Silver Medal for Talavera.*	From Ens. Sligo Militia;		...	Superseded July, 1813, being absent without leave.
ORR, John *Silver Medal for* 6, 12, 18, 19, 20, 22, 24, 25.	... Served with the Royal Fusiliers at the siege and capture of Copenhagen 1810; severely wounded at Albuera investment of Pampeluna, wounded in 1809; and in the Peninsula from the Esla and Ebro; affair at Osma; of Roncesvalles; the passage of the	28th AUG., 1804;	27th APRIL, 1809; in 1807; at the capture of Martinique by a musket ball in the leg; passage in the breast by a musket ball; pass Bidassoa, besides the various minor actions and skirmishes.	Major, 16th MARCH, 1815; placed on h. p. of the Regt., 25th Feb, 1816; retired April, 1826.
ORR, Martin *Silver Medal for* 12, 18, 19, 22, 24, 25, 26.	... Served with the Fusiliers from Feb. 1812, to the end of the war, including wounded in the left knee and elbow of Roncesvalles and Pampeluna, besides at Albuera; action of Osma; affairs was also at the capture of Paris in sides the various minor affairs. He 1815.	28th JUNE, 1810; to Aug, 1811, and again from April, siege of Badajoz, April and May, 1811; 29th July, 1862, 73rd Regt.;	28th Oct., 1831, 88th Regt.; exchd. to h. p, unatt., 23rd Feb., 1838;	Aptd. Staff Officer of Pensioners at London, 1st Oct., 1844; Bt. Major, 9th Nov., 1846; Bt. Lieut. Col., 20th June, 1854; died in Westbourne Place, London, 25th Oct., 1855.
ORRED, George Stanley	...	4th Sept., 1865, 73rd Regt.; exchd. to 7th, 6th FEB., 1866; 29th JAN., 1789;	...	Retired 21st Sept., 1874.
OSWALD, *Sir* John, G.C.B., G.C.M.G. *Gold Medal for* 1, 18, 20. Served in the expedition under Sir to Holland, 1799, present at the passage of the Helder, severely wounded at the battle of Maida; served in the Ionian Islands, 1809-10, present at the capture of Santa Maura. Served Placentia, at Osma, Vittoria, San in front of Bedart.	Feb., 1788, 23rd Regt.;		14th Jan., 1791, Indept. Comp.; aptd. to 35th Regt., 23rd March, 1791; of Martinique, St. Lucia, and Guadaloupe, 1794. Served in the expedition Chas. Grey. Present at the capture of terranean, present at the capture of Egypt in 1807, present at Alexandria and Rosetta. Served also in the In 1800 he embarked for the Mediterranean the 5th Division at Villa Morilla and Sebastian, Nivelle (attack of the outposts at St. Jean de Luz, when he established the posts of the division	Major, 1st Sept., 1795, 35th Regt.; Lieut. Col., 30th March, 1797, 35th Regt.; Col., 30th Oct., 1805; aptd. Col. of the 1st Greek Light Infantry, 25th Feb., 1811; Maj. Gen. 4th June, 1811, Lieut. Gen., 12th Aug., 1819; aptd. Col. of the 35th Regt., 9th Oct., 1819, Gen., 10th Jan., 1837; died at Dunikier, Co. Fife, 8th June, 1840.
OWEN, Humphrey	... America during the early portion of the American War; commanded the of Quebec.	27th FEB., 1761;	20th MAY, 1772;	Retired 1779; aptd. Adjt. Cinque Ports Batt., 23rd July, 1779; Capt. Lieut. Cinque Ports Batt., 5th April, 1780; reduced 1783.
PACK, Arthur John Reynell, C.B. *Medal for Sebastopol; Legion of Honour.*	9th Aug., 1833, 85th Regt.; Served the Eastern campaign from the Fusiliers at the assault of the	5th May, 1837, unatt.; exchd. to 7th, 26th JULY, 1838; Feb., 1855, at the siege of Sebastopol, Redan on the 18th June.	23rd JUNE, 1843; severely wounded when commanding	Bt. Major, 20th June, 1854; Major, 22nd DEC., 1854; Lieut. Col., 19th JUNE, 1855; retired on h. p. of the Regt., 27th May, 1856.
PADDON, Henry W. L. *Medal for N. W. Frontier.*	6th AUG., 1858; Served with the Fusiliers the Umbeyla Pass, and attack on sent at the defence of the Sungahs at and destruction of the village at the Dec.; also in the action at Umbeyla, sion of the hill tribes on the following rout of the enemy, and the submisday.	24th JUNE, 1862; Indian N.W. Frontier War of 1863 and storming of the Conical Hill, foot of the Bonair Pass on the 16th	23rd JUNE, 1869. with the Eusofzye Field Force, present at the destruction of Lalloo on the 15th Dec., which ended in the complete	
PAGE, William, K.H. Served as Adjutant with the 2nd French; remained prisoner at Bordeaux to the end of the war.	... From Sergt. Major 89th Regt.; Batt. in the Peninsula; wounded at	29th JAN., 1807; Talavera, and captured by the	25th MAY, 1812; exchd. to h. p. of Gren. Guards, 3rd April, 1823; exchd. to 80th Regt., 9th Nov., 1830; exchd. to h. p., unatt., 31st July, 1835;	Bt. Major, 22nd July, 1830; died 7th July, 1838.
PAGET, Catesby	8th Nov., 1827, 69th Regt.;	31st AUG., 1830;	9th MAR., 1839; exchd. to h. p. of Staff Corps, 26th Jan., 1844; exchd. to 14th Foot, 2nd Feb, 1849;	Retired 2nd Feb., 1849.
PAKENHAM, *Hon. Sir* Ed.M., K.B. Commanded the Fusiliers at the capture of Martinique; aptd. to the Staff in the Peninsula, where, or as a Brigadier, he served to the end of the war; aptd. to command the expedition to America in 1814.	...	...	...	Major, 6th Dec., 1794, 33rd L. D.; reduced 1796, but retained on f. p. of it; aptd. to 23rd L. D., 1st Jan., 1798; Lieut. Col., 17th Oct., 1799, 64th Regt.; aptd. to 7th, 5th MAY, 1804, Col., 25th Oct., 1809; Major Gen., 1st Jan., 1812; aptd. Col. 6th West India Regt., 21st May, 1813; killed before New Orleans, 8th Jan., 1815.
PALMER, Frederick	8th June, 1849, 58th Regt.;	18th July, 1851, 58th Regt.; exchd.to7th,26th MAR.,1852;	...	Retired 17th March, 1854.

Alphabetical List of Officers of the Royal Fusiliers.

NAME.	ENSIGN, &c.	LIEUTENANT.	CAPTAIN.	HIGHER RANKS AND REMARKS.
PAPLEY, Edward	37th Regt.;	26th Oct., 1777;	…	Died or retired 1779.
PARKE, Andrew	From Lieut. Sligo Militia;	16th June, 1808;	…	Died 1810.
PARKER, Gervase Served with the Regt. in the expedition to Cadiz and Vigo in 1702, war of the Spanish Succession.	…	17th May, 1697; and in the war of the Spanish Succession.	15th March, 1703;	; Lieut. Col., 11th Jan., 1715.
PARKER, Charles	14th May, 1707;	11th Jan., 1715.		
PARKINSON, John Served with the Regt. during the war of the Spanish Succession.	From Lieut. 1st West York Mil.;	4th May, 1808; exchd. to 90th Regt., 5th April, 1809;	…	Retired 1811.
PARKHURST, Charles	25th Dec., 1806, 35th Regt.;	28th May, 1807; aptd. to 1st Ceylon Regt., 18th Feb., 1808;	…	Retired 1812.
PARNELL, Alfred Bligh	24th Jan., 1865;	…	…	Died at Morar, Central India, 29th Dec., 1865.
PARSONAGE, John	12th March, 1794, 11th Regt.;	29th July, 1795;	25th Dec., 1801, 1st Foot;	Died 1805.
PARSONS, Laurence	3rd March, 1760, 10th Foot;	18th Feb., 1765, 10th Foot;	4th Dec., 1769, 10th Foot;	Major, 19th May, 1778; retired 29th Oct., 1778; died in Jermyn Street, 26th Sept., 1804.
PAULET, *Lord William*, G.C.B. *Medal for the Crimea; Legion of Honour; Commander, 1st Class, St. Maurice and St. Lazarus; 3rd Class of the Medjidie; Turkish Medal.* Served the Eastern campaign of 1854 as Assistant Adjt. Gen. of the Cavalry Division, including the battles of the Alma, Balaclava, and Inkerman, and siege of Sebastopol.	1st Feb., 1821, 85th Regt.;	23rd May, 1822;	12th Feb., 1825, unatt.; exchd. to 85th Regt., 21st April, 1825; retired on h. p., 28th Dec., 1826; exchd. to 63rd Regt., 29th March, 1827; aptd. to 21st Fusiliers, 4th Dec., 1828;	Major, 10th Sept., 1830, unatt.; exchd. to 68th Regt., 18th Jan., 1833; Lieut. Col., 21st April, 1843, 68th Regt.; exchd. to h. p. unatt., 31st Dec., 1847; Col., 20th June, 1854; Major Gen., 13th Dec., 1858; Col. of the 68th Regt., 9th April, 1864; Lieut. Gen., 8th Dec., 1867.
PAUNCEFORD, George	…	28th Feb., 1761; exchd. to h. p. of 108th Regt., Feb., 1767; aptd. to 1st Troop of Horse Guards, 4th Feb., 1767;	…	Retired 1769.
PAYNE, Richard Sowden	29th March, 1844, 40th Regt.;	7th May, 1847, 40th Regt.; exchd. to Ceylon Rifles, 1st Oct., 1847; aptd. to 7th, 9th May, 1851;	…	Retired 16th Sept., 1851.
PAYNE, Thos. Geo. Dupre *Medal for India.* Campaign of 1857-8, including the siege, assault, and capture of Delhi; Neijufghur.	16th Feb., 1849, 17th Regt.; aptd. to 61st Regt., 6th July, 1849;	25th Oct., 1850, 61st Regt.;	1st Oct., 1853, 61st Regt.; exchd. to 7th, 25th Feb., 1859; exchd. to 98th Regt., 11th Feb., 1860;	Retired 2nd Sept., 1862.
PAYNE, William Served with the Regt. throughout the Peninsular war; present at Busaco, Albuera, the affair at Aldea de Ponte, Vittoria, Pyrenees.	From Lieut. Worcestershire Militia;	12th April, 1809; exchd. to h. p. of Rifle Brigade, 16th March, 1820; aptd. to 75th Regt., 11th Aug., 1825; aptd. to 33rd Regt., 10th Aug., 1826;	4th Sept., 1827, unatt.;	Died at Northampton, 18th Sept., 1827.
PEACHEY, Edward	18th May, 1705;	20th Sept., 1705;		
PEACHEY, James	3rd Oct., 1787, 60th Regt.;	31st Oct., 1793;	29th July, 1795; 2nd batt., reduced 1796, but retained on f. p. of it; aptd. to 43rd Regt. 2nd Feb., 1797;	Died or retired 1800.
PEACHEY, John	…	16th June, 1719.		
PEACOCKE, George	…	2nd March, 1763, 78th Regt.; placed on h. p. of it, 1763; aptd. to 7th, 7th Jan., 1767; 4th April, 1851;	18th Jan., 1777;	Died in America, 1781.
PEARSON, Richard Lyons Otway *Medal for the Crimea; Sardinian Medal; 5th Class of the Medjidie; Turkish Medal.* Served the Eastern Campaign up of Sebastopol, attack of the Redan, 18th June, and expedition to Kertch.	3rd Dec., 1847, 32nd Regt.; aptd. to 95th Regt., 10th Dec., 1847;	to the 30th June, 1855, as aide-de-camp to Sir George Brown, including the	29th Dec., 1854; aptd. to Grenadier Guards, 20th July, 1855;	Bt. Major, 2nd Nov., 1855; Capt. and Lieut. Col., 27th Dec., 1864, Grenadier Guards.
PENNINGTON, John	…	…	21st June, 1685.	
PENRICE, Edward Served with the 2nd Batt. in the Peninsula, present at Albuera.	From Lieut. Worcestershire Militia;	10th April, 1809;	7th April, 1825; exchd. to h. p., unatt.; 8th Nov., 1827;	Died August, 1838.

Alphabetical List of Officers of the Royal Fusiliers.

NAME.	ENSIGN, &c.	LIEUTENANT.	CAPTAIN.	HIGHER RANKS AND REMARKS.
PENROSE, Henry F. Keane	23rd AUG., 1861 ;	5th APRIL, 1864 ; exchd. to 13th Foot, 25th April, 1865.		Retired 8th May, 1867.
PERCY, *Hon.* Francis John	…	30th JAN., 1806 ;	5th May, 1808, 9th Gar. Batt. ; aptd. to 23rd Regt., 18th Aug., 1808 ;	Died at Cuellar, 1812.
🎖 PERCY, *Hon.* Henry, C.B. Served with the 14th L. D. in the maimed in France until liberated by retreat from Burgos, 1812, and remained in France until liberated by the entrance of the allies into Paris in 1814. Placed on the staff in 1815 ; served with the Waterloo campaign ; as side-de-camp to the Duke he brought in the battle, and the despatches over to England the Eagles captured relating the triumph. Singularly enough one of his ancestors brought to England the intelligence of the victory of Blenheim.	…	16th AUG., 1804 ;	9th Oct., 1806, 6th West India Regt. ; aptd. to 7th, 6th Nov., 1806 ; exchd. to 14th L. D., 21st June, 1810 ;	Bt. Major, 16th Aug., 1810 ; Bt. Lieut. Col., 18th June, 1815 ; Major, 12th Oct., 1820, 14th L. D. ; retired 13th Sept., 1821 ; died in Portman Square, 15th April, 1825.
PERSSE, Dudley *Medal for the Crimea.* Severely wounded at the Alma.	16th June, 1848, 34th Regt. ;	5th April, 1850, 34th Regt. ; aptd. to 7th, 21st JUNE, 1850 ;	23rd SEPT., 1854 ;	Retired 20th March, 1855 ; aptd. Capt. in the Limerick City Militia Artillery, 18th July, 1855.
PETTYTOT, Stephen	…	6th FEB., 1718-19.		
PETTYTOT, Stephen	…	20th JUNE, 1727 ;	14th Nov., 1712 ;	Died Feb., 1730.
PETTY, George Speke	…	12th MAY, 1715 ;	… Aug., 1719, … Regt.	Aptd. Town Major of Dublin, May, 1735.
PHILLIPS, Harry Shakespear, C.B. *Medal for the Sutlege.* Served in the campaign on the Regt. in the battles of Buddiwal, Aliwal, and Sobroon, and a brigade in the army of the Sutlege during the occupation of the Punjaub.	8th Jan., 1824, 4th L. D.	12th May, 1825, unatt. ; exchd. to 7th, 19th May, 1825 ;	4th Feb., 1828, unatt. ; exchd. to 53rd Regt. ; 25th Nov., 1828 ;	Major, 1st Aug., 1838, 53rd Regt. ; Lieut. Col., 31st Mar., 1843, 53rd Regt. ; exchd. to 31st Regt., 15th April, 1846 ; placed on h. p. of it, Jan., 1847 ; exchd. to 57th Regt., 6th Aug., 1847 ; exchd. to h. p., unatt., 26th May, 1848 ; died at Malvern, 21st Nov., 1849.
PHILLIPS, Henry Brockolls	…	15th Nov., 1778 ;		
PHILLIPS, Thomas	…	…	20th DEC., 1687.	
PIERSON, Richard	…	…	11th JAN., 1715.	
PIGOTT, *Sir* George, *Bart.*	25th March, 1782, 52nd Regt. ;	15th MARCH, 1784 ;	…	Retired 1789.
PIGOTT, William	…	26th JAN., 1785 ;	…	Retired 28th April, 1794.
PILKINGTON, *Sir* Thomas, *Bart.*	…	…	1793 ;	Died at Chevet, Wakefield, 1811.
PILKINGTON, William *Silver Medal for 7, 9, 12.* Landed with the 2nd Batt. at Lisbon, 5th April, 1809.	15th Oct., 1803, 69th Regt. ;	27th Aug., 1804, 82nd Regt. ;	30th Feb., 1794, 21st Drags. ; 1st Dec., 1806, 8th Gar. Batt. ; exchd. to 56th Regt., 25th Sept., 1807 ; exchd. to 7th, 25th May, 1808 ; exchd. to 5th Gar. Batt., 11th June, 1812 ; reduced, placed on h. p. of it, 1814 ; aptd. to Newfoundland Vet. Comps., 25th July, 1824 ; aptd. to 3rd Vet. Batt., 2nd Sept., 1824 ; aptd. to 92nd Regt., 8th April, 1825 ;	Bt. Major, 12th Aug., 1819 ; Major, 18th May, 1826, unatt. ; retired March, 1827.
PINCHARD, Wm. Biddulph	31st AUG., 1855 ; aptd. to Ceylon Rifles, 21st Sept., 1855 ;	15th Oct., 1858, Ceylon Rifles ;	30th Oct., 1866, Ceylon Rifles ; exchd. to 70th Regt., 22nd June, 1867 ; retired on h. p. of it, 2nd July, 1870 ;	Died at Edmonton, 25th March, 1874.
PITCAIRN, Robert	19th Jan., 1826, Staff Corps, aptd. to 12th Foot, 5th Feb., 1829 ;	26th Oct., 1830, unatt. ; aptd. to 7th, 19th Nov., 1830 ; aptd. to 92nd Regt., 1st Feb., 1831 ;	6th Sept., 1839, 92nd Regt. ; exchd. to h. p. of 6th Gar. Batt., 27th Sept., 1844 ; aptd. Staff Officer of Pensioners ; retired on f. p. ;	Bt. Major, 11th Nov., 1851 ; Bt. Lieut. Col., 26th Oct., 1858 ; Col., 1st July, 1859 ; retired on f. p. ; died 27th Aug., 1873.
PITT, John Entered the Regt. as Lieut. to both in Ireland and Flanders, and afterwards under Marlborough.	… Capt. Beckman, became Captain of	14th JUNE, 1685 ; the Miners, and served with them	1688 ; throughout William's campaigns,	Left the Regiment with the Company of Miners.
PLENDERLEATH, Wm. Smyth	7th Nov., 1793, 60th Regt. ;	8th July, 1795, 60th Regt. ; aptd. to 7th, 29th JULY, 1795 ;	16th Feb., 1797, 81st Regt. ;	Major, 21st April, 1803, 81st Regt. ; exchd. to 100th Regt., 1st Jan., 1807 ; retired 9th June, 1808 ; died at Ramsgate, 5th June, 1863.

Alphabetical List of Officers of the Royal Fusiliers.

NAME.	ENSIGN, &c.	LIEUTENANT.	CAPTAIN.	HIGHER RANKS AND REMARKS.
PLUMMER, Heathcote *Medal for Sebastopol; Turkish Medal; Medal for India.*	15th DEC., 1854; Served with the Fusiliers in the Crimea from the 12th July, 1855, including the siege and fall of Sebastopol. Served with the 4th Punjaub Rifles in the successful attack on the topol. Served with the 4th Punjaub ber, 1859, and Jan., 1860; and as A. Q. M. General to the Tank Field the operations against the Mahsood tribe of Wuzeerees from April to Force, under Brig. Chamberlain, in burning of Makeen. the 22nd May, 1860, including the forcing of the Burrura Pass and	13th APRIL, 1855;	18th SEPT., 1859;	Major, 6th SEPT., 1873.
POCHIN, Norman	30th MAR., 1867;	28th OCT., 1871, 4th Foot; 31st May, 1831, aptd. to 7th, 21st JUNE, 1831;	23rd FEB., 1838;	Retired 1843; died on board his yacht, 25th June, 1855.
PONSONBY, W. Brabazon, *Lord*	13th DEC., 1827, 65th Regt.; aptd. to 4th Foot, 26th April, 1828;			
POPE, Richard Albert Verco	21st Dec, 1855, 39th Regt.;	23rd Oct., 1860, 39th Regt.; exchd. to 7th, 9th DEC., 1864; exchd. to 49th Regt., 7th Nov., 1868;	1st April, 1870, 49th Regt.; retired on h. p., 26th April, 1870;	
PORTER, Henry Aylmer	30th May, 1843, 44th Regt.;	11th June, 1844, 44th Regt.; aptd. to 7th, 22nd AUG., 1844;		Retired 1st Feb., 1850.
POTHAM, John *Medal for the Crimea; Turkish Medal; Medal for India.* Served the Eastern campaign of (wounded), and siege of Sebastopol. Frontier War of 1863 with the defence of the Sungahs at the Umbeyla Pass.	24th JUNE, 1862;	24th JAN., 1865; 1854-5, including the battle of Alma Served with the Fusiliers in the N.W. Eusafzye Field Force, present at the	1st APRIL, 1870; placed on h. p., 6th May, 1870.	
POWELL			Occurs as Capt., 1701.	
POWELL, James (? Henry)	25th MARCH, 1705.			
POWELL, Chas. Fredk.	...	19th Aug., 1864, 13th Foot; exchd. to 7th, 25th APRIL, 1865.	...	Retired 21st Aug., 1866.
POWELL, Thomas	11th JAN., 1715.			
POWER, Wm. Le Poer	19th JUNE, 1872;	12th JUNE, 1873; aptd. to 58th Regt., 22nd Jan., 1875.		
POWNALL, Edward	... Regt.;	3rd OCT., 1755.		
PRATT, Rupert	14th May, 1710,	13th JULY, 1718; Capt. Lieut., 9th FEB., 1751;	3rd JUNE, 1752;	Died in Ireland, June, 1753.
PRESCOTT, Edward Barker *Medal for Sebastopol.* Served at the siege of Sebastopol.	18th March, 1850, 87th Regt.;	8th APRIL, 1853; aptd. to 33rd Regt., 17th June, 1853;	26th Oct., 1855, 33rd Regt.;	Died at Deesa, Bombay, 21st Jan., 1862.
PRESCOTT, George Served with the 73rd in India; followed the marches of the Regt. death reached her, she braved the dangers of the fight, and recovered his body on the battle field.	1855, severely wounded on the 15th 5th May, 1799, 73rd Regt.; accompanied the 2nd batt. Fusiliers from the embarkation at Cork, and	4th June, 1801, 73rd Regt.; to the Peninsula. Mrs. Prescott had Aug. when the tidings of her husband's	27th Nov., 1806, 4th Gar. Batt.; exchd. to 7th, 25th SEPT., 1807;	Killed at Salamanca, 22nd July, 1812.
PRESCOTT, Richard				Major, 20th Dec., 1756; aptd. to 50th Regt., 11th Dec., 1759; Bt. Lieut. Col., 22nd Jan., 1761; Lieut. Col., 22nd May, 1761, 50th Regt.; aptd. to 7th, 19th Nov., 1761; Col., 22nd June, 1772; aptd. Col. of the Regt., 12th Nov., 1776; Major Gen., 29th Aug., 1777; Lieut. Gen., 26th Nov., 1782; died in Queen Anne Street West, Cavendish Square, 21st Nov., 1788.
PRESTON, Arthur John Present with the 2nd battalion at Busaco, and at the affair of Aldea de Ponte.	10th May, 1800, 56th Regt.;	18th SEPT., 1780; 15th Oct., 1803, 56th Regt.;		Died or retired 1786. Died at Falmouth, on his return from Portugal, May, 1812.
PREVOST, Henry Landed with the 1st battalion at Busaco.	Lisbon, July, 1810; present at 60th Regt.;	15th DEC., 1804;	15th Oct., 1807, 56th Regt.; exchd. to 7th, 18th AUG., 1808;	Died of wounds received at Albuera, 16th May, 1811.
PREVOST, John Augustus		1st MAY, 1782;	16th APRIL, 1795;	Major, 16th AUG., 1804; Lieut. Col., 27th Nov., 1806, 8th West India Regt.; aptd. to 56th Regt., 26th June, 1811; retired 17th Oct., 1811.
PRICE, John	...	18th Aug., 1708, Regt.; Capt. Lieut., Aug. 26th, 1737, Regt.	28th Aug., 1737, Regt.; aptd. to 7th, 25th MARCH, 1742;	Invalided 3rd June, 1752.
PRIDEAUX, Edmund	New Jersey Volunteers;	6th Nov., 1778;	...	Retired 20th Sept., 1780.

Alphabetical List of Officers of the Royal Fusiliers.

NAME.	ENSIGN, &c.	LIEUTENANT.	CAPTAIN.	HIGHER RANKS AND REMARKS.
PRINGLE, *Sir* James, *Bart.*	...	...	...	Major, 7th Dec., 1759, 59th Regt.; Lieut. Col., 21st March, 1765, 59th Regt.; retired 14th Dec., 1770; died at Stitehill, Berwick, 7th April, 1802.
PRITZLER, *Sir* Theophilus, K.C.B. Served under the command of Lord Mulgrave in Walcheren in 1794; in the campaign of 1794-5 in Holland and Germany; in St. Domingo from 1796 to 1798.	Jan., 1794, Indept. Comp.;	18th March, 1794, 85th Regt.; aptd. to 5th D. G., 27th Aug., 1794;	8th July, 1795, 5th D. G., exchd. to 21st L. D., 1st Sept., 1796;	Major, 1st SEPT., 1804; Bt. Lieut. Col., 16th April, 1811, 21st L. D.; aptd. to 22nd L. D., 4th June, 1813; Col., 4th June, 1814; aptd. to 13th L. D., 5th Nov., 1818; Major Gen., 19th July, 1821; Lieut. Gen., 10th Jan., 1837; died at Boulogne, 12th April, 1839.
PROBY, Thomas	...	...	Occurs 1724;	Out 4th Nov., 1724.
PROSSER, Frederick	22nd Dec., 1814, 30th Regt.; aptd. to 3rd D. G., 10th Jan., 1816;	18th Oct., 1816, 3rd D. G.;	1st Aug., 1822, 3rd D. G.; exchd. to h. p. of Gren. Guards, 27th Feb., 1823; exchd. to 7th, 3rd APRIL, 1823; retired on h. p. unatt., 2nd April, 1829;	Aptd. Professor at the Royal Military College, Sandhurst; died at Sandhurst, 7th Sept., 1844.
PYKE, W. A. Served with the Regt. as a volunteer at the capture of Martinique; Albuera.	...	3rd FEB., 1809; accompanied the 1st battalion to the Peninsula; present at Busaco and	...	Killed at Badajoz, April, 1812.
PYNYOT, Augustus	18th Oct., 1703, Regt.;	...	10th Sept., 1712, Regt.; aptd. to 7th, 26th DEC., 1726; 7th Aug., 1806, Cape Regt.; 14th Sept., 1695;	Retired 8th May, 1749.
RAINSFORD, Edward Mon.	...	28th JULY, 1803;		Not in Army List of 1809.
RAINSFORD, Francis	...	Occurs 1687; assault of the Castle of Namur, commanded a company in the expedition Spanish Succession.		Major, 11th JAN., 1715; Lieut. Col. 17
Served in the Regiment in the to Cadiz and Vigo, 1702, and served	Low Countries, wounded at the with the Regiment in the war of the	11th MAY, 1825; exchd. back to Rifle Brigade, 9th Nov., 1825;	8th April, 1826, unatt.; aptd. to 60th Regt., 12th April, 1827; exchd. to h. p. of 68th Regt., 4th Oct., 1831; exchd. to 7th, 9th MAR., 1839;	Retired 9th March, 1839; aptd. Lieut. Col. West Middlesex Militia, 22nd Jan., 1846; resigned 20th Oct., 1853.
RAMSDEN, Charles	29th Nov., 1821, 77th Regt.; exchd. to Rifle Brigade, 19th June, 1823;			
RANELAGH, Thos. Heron Jones, *Viscount*	3rd Sept., 1829, 1st L G.;	23rd Mar., 1832, 1st L. G.; aptd. to 7th, 24th JAN., 1834;	...	Retired 22nd July, 1836; aptd. Lieut. Col. Commd. of the 2nd Middlesex Rifle Vols., 30th Jan., 1860.
RAWDON, Marmaduke Served with the Regt. in the expedition to Cadiz and Vigo in 1702.	...	Capt. Lieut., 1695;	...	Left the Regiment, 10th June, 1703.
RAWSTORNE, James Served with the Regt. during the American War.	...	17th MAY, 1779;	...	Retired 11th Feb., 1785.
READE, Alfred J. M.	12th APRIL, 1864;	24th AUG., 1864; exchd. to 23rd Regt., 3rd Aug., 1809;	...	Retired 11th Dec., 1866.
REED, William	...	...	OCT., 1751.	Retired Oct., 1813.
REID	...	...	...	
REILLY, Edmund Geo.	6th July, 1870, 105th Regt.;	28th Oct., 1871, 105th Regt., aptd. to 7th, 4th OCT., 1873.	...	
REYNETT, Henry James	2nd Nov., 1778, 64th Regt.;	29th Nov., 1779;	8th Nov., 1792; exchd. to 81st Regt., 5th June, 1798;	Retired June, 1798; aptd. Paymaster of the 7th Regt., 27th JUNE, 1798; retired 23rd Nov., 1804.
RICE, Herbert Henry	24th MARCH, 1859;	...	...	Retired 31st Dec., 1859.
RICHARDSON, Thomas	Occurs 1687;	...	...	Out of the Regt. before 1695.
RICHARDSON, William	...	Occurs 1687;	...	Out of the Regt. before 1695.
RICHARDSON, Wm. E.	29th SEPT., 1865;	...	...	Retired 16th Sept., 1868.
RICHMOND, Chas., *Duke* of, K.G.	...	placed on h. p. of it, 1783; aptd. to 7th, APRIL, 1787;	29th Aug., 1787, 35th Regt.;	Capt. and Lieut. Col., 26th March, 1789, Coldstream Guards; Lieut. Col., 15th June, 1789, 35th Regt.; Col., 28th Jan., 1795; Major Gen., 1st Jan., 1798; Col. Comm., 5th Aug., 1799; aptd. Col. Comm. 35th Regt., 17th Mar., 1803; Lieut. Gen., 35th Regt., 1st Jan., 1805; Gen., 4th June, 1814; aptd. Governor of Hull; aptd. Governor of Plymouth; died at William Henry, Canada, 28th Aug.,

Alphabetical List of Officers of the Royal Fusiliers.

NAME.	ENSIGN, &c.	LIEUTENANT.	CAPTAIN.	HIGHER RANKS AND REMARKS.
RICKETTS, Charles	...	5th March, 1818, Coldstream Guards; placed on h. p. of it, 25th Dec, 1818; aptd. to 7th, 16th Nov., 1820;	24th May, 1822, h.p. of 72nd Regt.; aptd. to Rifle Brigade, 9th April, 1825;	Major, 20th Aug., 1826, unatt.; died 13th Nov., 1828.
RICKFORD, Charles W. H.	18th AUG., 1869;	28th OCT., 1871;	...	Retired 29th March, 1873.
RIDGWAY, Joseph	12th June, 1799, 53rd Regt.; aptd. to 11th Foot, 11th Jan. 1800; 23rd March, 1801; placed on h. p. of it, 1802;	21st JAN., 1805;	...	Retired 8th Sept., 1808.
RIDLEY, John Henry Ellis	23rd Sept., 1836, 60th Regt.;	12th JUNE, 1840; exchd. to 2nd D. G., 12th Oct., 1841;	...	Retired 5th Aug., 1848; aptd. Capt. 2nd Surrey Militia, 2nd Oct., 1852; Major, 16th Oct., 1854; Lieut. Col., 30th March, 1867.
ROBERTS, William Edward	11th MARCH, 1862;	19th JULY, 1864;	7th AUG., 1875.	Retired 1st May, 1866.
ROBINSON, Napier Douglas *Medal for Sebastopol.*	11th AUG., 1854; Served at the siege of Sebastopol the assault of the Redan on the 18th 60th Regt.;	12th JAN., 1855; from Feb. 17th, 1855; wounded at June.	28th AUG., 1857.	
ROBINSON, Robert	...	24th JUNE, 1795.	...	Died 4th Aug., 1833.
ROBINSON, William	...	12th Oct., 1795, 33rd Regt.; exchd. to h. p. of 90th Regt.; 3rd July, 1799; exchd. to 7th, 11th JULY, 1811; exchd. to h. p. of 47th Regt., 21st April, 1812;	...	
ROBISON, James *Served at the capture of Martinique.*	...	12th OCT., 1804;	1st JUNE, 1809;	Retired 20th June, 1822; died at Edinburgh, 4th July, 1832.
ROCHFORT, Henry Wollaston	25th JAN., 1859;	18th JULY, 1862;	...	
RODICK, Robert P. Birkett	9th FEB., 1870;	28th OCT., 1871.	7th FEB., 1871; placed on h. p. of the Regt., 19th Nov., 1873.	Died 1800.
ROEBUCK, William Henry	...	24th MAY, 1799;		Major, 19th AUG., 1855; retired 8th Aug, 1856.
ROSE, Eustace Henry *Medal for the Crimea.*	16th July, 1841, 60th Regt.; Served the Eastern campaign, including the battles of Alma and Inkerman (wounded) and siege of Sebastopol.	26th July, 1844, 60th Regt.;	28th Feb., 1851, 60th Regt.; aptd. to 42nd Regt., 21st Jan., 1853; exchd. to 7th, 20th MAY, 1853;	
ROSS, Robert Served the campaign in Holland, Accompanied the 20th Regt. to the Mediterranean, present with the at Maida. Served under Sir J. Moore he was appointed to command a in the Corunna expedition. Returned at San Sebastian, at Orthes, and the brigade of the 4th Division as a tured Washington.	1st Aug., 1789, 25th Regt.; and in the attack on Sir R. Abercrombie's lines, severely wounded expedition to Calabria; both he and to the Peninsula in 1812 with the Nive. At the termination of the war reward for his signal services. was appointed to command the expedition to America, in which he cap-	15th JULY, 1791;	19th APRIL, 1795; and thanked by the Com.-in-Chief the 20th Regt. greatly distinguished present at Vittoria, after which Greatly distinguished in the Pyrenees,	Major, 23rd Dec., 1795, 90th Regt.; reduced 1796, but retained on f. p. of it; placed on h. p. of it, 1798; aptd. to 20th Regt., 6th Aug., 1799; Bt. Lieut. Col. 1st Jan., 1801; Lieut. Col., 21st Jan., 1808, 20th Regt.; Col., 25th July, 1810; Major General, 4th July, 1813; killed by a rifle shot at Baltimore, U.S., 12th Sept., 1814.
ROSS, Robert	13th June, 1830, 50th Regt.; aptd. to 52nd Regt., 8th Feb, 1831;	11th JULY, 1834; aptd. to 96th Regt., 9th Jan., 1835;	14th Sept., 1838, 96th Regt.; aptd. to 36th Regt., 31st Dec., 1839; exchd. to h. p., unatt., 24th June, 1842; exchd. to 74th Regt., 1st Aug., 1848;	Retired 1st Aug., 1848; aptd. Barrack Master at Barbadoes, Jan., 1854; died there, 1st Nov., 1854.
ROTHES, Geo. Wm. Evelyn, *Earl of*	5th April, 1827, 81st Regt.;	12th DEC., 1827;	...	Retired 26th July, 1833; died 10th Mar., 1840.
ROUSSELET, John	...	28th JULY, 1781; exchd. to h. p., 1784.	9th MAR., 1803;	Retired 30th Aug., 1810.
ROWE, Hulton *Served with the Regt. at the capture of Martinique (wounded).*	...	12th JAN., 1796;	...	
ROWE, John	...	1st AUG., 1693;	...	Out of the Regt. before 1702.
ROWLAND, John *Served with the Regt. during the campaign in Flanders.*	...	7th Sept., 1756, 61st Regt.; placed on h. p. of it, 1763; aptd. to 4th Foot, 15th Aug., 1775;	3rd Nov., 1777, 22nd Regt.; aptd. to 7th, 15th Oct., 1780;	Retired 1783; aptd. Adjt. Merionethshire Militia, 4th Dec., 1793; Lieut. and Qr. Master, 25th Dec., 1793.

Alphabetical List of Officers of the Royal Fusiliers.

NAME.	ENSIGN, &C.	LIEUTENANT.	CAPTAIN.	HIGHER RANKS AND REMARKS.
ROWLEY, *Sir* Charles, *Bart.*	15th Jan., 1818, 68th Regt.;	30th SEPT., 1819;	13th June, 1822, 92nd Regt.; exchd. to 58th Regt., 12th Sept., 1822;	Major, 22nd April, 1826, unatt.; exchd. to 36th Regt., 12th June, 1828; Lieut. Col., 31st Aug., 1830, unatt.; exchd. to 9th Lancers, 28th Jan., 1842; retired same day.
RUDDUCK, William	...	14th MAY, 1710.	...	Out of the Regt., 8th May, 1749.
RUDYERD, Richard	...	11th APRIL, 1733;	31st MARCH, 1748;	Retired 1st April, 1859; aptd. Capt. Essex Rifles Militia, 14th Dec., 1872.
RUMBOLD, Henry E. W.	20th JULY, 1855;	9th Nov., 1855;	...	Bt. Major, 24th Jan., 1865; Bt. Lieut. Col., 1st April, 1874.
RUSSELL, Baker Creed, C.B. *Medal for India*; *Medal for Ashanti*. Was at Meerut with the Carabineers at the outbreak of the Sepoy Mutiny, and at Kernaul, when Col. Seaton's movable column at the action being killed, he commanded the squadron of his Regt., and a detachment of the 9th Lancers; on 17th Dec. commanded the cavalry at Putteali, where over 700 action and vigour in pursuit." Commanded Sepoys were killed. Thanked in manded the cavalry in pursuit. Commanded despatches "for his gallantry in Penny was killed and Bareilly taken; relief of Shahjehanpore, capture of destruction of the fort of Mahundee, present at the relief of Bareilly, with the fort of Remai and pursuit, with Fort Mitonlee, actions of Aligunge Russoolpore, attack and capture of of Tantia Topee; commanded a corps Showers, in Central India, in pursuit of natives in the Ashanti campaign;	2nd Nov., 1855, 6th D. G.;	1st Aug., 1856, 6th D. G.; bineers at the outbreak of the Sepoy Gerrard was killed; present with battle of Gungaree, where, his three Sepoys were killed; on where 250 of the rebels were killed; present at the relief of Bareilly, with Oude and actions of Mohudipore and Agra Field Force, under Brig.	24th Aug., 1858, unatt.; exchd. to 7th, 25th MARCH, 1859; exchd. to 18th Hussars, 3rd Oct., 1862;	
RUSSELL, *Hon.* Francis. Served with the Fusiliers in the Aide-de-camp to the Prince of Orange		27th June, 1811, 4th Batt.; exchd. to 7th, 18th JULY, 1811;	28th April, 1814, 2nd Gar. Batt.; reduced, placed on h. p. of it, 1814; exchd. to 57th Regt., 11th July, 1816; placed on h. p. of it; exchd. to 52nd Regt., 2nd Oct., 1817; aptd. to 12th Lancers, 23rd Sept., 1819; placed on h. p. of it, 1821;	Bt. Major, 21st Jan., 1819; Bt. Lieut. Col. and Inspecting Officer of Militia in Nova Scotia, 4th Oct., 1821; Lieut. Col., 7th July, 1825, Coldstream Guards; died in London, 24th Nov., 1832.
7th March, 1811, 2nd Foot; Peninsula and South of France; was at Waterloo.				
RUTHWIN, James	...	...	...	Died of wounds received at Landen on the 19th July, 1693.
RUXTON, Aug. Alex.	25th Aug., 1843, 16th Foot;	24th OCT., 1845;	...	Retired 25th Sept., 1849.
RYND, William Wolfe	15th MARCH, 1864;	14th OCT., 1868;	...	Retired 29th Dec., 1869.
ST. ANGE, Anthony De	...	...	9th JUNE, 1687;	Deprived of his command as a Roman Catholic, Nov., 1688.
ST. CLAIR, John	...	...	4th Jan., 1757, 77th Regt.; placed on h. p., 1763; aptd. to 7th, 13th DEC, 1765;	Bt. Major, 23rd July, 1772; retired 3rd June, 1774.
ST. CLAIR, John	...	Capt. Lieut., 20th July, 1692.	...	
ST. CLAIR, Robert	...	18th JUNE, 1685;	...	Major, 11th JUNE, 1685; Lieut. Col., 1st MAY, 1686; aptd. Governor of Tilbury Fort, 20th July, 1688;
ST. GEORGE WALDYVE, W.	14th FEB., 1865;	29th DEC, 1869;	...	Retired 23rd April, 1873.
ST. MAUR, Percy	16th SEPT., 1868;	28th OCT., 1871.	...	
ST. POL, Paul	...	8th MAY, 1806;	16th APRIL, 1812; Ponte.	Died of wounds received at Badajoz, 23rd April, 1812.
SALMON, Thomas. Landed with the 1st Batt. at Lisbon, July, 1810; present at Busaco, 26th Aug., 1799, 9th Foot;		Albuera, and the affair at Aldea de 21st May, 1801, 85th Regt.; placed on h. p. of it, 1802; re-aptd. to f. p. of it, 25th Nov., 1802;	21st MARCH, 1805;	Died in Lisbon, 31st Jan., 1811.
SALTER, Burridge	...	1st AUG., 1693.	...	
SALTER, John	...	18th JUNE, 1685;	Occurs 1695;	Died in the service before 1706.
SALTOUN, Alexander, *Lord*. Served during William's campaigns in Flanders, and also in the 11th Aug, 1837, 96th Regt.;		expedition to Cadiz and Vigo in 1702. 12th July, 1839;	8th OCT., 1844; exchd. to 28th Regt., 1st Aug., 1845;	Major, 16th July, 1852, 28th Regt.; retired 18th Oct., 1853.
SALUBERRY, Charles de, C.B. *Gold Medal for Chateauguay*. Served as Brigade Major in Canada; greatly distinguished himself in the action on the Chateauguay, where, while in command of the advanced pickets of the British, he checked the advance of the principal American and was afterwards conspicuous in bringing about the complete defeat column led by Major Gen. Hampton, 9th June, 1855, Bengal Army;	10th April, 1793, 60th Regt.;	25th Aug., 1794, 60th Regt.; aptd. to 7th, 29th JULY, 1795; re-aptd. to 60th Regt., 1796; of the enemy, Oct. 26th, 1813.	10th July, 1799, 60th Regt.	Bt. Major, 4th June, 1811; Bt. Lieut. Col., 24th Sept., 1812; Major, 18th Nov., 1813, 60th Regt.; aptd. to Canadian Voltigeurs, 1813; placed on h. p. of the Corps, 1813; retired Jan., 1826;
SANDYS, Thomas Myles		30th April, 1858, Bengal Army	9th June, 1867, Bengal Staff Corps; exchd. to 7th, 9th AUG., 1871;	Retired 21st July, 1875; aptd. Major, 3rd Royal Lancs. Militia, same day.

Alphabetical List of Officers of the Royal Fusiliers.

NAME.	ENSIGN, &C.	LIEUTENANT.	CAPTAIN.	HIGHER RANKS AND REMARKS.
SAUMAREZ, *Sir Thos., Kt.* Served with the 23rd Royal Welsh Fusiliers in America from 1775 to the termination of the war, and in which that regiment was engaged, he being principal actions attached to the 1st batt. of Grenadiers sent in the town and Yorktown, where he was taken prisoner. He was one of the officers selected for execution by order of Gen. Washington, when the lot fell on Sir Charles Asgill.	…	22nd Nov., 1777, 23rd Regt.;	13th Sept., 1779, 23rd Regt.; placed on h. p. of it, 1785; aptd. to 7th Regt., 13th JUNE, 1789;	Bt. Major, 1st March, 1794; Bt. Lieut. Col., 1st Jan., 1798; aptd. Inspector of Militia in Guernsey, 25th June, 1799; Col., 25th April, 1808; Major Gen., 4th June, 1811; Lieut. Gen. 19th July, 1821; Gen., 28th June, 1838; died at Guernsey, 4th March, 1845.
SAUNDERS, Robt. Erasmus	21st Sept., 1872, 13th Foot; aptd. to 7th, 23rd Nov., 1872.			
SAVAGE, Philip Chas. Coffin	20th July, 1855, Royal Canadian Rifles;	19th Feb., 1858, Royal Canadian Rifles;	1st April, 1870, h.-p. R. C. Rifles; aptd. to 7th, 10th DEC., 1873.	
SAWREY, John Gilpin	…	8th JULY, 1757;	…	Retired 1760; died at Broughton Tower, Lancashire, 3rd April, 1773.
SAXTON, John. Commanded the 45th Regt. in the American War from the commencement until his death.	…	14th MAY, 1759;	3rd Mar., 1760, 94th Regt., placed on h. p. of it; aptd. to 17th Regt., 25th Dec., 1765;	Major, 20th Oct., 1774, 45th Regt.; died in America in April or May, 1778.
SCOTT,	…	19th DEC., 1799;	…	
SCOTT, M. J.	Royal Nova Scotia Provincials;	20th JULY, 1795; exchd. to h. p. of 84th Regt., 14th Feb, 1797.	…	Died or retired 1802.
SCOTT, Ventris	Occurs 1687;	…	25th APRIL, 1741; Occurs 1694;	Left the Regt., 25th March, 1742.
SEATON, Patrick	23rd Jan., 1769, 24th Regt.;	25th DEC., 1770;	7th OCT., 1777;	Out before 1702. Retired 23rd April, 1788.
SELWYN, Henry Charles	…	Occurs 1695;	…	Out of the Regt., 30th Aug., 1695.
SENARGUS,	3rd Nov., 1846, 13th Foot;	29th DEC., 1848; exchd. to 59th Regt., 19th April, 1850;	…	Retired 10th Feb., 1852.
SENIOR, Stanton	…	31st MAY, 1810;	15th May, 1827, unatt.; aptd. to 35th Regt., 21st Feb., 1834;	Retired 5th Aug., 1836.
SETON, George Joined the 1st Batt. in the Peninsula, present at Busaco, Albuera (wounded), the affair at Aldea de Ponte (severely wounded).				
SEYMOUR, Hubert	Royal Nova Scotia Provincials;	24th JUNE, 1795; aptd. to 60th Regt., 17th May, 1796;	…	Died or retired 1801.
SEYMOUR, William	11th JUNE, 1685;	…	1st MAY, 1686;	"9th Feb., 1728, died William Seymour, Esq., Lieut. Gen. and Lieut. of the Band of the Gentlemen Pensioners."—*Hist. Register.*
SEYMOUR, William	July, 1792, 60th Regt.;	28th Nov., 1792;	20th APRIL, 1795; aptd. to 16th Regt., 1st Sept., 1795;	Died or retired 1797.
SHACKLETON, John	Aptd. Adjt., 23rd AUG., 1685;	29th OCT., 1688;	…	Out of the Regt. before 1695.
SHALES, John	16th JUNE, 1685;	…	…	Retired 1688.
SHAWE, Meyrick	…	23rd JUNE, 1814; aptd. to 30th Regt., 18th Jan., 1816; placed on h. p. of it, 25th Mar., 1817;	…	Died 1843.
SHEARS, Thomas	…	2nd MAY, 1751;	8th MAY, 1758; placed on h. p. of 107th Regt., 1763.	
SHEE, Charles. Served the early part of the campaign of 1809 in Portugal; and the Peninsular Campaigns of 1812, 13, 14 with the Portuguese army.		3rd SEPT., 1807; aptd. to 20th L. D., 26th Jan., 1809; latter end of 1809, 1810, 1811,	18th Nov., 1813, 12th Foot; placed on h. p. of the Regt., Feb., 1818; exchd. to 84th Regt., 18th Aug., 1825;	Major, 20th May, 1826, unatt.; aptd. to 60th Regt., 26th Oct., 1826; Lieut. Col., 5th April, 1831, unatt.; Col., 9th Nov., 1846; exchd. to 6th, D. G., 21st May, 1850; retired same day; died at Gravesend, 19th July, 1856.
SHEFFIELD, Chas. Hyde	9th AUG., 1864;	25th SEPT., 1869;	22nd Dec., 1803; 9th Batt. of Reserve;	Retired 26th March, 1873.
SHEKLETON, Charles Dixie	…	29th JULY, 1795;	54th Regt., 1804;	Bt. Major, 4th June, 1814; aptd. Major of Brigade at Quebec; died there, 1825.
SHERIDAN, Thomas	14th Oct., 1803, 10th L. D.;	17th DEC., 1803;	19th Sept., 1805, 27th Regt., h. p. of 20th Regt., 1807;	Died at the Cape, 12th Sept., 1817.

Alphabetical List of Officers of the Royal Fusiliers.

NAME.	ENSIGN, &c.	LIEUTENANT.	CAPTAIN.	HIGHER RANKS AND REMARKS.
SHIEL, Theobald *Silver Medal for Fuentes d'Onor.* Served in the rebellion in Ireland in 1798, present at Vinegar Hill. Served with the 18th Foot in the 12th L. D. at Walcheren, 1809, and with the 14th L. D. in the Peninsula— Torres Vedras, pursuit of Massena, affairs of Pombal, Redinha, Campo Mayor, siege of Ciudad Rodrigo (wounded), a horse shot under him in the wood of Especia, Nave de Ver (wounded); a horse shot under him at Fort Conception.	6th Feb., 1806, 12th L. D.;	30th March, 1808, 12th L. D.; exchd. to 14th L. D., 22nd June, 1809; exchd. to 7th, 1st Oct., 1812; superseded 1813; aptd. to 3rd Foot, 1st April, 1826; exchd. to h. p. of 60th Regt., 13th July, 1826;	...	Died 7th Jan., 1855.
SHIPLEY, Wm. Davies	3rd March, 1848, 95th Regt.; aptd. to 64th Regt., 31st March, 1848;	20th Aug., 1849, 64th Regt.; aptd. to 7th, 21st May, 1850; exchd. to 58th Regt., 26th March, 1852;	13th April, 1858, 58th Regt.	Major, 10th Nov., 1869, 58th Regt.; exchd. to 40th Regt., 30th Sept., 1874.
SHIPLEY, Reginald Yonge, C.B. *Medal for the Crimea; Sardinian Medal; 5th Class of the Medjidie.* Served the Eastern campaign of 1854, including the battles of Alma 26th Oct. Served in the N. W. Frontier War, 1863, with the Eusafzye Brigade from the 4th to the 14th Dec., and of the 1st Batt. Fusiliers at the siege of Sebastopol and sortie on the 26th Oct. Served in the N. W. Frontier War, 1863, with the Eusafzye field force in command of the 1st attack and storming of the Conical Hill, and the capture of Umbeyla.	5th Dec., 1843, 5th Foot; exchd. to 55th Regt., 3rd Jan., 1845;	11th Dec., 1846, 55th Regt.; and Inkerman (severely wounded), (mentioned in despatches).	30th April, 1852, 55th Regt.; exchd. to 7th, 24th Dec., 1852;	Bt. Major, 12th Dec., 1854; Major, 9th June, 1855; Lieut. Col., 27th May, 1856; placed on h. p. of the Regt., Nov., 1856; re-aptd. to f. p. of it, 29th May, 1857; Col., 31st Dec., 1861; retired on h. p. of the Regt., 20th June, 1865; aptd. to Woolwich Brigade depôt, 1st April, 1873; Maj. Gen., 10th Oct., 1874.
SHIREMAN, John	...	11th JAN., 1715.	...	...
SHRIMPTON, John Served in Flanders under William III.; wounded at Landen; commanded the Fusiliers at the capture of Namur; served during the War of Succession in Spain; commanded a brigade at Almanza, where he was taken prisoner, and released on parole.	...	...	...	Major, ... ; Lieut. Col, 1st Aug., 1692; aptd. to 7th, ; aptd. Major, 1st Guards, 1695; Major Gen., May, 1707; Lieut. Gen., ; M.P. for Christchurch; died 24th Dec., 1707.
SHULDHAM, Thomas	55th Regt.;	5th Nov., 1777;	...	Retired 15th Oct., 1778.
SHUTTLEWORTH, Edmund	...	9th April, 1777;	...	Died or retired 1783.
SHUTTLEWORTH, James	10th Dec., 1771, 13th Regt.;	21st July, 1779;	30th June, 1794;	Retired March, 1795.
SHUTTLEWORTH, John Ashton Served with the Fusiliers in America from the commencement of the war.	...	20th May, 1772;	10th June, 1778;	Retired 30th June, 1794; died at Hathersage Hall, near Sheffield, 16th July, 1794.
SHUTTLEWORTH, William	...	20th April, 1738; Capt. Lieut., 20th June, 1753;	4th Sept., 1754;	Retired 1756.
SIEVWRIGHT, Chas. Wightman	18th Jan., 1816, 25th Regt.; placed on h. p. of it same month; exchd. to Rifle Brigade, 25th Dec., 1817; placed on h. p. of it, 25th Dec., 1818; exchd. to 55th Regt., 23rd Dec., 1824;	8th April, 1825;	...	Retired 26th Sept., 1834; died 10th Sept., 1855.
SIMPSON, Christopher Joined the Regt. as Quartermaster, served with it during the campaigns	...	Capt. Lieut., 1st Aug., 1693; in Flanders, commanded a company	Occurs as Capt., 1702; in the expedition to Cadiz and Vigo.	Major, 25th Dec., 1704; Lieut. Col., out of the Regt., 21st Aug., 1707.
SINGER, James	...	14th June, 1801, 56th Regt.; placed on h. p. of it; to f. p., 31st Oct., 1802;	14th Nov., 1805;	Major, 9th Jan., 1812; killed at Badajoz, April, 1812.
SISSON, Joseph	...	29th Aug., 1756;	...	Died or retired 1765.
SKINNER, L. J.	30th April, 1873;	29th July, 1795.	...	
SKINNER, L. H. H. P.	3rd Oct., 1816, h. p. of 10th Foot; exchd. to 84th Regt., 20th Nov., 1823;	3rd March, 1825;	...	Retired 24th Mar., 1875.
SKYNNER, Aug. Chas.	...	...	12th April, 1827, 2nd West India Regt.; exchd. to 37th Regt., 28th June, 1827; exchd. to h. p., unatt., 7th Sept., 1832; exchd. to 1st Foot, 2nd Sept., 1836; exchd. to h. p. of 15th Hussars, 20th Dec., 1839; exchd. to 16th Lancers, 2nd July, 1847;	Bt. Major, 23rd Nov., 1841; retired 2nd July, 1847.

Alphabetical List of Officers of the Royal Fusiliers.

NAME.	ENSIGN, &c.	LIEUTENANT.	CAPTAIN.	HIGHER RANKS AND REMARKS.
SMITH, Francis	19th JAN., 1741;	25th APRIL, 1741;	7th July, 1747, 10th Regt.;	Major, 25th Sept., 1758, 10th Foot; Bt. Lieut. Col., 16th Jan., 1762; Lieut. Col., 18th Feb., 1762, 10th Foot; Maj. Gen., 19th Feb., 1779; aptd. Col. 11th Foot, 10th Aug., 1781; Lieut. Gen., 28th Sept., 1787; died in Lower Grosvenor Street, 7th Nov., 1791.
SMITH, James	...	19th JAN., 1740;	...	Died May, 1751.
SMITH, John Graydon	26th JAN., 1858;	12th JUNE, 1860;	12th JUNE, 1867; retired on h. p. of the Regt., 6th July, 1870;	Retired June, 1873; died 3rd Nov., 1873.
SMITH, John Sidney	16th Nov., 1860;	7th JUNE, 1864;	7th Nov., 1868, unatt.	
SMITH, Joseph	20th Feb., 1857, Mil. Train aptd. to 7th, 6th Nov., 1857;	12th JUNE, 1860;	1st APRIL, 1870, unatt.	
SMITH, Marcus Commanded the Regiment in the Mediterranean and at Minorca.	...	...	4th Nov., 1724;	Major, 13th FEB., 1741; Lieut. Col., 3rd JUNE, 1752; Col., 11th Nov., 1761, 60th Regt.; Major Gen., 10th July, 1762; died Nov., 1768.
SMITH, Matthew	...	7th JULY, 1747;	28th AUG., 1753; aptd. to 31st Regt., 2nd Sept., 1757; to Coldstream Guards, 5th May, 1761;	Capt. and Lieut. Col. Coldstream Guards, 1st May, 1777; died at the Tower, 18th Feb, 1812.
SMITH, William	26th Feb., 1806, 59th Regt.;	19th Nov., 1806; aptd. to 20th Regt., 14th April, 1808;	13th July, 1809, 90th Regt.;	Died or retired 23rd Aug., 1810.
SMITH, Thomas	21st SEPT., 1705;	...	1st JUNE, 1711.	
SMYTH, George Stracy Served at the capture of Martinique, St. Lucia, and Guadaloupe, under Sir Charles Gray. Served on the Staff at New Brunswick, and was Groom of the Bedchamber to H.R.H. the Duke of Kent. Served in the East Indies on the staff of Sir Alured Clarke.	18th Aug., 1780, 25th Regt.;	8th March, 1782, Indept. Compy.; aptd. to 7th, 25th SEPT., 1787;	16th Nov., 1794, 38th Regt.; aptd. to 7th, 17th APRIL, 1795;	Major, 6th Sept., 1798, 83rd Regt.; Bt. Lieut. Col., 1st Oct., 1799; exchd. to 3rd Gar. Batt., 9th May, 1805; made 1st 1814; Col., 25th Oct., 1809; Maj. Gen., 1st Jan., 1812; died at Fredricton, New Brunswick, 27th Mar., 1823.
SNOW, Sydenham	5th July, 1831, 67th Regt.;	12th April, 1833, 67th Regt.; exchd. to 7th, 26th DEC., 1837.	...	Retired 17th June, 1838.
SOMERSET, Lord Arthur	...	13th MAY, 1804;	26th June, 1806, 4th West India Regt.; exchd. to 91st Regt., 2nd Oct., 1806; exchd. to 19th L. D., 12th Sept., 1811;	Died at Lisbon, 4th May, 1816.
SOMERSET, Poulett G. H., C.B. Medal for the Crimea; 4th Class of the Medjidie; Turkish Medal. Served the Eastern campaign of 1854 as Aide-de-camp to Lord Raglan, including the battles of Alma, Balaclava, and Inkerman (horse killed by the explosion of a shell in him), and siege of Sebastopol.	29th March, 1839, 33rd Regt.;	1st May, 1840, Coldstream Guards;	28th Dec., 1846, Coldstream Guards; Capt. and Lieut. Col., 3rd March, 1854, Coldstream Guards;	Major, 17th Aug., 1841, 60th Regt.; Lieut. Col., 20th Dec., 1844, 60th Regt.; exchd. to 37th Regt., 9th May, 1845; exchd. back to Coldstream Guards, 30th Nov., 1849; retired 31st Oct., 1851; re-entered as Lieut. Col., 2nd FEB., 1858; Col., 2nd Feb., 1863; retired on h. p. of the Regt., 21st June, 1864; retired June, 1873; died at Dundrum, near Dublin, 7th Sept., 1875.
SOPER, Thomas	...	...	JUNE, 1685.	Major, 1st May, 1686; deprived of his command as a Jacobite, Nov., 1688.
SPARKS, Robert Watson	16th MARCH, 1855;	3rd AUG., 1855;	18th JULY, 1862.	
SPEARS, T.	...	2nd MAY, 1751.	...	
SPEEDY, Thos. Beckwith Medal for Jellalabad; Medal for Cabul. Served the campaigns of 1840-1 with the 13th Foot, present at the dulluk Pass, reduction of the Fort of Mamoo Khail, defence of Jollalabad general action and defeat of Ackbar Khan,	15th March, 1839, 13th Foot;	23rd Oct., 1841, 13th Foot; exchd. to 7th, 26th JUNE, 1846; storming of the Khoord Cabool Pass, March and 1st April, 1842, and 5th April, 1796, 27th L. D.;	17th Feb., 1854, unatt.; affair of Tezeen, forcing the Jugbad, and sorties on the 14th Nov.	Bt. Major, 6th June, 1856; Bt. Lieut. Col., 1st Jan., 1868; aptd. Secretary and Adjt. to the Royal Hibernian School.
SPENCER, Henry Leigh and 1st Dec., 1841, 11th and 24th	...	placed on h. p. of it, 1802 exchd. to 20th L. D., 3rd Feb, 1803;	28th SEPT., 1804;	Retired 5th March, 1812; died at Banstead Park, Surrey, 27th Aug., 1829.
SPRAGG, William	1st DEC, 1687;	...	...	Left the Regt. in 1695.

Alphabetical List of Officers of the Royal Fusiliers.

NAME.	ENSIGN, &c.	LIEUTENANT.	CAPTAIN.	HIGHER RANKS AND REMARKS.
SPROULE, Thomas	30th June, 1804, 34th Regt.;	28th DEC., 1804; exchd. to 16th Foot, 1st Sept., 1808;	…	Died at Veranda, near Swansea, Glamorganshire, 26th Feb., 1811.
SQUIRE, Tristrim Charnley *Medal for Ghuznee; Medal for Ava*.	24th April, 1809, 56th Regt.; Served the campaigns of 1810, 1811, and 1813 in the Peninsula; Burmese War of 1824, and was present at the taking of Cheduba; commanded the landing party and took the Chokey Stockade; was present as Major of three companies in storming the and succeeded to the command of Brigade at the storming of Ghuznee.	31st Jan., 1810, 34th Regt.; aptd. to 7th, 1st MAR., 1810;	18th OCT., 1821; placed on h. p. of the Regt., 25th Oct., 1821; exchd. to 13th Foot, 20th Dec., 1821;	Bt. Major, 10th Jan., 1837; Major, 21st April, 1839, 13th Foot; Lieut. Col., 2nd Aug., 1842, 13th Foot; retired 3rd Nov., 1846; died at Felpham, Sussex, 16th June, 1855.
SQUIRE, William Joseph	30th DEC., 1863;	12th JUNE, 1867.	…	
STAINFORTH, Chas. Edward	8th Sept., 1846, 97th Regt.;	14th Dec., 1849, 97th Regt.; exchd. to 7th, 2nd AUG., 1850;	…	Retired 4th April, 1851; aptd. Capt. 1st West York Militia, 17th Aug., 1853; died at Broad Lane House, Pontefract, 27th June, 1855.
STANHOPE, Russell Charles	23rd Feb., 1844, 56th Regt.;	27th FEB., 1846; exchd. to 13th Foot, 26th June, 1846;	…	Retired 24th Jan., 1851.
STANLEY, John	8th MAR., 1831, 70th Regt.;	11th Jan., 1833, 70th Regt.; aptd. to 7th, 12th APRIL, 1833;	…	Retired 9th Jan., 1838.
STEPHEN, Herbert Venn	15th Dec., 1840, 5th Foot;	28th JAN., 1842;	…	Retired 29th Dec., 1843.
STEPHENS, Geo. Bligh	1st DEC., 1863;	16th MARCH, 1867;	…	Retired 4th Oct., 1873.
STERLING, Alexander	…	16th July, 1794;	20th JUNE, 1799;	Died in 1800.
STEWARR, *Hon.* Charles	23rd Nov. 1768, 37th Regt.;	13th SEPT., 1770;	12th March, 1773, 35th Regt.;	Major, 8th Oct., 1775, 43rd Regt.; Lieut. Col., 26th Oct., 1777, 26th Regt.; Col. 20th Nov., 1782; to 101st, 29th July, 1784; regt. disbanded 1785, placed on h. p. of it; Major Gen., 12th Oct., 1793; aptd. Col. 26th Regt., 25th March, 1795; Lieut. Gen., 1st Jan., 1798; died at Richmond Lodge, Surrey, 25th March, 1801.
STEWARD, James Browne	9th April, 1812, 75th Regt.;	24th Nov., 1814; placed on h. p. of the Regt., 25th Feb., 1816; exchd. to 64th Regt., 9th May, 1816; exchd. to 10th Foot, 27th June, 1816; placed on h. p. of it, 29th Sept., 1818; 2nd FEB., 1844; exchd. to 52nd Regt., 10th May, 1844;	…	Retired June, 1827.
STEWART, John Henry Fraser	15th Jan., 1841, 24th Regt.;		16th June, 1848, 52nd Regt.;	Died at Subathoo, 20th Aug., 1855.
STODDARD, J. Herbert Randall	16th Nov., 1855, 2nd Drags.; aptd. to 12th Lancers, 22nd Aug., 1856;	10th Oct., 1857, 12th Lancers; exchd. to 7th, 11th JUNE, 1859;	…	Retired 23rd Aug., 1861.
STONE, John Served with the Regt. in the expedition to Cadiz and Vigo, 1702.		1st MARCH, 1693;	…	Out of the Regt. before 1706.
STONEMAN, Thomas	20th SEPT., 1705;	…	…	Out of the Regt. before 1715.
STOPFORD, *Hon.* Joseph Served with the Fusiliers in America during the Revolutionary war.	6th Nov., 1759, 18th L. D.;	…	22nd Oct., 1761, 107th Regt.; placed on h. p. of it, 1763; aptd. to 7th, 20th Nov., 1764;	Major, 27th OCT., 1772; Lieut. Col., 29th AUG., 1777; aptd. to 15th Foot, 31st Jan., 1778; Col., 20th Nov., 1782; died at Wexford, 29th June, 1786.
STRANGWAYS, Geo. Fox	5th Oct., 1820, 71st Regt.; placed on h. p. of it, Oct., 1821; reaptd. to f. p. of it, 16th May, 1822;	8th APRIL, 1825;	25th JUNE, 1829; exchd. to h. p., unatt., 8th June, 1838;	Died at Rewe, near Exeter, 15th April, 1852.
STRODE, John	…	13th FEB., 1757;	1767, 112th Regt.; placed on h. p., 1768;	Aptd. Col. Somersetshire Fencible Cavalry, 28th March, 1794; died at Southill, co. Somerset, 22nd Dec., 1807.
STRODE, John Purling Accompanied the Rifles to the Peninsula, and served with them until the period of his death.	…	17th APRIL, 1806; placed on h. p. of 96th Regt., March, 1807; aptd. to 95th Rifles, 30th March, 1809;	…	Died of wounds received at Cazal Nova, Portugal, in pursuit of Massena, 1811.
STRODE, Samuel	…	15th May, 1761; exchd. to h. p. of 12th Foot, 1st Sept., 1768.	…	

Alphabetical List of Officers of the Royal Fusiliers.

NAME.	ENSIGN, &c.	LIEUTENANT.	CAPTAIN.	HIGHER RANKS AND REMARKS.
STUART, *Lord* James Evelyn	2nd Dec., 1789, 6th Foot;	11th JUNE, 1790;	24th Jan., 1791, Indept. Comp.; reduced 1791; placed on h.p. of it, exchd. to Grenadier Guards, 30th April, 1793;	Major, 26th Oct., 1797, 66th Regt.; Lieut. Col., 1st Nov., 1797, 21st Regt.; aptd. to 22nd Regt., 25th June, 1802; retired 2nd Oct., 1806; died near London, 16th Aug., 1842.
STUART, John. *Medal for the Kaffir War.* Was twice complimented by Sir Harry Smith, for his gallantry in several engagements with the Kaffirs, while in command of a brigade.	22nd Jan., 1820, 46th Regt.;	26th March, 1823, 46th Regt.; exchd. to 7th, 5th JUNE, 1823;	13th AUG., 1825;	Major, 6th MAY, 1836; exchd. to 88th Regt., 20th March, 1840; exchd. to h.p. unatt., 12th May, 1843; Bt. Lieut. Col., 9th March, 1846; exchd. to 57th Regt., 21st May, 1847; exchd. to 6th Foot, 26th Sept., 1848; retired 26th Dec., 1851; died at Henley on Thames, 15th May, 1857.
STUART, John Morton	11th June, 1812, 77th Regt.;	6th JAN., 1814; placed on h.p. of the Regt., 25th March, 1817; exchd. back to f.p. of it, 10th Dec., 1818;	16th May, 1822, 37th Regt.; exchd. to h.p. of 12th Foot, 12th Sept., 1822; exchd. to 53rd Regt., 3rd Oct., 1823; exchd. to h.p., unatt., 22nd Sept., 1825;	Died 17th July, 1840.
STUART, Robert	23rd May, 1834, 44th Regt.;	11th June, 1837, 44th Regt.; aptd. to 7th, 11th MAY, 1838;	2nd DEC., 1842; exchd. to 41st Regt., 9th Sept., 1851;	Retired 25th June, 1852.
SUMYER, Edward	3rd April, 1806, 20th Regt.;	20th Aug., 1807, 20th Regt.;	24th SEPT., 1812; exchd. to Coldstream Guards, 23rd Sept., 1813;	Died 26th June, 1815, of wounds received at Waterloo on the 18th.
SUPPLE, John	25th Jan., 1856, 48th Regt.; aptd. to Canadian Rifles, 16th March, 1858;	11th AUG., 1716, 15th June, 1855, Canadian Rifles;	9th April, 1861, Canadian Rifles; exchd. to 7th, 18th JULY, 1862;	Brevet Major, 16th May, 1874.
SURMAN, Wm. Henry	1777, 40th Regt.;	5th OCT., 1777; 1st Oct., 1794, 6th Batt. Irish Brigade; disbanded 1798; placed on h.p. of it; aptd. to 7th, 25th APRIL, 1799;	...	Retired 28th June, 1783.
SUTHERLAND, John				Died in Halifax, Nova Scotia, 1800.
SUTTON, Ambrose	18th JUNE, 1685;			Out of the Regt. before 1695.
SUTTON, Daniel	...	28th APRIL, 1794;	17 ;	Retired Oct., 1751.
SUTTON	...	4th AUG., 1814; placed on h.p. of the Regt., 25th Feb., 1816; exchd. back to f.p. of it, 22nd April, 1819; exchd. back to h.p. of it, 16th Dec., 1819;	6th July, 1796, 58th Regt.;	Retired 18th Oct., 1802; died 1833.
SUTTON, Robert Nassau	...			Died at Huntingdon, 20th March, 1865.
SWEETING, George				
SWEETLAND, Thomas	7th Sept., 1858, 4th Foot; Served in Abyssinia as Aide-de-camp to Brig. Gen. Wilby; afterwards appointed Provost Marshal and Baggage Master 1st Brigade 1st Division; present at the action of Arogee and capture of Magdala; (mentioned in despatches and promoted Captain for service).	25th Feb., 1862, 4th Foot;	28th April, 1782, 60th Regt.; 2nd Sept., 1868, 4th Foot; placed on h.p. of it; aptd. to 7th, 6th JULY, 1870;	Retired 1783. Aptd. Adjt. 26th Kent Rifle Volunteers, 24th April, 1875.
SWENY, Geo. Augustus. *Medal for Abyssinia.*	11th Feb., 1848, 96th Regt.;	16th July, 1850, 96th Regt.; aptd. to 7th, 10th MARCH, 1854; exchd. to 11th Foot, 16th June, 1854; aptd. to 92nd Regt., 10th April, 1855;	13th March, 1857, unatt.; aptd. to Military Train, 11th Sept., 1857; exchd. to 100th Regt., 9th Nov., 1858;	Retired 12th June, 1860.
SWIFT, William Alfred				
SWINBURNE		25th AUG., 1804;	...	Retired 27th Nov., 1805.
SYMES, Charles Jeffereys		9th Nov., 1778;	...	Died in 1786.
TALBOT, *Hon.* Wellington P. M. Was appointed British Resident at Cephalonia, Sept., 1855.	19th DEC., 1834, 35th Regt.;	15th SEPT., 1837;	29th MAR., 1842;	Retired 1844; Lieut.-Col. 1st Staffordshire Militia, 4th March, 1853; Hon. Col., 26th April, 1873.
TALBOT, William Davenport	17th Feb., 1788, 2nd D.G.;	28th Oct., 1789, 2nd D.G.; exchd. to 7th, 11th JUNE, 1790;	14th April, 1791, Indept. Compy.;	Retired 1791; died in Old Burlington Street, 30th July, 1800.

Alphabetical List of Officers of the Royal Fusiliers.

NAME.	ENSIGN, &c.	LIEUTENANT.	CAPTAIN.	HIGHER RANKS AND REMARKS.
TALMASH, Thomas Served with the Guards at Tangiers in 1680; with the English Brigade in Holland until the Revolution; commanded a division under Marlborough in Ireland; led the assault of Athlone; served during the seige of Limerick, and at the surrender of the city was appointed governor. Commanded a division at Landen, 1693, and especially distinguished himself in conducting the retreat. In chief command of France.	…	…	…	Capt. and Lieut.-Col., 16th Jan., 1678, Coldstream Guards; aptd. to 7th, 11th June, 1685; retired and joined the Dutch service 1st May, 1685; aptd. Col. 5th Regt. 5th Oct., 1688; Maj.-Gen., 1689; died at Plymouth, 12th June, 1694, of wounds received in Camaret Bay, on the 8th.
TALMASH, Thomas Served with the Regt. in the expedition to Cadiz and Vigo in 1702.	14th APRIL, 1702.	…	…	…
TARLETON, Henry Served with the Fusiliers in the Vittoria, and in the Pyrenees; taken prisoner at Sauroren.	25th Feb., 1804, 1st D. G.; Peninsula; present at Busaco; wounded at Albuera; present at	19th Sept., 1805, 21st L. D.;	18th Aug., 1808, 4th Gar. Batt.; aptd. to 7th, 7th JUNE, 1810.	Major, 21st April, 1814, 60th Regt.; Lieut.-Col., 24th Feb, 1817, 60th Regt.; placed on h. p. of it, 25th March, 1817; died in Cheshire, Feb., 1829.
TAYLEUR, Charles	11th June, 1861, 8th Foot; aptd. to 7th, 6th AUG., 1861	…	…	Retired 1st March, 1864.
TAYLOR, Christopher	…	1st JUNE, 1796;	18th AUG., 1804;	Died 1806.
TAYLOR, Joseph	…	29th JULY, 1795;	17th AUG., 1804;	Killed on the heights of Surirey, Martinique, 2nd Feb., 1809.
TEIGHE, Matthew	…	9th March, 1797;	25th SEPT., 1800;	Died 1804.
TEMPLE, Frederick	21st Aug., 1799, 40th Regt.; exchd. to 29th L. D, 10th July, 1800;	10th Feb., 1802, 29th L. D.; made 25th, 1804;	27th Sept., 1809, 25th L. D.; exchd. to 7th, 18th Nov, 1808; placed on h. p. of it, 25th Feb., 1816;	Retired July, 1825.
TEMPLE, Henry Martindale	8th June, 1872, 4th Foot; aptd. to 7th, 6th SEPT., 1873;	6th SEPT., 1873 (comuission antedated, see *Gazette*, Sept. 18th, 1874);	…	Appointed a probationer for the India Staff Corps, 1875.
TENNISON, Thomas	…	29th JULY, 1757;	…	Died or retired 1759.
THACKWELL, E. L. R.	9th AUG., 1873, 106th Regt.; aptd. to 7th, 24th SEPT., 1873.			
TUFTON, *Hon.* Charles (*Thanet Earl of*)	21st Feb., 1787, 68th Regt.;	25th JUNE, 1788;	14th April,1793,Indept.Conpy.; aptd. to 93rd Regt., 30th Oct., 1793;	Major, 3rd Aug., 1796, 64th Regt.; retired 28th Aug., 1800; died at Hothfield Place, Kent, 20th April, 1832.
THOMAS, Charles	…	30th JULY, 1794;	…	Died Nov., 1797.
THOMAS, Nath. R.	…	17th August, 1797; exchd. to h. p. of 4th batt. Irish Brigade, 30th Oct., 1800;	…	Died or retired 1808.
THOMAS, Richd. Williams	18th Aug., 1848, St. Helena Regt.	7th MARCH, 1851;	29th DEC., 1854;	Retired 2nd Nov., 1855; died at Stonehouse, Devonshire, 12th April, 1869.
THOMPSON, Charles	…	7th APRIL, 1750;	…	Died or retired, 1756.
THOMPSON, Charles Farqthar	3rd Feb., 1804, 13th L. D.;	28th SEPT., 1804; aptd. to 14th L. D., 7th March, 1805;	10th July, 1806, 59th Regt.;	Dismissed the service, June, 1808.
THOMPSON, Thos. Peronet *Silver Medal for* 22, 24, 25, 26. Prior to entering the army was several years in the Royal Navy; served with the Rifles at the attack on Buenos Ayres, and was among the captured under Brig. R. Craufurd in the church of San Domingo Served the Pindaree and other campaigns in India from 1815 to 1819.	23rd Jan., 1806, 95th Rifles;	21st Jan., 1808, 95th Rifles; exchd. to h. p. of 47th Regt., 19th May, 1808; exchd. to 7th, 21st APRIL, 1812; exchd. to 14th L. D, 1st Oct, 1812	7th July, 1814, 50th Regt.; exchd. to 17th L. D, 20th Oct., 1814;	Major, 9th June, 1825, unatt.; exchd. to 65th Regt., 18th Jan., 1827; Lieut. Col. 24th Feb., 1829, unatt.; aptd. Lieut. Col., unatt., in the British Legion of Spain, 21st Dec., 1835; Col. 9th Nov., 1846; Major Gen., 20th June, 1854; Lieut. Gen., 27th Dec., 1860; Gen., 12th July, 1868; died at Blackheath, 6th, Sept., 1869.
THORNTON, Chas. Edmund	30th Dec., 1842, 56th Regt.;	20th Aug., 1844, 56th Regt.;	19th Sept., 1848, 2nd Foot; exchd. to 86th Regt., 6th July, 1849; exchd. to h. p. of 26th Regt., 28th Dec., 1855; aptd. to 7th, 23rd Oct., 1857; exchd. to h. p. unatt., 25th Mar., 1859; aptd. Staff Officer of Pensioners, 1st Jan., 1859; placed on h. p., 25th Mar., 1859.	Bt. Major, 3rd June, 1860; retired 17th April, 1867.
THUNDER, Geo. Francis	18th Nov., 1868, 38th Regt.;	27th April, 1870, 38th Regt.; aptd. to 7th, 24th Oct., 1873.		

Alphabetical List of Officers of the Royal Fusiliers.

NAME.	ENSIGN, &c.	LIEUTENANT.	CAPTAIN.	HIGHER RANKS AND REMARKS.
THURLOW, Hon. Thos. Hugh Hovel	26th Feb., 1836, 70th Regt.;	9th June, 1838;	9th May, 1843;	Retired 23rd Aug., 1844.
THURSTON, Henry Neville Cotton, Lieut. 3rd West York Mil., 11th Aug., 1854	22nd Dec., 1854;	13th April, 1855;	24th Dec., 1858; exchd. to 61st Regt., 25th Feb., 1859; exchd. to 13th Foot, 8th Feb., 1861;	Retired 1st April, 1862; died at Awebridge, near Romsey, Hants, 17th Oct., 1867.
THYNNE, Lord Edward	27th Mar., 1828, 60th Regt.;	25th June, 1829;		Retired 8th June, 1830.
THYNNE, Lord William	17th Aug., 1820, 78th Regt.;	6th June, 1822;	24th Feb., 1825, 27th Regt.; exchd. back to 7th, 21st April, 1825;	Major, 31st Aug., 1830; Lieut. Col., 31st Aug., 1838, unatt.; aptd. to 1st Foot Guards, 15th Oct., 1841; retired 16th Feb., 1844.
TIBEARDO, Anselm Lieut. 6th Lanc. Mil., 10th March, 1855;	9th Sept., 1855;	13th April, 1853;		Died on or about 17th Aug., 1863.
TICE, John	Lieut., 31st May, 1809, Surrey Militia;	9th May, 1811; exchd. to 4th Gar. Batt., 3rd Dec., 1812; made 2nd, 1814; placed on h. p. of it, 25th Dec., 1816;		Retired 1834.
TIPPING, Edward		22nd Jan., 1755;	6th Aug., 1803, York Rangers; aptd. to Nova Scotia Provincials, 24th Nov., 1803;	Died or retired 1757.
TONGE, Winckworth	12th May, 1783, 22nd Regt.;	31st Aug., 1785, 22nd Regt.; placed on h. p. of it, 2nd Sept., 1785; aptd. to Royal Nova Scotia Provincials, aptd. to 7th, 24th		Aptd. Town Major of Halifax, N.S., July, 1799; Town Adjt. of Cape Breton, 1803 retired June, 1811.
TORRINGTON, Geo., Viscount Was Governor and Commander-in-Chief of Ceylon from April, 1847, to October, 1850.	25th June, 1829, 60th Regt.;	June, 1795; 1st Nov., 1831;		Retired 4th Dec., 1832; aptd. Lieut. Col. of the West Kent Militia, 27th Feb., 1854; Hon. Colonel, 22nd May, 1869.
TOTTENHAM, Fred. St. Leger	29th May, 1869;	28th Oct., 1871.		
TRACY, Henry		13th Feb., 1757;	placed on h. p. of it, 1763.	
TRAHERNE, Llewellyn P.	29th Dec., 1854;	13th April, 1855;		Superseded, being absent without leave, 12th May, 1857.
TREVENES, William	1st Sept., 1848, 48th Regt.;	27th Aug., 1812;		Retired 18th April, 1816.
TRITTON, Geo. Sinclair	24th Jan., 1834, 73rd Regt.;	22nd Feb., 1850;		Retired 21st Nov., 1851.
TROUBRIDGE, Sir Thos. St. V. H. C., Bart., C.B. Served the Eastern Campaign of the Crimea.	1854, severely wounded at Inkerman—both legs amputated.	30th Dec., 1836;	14th Dec., 1841;	Major, 9th Aug., 1850; Bt. Lieut. Col., 12th Dec., 1854; Lieut. Col, 9th Mar., 1855; Col., 18th May, 1855; retired on h. p. of 22nd Regt., 14th Sept., 1855; died at Queen's Gate, Kensington, 2nd Oct., 1867.
TRYON, Thomas Medal for the Crimea.	12th May, 1848, 68th Regt.; Served the Eastern Campaign of the 28th October.	1st Feb., 1850; including the battle of Inkerman, siege of Sebastopol and sortie on	21st Sept., 1854;	Bt. Major, 6th June, 1856; Major, 20th March, 1857; Lieut. Col., 29th May, 1863; retired 1st Dec., 1863.
TUCKER, Sylvester	4th May, 1705.			
TUKE, Alfred John	15th Feb., 1850, 64th Regt.;	8th Jan., 1853, 64th Regt.;	18th Feb., 1862, 64th Regt.; exchd. to 7th, 3rd March, 1863.	Retired 24th Jan., 1865.
TUPPER, Charles William	8th Feb., 1839, 69th Regt.;	16th May, 1841, 69th Regt.; exchd. to 7th, 29th Dec., 1841;		Retired 5th Nov., 1847; aptd. Capt. in the Tower Hamlets Militia, 23rd Dec., 1842; retired 12th Feb., 1855.
TURNER, John	26th April, 1705.		12th Dec., 1694.	
TURNER, Ralph Served with the Regt. in Flanders,	19th Feb., 1841, 26th Reg.;	and commanded a company in the expedition to Cadiz and Vigo in 1702.		Died in the service between 1706 and 1715; supposed in Spain.
TURNER, Sir William West, C.B., K.C.S.I. Medal for China; Medal for the Crimea; Kt. of the Legion of Honour; 5th Class of the Medjidie; Turkish Medal; Medal for India; Medal for N. W. Frontier. Served with the 26th in China, present at defence of Ningpo, action and demonstration before Nankin; Fusiliers during the siege of Sebastopol, 7th June (in command of Regt. out of action); Karabelnaia, Sebastopol, from 3rd Dec., 1855 to June, 1856. Served in Field Force in the actions of Chanda, Umeerpore, and Sultaunpore, and Road near Sasseram, from 23rd July, Field Force at the assault and taking		27th Dec., 1842, 26th Regt.; pl. on h.p. of it, Sept., 1843; aptd. to 15th Foot, 19th Jan., 1844; of Tseke, storm and capture of Chapoo, with the 15th in Ceylon during the topol in 1855, including sorties of 5th storming party of Regt., slightly on 8th Sept. (in command of Regt. of the troops on the Grand Trunk 1858, to 10th July, 1859, including the	27th May, 1853, 15th Foot; exchd. to 7th, 15th Aug., 1854; Woosung, Shanghai, Chinkiangfoo, Kandian rebellion of 1848; with the April and 9th May, capture of Redan, 18th and wounded), commandant of the Bengal in 1857-8 with the Joumpore siege and capture of Lucknow, Employed on special duty in command actions of Suheipee, Nonadee, &c. of the Conical Hill and Lalloo, and capture of the Bonair Pass.	Bt. Major, 17th July, 1855; Bt. Lieut. Col., 2nd Nov., 1855; Major, 16th Nov., 1855, unatt.; aptd. to 97th Regt., 28th July, 1857; Col., 26th April, 1859; Lieut. Col., 4th June, 1859, 97th Regt., placed on h. p. of it, June, 1867; died at Naples, 9th July, 1871.

Alphabetical List of Officers of the Royal Fusiliers.

NAME.	ENSIGN, &c.	LIEUTENANT.	CAPTAIN.	HIGHER RANKS AND REMARKS.
TWEMLOW, Geo. Hamilton	11th Oct., 1844, 4th Foot;	16th May, 1846, 4th Foot; apt. to 64th Regt., 22nd Dec, 1848; 14th Oct., 1778;	16th Nov., 1855; exchd. to 16th Foot, 21st Jan., 1859;	Major, 1st April, 1870, unatt.; aptd. to 80th Regt., 10th May, 1871.
TWYSDEN, *Sir* William, *Bart.* Served with the Regiment during the American War.	...	...	...	Retired, Feb., 1784; died at Royden Hall, Kent, 3rd Feb., 1834.
UNDERWOOD, Caleb	2nd June, 1777, 10th Foot;	21st May, 1778;	...	Retired 19th Sept., 1779.
URMSTON, Geo. Cockburn	6th Mar., 1841, 3rd West India Regt.;	20th Aug., 1842, 3rd West India Regt.; exchd. to 7th, 17th April, 1843; placed on h. p. of 3rd Foot, 1st Nov., 1844;	...	Died at Ryde, Isle of Wight, 10th Mar., 1847.
USTICKE, William	9th June, 1758, 47th Regt.;	1st Mar., 1760, 47th Regt.;	22nd Mar., 1762, 47th Regt.; placed on h. p. of it, 1763; aptd. to 7th, 15th Dec., 1765;	Retired 25th Dec., 1770.
VANDELEUR, Thomas Burton	21st Sept., 1855;	23rd Oct., 1857;	21st June, 1864.	
VAUGHAN, Henry	... ... Regt.;	...	21st June, 1685.	
VEAICH, Charles	placed on h. p. of it;	9th Feb., 1751;	30th Aug., 1756, 67th Regt.;	Aptd. Quarter Master, 9th Jan., 1755; Major, 18th Feb., 1761, 67th Regt.; placed on h. p. of 105th Regt., 1764; died in Henrietta Street, Covent Garden, 27th Dec., 1786.
VEITCH, Henry	31st May, 1778, Royal Marines;	22nd Oct., 1780, Royal Marines; placed on h. p. 1783; aptd. to 7th, 23rd April, 1788;	28th Dec., 1791, Indept. Compy.;	Major, 24th Aug., 1795, 98th Regt.; Lieut. Col., 10th May, 1796, 98th Regt. reduced 1801, placed on h. p.; retired 1801; died 1st April, 1838.
VEREKER, John	21st Feb., 1828, 22nd Regt.;	24th Feb., 1832, unatt.; aptd. to 55th Regt., 30th March, 1832; exchd. to h. p. of 27th Regt., 13th Nov., 1832; aptd. to 7th, 29th Aug., 1834;	...	Retired 18th Mar., 1836; died at Kingston, near Dublin, Jan., 1840.
VERNER, John Donavan	24th Sept., 1841, 47th Regt.;	23rd Aug., 1844;	6th July, 1852; exchd. to 55th Regt., 24th Dec., 1852; exchd. to h. p. unatt., 10th Aug., 1855; aptd. to 4th West India Regt., 30th March, 1867;	Bt. Major, 24th July, 1864; Professor of Military Drawing, R. M. College; retired 30th March, 1867; died near Broadstairs, 5th May, 1868.
VINCENT, Edward		20th June, 1685.		
VOULES, Wm. James Lieut. Bucks Mil., 27th May, 1854;	... Jan., 1856, 30th Regt.; aptd. to 64th Regt., 5th Feb., 1858;	20th Mar., 1860, 64th Regt.;	12th June, 1867, 64th Regt.; exchd. to 7th, 25th Nov., 1868; placed on h. p. of the Regt., 24th Dec., 1873;	Aptd. Capt. North Durham Militia, 24th Dec., 1873.
WADHAM, Francis	22nd March, 1786, 37th Regt.;	20th Jan., 1790, 37th Regt.; aptd. to 7th,	21st April, 1795, Regt.; aptd. to Chatham Indept. Company, 8th July, 1795.	
WALKER, Alexander	14th Aug., 1775, 26th Regt.;	2nd Dec., 1777, 26th Regt.;	14th Feb., 1782, Indept. Compy., Aptd. to 7th, 3rd Mar., 1784;	aptd. Fort Major of Fort St. George, 1784; retired 8th Nov., 1792.
WALKER, Alexander	...	3rd May, 1796; placed on h. p. of the Regt., 1802;	...	Died at Bordeaux, 9th Feb., 1831.
WALKER, David	...	23rd Aug., 1804; aptd. to 1st West India Regt., 22nd Oct., 1807;	...	Resigned 14th March, 1809.
WALKER, Robert Previous to entering the army, viz.; rics, Canada, and Nova Scotia, and Brigade Major to the forces in Nova	13th May, 1776, 15th Foot; from February, 1772, to September, in the West Indies. From October, Scotia under H.R.H. the Duke of	20th April, 1778; 1775, served as Midshipman in the 1790, to April, 1795, he acted as Qr. Kent.	13th July, 1791; Royal Navy. Served in North America. R. F., and afterwards served as Mas.	Bt. Major, 1st Jan., 1798; Bt. Lieut. Col., 25th Sept., 1803; Major, 2nd June, 1804, 3rd West India Regt.; Lieut. Col., 25th Oct., 1805, 9th Vet. Batt.; battalion reduced, 10th July, 1814, retained on f. p. of it; aptd. Lieut. Gov. of Sheerness, 1814; died in Dublin, 23rd July, 1842.
WALKER, Samuel	10th Oct., 1822, 11th Foot;	12th May, 1825, unatt.; aptd. to 7th, 30th June, 1825;	1st Nov., 1827, unatt.; exchd. to 65th Regt., 15th May, 1828;	Major, 19th Sept., 1834, 65th Regt.; retired 17th April, 1840.

Alphabetical List of Officers of the Royal Fusiliers.

NAME.	ENSIGN, &c.	LIEUTENANT.	CAPTAIN.	HIGHER RANKS AND REMARKS.
WALKER, Wm. James Tyrwhitt	19th Aug., 1836, 61st Regt.;	31st. Dec., 1839, 61st Regt.; exchd. to 6th Drags., 26th Feb., 1841; exchd. to 7th, 8th Nov., 1842;	...	Retired 24th March, 1843.
WALLACE, Albany French *Medal for China*.	5th April, 1839, 26th Regt.;	29th Dec., 1840, 26th Regt.;	1st Oct., 1847, 26th Regt.; exchd. to 7th, 1st Dec., 1848;	Died in Varna in consequence of a fall from his horse, 4th June, 1854.
WALLACE, Geo. Thos. Wm. Embarked for India in 1802, and as a volunteer in the Peninsula.	4th Feb., 1803, 21st L.D.; served in the Mahratta War:	27th Nov., 1805; aptd. to 15th L.D., 6th Feb., 1806; aptd. to 17th L.D, 14th April, 1808;	...	Retired 30th March, 1809. Published his autobiography: London, 1821.
WALLACE, Hugh Ritchie *Silver Medal for 9, 12, 14, 15, 16, 25, 26*.	14th June, 1809, 1st Foot; Served with the Fusiliers in the Peninsula from the beginning to the end of the war.	16th Nov., 1809; exchd. to h. p. of the Regt., 9th July, 1818;	...	Died 2nd March, 1870.
WALLACE, William Edward	3rd Sept., 1847, 1st D. G.; aptd. to 26th Regt., 1st Oct., 1847;	9th Nov., 1849; reaptd. to 26th Regt., 21st May, 1850;	9th July, 1854, 20th Regt.; aptd. Adjt. of 1st Depot Batt., 15th April, 1859;	Bt. Major, 15th April, 1865; placed on h. p. same day.
WALLER, Edmund	16th Nov., 1855;	30th July, 1858;	1st May, 1866; 20th Mar., 1857;	Died at 16, Eaton Square, 6th Feb., 1871.
WALLER, Geo. Henry *Medal for the Crimea; Legion of Honour; Turkish Medal*.	10th Aug., 1854; Served with the Fusiliers in the siege of Sebastopol, sortie of the 9th of the Redan, 18th June (wounded).	22nd Dec., 1854; Crimea from the 21st Nov., 1854, to May, attack and capture of the Quarries and second assault on the 8th Sept.	the end of the war, including the assault ries, 7th June (wounded),	Major, 21st June, 1864; Lieut. Col., 28th Oct., 1871.
WALPOLE, Thomas B.	17th April, 1804; 3rd Drags.;	26th Dec., 1805, 3rd Drags.; exchd. to 7th, 15th Jan., 1807;	...	Superseded, June, 1809.
WALSH, William	30th Nov., 1815, 11th Foot; placed on h. p. of it, 25th March, 1816; aptd. to 3rd Vet. Batt., 16th Nov., 1823; aptd. to 35th Regt., 7th April, 1825;	30th March, 1826, 3rd Foot; aptd. to 50th Regt., 25th Sept., 1826; exchd. to 7th, 28th March, 1834; exchd. to 45th Regt., 5th Feb., 1836; placed on h. p. of it, 25th May, 1838;	...	Died in Kent, 21st April, 1839.
WARD, Charles	...	12th Jan., 1757; Capt. Lieut., 3rd April, 1767;	...	
WARD, Nicholson	...	5th July, 1787, Regt.; aptd. to 7th, 10th Aug., 1787; aptd. to Invalids, 23rd March, 1740.	...	Retired 25th Dec., 1770.
WATKINS, George	...	26th Dec., 1726;	...	
WATSON, Brereton	26th Jan., 1797, 23rd Regt.;	1st Nov., 1799, 20th Regt.; placed on h. p. of it; exchd. to 30th Regt., 1st April, 1805;	29th Jan., 1807; exchd. to 56th Regt., 18th Aug., 1808;	Retired 1810.
WATSON, Chas. Edward *Medal for the Crimea; 5th Class of the Medjidie; Turkish Medal*.	13th Oct., 1843, 71st Regt.; Served with the Fusiliers the Eastern campaign of 1854, severely	5th Aug., 1845; wounded at Alma.	24th Feb., 1854;	
WATSON, Musgrave	27th July, 1855;	17th Nov., 1855, 24th Regt.; exchd. to 76th Regt., 7th Oct., 1851;	1st Dec., 1863; 2nd Feb., 1858; aptd. Staff Officer of Pensioners, Manchester, 1st Jan., 1868, in the N.W. Frontier, 1863, with the	Bt. Major, 2nd Nov., 1855; Major, 8th Jan., 1856; Lieut. Col., 21st Nov., 1862, unatt.; aptd. to 18th Foot, 9th Nov., 1866; retired same day.
WEDDERBURNE, Geo. Webster *Medal for the Punjaub; Medal for N.W. Frontier*. Served with the 24th the Punjaub Eusafzye Field Force, present at the 15th and 16th December, which	3rd Dec., 1847, 53rd Regt.; aptd. to 24th Regt., 14th Jan., 1849; campaign of 1848-9, present at defence of the Sungahs at the Umbeyla Pass and the attack on the	21st Dec., 1849, 24th Regt.; Goojerat. Served with the Fusiliers Conical Hill, and the affairs of the		Retired 15th March, 1864. Bt. Major, 5th July, 1872; died at Northampton, 20th Aug., 1875.
WEEKS, John	...	1st July, 1795;	16th Aug., 1804; exchd. to 7th West India Regt., 28th Jan., 1808; placed on h. p. of it, 1816;	Bt. Major, 4th June, 1814; died at Nassau, New Providence, 3rd April, 1826.
WEEKS, Joshua Wingate	Capt., 25th Sept., 1803, Nova Scotia Fencibles;	11th Feb., 1807;	15th May, 1812; exchd. to Nova Scotia Fencibles, 6th May, 1813; placed on h. p. of it, 25th Sept., 1816;	Aptd. Town Adjutant of Cape Breton, 25th Oct., 1819; died at Cape Breton, 23rd June, 1824.

Alphabetical List of Officers of the Royal Fusiliers.

NAME.	ENSIGN, &c.	LIEUTENANT.	CAPTAIN.	HIGHER RANKS AND REMARKS.
WELLWOOD, Andrew	2nd June, 1781, 81st Regt. ;	10th Dec., 1781, 81st Regt. ; reduced 1783 ; placed on h. p. of it ; exchd. to 7th, 15th MARCH, 1786 ;	…	Retired 9th Jan., 1793.
WEMYSS, Charles J.	…	27th MARCH, 1806 ;	18th JULY, 1811 ;	Died at Sauroren of wounds received in action at that place, 28th July, 1813.
WESTCORR, John Hancock Served in America, present at the attack of New Orleans, 8th January, 1815 ; served with the army of occupation in France until 1817.	20th July, 1809, 3rd Gar. Batt. ;	12th Aug., 1812, 73rd Regt. ; exchd. to 7th, 26th NOV., 1812 ; placed on h. p. of the Regt., 25th March, 1817 ;	…	Died 28th Jan., 1849.
WESTENRA, Hon. Richard	27th April, 1815, 94th Regt. ; placed on h. p. of it, 25th Dec., 1818 ; exchd. to 70th Regt., 4th Jan., 1821 ;	8th APRIL, 1825 ;	10th June, 1826, unatt. ; exchd. to 8th Foot, 27th Jan., 1837 ;	Retired 3rd Feb., 1837 ; died at Balyleck, Co. Monaghan, 9th June, 1838.
WEST, John Wade	16th Dec., 1795, 22nd Regt. ;	4th Jan., 1797, 22nd Regt. ; placed on h. p. of it ; exchd. to 7th, May, 1807 ; aptd. to 4th Gar. Batt., Sept., 1807 ; exchd. to 2nd Gar. Batt., 17th May, 1810 ; placed on h. p. of it, 1814 ; to 14th Regt., 7th Sept., 1815 ; placed on h. p. of it, 25th March, 1816 ;	…	Died 17th May, 1845.
WESTMORELAND, John, Earl of, G.C.B., G.C.H. Silver Medal for 2, 3, 7, 9 ; Knight of Maria Theresa ; Grand Cross of St. Ferdinand ; Grand Cross of St. Joseph. attack and siege of that place, with by Sir A. Wellesley ; in the affair of retreat to Torres Vedras, and advance Schwarzenberg, in Germany. Served Brienne, capture of Troyes, affairs of Aube, affair on the Barce, re-capture Envoy Extraordinary at the Court of tino and Marcerata. Signed, in conjunction with Marshal Bianchi, who was restored to Ferdinand.	17th Dec., 1803, 11th Foot : Served in 1805-6 as A.-de-C. to Gen. in Sicily ; on board Ad. Sir J. Turkish fleet ; actions before Constantinople in Portugal as Assist. Adj. Gen. under Maj. Gen. Obidos ; in 1809 served as extra to Santarem. In Sept., 1813, promoted the siege of Huningen, and campaign of Morman and Nangis, Bray, defence Mormant and Nangis, Bray, defence of Troyes, battles of Arcis-sur-Aube Tuscany, served with the Austrian junction with Marshal Bianchi, who	Lieut. Gen. Don the expedition to Duckworth's fleet at the passage of stantinople at Prota, and repassage Wauchope, at the first storming of In 1808 served in Portugal as Assist. A.-de-C. to Wellington. In 1810 ceeded as Military Commissioner to paign of 1814, including taking of Langres, battles of La Rothiere and parte, 23rd Feb. ; battle of Bar-sur-and Fere Champenoise, of Paris, and army of that city. As His Majesty's in 1815, including battles of Tolentino Military Convention by which Naples	3rd May, 1805, 23rd Regt. ; aptd. to 3rd D. G., 1st Nov., 1805 ; Hanover. In 1806-7 as Assist. Adj. of the Dardanelles. In Egypt as Rosetta, and retreat ; in second Adj. Gen. in the army commanded with 3rd D. G., in Portugal, including head-quarters of the allies, under capture of that city. As His Majesty's commanded the Austrian army, the	Major, 20th Dec., 1810, 83rd Regt. ; placed on h. p. of the 91st Regt., 21st March, 1811 ; exchd. back to 7th, 10th DEC., 1811, 63rd Regt. ; Col., 4th June, 1814 ; placed on h. p. of it, 25th Dec., 1814 ; Major Gen., 27th May, 1825 ; Lieut. Gen., 28th June, 1838 ; aptd. Col. of the 56th Regt., 17th Nov., 1842 ; Gen., 20th June, 1854 ; died at Apthorpe House, Northampton, 16th Oct., 1859
WETHERALL, F. Augustus	…	…	…	Major, ; Lieut. Col., ; killed at Landen, 19th July, 1693.
WHALLEY, Thomas	…	29th JULY, 1795 ; exchd. to h. p. of 6th Regt. of Irish Brigade, 1798.	13th JUNE, 1685 ;	
WHARNCLIFFE, Lord, James Archibald Stuart-Wortley Embarked for Canada in 1792 ; returned home in 1795 ; accompanied the 98th Regt. to the Cape of Good Hope, whence he returned in 1796 with dispatches from Earl Macartney.	19th Nov., 1790, 48th Regt. ;	11th May, 1791 ;	15th Feb., 1794, 98th Regt. ;	Major, 22nd Dec., 1794, 98th Regt. ; Bt. Lieut. Col., 15th April, 1795 ; Lieut. Col., 10th May, 1796, 98th Regt. ; aptd. to 1st Foot Guards, 27th Dec., 1797 ; retired 3rd July, 1801 ; aptd. Lieut. Col. Commd. South West Yorkshire Yeomanry, 15th May, 1810 ; died in London, 19th Dec., 1845.
WHIGHAM, Robert Medal for the Crimea ; Turkish Medal.	6th June, 1854, 42nd Regt. Served with the 42nd Highlanders including the expedition to Kertch, assault of the outworks on the 18th	8th Dec., 1854, 42nd Regt. ; in the Crimea from 2nd Dec., 1854, siege and fall of Sebastopol, and June.	12th Sept., 1856, 42nd Regt. ; placed on h. p. of it, Dec., 1856 ; aptd. to 7th, 31st Dec., 1857 ; exchd. to 16th Lancers, 9th Oct., 1863 ;	Bt. Major, 5th July, 1872 ; Major, 16th Aug., 1873, 16th Lancers.
WHITEHEAD, Fredk. Jno. Geo.	25th Nov., 1842, 14th L. D. ; exchd. to 13th L. D., 14th April, 1843 ;	8th OCT., 1844 ;	25th MARCH, 1853 ; exchd. to 42nd Regt., 27th May, 1853 ;	Retired 28th July, 1854 ; aptd. Major in the Essex Rifle Militia, 6th June, 1857 ; Lieut. Col., 7th Dec., 1870.

Alphabetical List of Officers of the Royal Fusiliers.

NAME.	ENSIGN, &c.	LIEUTENANT.	CAPTAIN.	HIGHER RANKS AND REMARKS.
WHITTINGHAM, Ferdinand, C.B. *Medal for China.* Served as Aide-de-Camp to Sir Hugh Gough throughout the operations in China, 1842; present at Segoan, Chapoo, Woosung, Shanghai, and Chin Kiang Foo.	2nd Nov., 1832, 83rd Regt. ;	19th FEB., 1836; exchd. to 67th Regt., 26th Dec., 1837 ;	30th April, 1841, 80th Regt. ; aptd. to 26th Regt., 18th May, 1841 ;	Bt. Major, 23rd Dec., 1842 ; Major, 1st Oct., 1847, 26th Regt. ; Bt. Lieut. Col., 20th June, 1854 ; Lieut. Col., 29th Aug, 1856, unatt. ; Col., 26th Oct., 1858 ; Maj. Gen., 7th April, 1865 ; retired on f. p.
WHITMORE, Mortimer, R.S.	26th June, 1827, 49th Regt. ;	5th Aug., 1828, 49th Regt. ; aptd. to 7th, 28th AUG., 1828;	16th FEB., 1838 ; exchd. to h. p. of 19th L.D., 23rd June, 1843; aptd. Staff Officer of Pensioners, 11th Oct., 1842 ; retired on f. p., 1st Oct., 1871 ;	Bt. Major, 11th Nov., 1851 ; Bt. Lieut. Col., 22nd March, 1858 ; Col., 13th Aug., 1862 ; Major Gen., 1st Oct., 1871 ; retired on f. p. same day.
WILBRAHAM, Sir Richd., K.C.B. *Medal for Syria; Medal for the Crimea; Legion of Honour; 3rd Class of the Medjidie; Turkish Medal.* Served the Syrian Campaign of 1840-1, including the advance on Gaza and affair near Askelon; served the Eastern Campaign of 1854-5 as Assist. Adj. Gen., including the battles in the Crimea and siege of Sebastopol.	25th March, 1828, Rifle Brigade ;	25th May, 1833, Rifle Brigade ;	22nd July, 1836, 34th Regt. ; exchd. to h. p., unatt. 29th July, 1836 ; exchd. to 7th, 5th APRIL, 1839 ;	Local rank of Lieut. Col. in Persia, 2nd June, 1837 ; Bt. Major, 31st Dec., 1841 ; Major, 19th JAN., 1844 ; Bt. Lieut. Col., 11th Nov., 1851 ; Lieut. Col., 12th Dec., 1854, unatt. ; Col., 28th Nov., 1855 ; Major Gen., 26th Jan., 1866 ; Hon. Col. 5th Cheshire Rifle Vols., 30th Jan., 1867 ; Lieut. Gen., 21st March, 1874.
WILBY, William Henry. In 1809 and 1810 he acted as Military Secretary and Aide-de-Camp to Sir Geo. Beckwith on the staff in the West Indies, and was the bearer of the dispatches and of the Eagles taken from the enemy at the capture of Guadaloupe.	26th Sept., 1801, 47th Regt. ; placed on h. p. of it; exchd. to 7th, 3rd MARCH, 1803 ;	24th Dec., 1802, 52nd Regt. ; placed on h. p. of it; exchd. to 7th, 3rd MARCH, 1803 ;	21st Jan., 1806, 90th Regt. ; exchd. to h. p. of 31st Regt., 19th Oct., 1820 ;	Bt. Major, 15th March, 1810 ; Bt. Lieut. Col., 12th Aug., 1819 ; died at Bishop's Stortford, 6th May, 1831.
WILKINSON, Thomas	...	3rd JUNE, 1742;	1st Dec., 1745, Jeffrey's Regt.	
WILKINSON, William *Silver Medal for 14, 15, 18, 19, 22, 24.*	...	29th AUG., 1807 ;	2nd SEPT., 1813 ; exchd. to 60th Regt., 16th Dec., 1813 ; placed on h. p. of it, 25th March, 1818 ; aptd. to 8th Vet. Batt., 24th Feb., 1820 : disbanded 1821 ; retained on f. p. of it ; aptd. to 3rd Vet. Batt., 25th Dec., 1821 ; placed on retired f. p. of it, 1826.	Died 14th March, 1848.
WILLETT, William Saltren Served with the 34th Regiment in the Peninsula.	3rd Foot ;	19th SEPT., 1804 ;	2nd Dec., 1806 ; 8th Gar. Batt., exchd. to 34th Regt., 10th Nov., 1807 ; exchd. to h. p. of 23rd Regt., 18th May, 1815 ;	Died at St. James's Abbey, near Exeter, 17th Feb., 1823.
WILLIAMS, Charles	...	25th August, 1746.		
WILLIAMS, David	14th June, 1685 ;	...	...	Out of the Regt. before 1695.
WILLIAMS, David	19th May, 1794, 103rd Regt.	14th Jan., 1795, 111th Regt. ; exchd. to 99th Regt., 31st Aug., 1795 ;	25th May, 1798, 11th West India Regt. ; exchd. to 29th Regt., 5th Feb., 1801 ; placed on h. p. of it, 1802 ; aptd. to 7th, 25th MAY, 1803 ; exchd. to Staff at Army Depot, 17th Dec., 1803 ; placed on h. p. of it, 25th Dec., 1825 ;	Bt. Major, 25th April, 1808 ; Bt. Lieut. Col., 4th June, 1814 ; aptd. Inspecting Field Officer of the Cork Recruiting District, 1834 ; Col., 10th Jan., 1837 ; aptd. to 17th Foot, 22nd June, 1838 ; retired next day ; died 1849.
WILLIAMS, Edwd. Wilmot	18th JULY, 1862 ;	...	...	Retired on appointment as Dep. Asst. Com. Gen., 10th July, 1866.
WILLIAMS, John Bythesea	28th Jan., 1826, Rifle Brigade	27th March, 1827, unatt., aptd. to 7th, 15th MAY, 1827 ;	...	Died at Malta, 6th May, 1829.
WILMOT, Eardley	11th March, 1819, 35th Regt. ; aptd. to 2nd Foot, 8th Mar., 1821 ;	11th JULY, 1822 ;	12th May, 1825, unatt. ; exchd. to 85th Regt., 25th June, 1825 ;	Major, 21st June, 1831, unatt. ; Bt. Lieut. Col., 9th Nov., 1846 ; Col., 20th June, 1854 ; Major Gen., 1st May, 1861 ; Lieut. Gen., 19th Nov., 1870.
WILSON, Edmund Served the campaign in Holland ; severely wounded at Landen.	...	...	1685 ;	; Lieut. Col.,
WILSON, George	20th JULY, 1692 ;	...	...	Major 1st August, 1693.
WILSON, Geo. Christian	15th Dec., 1840, 38th Regt. ;	19th MAY, 1843 ;	25th DEC., 1704.	
WILSON, Thomas	...	9th JULY, 1729.	9th AUG., 1850 ;	Retired 7th March, 1851.

Alphabetical List of Officers of the Royal Fusiliers.

NAME.	ENSIGN, &c.	LIEUTENANT.	CAPTAIN.	HIGHER RANKS AND REMARKS.
WILSON, Wharton	25th March, 1705.			
WILSON, Wm. Horace	3rd Dec., 1863;	30th March, 1867; exchd. to 87th Regt., 15th July, 1868;	31st Oct., 1871, 87th Regt.	Out of the Regt. 1688.
WINDEBANK, Sir Francis	... ...	Occurs 1687;		
WINGFIELD, Thos. Henry	... ...	11th Nov., 1813; placed on h. p. of the Regt. 1816; exchd. back to f. p. of it, 6th June, 1816; aptd. to 32nd Regt., 15th May, 1817	12th Sept., 1822, 32nd Regt.;	Major, 3rd June, 1828, 32nd Regt.; Lieut. Col., 19th Jan., 1839, 32nd Regt.; retired 22nd July, 1842; died 8th May, 1858.
WINNE	Occurs 1695.			
WINTER, Henry Burton	11th Feb., 1862;	21st June, 1864.		
WITHERS, Hunt Served with the Regt. during the campaign in Flanders, commanded a company at Landen (wounded), and Regt. during the War of the Spanish Succession.			Occurs as Capt. 1693; as Major in the expedition to Cadiz	Major, Lieut. Col., 24th Dec., 1704.
WOOLDRIDGE, Thos. Thornbury, K.H. Silver Medal for 6, 9, 12;	17th March, 1793, 30th Regt.;	5th July, 1794, 30th Regt.;	25th Nov., 1802, Army Depôt, exchd. to 7th, 17th Dec., 1803;	Major, 10th June, 1811; exchd. to h. p. of 91st Regt., 10th Dec., 1811; Bt. Lieut. Col., 12th Aug., 1819; Col., 10th Jan., 1837; Major Gen., 9th Nov., 1846; died in Liverpool, 9th March, 1848.
WOOLLERY, R. Theodore	... ...	18th June, 1801; 1798.		Retired Dec., 1804.
WOOLLEY, George	... ...	23rd Aug., 1685;		
WORTHEVALE, Christopher Appointed Adjutant of the Regiment at its formation; served with it and Vigo, 1702.		during the Campaign in Flanders		Major, 1st Aug., 1693; Lieut. Col. out of the Regt., 24th Dec., 1704.
WORTHINGTON, Francis	14th Oct., 1868;	16th Aug., 1842, 86th Regt.; exchd. to 3rd Foot, 18th Aug., 1843; aptd. to 7th, 1st Nov., 1844;		Retired 24th July, 1869.
WOULFE, Stephen Roland	31st Jan., 1840, 54th Regt.; aptd. to 86th Regt., 17th Sept., 1841;			Retired 24th Oct., 1845.
WRAY, Thomas Fawcett	From Lieut. North York Mil.;	13th April, 1809;		Killed at Badajoz, April, 1812.
WREY	... ...		Occurs as Capt., 1693;	Left the Regt., 20th May, 1693.
WRIGHT, George	... ...	24th Sept., 1799, Regt.; aptd. to Wagon Train, 28th May, 1803; placed on h. p. of it; exchd. to 7th, 21st May, 1807; exchd. to h. p. of 20th Regt., 1807.		
WRIGHT, Thomas	10th April, 1825, 15th Regt.;	4th Dec., 1832; aptd. to 60th Regt., 14th June, 1833; exchd. to 89th Regt., 26th Feb. 1836;		Retired 10th March, 1837.
WRIGHT, William, L. L. G.	5th Nov., 1854;	9th March, 1855;		Killed in the attack on the Redan, 8th Sept., 1855.
WYBAULT, Jacques Appointed to the Fusiliers while served with them in the expedition	they were in service in Flanders; to Cadiz and Vigo in 1702.	15th Sept., 1695; aptd. to Capt. Lucas's Company, 10th April, 1701.		
WYLLY, Alex, Campbell, C.B. Served in the Peninsula as Aide de Camp to Major Gen. Pakenham, Pakenham died in his arms; brought home the dispatches from Sir John Lambert.—See U. S. Mag., July, 1843, p. 459.		11th July, 1805; present at New Orleans, where Gen.	19th June, 1811;	Bt. Major, 16th Mar., 1815; Bt. Lieut. Col., 18th June, 1815; Major, 26th June, 1823; Lieut. Col., 8th July, 1825; died at Malta, 10th Nov., 1827.
WYKE, Chas. Lennox	6th Feb., 1835, 35th Reg.;	9th, Jan., 1838;		Retired 9th Aug., 1839.
WYNCH, Alex. John	... ...	9th April, 1812;		Retired 13th June, 1816.
WYNN, Herbert Watkin Williams	5th July, 1839, 10th Foot;	24th Sept., 1841;	28th April, 1846;	Major, 1st April, 1853, 2nd West India Regt.; retired 31st Aug., 1855; aptd. Major 1st Flint Rifle Volunteers, 14th Aug., 1860; died at Cefn, St. Asaph, 22nd June, 1862.
WYNN, Thomas	... ...	3rd Oct., 1735.		
WYTHE, George	2nd April, 1807, 62nd Regt.;	20th April, 1808, 62nd Regt.; exchd. to 7th, 2nd Nov., 1809; exchd. to 2nd Gar. Batt., 2nd Oct., 1812;		Died 12th Oct., 1814.

Alphabetical List of Officers of the Royal Fusiliers.

NAME.	ENSIGN, &c.	LIEUTENANT.	CAPTAIN.	HIGHER RANKS AND REMARKS.
YEA, Lacy Walter Giles Commanded the Regiment throughout the Eastern Campaign, including Alma, Inkerman, and siege of Sebastopol.	6th Oct., 1825, 37th Regt.;	19th Dec., 1826, unatt.; aptd. to 5th Foot, 13th March, 1827; exchd. to 7th, 13th March, 1828;	30th Dec., 1836;	Major, 3rd June, 1842; Lieut. Col., 9th Aug., 1850; Col., 28th Nov., 1854; killed in the attack on the Redan, 18th June, 1855.
YEA, Raleigh Henry	13th Mar., 1835, 18th Foot;	23rd Feb., 1838; exchd. to 4th Foot, 15th June, 1838; aptd. to 98th Regt., 23rd Aug., 1839;	...	Retired 29th Jan., 1841;
YOUNG, Plomer John Medal for Sebastopol; Turkish Medal. Present at the fall of Sebastopol.	11th May, 1838, 88th Regt.;	1st Nov., 1839, 88th Regt.; exchd. to 7th, 23rd July, 1844;	25th March, 1853, unatt.; aptd. to 14th Foot, 7th July, 1854;	Retired 3rd Oct, 1862.

PAYMASTERS.

ARMSTRONG, John, from Capt. 64th Regt.; 23rd Nov., 1804; retired on h. p. of the Regt., 11th March, 1813; died 1833.
Served with the Regiment in the Peninsula.

BERKELEY, Thomas, 13th June, 1805; retired 26th March, 1812; died at Brussels, 1836.
Served with the Regiment in the Peninsula.

BLAKE, Stephen, Ens., 3rd Feb., 1814, 37th Regt.; Lieut., 3rd Sept., 1818, 37th Regt.; placed on h. p. of it, 25th Dec., 1818; aptd. Paymaster 1st Foot, 25th Feb., 1822; aptd. to 42nd Regt., 3rd July, 1828; exchd. to 7th, 23rd Aug., 1833; aptd. to 65th Regt., 6th Aug., 1838; aptd. to Canadian Rifles, 20th March, 1846; exchd. to 93rd Regt., 20th July, 1847; Hon. Major, 1st Jan., 1860.

BRENAN, Justin, 14th March, 1813; exchd. to h. p. of 88th Regt., 5th Nov., 1818; died 10th Dec., 1845.
Served with the Regiment in the Peninsula.

BUCHANAN, Wm. Handasyde, 19th Nov., 1858; Hon. Major, 19th Nov., 1873.

DIXON, Henry, Ens., 6th Feb., 1847, 41st Regt.; Lieut., 29th Dec., 1848; aptd. Paymaster of the Regt., 29th Oct., 1852; aptd. to 1st Drgs., 5th Feb., 1856; Hon. Major, ; retired on h. p. of 1st Drgs., 28th May, 1870.
Served the Eastern Campaign of 1854-5, including the battles of Alma and Inkerman, and siege of Sebastopol.

EMLY, Henry Francis, Ens., 19th July, 1855, 57th Regt.; Lieut., 29th Dec., 1860, 57th Regt.; retired 4th April, 1865; aptd. Paymaster of the 7th, 1st Aug., 1868; died at Aden, 24th Sept., 1870.

GILLEY, Thomas, Lieut., 9th Nov., 1830; Capt., 3rd Nov., 1834, unatt.; aptd. Adjt. of a Depôt Batt.; aptd. to 7th, 23rd Oct., 1857; aptd. Paymaster of the Regt., 11th May, 1838; retired on h. p. of it, 29th Oct., 1852; aptd. to 78th Regt., 10th Dec., 1852; Bt. Major, 26th Dec., 1856; retired 31st Aug., 1858; died at Castle Connell, 28th March, 1869.

McDOUGALL, William Adair, 1st July, 1813, 88th Regt.; placed on h. p. of it, 25th March, 1816; exchd. to 7th, 5th Nov., 1818; exchd. to 42nd Regt., 23rd Aug., 1833; retired on h. p. of it, 1st Oct., 1828; died 27th Jan., 1841.

MANNING, Charles Downes, 23rd March, 1867, 38th Regt.; aptd. to 7th, 28th Oct., 1871; placed on h. p, 1st July, 1872.

MOORE, Fred. Geo. Furlong, Ens., ; Lieut., 8th Foot; aptd. Paymaster of the 107th Regt., 23rd Aug., 1864; aptd. to 7th, 16th Dec., 1874.

MOSLEY, Godfrey Goodman, Ens., 1st May, 1846, 59th Regt.; Lieut., 11th May, 1849, 59th Regt.; exchd. to 7th, 19th April, 1850; aptd. Paymaster of the 20th Regt., 11th Oct., 1853; aptd. to 7th, 11th Nov., 1857; placed on h. p. as a Lieut. of the Regt., 19th Nov., 1858; aptd. to 75th Regt., 29th March, 1861; retired same day.
Medal for the Crimea.
Served with the 20th Regt. in the Eastern Campaign of 1854-5, including the battles of Alma and Inkerman, and siege of Sebastopol.

MURTON, George, Lieut., 25th Aug., 1807; aptd. Paymaster of the Regt., 26th March, 1812; placed on h. p. of it, 25th Feb., 1816; died in Drummond Street, Euston Square, 12th March, 1833.

REYNETT, Henry James, Ens., 2nd Nov., 1778, 64th Regt.; Lieut., 29th Nov., 1779; Capt., 8th Nov., 1792; exchd. to 81st Regt., 5th June, 1798; retired June, 1798; aptd. Paymaster of the 7th, 27th June, 1798; retired 23rd Nov., 1804.

SCOTT, John Mortimer, Quartermaster, 18th Aug., 1854; aptd. Paymaster, 15th Feb., 1856; placed on h. p. of it, 1st Aug., 1868; aptd. to 15th Foot, 22nd Feb., 1871; Hon. Major, 24th Feb., 1872.
Medal for the Crimea; Turkish Medal.
Served the Eastern Campaign of 1854-5, including the battles of Alma and Inkerman, and siege of Sebastopol.

SPILLER, Augustus, Ens., 3rd Aug., 1855, 56th Regt.; Lieut., 11th Jan., 1859, 56th Regt.; aptd. Paymaster 56th Regt., 9th April, 1861; aptd. to 7th, 4th Feb., 1871; Hon. Major, 9th April, 1871; died 16th Sept., 1871.

STAUNTON, , 1805; resigned 13th June, 1805.

Alphabetical List of Officers of the Royal Fusiliers.

QUARTERMASTERS.

AMES, William, 19th Oct., 1872. *Medal for the N. W. Frontier.*

BORTH, Lees, 18th April, 1749.

BULBRIDGE, Samuel, 15th March, 1703.

CAMPION, Robert, 1st Aug., 1692; Lieut., 1st Aug., 1693.

COOPER, John, 10th May, 1692.

CHILLCOTT, J. Congreve, occurs 1727; Lieut., 18th Jan., 1740; Capt., 16th Dec., 1752; exchd. to h. p. as Quartermaster, 25th March, 1755.

CRAUFURD, 14th April, 1808; died 1814.
Landed with the 1st batt. in the Peninsula; present at Busaco and Albuera.

DONDE, Peter, Ens., 27th Aug., 1756, 53rd Regt.; Lieut., 11th Aug., 1759; aptd. Quartermaster, 11th Nov., 1761; Capt., 25th Dec., 1770; retired 19th Feb., 1777.

DONELLAN, Ralph, Lieut., 24th April, 1755; 19th Feb., 1757; aptd. to 92nd Regt., 29th Jan., 1760; placed on h. p. of it, 1763.

GREENWOOD, William, 14th July, 1814; placed on h. p. of the Regt., 25th Feb., 1816; died 1818.

HARGRAVE, Thomas, Lieut., 9th Oct., 1747; aptd. Quartermaster, 25th March, 1755.

HARRISON, John, Ens., 21st May, 1761, 51st Regt.; Lieut., 31st March, 1763, 51st Regt.; placed on h. p. of it, 1763; exchd. to 7th, 4th Feb., 1767; aptd. Quartermaster, 25th March, 1771; Capt., 25th March, 1777; retired 1781.
Served with the 51st in Germany during the Seven Years' War, and with the Fusiliers in America during the Revolutionary War; taken prisoner at Fort Chambly.

HOGAN, John, 25th Sept., 1806; exchd. to h. p. of 14th Regt., 5th Nov., 1818; Ens., 3rd Feb., 1820, 9th Vet. Batt.; aptd. to 2nd Vet. Batt., 25th Dec., 1821; placed on r. f. p. of 9th Vet. Batt., 1802; died in Dublin, 24th Feb., 1825.
Landed with the 2nd batt. in the Peninsula, and served with it throughout the whole war.

HOGAN, John, 1st Oct., 1847; died at Monastir Camp, Turkey, 26th July, 1854.

LAMBERT, Luke, 29th Jan., 1807, 5th Gar. Batt.; aptd. to 14th Foot, 21st Nov., 1811; placed on h. p. of it, 30th July, 1818; exchd. to 7th, 5th Nov., 1818; died at Chatham, 11th April, 1824.

LEDSAM, John, 20th April, 1826; retired on h. p. of the Regt., 1st Oct., 1847; aptd. a Military Knight of Windsor; died at Windsor, 1st *Silver Medal for 9,* 12, 16, 18, 19, Dec., 1855. 25, 26.
Served with the Fusiliers in the expedition to Copenhagen, 1807; and in the Peninsula from July, 1810, to the end of the war, including the action at Pampeluna; present at the attack on New Orleans, 1815. Served also with the Army of Occupation in France.

LOWE, John, 15th Aug., 1695; became a Lieut. in the Regt.

McLAGAN, Charles, 22nd Oct., 1861, 74th Regt.; exchd. to 19th Foot, 16th May, 1865; exchd. to 7th, 31st Oct., 1871; died at Portsmouth, *Medal for the Kaffir War; Medal for* 11th September, 1872. *India.*
Served with the 74th Highlanders in the Kaffir War of 1851-3; also in the Indian Mutiny Campaign of 1868; present at the storm and capture of Shorapore.

METCALFE, Timothy, Ens., 7th Dec., 1855, 49th Regt.; aptd. to Quartermaster 7th *Medal for the Crimea;* Fus., 28th Oct., 1857; exchd. to 38th, 12th Feb., 1873; *Turkish Medal.* transferred to 58th Brigade Depôt, 26th July, 1873; retired on h. p., 31st Oct., 1874.
Served with the 49th throughout the Eastern Campaign of 1854-5, including the battles of Alma and Inkerman, siege and fall of Sebastopol, sortie of the 26th Oct., and assaults of the Redan on the 18th June and 8th Sept.

MURPHY, Thomas, 4th April, 1856; exchd. to 19th Foot, 31st Oct., 1871; retired *Medal for N.W.* on h. p., 9th Aug., 1873. *Frontier.*
Served with the Fusiliers in the N.W. Frontier War of 1863 with the Eusafzye Field Force, present at the defence of the Sungehs at the Umbeyla Pass, and at the attack on and storming of the Conical Hill, and destruction of Lalloo on the 15th Dec.; also in the action at Umbeyla and destruction of the village at the foot of the Bonair Pass on the 16th Dec, which ended in the complete rout of the enemy and submission of the hill tribes.

NEAL, 12th Oct., 1804.

ODIAM, Gregory, 21st April, 1701; Capt., 30th Sept., 1707.

OWEN, Humphrey, 20th Jan., 1759, became a Capt. in the Regt.

PARKES, James, 15th April, 1796; died 1806.

ROGERS, Thomas, 11th Jan., 1715.

SCOTT, John Mortimer, 18th Aug., 1854; aptd. Paymaster, 15th Feb., 1856; placed *Medal for the Crimea;* on h. p. of it, 1st Aug., 1868; aptd. to 15th Foot, 22nd Feb., *Turkish Medal.* 1871; Hon. Major, 24th Feb., 1872.
Served the Eastern Campaign of 1854-5, including the battles of Alma and Inkerman, and siege of Sebastopol.

SELWYN, Henry Charles, Ens., 23rd Jan., 1769, 24th Regt.; Lieut., 25th Dec., 1770; aptd. Quartermaster, 12th May, 1773; Capt., 7th Oct., 1777; retired 23rd April, 1788.

SIMPSON, Christopher, occurs 1687; became Lieut. Col., and was out of the Regt., 21st Aug., 1707.
Served with the Regt. during the campaigns in Flanders; commanded a company in the expedition to Cadiz and Vigo in 1702.

SIMPSON, Thomas, 15th April, 1824; aptd. Ens. 5th Foot, 20th April, 1826; aptd. to 95th Regt., 18th May, 1826; died at Lancaster, 19th June, 1831.

SLATTERY, Matthew, 23rd July, 1858, 58th Regt.; aptd. to Depôt Batt., 20th April, *Medal for New* 1860; exchd. to 38th Regt., 24th June, 1862; exchd. to 7th, *Zealand.* 12th Feb., 1873.
Present with the 58th at the taking and destruction of Pomare's Pah, 30th April, 1845; attack on Heki's Pah; destruction of the Waikiri Pah; storming of Kawitti's Pah; capture and destruction of Rhuapekapeka, 11th Jan., 1856.

TAYLOR, Nathaniel, 22nd Sept., 1781.

TAYLOR, Thomas, 29th Nov., 1777.

VEAITCH, Charles, 9th Jan., 1755, became a Capt. in the Regt.

WALKER, Robert, 13th Oct., 1790, became a Capt. in the Regt.

Alphabetical List of Officers of the Royal Fusiliers.

SURGEONS.

NAME.	ASSIST. SURGEON.	SURGEON.	NAME.	ASSIST. SURGEON.	SURGEON.
ADAMS, W.	...	21st MAY, 1807; aptd. to 9th L. D., 5th May, 1808; Staff Sur., 15th June, 1809; placed on h. p.; died at Calais, 15th Dec., 1829.	DUIGAN, Philip, M.D. Served with the Regiment in the Peninsula.	16th Nov., 1809;	19th Nov., 1821, 2nd West India; died at Sierra Leone, 5th June, 1823.
ARMSTRONG, William *Silver Medal for* 6, 9, 12, 14, 15.	16th May, 1805;	29th Aug., 1811; retired 15th July, 1813.	FERON, Thomas	6th Drags.;	19th FEB., 1801; aptd. to 3rd Gar. Batt., 25th Sept., 1806.
ATKINS, Charles Alfred *Medal for Ashanti.*	30th Sept., 1863; aptd. to 7th, 1st MAY, 1867;	Surgeon, 30th Sept., 1863.	FISHER, Henry, M.D. Served with the Regiment in the Pyrenees and South of France.	3rd JUNE, 1813; to 63rd Regt., 18th Jan., 1816; exchd. to h. p. of 19th Lancers;	Died 1832.
BATT, Thomas *Silver Medal for* 3, 11.	25th April, 1806, Regt.; aptd. to 67th Regt., 9th Oct., 1806; aptd. to 2nd Regt., 12th Nov., 1807; aptd. to 5th Vet. Batt., 28th May, 1812;	15th JULY, 1813; placed on h. p. of the Regt., 25th Feb., 1816; died at Brecon, 13th Jan., 1848.	FRYER, George	...	4th Jan., 1749-50; out of the Regt, 29th March, 1760.
			GIBBON, Edward Acton	1st Sept, 1858, Staff; aptd. to 7th, 1st Oct., 1858; aptd. to Staff, 8th Nov., 1861; aptd. to Royal Artillery, 3rd April, 1867;	Sur. Major, 1st April, 1873.
BUFFA, John	...	7th April, 1795, 24th Regt.; aptd. to 7th, 9th June, 1800; died at Faversham, 3rd July, 1812.	GILES, Adam	Occurs 1754.	
CAREY, Thomas *Medal for Persia; Medal for India.*	24th Jan., 1851, 64th Regt.;	26th Jan., 1858, Staff; aptd. to 87th Regt., 24th May, 1861; placed on h. p. of it, 22nd May, 1866; aptd. to 7th, 29th May, 1867; Sur. Major, 31st Jan., 1872; aptd to 2nd (Carlisle) Brigade Depôt, June, 1873; retired on h. p.	V. C. HALE, Thomas Egerton, M.D. *Medal for Sebastopol; Turkish Medal.* Served with the Fusiliers in the trenches including duty in the trenches as also the assaults of the Redan of a field force, under Col. Blunt, Indus Frontier during the hot season of 1857.	2nd March, 1855, Staff; aptd. to 7th, 15th June, 1855; Crimea from the 25th Jan., 1855, during the bombardments of on the 18th June and 8th September, during the Indian Mutiny, de-	Sur. Major, 4th Oct., 1867; 23rd Oct., 1867, Staff; exchd. to 43rd Regt., 27th Feb, 1869; exchd. to 94th Regt., 26th June, 1872. Sebastopol in April and June, ber. Served in medical charge tached from Lahore to the trans-
			HALL, Hannibal	...	5th April, 1694; left the Regt., 24th June, 1709.
COLLINGS, Adolphus, M.D. Served with the 64th the Persian storm and capture of Reshire, and battle of Kooshab. Served in suppressing the mutiny in men, being the head quarters of actions of Futtehpore, Aoung, Busserut Gunge (first and second), garwar, Alumbagh, and first re-column; present in three sorties wounded; a year's service for Lucknow. Campaign of 1856-7, including surrender of Bushire, night attack in Bengal and N. W. Provinces 1857-8, in medical charge of 500 the Regiment, present at the Pandoo Nuddee, Cawnpore, Onao Boorbeakechowkee, Bithoor, Munlief of Lucknow with Havelock's from the Residency; also at the defence of Cawnpore, severely	26th Feb., 1841, Staff; aptd. to 7th, 16th APRIL, 1841;		HANKELL	...	17th Dec., 1794; aptd. Sur. to Annapolis Royal, Oct., 1796.
			HAZELTON, George	...	29th April, 1779; aptd. to Staff in Lower Canada, 1794.
CONNELLAN, Edward	2nd Oct., 1865, Staff; aptd. to 7th, 23rd OCT., 1867; aptd. to Staff, 25th Jan., 1867;	20th Nov., 1846, 2nd West India; Staff Sur., 2nd Class, 18th Feb., 1848; aptd. to 40th Regt., 12th March, 1852; placed on h. p. of it, 24th Aug, 1858; died at Grange Hill, Guernsey, 1st Dec., 1871.	HENDLEY, John *Medal for the N. W. Frontier.* Present in an engagement between the British troops and the Mahometans of Coombo in the and received contusions on the English on the 4th August followed on the 7th July, 1855, destroyed. Served in the 7th Ensafzye Field Force, present at the defence of the Sungrahs at attack on and storming of the Conical Hill and destruction of the action at Umbeyla and destruction of the village at the 15th, which ended the war.	14th March, 1851, Staff; tween the British troops and the Gambia, on the 7th July, 1855, chest and forehead from musket balls. Served also with the com owing, when the stockaded iron Fusiliers in the Indian N.W. the Umbeyla Pass, and at the Lalloo on the 15th Dec.; also in foot of the Bonair Pass, Dec.	5th Dec., 1856, Staff; aptd. to 7th, 9th JAN., 1863; Sur. Major, 14th March, 1871; aptd. to Staff, 18th Nov., 1871. of Sabajee was taken and Frontier War of 1863 with the
COPELAND, Joseph	15th JUNE, 1826;	Oct., 1796; died 1800.	HERIOT, Andrew	...	11th June, 1685.
DAVEY, Henry W. Robert	...	Resigned 4th Jan., 1833.	HIGGINS, Edward	...	20th June, 1727.
DAWSON, Richard	6th AUG., 1807.		HUDDLESTONE, Richard	...	6th Dec., 1770; aptd. to Hospitals in North America, 1779.
DOCKER, Edward Scott	29th Dec., 1840, 53rd Regt.; aptd. to 54th Regt., 26th Jan., 1841; aptd. to 60th Rifles, 6th June, 1845; aptd. to 2nd Regt., 15th Jan., 1847;	14th March, 1851, 5th Regt.; aptd. to Staff, 18th Sept., 1857; aptd. to 7th, 23rd Oct., 1857; aptd. to 18th Hussars, 13th Aug., 1858; exchd. to Staff, 4th Sept., 1860; Surg. Major, 29th Dec., 1860; placed on h. p, 2nd March, 1866; Hon. rank of Dep. Insp. Gen., same day	HUME, William Henry, M.D.	24th Feb., 1814, Regt., to 7th, 26th MAY, 1814; aptd. to Staff, 13th July, 1815;	4th May, 1826, Staff; died at Barbadoes, 18th Nov., 1827.
			IRVING, Charles	12th JUNE, 1835; aptd. to 68th Regt., 1st April, 1836;	Died at Annan, 13th March, 1845.

Alphabetical List of Officers of the Royal Fusiliers.

NAME.	ASSIST. SURGEON.	SURGEON.	NAME.	ASSIST. SURGEON.	SURGEON.
IRWIN, John	21st Dec., 1797;	9th June, 1800, 24th Regt.; aptd. to 1st Drags., 31st Dec., 1803; Staff Sur., 29th June, 1809; died 22nd April, 1810.	MOORHEAD, Thomas, M.D. *Medal for the Crimea; Turkish Medal; Medal for Abyssinia.* Served in the Crimea from the Fusiliers, at the capture of the Redan; served as Sanitary Officer to the British troops in 1868.	24th Oct., 1845, 54th Regt.; aptd. to Staff, 2nd Dec. 1853;	Staff Surg, 2nd Class, 3rd Nov., 1854; aptd. to 7th, 11th May, 1855; aptd. to Staff 9th Jan., 1863; Surg. Major, 24th Oct., 1865.
JAMES, Isaac	19th Nov., 1821; aptd. to Staff, 12th Sept., 1824;	Died at Malta, 19th July, 1825.		4th Nov.,1854; and with the Royal Quarries, and both assaults of the Fusiliers, at the capture of the Royal Quarries, and both assaults of the British troops in 1868.	
JONES, William Phillipson	19th Feb., 1801;	Died 1804.	MOORE, John, M.D.	4th OCT., 1839; aptd. to 4th L. D. 6th Oct., 1843;	24th Dec., 1847, 72nd Regt.; aptd. to 11th Hussars, 14th Oct., 1851; aptd. to 15th Hussars, 3rd June, 1853; Staff Sur. 1st Class, 6th July, 1855; aptd. to 7th D. G., 21st Nov., 1865; aptd. Dep. Insp. of Hospitals, 7th August, 1867; retired on h. p.
LANGHAM, John Phillipson	28th MARCH, 1854;	Died at sea, 3rd Feb., 1855.			
LOCKWOOD, Augustus Purefoy *Medal for the Crimea; Legion of Honour.* Served with the Fusiliers the including the affair of Bulganak Alma, capture of Balaclava, Inkerman, and siege of Sebastopol; was present with the 8th Hussars at the battle of the Tchernaya.	17th Sept., 1841; Staff; aptd. to 30th Regt, 5th Oct., 1841; Eastern Campaign of 1854-5, including the affair of Bulganak and McKensie's Farm, battle of Inkerman, and siege of Sebastopol; was present with the 8th Hussars at the battle of the Tchernaya.	Staff Sur. 2nd Class, 21st Sept., 1852; aptd. to 7th, 6th JAN., 1854; aptd. to 8th Hussars, 11th May, 1855; exchd. to 2nd Drags., 31st Aug., 1858; Sur. Major, 17th Sept., 1861; placed on h. p. of the Regt., 4th April, 1865; died 20th July, 1858.	O'BRIEN, John, M.D.	18th OCT., 1827;	Died at Canterbury (? Clapham), 1st April, 1841.
			OKEY, William	...	30th JULY, 1703.
McARTHUR, Alexander, M.D. *Medal for the Crimea.*	3rd April, 1849, 1st West India; aptd. to 66th Regt., 11th March, 1853; aptd. to 7th, 24th MARCH, 1854;	Staff Sur. 2nd Class, 11th May, 1855; aptd. to Military Train, 31st Oct., 1856; Sur. Major, 10th Jan., 1869; aptd. to Staff 16th March, 1870; died at Shooter's Hill, Kent, 26th Jan., 1871.	O'REILLY, John	9th Nov., 1815, 1st Regt.; placed on h. p. of it, 25th Dec., 1818; aptd. to 7th, 12th SEPT., 1824; exchd. to Staff, 17th Feb., 1825.	Died at Hythe Barracks, 15th Nov., 1825.
MACKIE, David, M.D.	1st Oct., 1862, Staff; aptd. to 7th, 5th MAY, 1863;	Surgeon, 1st Oct., 1862.	PARKER	...	3rd Sept., 1794; out of the Regt., 17th Dec., 1794.
MAHONEY, Montague Martine, M.D. *Silver Medal for 7, 9, 12, 14, 15, 16, 18, 19, 20, 22, 24, 25, 26.* Served in the Peninsula from war, including the passage of the Douro; taken prisoner at Talavera, and marched to Verdun.	29th SEPT., 1808; April, 1809, to the end of the war, including the passage of the Douro; taken prisoner at Talavera, and marched to Verdun.	3rd JUNE, 1813; Surgeon to the Forces, 11th Aug., 1835; Asst. Inspector, 30th Aug., 1839; Dep. Insp. Gen., 29th Oct., 1841; Inspector General, 19th Jan., 1849; placed on h. p., same day; died at 1, Walpole Street, Chelsea, 25th Jan., 1868, aged 77.	PHILLIPS, George	11th SEPT., 1800.	
			PILKINGTON, Edward	16th May, 1811, 5th Gar. Batt.; aptd. to 19th L. D., 19th Aug., 1813; exchd. to h. p. of 73rd Regt., 25th Sept., 1817; aptd. to Staff, 18th Nov., 1824; exchd. to 7th, 17th FEB, 1825;	30th August, 1827, Staff; placed on temporary h. p. of it, 1829; aptd. to 21st Fusiliers, 17th Aug., 1832; exchd. to 17th Lancers, 24th Sept., 1841; aptd. Staff Surgeon 1st Class, 2nd Feb., 1844; placed on h. p.; died at Ruthin, 28th July, 1851.
MANDEVILLE, Edw. W. Thos. *Medal for the Kaffir War.* Served during the whole of the campaign, under Sir George Berkeley, against the Kaffirs in native lines. Accompanied the expedition in 1848 against the rebel Boers. Served also in the Kaffir War of 1850-1, present at Fort Brown on the 1st Oct, 1851, when a combined force of Kaffirs in their attempt to capture the cattle belonging to the Fort.	25th Sept., 1846, Staff; aptd. to 66th Regt., 9th July, 1852;	16th Feb., 1855, Staff; aptd. to 7th, 13th AUG., 1858; Sur. Major, 25th Sept., 1866; died 1st April, 1867.	QUINLAN, Michael	8th Dec., 1857, Staff; aptd. to 7th, 26th JAN., 1858; aptd. to Staff, 1st May, 1863.	
			REID, William	...	21st JAN., 1765; retired 11th Jan., 1769.
MITCHELL, John, M.D.	13th Nov., 1832, Staff; aptd. to 86th Regt., 31st May, 1833; aptd. to 48th Regt., 9th June, 1837; reaptd. to Staff, 28th June, 1839; aptd. to 78th Regt., 20th Jan., 1843;	12th JAN., 1844; Staff Sur. 1st Class, 6th Jan., 1854; died at Balaclava, 24th Sept., 1854.	RICKETTS, Charles *Medal for the Crimea; Turkish Medal; Medal for N. W. Frontier.* Served in the Crimea, including sortie of the 26th Oct., and capture of Kertch and Yenikale. N. W. Frontier war of 1863, with Eusafzye Field Force, present at Umbeyla Pass, and at the attack on and storming of the Conical Umbeyla Pass, and at the attack Dec. 15th, also in the attack at Pass, Dec. 16th, which ended in the complete rout of the enemy, Dec. 16th, which ended in the destruction and submission of the Hill tribes.	28th April, 1854, Staff; aptd. to 7th, 29th JUNE, 1855; aptd. to Royal Artillery, 5th Aug., 1864;	20th June, 1865, Staff; reaptd. to Royal Artillery same day.
			ROBINSON, Henry	8th May, 1801, 64th Regt.; aptd. to 7th, 15th JUNE, 1804;	kerman, siege of Sebastopol. Served with the Fusiliers in the defence of the Sungahs at the Hill, and destruction of the Bonair village at the foot of the Bonair and submission of the Hill tribes. 15th DEC., 1804; retired Oct., 1811.
MONRO, James, M.D.	2nd Nov., 1832, Staff; aptd. to 7th, 4th Jan., 1833; aptd. to 2nd Drags., 15th May, 1835; exchd. to Coldstream Guards, 27th Aug., 1841;	Batt. Surg., 4th April, 1851, Coldstream Guards; Sur. Major, 20th Feb., 1853; retired on f. p. of the Regt., 9th Jan., 1863; died in London, 3rd, Nov., 1870.	RUDD, Thomas, M.D. *Medal for India.* Served with the 8th Hussars during the Indian Mutiny in 1857-8, present at the capture of Kotah, battle of Kotaria and Kooshana (mentioned in dispatches).	1st Aug., 1857, Staff; aptd. to 8th Hussars, 18th Sept., 1857; aptd. to 2nd Drags., 2nd Dec., 1859;	Sur. Major, 18th Nov., 1871, Staff; aptd. to 7th, same day.

Alphabetical List of Officers of the Royal Fusiliers.

NAME.	ASSIST. SURGEON.	SURGEON.	NAME.	ASSIST. SURGEON.	SURGEON.
SABINE, Edward	... ...	11th Jan., 1769.	TIPPETTS, Alfred Malpas Medal for the Crimea; Turkish Medal. Served the campaign of 1854-5 with the Fusiliers, including the affair of Bulgunac, battles of Alma and Inkerman, and siege of Sebastopol.	7th April, 1854, Staff; aptd. to 7th, 28th APRIL, 1854; aptd. to 16th Lancers, 29th June, 1855; aptd. to Staff, 2nd Nov., 1855;	18th Oct., 1864, Staff; aptd. to 5th Regt., 15th June, 1866; Sur. Major, 18th Oct., 1864.
SAUNDERS, Wm. Sedgwick, M.D.	6th Nov., 1846, 1st West India; aptd. to 7th, 20th Nov., 1846; aptd. to Staff, 2nd Aug., 1850.				
SHEAN, Robert, M.D. Silver Medal for 18, 19, 24. Served in the Peninsula from war.	28th JAN., 1813; March, 1813, to the end of the	26th OCT., 1830; placed on h. p., 12th Jan. 1844; died 1858.	TRAVIS, Henry	4th AUG., 1804; aptd. to 4th Gar. Batt., 25th Dec., 1806;	Retired ; died at Rothbury, Northumberland,
SHEEHY, Thomas, M.D.	29th JUNE, 1855; re-aptd. to 7th, 15th MAY, 1857;	1st May, 1867, Staff.	WALLACE, William Served with the Regiment in the Peninsula.	... ...	5th MAY, 1808; Staff Sur. 17th Aug., 1809; placed on h. p., 1816; died 6th Aug., 1844.
SIDNEY, John	... ...	29th MARCH, 1760; out of the Regt., 21st Jan., 1765.			
SMYTH, James	... ...	24th June, 1700.	WALTERS, William	26th Nov., 1807; aptd. to Staff at Gibraltar, 1810; Dec., 1806.	Died 1813.
STONE, John	... ...	12th AUG., 1741; resigned 4th Jan., 1749-50.	WATERS, William		
SUNTER, Thomas Moore, M.B. Medal for the Crimea; Turkish Medal.	6th OCT., 1843; Served in the Crimea during the siege of Sebastopol from the 29th July, 1855.	Staff Sur. 2nd Class, 28th March, 1854; placed on h. p., 8th July, 1862.	WATTON, William		25th SEPT., 1806.
			WILLIAMS, William Served with the Regiment in the Peninsula.	29th Aug., 1811; 1st Vet. Batt.	Discharged the service, 20th May, 1814.
SWEENEY, Michael, M.D. Served with the Regiment in the Peninsula.	26th JULY, 1810; placed on h. p. of the Regt., 25th Dec., 1818;	Staff Sur., Physician, 7th Dec., 1826; Dep. Insp., 31st July, 1828; died at Cork, 13th Jan., 1839.	WILLIAMSON, James, M.D. Served with the Regiment in the Peninsula.	28th Regt.	23rd Nov., 1809; Staff. Sur., 3rd June, 1813; placed on h. p. ; died at Banff, 31st March, 1833.

INDEX.

	PAGE.
Aden, 1st Battalion Stationed in	216
Albuera, Battle of	105
Aldea de Ponte, Affair at	112
Alma, Battle of	176
,, Losses at	180
Amboy, The Regiment Stationed at	71
America, Embark for	66, 144
Armament of the Regiment	1, 8
Arras, Band Contest at	150
Ashanti, Volunteers for	223
Badajoz, Second Siege of	105
,, Third Siege of	115
Barcelona, Siege of	38
Bath, Guard of Honour at	53
Berri, Duc de, Guard of Honour to	143
Book of Merit Started	92
Bouljanak, Affair at	176
Bristol Riots, Depôt Sent to	159
Burlada, Affair at	103
Busaco, Battle of	102
Byng's Action, Serves in	63
Cadiz, Expedition to	34
Cambrai, Encamped at	150
Canada, Fenian Raid into	214
Canrobert, Regiment Inspected by	174
Castrejon, Affair at	118
Chamblée Attacked	67
Charlestown, Siege of	75
Chobham, Camp at	171
Clarke, Sir Alured, Presents Plate to the 2nd Battalion	160
Colours Embroidered by the Princesses	160
,, Presentation of, by Lady Fitzclarence, at Malta	158
,, ,, ,, at Portsmouth	170
,, Restoration of	223
Condom, Ball at	137
Copenhagen, Expedition to	87
Corfu, Stationed at	157
Cork and Kinsale, Capture of	17
Cowpens, Action at	76
Crimea, Land in	175
Crowder, Captain, Distinguished at Vittoria	119
Ciudad Rodrigo, Siege of	114
Depôt Company System Adopted	156

	PAGE.
Discontent in the Regiment	10, 11
Distinctive Badges Awarded	60
Echallar, Combat of	131
First List of Officers	4
Fisher, Colour Sergeant, Distinguishes Himself	186
Fitzclarence, Lady, Presents New Colours	158
Fort, St. John's, Besieged	66
French Siege Park, Crimea, Explosion in	196
Fund Raised for the Families of Sick Soldiers	159
Gibraltar, Embarks for	54, 64, 80, 165, 208
,, Returns from	57, 64
Ghent, Quartered in	22, 25, 31
Halifax, Stationed in	82, 88, 91, 169
Hay, Lieutenant, Complimentary Mention of	137
Hibbert, Captain, Promoted for Gallantry	195
Holland, Embark for	15, 17
,, Return Home from	16
Hope, Lieutenant W., Gallantry of	197
Hounslow Heath, Encamped at	5, 7, 10
India, The Regiment Embarks for	205
,, Stations in :—	
Ferozpore	211
Jhelum	208
Meean Meer	207, 211
Nowshera	210
Peshawur	209
Poona	223
Rawul Pindee	208
Saugor	214
Inkerman, Battle of	181
,, Losses at	182
Ionian Islands, Embark for	156
La Bougé, Attack of	26
Landen, Battle of	23
Legion of Honour, Recipients of	198
Lerida, Siege of	39
Madrid, Entry into	122
Malta, Stationed at	158, 213
Marmont, Marshal, Regiment Reviewed by	161

INDEX.—Continued.

	PAGE.
Martini-Henry Rifles Issued	224
Martinique, Capture of	88
Medals, Distinguished Conduct, Granted	187, 198
Miners Separated from the Regiment	13
Minié Rifles Issued	173
Minorca, Stationed in	43-46
Monck, Captain, Death of	178
Montevite, Affair at	124
Montreal Captured	68
Murphy, Quarter-Master, Testimonial Presented to	204
Myers, *Sir* W., Killed	106
Namur, Defence of	19
,, Siege of	26
Newark, U.S., Affair at	71
Newhaven, Affair at	73
New Orleans, Attack of	144
New York, Head Quarters at	70, 73, 78
Nivelle, Battle of	133
Norwalk, Affair at	74
Olivenza Captured	104
Oporto, Capture of	95
Order of Merit Established	80
Orthes, Battle of	135
Pakenham, Colonel, Sword Presented to	93
,, ,, His Portrait Taken	93
,, ,, Killed	146
Paris, Entry into, after Waterloo	149
Persia, Shah of, Visits England	221
Philadelphia, Stationed at	72
Picket House, Affair at	193
Portugal, 1st Battalion Embarks for	99
,, ,, Returns from	143
,, 2nd Battalion Sails to	94
,, ,, Returns from	110
Prussia, King of, Reviewed by	151
Pye, Corporal, Distinguished at the Alma	179
Quarries, Attack and Capture of	188
Quebec Besieged	68
,, Embark for	81
Redan, Assaults of	190, 193
Roman Catholic Officers Dismissed	12
Russia, Emperor of, Visits England	224
Salamanca, Battle of	119
Salisbury Plain, Manœuvres on	219
San Sebastian, Storming of	132
Santa Maura, Stationed at	157

	PAGE.
Sauroren, Combat of	129
Scutari, Embarks for	172
Sebastopol, First Bombardment of	181
,, Second Bombardment of	187
,, Detail of Duties at	200
,, Return from	204
Second Battalion Raised	82, 85, 206
,, ,, Reduced	83, 149
Second Lieutenants Abolished	49
Sicily, Service in	46
Snider Rifles Issued	219
Snowstorm on Dartmoor, Men Lost in	171
Sortie of the 22nd March, 1855	185
,, 1st September	193
Spain, Embarks for	37, 42
,, Returns from	41
Stations in the Peninsula, Register of	138-143
Stations of the Regiment in Great Britain :—	
Aberdeen	79
Aldershot	204, 209, 217
Barnet	13
Berwick	65
Bolton	164
Brighton	154
Bristol	53, 62
Bury	215
Chatham	64, 65, 153, 154
Clonmel	94
Cork	47, 48, 60, 61
Colchester	225
Dover	62, 222
Dundee	79
Dublin	49, 60, 86, 152, 165
Edinburgh	65, 153
Exeter	53
Fermoy	220
Glasgow	65, 80, 153
Gloucester	64, 79
Guernsey	32
Harwich	15, 154
Hounslow Heath	5, 7, 10
Jersey	32, 110
Kilkenny	165
Kinsale	57
Lewes	87
Limerick	48, 61
Liverpool	215
London	4, 6
Londonderry	60
Manchester	155, 172
Marlborough	51
Newcastle	153

INDEX.—*Continued.*

	PAGE.
Stations of the Regiment in Great Britain.—*Continued.*	
Norwich	13
Perth	65
Portsmouth	36, 65, 87, 144, 161, 170, 205
Preston	208
Plymouth	37, 54, 79, 171
Reading	36
Ringwood	36
Salisbury	16, 51
Sheerness	4, 153
Southwark	16, 32
Taunton	36, 41, 47
Tavistock	37
Wakefield	85
Waterford	48, 61
Weymouth	86, 218
Winchester	36, 86, 155, 162, 170
Windsor	153, 154, 162
Yarmouth	13
Steinkirk, Battle of	20
Subalterns to be Lieutenants	2
Surirey, Heights of, Carried	89
Talavera, Battle of	96

	PAGE.
Tarragona, Regiment Encamped at	43
Torres Vedras, Lines of	102
Toulouse, Battle of	136
Umbeyla, Affair at	212
Uniform, Description of	4
Walcourt, Battle of	15
West Indies, Proceed to	85, 167
William IV., Vase Presented by	163
Wilson, *Sir* Robert, Compliments the Regiment	166
Winchester Cathedral, Monument in	205
Windmill Hill, Fusiliers Make the Roads on	167
Varna, Proceeds to	173
Victoria Cross, Recipients of	199
Vigo Captured	35
Vittoria, Battle of	125
Volunteer Sharp-Shooters at Sebastopol	181
Yea, Colonel, at the Alma	177
,, His Devotion to the Regiment	184
,, His Death	190
,, Epergnes in Memory of	218

www.ingramcontent.com/pod-product-compliance
Lightning Source LLC
Chambersburg PA
CBHW080846010526
44114CB00017B/2384